D1227873

Jesuit Colleges and Universities
in the United States

Jesuit Colleges and Universities in the United States: A History

Michael T. Rizzi

The Catholic University of America Press
Washington, D.C.

∞

Names: Rizzi, Michael T., author.

Title: Jesuit colleges and universities in the United States : a history /
Michael T. Rizzi.

Description: Washington, D.C. : The Catholic University of America Press,
[2022] | Includes bibliographical references and index.

Identifiers: LCCN 2022026146 | ISBN 9780813236162 (paperback) |
ISBN 9780813236179 (ebook)

Subjects: LCSH: Jesuit universities and colleges--United States--History.

Classification: LCC LC493 .R59 2022 | DDC 378/.0712--dc23/
eng/20220718

LC record available at https://lccn.loc.gov/2022026146

*To my parents, Theodore and Janice Rizzi,
and to my sister, Jennifer Rizzi, for their love and support.*

Table of Contents

Preface

When I first became interested in the history of Jesuit colleges and universities, I was surprised to learn that no single book told their collective story. The history was available piecemeal—in the many books about individual colleges or about the work of the Jesuit order as a whole (which extends far beyond higher education). As I read those sources, it became clear that I was reading the same story told from different vantage points. The same characters appeared repeatedly in different contexts. A Jesuit who served as president of one university also, at a different point in his career, served as president of another. Buildings on Jesuit campuses thousands of miles apart shared the same name, because both were built to honor the same transformative leader. Changes in American higher education, as well as decisions from Jesuit headquarters in Rome, affected all of the universities simultaneously. Seeing how each university responded to these common challenges, trends, and opportunities was like listening to different members of one extended family on Thanksgiving describing what it was like to grow up in the same household.

My goal in this book is to weave these different perspectives together into something resembling a coherent narrative. While each institution is distinctive, Jesuit colleges and universities operated as a fairly cohesive unit for most of their existence. The history of Boston College is deeply intertwined with the history of Georgetown University. Decisions made at Saint Louis University directly affected Marquette University. Neither the University of San Francisco nor Loyola Marymount University would exist today if not for Santa Clara University, and Santa Clara almost sacrificed its life to save those two sister institutions. These connections are easy to forget at a time when Jesuit universities are mostly independent of each other, but the story of their mission, identity, and origin is so interwoven that it deserves to be told as one.

I do not claim to be a trained historian. My doctoral degree is in education, and most of my experience and academic writing is in higher education management. This perspective gives me a bias toward the administrative side of university life, which I am sure will become apparent as the story unfolds. In researching this book, I have done archival research to fill in gaps, but most of my sources are secondary—the work of historians far more competent than I. My hope is that I have taken their outstanding work, all of which focused on a small portion of this history, and synthesized it to highlight common themes—showing how Jesuit colleges responded to the evolving needs of the United States and American Catholics over more than two centuries.

At a time when Jesuits themselves are becoming scarcer on campus, it is up to the current members of the campus community—including many who are lay and not

Catholic—to preserve the unique spirit and mission of Jesuit higher education. I firmly believe that today's stakeholders in Jesuit colleges and universities can, should, and will keep that spirit alive regardless of the number of Jesuits living and teaching among them. To do so, they must first understand their shared origins. At the same time, I hope that this book is a good introduction to Jesuit education for anyone interested in the history of American colleges and universities. It does not assume any prior knowledge of the Jesuits and is written to give a broad, but hopefully thorough overview of this important slice of the American higher education sector.

Scholarly readers should think of this book as an extended literature review, summarizing and seeking out common themes in the hundreds of different sources that have, until now, told this history in a more localized way. The scholarly community deserves a professional, archival-based history of Jesuit higher education as a whole. That book has yet to be written, and as I researched this much humbler book, I came to understand why. It would be an almost superhuman undertaking to sift through the archives of the (literally) hundreds of colleges, high schools, churches, dioceses, and Jesuit provinces across the country that contain the sources for such a history. A definitive history of Jesuit higher education in America will be written someday by a scholar with far greater skills than mine. My hope is that, by situating the existing academic literature in context, this book will encourage future scholarly research by putting this complicated, multi-tiered story into something that makes sense as a meta-narrative. I believe that there is value in collecting this information in one place, and I encourage readers to dig deeper into these excellent sources for an even richer understanding of this complex history.

In the meantime, I hope that readers enjoy this introduction to a fascinating, important, influential, and largely underappreciated story in American education.

A Note on Style and Organization

This book is organized chronologically into seven main sections covering the Jesuits' early history and the periods 1789–1865, 1865–1918, 1918–1945, 1945–1990, and 1990–present. Each section begins with a short overview of the period, and then tells the story of the American Jesuit colleges and universities founded in that era. The remainder of each section analyzes and explores the shared themes, common challenges, and external influences that shaped those colleges as they evolved during that era.[1]

When I introduce a new theme or idea, I often try to follow it to its conclusion—even if that conclusion extends beyond the time period in question. My purpose in doing so is to tell a complete story, without asking the reader to jump from one section to another to see how a particular problem was resolved years later. When it comes to certain "big" themes like anti-Catholic discrimination in the United States, however, I separate the story into different entries for each section to show how the situation evolved over time. Naturally, this results in some repetition, but I have tried to keep that to a minimum. Hopefully this approach makes the complete story easier to understand.

Some Jesuit schools, including Saint Louis University, Saint Peter's University, and Saint Joseph's University (Philadelphia) prefer to spell out the word "Saint" in their names rather than using the abbreviation, "St." In keeping with their custom, I do so here as well, although I use the shortened "St." in other circumstances. For example, in this manuscript "Saint Louis" refers to the university whereas "St. Louis" refers to the city.

---

1. This chronological breakdown draws loosely on a conceptual chart that I developed in 2018. See Michael Rizzi, "We've Been Here Before: A Brief History of Catholic Higher Education in America," *Journal of Catholic Higher Education* 37, no. 2 (Summer 2018): 154–155.

Introduction

How can we measure the impact the Jesuits have had on education? During the past five centuries, no single organization—no government, no charity, no wealthy philanthropist, and no other branch of the Catholic Church—has opened and operated more schools in more places than the dedicated group of educators known formally as the Society of Jesus. Universities, high schools, and elementary schools with Jesuit origins can be found on every continent except Antarctica—and it is a safe bet that, if Antarctica ever needs schools, the Jesuits will soon be there. Their work has touched the very rich and the very poor, from the children of European kings to the children of penniless street urchins from the lowest castes of India. It has changed the lives of Catholics and non-Catholics alike, from Chicago to Shanghai, and from Mexico to Nigeria.

Before there was a Peace Corps, AmeriCorps, or any of the other secular organizations that fill a similar role today, there were the Jesuits. For centuries, the Society of Jesus provided a vehicle for idealistic young volunteers to make an impact on the world, work with immigrants in inner-city schools, and travel to remote places around the globe to serve communities in need. A young man who joined the Jesuits in the nineteenth century was joining one of the world's largest and best-organized service corps—but unlike modern-day volunteers, who make only a two-year commitment to the Peace Corps or Teach for America, a vocation to the Jesuits was a lifetime sacrifice.

There are twenty-seven Jesuit colleges and universities in the United States today—representing roughly one out of every six American Catholic colleges. Even that number underestimates their impact, as their size and influence are far greater. More than one out of every five students in American Catholic higher education are enrolled at a Jesuit institution. Jesuit universities are home to fourteen law schools and four medical schools, representing 50% of the JD programs and 100% of the MD programs at American Catholic universities. No other single Catholic religious order comes close to this level of impact.

For generations of Americans (especially, but not exclusively, men), a Catholic education simply *was* a Jesuit education. Jesuit schools were located in the country's biggest cities; they fielded football and basketball teams that made headlines from coast to coast; and they often had a reputation for attracting the brightest and most talented Catholic students. Before long, the names of these small academies became known nationally and internationally—names like Georgetown, Boston College, Fordham, Santa Clara, Loyola, Marquette, Gonzaga, Creighton, Xavier, and Holy Cross, among others.

Most American Catholics who emigrated from Europe in the nineteenth or twentieth centuries—or who trace their roots to that generation—lived in the shadow of a Jesuit college. At Catholic dinner tables and parish halls, women's guilds and summer festivals, the gossip and buzz was the same: those who wanted the best possible education for their sons should send them to the Jesuit school down the street. For millions of Catholic immigrants shut out of American elite society, unwelcome at schools like Harvard and Yale and struggling to assimilate into their new culture, a Jesuit college diploma represented the highest possible educational attainment and the only realistic path to self-improvement.

As important as the Jesuits were to American Catholics, the impact of their work stretched far beyond Catholic circles. From their very beginnings, American Jesuit colleges enrolled diverse student bodies that included Protestants, Jews, and international students of every creed. A Jesuit university (Georgetown) was the first American university to hire a full-time Muslim campus minister in the 1990s. Most Jesuit schools have, at one point or another, enrolled a student body that was primarily non-Catholic. They have always reflected, and contributed to, the diversity of America. This is not some recent development brought on by changing demographics, but a classic feature of Jesuit education that was as true in the nineteenth century as it is today.

At times, this dual mission—as Catholic universities dedicated to the traditions of the Church and American universities immersed in the realities of American culture—has left Jesuit schools in a kind of limbo, attempting to belong fully to two camps but unwilling (or unable) to sacrifice the values of either. American Jesuit universities are like acrobats walking a tightrope, balancing tradition and practicality. In the United States, Jesuits were forced to adapt their classical, European curriculum to the needs of a growing country where the middle class was mobile and elite education demanded more than just memorization of Latin and Greek. They competed with Protestant and public universities, trying to live up to those schools' academic standards while still offering an experience that was distinctively and identifiably Catholic in its tradition and scope. This mission gave Jesuit universities an awkward dual purpose: "preventing cultural assimilation while promoting economic assimilation" for American Catholic immigrants.[2]

Serving two masters was a big challenge, and one that American Jesuit schools could hardly afford to get wrong. The Catholic Church provided them with resources like faculty, staff, and land for their campuses; the secular government controlled their charters, their ability to grant degrees and (eventually) the lion's share of their funding. At times, the Roman hierarchy criticized Jesuit schools for being too "Americanized"—yet it relied on them to train many of the priests, missionaries, and laypeople who led the Catholic Church in America. Federal and state governments were often openly hostile to the schools' Catholic identity and pressured them to conform to the

2. Michael Rizzi, "A Typology/Change Model for US Catholic Universities: Expressing a Catholic, American Identity," *Journal of Catholic Higher Education* 36, no. 2 (Summer 2017): 180.

secular standards of American higher education—yet they readily called upon the Jesuits and their students for support during times of crisis, such as the Civil War and World Wars I and II.

In return, American Jesuit colleges and universities did much to shape the Church and the country that shaped them. Jesuit higher education had a profound impact on American Catholicism and how American Catholics saw themselves. As the chapters ahead will show, many common Catholic practices—like the veneration of the Virgin Mary during the month of May (first introduced at Georgetown)—originated on Jesuit campuses.[3] In the secular government, Jesuit-educated recruits from Fordham, Georgetown, and elsewhere were so numerous that they formed significant subcultures within the CIA, State Department, and J. Edgar Hoover's FBI during the height of the Cold War.

Jesuit colleges and universities also had a major (and underappreciated) impact on American higher education as a whole. From the country's first college west of the Mississippi to its first professional school of international affairs, and from great scientific discoveries in astronomy to seismographic experiments that changed our understanding of earthquakes, Jesuit colleges in the United States have given as much as they have taken. American higher education, it might be said, after centuries of moving in the opposite direction, is now becoming more "Jesuit" in its approach. When colleges embrace "new" ideas about interdisciplinary learning, and when they respond to the #MeToo movement by thinking seriously about their responsibility for the moral—not just intellectual and professional—growth of their students, they are moving toward a model that the Jesuits embraced centuries ago.

For most of their existence, Jesuit colleges were not independent. They were—in practice and sometimes in law—part of a single network. They awarded degrees in each other's names. Decisions affecting all of the colleges were made at the Jesuit headquarters in Rome. Individual Jesuit professors transferred regularly from one college to another, meaning that students at the University of Scranton could easily be taught by a priest who, just a year earlier, had been on the faculty at Georgetown. Especially talented Jesuits served as president of more than one college during their lifetimes. Far from being autonomous, the colleges were part of a vast network of Jesuit enterprises, including high schools, parishes, hospitals, and missions—all run centrally by a surprisingly small group of priests who kept all of those projects afloat even as they kept expanding.

This is a story of thousands of priests and brothers who dedicated their lives to teaching and gave up large measures of their own freedom to go wherever they were needed, leaving a lasting impact on the United States from Atlantic to Pacific. It is the story of the schools they collectively built: small academies that were initially little more than glorified high schools, but which evolved into some of the largest and best modern research universities that America has to offer.

---

3. John M. Daley, SJ, *Georgetown University: Origin and Early Years* (Washington: Georgetown University Press, 1957), 164.

It is the story of missionaries who dared to open schools in remote places that even the federal government would not touch. It is the story of visionaries who saw the potential in New York City, St. Louis, San Francisco, Seattle, Denver, and Washington when those cities were barely more than small towns on the edge of the country—and who bought, at bargain prices, prime downtown real estate that would eventually be worth millions of dollars for their schools' campuses.

It is the story of schools where, even today, European royalty sit in classrooms next to first-generation college students who grew up poor in the inner city, and where dedicated professors share their expertise equally with bureaucrats at the World Bank and with inmates at the state penitentiary. It is the story of a single educational network that has equally served Wall Street financiers and orphans from rural Appalachia, producing graduates who would go on to lead everything from small businesses to entire countries.

It is a story that contains failures as well as successes. Jesuit spirituality emphasizes reflection and honest assessment of one's own faults, so any history of Jesuit education cannot overlook its many mistakes. Jesuit leaders made decisions, both good and bad, that helped and harmed the colleges and the communities they served. Their story is replete with human imperfections—of prejudice as well as tolerance, of poor leaders as well as great ones, and of missed opportunities as well as remarkable achievements. In short, it is a human story—both quintessentially American and quintessentially Catholic.

Most of all, it is the story of hundreds of thousands of students whose lives were shaped by a philosophy, a spirituality, and an approach to learning that remains as appealing today as it was five centuries ago, giving them the right to join millions of people across the tide of history in saying, "I am Jesuit-educated."

Part I:

Jesuit Higher Education in America:
An Overview

Terminology

The Society of Jesus is the largest all-male religious order within the Catholic Church, currently with more than 17,000 members worldwide. Under Catholic canon law, it is an *exempt* order, meaning that Jesuits answer to their own hierarchy and are not directly under the authority of the local bishops. As a result, bishops can invite Jesuits into their dioceses and ask for their cooperation in Church activities, but cannot order them to do so. Whenever the Jesuits sought to assume control of a college, the process necessarily involved negotiations between Jesuit authorities and the bishop in whose diocese the college was located.[1]

The Society is led by a *superior general*—a Jesuit elected to that position by his peers, and who, from Rome, has ultimate authority over all Jesuit ministries around the globe. Those ministries—including schools, churches, social work agencies, and other activities—are organized geographically into *provinces*, each led by a *provincial* who appoints the Jesuits under his jurisdiction to serve where they are needed. Jesuits assigned to work at a specific institution traditionally live on-site, and the local community is led by a *superior* (also known as a *rector* if it is an academic ministry, like a college.)

Each province is responsible for multiple schools and other ministries, but is still typically expected to spare some of its manpower for *missions*—outposts of Jesuit activity in distant parts of the world where the poor are in need of their services. American provinces have operated missions in the Philippines, Belize, Micronesia, and many other locations, sending Jesuits to serve as teachers, health care workers, and missionaries in remote (even dangerous) areas. Many Jesuit provinces in the United States began as missions of established European provinces before they grew large enough, and self-sustaining enough, to be elevated to provinces in their own right.

The large majority of Jesuits are ordained Catholic priests, though it is possible to be a Jesuit without being ordained; such men are known as Jesuit *brothers* and live in community with the others, but do not say Catholic Mass, hear confessions, or perform other priestly functions. All Jesuits—priests and brothers alike—take vows of poverty, chastity, and obedience. Most take a fourth vow of obedience to the pope, indicating their willingness to go anywhere in the world they are needed.

The process of becoming a Jesuit can stretch over more than fifteen years, during which most men earn multiple academic degrees in theology and other disciplines, while also receiving intense spiritual training through month-long retreats, meditative

---

1. For more, see Thomas Worcester, ed., *The Cambridge Companion to the Jesuits* (Cambridge: Cambridge University Press, 2008).

exercises, and other processes that develop both their intellect and their spirituality. Although there are several different stages, including an initial two-year period in which they are known as *novices*, Jesuits-in-training are known for most of this time as *scholastics*, and they are considered members of the Society of Jesus even as they move through the multiple steps necessary to become a fully-formed Jesuit.

If the decade-plus period of Jesuit formation seems excessive, consider that most modern-day college faculty go through a similarly lengthy period of training to become professors. Compared to the tenure process at most universities, the fifteen years of Jesuit formation seem reasonable. Many aspiring academics today will spend six to ten years enrolled in a PhD program, followed by a year or two in a postdoctoral fellowship. Those who survive that lengthy training process are faced with another six or more years as junior faculty members working toward tenure, under intense pressure to research and publish. After achieving tenure, they are called to become deans, mentor younger faculty, and take on other leadership roles comparable to those that might have been assigned to fully-formed Jesuits in years past.

Much like a Jesuit scholastic, a modern graduate student will study under the mentorship of a senior professor, live on little to no income, and help to teach when needed. A modern-day PhD graduation ceremony even bears some resemblance to an ordination ceremony; just as a bishop lays his hands on a priest to confer holy orders, senior faculty mentors confer doctorates on their graduate students by placing the doctoral hood around their necks.

In a sense, college faculty in the United States today have become a kind of secular priesthood, and their period of formation is no shorter or less intense than that of a Catholic priest. Imagine, however, if modern-day college professors were, in addition to their teaching duties, also called upon regularly to minister to the sick at local hospitals, visit prisons, supervise their students 24 hours per day, and perform weekly (if not daily) religious ceremonies outside of the classroom. Imagine, moreover, that those same faculty were required to live on campus with all other professors, always with the knowledge that they could be transferred to another university hundreds of miles away at any time, and at the sole discretion of their supervisor. This thought experiment can help us understand—if not fully appreciate—the sacrifices and dedication of Jesuit educators throughout history.

A List of Jesuit Colleges and Universities in the United States

It is not easy to count exactly how many colleges and universities the Jesuits have operated in the United States. The definition of a "college" has changed over time, as have the eligibility requirements for a school to confer college degrees. Some Jesuit schools (especially in the nineteenth century) described themselves as "colleges" even though they were really more like modern-day high schools. During their history, the American Jesuits have operated at least five degree-granting colleges that later became high schools, and at least seven "high schools" that they tried unsuccessfully to develop into full-fledged colleges. They even had an official term—*collegium inchoatum*—that they used to describe colleges-in-the-making. In most cases, a *collegium inchoatum* was essentially a high school to which the Jesuits intended to add college-level coursework as the students progressed. Some of these "proto-colleges" (like Tampa College in Florida and Regis College in Illinois) publicly advertised themselves as colleges and obtained a legal charter to grant degrees even though they never actually enrolled college-age students.

Using a liberal definition of what counts as a "college," the Jesuits have operated a total of 54 colleges and universities across 25 states and the District of Columbia. This number includes every Jesuit school that publicly described itself as a "college" and enrolled lay students who were not seeking to become Jesuit priests. It does not include the many seminaries founded specifically to train Jesuits themselves, nor does it include the more than 100 "true" high schools, middle schools and other kinds of educational institutions that have been affiliated with the Jesuits over the years. Although the line between high school and college was blurry for the first century of American history, at least 54 Jesuit schools qualify as "colleges" in the modern sense of the word, meaning that at one point of another, they either granted bachelor's degrees to non-seminarians or at least took steps to do so.

Most of these 54 schools were legally accredited to grant college degrees, although a few were not, mainly due to the circumstances of the time. For example, St. Joseph's College (1843–1849) was located in what is today Oregon, but for most of its short life, there was no organized government in Oregon capable of accrediting it. When Catholic pioneers settled in Oregon, the Jesuits supported a school in the community even before the government did. Although the definition of a college has changed over time, if a Jesuit school would have been considered a "college" by its local community at the time it existed, I include it in this narrative.

Of those 54 schools, 27 still operate as Jesuit colleges or universities today. One (Wheeling University) still operates as a Catholic university, but no longer under Jesuit auspices. One (Las Vegas College) merged with another Jesuit institution (Regis University). Six no longer offer college degrees, but have reinvented themselves as Jesuit high schools. Another three still house Catholic high schools on or near their original campuses, but are no longer sponsored by the Jesuits. Only sixteen have closed their doors for good, their campuses sold or repurposed for other projects. Most of those "closed" colleges only existed for a very short time—some for less than a decade—before the Jesuits had to abandon them.

Philip Gleason, a distinguished historian of American Catholic higher education, observed that most Jesuit colleges were founded on a hub-and-spoke model. The pattern was consistent: in any given region of the United States, Jesuit missionaries first built a single college to serve as their base of operations, and as that college matured, whatever faculty it could spare were sent forth to establish other schools in nearby cities.[2]

---

2. Philip Gleason, "The First Century of Jesuit Higher Education in America," *US Catholic Historian* 25, no. 2 (Spring 2007): 37–52. Much of this section is based on Gleason's article, although Gleason

In total, there were five "core" schools, each of which was founded through the efforts of Jesuits from one of five different European immigrant groups. Gleason refers to these five epicenters as the "nucleus" or "staging areas" of Jesuit education.[3] The 54 colleges that grew out of those staging areas would almost all eventually become independent institutions in their own right, but many were at first (in effect, and sometimes in law) branch campuses of the original schools. This means that there is a clear "family tree" of Jesuit colleges and universities, in which five schools essentially "gave birth" to the others. Figure One shows approximately what this family tree would look like.

Base One: Georgetown University, Washington, DC (English Jesuits)

The story begins with English Jesuits, who settled in Maryland during the colonial era and whose heirs eventually established **Georgetown University** in 1789. Their first attempts to expand in the early 1800s were less than successful, leading to a series of three failed colleges in New York City, northern Maryland, and downtown Washington, DC. By the mid-1800s, however, Georgetown faculty and alumni successfully founded the **College of the Holy Cross** in Massachusetts (1843), **Saint Joseph's University** in Philadelphia (1851), **Loyola University** in Baltimore (1852), and **Boston College** (1858). The twentieth century saw further growth in the northeast, as Jesuits from these schools founded or assumed control of the **University of Scranton** (1942), **Fairfield University** (1942), and **Wheeling University** (1954).

Base Two: Saint Louis University, St. Louis, Missouri (Belgian Jesuits)

What the Maryland Jesuits did for East Coast Catholics living between Washington and Boston, the Missouri Jesuits did for Midwestern Catholics of the Great Lakes and Great Plains. From their base at **Saint Louis University**, the Missouri Jesuits became prolific college-builders, more than matching their Maryland counterparts in scope and importance.

Initially, the Jesuit mission in Missouri consisted of Belgian priests who came to the area to serve the small, French-speaking Catholic settlements along the Mississippi River. St. Louis, newly acquired by the American government as part of the Louisiana Purchase, was at the time primarily Catholic and Francophone. Between 1826 and 1829, the Belgian Jesuits assumed control of Saint Louis College, which had been founded by the Bishop of Louisiana in 1818 to serve one of the most isolated Catholic

---

focuses solely on the nineteenth century and therefore omits colleges founded later. He also omits a number of colleges with nineteenth century origins, presumably because they were small or short-lived: St. Mary's (Texas), St. Joseph's (Oregon), St. Joseph's (California), both colleges in Louisville, and the proto-colleges in Maryland, Kansas, Florida, and Louisiana. I include these schools because most were "colleges" in the eyes of the law and/or the public.

3. Ibid., 40–43.

settlements in the country. It was the only college of any kind in the vast wilderness of the west, located in a remote European outpost surrounded by Native Americans.

The Missouri Jesuits' first permanent foray from Saint Louis brought them to Cincinnati, where they assumed control of what is today **Xavier University** (1840). Prior to the Civil War, they operated two schools in Kentucky (**St. Joseph's College** in Bardstown and **St. Aloysius College** in Louisville), but abandoned both by the end of the 1860s. Slightly more successful was **St. Mary's College** in Kansas, which grew out of a mission school the Jesuits founded in 1848 to evangelize the Potawatomi Indians. Located 90 miles west of Kansas City in an area of the Great Plains that (even today) qualifies as remote, St. Mary's continued to operate as a college until 1931, when it closed its doors as a casualty of the Great Depression.

The Catholic population of the Midwest boomed in the late 1800s, as the steel-making and meatpacking industries brought a surge of German, Italian, Polish, and other immigrants to the industrial cities around the Great Lakes. The Missouri Jesuits were quick to respond to these developments. In a forty-year burst of expansionist energy, they founded **Loyola University** in Chicago (1870), the University of Detroit (now the **University of Detroit Mercy**) in Michigan (1877), **Creighton University** in Omaha (1878), **Marquette University** in Milwaukee (1881), and **Rockhurst University** in Kansas City (1910), while briefly dabbling with other unsuccessful college projects in Illinois, Kansas, and Wisconsin.

The educational projects of the Missouri Jesuits covered an enormous amount of territory. The Maryland Jesuits' work was concentrated in a northeastern corridor of the country that benefitted from comparatively easy transportation and shorter distances between cities. By contrast, the Missouri Jesuits established a presence from Ohio to the Rocky Mountains in an era when horseback, riverboat, and the most rudimentary railroads were the only means of connecting one school to another.

Base Three: Santa Clara University, Santa Clara, California (Italian Jesuits)

Even before Oregon was definitively part of the United States, Jesuit missionaries from Missouri established a headquarters in the Willamette Valley to evangelize Native Americans and minister to Catholic squatters who were arriving in their covered wagons. As part of these efforts, the Jesuits taught at **St. Joseph's College** in the small Catholic farming community of St. Paul, about 30 miles south of modern-day Portland. The school opened in 1843 but closed just six years later after most of the local settlers abandoned Oregon and moved to California to take advantage of the 1849 Gold Rush. The Jesuits, too, soon discovered that their services were more urgently needed a few hundred miles to the south.

By the 1850s, the chaos of the Mexican War had left a small population of Catholics stranded in the northern part of California, which had suddenly become an American state after decades of Mexican rule. The San Francisco Bay Area was home to a polyglot mix of Spanish-speaking Mexican-Americans, Native Americans, and a

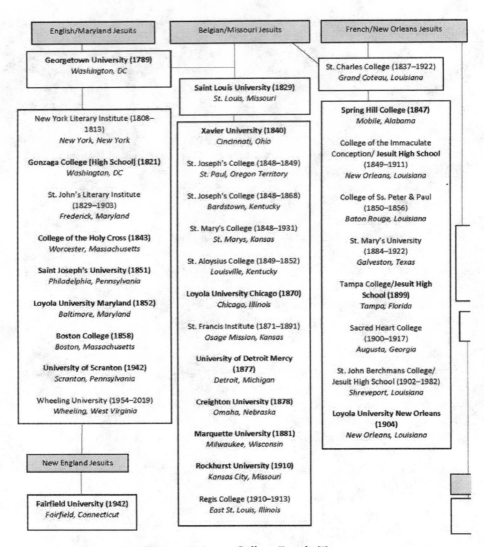

FIGURE 1. Jesuit College Family Tree

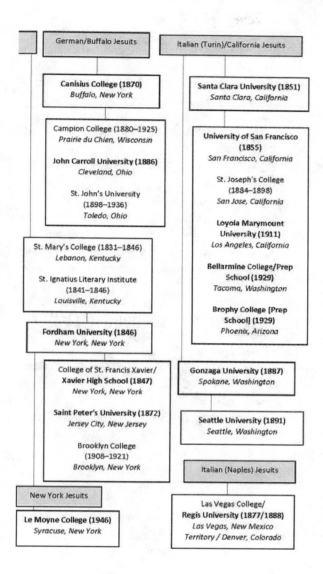

German/Buffalo Jesuits

Italian (Turin)/California Jesuits

Canisius College (1870)
Buffalo, New York

Santa Clara University (1851)
Santa Clara, California

Campion College (1880–1925)
Prairie du Chien, Wisconsin

John Carroll University (1886)
Cleveland, Ohio

St. John's University
(1898–1936)
Toledo, Ohio

University of San Francisco
(1855)
San Francisco, California

St. Joseph's College
(1884–1898)
San Jose, California

Loyola Marymount
University (1911)
Los Angeles, California

Bellarmine College/Prep
School (1929)
Tacoma, Washington

Brophy College [Prep
School] (1929)
Phoenix, Arizona

St. Mary's College (1831–1846)
Lebanon, Kentucky

St. Ignatius Literary Institute
(1841–1846)
Louisville, Kentucky

Fordham University (1846)
New York, New York

College of St. Francis Xavier/
Xavier High School (1847)
New York, New York

Saint Peter's University (1872)
Jersey City, New Jersey

Brooklyn College
(1908–1921)
Brooklyn, New York

Gonzaga University (1887)
Spokane, Washington

Seattle University (1891)
Seattle, Washington

Italian (Naples) Jesuits

New York Jesuits

Le Moyne College (1946)
Syracuse, New York

Las Vegas College/
Regis University (1877/1888)
Las Vegas, New Mexico
Territory / Denver, Colorado

growing number of English-speaking Gold Rush forty-niners. Sensing an educational vacuum, Jesuit missionaries from Oregon opened a school on the grounds of a deteriorating Spanish mission church in the valley outside San Jose. Thus was born in 1851 **Santa Clara University**—the second oldest college (of any kind) in California, and the first American college (of any kind) to confer a bachelor's degree on the West Coast.[4]

Italian Jesuits from Turin soon took formal control of Santa Clara. Even before the first Santa Clara students graduated, the Turin Jesuits opened a second California college, known today as the **University of San Francisco,** in 1855. From 1884 to 1898, a third Jesuit school, **St. Joseph's College**, operated in nearby San Jose.

Despite the importance of their California projects, these Italian missionaries did not neglect the Jesuits' original focus on the Pacific Northwest. Throughout the late 1800s they staffed dozens of missions, churches, and Indian schools, and in 1887 those efforts coalesced with establishment of **Gonzaga University** in Spokane, Washington. Characteristically feeling a need to be present in their region's dominant city, Jesuit faculty from Gonzaga quickly branched out to open **Seattle University** in 1891.

Maintaining four western colleges was already a tax on their resources, but the Jesuits soon encountered another expansion opportunity too good to ignore. By the early twentieth century, Los Angeles had transformed from a frontier town populated mostly by tumbleweeds into one of the most important cities on the West Coast. Under pressure from the local bishop, the Santa Clara Jesuits agreed to open what is today **Loyola Marymount University**. The school opened in 1911, largely with faculty and funds on loan from Santa Clara. Although Santa Clara itself was struggling at the time and had few resources to spare, in Jesuit history, practical considerations sometimes lost out to missionary imperatives. It was neither the first nor the last time that the Jesuits over-extended themselves and sacrificed the well-being of one college to establish another.[5]

In 1929, western Jesuits founded two proto-colleges that they never fully developed: **Brophy College** in Phoenix, Arizona and **Bellarmine College** in Tacoma, Washington. Both were legally chartered to grant degrees by their respective state governments, and Brophy enrolled undergraduate students for a short time in the 1930s. The two schools are still in Jesuit hands today, and although they operate strictly as prep schools, their campuses rival those of some full-fledged colleges.

Base 3.5: Regis University, Denver, Colorado (Italian Jesuits)

While their colleagues from Turin were building colleges on the Pacific coast and the northern Rockies, a second group of Italian Jesuit missionaries (from Naples), independently came to the United States in the 1860s to serve the southern Rockies.

---

4. Gerald McKevitt, SJ, *The University of Santa Clara: A History, 1851–1977* (Palo Alto: Stanford University Press, 1979), 14–20.

5. Ibid., 158–165.

This group, the smallest in the American Jesuit family tree, established **Las Vegas College** in New Mexico (1877) and **Sacred Heart College** in Colorado (1884). Those two schools eventually merged to create what is today **Regis University** in Denver (1888).

Base Four: New Orleans, Louisiana (French Jesuits)

French Jesuit missionaries served in the American South. Although they were based mainly in New Orleans, through the 1920s they operated (or attempted to operate) colleges in Alabama, Florida, Georgia, Kentucky, Texas, and four different locations in Louisiana.

Their original flagship schools were the now-defunct **St. Charles College** (1837–1922) in rural Grand Coteau, Louisiana, and **St. Mary's College** (1831–1846) in central Kentucky. Like St. Charles and St. Mary's, virtually all of the Jesuits' Southern colleges failed due to a combination of strong anti-Catholic prejudice in the region, relatively small local Catholic student populations, and ill-timed natural disasters. **St. Mary's University** (1884–1922) in Galveston, Texas and **Sacred Heart College** (1900–1917) in Augusta, Georgia were modestly successful, but the former was destroyed by a hurricane and the latter fell victim to a flood, after which neither ever fully recovered. The **College of the Immaculate Conception** (1849–1911) served generations of commuter students in New Orleans before the Jesuits reconfigured it as a high school. Other brief college projects in Baton Rouge, Tampa, and Shreveport were likewise abandoned or reimagined as prep schools.

Today, **Loyola University** in New Orleans (founded 1904) and **Spring Hill College** in Mobile (in Jesuit hands since 1847) are the only remnants of what was once a much larger Southern network.

The French Jesuits made their most lasting contribution far outside of their traditional Southern territory. It was they who brought **Fordham University** into the Jesuit fold in 1846, after circumstances forced them to withdraw from one of their early college projects in Kentucky and relocate its faculty to New York. By 1910, Fordham would go on to become the mother institution of three other Jesuit colleges in the New York City area, including the **College of St. Francis Xavier** in Manhattan (now a high school), **Brooklyn College** (now closed), and **Saint Peter's University** in New Jersey (which survives as a college today). Much later, in 1946, Jesuits from New York expanded Upstate with the founding of **Le Moyne College** in Syracuse.

Base Five: Canisius College, Buffalo, New York (German Jesuits)

The final branch of the American Jesuit family tree consisted of German refugees who arrived in Buffalo and founded **Canisius College** in 1870. This small group would eventually establish **John Carroll University** (1886) in Cleveland, as well as the now-defunct **Campion College** (1880–1925) in Prairie du Chien, Wisconsin and **St. John's University** (1898–1936) in Toledo, Ohio.

Summary and Reflections

As this family tree indicates, Jesuit expansion in the United States was not a mono-lithic enterprise. Although everything the Jesuits did was ultimately controlled from Rome, the actual work of building colleges fell upon five different immigrant groups that splintered into a complicated web of missions. The English Jesuits in the northeast, the Belgian Jesuits in the Midwest, Italian Jesuits in the far west, French Jesuits in the Gulf Coast and New York City, and German Jesuits in the Great Lakes all built a portion of what would become a national network of schools. The five "core" institutions (George-town University, Saint Louis University, Santa Clara University, Canisius College, and, to some extent, Fordham University) all created new colleges in their own image and lent their faculty to these expansion efforts, often at great cost to themselves.

Today, the twenty-seven remaining Jesuit colleges and universities collectively enroll over 200,000 students, ranging in size from fewer than 1,500 (Spring Hill) to more than 19,000 (Georgetown). Eleven of the 20 largest metropolitan areas in the United States are home to Jesuit colleges or universities; seven of the remaining nine are home to Jesuit high schools. With few exceptions, Jesuit educators built schools wherever American Catholics settled in numbers large enough to need their services, and what they were able to accomplish with few resources beyond their own sweat is nothing short of remarkable.

What patterns can we extrapolate from this long list of schools, successful and unsuccessful? There are a few universal characteristics of Jesuit education that stand out:

Urban Character

First, Jesuit schools were predominantly **urban institutions**. Jesuits sought to meet the people where they were, and built schools that were conveniently located for the millions of poor immigrants flooding America's cities in the nineteenth century. There was strong desire to establish a Jesuit presence in any city that became big enough to play a major role in American history, and hardly any large city escaped the Jesuits' attention. The few rural schools that the Jesuits did sponsor (in places like St. Marys, Kansas; Grand Couteau, Louisiana; Bardstown, Kentucky; and Prairie du Chien, Wisconsin) all closed or were abandoned. The Jesuits sought to concentrate their manpower where they could serve the largest number of people.

These urban schools did not have sprawling, idyllic campuses like those of many state universities; to the contrary, they often consisted of one or two buildings in the heart of downtown. This was convenient in the nineteenth century, when their urban locations made them accessible to commuters, but it would become a liability in the twentieth century, as expectations for college education evolved and students began to demand amenities like dorms, fitness centers, and green space. Many Jesuit schools, including Boston College, Loyola (Baltimore), Saint Louis, Canisius, Xavier, and John Carroll (among others) abandoned their original buildings and built new cam-puses from scratch in the suburbs. In New Orleans, the Jesuits simply built a new college (Loyola) when the old one (Immaculate Conception) proved too hard to expand in its original location.

Day Schools and Boarding Schools

Second, there were two kinds of Jesuit colleges in the nineteenth century: day schools and boarding schools. The boarding schools required a significant investment of resources, since they needed to be staffed by enough Jesuits to provide 24/7 supervision over rambunctious teenagers. Day schools catered to commuter students and were generally much cheaper to operate. They were often deliberately located in downtown neighborhoods accessible to public transit, which only exacerbated their challenges when it came time to expand.

Of course, boarding schools would often accept day students who lived in the immediate area and did not need accommodations on campus. However, they at least had the capacity to house students when the need arose. Figure 2 shows the main Jesuit boarding schools in the nineteenth century, omitting some schools that lasted only a few years under Jesuit leadership.

As the chart shows, in many cases, the Jesuits built day schools in close proximity to their boarding schools. In the District of Columbia, the day school was Gonzaga College, less than four miles from the boarding school at Georgetown. In New York, it was St. Francis Xavier College, fourteen miles from Fordham. In Massachusetts, it was Boston College—located near the center of Boston even though Holy Cross was less than a day's journey to the west. In California, the University of San Francisco filled the same role just up the peninsula from Santa Clara. In New Orleans, the College of the Immaculate Conception was a downtown counterpart to rural St. Charles College. In Washington State, Seattle University served students who could not travel to Gonzaga University in Spokane. Rockhurst University was, in effect, a downtown-Kansas City counterpart to St. Mary's College. The only major exceptions to this rule were Saint Louis and Xavier Universities, both of which were boarding schools but were also located in the middle of their respective cities, easily accessible to commuters. Xavier, however, ceased being a boarding school early in its history and became strictly a day school by the time of the Civil War, and Saint Louis briefly stopped accepting boarding students after it moved to a new campus in 1889.

On the surface, this pattern seems counter-productive at best and self-defeating at worst. Why would the Jesuits double their investment in every city and build schools in such close proximity that they would inevitably compete for students? There were indeed times when the presence of a downtown day school retarded the growth of the main boarding school; St. Francis Xavier College in New York had a larger student population and arguably a better reputation than Fordham for most of the nineteenth century.[6]

---

6. Gleason, "First Century," 43. Thomas J. Shelley, *Fordham: A History of the Jesuit University of New York, 1841–2003* (New York: Fordham University Press, 2016), 102.

FIGURE 2. Jesuit College Boarding Schools and Nearby Day Schools

Principal Boarding Schools	Originally Founded as Day Schools	Distance from Nearest Boarding School
Maryland Branch		
Georgetown University (1789) *Washington, DC*	New York Literary Institute (1808) *New York, NY*	230 miles
	Gonzaga College (1821) *Washington, DC*	3 miles
	St. John's Literary Institute (1829) *Frederick, MD*	43 miles
	Loyola University Maryland (1851) *Baltimore, MD*	42 miles
	St. Joseph's University (1852) *Philadelphia, PA*	108 miles (to Fordham)
College of the Holy Cross (1843) *Worcester, MA*	Boston College (1858) *Boston, MA*	47 miles
Missouri Branch		
Saint Louis University (1823) *St. Louis, MO*	Loyola University Chicago (1870) *Chicago, IL*	313 miles
	University of Detroit Mercy (1877) *Detroit, MI*	520 miles
	Marquette University (1881) *Milwaukee, WI*	380 miles
St. Joseph's College (1848) *Bardstown, KY*	St. Aloysius College (1849) *Louisville, KY*	40 miles
St. Mary's College (1848) *St. Marys, KS*	Creighton University (1878) *Omaha, NE*	160 miles
	Rockhurst University (1910) *Kansas City, MO*	90 miles
French/New Orleans/New York Branch		
St. Mary's College (1831) *Lebanon, KY*	St. Ignatius Literary Institute (1841) *Louisville, KY*	60 miles
Fordham University (1846) *Bronx, NY*	St. Francis Xavier College (1847) *New York, NY*	14 miles
	St. Peter's College (1872) *Jersey City, NJ*	23 miles
	Brooklyn College (1908) *Brooklyn, NY*	19 miles
St. Charles College (1837) *Grand Coteau, LA*	College of the Immaculate Conception (1849) *New Orleans, LA*	144 miles

(continued on next page)

FIGURE 2. Jesuit College Boarding Schools and Nearby Day Schools (*continued*)

Principal Boarding Schools	Originally Founded as Day Schools	Distance from Nearest Boarding School
California/Rocky Mountain Branch		
Santa Clara University (1851) Santa Clara, CA	University of San Francisco (1855) San Francisco, CA	45 miles
	St. Joseph's College (1884) San Jose, CA	7 miles
	Loyola Marymount University (1911) Los Angeles, CA	347 miles
Gonzaga University (1887) Spokane, WA	Seattle University (1891) Seattle, WA	279 miles
Buffalo Branch		
Canisius College (1870) Buffalo, NY	John Carroll University (1886) Cleveland, OH	180 miles
	St. John's College (1898) Toledo, OH	315 miles

The answer lies in the Jesuit ethos of education. As in Europe, the American Jesuits served both the elite of society and the very poor. The downtown day schools were tuition-free; indeed, for much of the nineteenth century Jesuit schools were forbidden to charge tuition as a matter of policy set by Rome. The boarding schools could circumvent this prohibition by charging a fee for room and board, but this meant that they became elite schools accessible primarily to the wealthy. Even though Jesuits did waive the fees liberally and often allowed students to pay for their room and board with alternative forms of currency (like crops or food donations), the Jesuits' desire to make their brand of education accessible to everyone led them to open free day schools like Saint Joseph's in Philadelphia, Loyola in Baltimore, and Boston College. The same education available to elites in the suburbs would be available to the urban poor in the inner city. In many cases, revenue generated by the boarding schools (little though it was) supported the day schools, since they were all part of the same provincial network.

Ironically, many of the boarding schools that were once considered remote and inaccessible to the average student are now in the hearts of the busiest metro areas in the country. Santa Clara's campus, once surrounded by farmland, is now near the center of Silicon Valley. The property that the Jesuits acquired in and around Santa Clara Mission would be worth tens of millions of dollars if purchased today. Georgetown, which was originally on the outskirts of a small tobacco port, is now in one of the most expensive neighborhoods of the nation's capital. Urbanization and railroads have erased the distance between Fordham's Bronx campus and Manhattan. Whether through shrewdness or dumb luck, the Jesuits acquired property that became so valuable over time that many governments and investors have tried to take it from them; New York City commandeered a portion of Fordham's campus through eminent domain to create the New York Botanical Garden, and various government agencies have sought to acquire property from Holy Cross and Georgetown for transportation projects.[7]

A Midcentury Shift

Broadly speaking, as Philip Gleason observed, Jesuit colleges founded before 1850 were located in the South and in the Mississippi or Ohio River valleys—the two places where the earliest American Catholics settled. Those schools, moreover, were generally not founded by Jesuits but were simply handed over to them, after being originally established by local bishops and dioceses. After the 1850s, the pattern changes noticeably, with most Jesuit colleges located in industrial urban areas in the north, and founded directly by Jesuits from the beginning. As such, the colleges mirror the dramatic change that took place in American Catholicism, which transformed from a rural, mostly Southern religion into a working-class, northern, metropolitan one.[8]

As was the case elsewhere in the world, Jesuits responded and adapted to the needs of American Catholics as their character, demographics, and social role evolved over time. To understand the growth in Jesuit education is to understand the growth of American Catholicism. That pattern would continue into the twentieth century as Catholics—and Catholic education itself—continued to evolve from a culture on the American periphery to one that was increasingly mainstream. As the Catholic Church grew from an immigrant church to an American one, from a missionary organization to a social service one, and from a small-town church centered in places like Bardstown and Mobile to a big-city one centered in places like New York and Chicago, the Jesuits were always there.

---

7. Anthony J. Kuzniewski, SJ, *Thy Honored Name: A History of the College of the Holy Cross, 1843–1994* (Washington: Catholic University of America Press, 1999), 326. Shelley, *Fordham,* 128.

8. Gleason, "First Century," 44–45.

Part II:

European Origins

Every institution has an origin story that defines its identity. For American Jesuit colleges and universities, the origin story properly begins on the other side of the Atlantic. By the time they brought their trade to the United States, the Jesuits had over two centuries of experience operating schools in Europe, Asia, and elsewhere in the Americas. The US schools that they built in the 1700s and early 1800s were self-conscious replicas of the Jesuit educational projects elsewhere.

The schools were, initially, a European educational tradition transplanted onto American soil. Most of the early Jesuits who led and taught at these schools were Europeans who had left their homelands to become missionaries or to flee civil conflicts.[1] The relatively few nineteenth-century Jesuits born in the United States were often educated in Europe. They built their schools around European customs that were still standard practice in American education during the early 1800s, and they often continued to hold onto those traditions more than a century later, long after American higher education as a whole had begun to do things quite differently.

What is it that made Jesuit schools tick, then and now? In June, 1989, Jesuits from around the world gathered at Georgetown University to mark the 200th anniversary of Jesuit education in the United States. Speaking at the conference, the superior general of the Society of Jesus, Peter Hans Kolvenbach, SJ, defined Jesuit education simply and concisely: "It is education which is inspired by the spirituality of Ignatius Loyola."[2] Therefore, the first step in understanding the Jesuits' unique approach to education is to understand the life, legacy, and spirituality of their founder.

The Founder: St. Ignatius of Loyola

Iñigo Lopez de Loyola (known today as St. Ignatius of Loyola) was born in 1491 to a Basque family in northern Spain, the youngest of a large group of siblings. As the "de" in his name indicates, he was noble—growing up in the medieval Castle of Loyola to wealthy, landowning parents who boasted the coveted titles "Don" and "Doña" that Spanish society reserved for elites.[3]

The word "Loyola" itself is a contraction of the Spanish "lobo y olla," or "wolf and kettle." The image of two wolves dancing around a large black pot was part of the Loyola family crest, and that same image has become a symbol of the Jesuit order

---

1. Gleason, "First Century," 45.

2. William C. McFadden, SJ, "Introduction," in *Georgetown at Two Hundred: Faculty Reflections on the University's Future*, ed. William C. McFadden (Washington: Georgetown University Press, 1990), xv.

3. For more details, read *The Autobiography of St. Ignatius of Loyola*, ed. John C. Olin (New York: Fordham University Press, 1992).

today. Many American Jesuit colleges and universities incorporate the wolves and kettle into their own corporate seals: Gonzaga, Detroit Mercy, John Carroll, Saint Joseph's, San Francisco, Scranton, Seattle, and (not surprisingly) all three of the schools actually named "Loyola University." Four Jesuit Universities—Loyola (Chicago), Loyola (New Orleans), John Carroll, and Scranton—take the imagery even further and use the wolf as their athletic mascots.

Iñigo was, at first blush, an unlikely spiritual leader. Vain, fond of luxurious clothing, a notorious socialite, and in trouble with the law more than once during his teens and twenties, he stood a diminutive 5'2" and was bald by adulthood. His life was shaped by the circumstances of his time. King Ferdinand and Queen Isabella (best known for financing Christopher Columbus's voyage) were on the Spanish throne during Iñigo's formative years, and under their leadership, the modern country of Spain took shape—often through conquest and violence. During his lifetime, Iñigo would experience the Protestant Reformation in real time and would see firsthand the corruption of the Renaissance-era Catholic Church. However, unlike his contemporaries, Martin Luther and John Calvin, he sought to reform the Church from within, re-energizing it with a fresh spirituality without breaking from it.

During Iñigo's childhood, Spain was emerging from 700 years of Muslim rule and was frequently in a state of war, as Ferdinand and Isabella expelled the last remaining Muslims from the south and fought sporadically with the Bourbon kings of France to secure their northern border. One of the disputed territories claimed by both France and Spain was the Basque region—Iñigo's homeland. In 1521, at age 30, Iñigo fought for the Spanish at the battle of Pamplona—still one of the largest cities in the Basque region. During the battle, a French cannonball struck him directly, shattering the bones in one leg and seriously wounding the other.

The Shot Heard Round the World

That direct hit set off a chain of events that drastically changed Iñigo's life, and all of Catholicism in the process. Recuperating for months in the Castle of Loyola, Iñigo endured all of the pain inherent in sixteenth-century medicine as well as the psychological trauma of knowing that his luxurious, courtly life as a soldier was likely over. Twice, he ordered the doctors to re-break the leg in the hope of straightening it so that his disfigurement would not prevent him from wearing the fine clothes and armor he valued so much. It was not to be. The best efforts of the doctors still left him with a permanent limp and one leg that was forever shorter than the other.

Confined to his sickbed and with nothing better to do, Iñigo read the only books available to him: *The Life of Christ* by Ludolph the Carthusian and *Flos Sanctum*, a book about the lives of the saints. Anyone who has ever doubted the power of the printed word to change history need look no farther than its impact on Iñigo. Overcome by the heroic tales of sacrifice and honor, he began to see parallels between his own life as a soldier in service to the king and the lives of the saints who served an even higher power. Having nearly died for the cause of expanding Spain's territory, he began to contemplate whether he might dedicate himself to a nobler spiritual cause, and whether he could contribute more to the world by saving souls than by taking lives.

Having finally recuperated after more than a year, Iñigo entered a depressive and uncertain stage of life in which he lived for months as a reclusive hermit near the Spanish town of Manresa. Periods of intense thought and reflection left him ashamed of his youthful indiscretions, considering suicide, and seeking a new path that would allow him to serve the world more fully and meaningfully. In 1523, he came to the conclusion that his true calling was to go to the Holy Land and preach the Gospel in a region that was then under Turkish rule.

After traveling to Jerusalem, he met with the Franciscan priests who (then as now) serve as custodians of the ancient Christian holy sites. Much to his surprise, they advised him that his plan to act as a missionary to Muslims would only cause trouble for himself and for the (generally tolerated) Christian minority in the Turkish Empire. After only three weeks in the Middle East, demonstrating an adaptability and open-mindedness that would become a hallmark of the Jesuit spirit, Iñigo accepted the Franciscans' advice and returned to Spain, concluding that he had misinterpreted God's plan.[4]

Education Shows the Way

But if Iñigo was not meant to be in Jerusalem, where did he belong? More soul-searching led him to conclude that his lack of education was preventing him from serving God and the world as effectively as he should. In 1524, at age 33, he enrolled himself in school at Barcelona, and sat in classes alongside boys in their early teens and even younger.

Over the next three years, Iñigo bounced from one Spanish school to another, enrolling briefly at universities in Alcalá and Salamanca while also preaching in those communities. His evangelical work caught the attention of the Spanish Inquisition, which threw him in prison more than once while it investigated his theology. Ultimately, he was acquitted, as the investigations determined that his message, while novel in its approach, was not out of step with established Catholic teaching.

Leaving Spain in search of a more tolerant environment in 1528, Iñigo enrolled at the most prestigious university of his day—the University of Paris—where the 37-year-old at last settled into an atmosphere that seemed a good fit for his intellect and spirituality. He would spend seven years at the University, earning a master's degree and changing his name to the Latin "Ignatius."

In Paris, Ignatius would also build a social network that led directly to the founding of the Society of Jesus. He lived with two fellow university students (his "college roommates," if you will): a Spaniard, Francisco Javier (known today as St. Francis Xavier), and a Frenchman, Pierre Favre (known today as St. Peter Faber). Both men

---

4. David Mitchell, *The Jesuits: A History* (New York: F. Watts, 1981), 28.

were in their early twenties, roughly 15 years Ignatius's junior, and looked up to their older roommate as both a father figure and a spiritual guide. Ignatius taught them the spiritual practices he had learned during his years as a recluse, and they in turn influenced Ignatius's thinking with their bright minds and missionary zeal.

The Founding of the Order

Many college friends today join fraternities to cement their bonds to each other. In 1534, Ignatius and his followers (the group had grown to seven by that time) did something more profound: they took vows of poverty, chastity, and obedience at a chapel in Montmartre, France. That moment marks the de facto founding of the Society of Jesus. Six years later, the group had grown to eleven members, and Pope Paul III (after much lobbying in Rome) granted them official recognition as a religious order.

An immediate issue facing the group was what to call itself. Ultimately, the group reasoned that they were companions on a journey, a companionship cemented by their companionship with Jesus, and so they chose as their name (in Spanish) *la Compañía de Jesús*. This translated imperfectly into official Latin documents as *Societas Jesu*—hence the "S.J." that Jesuits write after their names. The fact that "S" and "J" are also the initials of the "Society of Jesus" in English is mere etymological coincidence.[5]

The name was controversial. More established religious orders like the Franciscans and Dominicans scoffed at its audacity. Who were these upstarts who dared to name their order after Jesus Himself? The term "Jesuit" was initially applied to the order by these other groups as a pejorative, but Ignatius's companions soon embraced it as their own.

The new order did many things outside the usual mold. Unlike other orders, the Jesuits did not wear a distinctive habit. While Franciscans and Dominicans could be easily identified by their belts, cowls, and other attire, Ignatius ordered his followers to dress in the standard priestly fashion of the day, which consisted of a black, floor-length cassock with sleeves and a square cap called a biretta (but without a tuft on top, as tufts were the mark of diocesan clergy). Even after the cassock had fallen out of fashion in Europe, many Jesuits continued to wear it; ironically, it became a kind of distinctive Jesuit "uniform" simply because other priests had largely abandoned it. In the nineteenth century, as Jesuit missionaries explored the American west, Native American groups commonly referred to them as the "blackrobes" because of their old-fashioned attire.

Even more significant than their style of dress was the Jesuits' unique approach to evangelization. Older orders like the Benedictines often shunned the world as corrupt, removing themselves from society and building isolated monasteries far from civilization. Ignatius's group intended from the beginning to be different: they would engage the world, be present with the people, and take their message to population

---

5. Ibid., 43.

centers, whether at home in Europe or overseas as missionaries. Believing that they could save souls most effectively by meeting the people where they were, they began to focus their work in the cities and towns, choosing to be *of* the cosmopolitan society they were trying to help rather than *apart* from it. The earliest Jesuits set a brave example: Francis Xavier traveled to India, China, Japan, and the East Indies. Peter Faber traveled throughout Europe, teaching and preaching in Spain, Italy, Germany, and elsewhere.

An Elite Corps

Older and frailer than his companions, Ignatius kept an eye on the practicality of his endeavors and cultivated sponsors for the Society.[6] His own background as a noble courtier helped him to charm wealthy Europeans, many of whom not only donated to the new missionary corps, but joined it themselves. Despite the vows of poverty that came with a Jesuit vocation, many wealthy young men were attracted to the new Society because it would enable them to live out their piety in cities they knew well and wanted to serve.

In part because of their appeal to the upper classes, Jesuits soon developed a reputation (not always fair) as elites who ministered to the rich and powerful. In European courts, they became spiritual advisors to royalty and confessors to kings and princes (who were, after all, sometimes related to them). Having the ears of so many heads of government gave the Jesuits an outsized influence on European politics and diplomacy. Within a century the Jesuit superior in Rome became known derisively as the "black pope"—a reference to the fact that he wore black in contrast to the pope's white, and held arguably as much real power.[7]

The missionary zeal of the Jesuits became legendary and almost militaristic in nature. Ignatius referred to himself and his followers as "soldiers of Christ," and often used metaphors from his own military background to describe their work. Jesuit missionaries helped to slow the progress of the Protestant Reformation, not only by lobbying kings and queens to remain loyal to the pope, but also by counterbalancing some of the appeal of Protestantism among the masses. Many regions of Poland, Lithuania, Spain, and Germany are (even today) much more Catholic and less Protestant than they otherwise might have been because of the efforts of those sixteenth-century Jesuit missionaries.

The Spiritual Exercises

The foundational document for Ignatius's particular brand of spirituality was the *Spiritual Exercises*. (In the original Spanish, the title has more satisfyingly alliterative balance: *Ejercicios Espirituales*.) Ignatius began work on the *Exercises* during his hermit

---

6. Ibid., 47.
7. Ibid., 47.

days in Manresa and continued to update them throughout his life; they are so central to the Jesuit experience and worldview that no description of Jesuit education could be complete without them. All Jesuits throughout history have been intimately familiar with the *Spiritual Exercises*, and the book had a profound influence on the Jesuit approach to teaching and learning.

The prose of the *Spiritual Exercises* is not particularly gripping. Ignatius was not a gifted writer; his words are dry and his sentences are short. That, combined with his frequent use of bullet points and sub-headings, makes the *Exercises* a quick read. The book resembles an instruction manual—and that was precisely its intent. It is not a work of theology, but a guidebook meant to show Jesuits how to lead others on their own spiritual journeys—full of practical advice about how to bring people to God and awaken within others a greater understanding of their own spiritual identity. In many ways, it is the corporate handbook of the Jesuit order.

The bulk of the *Spiritual Exercises* provides instructions for a Jesuit leading someone on a month-long spiritual retreat. Ignatius describes, week-by-week, what the Jesuit should do to help the retreatant grow in spiritual awareness. As such, the *Exercises* are not so much meant to be read as to be experienced. Ignatius takes a visceral, human approach to spirituality, inviting his readers to insert themselves into Biblical situations and visualize what it must have felt like to watch Jesus die on the cross or to journey with Mary and Joseph to Bethlehem, experiencing the fear and uncertainties they would have felt, and imagining the smells and sounds that would have been part of the experience.

While the *Exercises* are structured, they are not rigid; Ignatius cautions Jesuits to act as tutors rather than teachers, nudging others in the direction they need to go, but allowing them to make their own discoveries without being spoon-fed conclusions. Ignatius acknowledges that not everyone will progress at the same pace, and not everyone will complete the full course in a month. Jesuits are taught to be sympathetic to these individual differences and to adapt the pace to the level and needs of the person under their care.

The *Exercises* are full of gems of wisdom that remain as relevant today as they were centuries ago. Although it is impossible to summarize the *Exercises* in a page or two, there are broad themes that characterize Ignatian spirituality:[8]

- **Finding God in All Things.** For Ignatius, people are put on earth to bring glory to God, and to help others do the same. The Jesuit motto, *Ad Majorem Dei Gloriam* ("For the Greater Glory of God," often abbreviated as AMDG) stems from this principle. Ignatian spirituality holds that all parts of God's creation can be appropriated toward this end, and all forms of work can contribute to it. If we are adrift or unsatisfied with our lives, we must ask ourselves what we have done, and can do,

---

8. Margaret Gorman, "Influence of Ignatian Spirituality on Women's Teaching Orders in the United States," in *The Jesuit Tradition in Education and Missions*, ed. Christopher K. Chapple (Scranton: University of Scranton Press, 1993), 185–186.

to bring greater glory to God through improving the well-being of creation. A Jesuit can sense God's presence in everything, from the beauty of the night sky to the creative process that inspires artists to paint or musicians to compose.

- **Contemplation in Action.** Although this exact phrase does not appear in Ignatius's writing, Jesuits often use it to represent the Ignatian practice of putting one's prayer, intellect, and talents to practical use in the world. For Ignatius, prayer is not simply a conversation between a person and God during church services. All activities throughout the day—including the act of teaching, the act of learning, or the act of studying—can be a form of prayer. When we are honest in our business endeavors, when we use our position to help others, or when we simply work hard and do a good job in whatever task is required of us, we are in communication with our Creator and coming to a better realization of God's will and plan. Our contribution to the world professionally and personally represents an ongoing conversation with the God who put us on the earth for those very purposes.

  In the twentieth century, Pedro Arrupe, SJ, Superior General of the Society of Jesus, summarized this ancient practice in modern terms: "The paramount objective of Jesuit education must be to form men and women for others."[9] The phrase, "men and women for others" or "people for others" has become almost a universal mission statement for Jesuit schools, emphasizing that the privilege of education carries with it a responsibility to use one's knowledge for the broader benefit of society. Education does not exist for its own sake, but should be transformed into purposeful action. Those fortunate enough to possess knowledge and wisdom must put those virtues to use in service to others.

- **Discernment.** Fortunately, Jesuit tradition does not call for "contemplation in action" without giving some advice about "contemplation" itself. Several sections of the *Exercises* contain guidance on how to choose the right path when faced with a major decision. Ignatius encourages anyone making a difficult choice to imagine themselves on their deathbed, many years older and wiser than they are now. Which decision would they wish they had made? Which decision would give them the most peace of mind in the twilight of their lives? Similarly, he advises his readers to step back and view their own situation as if they were objective outsiders. What advice would they give, as a disinterested third party, to someone else in the same situation who sought their help?[10]

  For Ignatius, true discernment requires constant introspection and self-reflection. He encouraged all Jesuits to pray a nightly prayer he called the *Examen*, in which they mentally review their experiences of the day, recall their emotions, and reflect on what those emotions told them about God's plan in their lives. True fulfillment and contentment come from God; empty pleasures and fleeting joy are distractions to be avoided.

---

9. This quote is inscribed on the walls of Arrupe Hall at Georgetown University.

10. George Ganss, *The Spiritual Exercises of St. Ignatius: A Translation and Commentary* (Chicago: Loyola Press, 1992), 79. Much of this is section is based on the Ganss translation.

Befitting his background as a soldier, Ignatius often speaks of this struggle between good and evil—between the right choice and the wrong choice—in military imagery. Ignatius describes evil as "the Enemy," much like an adversary to be defeated on the battlefield. Soldiers of Christ, like all good soldiers, achieve victory over "the Enemy" by discerning their true marching orders and ignoring traps and false paths designed to lead them astray. In the conflict between good and evil, God always leads to the right path, while "the Enemy" attempts to derail God's plan and tempt us to stray from it.

- **Indifference.** Effective discernment requires objectivity. Like the great Stoic philosophers (including his fellow Iberian, Seneca), Ignatius promotes a sense of indifference to the ups and downs in life—avoiding over-attachment to joy or over-aversion to pain. He advises his followers to discern a deeper meaning in whatever successes or failures they experience, viewing both as steps on the path to a complete, meaningful life. Such detachment, sometimes dubbed **Ignatian Indifference,** is necessary for a truly complete understanding of one's own self. For Ignatius, all experiences, good and bad, can be an occasion to draw closer to God and realign one's life toward the correct path. This is not to say that all things happen for the best, but that even tragedies like the loss of a loved one can be an impetus to deepen our spirituality and discern the proper path for us.

- **Magis.** Translated as "more," *magis* is the Ignatian principle of striving for constant improvement, of never being satisfied with the status quo, and of constantly seeking something better. Considering the rapid pace at which Jesuits have always opened schools and other ministries, it is clear that at least some took this advice literally. However, at its core, the concept of *magis* is one that drives Jesuits to strive, internally and externally, ever closer to a full understanding of God's plan for the world.

- **Adaptability.** People are different, and Ignatius shuns a one-size-fits-all approach to spirituality. His is an empathetic spirituality, cognizant of human imperfections and individuality. The *Exercises* make many allowances for the different needs of retreatants, and leave a great deal to the discretion of the Jesuit leading the retreat. The Jesuits adapted their work to the circumstances and needs of the people they were helping.

Ignatius and his followers gave the *Spiritual Exercises* to anyone willing to participate, helping princes and paupers alike to develop their spirituality in the same way that a physical trainer might develop an athlete's muscles. Ignatius's handbook became a powerful weapon in his soldiers' evangelization campaigns.

The Spiritual Exercises and Education

It is easy to see how these spiritual principles translate into a philosophy of education. Striving constantly to improve; relating all learning to its ultimate purpose; transforming one's knowledge into purposeful action; seeking out the good in all things; empathizing with others; objectively discerning one's own talents; reflecting on what one has learned in search of true wisdom—these are the hallmarks of a Jesuit college experience. Indeed, they should be the hallmarks of any college education, and even non-Jesuit colleges increasingly recognize their value. Ignatius was not the only philosopher ever to discover these truths; many new-age secular philosophies, like Mindfulness, offer similar advice about reflection, contemplation, indifference, and self-awareness. These modern-day philosophies are largely offering a secularized version of the principles Ignatius and other religious thinkers discovered centuries ago.

Ignatius's approach to decision making is an ideal tool for guidance counselors, advisors, or anyone mentoring a young person in the formative stages of life. His philosophies about adaptability read like a primer on the tutorial process; any good tutor knows that it is often better to empower students to make their own discoveries than to spoon-feed them information. These spiritual techniques translate naturally into a classroom pedagogy and an approach to learning that emphasizes the unique needs of each individual.

Most specifically, an Ignatian pedagogy is one that embraces the care of the whole person—the Jesuit principle of *cura personalis*. Jesuit education acknowledges that people are multi-dimensional beings who need to be nurtured from all angles—intellectually, socially, emotionally, spiritually, and even physically. The purpose of a Jesuit school is not simply to develop the mind but also to develop a student's moral character, cultivating not just scholars but also upstanding citizens capable of becoming productive members of society and of their own families. A Jesuit college is in the business not just of imparting knowledge but of forming a virtuous human being. The phrase "cura personalis" does not appear in Ignatius's writings (or in any Jesuit document prior to 1934), but it gained popularity in Jesuit education in the 1980s and 1990s, and today serves as a kind of common mission statement for all Jesuit schools.[11]

Directly related to the principle of *cura personalis* is another traditional Jesuit principle, *Mens sana in corpore sano*—a phrase from the Roman poet Juvenal, translated as "a healthy mind in a healthy body." As might be expected in an all-male environment, early Jesuit schools emphasized athletics, often incorporating time for recreation. As intercollegiate athletics took shape in the nineteenth century, Jesuit colleges were known for their sports programs and competed successfully with state universities many times their size. It is no accident that, even today, twenty of the twenty-seven Jesuit colleges sponsor NCAA Division I athletics programs, even though most enroll far fewer students than the Division I average.

The First Jesuit Schools

Education was not, initially, one of Ignatius's goals for his Society. The first Jesuits saw themselves as missionaries whose most important goal was evangelization. However,

---

11. Barton T. Geger, SJ, "Cura Personalis: Some Ignatian Inspirations," *Jesuit Higher Education* 3, no. 2 (2014): 7–8.

as his own life neared its end and as the Society of Jesus matured, Ignatius and others began to realize that education could be an important element of their evangelism.

Exactly what constitutes the "first" Jesuit school is ambiguous. In 1546, a Jesuit who would eventually be known as St. Francis Borgia (of the noble Borgia family) opened a school in Gandía, Spain, which the pope declared a university a year later. Its purpose was to train Jesuits, although some non-Jesuit students were apparently enrolled there from the beginning.[12] While Gandía has claim to being the world's oldest Jesuit college, the historian Paul Grendler describes it as "little more than a paper university" because its instruction was extremely limited and only 13 Jesuits (including both teachers and students) lived there two years after its founding.[13]

The first Jesuit school founded explicitly to teach lay students came in 1547 in Messina, in northeastern Sicily. It was, initially, comparable to what we today would call a high school. The citizens of Messina had asked Ignatius to send five Jesuit teachers to staff a school for local boys; in exchange, the city would cover expenses and allow up to five young Jesuits to enroll as students. Ignatius, ever the pragmatist, accepted the generous offer after some lobbying by a Jesuit named Domenech, who had been doing missionary work in Sicily and seems to have been an advocate for the plan. We know relatively little about Domenech, but his humble efforts planted the seeds of a global trend, and Messina is commonly considered the "first" Jesuit school in the world. The Jesuits would soon open another school a few miles away in Palermo, and, in 1552, yet another in Rome. The Roman College (known today as the Gregorian University) was intended to be a higher-level school that went beyond the curriculum of the others, so it can be considered the first true Jesuit university.[14]

Historian John O'Malley, SJ has described the Jesuits as "the first teaching order within the Catholic church."[15] This is not to say that other orders did not teach; individual Franciscans and Dominicans were working as professors at the University of Paris and other medieval schools long before the Jesuits existed. But the Jesuits were, according to O'Malley, the first order of priests in Catholic history (1) to build a new network of schools from the ground up, (2) to open schools primarily for the purpose of teaching lay students, and (3) explicitly to designate "the staffing and management of schools (as) a true ministry of the order, indeed its primary ministry."[16] For other orders, teaching was a superfluous activity; for Jesuits, it became the Society's *raison d'etre*.

---

12. Claude Nicholas Pavur, *The Ratio Studiorum: the Official Plan for Jesuit Education* (St. Louis: Institute of Jesuit Sources, 2005), 217.

13. Paul F. Grendler, *The Jesuits and Italian Universities, 1548–1773* (Washington: Catholic University of America Press, 2017), 43.

14. John W. O'Malley, SJ, "How the First Jesuits Got Involved in Education," in *The Jesuit Ratio Studiorum: 400th Anniversary Perspectives*, ed. Vincent J. Duminuco, SJ (New York: Fordham University Press, 2000), 7. https://www.bc.edu/content/dam/files/top/church21/pdf/HowtheFirstJesuits BecameInvolvedinEducation.pdf

15. Ibid., 1.

16. Ibid., 3.

A letter from Jesuit headquarters in 1560 acknowledged what had by then become reality: that education was now the order's first priority and its main focus.[17] In stating this, the Jesuits were not abandoning their original purpose as missionaries, but refocusing that effort through different means. Ignatius and his companions had come to realize that educating the young was the most effective way to achieve their evangelical goals. Jesuits continued to serve as missionaries, but from this point on, opening a school was seen as a natural part of their missionary strategy wherever they went.

By 1579, the Jesuits were operating 144 educational institutions. By 1749, the number had grown to nearly 700[18] and had passed the 800 mark by the 1770s.[19] It was "the most immense (educational network) operating under a single aegis on an international basis that the world had ever seen."[20]

The Plan for Jesuit Education: *The Ratio Studiorum*

Such a large network of schools needed some form of quality control. Ignatius based the curriculum of his early colleges on the one he himself had followed during his student days at University of Paris. The colleges at Messina and Rome exchanged faculty and curriculum ideas almost from the time of their founding, so there was significant collaboration from the start.[21]

Beginning in 1584, almost three decades after Ignatius's death, a committee of six Jesuits met daily for about six months to draft a standard curriculum for all Jesuit schools. Early drafts were circulated in 1586 and 1591, and after feedback from Jesuit teachers around the world, a final version was published in 1599.

The *Ratio Studiorum*, as it was called, laid out a sequential, logical plan of study that allowed students to progress from one grade level to another, with more advanced work introduced every year. This seems perfectly normal to modern eyes, but in the sixteenth century, when education was often haphazard and unregulated, it was truly novel. In many respects, modern educators can thank the Jesuits for popularizing the idea of distinct "grades" in which students progress "up" to the next level at the end of each year.[22]

The *Ratio* envisions a seven-year plan of study, roughly corresponding to what we today would call a high school and college education combined. Most students would start the program in their early or mid-teens and finish in their twenties. The age of a student, however, was less important than his ability level; a grown man with

---

17. Ibid., 8.

18. Christopher K. Chapple, "Introduction," in *The Jesuit Tradition in Education and Missions*, ed. Christopher K. Chapple (Scranton: University of Scranton Press, 1993), 7.

19. O'Malley, "First Jesuits," 8.

20. Ibid., 8.

21. Pavur, *Ratio Studiorum*, 217–218. Kuzniewski, *Thy Honored Name*, 6.

22. O'Malley, "First Jesuits," 6.

no education would start at the beginning, even if this meant sitting in class with much younger boys. Moreover, progressing from one grade to another was not automatic; anyone who failed to master the material would be held back and forced to repeat the year.[23]

Just as we use the terms "freshman, sophomore, junior, and senior" to refer to the four years of high school, Jesuit schools used nicknames for each grade level. There were variations over time and place, but generally, the years were (with the rough modern-day equivalents in parentheses):

Year 1: Rudiments (freshman/sophomore year of high school)
Year 2: Third Humanities (junior year of high school)
Year 3: Second Humanities (senior year of high school)
Year 4: First Humanities (undergraduate year one)
Year 5: Poetry (undergraduate year two)
Year 6: Rhetoric (undergraduate year three)
Year 7: Philosophy (undergraduate year four, or graduate school)[24]

This nomenclature did vary over time and place, and at least some Jesuit schools referred to the lower grades as "First, Second, and Third Grammar," or made substitutions in the middle grades.[25] It is also important to remember that boys as young as eight or ten were sometimes admitted to the lower grades, allowing them to finish the full "college" course of study by their late teens. The notion that "college" study should take place between the ages of 18 and 22 is unique to the present day and was not widespread, even in America, until the twentieth century. Colleges like Yale commonly admitted boys aged 16 or younger for most of the nineteenth century and earlier.

Not all Jesuit schools offered the full seven-year course of study. Some were essentially "prep" schools that offered only the first few years of the curriculum, after which a student would be expected to move up to a higher school. Many students ended their education after year six or earlier, if for no other reason than their school did not offer anything further. Only the finest Jesuit universities offered year seven, philosophy, which was often reserved for students seeking the priesthood.

The *Ratio* emphasized Latin and Greek, and it required students to spend a good deal of time translating ancient texts and declining verbs. It even specified which authors (Homer, Vergil, Cicero, etc.) should be introduced and when. Ample time was devoted to mathematics and "natural philosophy" ("science," in today's language). The writings of St. Thomas Aquinas, the great medieval Dominican theologian, were given pride of place in philosophy courses. Befitting a Renaissance education, this cur-

---

23. Robert Emmett Curran, *A History of Georgetown University, Volume I* (Washington: Georgetown University Press, 2010), 45.

24. Edward J. Power, *Catholic Higher Education in America: A History* (New York: Appleton Century Crofts, 1972), 135–136.

25. Kuzniewski, *Thy Honored Name*, 7.

riculum was designed to exercise the mind through increasingly challenging grammar puzzles, texts, and memorization.

The most-valued skill a student could develop in the *Ratio* curriculum was public speaking—the Jesuit ideal of *eloquentia perfecta*. Oratorical exercises were standard fare in the classroom and a major part of how students were evaluated. Oral exams were the norm, and students frequently stood in front of their Jesuit teachers to perform speeches in Latin. Persuasive, fluent, articulate speech was the goal.

To our modern ears, this curriculum sounds archaic, but, in the Renaissance, it was a career-oriented form of education.[26] Anyone who wanted to participate in European elite society had to master the classical languages and public speaking; these were the hallmarks of a learned man. European nobles had long acquired these skills through private tutors, but the Jesuits were now democratizing them, making them available to all classes of society—a fact underscored by Ignatius's directive that Jesuit schools must not charge tuition. The Jesuits' insistence on teaching the trappings of elitism to everyone—both rich and poor—drew criticism from aristocrats who resented the notion that peasants were being trained to talk and walk with kings.[27] Among the prominent Europeans educated by the Jesuits in this era were Descartes, Molière, and Voltaire. (All three had disagreements with the Catholic Church later in life, but they developed their legendary intellects in Catholic school environments.)

Like Ignatius's *Spiritual Exercises*, the *Ratio Studiorum* makes allowance for individual differences. It provides order by prescribing specific lessons at sequential points in the process, but leaves room for creativity in presenting those lessons; teachers generally introduced the material as required, but adapted the pace to the needs and abilities of their class.[28] Like Ignatian spirituality in general, the *Ratio* was regimented but not rigid, structured but not inflexible—all in all, a humane approach to learning.

The *Ratio* also provides guidance on how to manage the schools administratively, addressing everything from the proper way to proctor exams to dealing with absenteeism. The administrative structure of a Jesuit school was standardized: the head of the college was the **rector,** who also served as the superior of the community of Jesuits. The number-two position was that of the ***prefect of studies***—roughly the equivalent of a modern-day dean, with responsibility for day-to-day curriculum implementation and student discipline. The remaining Jesuits primarily served as classroom teachers, though everyone in the community shared in the general business of maintaining the buildings, grounds, etc. In this structure, a team of five to ten Jesuits could easily manage a small school of a few dozen students. With a lean staff composed entirely of men who had taken a vow of poverty and worked for no pay, the schools could survive on a few donations without charging tuition.

---

26. Philip Gleason, *Contending with Modernity: Catholic Higher Education in the Twentieth Century* (New York: Oxford University Press, 1995), 5.

27. O'Malley, "First Jesuits," 9–10.

28. Shelley, *Fordham*, 74–75.

Another hallmark of Jesuit education prescribed in the *Ratio* is the awarding of prizes. The Jesuits emphasized competition among students as a learning tool, and contests were held for the best oration, best translation of a Latin text, etc.[29] Award ceremonies were important occasions and winners were held in high esteem. The *Ratio* directs: "(W)ith as much ceremony and in the presence of as large an assembly as possible, the names of the winners should be announced publicly, and their prizes should be given out in a dignified way to each of them as they proceed to center stage."[30] By the time Jesuit education had reached America, these ceremonies had become ritualized; students at the top of the class were honored, and those at the bottom were publicly shamed in front of their classmates as a form of motivation.

In short, the *Ratio Studiorum* was a Renaissance-era attempt to provide structure and order to the largest global network of schools that had ever been created to that point. It was revolutionary in the degree to which it made education widely accessible, and it nurtured the intellectual and spiritual growth of students through the most sophisticated means available at the time—heavily grounded in the humanities and classical languages, but also cutting-edge in the embryonic fields that would eventually be recognized as "science." Its ultimate goal, however, remained the evangelization and salvation of souls; for Jesuits, education was always a means to an end, never an end unto itself. Historian Gerald McKevitt, SJ summarizes it this way:

> The ambitious objective of Jesuit pedagogy, as formulated in the Ratio Studiorum . . . was "the full and harmonious development of all those faculties that are distinctive of man." In this plan, the development of the "whole man" was held up as the end and essence of education. The Jesuit system aimed not at vocational training, as its practitioners never tired of explaining, nor did it seek the "mere accumulation of learning": its goal was the development of the student's "faculties" and the "training of his character." "The acquisition of knowledge, though it necessarily accompanies any right system of education, is a secondary result of education. Learning is an instrument of education, not its end. The end is culture, and mental and moral development."[31]

Jesuits Arrive in the New World

Ignatius had founded a missionary order at the exact moment that Europeans were becoming aware of an entirely new world on the other side of the Atlantic. It was inevitable that Jesuits would find their way to the Americas. The first to arrive landed in the Portuguese colonies of Brazil in 1549. Before the end of the sixteenth century, other Jesuits would establish missions in the two main population centers of the New World: Peru and Mexico. Their most significant contributions to the Spanish Empire would

---

29. Pavur, *Ratio Studiorum*, 133–136.
30. Ibid., 136.
31. McKevitt, *University of Santa Clara*, 56.

come in Paraguay, where Jesuit mission communities known as *reducciones* became major staging grounds for evangelizing the indigenous people of South America.[32] Perhaps the most notable Jesuit in the Spanish colonies was St. Peter Claver, SJ, who arrived in what is today Colombia in 1610 and is best known for his ministry to slaves.

French Jesuits played a major role in the exploration of North America. The first arrived in what is today Canada in 1611, and true to form, established a school 24 years later.[33] Between 1642 and 1649, a total of eight French Jesuit missionaries, known collectively as the North American Martyrs, were captured and killed by the Iroquois nations of what is today Upstate New York; all are now recognized as saints. They are memorialized on the campuses of several Jesuit universities: a dormitory at Fordham is named Martyrs' Court in their honor, as is Georgetown's Copley Crypt Chapel of the North American Martyrs. The best-known of the eight martyrs, St. Isaac Jogues, SJ, is the namesake of a retreat house owned by Creighton University, and is depicted in stained glass windows from Georgetown to Loyola Marymount.

As the French expanded their influence over North America, a Jesuit, Father Jacques Marquette, SJ, co-led the first European expedition to the Mississippi River in 1673. Father Marquette founded two towns in what is today the Upper Peninsula of Michigan, both of which have unambiguously religious names that betray their Jesuit roots: Sault Ste. Marie and St. Ignace. Many parks, streets, and cities in the Midwest are named in Father Marquette's honor, as, of course, is the Jesuit university in Milwaukee.

Jesuits in the Thirteen Colonies

On March 25, 1634, nearly two hundred English settlers landed on the southern tip of what we today call Maryland. Like the Puritans who had landed on Plymouth Rock fourteen years earlier, and like the employees of the Virginia Company who had settled at Jamestown 27 years earlier, this hardy group had endured nearly five months at sea, crammed into tiny boats that they shared with horses, pigs, and not a few rats.

But there was something different about this group of settlers, compared to the few who came before them and the many who would come after. They were English Catholics, and they had come to the New World with the intention of founding a Catholic colony where they could practice their faith. Their voyage came exactly 100 years after Henry VIII had broken away from the Catholic Church, and by then, it was clear that Catholics in England were on the losing side of history.

The first settlers of Maryland included two priests: Fathers Andrew White, SJ, and John Gravenor, SJ. Both of these men, along with their companion, Brother Thomas Gervase, SJ, were members of a small, brave group of English Jesuits who put

---

32. Chapple, "Introduction," 8.
33. Ibid., 8.

themselves at some risk by ministering to the dwindling number of Catholics in their home country. Now, thanks to the help of a wealthy Catholic benefactor—Lord Baltimore, who had provided the money and the land for this voyage—they hoped to start anew.

One thing they forgot to bring with them was an appropriate crucifix; so, after landing, they quickly constructed a makeshift cross out of spare iron from the ship. This simple cross stood over them as Father White celebrated the first Catholic Mass ever said in the English colonies. Today, that same cross, inscribed in Latin, hangs behind glass in Georgetown University's Dahlgren Chapel.

They named their capital St. Mary's City, and their colony, Maryland. Officially, the colony was named after Henrietta Maria, the Catholic wife of King Charles I. Historians have debated whether the name "Maryland" was truly meant to honor "Henrietta Maria" or the Virgin Mary. This author, for one, finds it impossible to believe that a group of devout Catholics, who had great devotion to the Virgin Mary and unapologetically named their capital city "St. Mary's," would somehow choose the name "Maryland" to refer to anyone else. Of course, openly naming an English colony after a Catholic religious icon would have raised eyebrows in Protestant England, and the Queen's second name provided a plausible justification.

The Jesuits are the only Catholic religious order that can claim to have had a significant impact in the thirteen English colonies that eventually became the United States. The small Catholic population of the colonies was confined almost exclusively to Maryland, but even there, in a colony designated specifically for them, Catholics did not have complete freedom. Shortly after Maryland was established, the Puritan radical Oliver Cromwell seized power in London and soon cracked down on Catholic religious practice as well as Catholic education. His prohibitions applied in the English colonies just as they applied in England, which meant that Catholic education was almost immediately illegal in the Catholic colony.

Maryland Jesuits skirted these laws and established underground schools, which represent the beginnings of Catholic education in the United States. Some teaching and preaching took place at St. Mary's City as early as 1634, and eventually, short-lived schools opened on plantations in Calverton Manor (1640), Newtown Manor (one in 1650 and another in 1677), and Bohemia Manor (1745). Another briefly operated in New York in the late 1680s.[34] None of these academies would have qualified as a college by any definition—they were simply rooms in farmhouses—although the basic curriculum they offered would have been based on the *Ratio Studiorum*. Nearly 300 years later, the president of Georgetown University, W. Coleman Nevils, SJ, would argue that the early Maryland Jesuit academies were intrinsically linked to Georgetown's history and that 1634 should be considered the true founding date of the University, stretching its origin all the way back to the beginnings of the Jesuit

---

34. Arthur A. Weiss, SJ, "Jesuit Mission Years in New York State 1654–1879," *Woodstock Letters* LXXV, no. 1 (1 March 1946): 14–16.

educational experiment in America. Conveniently, this would have made Georgetown the oldest university in the country, beating Harvard by two years. Nevils went so far as to inscribe his version of history in stone above the front entrance of Georgetown's White-Gravenor Hall, which states that the University was "Founded 1634" and "Established 1789."[35]

Early Jesuit academies were not located on plantations by accident. Unlike neighboring Virginia, which supported the Anglican Church through tax dollars, Maryland had no established church and gave no money to Catholics. The Jesuits had to raise their own funds, and they did so in one of the only economically viable ways available to them in a rural southern colony: agriculture. They acquired vast estates with thousands of acres of farmland; one of the first (in 1636) was named St. Inigoes Manor and was located in close proximity to St. Mary's City. A gift from the chief of the Patuxent Indians deeded the Jesuits a significant amount of property at Mattapany in 1639.[36] Over the next century, the Jesuits acquired many plantations, the largest of which were St. Thomas Manor in the Port Tobacco area, Newtown Manor in the south near St. Mary's, and Whitemarsh in Prince George's County.[37] Their lands ranged throughout southern Maryland and the Eastern Shore. Some of that property remained under Jesuit ownership until 2009, when the Maryland Province of the Society of Jesus sold more than 4,400 acres in St. Mary's and Charles Counties to the State of Maryland for $57 million, intending to use the proceeds to care for aging Jesuits.[38]

These plantations could not have been sustainable or profitable if not for slave labor. Like other colonial Southerners, early Jesuits used slaves to work their fields. Over the course of two centuries, the Maryland Jesuits would come to own hundreds of men and women, most of whom lived on the plantations and were sometimes exchanged between one plantation and another.[39] They baptized their slaves and presided over slave wedding ceremonies, although this recognition of the slaves' humanity is, to modern eyes, hard to reconcile with the condition of slavery itself.[40] The long history of Jesuit slave ownership would eventually drive a wedge between the Jesuits themselves, especially in the years leading up to the Civil War, when many Jesuits came to recognize slavery as unjust. That story will be told in more detail in the chapters ahead.

---

35. Robert Emmett Curran, *A History of Georgetown University, Volume II* (Washington: Georgetown University Press, 2010), 147.

36. William Warner, *At Peace with All Their Neighbors: Catholics and Catholicism in the National Capital, 1787–1860* (Washington: Georgetown University Press, 1994), 37.

37. Ibid., 47.

38. "State Buys 4,400 Acres of Waterfront from Jesuits," *Washington Examiner*, January 29, 2009. https://www.washingtonexaminer.com/state-buys-4-400-acres-of-waterfront-from-jesuits

39. Edward F. Beckett, SJ, "Listening to Our History: Inculturation and Jesuit Slaveholding," *Studies in the Spirituality of the Jesuits* 28, no. 5 (November 1996): 13.

40. Warner, *At Peace*, 89.

The Jesuit manor houses became de facto chapels (since Catholics who worshiped in the privacy of their homes were tolerated under English law), and Catholic colonists from the immediate area traveled on horseback to the plantations for Sunday Mass. However, the Catholic population of Maryland was so diffuse that Jesuits frequently had to travel hundreds of miles to visit parishioners, many of whom were lucky to see their priest for Mass and confession once per month.[41] Proceeds from the plantations were used not simply to enrich the Jesuits, but to finance this travel and to provide books, tutoring, and other services to colonial Catholics.[42]

The Catholic (and Jesuit) contribution to the thirteen colonies is in many ways a typical American story, but also underappreciated, even by Catholics themselves. What Plymouth Rock is to American Protestants, St. Mary's City is to American Catholics; the role of the *Mayflower* in US history is comparable to the role of the Jesuits' two ships, the *Ark* and the *Dove*. Although the Maryland Jesuits in later years made some effort to promote the study of their history (Georgetown held an elaborate celebration marking the tercentennial of the landing in 1934, for example),[43] the Catholic experience never quite entered into the American creation story as widely as did the story of the Puritans and the *Mayflower*. Part of the reason for this, no doubt, is the important role that Harvard and other Boston institutions played in the writing of American history; Harvard faculty naturally emphasized the history of their own home state, Massachusetts. However, it also reveals anti-Catholic bias among early American historians, who largely overlooked the contributions of colonial Catholics. Today, although it is far less well-known than, say, Colonial Williamsburg, historic St. Mary's City is maintained as a historic park by the State of Maryland.

Feeder Schools: Newtown Manor, Bohemia Manor, and St. Omer's

Since the Maryland Jesuits were English, they fell under the authority of the English Jesuit province. Due to the difficulties of operating a Catholic school in their own country, the English Jesuits opened a college in what is today Belgium in 1593. Officially called "The English Jesuit College of St. Omer," it offered the *Ratio Studiorum* curriculum to expatriate English boys who were willing to cross the English Channel. Though instruction was in Latin, the students and faculty commonly spoke English to each other outside of the classroom.

St. Omer's was therefore the college that a young Maryland Catholic boy would aspire to attend. For a generation of colonial Marylanders who could afford such a

---

41. Georgetown University Library, "The American Mission: Maryland Jesuits from Andrew White to John Carroll," undated, https://www.library.georgetown.edu/exhibition/american-mission-maryland-jesuits-andrew-white-john-carroll

42. Warner, *At Peace*, 12.

43. Curran, *History of Georgetown Vol. II*, 148.

privilege, St. Omer's was the destination after a boy had exhausted the resources of the tiny Jesuit academies in the colonies.

By the 1700s, as the colony was beginning to mature, this process had settled into something of a routine. The eighteenth-century Jesuits operated academies at two Maryland farmhouses: Newtown Manor (non-continuously from about 1650 to 1704) and at Bohemia Manor (founded sometime around 1745 and closed around a decade later). These schools offered a rudimentary elementary education resembling the first few years of the *Ratio Studiorum*, after which the most promising students were sent across the sea to complete their studies at St. Omer's. Some of the most important leaders of the early American Church were educated this way; in their boyhood, John Carroll, Leonard and Francis Neale, and other founding fathers of American Catholicism enrolled at Bohemia Manor during its short life.

There was only one problem: all of this was illegal in Maryland. By the 1700s, Catholics were an openly oppressed minority in their own colony. At the time of its founding, Maryland was ahead of its time in that its original Catholic settlers established no official state religion. (This was a matter of enlightened tolerance as well as enlightened self-interest, since any colony that was officially Catholic would have struggled to find support in the English government.) However, that decision would come back to haunt the Catholics generations later, as Protestant settlers came to outnumber them and took control of the Maryland government.

The Protestant majority came to resent the fact that Catholics had something resembling a formal school system, making them generally better educated than their Protestant neighbors.[44] In 1704 and 1756, the Maryland Legislature passed discriminatory laws that forced the closure of the Jesuit academy at Newtown Manor and fined any Catholics who sent their sons to Europe for a Catholic education. Catholics also paid double taxes on their property and were forbidden to inherit land unless they swore an oath of allegiance to the English king. Their taxes were used to fund Protestant churches, while the Jesuits of Maryland were left to fend for themselves and raise all of their money through their plantations. As a final indignity, Catholics were denied the vote.[45]

For all of these reasons, it is not surprising that the Jesuit academy at Bohemia Manor was located deep in the Maryland wilderness, just a stone's throw away from the Pennsylvania border. Georgetown historian John Daley, SJ cites research speculating that the Jesuits deliberately built their school in that remote location to avoid scrutiny. Moreover, they could easily escape into more tolerant Pennsylvania if the authorities ever came knocking.[46] It is also not surprising that Catholics in general supported the American Revolution and its promise of religious freedom.[47]

---

44. Warner, *At Peace*, 16.
45. Daley, *Georgetown University*, xv–8.
46. Ibid., 4–5. Georgetown University Library, "American Mission."
47. Georgetown University Library, "American Mission."

Two Worlds Turned Upside Down:
Suppression in Rome and Revolution at Home

In 1773, on the eve of the Revolutionary War, there were twenty-three Jesuits in the thirteen colonies—concentrated in Maryland and Pennsylvania.[48] They represented virtually all of the Catholic priests in the English-speaking part of North America. That year, while most of the colonies were preoccupied with the looming conflict with the British, the Maryland Jesuits received news that must have shaken them to their core: the Society of Jesus was no more. It had been suppressed by Pope Clement XIV, and the Jesuits were, by order of Rome, disbanded worldwide. All Jesuit priests would be forced to sign a document stripping them of their membership in the Society, and while they would remain Catholic priests, they would no longer be formally tied to the Jesuit tradition or to each other.

This decision by the pope deserves some explanation. At first glance, it seems self-defeating for the Catholic Church to cut off its most visible and influential branch. By the eighteenth century, the Jesuits were the largest single order of Catholic priests and were spreading Catholicism effectively as missionaries from Asia to the Americas. Their suppression would be a massive and costly undertaking, resulting in the uprooting or reorganization of hundreds of parishes, schools, and other ministries across five continents. The reasoning behind that decision was as complex and diverse as the Jesuit influence itself.

The first issue was political. European royalty felt threatened by the Society's influence over average citizens, and the pope was under increasing pressure to step in and curtail Jesuit power. Even before the Society was suppressed worldwide, individual heads of state expelled the Jesuits wholly or partly from their territories—first in Portugal, then in France (including the French colony of Louisiana), Spain, Naples, and Parma.[49] Of particular concern to these secular rulers was the Jesuits' growing power in non-spiritual matters; the Society had virtually monopolized foreign trade on the Caribbean island of Martinique and was dominating commerce with Japan. In an age of exploration, Jesuits developed a reputation as greedy merchantmen amassing riches that the royals wanted for themselves.[50]

Compounding this issue was the characteristic Jesuit pride, which an eighteenth-century Italian Jesuit, Giulio Cesare Cordara, SJ, described as "the hidden sore spot for the Society."[51] Arrogance ran high in the ranks of the Church's largest order, which often preached its own superiority as fervently as it preached the Gospel. In the eyes of many observers, the Jesuit order was too preoccupied with its own growth and

---

48. Ibid.

49. Daley, *Georgetown University*, 17.

50. Giulio Cesare Cordara, SJ, *On the Suppression of the Society of Jesus: A Contemporary Account*, trans. John P. Murphy, SJ (Chicago: Loyola Press, 1999), 172.

51. Ibid., 178.

glory, leaving it susceptible to criticism that it was acting in its own best interest instead of the Church's. In other words, Jesuits were accused of being not "Catholic" enough. Cordara wrote in the 1700s:

> Many accuse the Jesuits for propounding moral teaching that was too lax and too accommodating to human passions. By this device, they kept saying, Jesuits inveigled entrance into the courts of monarchs, attracted large followings for themselves, and everywhere subjected people to their influence.[52]

There was some validity to this argument. Some of the Jesuits' popularity did indeed stem from the permissive, worldly version of Catholic theology that they preached, and in some of their missionary work, Jesuits took generous liberties with Catholic theology as they tried to adapt its core principles to other cultures. The most notorious such case took place in China, where Jesuit missionaries combined elements of Christianity with the native Confucian and Buddhist traditions—drawing sharp criticism from Popes Clement XI and Benedict XIV.

In his account of events, however, Cordara, defended Jesuit "laxity" in doctrinal matters by arguing that most Jesuits had done nothing more than emulate the merciful example of Christ Himself. What was perceived as doctrinal laxity was, in his view, Christian mercy:

> While Jesuits professed kindness toward their neighbor, it was the kindness which our Divine Teacher taught by word and deed. They condemned severity, but only the severity which Christ himself reproached in the Pharisees who demanded that the minutest detail of the law be observed. They exhorted to the more perfect, they did not require it. . . . They denied the sacraments to no one provided he was penitent and sorrowful. They drove no one to despair over the forgiveness of his sins and hope for his salvation. For that reason great throngs of penitents flocked to them.[53]

Other Catholic religious orders of the day often harbored jealousy toward the Jesuits and pushed for their suppression. Cordara writes that Rome was full of "very many from every order, but especially from the monks who either openly or secretly were striving for our destruction."[54] Naturally, there was always rivalry between the Jesuits and other religious orders, but by the 1700s, it had grown into a competition that the Jesuits were clearly winning in terms of numbers and influence. This eventually united the other orders against them. As members of these other orders ascended in the church hierarchy, they brought their prejudices with them, resulting in a strong anti-Jesuit sentiment within the power centers of the Church.

---

52. Ibid., 174.
53. Ibid., 174.
54. Ibid., 168.

St. Ignatius had discouraged his Jesuits from seeking positions in the church hierarchy, which he saw rightfully as corrupt. Indeed, despite the Jesuits' huge influence over Catholicism, no Jesuit ever served as pope until 2013, when the Argentine Jorge Bergoglio, SJ became Pope Francis. This meant both that Jesuits tended to operate outside of the hierarchy and that they were not well-represented within it. While Benedictines and Dominicans rose through the ranks to become members of the Roman curia and even popes, there were few if any Jesuit voices at the table. Pope Clement XIV was himself a Franciscan.

Effects of the Suppression in Maryland

For the twenty-three ex-Jesuits in the English colonies, the suppression had a number of immediate effects. First was a secular legal matter. Since the Society of Jesus no longer existed as a corporate entity, all of its vast property in Maryland was in limbo. In most cases, at least initially, individual priests simply took control of the various plantations and held them legally in their own names. Eventually, the ex-Jesuits formed a corporation, the Corporation of the Roman Catholic Clergy of Maryland, to hold the land. They continued to live and work on the estates, but they met as a group regularly on the plantation in Whitemarsh, Maryland, to make decisions. Although these men were no longer Jesuits bound by vows to each other, they in many ways still acted as if they were, and managed Church assets collectively. It was a quasi-democratic beginning for the American clergy, and Whitemarsh became a kind of quasi-capital for Catholic activity in the emerging United States.

There was almost immediately a dispute among the ex-Jesuits about what to do with their property. Some held out hope that the pope's suppression was only temporary, and felt that all estates should be held intact so that they could be returned to the Society of Jesus if and when the Society was ever restored. Others believed that the land should be used to support the embryonic Catholic Church in the new country—whether by selling it to raise money, or by building churches on the property. The plantations were effectively the only major assets the American church had, and there were heated arguments at Whitemarsh about whether the clergy should be in the business of managing farms or building proper worship facilities for the faithful.[55]

A second issue was where the twenty or so Catholic priests in America belonged within the worldwide Church. Although they were no longer Jesuits, they were still ordained Catholic clergy. But in the upheaval of the American Revolution, it was unclear whether they were even living in a legitimate country, let alone which Catholic bishop in Europe should have jurisdiction over their mission. Their former superiors, the English Catholic hierarchy in London, more or less washed their hands of any responsibility for the rebellious Americans.[56]

---

55. Daley, *Georgetown University*, 25–28.
56. Ibid., 22.

In the resulting power vacuum, the man who had been acting as the superior of the Jesuit community before suppression, Father John Lewis, SJ, became the de facto leader of the small band of priests. The double blow of canonical upheaval in Rome and political upheaval in the colonies had left the American ex-Jesuits orphaned on both sides, and the future of American Catholicism was in doubt. As Daley has written, "The Church in the United States could scarcely ever be placed again in so perilous a position as that which it faced at the time of the suppression of the Jesuits in 1773."[57]

Hope for the Future

Yet there was hope. As it happened, the Jesuits were not suppressed worldwide—not completely. A small remnant found refuge in an unlikely place: Russia. At the time, the Russian Empire included several predominantly Catholic territories in what is today Poland, Lithuania, and Belarus, where the Jesuits provided most of the free schooling. Seeing the importance of the Jesuits to her country's education system, Russian Empress Catherine the Great refused to accept the pope's order of suppression. She decreed that the Jesuit order would remain alive and well in lands under her jurisdiction. Thus, a Catholic religious order that had been shunned by Catholic monarchs was protected from total obliteration through the efforts of an Orthodox Christian empire led by a woman who had been raised as a German-speaking Lutheran. It was a tenuous lifeline, but one that kept hope alive in Maryland and elsewhere. Somewhere in the world, there were still Jesuits teaching and preaching as they always had.

Years later, in 1801, Pope Pius VII would recognize the Russian branch of the Society of Jesus as legitimate. This meant that the Jesuits still technically existed, and it was possible for any priest—anywhere in the world—to become a Jesuit by affiliating with the Russian order. This was all the ex-Jesuits in Maryland needed to hear. In 1802, a group of thirteen aging Maryland priests formally petitioned to rejoin the Jesuits via the Russian loophole. Three years, later, the superior of the Jesuit order in Russia formally accepted them. The joy they must have felt, learning that their identity had been officially restored almost thirty years after it been wiped away, must have been overwhelming. They were Jesuits again! By 1814, even that tenuous lifeline was no longer necessary. That year, in the reactionary spirit that characterized the early nineteenth century and foretold a return to the old ways in post-Napoleonic Europe, Pope Pius VII fully restored the Society of Jesus worldwide.[58]

A second cause for hope came from closer to home, in the form of a competent American leader. John Carroll, the first Catholic bishop and later archbishop of the United States, had the unenviable task of leading the American church at a time when the nation's government and its small corps of Catholic clergy were both in disarray. Simultaneously, the American Revolution and the suppression of the Jesuits had sev-

---

57. Ibid., 21.
58. Ibid., 121–123.

ered most of the important political and religious ties that connected American Catholics to their roots in Europe. Amid heated debates about the future of the country in Philadelphia and about the future of the Church in Whitemarsh, Carroll proved himself to be the right man for his time. He made sense of the chaos and planted the seeds of a fully functioning Catholic Church in the young United States.

John Carroll—Marylander, ex-Jesuit, alumnus of the Jesuit academy at Bohemia Manor, and founder of Georgetown University—belongs in the pantheon of founding fathers like Washington, Franklin, and Jefferson who set in motion the institutions that would shape the emerging American culture. It is with him that the story of Jesuit education in America truly begins.

Part III:

Pioneer Colleges (1789–1865)

Overview, 1789–1865

The roughly seven decades between the founding of Georgetown University in 1789 and the end of the Civil War in 1865 were a period of some instability but relative prestige in American Jesuit higher education. During this time, the Jesuits founded or assumed control of twenty-five colleges, fourteen of which survive (in one form or another) to the present day. Among the modern-day Jesuit colleges and universities that trace their roots to this early era are Saint Louis, Holy Cross, Xavier, Spring Hill, Fordham, Santa Clara, Saint Joseph's (Philadelphia), Loyola (Maryland), the University of San Francisco, and Boston College.

At a time when America's largest cities were only small towns by modern standards, and when frontier settlers were pushing American influence further west, the Jesuits often arrived in new settlements in lockstep with the pioneers. The colleges they built were typically the first, and in some cases only, schools of any kind in their frontier communities.

On the East Coast, what was left of the historic Jesuit mission in Maryland survived the forty-year suppression by the Holy See, and the aging priests reentered the Jesuit order as soon as it was possible for them to do so. In 1814, the reestablished Society of Jesus took formal ownership of Georgetown after having held de facto control over it since its inception in 1789. In time, these East Coast Jesuits expanded their network, building sister colleges in New York, Massachusetts, Maryland, Pennsylvania, and downtown Washington, DC.

Meanwhile, another historic base of Jesuit activity—Louisiana—was reinvigorated with new French missionaries who not only built colleges in and around New Orleans, but also assumed control of Catholic colleges in Kentucky, Alabama, and New York City.

On the western frontier, new waves of European Jesuit missionaries arrived to evangelize the Native Americans and serve the Catholic settlers, building some of the region's first colleges in the process. The first American college of any kind to grant a bachelor's degree west of the Mississippi (Saint Louis University) and the first to grant a bachelor's degree on the West Coast (Santa Clara University) were both Jesuit projects. The pioneers who staffed those schools, mostly from Belgium and Italy, respectively, were among the first Europeans to visit the American west, the first to map the territory, and the first to have contact with the region's indigenous people.

None of this expansion came easily. The fledgling Jesuit colleges struggled financially and there were many false starts. Schools in New York City, downtown Washington, and Kentucky either closed for good or suspended operations for years at a time. Those schools that did survive were often beset by debt, a chronic shortage of faculty, and internal disagreements about how they should be run.

Where they did take root on the American frontier, Jesuit schools enjoyed a strong reputation. Indeed, because they were often the only colleges for miles around, Americans of all religious stripes—Catholics, Protestants, Jews, and others—sought to enroll their sons. The schools' student populations were small, but heavily international in nature. Georgetown enrolled many students from the Caribbean; Santa Clara enrolled students from Mexico and other parts of Latin America. At Saint Louis, French speakers outnumbered native English speakers for a whole generation. By and large, the Jesuit faculty at these colleges were European immigrants—not just from places like France, Ireland, and Italy, but from as far away as Poland and the Russian Empire. Jesuit colleges were some of the most cosmopolitan intellectual communities in America during the early 1800s.

The Jesuits' openness to the diversity of American society was not usually reciprocated. Anti-Catholic bigotry ran strong in America during this era, and riots broke out in Cincinnati, Boston, Philadelphia, and other places where Jesuits tried to establish a presence. Americans violently protested the growing influence of the Catholic Church and the waves of Irish immigrants rapidly changing the religious composition of the young country. Catholics were often physically unsafe in communities where explicitly anti-Catholic political parties (like the Know-Nothing Party) took control of local governments, and mobs and gangs took into their own hands what the politicians could not achieve through legal means. In this environment, Jesuit schools not only provided an alternative education for Catholics excluded from mainstream American colleges, but also provided a refuge where those students could feel safe in a society that openly discriminated against them.

The Jesuit curriculum at the time was roughly comparable to the curriculum offered elsewhere in America. The *Ratio Studiorum*'s emphasis on the rote study of Latin and Greek was not terribly different from the classical education offered at Protestant colleges like Yale and Princeton. Jesuit colleges arguably offered a better education than their Protestant counterparts, since their course offerings included electives like French and German at a time when most colleges generally ignored modern languages. Jesuit schools also offered what was, for the nineteenth century, a cutting-edge science education. Science in Italy and France was far ahead of anything offered in the United States at the time, and Jesuit colleges benefitted from the European roots of their faculty, who brought expertise in astronomy and chemistry along with the latest European books and lab equipment across the Atlantic.

Graduate school was, for the most part, a consideration for the future. This was a period in which undergraduate education reigned supreme. However, it was not undergraduate education as we understand it today. The minimum age of entry for most Jesuit colleges was around eight, and only a tiny handful of students successfully completed the six- or seven-year curriculum leading to the bachelor's degree. A majority of students enrolled for only a year or two at a time, meaning that these "colleges" were more like transient high schools than any college that we would recognize today.

Again, this was not unusual at a time when most American "colleges" catered to teens and preteens. Education as a whole was neither universal nor standardized in the antebellum United States. Both on the frontier and on the East Coast, it was a rare privilege to have any education outside the home. Public schools and community schoolhouses did not exist in most cities, let alone in rural areas. Those who could afford the privilege hired private tutors to teach their children at home, but the next best option was often to send a child away to one of the few functioning schools that actually existed.

In short, Jesuit colleges, while at the forefront of higher education at the time, were almost nothing like the institutions they would one day become. They were essentially high schools in which a dozen or so Jesuit priests, brothers, and scholastics watched over a small student body that rarely exceeded 200, comprised almost entirely of young teenagers. Their "campuses," such as they were, usually consisted of one or two buildings in which faculty and students both lived and studied.

Lastly, most of the Catholic story at this stage in history took place in the American South. Although the Jesuits' tolerance for ethnic and religious diversity was well ahead of its time in an era when the country was starkly divided along those lines, that tolerance did not always extend to race. Fourteen of the twenty-five Jesuit colleges founded before the Civil War were located in places where slavery was legal: Alabama, Kansas, Kentucky, Louisiana, Maryland, Missouri, and the District of Columbia. Catholicism at the time was primarily a Southern religion, with all the trappings of Southern life, including slave ownership. Slavery has been called America's original sin, and Jesuit colleges were touched by that sin as much as any institution in the antebellum United States.

The story of Catholic and Jesuit higher education in America properly begins with Georgetown University and its founder, Archbishop John Carroll, just after the American Revolution opened the door for Catholics to open schools legally in the United States.

John Carroll and Georgetown University (1789), Washington, DC

John Carroll was born in Maryland in 1735 to one of the wealthiest, most prominent Catholic families in the thirteen colonies. His cousin, Charles Carroll, was the only Catholic to sign the Declaration of Independence; his brother, Daniel Carroll, signed the US Constitution and represented Maryland in the US House of Representatives. Another cousin, Daniel Carroll of Duddington, owned much of the land that eventually became the District of Columbia and donated to the federal government the property on which the US Capitol sits today.[1]

John was educated at the illegal Jesuit academy at Bohemia Manor (where he appears on the rolls as "Jacky Carroll")[2] until age thirteen. Then, like other Maryland

---

1. Warner, *At Peace*, 16, 62–65.
2. Daley, *Georgetown University*, 13.

Catholics lucky enough to have that unique combination of ability and wealth, he was sent off to the English Jesuit College of St. Omer's in Belgium. He would live in Europe for the next twenty-six years, during which he entered the Society of Jesus and began what looked, at first, like a comfortable career as a teacher in European Jesuit schools.

But circumstances were not on John's side. In 1773, just two years after he made his final vows as a Jesuit, news of the Jesuit suppression came from Rome. Uprooted from his order, and hearing news about the coming war for independence in the land of his birth, Carroll set sail for the colonies in 1774. (There is an apocryphal story that Carroll's own mother did not recognize him when he finally came back to her as a grown man more than two decades after she sent him off to Europe as a thirteen-year-old.)[3]

A strong supporter of the revolution, Carroll contributed to the war effort by joining his cousin, Charles, along with Benjamin Franklin and Samuel Chase, on a diplomatic mission to Québec during the early days of the conflict. Their objective was to convince the French-speaking Catholics in Montréal, who had themselves lived under British rule since the end of the French and Indian War, to join in the revolution. Had they succeeded in convincing Québec to become the fourteenth American state, the consequences to world history would have been enormous; Canada as we know it might never have existed. The colonists in Québec, however, were not convinced that their fate would be any better as citizens of a Protestant, English-speaking United States than of a Protestant, English-speaking British Empire, and they chose not to join their neighbors in rebelling.

The Québec mission, although a failure, left a lasting impact on Carroll's life. Years later, when Benjamin Franklin was serving as the US Ambassador to France, word came that the pope was in search of a bishop to lead a new diocese in the independent United States. Franklin, who like most ambassadors in Paris had the ear of the Church hierarchy, recommended his old friend, John Carroll. The Church had some reservations about appointing an American, rather than a European, to this unprecedented post in the newly independent country, but Franklin convinced the Roman Curia that the US government would not interfere in ecclesial matters and the loyalty of an American-born bishop would not be suspect.[4] In 1789, Carroll became the first bishop of the Diocese of Baltimore—a single diocese that covered the entire country.

The task before Carroll was immense. He had only twenty-four priests under his jurisdiction, most of them aging ex-Jesuits, to serve an area from that stretched from modern-day Maine to Georgia. The priests were concentrated in the mid-Atlantic states; nineteen ex-Jesuits lived in Maryland, and the other five were in Pennsylvania.[5] Unfortunately, the Catholic population they served, while not geographically dispersed, was already larger than they could handle and likely to grow. Carroll estimated

---

3. Ibid., 14.

4. Curran, *History of Georgetown Vol. I*, 11.

5. Warner, *At Peace*, 9.

that there were 25,000 Catholics living in Maryland, Pennsylvania, and New York, many of them a day's journey or more from the nearest priest.[6]

More forward-thinking than his contemporaries, Carroll saw clearly what should have been obvious to all ex-Jesuits in the former colonies: American Catholics needed a school if they were to survive and thrive. The Diocese of Baltimore would have to educate its own, home-grown clergy or else it would remain reliant on European missionaries; lay Catholics would have to be educated if they were to contribute to American society as equals to Harvard- and Yale-educated Protestants. In short, Carroll's proposed Catholic college would fulfill the same role that the English Jesuit College at St. Omer's had filled during the colonial days—without requiring a weeks-long trip to Belgium.

Before becoming bishop, Carroll had had a difficult time convincing his fellow priests of the importance of this long-term vision. The elderly ex-Jesuits of Maryland were preoccupied with managing their 12,677 acres of plantations.[7] There was a clear power vacuum and an ambiguous chain of command in their ranks. Father John Lewis, the former superior of the Maryland Jesuits, still held some informal authority, but the real power was in the quasi-democratic government the priests set up in Whitemarsh, Maryland. Their periodic meetings at Whitemarsh between 1783 and 1784 had turned into something like a Catholic version of the Continental Congress, in which America's few remaining priests elected representatives to manage their assets and govern themselves.

All of this would change when Carroll was appointed "Superior of the Mission in the United States" in 1784 and then bishop in 1789.[8] Carroll had long been one of the most active voices at Whitemarsh;[9] now, he was unquestionably in charge, and spoke with all the authority of the pope's representative. He was excited by the possibilities the new republic offered to Catholics. For the first time since the 1600s, Catholics in America could vote, hold elected office, and open schools legally without constant threat of supervision by the state. Carroll intended to take full advantage of these freedoms.

The Plan for Georgetown

Even as Carroll dealt with the many issues on his plate as the first head of the American Church, his proposal for a college remained a priority—so much so that he described it in 1785 as "the object nearest my heart now."[10] His goal was to establish two schools: one general college that would prepare boys for every profession, and a seminary, which would specialize in the training of priests. The most promising boys from the college would graduate and move on to specialized study in the seminary;

---

6. Curran, *History of Georgetown Vol. I*, 10.
7. Ibid., 10–11. Warner, *At Peace*, 9.
8. Warner, *At Peace*, 9.
9. Daley, *Georgetown University*, 24–25.
10. Curran, *History of Georgetown Vol. I*, 14.

after being ordained priests, they would be available to teach in the college, so the two institutions would mutually reinforce each other in a perpetual cycle.

To modern ears, this doubling of the investment sounds like a waste of resources. Why build two schools instead of one, and why separate the seminarians from the other students? American Protestants had long trained ministers and laypeople on the same campuses at Princeton, Yale, and elsewhere. However, Catholic custom required Carroll to do things differently. During the Protestant Reformation, Catholics at the Council of Trent had resolved to do more to educate and profession-alize the clergy. As a result, since the 1500s it had been standard practice for most Catholic dioceses to sponsor stand-alone seminaries. These were often separate from "regular" colleges and located near the seat of the bishop, both to ensure quality and to cultivate an intense spiritual environment for the students. In this respect, by sep-arating his seminary from his college, Carroll was simply following Catholic custom.

Almost immediately, however, there were kinks in Carroll's plan. For one, it proved difficult to find faculty for two new schools simultaneously. Carroll at first had been optimistic that his old faculty colleagues from St. Omer's could send some Eng-lish ex-Jesuits as teachers. However, the College at St. Omer's had recently been shut down by Habsburg authorities and its faculty were still scrambling to regroup and staff another school in the Belgian town of Liège. They had no one to spare.[11]

A second problem came from the council at Whitemarsh. To fund the construc-tion of the two schools, Carroll had proposed selling some of the ex-Jesuit plantations in Maryland. But the elderly ex-Jesuits, led by the conservative Father Leonard Neale, refused to part with their cherished land, still hoping that it would one day be returned to a restored Society of Jesus.[12] (These political complications also help to explain why Carroll did not simply build a college campus on one of those plantations, as might have been logical.) Although the Whitemarsh priests did pass a resolution authorizing Carroll to establish a college, it would have to be funded through other means.

For the undergraduate college, Carroll identified Georgetown, Maryland as an appropriate location. Construction of the first building commenced in 1788, even before the deed to the property was formally transferred to Carroll on January 23, 1789—a date still recognized by Georgetown University as its formal "founding." At the time, the city of Georgetown was simply a tobacco port; the United States government had not yet decided where it would build a permanent capital. Carroll selected the location in part because Georgetown was easily accessible by water for most of the Catholics living in Maryland and Pennsylvania and because, ironically, he believed that it would offer a comparatively lower cost of living and less pollution than the bigger cities.[13] When word came in July of 1790 that Congress had carved the District of Columbia out of 100 square miles of Maryland and Virginia, bringing a purpose-built capital right to the col-

---

11. Ibid., 14.
12. Ibid., 14.
13. Ibid., 23.

lege's doorstep, no one was more surprised than Carroll. However, he was happy that his fortuitous decision had positioned his college so close to the seat of American power. Although there is no direct evidence that Carroll himself influenced the location of the District of Columbia, his cousin, Daniel Carroll of Duddington, was the largest landowner in the area and served on the commission that selected the site.[14]

And a splendid location it was, with or without the nation's capital. The high bluff overlooking the Potomac River, on a green, rolling hilltop convenient to, but not surrounded by, the city of Georgetown was a charming setting for a school. Carroll himself described it as "one of the most lovely situations, that imagination can frame." He added that, "On this Academy is built all my hope of permanency and success to our H(oly) Religion in the United States."[15]

The first building (later to be called "Old South") was small, built in the colonial style, and oriented with a beautiful view of the Potomac. It was followed by a much larger, similarly-designed colonial building ("Old North") in 1795. They were larger versions of the kind of structures in which most Maryland Catholics had lived since the 1600s and would have looked familiar to anyone raised in that culture, giving Georgetown "the composite air of a Southern plantation."[16]

The human infrastructure of the school was more difficult to build than the physical. Rebuffed in his efforts to recruit European teachers, Carroll was forced to draw his faculty from the tiny ranks of ex-Jesuits in Maryland. Unfortunately, most of them were elderly and unqualified to lead an academic institution. After some struggles, Carroll finally recruited Father Robert Plunkett, a thirty-nine-year-old ex-Jesuit who had recently arrived at Whitemarsh from England, to serve as the academy's first president. Plunkett thus has the distinction of being the first president of an American Jesuit college, even though his eighteen-month tenure in the position was otherwise unremarkable. As many historians have noted, Plunkett came to America to be a missionary, not an educator, and he was a better pastor than an academic.[17] He was succeeded by Father Robert Molyneaux, a 55-year-old ex-Jesuit who had ministered in parishes in Maryland and Pennsylvania.

The Seminary

By 1792, classes were finally underway at Georgetown, and Carroll had already begun to focus on the second half of his plan: a seminary. Carroll initially wanted to delay the opening of the seminary until the first Georgetown graduates were in a position to enroll, but circumstances provided him with an opportunity ahead of schedule that he could not pass up.

---

14. Ibid., 23–24. Warner, *At Peace*, 62–65.

15. As quoted in Daley, *Georgetown University*, 47.

16. Joseph T. Durkin, SJ, *Georgetown University: The Middle Years (1840–1900)* (Washington: Georgetown University Press, 1963), 1.

17. Curran, *History of Georgetown Vol. I*, 34–35. Daley, *Georgetown University*, 61–62.

By 1789, the revolutionary spirit that began in America had spread to France. In the chaos of the French Revolution, large numbers of French Catholic priests were killed or expelled. One group in peril was the Society of St. Sulpice, better known as the Sulpicians. The Sulpician order is unusual among Catholic religious orders in that its priests focus their ministry on the education of other priests. They did—and still do—operate seminaries.

Carroll was visiting England in 1790 to be formally consecrated as a bishop when he met James Andrew Emery, SS, superior general of the Sulpicians. Emery asked Carroll whether the new American diocese would be willing to give refuge to a group of Sulpicians fleeing France. Carroll was at first hesitant; his seminary was not ready to get off the ground just yet. But the availability of a group of priests who specialized in seminary education was too fortuitous to pass up, and in 1791, a group of nine Sulpicians—four priests and five seminarians—arrived in Baltimore.[18]

Several Sulpicians would teach at Georgetown during the early years of the school. In fact, Sulpicians outnumbered ex-Jesuits on Georgetown's small first faculty by a count of four to three.[19] However, their main objective remained the seminary. St. Mary's Seminary opened in Baltimore in 1791, a bit earlier than Carroll would have liked. Since there were as yet few candidates for the priesthood in America, Carroll gave permission for the seminary to open a college division, despite the fact that it would be competing directly with Georgetown for students. The hope was that the lay college students could temporarily keep the Baltimore school afloat until the day finally came when St. Mary's had enough seminarians to focus entirely on educating priests.

As it happened, that "temporary" college at St. Mary's lasted more than fifty years until 1852, and the competition for students prevented Georgetown from growing as quickly as it might have otherwise. In part, this was because fewer Georgetown graduates entered the priesthood than Carroll originally hoped; the seminary would not have been financially viable without its college division for decades. However, another factor was the rivalry between the ex-Jesuits and the Sulpicians, which manifested itself in the rivalry between the two schools located less than fifty miles apart.

The ex-Jesuits at Whitemarsh who still controlled Georgetown's board of directors never fully accepted the Sulpicians in their midst. The rivalry had as much to do with nationality (French against English) as it did with seniority (old Maryland establishment against newly arrived European upstarts).[20] It came to a head most directly in the clash over Georgetown's first and only Sulpician president, Guillaume DuBourg, SS.

---

18. Daley, *Georgetown University*, 73–75.
19. Curran, *History of Georgetown Vol. I*, 35.
20. Ibid., 54.

Guillaume DuBourg: Georgetown President and Founder of Saint Louis University

The Sulpician Father Guillaume DuBourg, SS had more impact on the first few decades of American Jesuit education than perhaps any other non-Jesuit. He is a founding father of the American Church; in addition to succeeding Robert Molyneaux as the third president of Georgetown, he also served as the first Catholic bishop (in effect) of both New Orleans and St. Louis, in which capacity he founded the second-oldest Jesuit college in the United States, Saint Louis University. The main building at Saint Louis University, DuBourg Hall, is named in his honor.

DuBourg, a Frenchman born in colonial Haiti, became president of Georgetown in 1796 and made a considerable impact on the school despite a tenure of only two years. He helped to establish Georgetown as a bedrock cultural institution in the nation's capital. During his presidency, George Washington's nephews (Augustine and Bushrod) enrolled at the college, and DuBourg himself was invited to Mount Vernon as a dinner guest. In 1797, Washington paid a return visit and addressed the student body (including his nephews) from the steps of the Old North building, becoming the first of more than a dozen US presidents to visit the Georgetown campus.

Under DuBourg's leadership, the college greatly expanded its reputation, facilities, faculty . . . and debt. A spendthrift fond of extravagant purchases, DuBourg soon irritated the ex-Jesuits at Whitemarsh who ultimately had to pay for it all. The situation was exacerbated in 1798, when the State of Maryland acknowledged legally that Georgetown College was the property of the Corporation of Roman Catholic Clergyman headquartered at Whitemarsh. Flexing their muscles as the legal owners of the college, the Whitemarsh ex-Jesuits micromanaged DuBourg to such an extent that he resigned later that year.[21]

After leaving Georgetown, DuBourg served as an effective president of St. Mary's College in Baltimore (the ultimate revenge against the ex-Jesuits who had all but ousted him), but he was destined for even higher office. His unique résumé as a native French-speaker intimately familiar with American culture caught the eye of Church authorities in Rome, especially after the Louisiana Purchase of 1803 transformed thousands of French Catholics in the Mississippi valley into American citizens overnight. In 1815, DuBourg was named bishop of "Louisiana and the Floridas," a diocese that stretched over tens of thousands of miles of newly acquired American territory.

Origins of Saint Louis University (1818), St. Louis, Missouri

To the surprise of most Catholics in Louisiana, the newly promoted Bishop DuBourg chose not to live in the largest city under his jurisdiction—New Orleans—and settled instead in St. Louis, then a much smaller frontier town. New Orleans at

---

21. Ibid., 50–54.

the time was a literal and figurative swamp—full of malaria and decades of entrenched corruption—and DuBourg felt that St. Louis offered a better blank slate on which to build a diocese.[22]

Like Carroll in the east, DuBourg prioritized education and sought to open both a seminary and a college. Saint Louis College opened inauspiciously in 1818, housed in the home of a local widow of Spanish descent, Mrs. Alvarez.[23] At first, the college enrolled both seminarians and lay teens, though the seminarians were soon concentrated at the newly opened St. Mary's Seminary in Perryville, Missouri. By the time Missouri achieved statehood in 1821, Saint Louis College, now strictly a school for the laity, had moved into a two-story brick building of its own.[24]

Saint Louis College was not yet a Jesuit school—the Jesuits were still officially suppressed everywhere but Russia—so it operated under the control of a handful of diocesan priests and some Vincentian missionaries. Father Francois Niel, a French immigrant ordained by DuBourg in St. Louis, served as its first president, leading a faculty that included three other priests and one seminarian. Even though its student body was small, the clergy alone were unable to staff the school, and four lay teachers rounded out the faculty.[25]

Just five years after its opening, in 1823, Saint Louis College made a historic hire: Elihu Shepard. Shepard, a Protestant, holds the distinction of being the first non-Catholic to teach at one of the twenty-seven Jesuit colleges in the United States. His appointment was partly a matter of necessity, since there were so few educated men on the frontier capable of teaching at the college level. He was also the only native English speaker on the faculty—an important asset to the school at a time when all other professors and most students spoke French.[26]

As the only college in the largest US city west of the Mississippi, Saint Louis saw itself as a community asset, offering free education to the city's poorest boys as well as enrichment programs for adults. As early as the 1820s, it was already offering night classes for grown men not seeking a formal degree; this evening lecture series grew into a major part of the city's social and intellectual scene throughout the 1800s.[27] The model was so successful that the Missouri Jesuits repeated it in Cincinnati, Detroit, and other cities in which they opened colleges later in the century. Evening lectures— an early version of night school—became a popular option for local students seeking to build their professional skills long before community colleges were mainstream.[28]

---

22. William Barnaby Faherty, SJ, *Better the Dream: Saint Louis University and Community, 1818–1968* (St. Louis: Saint Louis University, 1968), 8.

23. Ibid., 8.

24. Ibid., 11.

25. Ibid., 10.

26. Ibid., 15.

27. Ibid., 12.

28. Lee J. Bennish, SJ, *Continuity and Change: Xavier University, 1831–1981* (Chicago: Loyola University Press, 1981), 95. Herman J. Muller, SJ, *The University of Detroit, 1877–1977: A Centennial History* (Detroit: University of Detroit, 1976), 77–79.

Saint Louis College was so important as a cultural hub for its frontier community that the St. Louis city government supported it with tax money. Catholics and Protestants alike contributed to the college financially.[29] More than any other Catholic college before the Civil War, Saint Louis developed a reputation for innovation that kept it on the cutting edge of American higher education. In addition to granting the first bachelor's and master's degrees west of the Mississippi, it would also become the nation's first Jesuit college to sponsor a medical school.

All of this, however, was far into the future while DuBourg was bishop. DuBourg eventually moved his diocesan headquarters to New Orleans where it logically belonged, but he visited St. Louis often. During one such visit in 1825, he found the college in such bad condition that he ordered it to be closed. Several professors left the college that year, including Elihu Shepard, who opened a competing school and brought many of his favorite students with him.[30]

When DuBourg left St. Louis after his final inspection, he sincerely believed that his order to shut down Saint Louis College had been obeyed. However, with DuBourg out of sight and out of mind, the college president, Father Edmund Salnier, ignored the bishop's directive and kept the school open with twelve students and one faculty member.[31] That act of disobedience was sufficient to keep the small college afloat until the Jesuits could take over three years later.

If DuBourg harbored any grudge toward the ex-Jesuits who had made his life so difficult at Georgetown, he did not let it impede his judgment as bishop. It was at his invitation that the Jesuits first arrived in Missouri, which would become their toehold for future expansion throughout the Midwest. After the Jesuits were restored worldwide in 1814, DuBourg reached out to his old Jesuit contacts in Maryland and offered them land on which to open a college in St. Louis on three separate occasions.[32] The Maryland Jesuits were at first too preoccupied with their work on the East Coast to accept.

But by 1823, circumstances had changed. A small group of Belgian Jesuits had just arrived in Maryland, hoping eventually to become frontier missionaries in the American west. They had crossed the Atlantic at the invitation of Father Charles Nerinckx, a pioneering Belgian missionary who had worked in Kentucky and, appalled by the scarcity of priests on the frontier, traveled twice to his home country to recruit more. Though Nerinckx was not himself a Jesuit, he convinced a group of young Belgian Jesuit seminarians to complete their studies at Georgetown rather than in Europe, with the goal of eventually serving on the frontier. Although they took up residence temporarily on the Whitemarsh plantation after arriving in the United States, this youthful group was eager to go west and follow in Nerinckx's footsteps.[33]

---

29. Faherty, *Better*, 18–20.

30. Ibid., 19.

31. Ibid., 19.

32. Ibid., 12. Gilbert J. Garraghan, SJ, *The Jesuits of the Middle United States Volume I* (Chicago, Loyola University Press, 1983), 269–270.

33. Garraghan, *Jesuits of the Middle U.S. Vol. I,*, 11–14.

The funding for their mission came from an unlikely source: the federal government. Seeking to spread US cultural influence west of the Mississippi, Congress had just appropriated some money to support Christian missionaries who promised to work with the western Indians. DuBourg applied for the funds to help bring the Jesuits to his diocese, and his proposal was approved by President James Monroe and Secretary of War John C. Calhoun.[34] Calhoun was a Protestant, but he had a soft spot for Catholicism. During his time in Washington, he developed a friendship with a Georgetown Jesuit, Father Francis Dzierozynski, SJ, who tutored him on Catholic philosophy. It is unclear whether Father Dzierozynski influenced Calhoun's decision to fund the Jesuit missionaries, but the friendship between the two men certainly did not hurt the cause.[35]

Federal money in hand, twelve Belgian Jesuits left Maryland for Missouri, bringing with them six slaves (three married couples). The travel party of eighteen people, led by thirty-four-year-old Father Charles Van Quickenborne, SJ, completed the 800-mile overland journey to St. Louis in 1823—often traveling on foot and staying overnight at the homes of charitable Catholic families.[36] Upon their arrival, their initial objective was to evangelize the local Native Americans, not to become college professors, and their first project was an Indian mission school in Florissant, Missouri, just outside the city. However, in 1828, they agreed to assume control of Saint Louis College, which was still limping along under diocesan control. Saint Louis thus became the second Jesuit college in the United States.[37]

DuBourg, unfortunately, was not there to witness it. Two years earlier, in 1826, he had left the United States for good and returned to France, where he served as bishop in two French cities before his death in 1833. These "retirement" posts were far more comfortable than his long career in hardscrabble frontier settlements in America. Although DuBourg had opened Saint Louis College and had brought the Jesuits to Missouri, he never brought the two together during his time as bishop. Serendipitously, his two unrelated projects came to reinforce each other, as the Jesuits saved the struggling college and the college became the Jesuits' key asset on the frontier. For the rest of the century, Saint Louis University would serve as home base for Jesuit missionary work and academic work in the Midwest.

Connection in Seals

The historical connections between Georgetown and Saint Louis Universities are evident in the universities' seals. Georgetown's seal, originally designed by DuBourg

---

34. Faherty, *Better*, 11.

35. Anthony J. Kuzniewski, SJ, "'Our American Champions': The First American Generation of American Jesuit Leaders after the Restoration of the Society," *Studies in the Spirituality of Jesuits* 46, no. 1 (Spring 2014): 13.

36. Garraghan, *Jesuits of the Middle U.S. Vol. I*, 79–84.

37. Faherty, *Better*, 16.

during his term as president, is based closely on the seal of the United States and features the federal eagle with its wings outstretched. It is almost identical to the federal insignia on the back of most dollar bills, but instead of the familiar olive branches and arrows, the eagle holds in its talons a cross (symbolizing religious faith) and a globe and calipers (representing the sciences.) The banner in the Georgetown eagle's mouth reads, "Utraque Unum," a Latin phrase that comes from St. Paul's letter to the Ephesians in the New Testament. Loosely translated, it means, "both one," or "unity between two things that might at one time seem separate." In the case of Georgetown, this refers to the unity between faith and reason, or religion and the sciences.

The Saint Louis University seal also features the federal eagle, although the stars and stripes on its breastplate have been replaced by the Jesuit symbol "IHS"—an abbreviation of the Greek spelling of Jesus. The Saint Louis eagle, like Georgetown's, holds a cross in its talons, symbolizing the unity of faith and patriotism. Later in the nineteenth century, other Jesuit schools—including Santa Clara University, Gonzaga University, and Gonzaga College (DC)—adopted similar imagery in their own seals.

By combining symbols of the United States and Christianity, these seals reflected patriotism and optimism that the young country would be a welcoming place for Catholics—a place where they could unite the practice of their faith with the study of the modern arts and sciences in ways never possible in Europe. Today, apart from Georgetown, Saint Louis, and to a limited extent Santa Clara, the only other American colleges that use a stylized version of the federal seal as their own are the service academies.

Benedict Flaget and St. Joseph's College (1819), Bardstown, Kentucky

Nearly twenty years after John Carroll became bishop of Baltimore, it was no longer feasible for the entire United States east of the Mississippi to remain a single Catholic diocese. In 1808, the Diocese of Baltimore was subdivided and four new dioceses were carved from parts of its former territory: the Dioceses of Boston, New York, Philadelphia, and Bardstown in Kentucky. Baltimore was elevated to an archdiocese, which "supervised" the four suffragan dioceses.

Bardstown, geographically the largest diocese and the most difficult to govern, stretched across the entire American frontier from the Allegheny Mountains to the Mississippi River. The first bishop to lead it was Benedict Joseph Flaget, SS—one of the French Sulpicians who had come to the United States at Carroll's invitation in 1791. Like his friend and fellow Sulpician, Guillaume DuBourg, Flaget had taught at Georgetown, though he never served as its president. Flaget and DuBourg both served on the faculty at St. Mary's Seminary in Baltimore and had gone on mission trips together between teaching assignments; Flaget was thus accustomed to life in hardscrabble frontier conditions.

Bardstown today is a small village in central Kentucky almost fifty miles from Louisville. In the early 1800s, however, it had a booming Catholic population and seemed a logical place to put the seat of the western diocese. Located almost due west of Maryland, Kentucky was an attractive place for Maryland Catholics to resettle as they (like the rest of the country) expanded west in search of new land and new opportunity. The climate and seasons of Kentucky were similar to those of Maryland, and the bluegrass soil was even more fertile. A slave state, it also allowed the former Marylanders to bring their human property with them. As a result, Bardstown and central Kentucky soon became one of the few English-speaking centers of Catholic culture on the frontier.

Flaget, like Carroll and DuBourg, made education a top priority. In 1815, he invited the Georgetown Jesuits to send teachers and open a school in Bardstown. Unfortunately, as will be explained in detail later, the Maryland Jesuits were contracting their ministries at the time and were in the process of closing an ill-fated college in New York City. Keeping Georgetown afloat required all of their available manpower, and they had no one to spare for an excursion into rural Kentucky.

Rebuffed, Flaget opened a college anyway with his own resources in 1819. St. Joseph's College in Bardstown was initially staffed by diocesan priests, but Flaget understood that those priests were only a temporary solution. They would soon be needed for parish work, and the long-term survival of the college would only be secure if it could be handed over to a religious order that could give it full-time attention. For over a decade he offered the college to Irish, French, and English Jesuits in Europe, all to no avail.[38]

The Jesuits Come to Kentucky, but Are They Wanted?

What followed is a classic example of corporate miscommunication. At a time when mail between Europe and America sometimes took months to reach its destination (if it arrived at all), a group of French Jesuits decided to accept Flaget's offer in 1830, more than three years after first receiving it. They were suddenly available to cross the Atlantic because the French government, still reeling from revolutionary instability, had forcibly closed all Jesuit colleges in 1828 and formally banned the Jesuits from operating schools in 1830. With nothing better to do, the now-unemployed teachers dusted off Flaget's old letter and, "without checking to see if the bishop's invitation was still on the table," set off for America.[39]

Four French Jesuits arrived in New Orleans in 1830. Two decided to stay in Louisiana, as their pastoral services were needed there, but the other two continued up the Mississippi and Ohio Rivers en route to Bardstown. The very idea that two men expected to operate an entire college by themselves seems astonishing from a modern perspective, but such was the nature of higher education in the early nineteenth century. When they arrived, they were shocked to discover that the diocesan priests in

---

38. Shelley, *Fordham*, 32.
39. Ibid., 32.

charge of St. Joseph's College no longer had any intention of handing it over to them. St. Joseph's had operated just fine without Jesuit interference for eleven years, and the diocesan clergy resisted the French outsiders' intrusion on their territory.

Bishop Flaget was caught between a rock and a hard place. On one hand, he would have liked nothing more than to entrust St. Joseph's to the Jesuits; it would have freed his own clergy to do much-needed pastoral work across his vast diocese, and the financial condition of the college was so poor that it would have been a relief to rid himself of the problem. On the other hand, he had dissent in his ranks, and it would be an unpopular decision to take the college away from diocesan priests who had invested years of work into it and come to love its students.

Flummoxed, Flaget prayed a novena to St. Ignatius Loyola for guidance. On the final day of the novena, the story goes, he got a clear and providential answer. There was a second school in the Diocese of Bardstown—Mount St. Mary's Seminary near the small town of Lebanon, Kentucky, about 25 miles away—that had operated in the most rudimentary conditions since 1821. For a decade it had been run almost single-handedly by a diocesan priest, Father William Byrne, who not only oversaw instruction but also managed a 500-acre working farm on the property. The college's students doubled as farmhands and, at times, as faculty, teaching their classmates when Father Byrne was unavailable.[40] Byrne had briefly attended Georgetown in his youth and at one time even sought to become a Jesuit, but had found his true calling on the frontier.[41]

Even though Father Byrne's college was so geographically close to St. Joseph's College, it was surprisingly successful, enrolling by one (probably exaggerated) estimate 1200 students over twelve years.[42] Byrne told Flaget that he would be willing to entrust his beloved school to the Jesuit newcomers on the condition that they allow him to remain president for a short while to ease the transition. Tragically, in 1833, at the end of the school year in which he planned to step down, Byrne died of cholera. The Jesuits then assumed full control. Under their leadership, Mount St. Mary's Seminary became known as St. Mary's College.[43]

Thus, by 1833 the Jesuits had established schools in three of America's six original dioceses: the old bedrock Maryland Jesuit community was operating in the Archdiocese of Baltimore, while Belgian Jesuit missionaries had put down roots in St. Louis and French Jesuit missionaries had settled in Bardstown. Of the country's original six dioceses, only New York, Philadelphia, and Boston remained without a functioning Jesuit educational institution. Before the end of the Civil War, the Jesuits would be managing colleges in those cities as well.

Although the Jesuits' arrival in Kentucky seemed to have a lot of potential, their relationship to the Bluegrass State for the rest of the nineteenth century would be

---

40. Ibid., 34.
41. Ibid., 33.
42. Ibid., 34.
43. Ibid., 35.

complicated. As will be discussed later, the Jesuits would operate four different Kentucky colleges before the Civil War, none of which survived. St. Mary's College holds an important place in Jesuit history, not only because it was the first of these Kentucky schools, but because it was the direct ancestor of Fordham University in New York City. Just twelve years after arriving at St. Mary's, the French Jesuits would abandon the small Kentucky college and relocate to (metaphorically) greener pastures in New York, where they formed the core of the first Jesuit faculty at Fordham. New York's Jesuit school thus has some decidedly Bluegrass roots.

Although little Bardstown ultimately proved unable to sustain any Catholic colleges, and although Bishop Flaget moved the seat of the diocese from Bardstown to Louisville in 1841, this tiny village in central Kentucky still relishes its role in American history as one of the original epicenters of American Catholic life. As historian Thomas Shelley has observed, Kentucky Catholics still refer to Nelson and Washington Counties as "the American Holy Land" due to their high concentration of historic churches and convents.[44] Towns in the countryside around Bardstown are peppered with names like St. Mary, Nazareth, Loretto, St. Francis, Nerinx (sic) and other reminders of the outsized role this rural area once played in American Catholic history.

Georgetown, the Jesuit Restoration, and the War of 1812

Even before its former faculty-members-turned-bishops, Guillaume DuBourg and Benedict Flaget, began to build new colleges on the frontier, Georgetown was facing challenges of its own. The college and its founder, Archbishop Carroll, were busily trying to ensure the growth of the Catholic Church in its original Maryland heartland, but they had to do so in the face of personnel shortages, ecclesial politics, ethnic rivalries among the Jesuits themselves, and the British invasion of Washington, DC, during the War of 1812.

After forcing DuBourg out of the Georgetown president's office, the ex-Jesuits at Whitemarsh promoted some of their own to lead the college. Georgetown's presidents during this period included the ultra-conservative Neale brothers: Leonard (president from 1798 to 1806) and Francis (president from 1808 to 1812, with a few months' absence in 1809). Both men were staunch traditionalists who enforced such harsh discipline that many boys chose to enroll instead at St. Mary's College in Baltimore, or the newly established Mount St. Mary's College in Emmitsburg, Maryland.[45] The Neales' strict approach to education caused them to clash with the more liberal-minded Carroll, who felt that sheltering students in an impenetrable disciplinary bubble was not an ideal way to form moral gentlemen capable of making their own

---

44. Ibid., 31.
45. Curran, *History of Georgetown Vol. I*, 69.

decisions. Unusually open-minded for his day, Carroll believed that strict discipline would ultimately be counter-productive to its own intentions. He wrote,

> Indeed it is a difficult problem to solve, what degree of it (liberty) should be allowed in literary establishments, and never have I been able to satisfy my own mind on this subject, though it has been much employed in thinking of it. Theory and experience are constantly at variance in this case; for though the principles of religion and morality command, or seem to command, the instructors of youth to restrain their pupils from almost every communication with the men and things of the world, yet that very restraint operates against the effects intended by it, and it is too often found that on being delivered from it, young men, as when the pin that confines a spring is loosened, burst out of confinement into licentiousness, and give way to errors and vices, which with more acquaintance with the manners and language of the world they would have avoided. . . .[46]

The Neales were also busy men, and the presidency of the college was something of a part-time job for them. Francis Neale simultaneously served as the pastor of Holy Trinity Church in Georgetown, the first Catholic Church in the District of Columbia, located just steps away from the college campus. In that capacity, he visited parishioners across the region so often that he became essentially an absentee president "on horseback."[47] The dearth of priests in the United States also forced Neale to serve as pastor of St. Mary's Church in distant Alexandria, Virginia—a heavy extracurricular workload for a college president, even then.

The Restoration of the Jesuits

Between 1773 and 1814 the Jesuits existed only in the Polish-Lithuanian portion of the Russian Empire, where Catherine the Great ignored the papal directive suppressing the order. Although that sole remaining Jesuit province was based in Russia, it was polyglot in its membership; it included Italians, Germans, Poles, and numerous other nationalities. The priests were "Russian" only in the sense that they lived in Russian territory.

In 1801, Pope Pius VII recognized that vestigial Jesuit cell as legitimate and opened the door for any priest worldwide to affiliate with the Russian branch of the Society of Jesus. In 1814, the forty-one-year-old suppression was formally lifted and the Society of Jesus was officially restored worldwide. News of the restoration was a cause for celebration among the Maryland Jesuits, but it was not universally welcomed in the United States. Many American Protestants feared the effect that the resurrection of the old missionary order would have on their country. Would the Jesuits come to America in large numbers seeking to convert Protestants to Catholicism? Would

---

46. As quoted in Daley, *Georgetown University*, 114.
47. Curran, *History of Georgetown Vol. I*, 69.

they infiltrate the American government as they had so many European monarchies? Would they reach the Native Americans in the west before Protestant missionaries did? Former president John Adams, by then retired to his farm in Massachusetts, wrote to his old friend and rival, Thomas Jefferson in 1816:

> If ever any Congregation of Men could merit eternal Perdition on Earth and in Hell, according to these Historians, though like Pascal true Catholics, it is the company of Loyola. Our system of Religious liberty must afford them an asylum. But if they do not put the purity of our Elections to a severe trial, it will be a Wonder.[48]

Effects of the Jesuit Restoration on Georgetown

From 1789 to 1808, Georgetown was essentially the only Jesuit school in the United States. It was "Jesuit" only in the sense that its legal owners and many of its faculty were ex-Jesuits who had been trained in the Ignatian tradition and were familiar with Ignatian spirituality and pedagogy. During its first decade or so of existence, Georgetown was at least a Jesuit school in spirit, if not in name, and it benefitted from its ties to the vestigial Society in Russia. In 1805, with John Carroll's approval and assistance, five of the ten ex-Jesuits still living in Maryland re-entered the Society under the authority of Gabriel Gruber, SJ, the Austrian-born Jesuit superior in St. Petersburg. The Maryland Jesuits became technically a "mission" of the Russian order, and Georgetown was their central ministry.

To support their new colleagues, the Russian Jesuits sent a total of five men to Maryland in 1805 and 1806.[49] In addition, eleven American men entered the Maryland mission and became Jesuits. That group included a veritable who's who in the history of US Catholicism. Among the new American recruits was Francis Neale, who was by then already an experienced priest and educator, but who had never officially joined the Jesuits before their suppression. Joining Father Neale as novices were three of his parishioners at Holy Trinity, all of whom were Georgetown alumni: John McElroy and a pair of siblings, Enoch and Benedict Fenwick.

All three young men went on to impressive careers. Enoch Fenwick became president of Georgetown in the 1820s; his brother Benedict served twice as Georgetown's president before being named the second Bishop of Boston—in which capacity he would found the College of the Holy Cross in Massachusetts. John McElroy eventually founded two American colleges: St. John's Literary Institute in Frederick, Maryland, and Boston College.[50]

This group of American novices and European transplants gathered at Holy Trinity Church on October 10, 1806 for a Mass of celebration, beginning their journey as Jesuits together. The collective historical significance of these men, all in one

---

48. As quoted in Bennish, *Continuity*, 25.
49. Curran, *History of Georgetown Vol. I*, 63.
50. Warner, *At Peace*, 99.

place at one time, is remarkable to consider. In the church that day, praying together, were the founding fathers of Georgetown, Boston College, and Holy Cross; these were men who would teach at Jesuit schools for the next fifty years, and train students who went on to establish still more colleges in Baltimore and Philadelphia. Nearly every Jesuit college on the East Coast can trace its roots directly or indirectly to the small group of priests who entered or re-entered the Society that year, and who celebrated their bond to each other and to the Ignatian tradition that day at Holy Trinity.

John Carroll, too, was present for the Mass. He could not have known that the men with whom he shared the pews that day would fulfill his vision and build a Church capable of serving their vast country—but he must have smiled at the potential. The young men entering this new, American branch of the Society of Jesus were the very embodiment of his dream: sons of Georgetown who would use their education to bring their faith and its traditions far from its historic home in Maryland. Although Carroll himself never re-entered the Society of Jesus, he maintained a soft spot in his heart for his former order throughout his life. That affinity helped him to navigate some looming conflicts in the years ahead, as he argued with the Jesuits in his diocese about how Georgetown should be managed, among other priorities. [51]

Conflict in the Ranks

Despite the good feeling during the Mass on October 10, there was conflict almost immediately between the upstart American Jesuits and the new reinforcements from Europe. The Europeans were outsiders, coming to a country that already had its own elite cadre of Catholic clergymen. Among the Americans were priests like the Neale brothers, born into wealth and power in the colonial era and accustomed to getting their way, no matter what their position in the formal hierarchy. But now, technically, the American Jesuits were a branch of the Russian province and were under European supervision. This awkward power dynamic played out in a number of ways, most especially when it came to the training of the next generation of Jesuits.

In 1806, Father Francis Neale was an elder statesman of the American Church, pastor of the most important parish in the city, and brother of the sitting president of Georgetown College. Even though he was only a novice himself, he asked to be put in charge of the other, younger Jesuit novices and to be responsible for directing their training. This did not sit well with the new arrivals from the Russian province, who objected to the idea that any priest—even one as distinguished as Father Neale— could train aspiring Jesuits in the Ignatian tradition without ever having been through such training himself. [52]

The strongest voice in opposition was that of Anthony Kohlmann, SJ, an Alsatian-born priest who arrived in Maryland in 1806. Kohlmann was an agitator who was

---

51. Gleason, "First Century," 47.
52. Warner, *At Peace*, 97–99.

disturbed by the state of the Catholic Church in Maryland, and who apparently did not hesitate to point out the flaws he saw in the Americans' way of doing things. He considered Washington, DC a rural southern backwater and questioned openly why the Jesuits would maintain their only college in such a city. The real potential for growth, he believed, was in New York City—already overtaking Philadelphia as America's commercial capital and the largest city under the jurisdiction of the Baltimore Diocese.

Anthony Kohlmann, SJ, and the New York Literary Institute (1808–1813)

For most of his career in America, Anthony Kohlmann would be a thorn in John Carroll's side. By 1808, after extensive badgering, Kohlmann had convinced Carroll that a Jesuit college in New York would be in the country's and the Church's best interests. To allay fears that such a college would compete with Georgetown for students, Kohlmann initially sold it as a "prep school" for Georgetown—one that would only offer the first few years of the *Ratio Studiorum* and then send its most promising students south to Washington. Privately, however, Kohlmann's own writings show that he had doubts about Georgetown's long-term viability, and viewed it as nothing more than the second-best Catholic college in the country after St. Mary's in Baltimore. The Jesuits, he thought, could do better.[53]

During its short life, Kohlmann's school, the New York Literary Institute, was successful by nineteenth-century standards. It developed a strong local reputation, and its healthy initial enrollment of around fifty students soon grew to over 100.[54] Most of those students were Protestant, since the Catholic population of New York City was not yet large enough or wealthy enough to demand higher education in large numbers.[55] As a sign of their important role in the New York cosmopolitan scene, Kohlmann and his Jesuit colleagues were invited into the social circles of the faculty at Columbia University, and developed a collegial relationship with the institution across town.

What doomed the New York Literary Institute was not a dearth of students or reputation, but a lack of faculty. There simply were not enough Jesuits in the United States to operate two colleges at once. Kohlmann fought hard to keep his pet project open, convinced that New York was a vastly superior location to Maryland, which he described as the "poorest and most beggarly (state) of the whole union."[56] But in a diocese based in Baltimore and dominated by old Maryland families with deep roots in the state, it is not hard to see why many of Kohlmann's fellow Jesuits took a different view.

---

53. Curran, *History of Georgetown Vol. I*, 65.
54. Daley, *Georgetown University*, 158.
55. Curran, *History of Georgetown Vol. I*, 65–66.
56. As quoted in Daley, *Georgetown University*, 180.

Father Francis Neale, who was by then president of Georgetown, viewed Kohlmann as a nuisance and worked hard to convince his fellow Marylanders that the Alsatian in their midst was actively conspiring to undermine their life's work by weakening Georgetown.[57] It soon became clear that most American Jesuits were siding with Neale. Kohlmann made a number of last-ditch efforts to save the New York Literary Institute, and even proposed that Georgetown be converted into a seminary so that the two schools could serve different audiences. It was all to no avail. In Carroll's mind, and in the minds of the Jesuits still loyal to their Maryland roots, "if only one of them could be chosen—Georgetown or the Literary Institute—there must be no hesitation."[58] The New York school closed in 1813, just five years after it opened, and Kohlmann was recalled to Maryland, where he was assigned to train Jesuit novices at Whitemarsh and continued to lobby for Georgetown's closure.

Although Kohlmann did not create a lasting Jesuit presence in the Empire State, today's New York Jesuits still recognize him as the de facto founder of the Archdiocese of New York and as the first Jesuit to establish a meaningful presence in America's largest city. He erected the first St. Patrick's Cathedral (now known as the Basilica of Old St. Patrick's Cathedral on Mulberry Street in Manhattan).[59] Even though he had no direct ties to Fordham University (founded more than thirty years after he left New York), Kohlmann Hall, a Jesuit residence on the Fordham campus, is named in his honor.

Whether Kohlmann was a troublemaker or a visionary, his wings were effectively clipped for the time being. Still, many of the criticisms Kohlmann lobbed at Georgetown and at the city of Washington, DC were perfectly valid. Georgetown survived this period because it had the absolute commitment of its founders and a coterie of Jesuits dedicated to its success, but it was not a healthy, stable college in the early 1800s. Faced with competition from St. Mary's College in Baltimore and Mount St. Mary's College in Emmitsburg, Georgetown was teetering on the verge of collapse at the turn of the century, as was the city of Washington overall. Citizens of the District of Columbia lived in constant fear that their city's status as the US capital would be revoked and that the federal government would return to better-established cities like Philadelphia or New York.[60] Downtown Washington was still rural and disconnected, home to only a handful of purpose-built government buildings and hardly any infrastructure. It was a sleepy southern town, nothing like the booming metropolis it would one day become.

---

57. Curran, *History of Georgetown Vol. I*, 66.
58. Daley, *Georgetown University*, 179.
59. Shelley, *Fordham*, 29.
60. Warner, *At Peace*, 158, 174, 185–186.

Giovanni Grassi, SJ, and Georgetown during the War of 1812

At no time was the status of Georgetown and Washington more insecure than during the War of 1812, when the British destroyed most of the capital city's embryonic government buildings and set fire to the newly constructed White House and Capitol. Although Georgetown was about four miles removed from the fighting and was not directly targeted by the British, the raging fires were easily visible from its hilltop campus. In an oft-quoted passage, Father John McElroy, SJ, Georgetown's financial manager (and future founder of Boston College), wrote in his diary that the flames "were so great that a person could read at the college."[61]

Georgetown survived this challenge largely because of the effective leadership of Giovanni Grassi, SJ, its president from 1812 to 1817. An Italian by birth, Father Grassi was part of a second group of European reinforcements sent by the Russian province in 1810. Having previously served as the rector of a Russian Jesuit college at Polotsk in modern-day Belarus, he brought years of experience in higher education as well as the latest European books and scientific equipment. Under his leadership, first as vice president and then as rector, Georgetown flourished. During the War of 1812, Grassi refused to abandon the campus, sheltering his students in place. The college was a beacon of stability in the devastated city. Grassi's patience during the height of battle was rewarded when a providential thunderstorm doused the fires before they could do much damage outside of Capitol Hill.[62] Georgetown escaped the war untouched by the destruction at its doorstep.

Grassi knew how to run a college, and he assembled a strong cadre of Jesuit faculty, including both native-born Americans and European reinforcements. He also knew that, to be successful, the college must have legal recognition. For the first two decades of its life, Georgetown had operated without a charter. Typically, state governments were responsible for chartering colleges, but since Georgetown was located in the federally administered District of Columbia, the only legislature with jurisdiction over it was the United States Congress itself. Through the efforts of Georgetown's first student, William Gaston (by then a Congressman from North Carolina), and with the support of President James Madison, America's first Catholic college was legally chartered by an act of Congress in 1815.[63]

The Death of John Carroll

It was during Grassi's tenure as president that the father of Catholic and Jesuit education in America, John Carroll, died on December 3, 1815. Knowing that the arch-

---

61. Daley, *Georgetown University*, 185.
62. Curran, *History of Georgetown Vol. I*, 77–79.
63. Daley, *Georgetown University*, 189–190.

bishop's death was near, Grassi had journeyed to Baltimore to visit Carroll on his sickbed just days earlier. As Georgetown historian John M. Daley, SJ recounts the event,

> Here was Georgetown's founder on his death-bed in conversation with the beloved academy's second founder. What did they talk about? Is it mere conjecture to imagine that the words "Georgetown" and "my hopes" could have been overheard? Did he tell Grassi about the chance he took in raising the building before he possessed the deed for the ground? Did he tell him of his begging tours for the college? Did he ask him if he had followed his suggestion and obtained a new college cook? Did he smile and say, "Now, don't be a Neale with the boys"? One thing we know he did say. He confided to Grassi that "of those things which give me most consolation at the present moment is, that I have always been attached to the practice of devotion to the Blessed Virgin Mary, that I have established it among the people under my care, and placed my diocese under her protection." We can be certain that Georgetown's founder had placed the college also under her protection.[64]

Carroll had taken on a herculean task—building a Catholic Church in the United States almost from scratch—and succeeded remarkably well. The infrastructure he created during his lifetime transformed American Catholicism from a loose confederacy of about two dozen itinerant priests into a solid, if not yet strong, institution capable of welcoming and serving generations of immigrants to come.

Carroll had lived long enough to see his beloved academy at Georgetown survive for more than three decades, and had lived to see the Jesuit order, suppressed when he was in his thirties, resurrected. He knew at the time of his death that his two great loves, the Jesuits and Georgetown, were permanently in each other's care. He did not, however, live to see the enormous national education network that Georgetown, its faculty, and alumni would spawn from Atlantic to Pacific. Their canvas was the entire United States; Carroll had given them the tools with which to paint.

Carroll was succeeded as Archbishop of Baltimore by Leonard Neale, SJ, with whom he had clashed so often over the management of Georgetown. But the aging Neale was in declining health and his own death came just two years later, in 1817.

Changes (and a Power Grab) at Georgetown

It was during Grassi's tenure that the Society of Jesus was fully restored in 1814. Although it would take years to iron out the legal details, this meant that Georgetown could finally be owned and operated directly by the Jesuits, rather than by the independent Corporation of Roman Catholic Clergymen—which, in the eyes of the state, still legally controlled most of the old Jesuit property. It also meant that, moving forward, ultimate authority for Georgetown would not be at Whitemarsh but in Rome.

---

64. Ibid., 192.

The first superior general of the restored Jesuit order, the Polish-born Tadeusz Brzozowski, SJ, would now have final say over all Jesuit activity in the United States. With respect to Jesuit colleges, Brzozowski had authority over the minutest details, from campus construction to curriculum changes.

Despite Grassi's many accomplishments as Georgetown's president, the Jesuit bureaucracy cut his tenure short. During a routine visit to Rome in 1819, during which he hoped to raise funds and faculty for the Maryland mission, Grassi fell and suffered what was determined to be an inoperable hernia. He was advised that his health was too poor to attempt a transatlantic voyage back to America.[65] Instead, Father Brzozowski named Anthony Kohlmann the new head of the Maryland mission. Kohlmann immediately appointed himself president of Georgetown. Suddenly, Georgetown was in the hands of a man who had spent years advocating for its closure.

Fortunately, there were checks and balances in place that would have made any dramatic decision like the closure of the college difficult for Kohlmann. In the eyes of the Church, Georgetown was now a Jesuit college, but its civil assets remained under the control of the old Corporation of Roman Catholic Clergymen. In practice, power now resided in the hands of the Jesuit hierarchy, but in the event that Kohlmann ever tried to shut down the college, the Whitemarsh council theoretically could have exercised its civil authority over the institution to stand in the way.[66]

Nonetheless, Kohlmann's leadership was a blow to Georgetown's stability—so much so that Georgetown historian Robert Emmett Curran describes the Kohlmann years as "a disaster."[67] A strict disciplinarian like his arch-rivals the Neales, Kohlmann liberally expelled misbehaving students (even at a cost to the college's tuition revenue), and enrollment fell. Morale was so low that students planned a riot, and those who were not expelled by force often withdrew voluntarily. The reputation of the college began to suffer, as it drifted away from being the preeminent civic institution it had become under Father Grassi, and toward a narrow sectarianism.[68]

Why was Kohlmann appointed to such an important leadership role, given his history? Kohlmann had clashed with almost everyone he encountered, including Archbishop Carroll and the Neales. He was opinionated and headstrong, seemingly convinced that he was always the smartest person in the room. (One has to wonder if the Russian province originally sent him to America at least in part to make him someone else's problem.) But he was also an erudite scholar and a respected educator—two qualities that could not be taken for granted in the young United States. Some of his ideas, if followed, could have resulted in success, and he is still fondly remembered for his pioneering work in New York City. He was correct in his assessment that the future of the Jesuits was in large urban areas, and not in the rural south-

---

65. Curran, *History of Georgetown Vol. I*, 90; Daley, *Georgetown University*, 206.
66. Kuzniewski, "Our American Champions," 5.
67. Curran, *History of Georgetown Vol. I*, 91.
68. Ibid., 91.

ern plantations where many of them still lived, jealously guarding a colonial-era lifestyle that was fast becoming anachronistic. Had he been more tactful, he might have convinced his American colleagues to support his vision. On the other hand, Kohlmann vastly underestimated Washington, DC's long-term potential both as a city and as a setting for a college, and he was wrong in his assessment that the future of American higher education was in European-style, downtown commuter schools rather than in boarding schools with large campuses.

There was also at least some hope that Kohlmann's appointment would only be temporary, and that Grassi would eventually recuperate enough to return. From Italy, Grassi continued to support the college, sending books and art for its library. Kohlmann himself publicly expressed the belief that his tenure as president would be brief; on September 15, 1818, he put a notice in the Washington newspapers that "The Rev. Dr. Grassi being daily expected from Europe to resume the presidency, the subscriber will, in the meantime, supply his place."[69]

And yet, Kohlmann did not behave as if he truly believed that he was in a temporary caretaker role. He dismissed many of the outstanding faculty that Grassi had assembled, including the talented Benedict Fenwick, SJ, whom Grassi had deliberately left in charge of the college when he departed for Europe.[70] Kohlmann quickly emptied the faculty of anyone with whom he had quarreled and, in their place, appointed strict disciplinarians like himself. Fenwick accepted an assignment in South Carolina, where he became vicar general of the newly created Diocese of Charleston.

Georgetown historians differ on how much Kohlmann should bear the blame for this. John Daley, SJ gives Kohlmann some benefit of the doubt, pointing out that Fenwick and many of the other departed Georgetown faculty were badly needed in the expanding church hierarchy, and it was only a matter of time before these talented men were poached from the college for higher office. As much as Fenwick could have contributed to Georgetown, he was needed even more in Charleston.[71] Indeed, after his experience in South Carolina, Fenwick became the second Bishop of Boston, in which capacity he founded the College of the Holy Cross. However, Daley does acknowledge that Kohlmann did little to stop the poaching of his best professors and even lobbied the Archbishop of Baltimore to keep Fenwick and the other Grassi-era faculty away from the college.[72] Moreover, despite being given many opportunities to return to Georgetown over the years, Fenwick respectfully declined to work with Kohlmann: "So long as Anthony Kohlmann was superior, Fenwick continued to plead Charleston's pastoral needs as his excuse for not returning to the District."[73]

---

69. Daley, *Georgetown University*, 205 (n. 40).
70. Curran, *History of Georgetown Vol. I*, 90.
71. Daley, *Georgetown University*, 205, 211.
72. Ibid., 211.
73. Curran, *History of Georgetown Vol. I*, 97.

Peter Kenney, SJ, Arrives (1819)

In September, 1819, a forty-one-year-old Irish Jesuit arrived in Annapolis after a weeks-long sea voyage from Europe. The man was Peter Kenney, SJ, sent by Jesuit Superior General Brzozowski to inspect the American mission and report back on what he found. His title was "Special Visitor of the Society" and he was to be Brzozowki's eyes and ears on the ground. Word of the personality conflicts in Maryland had reached Europe, and Kenney was assigned to be an objective observer. Were the European-born and American-born Jesuits really at each others' throats? Was the Maryland mission truly paralyzed by ethnic rivalries? Was Kohlmann's management of Georgetown as bad as had been reported? Brzozowski wanted an unbiased third-party whose opinion he valued to judge the situation. Kenney had already served successfully as head of the Jesuits' Irish mission and as president of two Jesuit colleges in Ireland.[74]

Fortunately, after meeting with the various Jesuits in the Maryland mission, Kenney reported back that "Matters are not so bad as they were made to appear" and the "poor general has been more plagued than he ought to have been" by complaints.[75] However, Kenney did judge that Anthony Kohlmann was the wrong man to lead Georgetown. The German's impetuousness had led to multiple bad decisions, and the fact that Kohlmann was widely disliked by other Jesuits had leaked outside of Jesuit circles, damaging the reputation of the college.[76]

Kenney recommended that Enoch Fenwick, SJ—Benedict's brother—be recalled from pastoral work in Baltimore and appointed president of Georgetown. This led to the question of what to do with Kohlmann. Kenney's erudite solution was to relieve Kohlmann of the Georgetown presidency but assign him to start a seminary for aspiring Jesuits. Kohlmann would live at the seminary and would serve as master of the Jesuit novices—a role in which his hard-handed approach to discipline would be more appropriate and even expected. The new school was to be called the Washington Seminary and would be located in downtown Washington in a building the Jesuits already happened to own. Finally, Kohlmann would be forced to step down as superior of the Maryland mission and would be replaced by an American, the elderly Charles Neale, SJ (brother to Francis and Leonard).

It was a reasonable solution that demonstrated Kenney's diplomatic skills. The best way to save Georgetown from Kohlmann's erratic leadership was to create a new school for him to run, hopefully satisfying his ego and keeping him quiet. Father Charles Neale was solidly in the "American" camp, so his appointment as superior of the mission satisfied the Americans. However, since Neale was old and increasingly ill, his appointment would clearly be temporary. To assist Neale, Rome sent a well-respected Polish Jesuit, Francis Dzierozynski, SJ, first to act as Neale's assistant and,

---

74. Ibid., 95–96.
75. Daley, *Georgetown University*, 209.
76. Ibid., 210.

after Neale's death (which occurred in 1823), to become the acting head of mission.[77] In this way, titular power was in the hands of an American, but a European would have real influence and would be the presumptive heir.

Father Dzierozynski was the right man for the job. During his roughly thirty-year career in the United States, he became a beloved professor at Georgetown (where the students affectionately knew him as "Father Zero") and developed a reputation as a saintly figure throughout Maryland, where he was often sought out as a spiritual advisor.[78] Kenney had known Dzierozynski when both men were stationed at the Jesuit college in Bologna, and historians have suggested that Kenney may have had Dzierozynski in mind when he recommended this solution. It was under Dzierozynksi's leadership that the old Corporation of Roman Catholic Clergymen finally folded into the governing structure of the restored Society of Jesus.[79] A Jesuit journal, published in 1933, declares: "The Jesuits of the East owe much to Father Dzierozynski, and his name should never die out among us."[80]

However, part of Kenney's plan backfired. Kohlmann took liberties with his new position as head of the Washington Seminary to create a competing college that continued to damage Georgetown. Did he do this partly out of spite for the Marylanders with whom he had clashed so often? We can only guess at the motivations behind his actions, but it soon became clear that he wanted the Washington Seminary to be more than just the house of formation for Jesuits that Peter Kenney envisioned.

Anthony Kohlmann, SJ and Gonzaga College (1821), Washington, DC

Kohlmann remained unconvinced that Georgetown would ever be viable. He preferred schools that were located downtown, close to the people, not literally and figuratively on a hill removed from the population center. After stepping down from the Georgetown presidency in 1820 and assuming the leadership of the Washington Seminary in 1821, he resolved to turn the Seminary in to just such a college.

A year after the Seminary opened, Kohlmann expanded its enrollment to include students not seeking the priesthood, opening the equivalent of a high school on-site and using the seminarians as faculty. At the time, the school offered only the first few years of the *Ratio Studiorum* curriculum, so it was not directly competing with Georgetown except at the lowest levels. It was strictly a day school and did not enroll boarders, so on paper the two colleges served different audiences. Talented students who wished to continue their education past what the Seminary offered would have

---

77. Kuzniewski, "Our American Champions," 10–11.

78. Curran, *History of Georgetown Vol. I*, 98.

79. Ibid., 107–108; Kuzniewski, "Our American Champions," 11.

80. Edward I. Devitt, SJ, "History of the Maryland-New York Province IX: The Province in the Year 1833," *Woodstock Letters* LXII, no. 3 (1933): 315.

to enroll at Georgetown. In today's terminology, it might be said that Kohlmann founded a community college or a prep school—just as he had done fourteen years earlier at the New York Literary Institute.[81]

Nonetheless, the Washington Seminary did ultimately weaken Georgetown. Kohlmann's own public statements indicate that he intended the school to become more than just a junior college; he wanted it to develop into a full-fledged university in its own right.[82] Georgetown had always drawn a considerable number of students from the Washington area, and its enrollment in 1821 (after three years of Kohlmann's leadership) was shrinking. Inevitably the new college siphoned off some local boys who otherwise would have paid tuition to Georgetown. Even if the impact was initially felt only in Georgetown's lower grade levels, it was still significant.

The damage to Georgetown's bottom line soon evolved into something more than just opportunity cost. A dispute quickly arose because Kohlmann wanted the Washington Seminary to charge tuition. Since the days of St. Ignatius, Jesuit schools had been forbidden to do so. For its first thirty years, Georgetown had gotten away with charging tuition because it was not technically a Jesuit institution, as the Jesuits did not formally exist in America. However, now that the Society of Jesus was back and irrefutably in charge, Jesuit schools around the world had to operate on Jesuit norms.

When Kohlmann petitioned Rome for a dispensation to charge tuition, he brought this issue to the attention of the Jesuit authorities, who not only refused to grant Kohlmann what he wanted, but also ordered their Maryland colleagues to cease charging tuition at *both* of their schools.[83] Georgetown thus lost its most important source of operating income. It could still charge room and board for those who lived on campus, but there were not nearly enough boarders to finance the entire institution comfortably. Meanwhile, the Washington Seminary proved impossible to operate without tuition income, and the Jesuits abandoned it after just six years. It had lasted only one year longer than Kohlmann's earlier project in New York.

The Jesuit prohibition on charging tuition was eventually relaxed in America in 1833, but much damage had been done. After a decade of reduced income, the Maryland Jesuits' finances were strained, leading in part to one of the most controversial decisions in their history—the sale of more than 270 slaves in 1838, in an attempt to pay off the province's debts.

The Aftermath: Gonzaga College High School

After leaving the Washington Seminary, Kohlmann returned to Europe, where he became a professor at the prestigious Jesuit school in Rome, the Gregorian University. Although he had been sent to the United States to support the fledgling Ameri-

---

81. Curran, *History of Georgetown Vol. I*, 100.
82. Ibid., 100.
83. Ibid., 101.

can Jesuit college at Georgetown, virtually everything he did during his roughly two decades on this side of the Atlantic served to weaken it. Georgetown survived in spite of, not because of, his efforts.

As for the Washington Seminary, the departure of the Jesuits in 1827 did not lead to the school's permanent closure. It operated sporadically in a building owned by St. Patrick's Church, under the direction of diocesan clergy. For years, diocesan faculty begged the Jesuits to send teachers to the struggling school, and in 1848, those pleas were finally answered. The Jesuits returned and, a decade later, renamed the seminary Gonzaga College after the sixteenth-century Italian Jesuit, St. Aloysius Gonzaga, SJ. The mission of the school was now even more explicitly comparable to that of a modern-day community college; it would be a feeder school for Georgetown as well a more affordable alternative for those who could not pay Georgetown's tuition. By the 1850s, unlike thirty years earlier, the population of Washington, DC was big enough to justify two colleges and sustain both comfortably. Gonzaga was chartered as a college in 1858 by act of Congress, and offered bachelor's degrees for most of the rest of the nineteenth century—always self-consciously as a junior partner to Georgetown.

When the delineation between high school and college became more regulated at the turn of the twentieth century, Gonzaga abandoned its undergraduate degree programs and redefined itself strictly as a Jesuit high school. Today, Gonzaga College High School enrolls just under 1,000 all-male students in grades 9–12. The age of its students has remained fairly consistent over the years; even when it was a "college," it still enrolled mainly teenagers. What have changed are American's expectations about the kind of education appropriate for teens and the ages appropriate for undergraduate study.

However, Gonzaga's 1858 charter as a college has never been revoked, and it retains the legal ability to grant degrees. It still awards honorary doctorates to distinguished guests. The historic relationship between Georgetown and Gonzaga remains strong, and many Gonzaga alumni are admitted to the crosstown university every year to continue their Jesuit education. In 2019, the ongoing camaraderie between the two institutions proved to be mutually beneficial when Georgetown signed an 85-year lease on property owned by Gonzaga for the purpose of building a new dorm, expanding the university's housing options while providing the high school with a steady revenue stream.

Whatever Kohlmann's original motivation in founding it, Gonzaga College High School has served generations of boys and changed tens of thousands of lives. It never developed into the university its founder envisioned, but it is one of the city's premiere high schools and today, at long last, it finally serves to support Georgetown.

Peter Kenney, SJ, and the Next Generation

After his first visit to the United States, Father Peter Kenney also (logically) recommended that the Jesuit mission in Maryland should do more to train its own next generation of leaders. He advised the American Jesuits to send their most promising young scholastics off to Rome for advanced study, after which they would presumably return to the United States with impeccable Ignatian credentials. He identified six young men—all Georgetown alumni, and all of whom had studied under Anthony Kohlmann—for the honor. That small group left Maryland in 1820 and arrived in Italy by way of Gibraltar, where they planned to rendezvous with Giovanni Grassi and two other students he had already brought to Rome during his Georgetown presidency. There were now eight Americans studying for the Jesuit priesthood in Italy.

This group of eight students constituted what might be called the "second generation" of American Jesuit educators. The "first generation" consisted of that group of men—including John Carroll, Benedict Fenwick, Enoch Fenwick, Leonard Neale, Francis Neale, Anthony Kohlmann, and John McElroy—who had celebrated that fateful Mass together at Holy Trinity in Georgetown on October 10, 1806. This "second generation" was to be just as important as the first. Five of the eight scholastics returned to America at the conclusion of their studies in 1828 and 1829:

- **James Ryder, SJ.** Born in Dublin, Ryder came to the United States as a boy. Considered the brightest of the bunch, he would serve twice as president of Georgetown (1840–1845 and 1848–1851). In between those two terms, he served as the second president of Holy Cross (1845–1848). At the end of his career, he led Saint Joseph's University in Philadelphia as president from 1855 to 1858.[84]

- **George Fenwick, SJ.** The younger brother of Benedict and Enoch would become a renowned professor of classics at both Georgetown and Holy Cross, where his affable manner made him a father figure to the boys and earned him the nickname "Dad Fenwick."[85]

- **Thomas Mulledy, SJ.** The hot-headed Virginian would serve twice as Georgetown's president (1829–1838 and 1845–1848), as the founding president of Holy Cross (1843–1845), and as president of the St. John's Literary Institute (1850–1853) before finishing out his career on the faculty at Holy Cross and Saint Joseph's University in Philadelphia. Like his old mentor, Anthony Kohlmann, Mulledy firmly believed that the Jesuits needed to get out of the agriculture business, sell off the old Maryland plantations, and focus their ener-

---

84. Kuzniewski, "Our American Champions," 32–33. Devitt, "History of the Maryland-New York Province IX," 311.

85. Kuzniewski, "Our American Champions," 36–38.

gies on the cities. In 1838, he masterminded the highly controversial decision to sell more than 270 of the Jesuits' slaves.

- **William McSherry, SJ.** Considered an average student, McSherry made up for whatever skill he lacked in the classroom with his charming nature. Well-liked by his peers, he became the first head of the Maryland Jesuit Province at age 33 and briefly served as president of Georgetown from 1838 to 1839.[86]

- **Aloysius Young, SJ.** Unlike most of his colleagues, Young remained mainly in the classroom and did not assume any major leadership positions, instead teaching at Georgetown and St. John's Literary Institute.[87]

Of the three other scholastics who went to Rome, one (John Smith, SJ) tragically died young in Europe. Another, Charles Pise, left the Jesuits to become a diocesan priest. He served much of his career as pastor of St. Patrick's Church in Washington (the same church that kept Gonzaga College High School alive in the 1840s), and was such a respected orator that he was invited to preach at the dedication of the College of the Holy Cross in 1843.[88] The third, James Neil, SJ (who had gone to Rome with Grassi earlier than the others) became a pastor at Jesuit plantation parishes in southern Maryland.[89]

When the group arrived in Italy, Anthony Kohlmann wrote to Giovanni Grassi with some opinions about each of his former mentees. Historian Anthony Kuzniewski, SJ summarizes the contents of the letter in this way:

> Mulledy was "subject to very strong passions of pride and anger" but was "open, candid, nobleminded (sic) and possessing excellent talents." Smith and McSherry were "fine young men" with leadership potential. Ryder and Pise were the most intellectually gifted, but "mighty young, light and naturally dissipated." Fenwick had "middling talents" and a tendency to laziness.[90]

With all of their very human strengths and weaknesses, these five men would lead American Jesuit education for the next thirty years, and would help to build an unprecedented network of colleges and universities on the East Coast that is still in operation today. Georgetown, Holy Cross, Saint Joseph's (Philadelphia), and to a large extent Loyola (Baltimore) and Boston College owe their very existence to this small group of teens and twentysomethings who set sail for Europe in 1820. They, and the many students they would teach during their careers, left a collective impact on American higher education that few others would ever match.

---

86. Ibid., 22.
87. Ibid., 39–40.
88. Ibid., 39–41.
89. Curran, *History of Georgetown Vol. I*, 124–125.
90. Kuzniewski, "Our American Champions," 9.

Peter Kenney, SJ Returns

Father Kenney's recommendations were widely accepted by the American Jesuits, and they seemed at first to solve the issues the Maryland mission was facing. So it must have come as a surprise to Kenney when, just a decade later, he was asked to return to the United States and put out more fires. His original plan had worked just fine; most of the young men who had been sent to Rome did indeed return to America and had assumed important leadership roles. But now, their leadership style was proving to be just as abrasive and controversial as their predecessors'.

By then, the Jesuits had elected a new Superior General in Rome: Jan Roothaan, SJ—a Dutchman who would serve in that office from 1829 to 1853. Because his tenure coincided with the first major era of Jesuit expansion in the United States, Roothaan's decisions significantly impacted American Jesuit higher education.

Chief among Roothaan's concerns was the issue of slavery and the plantations. The hotshot young Jesuits just returned from Europe had been pushing, in Curran's words, "grand plans" to sell off most of the old farms, leaving the older Jesuits feeling "scandalized."[91] It was the Kohlmann-Neale debate all over again, but this time, it was one generation of priests against another. The older Jesuits were defensive about their traditional lifestyle, which, it was increasingly obvious, was on the wrong side of history. Opposition to slaveholding was mounting, not only in the ranks of the Jesuits, but worldwide; the British Empire outlawed slavery in 1833 and the French Empire did the same in 1848. In America, the issue was still three decades away from a resolution, and its divisiveness within the Jesuit order reflected its divisiveness nationwide. The Jesuits' old colonial-era practice of financing their ministry through agriculture seemed anachronistic as America's Catholic population became more northern and more urban. The younger generation of Jesuits had no patience for the plantation lifestyle and wanted to rid itself of that vestige of the past.

Second among Roothaan's concerns was the conduct of Father Thomas Mulledy. After assuming the presidency of Georgetown in 1829 at age 35, Mulledy developed a reputation for brashness and stubbornness that was off-putting to some. During his student days in Italy, Mulledy was known as a jingoistic hothead who would readily debate any European who dared question the virtues of the United States.[92] He was a man of contradictions. He had exceptional academic talents and a skill for writing beautiful poetry, but he also had a temper and a drinking problem that made him difficult to work with.[93] His scholarly gifts and his propensity to defend the honor of his homeland had made him the de facto leader of the eight American scholastics in Italy.[94]

---

91. Curran, *History of Georgetown Vol. I*, 121.
92. Ibid., 116.
93. Kuzniewski, "Our American Champions," 30.
94. Ibid., 17.

His high profile made him a natural choice for the Georgetown presidency when the group returned, but his leadership alienated many in the old guard.

In the summer of 1829, Peter Kenney was in Rome, participating in the assembly that elected Roothaan superior general. It was there that he learned Roothaan would be sending him back to Maryland. Kenney was apparently hesitant to accept the job, but had little choice in the matter.[95] Roothaan was aware of Mulledy's reputation as a hothead; he instructed Kenney to "keep a careful eye on Mulledy's work as rector of Georgetown"[96] and, in other correspondence, warned Mulledy's superior, Father Francis Dzierozynski, to "let him not do everything as he pleases. . . ."[97]

In 1830, Kenney arrived in Maryland for the second time. The Jesuit mission he was inspecting now included 41 priests and seven scholastics. Those men collectively staffed Georgetown College (along with its associated Holy Trinity Parish), and the embryonic St. John's College in Frederick, Maryland (which will be discussed in later chapters). They also managed six plantations in Maryland—St. Thomas, Whitemarsh, Newtown, St. Inigoes, Bohemia, and St. Joseph's—each of which functioned as both a farm and as a parish or house of formation for novice Jesuits, and four farms/parishes in Pennsylvania (at Conewago, Goshenhoppen, Philadelphia, and Lancaster).[98]

In addition, a pocket of Belgian Jesuits, new to the United States since Kenney's previous visit, now operated hundreds of miles away in St. Louis, where they had just taken control of Saint Louis College and were actively opening missions among the Plains Indians. This group had been operating technically as a branch of the Maryland mission for a decade, but the huge distance between the two epicenters of Jesuit activity meant that the St. Louis priests had a great deal of autonomy. Recognizing this, Roothaan formally separated the Maryland and Missouri missions in 1830.[99] Father Kenney was assigned to report on the status of both.

This time around, Kenney carried an extra badge of authority. In addition to being Jan Roothaan's official visitor, he also brought paperwork showing that Roothaan had appointed him the temporary head of the Maryland mission. This apparently came as a surprise to Father Francis Dzierozynski, who had been the acting head of the mission since Charles Neale's death in 1823, but Dzierozynski accepted the arrangement.[100]

On the issue of the plantations, it was clear where Kenney stood. During his first visit, he described Jesuit slaveholding as scandalous, and we can assume that his opinion did not change as he inspected the slaves in Maryland and Missouri on his second.[101] Halfway through the second visit, however, he received a letter from Rome

95. Curran, *History of Georgetown Vol. I*, 121–122.
96. Kuzniewski, "Our American Champions," 19.
97. Curran, *History of Georgetown Vol. I*, 121.
98. Devitt, "History of the Maryland-New York Province IX," 309.
99. Faherty, *Better*, 29.
100. Daley, *Georgetown University*, 269.
101. Kuzniewski, "Our American Champions," 7.

stating that Roothaan had already decided *not* to sell off the plantations. Apparently the older American Jesuits had written to Roothaan behind Kenney's back, pleading to keep the plantations intact on the grounds that they could continue to minister spiritually to the slaves who lived there. The slaves would be better off under Jesuit care than under the care of some unknown buyer, they argued. The letter and Kenney had crossed each other in the Atlantic. This rendered Kenney's opinion on the matter moot; a decision had already been made. No doubt it frustrated him and the younger Jesuits, who fully anticipated that Kenney would take their side and recommend selling off the old plantations.[102]

Kenney judged Mulledy, the young college president, to be imperfect but energetic. While acknowledging the young man's impetuousness and his other character flaws, Kenney saw Mulledy as the right man for the Georgetown presidency, and felt that some of Mulledy's brashness had mellowed as he matured. He recommended against removing Mulledy from his position.[103] In addition, Kenney recommended that the Jesuits allow Georgetown and Saint Louis Universities to charge tuition, and that Georgetown be granted a pontifical charter—giving it the right to confer theological degrees in the name of the pope. Both of these requests were approved in 1833.[104] Georgetown retains its status as a pontifical university to this day, although it has not actually utilized the power to grant papal degrees for some time.[105]

Kenney's second visit also indirectly laid the groundwork for Saint Joseph's University in Pennsylvania. Kenney negotiated with Bishop Francis Kenrick of Philadelphia to return St. Joseph's Church, the city's oldest Catholic parish, to Jesuit control.[106] Small as it was, that church would eventually serve as the first "campus" of the Jesuit college in Philadelphia. As it matured into the university that it is today, that college retained the name, "Saint Joseph's" in homage to the city's oldest Catholic parish.

Peter Kenney, SJ, in St. Louis

Having inspected the Maryland mission, Father Kenney set out on the long journey to St. Louis, bringing one Marylander, Father William McSherry, with him. Also joining them was Father James Van de Velde, for whom the journey would be a one-way trip. Van de Velde had been teaching French and calligraphy at Georgetown but, largely because of his Belgian nationality, was being transferred to Saint Louis. At the time of Kenney's second visit, there were five Belgian Jesuits working in Maryland (mostly on the Georgetown faculty) but Roothaan had decided that they "properly"

---

102. Kuzniewski, "Our American Champions," 20. Curran, *History of Georgetown Vol. I*, 121.

103. Kuzniewski, "Our American Champions," 19.

104. Curran, *History of Georgetown Vol. I*, 122–123.

105. Joseph T. Durkin, SJ, *Georgetown University: First in the Nation's Capital* (Garden City, New York: Doubleday & Company, 1964), 27.

106. Kuzniewski, "Our American Champions," 20.

belonged with their countrymen in Missouri. Mulledy objected strongly to this blow to the Georgetown faculty, but he was powerless to stop it.[107]

Van de Velde would go on to become a major figure in the frontier church. He taught at Saint Louis University for nearly a decade and served as a recruiter for the university in Louisiana, where he became widely known as a popular bayou preacher. He would also serve as Saint Louis's president from 1840 to 1843, during which time, according to one historian, he was "the best-educated college president in the United States. . . . He read and spoke Latin and was fluent in Flemish, English, French, Italian, and Spanish. He gave public addresses in all these languages. . . . He brought Saint Louis University to a position of eminence it never again matched in that century, and perhaps in all its history."[108] After leaving the university presidency, he eventually served as the second Bishop of Chicago (1849–1852).

All of this was many years in the future, however, when Van de Velde and his two companions left Georgetown in 1831. En route to St. Louis, the trio stopped in Cincinnati, where a new diocese had recently been erected under the leadership of Bishop Dominic Fenwick (a cousin of Benedict, Enoch, and George, and yet another prominent member of the Maryland Fenwick family).[109] By that time, Bishop Fenwick was already laying the groundwork for the college that would eventually become Xavier University—but that school would not be handed over to the Jesuits for another decade.

For Kenney, McSherry, and Van de Velde, the stop in Cincinnati proved memorable mainly because they were victims of thieves. McSherry's cane and boots were stolen, as were Kenney's glasses. As Xavier University historian Lee Bennish, SJ observed, tongue-in-cheek, the Jesuits "probably breathed a sigh of relief when they finally arrived in the more honest and law-abiding city of St. Louis."[110]

In Missouri, Kenney met Belgian-born Father Peter Verhaegen, SJ, the second Jesuit to serve as president of Saint Louis College. Verhaegen had assumed the presidency at the young age of twenty-nine.[111] At the time of Kenney's visit, the college was educating 150 boys, 51 of them non-Catholics, with a teaching staff of seven priests, one scholastic, and three brothers. Kenney openly questioned whether a college serving such a large percentage of Protestants was the best use of Jesuit resources on the American frontier. With tens of thousands of potential Native American converts at their doorstep, not to mention a smattering of Catholic settlers on the prairie who often went months without access to a priest, was it wise for so many of the Missouri Jesuits to concentrate their work on a single college?[112]

---

107. Garraghan, *Jesuits of the Middle U.S. Vol. I*, 315, 317.

108. William Barnaby Faherty, SJ, *Saint Louis University: A Concise History* (St. Louis: Gas House Books, 2009), 8.

109. Early American Catholic history certainly reads like a family affair at times.

110. Bennish, *Continuity*, 27.

111. William Barnaby Faherty, SJ, "Nativism and Midwestern Education: The Experience of Saint Louis University, 1832–1856," *History of Education Quarterly* 8, no. 4 (Winter, 1968): 449.

112. Faherty, *Better*, 34–35. Garraghan, *Jesuits of the Middle U.S. Vol. I*, 323–324.

Kenney was surprised to find that Verhaegen was taking liberties with the traditional Jesuit plan of study, the *Ratio Studiorum*. The curriculum at Saint Louis included many concessions to modernity, and was much more progressive than that of Georgetown. Only eight of the 150 boys were studying Latin, and Kenney found their knowledge of the language to be sub-par. In Rome, Roothaan was scandalized by these discoveries.[113] Verhaegen responded to the criticism by arguing that his scrappy band of frontier Jesuits had an obligation to meet the needs of the people as they were, and if a classical education in Latin and Greek was not in high demand among Midwestern farmers, the Jesuits would offer the kind of practical education in English and French that *was* needed.[114] He framed the concessions as a temporary measure to ensure the college's survival. Eventually, he promised, the city of St. Louis would become more sophisticated and the classics would find an audience.[115]

Kenney left St. Louis with a relatively poor opinion of both the college and the city. He criticized the gamey food, dirt roads, and the semi-lawless atmosphere on the frontier, and complained about the harsh Midwestern weather that aggravated his asthma and temporarily stranded him in the city when the Mississippi River—his highway home—froze over.[116] Most of his recommendations to Verhaegen focused on making life more comfortable for the students and faculty in these rough-and-tumble conditions. To Roothaan, he wrote that the Jesuits should avoid opening more colleges in places so far on the fringe of western civilization:

> "I should not readily advise that colleges of this kind be opened by ours in similar localities. For I doubt whether the results will answer to the labor entailed. Is it in the interest of the common good that our priests wear out their strength and spend their days in the management of colleges such as this?"[117]

Verhaegen took some of Kenney's advice to heart, and the food and facilities at Saint Louis improved. However, he clearly ignored Kenney's advice against further expansion on the American frontier and became one of the Jesuits' most prolific expansionists. Before the next decade was over, Verhaegen would personally oversee the Jesuit acquisition of Xavier University in Cincinnati and St. Joseph's College in Kentucky, and even orchestrated a brief foray into Louisiana. It was on his watch that Saint Louis College received a charter from the Missouri legislature in 1832 (the first such charter west of the Mississippi), elevating it to university status.

---

113. Garraghan, *Jesuits of the Middle U.S. Vol. I*, 324–325.
114. Faherty, *Better*, 38.
115. Garraghan, *Jesuits of the Middle U.S. Vol. I*, 325.
116. Ibid., 326. Faherty, *Better*, 33.
117. As quoted in Faherty, *Better*, 35.

Peter Kenney's Parting Gift (1833)

His work complete, Father Peter Kenney left the United States in 1832, but he returned briefly in 1833 to say one final goodbye to the men he had come to know so well. On July 8th of that year, the Georgetown community gathered at 6 p.m. to hear Father Kenney tearfully announce that the Maryland mission had been elevated to the status of a province—a major honor and a recognition that it had grown strong enough to sustain itself. Father William McSherry, SJ, who had studied in Rome on Kenney's recommendation and later joined him on that difficult trip to St. Louis, was appointed its first provincial. As he prepared to leave America for the last time, Kenney became emotional and said,

(For) so many dear Fathers and Brothers who for three years have never given me the least cause of trouble and have afforded in innumerable kindnesses, the sincere evidence of their respect and charity for me. When I think of the state in which I saw these missions fourteen years ago, and that in which they are now, is not the consolation thence derived a new cause of regret, that I am no more to witness the progress of their prosperity? Those who were then sent to Rome are now the able and indefatigable Superior and Operarii; and the last consoling duty of my ministry was to induct Father McSherry, one of their number into the office of Provincial, and promulgate the General's degree by which the new Province of Maryland is erected. . . . I know I shall be happy in Ireland. Everything has its time. I am not now rejoicing in hopes of seeing Ireland; I am mourning, as far as I dare, for leaving America."[118]

The admiration was mutual. Whatever combination of diplomatic and managerial skill Peter Kenney possessed, his leadership was the one thing the usually fractious American Jesuits could agree upon. As one Jesuit wrote in Georgetown's diary in 1833, "This morning, July 11, 1833, we all embraced for the last time our beloved and honored Fr. Kenney. He himself was very much moved at his leave-taking. Never has a man lived among us whom all without exception so loved and reverenced."[119] In Missouri, Peter Verhaegen wrote, "alas! In losing today our excellent Father Visitor, we lose a treasure."[120] During his brief stopover in Cincinnati, Kenney apparently made such a positive impression on Bishop Dominic Fenwick that Fenwick lobbied hard to make Kenney his assisting bishop.[121] Even 100 years later, a Jesuit historian wrote that "friends and foes alike had to yield to (Kenney's) charm and eloquence. His Visitation of the Province was hailed as a blessing from God."[122]

---

118. As quoted in Devitt, "History of the Maryland-New York Province IX," 346.
119. "The Jubilee of the Province, 1833," *Woodstock Letters* XII, no. 2 (1883): 207.
120. Garraghan, *Jesuits of the Middle U.S. Vol. I*, 327.
121. Ibid., 328–329.
122. Devitt, "History of the Maryland-New York Province IX," 345.

At the end of Kenney's first visit, even Anthony Kohlmann had asked for Kenney to stay in America and become superior of the Maryland mission.[123] (And it certainly speaks volumes that the usually headstrong Kohlmann wanted Kenney to be his boss, even declaring him "the best Orator that ever was heard in this country.")[124] Georgetown historian Richard Daley, SJ speculates: "Had this request been granted, it is more than likely that Georgetown's history for the period 1820–1830 would have been vastly different. The problem of manpower would have vexed any superior, but Peter Kenney would have taken vigorous steps to provide some remedy."[125]

Unfortunately, Kenney's skills were in high demand elsewhere. American bishops (among them Guillaume DuBourg in New Orleans) lobbied to have Kenney appointed bishop of New York or Philadelphia. In Kenney's homeland, the Irish were agitating to appoint him bishop in their own country.[126] In 1833, the pope came close to appointing him Bishop of Cincinnati. But Kenney was humble and preferred pastoral work, despite his outstanding managerial skills. The idea of being sent back to Cincinnati at age 54, especially when he had loathed so much about the frontier lifestyle he had observed in St. Louis, terrified him. Ultimately, he was spared the assignment through the intervention of Jan Roothaan.[127] Kenney spent most of the rest of his life as a pastor in Europe before dying in 1841 at the age of 62.

A Living Link to the Past

When Kenney announced the creation of the Maryland Province, he was courteous enough to send the first notice to Father Francis Neale, SJ, who was by then in the twilight of his life.[128] As a young man in Europe in 1773, Neale had been denied the right to enter the Jesuits because the order was suppressed shortly before he was scheduled to take his vows. In America, he and his brothers, Leonard and Charles, had led the efforts to restore the Jesuits, first via the Russian loophole in 1805, and then permanently in 1814. (In total, there were seven Neale brothers, all but one of whom became or at least tried to become Jesuits. Two of them, Joseph and Oswald, died before fully completing their studies at St. Omer's.)[129]

Francis Neale's career in the United States was controversial; his presidency of Georgetown was largely ineffective, and he, along with his brothers, had fought hard to keep the old plantations in Jesuit hands even after it was clear that they had become an outdated relic of a bygone era. Nonetheless, the youngest of the Neale brothers was a living link to the past. Of the Maryland Jesuits alive in 1833, he alone had experi-

---

123. Daley, *Georgetown University*, 269.
124. As quoted in Kuzniewski, "Our American Champions," 6.
125. Daley, *Georgetown University*, 269.
126. Ibid., 268–269.
127. Garraghan, *Jesuits of the Middle U.S. Vol. I*, 328, 330.
128. Daley, *Georgetown University*, 275.
129. Devitt, "History of the Maryland-New York Province IX," 326–327.

enced firsthand the discriminatory atmosphere of the colonial era, along with the suppression, restoration, and ultimately, the rise of the Jesuit order in America. For the
old man, news that Maryland was now a province in its own right must have seemed
like vindication of his life's work. As Daley writes, "The joy of this made the years
since 1773 seem few."[130]

When Francis Neale, SJ died in 1837, it symbolically marked the end of the old
order in American Catholicism. It was the curtain call of an era in which the American Church was dominated by old Maryland families (particularly the Neales, Car-
rolls, and Fenwicks), and by bishops who had come of age before the Revolutionary
War. Although there were plenty of Fenwicks still teaching at Jesuit colleges or serving as bishops, Francis Neale was the last major survivor of the generation of boys
who, like John Carroll, had been educated at the illegal Jesuit academy in Bohemia
Manor, then gone off to complete their degrees at St. Omer's in Belgium. Those
American men had, for all their efforts, successfully built and sustained only one true
Jesuit college in America, literally and figuratively at the center of American power in
Washington, DC. It was only through the efforts of Belgian reinforcements that the
Jesuits had established a second college in Missouri. It would now be up to their stu-
dents—the "second generation" of American Jesuits—to carry on their work and
expand Jesuit education to the rest of the country, as Catholics began to immigrate to
the United States in droves and the American Church continued to grow.

John McElroy, SJ, and St. John's Literary Institute (1829), Frederick, Maryland

The St. John's Literary Institute in Frederick, Maryland was founded in 1829, on
the eve of Peter Kenney's second visit. The driving force behind it was Father John
McElroy, SJ, an alumnus of Georgetown and the future founder of Boston College.
This makes St. John's the first American college to be founded by a Jesuit who was,
himself, the product of an American Jesuit education.

McElroy was an Irish immigrant who crossed the Atlantic at age twenty and settled in the Georgetown neighborhood, where he worked as a merchant. There, he
became a regular parishioner at Holy Trinity Church and eventually enrolled at
Georgetown College. When the restored American Jesuits celebrated Mass together
that fateful day in October, 1806, McElroy was one of the original recruits. He initially entered the Society as a brother, in which capacity he performed the kinds of
administrative tasks often assigned to brothers, serving mainly as Georgetown's
bookkeeper. This low-level assignment probably reflected his working-class background more than his raw skill, because when Giovanni Grassi became head of the
college, he recognized McElroy's potential and encouraged him to pursue further
studies toward the priesthood. McElroy completed his theological training at

---

130. Daley, *Georgetown University*, 275.

Georgetown while still maintaining his responsibilities for the college's finances, and in 1817, he was ordained.[131]

McElroy served as pastor of Holy Trinity Church in Georgetown before being transferred to Frederick, Maryland, where he assumed responsibility for St. John's Church. Only a young, energetic man could have handled such an assignment; McElroy almost single-handedly served a huge territory in northern Maryland, making regular home visits to Catholic families as far away as the western panhandle. As pastor, he oversaw the construction of a beautiful new church building and established free schools in the city for both girls and boys. The girls' school was run by the Sisters of Charity, while McElroy recruited some fellow Jesuits from Georgetown to staff the boys' school.

Once again, using modern terminology, the closest equivalent to what McElroy founded would be a community college. It was meant to serve poor children from northern Maryland who lacked the means to travel and attend Georgetown, and initially it offered only the first few years of the *Ratio Studiorum* curriculum. Its best students were expected to complete the full seven-year course of study at Georgetown. In time, however, it began to attract students from out of town who boarded with local families, and in 1850, St. John's received a state charter to award degrees in its own name.

McElroy was not there to celebrate that milestone. In 1847, he had been called into military service during the Mexican War. President James K. Polk was eager to appoint Catholic chaplains to the Army as a way to bolster the war's popularity among Catholic voters and to avoid any perception that the conflict was a sectarian war between a Protestant country and a Catholic one. The Jesuits were asked to provide two such chaplains to the war effort, and they selected McElroy for one of the posts.[132]

The school at Frederick was largely built around McElroy himself, and its collegiate ambitions did not long survive his departure. In McElroy's absence, St. John's passed into the hands of the notoriously stubborn Thomas Mulledy, SJ. In 1853, Mulledy expelled a group of students for participating in a campus riot, including nearly everyone who had been on track to graduate with the school's first bachelor's degrees. Although some of those students went on to graduate from Georgetown, their mass expulsion from St. John's marked the beginning of the end of the Frederick school as a "college." St. John's continued to enroll seminarians and occasional lay students in its upper divisions, but the Jesuits deliberately scaled back its course offerings.[133] Though, on paper, it remained a college, the Jesuits stopped advertising it as such, and by the end of the 1850s it became primarily a grammar school. At that time, the Maryland Province was staffing colleges in Baltimore and Worcester and was struggling to get new colleges off the ground in Philadelphia and Boston, all of which were higher priorities than the junior college in Frederick.

---

131. "Death of Father John McElroy," *Woodstock Letters* VI, no. 3 (1878): 178–180.

132. Ibid., 178–180.

133. John J. Ryan, SJ, "St. John's College, Frederick: Half a Century Ago," *Woodstock Letters* XXX, no. 2 (1901): 231–246.

Meanwhile, McElroy remained enlisted in the Army and was assigned to a regiment in Boston. There, after his discharge, he took control of St. Mary's Church and built the original campus of Boston College in the late 1850s. He worked diligently in Boston until his health would not allow him to continue. Blind and frail, he was sent back to Frederick where he died in 1877, reportedly still saying Mass daily from memory.[134] His obituary read:

> This pile of buildings (at Boston College), magnificent in its proportions, and still more so in the results which are being there achieved for the Church in New England, is the noblest monument of his zeal. When he had finished it, the work of his life was done. His sight failed, and his frame, gigantic though it was, could no longer withstand the effects of nearly three quarters of a century spent in unflagging toil in the service of God.[135]

McElroy had served ably at Georgetown and had founded two colleges, one of which would eventually rank among the largest and most prominent Jesuit universities in the world. (That story will be told in more detail in later chapters.) Although Boston College was unquestionably McElroy's greatest accomplishment, his earlier contributions in Maryland were still significant. His influence spread throughout the Maryland Province by way of the students he educated. Two of his mentees at Frederick would go on to become major figures in Jesuit education in their own right: Bernard Maguire, SJ served twice as President of Georgetown, and John Early, SJ led both Georgetown and Holy Cross and served as the founding president of Loyola University (Baltimore).

As for St. John's Parish in Frederick, the Jesuits continued to operate the church and its associated grammar school until 1903, when they withdrew permanently. The church and school were then transferred to the Archdiocese of Baltimore. A coeducational Catholic high school still operates near the site today: St. John's Catholic Prep. It is the spiritual successor to the schools that John McElroy founded in Frederick nearly two centuries ago.

The Jesuits Return to Louisiana

One puzzle of American Catholic history is why it took so long to establish a successful Catholic college in Louisiana. No US state had a larger Catholic population in the early 1800s. Louisianan culture is replete with Catholic influence; even the state flag features the image of a pelican in its nest—a traditional Catholic symbol representing self-sacrifice, based on the medieval legend that a pelican pierces its own breast to feed its young. The pelican symbol is common in Catholic churches around the

---

134. Woodstock Letters, "Death of Father John McElroy," 184.
135. Ibid., 184.

world, and Louisiana's nickname, "the Pelican State," can be construed as a subversive way of calling it, "the Catholic state."[136]

The 1830s saw the arrival—or, more correctly, the return—of the Jesuits to Louisiana. French Jesuits first came to the Louisiana colony in 1700, sixty-six years after the English Jesuits arrived in Maryland. Like their Maryland counterparts, the Louisiana Jesuits operated a large plantation for income and owned slaves. They evangelized local Native Americans (who killed at least three of the French priests) and were in the planning stages for a proposed Jesuit college in New Orleans when European politics intervened. In 1763, the French government ejected the Jesuits from all of its territory (including colonies) as part of the political upheaval leading to the worldwide Jesuit suppression in 1773.[137] After that, the Jesuit presence in Louisiana was negligible until 1830, when, as described in earlier chapters, a small group of four French Jesuits landed in New Orleans en route to Bardstown, Kentucky, where they mistakenly believed that they would take control of St. Joseph's College.

There were certainly attempts to found a college on the bayou. In 1832, Bishop Leo de Neckere of New Orleans (an alumnus of Saint Louis College) asked the Jesuits at his alma mater to open a school in Louisiana and even offered land for that purpose. Unfortunately, Saint Louis had no faculty to spare, but President Peter Verhaegen referred the matter to Superior General Jan Roothaan in Rome. Verhaegen committed to loan some Jesuits from the Missouri mission if Roothaan could make a comparable commitment by sending three Jesuit professors from Europe. It was not to be; in 1832, Roothaan had just formally approved the Jesuit takeover of St. Mary's College in Kentucky, and he was determined to fulfill that commitment without spreading his resources too thin.[138]

Paradoxically, even after the French Jesuits reestablished a meager presence in Louisiana in 1830, their major ministry for more than five years was St. Mary's College, located hundreds of miles away. Only a skeleton crew remained in New Orleans, while most money and personnel went to the Kentucky school. In addition to providing financial subsidies, between 1830 and 1839 the French province sent fifteen Jesuits to St. Mary's, who were supplemented by twenty Americans who entered the Society through the college.[139]

For the time being, Louisiana boys would simply have to go to St. Louis, Kentucky, or Georgetown for their education, and many did. Louisiana plantation owners

---

136. Pelicans regurgitate fish from their pouches to feed their young. From a distance, this looked, to medieval observers, as if the birds were pecking at their own bodies and drawing blood to bring their dead chicks back to life. Christians saw parallels between this legend and Christ's sacrifice and resurrection, and St. Thomas Aquinas compared Jesus to a pelican. In medieval art, a pelican is depicted "in her vulning" (pecking at her breast) or "in her piety" (feeding blood to the chicks).

137. Bernard A. Cook, *Founded on Faith: A History of Loyola University New Orleans* (New Orleans: Loyola University, 2012), 8–16. Walter B. Posey, Review of *The French Jesuits in Lower Louisiana (1700–1763)* by Jeane Delanglez, *Church History* 4, no. 4 (December, 1935): 314–315.

138. Faherty, *Better*, 44.

139. Shelley, *Fordham*, 36, 41.

who could afford the privilege sent their sons on the long journey along the coast to Washington or up the Mississippi. Louisiana was so important as a source of students that Saint Louis College sent Jesuits to New Orleans as recruiting agents. One of the most important of these agents was Father James Van de Velde, SJ, the former Georgetown professor who had accompanied Peter Kenney on his visit to St. Louis. As a recruiter, Van de Velde toured the bayous and preached at churches on Sundays, identifying promising students whom he then chaperoned on the long boat voyage back up the Mississippi to St. Louis.[140] Although Georgetown did not send actual recruiters to Louisiana, it printed advertisements in French and developed a strong reputation in the Catholic community there. By the middle of the 1800s, Louisiana was sending more students to Georgetown than any other southern state except Maryland—even more than neighboring Virginia.[141]

Nicholas Point, SJ, and St. Charles College (1837–1922), Grand Coteau, Louisiana

The most prominent of the French Jesuits sent to St. Mary's College in Kentucky was Father Nicholas Point, SJ. After concluding a teaching stint at St. Mary's that lasted only a year, Point was named head of the New Orleans Mission, in which capacity he was approached by the new Archbishop of New Orleans, Antoine Blanc, in 1835 about opening a college. The archbishop offered land in Iberville (near Baton Rouge), but Father Point declined.[142] He set his sights instead on Donaldsonville, just a few miles away, but he encountered opposition from anti-Catholic bigots in the area, who organized an eleventh-hour campaign to block the Jesuit college.[143]

Frustrated, Father Point settled instead on a more isolated town farther inland, Grand Coteau, in 1837. In French, Grand Coteau means, "big hill," and it is exactly that—a rough circle of earth that rises above the marshy lowlands around it. Its population at the time numbered some 8,000, including both Catholic Cajuns and a significant number of Catholic pioneers from Maryland who had chosen to settle there as part of their migration west. The remote location caught Father Point's attention because a women's religious order, the Religious of the Sacred Heart of Jesus, had been operating a successful girls' school there for seventeen years.[144]

The abandoned site in Donaldsonville had been attractive mainly because it was on the Mississippi River and easily accessible to Louisiana's two major cities: New Orleans and Baton Rouge. Grand Coteau was very much the opposite. The closest

---

140. Faherty, *Better*, 44.

141. Curran, "Wave her Colors Ever: Writing Georgetown's History," *US Catholic Historian* 28, no. 3 (2010): 74.

142. R. Eric Platt, *Sacrifice and Survival: Identity, Mission, and Jesuit Higher Education in the American South* (Tuscaloosa: University of Alabama Press, 2014), 59.

143. J. Maitrugues, SJ, "St. Charles College, Grand Coteau, La.," *Woodstock Letters* V, no. 1 (1876): 19.

144. Ibid., 18.

city of any meaningful size was Opelousas, and getting to the Jesuit college from New Orleans required four or five days of travel. There were two main routes: one by water and one overland. The all-water route required students to travel by boat up four different rivers: the Mississippi, the Red, the Atchafalaya, and the Bayou Courtanbleau. Travelers had to camp overnight on the riverbanks, and for a few months every year, when the water levels fell, this route was completely inaccessible. The second (overland) route required travel by stagecoach, steamboat, and (in later years) railroads, but still necessitated multiple overnight stays.[145]

Father Point named his school St. Charles College. Despite its remoteness, it welcomed an entering class of more than 60 boys in 1837.[146] Over the course of its history, St. Charles would be mildly successful, but its facilities were always meager and its enrollment never exceeded 200. In the end, its remote location doomed it, but a number of quirky accidents artificially prolonged its life.

In 1838, barely a year after it was founded, St. Charles College changed hands. The French Jesuit missionaries led by Father Point turned it over to the Missouri Jesuits based out of St. Louis, who were then led by Father Peter Verhaegen. This allowed the French Jesuits to concentrate their limited personnel on St. Mary's College in Kentucky (which they still envisioned as their main ministry in the United States) and satisfied Verhaegen's desire to expand. St. Charles thus became the first of many branches of the Saint Louis University family tree. Ten years later, in 1848, the Missouri Jesuits withdrew from Grand Coteau and another wave of French Jesuit missionaries from Lyon took over St. Charles College.[147]

Almost immediately, the French Jesuits from Lyon recognized the flaws in the college's location. In 1849, they made plans to abandon St. Charles and replace it with two new Louisiana colleges: a day school in New Orleans and a boarding school in Baton Rouge, where there were more students to serve. The Baton Rouge school was known the College of Saints Peter and Paul, but it never amounted to much; it opened in 1850 but closed six years later due to local Protestant opposition and an unfortunately timed yellow fever outbreak in the city. Their foray into Louisiana's capital city a failure, the Jesuits returned to Grand Coteau and reopened St. Charles.[148]

The day school in New Orleans was more successful. Founded by Jesuit astronomer John Cambiaso, SJ, the College of the Immaculate Conception served commuter students in the Crescent City for more than five decades and became a convenient alternative for those who could not afford the journey to Grand Coteau. Technically speaking, the College of the Immaculate Conception shut its doors in 1911 and became what is known today as Jesuit High School in New Orleans. However, it was in effect the ancestor of today's Loyola University of New Orleans, founded to replace it in 1904.

---

145. Ibid., 17. Platt, *Sacrifice*, 63–64.

146. Maitrugues, "St Charles College," 21.

147. Garraghan, *Jesuits of the Middle U.S. Vol. II* 140.

148. Platt, *Sacrifice*, 66.

St. Charles College survived another brush with death in 1869. That year, it was inspected by a Jesuit visitor from Europe, who judged it to be a waste of resources and recommended its closure so that the Jesuits could focus their limited manpower on rebuilding Southern communities devastated by the Civil War. That same year, however, a fire broke out at the Jesuits' Spring Hill College in Mobile, Alabama. With their facilities destroyed, the faculty and students at Spring Hill relocated to Grand Coteau to continue their studies uninterrupted.[149] The temporary influx of refugees from Mobile breathed life into St. Charles College, but after Spring Hill was rebuilt, enrollment at Grand Coteau fell once more.

St. Charles again avoided total closure, in part, because the New Orleans Jesuits decided to locate their seminary on its grounds. The seminarians combined with the lay students provided enough justification to keep the campus open, but the Jesuits continued to search for a more accessible location.[150] Unfortunately, although maintaining the remote school at Grand Coteau was always a significant drag on Jesuit resources, the alternative—building a new college from scratch—invariably proved to cost even more. As a result, St. Charles limped along well into the twentieth century. Fires destroyed the main building in 1900 and 1907, and after the latter, Spring Hill College repaid the favor that had been extended to it thirty-eight years earlier, taking in faculty and student refugees from St. Charles. The small college at Grand Coteau chugged along until a European Jesuit visitor, Father Norbert de Boynes, SJ, inspected it in 1921 and recommended its closure the following year.

While 1922 marked the end of St. Charles as a college for lay students, the New Orleans Jesuits continued to educate their seminarians there, and do so to this day. The isolated (rebuilt) campus is often described as idyllic and perfect for spiritual reflection. Since 1972, the site has also been home to the Jesuit Spirituality Center, a retreat facility in which resident Jesuits and seminarians offer St. Ignatius's *Spiritual Exercises*. Grand Coteau thus remains an integral part of the Jesuits' ministry, and they have never parted with it.

The college's founder, Father Nicholas Point, remained at Grand Coteau long enough to ensure that St. Charles had gotten off the ground, but in 1841 he moved west in pace with the expanding American frontier. He became part of the next chapter in Jesuit history as a missionary in the Rocky Mountains, serving the Native Americans in Montana, Idaho, and the Pacific Northwest. That mission helped to give birth to most of the western Jesuit colleges, including Gonzaga, Seattle, and Santa Clara. Point is remembered as one of the first Europeans to map and document much of the Rocky Mountain region.[151]

---

149. Ibid., 68.
150. Ibid., 64.
151. Shelley, *Fordham*, 40.

Conditions in the 1830s and 1840s

Cholera

Grand Coteau seemed appealing as a location for a college in 1837 because its isolation provided some protection from disease. This was a serious concern in the 1830s because a cholera epidemic had broken out across the United States, and densely populated cities were most affected.

Nearly all colleges operating in the 1830s were in some way affected by cholera. The disease claimed the lives of Father William Byrne, founder and president of St. Mary's College in Kentucky, and Bishop Dominic Fenwick, founder of Xavier University, before either school was in Jesuit hands. An 1849 outbreak in Cincinnati devastated the city, claiming the lives of 4,600 people, including several Jesuits who died after ministering to infected patients in local hospitals.[152]

In St. Louis, the epidemic forced boarding students to relocate temporarily to the more isolated Jesuit mission at Florissant, Missouri. The preventative measure worked; no students or faculty died, despite a high casualty rate in the city proper. At Georgetown, a number of Jesuits were stricken with cholera, including President Thomas Mulledy, SJ, but there were few deaths. Although the city of Washington was severely affected with nearly 2,000 cases, the still-separate city of Georgetown was relatively spared, with only 400. Nonetheless, the epidemic did affect enrollment, as many parents kept their sons home.[153]

First Government Investment

The 1830s saw the first major government investment in Jesuit education. In 1833, the United States Senate (by vote of 14 to 13) granted $25,000 worth of city lots in the District of Columbia to Georgetown, expecting the college to sell them to raise funds. President Andrew Jackson, who approved the deal, and future President John Tyler, who voted for it as a US Senator from Virginia, both had a favorable opinion of Georgetown. Jackson enrolled his ward and Tyler enrolled his son at the college.[154]

When word of the government grant reached St. Louis, the Missouri Jesuits sought a similar arrangement; after all, theirs was the only chartered college on the frontier, and it had benefitted from local tax dollars almost since its inception. Federal investment seemed like a logical next step. Senator Thomas Hart Benton of Missouri argued in favor of providing federal funds to Saint Louis University, but the measure was ultimately tabled on Capitol Hill. The votes were split along geographic lines, with newer Midwestern states in support and older East Coast states

---

152. Ibid., 35. Bennish, *Continuity*, 53–54.
153. Faherty, *Better*, 46. Daley, *Georgetown University*, 278. Curran, *History of Georgetown Vol. I*, 190–191.
154. Curran, *History of Georgetown Vol. I*, 175.

opposed. The easterners objected mainly because of the French-speaking character of the college. The student body at Saint Louis at the time was basically trifurcated among French-speaking Louisianans, Spanish-speaking Mexicans, and native Missourians, many of whom were still Francophone.[155] As a result, while Georgetown's close ties to the American establishment were enough to overcome anti-Catholic prejudice in the federal government, the same level of tolerance did not apply to the more Continental European Catholic cultures that still dominated the former Louisiana Territory.

First Graduate and Medical Schools

Graduate education in antebellum America differed drastically from today's. By convention, master's degrees were not taught; any man could be awarded a master's degree if he already possessed a bachelor's degree and could credibly demonstrate at least a year of meaningful, independent study of a subject. A master's degree was effectively an honorary degree given to lifelong learners. This was not just a practice at Catholic schools; Harvard, Yale, and Princeton did not start to award master's degrees for actual classroom work until the 1870s.[156]

Sources differ as to when Jesuit colleges first started offering master's degrees, but the phenomenon began roughly in the 1830s. Georgetown awarded four master's degrees in that decade, though it also awarded one in 1826 and possibly another as early as 1817.[157] The real credit for systematizing graduate education, however, goes to Saint Louis, which advertised the criteria for a master's degree in 1838: "The degree of A.M. is given to alumni who, after having received the degree of A.B., shall have devoted two years to some literary pursuit." In the 1860s, Saint Louis raised the bar slightly and began requiring either one year of on-campus study or two years of demonstrated work in a "learned profession."[158] Nonetheless, many Jesuit colleges, including Xavier and Fordham, continued to advertise the old-fashioned master's degree, requiring little but the student's word, for decades.[159]

Medical school, too, was vastly different in the early 1800s. A bachelor's degree was not required for admission, and most medical schools were more like apprenticeship programs, run part-time by practicing doctors who lectured in the evenings. When Father Peter Kenney visited the United States for the second time, Roothaan asked him to consider whether Georgetown should establish a medical school, but nothing immediate came from that inquiry.[160] The first Jesuit medical school—in fact, the first professional school of any kind at a Jesuit university—was at Saint Louis.

---

155. Faherty, *Better*, 54, 67–69.
156. Power, *Catholic Higher Education*, 339.
157. Ibid., 337. Curran, *History of Georgetown Vol. I*, 362.
158. Power, *Catholic Higher Education*, 338.
159. Ibid., 339.
160. Curran, *History of Georgetown Vol. I*, 123.

As president of Saint Louis University, Father Peter Verhaegen proactively asked local physicians to open a medical department at the university in 1835. Verhaegen promised the doctors near-full autonomy in governing the school; the Jesuits would merely provide the facilities and, through their state charter, the right to grant degrees. Planning was slow. Saint Louis granted its first medical degree—the first medical degree ever awarded in the region—in 1839, before the medical school officially existed. The honorary degree went to Dr. B.B. Brown, a local dentist who had completed all of his training as an apprentice.[161] The medical school properly opened in 1842, with a faculty that was almost entirely Protestant and a governing board that represented many different religious denominations.[162]

Despite its ecumenism, the Saint Louis medical school fell victim to anti-Catholic bigotry. As more Americans from the east settled in Missouri, the state's demographics changed, and it ceased to be the overwhelmingly Catholic enclave it had been since the colonial days. Anti-Catholic mob violence was directed at the medical school so often that its faculty voted to dissociate the school from the university in 1848. That story will be told in the chapters ahead. It would be another half-century before medical education would return to Saint Louis University in 1903.

Notable Visitors in the Antebellum Years

Both Georgetown and Saint Louis Universities played host to prominent civic figures in the antebellum years. President Martin Van Buren enrolled his son at Georgetown, and spoke at Saint Louis shortly after his term in the White House ended.[163] Presidents Washington, John Quincy Adams, Jackson, Tyler, Polk, Taylor, Pierce, Buchanan, and Lincoln all visited the Georgetown campus before or during the Civil War.

Charles Dickens visited both major Jesuit schools as part of his six-month tour of the United States in 1842, and he commented on both of them in his "American Notes" published later that year. In describing Washington, he wrote:

> At George Town, in the suburbs, there is a Jesuit College; delightfully situated, and, so far as I had an opportunity of seeing, well managed. Many persons who are not members of the Romish Church avail themselves, I believe, of these institutions, and of the advantageous opportunities they afford for the education of their children. The heights in this neighbourhood, above the Potomac River, are very picturesque; and are free, I should conceive, from some of the insalubrities of Washington. The air, at that elevation, was quite cool and refreshing, when in the city it was burning hot.[164]

---

161. Faherty, *Better*, 62.
162. Faherty, "Nativism," 450.
163. Faherty, *Better*, 64. Curran, *History of Georgetown Vol. I*, 175.
164. Charles Dickens, *American Notes* (New York: St. Martin's Press, 1985), 112.

Of Saint Louis, he wrote:

> The Roman Catholic religion, introduced here by the early French settlers, pre-
> vails extensively. Among the public institutions are a Jesuit college; a convent for
> 'the Ladies of the Sacred Heart;' and a large chapel attached to the college, which
> was in course of erection at the time of my visit, and was intended to be conse-
> crated on the second of December in the next year. The architect of this building,
> is one of the reverend fathers of the school, and the works proceed under his sole
> direction. The organ will be sent from Belgium.
>
> In addition to these establishments, there is a Roman Catholic cathedral, dedi-
> cated to Saint Francis Xavier; and a hospital, founded by the munificence of a
> deceased resident, who was a member of that church. It also sends missionaries
> from hence among the Indian tribes.[165]

At the time of Dickens's visit, Jesuits operated six American colleges, all but one
of which were culturally, if not geographically, in the South. The Southern schools
included Georgetown (DC), Saint Louis (Missouri), St. Mary's (Kentucky), St.
Charles (Louisiana), and the rudimentary St. John's (Maryland). The only Jesuit college solidly in the northern United States was in Cincinnati, where the Missouri
Jesuits had recently expanded to take control of what is now Xavier University.[166]
(Dickens did stop in Cincinnati during his American tour, but he made no mention
the fledgling Xavier in his notes.)[167]

Across the Atlantic, the American Jesuits were already developing a reputation as
the leading Catholic educators in the United States. European Catholic missionaries
looked to the Jesuits as an example in setting up their own American colleges and missions. Boniface Wimmer, a German monk who brought the Benedictine order to the
United States and founded America's first Benedictine school, St. Vincent College
near Pittsburgh, wrote in 1845:

> The (American) Jesuits devote their energies principally to teaching in colleges;
> their students are mostly from the higher classes of society and many of them
> belong to Protestant families. Many Jesuits are also doing excellent work among
> the Indians. . . . (The) Jesuits generally receive only the children of rich families,
> many of whom are Protestant, into their institutions, because they depend on
> them for sustenance. . . .[168]

Wimmer's mildly tongue-in-cheek criticism of the Jesuit penchant for educating
the rich underscored an Achilles heel that haunted Jesuit higher education for cen-

---

165. Ibid., 159.
166. Faherty, *Better*, 50, 61.
167. Bennish, *Continuity*, 38.
168. Boniface Wimmer, "Concerning the Missions," in *Boniface Wimmer: Visions of a Founder*
(Latrobe, PA: St. Vincent College, undated), 7–8.

turies. The Jesuits needed money, and they did not have nearly enough resources to finance their ambitious expansion plans or serve all of the students who, they felt, needed access to a Jesuit education. This paucity of funds led to one of the most controversial decisions in Jesuit history, bringing to a head an internal debate over slavery that had divided the Jesuits almost from the very beginning of their ministry in the United States.

The 1838 Slave Sale

The darkest year in the history of the American Jesuits was 1838, when the decades-long debate about the old colonial-era plantations in Maryland, what to do with them, and whether they should continue to exist, reached its climax. The culmination of this conflict, which resulted in the sale of more than 270 Jesuit-owned slaves from Maryland to a buyer in Louisiana, ultimately did little to resolve any of the issues that had been debated for the previous half-century, but did inflict harm on hundreds of people and cause serious conflict among the Jesuits themselves. Indeed, the decision made by the notoriously headstrong Thomas Mulledy, SJ during his first year as provincial of the Maryland Province represented arguably the worst of all possible outcomes.

It is helpful to review how the Jesuits came to own slaves in the first place. As mentioned previously, the Jesuits and the small handful of settlers they served constituted the only significant Catholic population in the thirteen English colonies during the 1600s and 1700s. Despite having helped to found the Maryland colony, Catholics represented no more than one-twelfth of its population for most of the pre-Revolutionary War era. They were soon subject to open discrimination by anti-Catholic laws passed both in London and in Maryland's own Protestant-dominated legislature.[169] Unlike other colonies like Massachusetts and Virginia, which supported their established churches (Puritanism and Anglicanism, respectively) through tax money, Maryland never provided any government support to Catholicism. As a result, the Jesuits had to raise their own money, and they relied on farming to do so.[170]

At first, indentured servants worked on the Jesuit plantations in Maryland, but like other colonists engaged in agriculture, the Jesuits soon turned to slavery. The date of the first slaves' arrival on Jesuit plantations is unclear, but by the eve of the Revolutionary War, the roughly two-dozen Catholic priests in America collectively owned about 200 slaves, some of whom were likely purchased, and some of whom were likely donated by wealthy Catholics.[171] The priests were like the other members of the landed gentry in the American South, presiding over manor houses and engaging in normal trades of the time, like shoemaking and blacksmithing. But unlike most plan-

---

169. Beckett, "Listening," 4.
170. Ibid., 4–5.
171. Ibid., 7.

tation owners, they also ministered on horseback to Catholics throughout the area, visiting homes many miles away to say Mass, hear confessions, and deliver the sacraments.[172] Income from the farms made these ministries possible.

Slaveholding was not forbidden by Catholic moral teaching at the time. Slavery was practiced in the Roman Empire, so the Catholic Church came of age in a slave-owning society. As historian Edward Beckett, SJ explained, "Millions of Catholics throughout history, including innumerable popes, bishops, priests, and religious were slave owners."[173] By the time the Jesuits arrived in Maryland, there were already Jesuit-owned slaves throughout the Spanish and Portuguese colonies in the New World. Indeed, the Latin American slave plantations run by Jesuits initially dwarfed those in the United States.[174] As the years progressed and other Catholic religious orders arrived in America, they, too, participated in the slave economy. Among the other orders of priests and nuns that owned slaves in the United States were the Carmelites, Daughters of Charity, Dominicans, Religious of the Sacred Heart, School Sisters of Notre Dame, Sisters of Charity, Sisters of Loretto, Sisters of Mount Carmel, Sulpicians, Vincentians, Visitation Sisters, and Ursulines.[175]

Since the Jesuit plantations doubled as Catholic "churches," the slaves were active members of the congregations. While eighteenth-century Catholic doctrine tolerated slavery, it also taught that slaves were human beings with souls to be saved. The Jesuits baptized their slaves, presided over slave marriages, and gave last rights to the dying slaves, just as they would for any other Catholic. In the 1760s, the list of parishioners at St. Inigoes Plantation included 166 whites and 33 slaves.[176] At Holy Trinity Church in Georgetown, African-Americans (both free and enslaved) represented 30% of the congregation from the 1790s through the Civil War.[177] As William Warner has observed, Blacks routinely served as godparents at Holy Trinity baptisms and engaged in other social activities that demonstrate active participation in parish life. At least in the early nineteenth century, Black and white worshippers attended the same Sunday services, although the congregation was racially segregated, with whites in the lower pews and Blacks sitting in a balcony that could only be accessed by an exterior stairway.[178] In Missouri, the Jesuits at Saint Louis University built a chapel for Black worshippers within St. Francis Xavier College Church in 1858. They later assumed responsibility to manage St. Elizabeth's Parish, the city's main Catholic parish for free Blacks, in 1873.

---

172. Ibid., 6. Warner, *At Peace*, 85–86.

173. Beckett, "Listening," 9.

174. Nathaniel Millett, "The Memory of Slavery at Saint Louis University," *American Nineteenth Century History* 16, no. 3 (2015): 331.

175. Beckett, "Listening," 45 (n. 185). Susan Nalezyty, "The History of Enslaved People at Georgetown Visitation," *US Catholic Historian* 37, no. 2 (2019): 28.

176. Beckett, "Listening," 10.

177. Warner, *At Peace*, 31.

178. Ibid., 91–92.

In the Maryland Province, John McElroy, SJ founded a Sunday school for Black children in 1819; another Jesuit, Thomas Lilly, SJ, taught slaves in Frederick and attempted to build a school for free Black students in Philadelphia during the 1830s.[179] In Kentucky, records show that Catholic slave owners sent enslaved children to the Jesuits for religious instruction.[180] Baptismal records and other documents (while incomplete) sometimes list the slaves *by name* at a time when the US census listed them only as nameless property. The lives and identities of slaves associated with the Jesuits, therefore, are somewhat better documented than what was typically the case in Protestant America.

Partly as a result of this documentation, we also know that there was cruelty on the plantations. Some Jesuits used corporal punishment against their slaves—a practice that Peter Kenney, SJ severely restricted (but did not completely ban) after his first visit. Whippings and other forms of punishment were most often enacted by the lay Jesuit brothers who managed the farms rather than by the priests themselves, but they certainly took place.[181] Jesuit-owned slaves often lived and slept in painfully inhumane conditions.

Slaves were sometimes relocated from one Jesuit property to another, presumably without their consent. When the Belgian Jesuits initially set out for Saint Louis in 1823, they brought six slaves from the Whitemarsh Plantation who had previously labored in Maryland. Those six slaves—three married couples whose names are recorded as Thomas and Polly (or Molly) Brown, Moses and Nancy Queen, and Isaac and Suzzy Hawkins (or Queen)—and their eventual children formed the basis of Jesuit slaveholding in Missouri.[182] Some of these slaves sent letters back to Maryland. In 1833, Thomas Brown wrote to Father William McSherry, head of the Maryland Province. In the letter, he speaks of his three decades of service to the Jesuits, states that his living conditions in Missouri have become dangerously unhealthy, and offers to buy his own freedom (and his wife's) for the price of $100.[183] Heartbreaking stories like this reveal the inherent cruelty of slavery. There is no evidence that Thomas Brown ever received a reply from Father McSherry, who at any rate, had little power to intervene, because as of three years earlier, the Missouri Jesuits were no longer under the jurisdiction of their Maryland counterparts.

---

179. Ibid., 92. Beckett, "Listening," 38.

180. Shelley, *Fordham*. 39.

181. Beckett, "Listening," 24.

182. Millett, "Memory," 339. Kelly L. Schmidt, Sean Ferguson, and Claire Peterson, "Enslaved People in the Jesuits' Missouri Province," Slavery, History, Memory, and Reconciliation Project, 2020, https://www.jesuits.org/our-work/shmr/what-we-have-learned/missouri/.

183. Thomas Brown, "Letter from Thomas Brown, an Enslaved Man at St. Louis University, 1833," The Georgetown Slavery Archive, Georgetown University, https://slaveryarchive.georgetown.edu/items/show/39.

A House Divided

By the 1830s, opinions on slavery within the Jesuit order were as sharply divided as in the country at large, perhaps even more so. Many nineteenth-century Jesuits were outraged that the Society would participate in the unjust practice of slavery, while others accepted it as a reality of American life. Four of the five Jesuit colleges that existed in 1838 were located in the border states of Maryland/DC, Missouri, and Kentucky—places where slavery was legal, but that chose to remain part of the Union during the Civil War. Nowhere else in America were opinions on slavery so evenly split. Since most American Catholics were Southerners and were themselves an oppressed minority in their country, many were hesitant to speak out against slavery for fear of drawing attention to themselves as foreigners or outsiders. Abolitionists in America were overwhelmingly northern Protestants, many of whom were as violently anti-Catholic as they were anti-slavery; they viewed both the hierarchical Church and the hierarchical slave economy as incompatible with American liberty. In their efforts to assimilate into US society, Catholics generally kept a low profile and bishops avoided taking a public position on slavery.[184]

Planning for the Sale

In 1835, ten Maryland Jesuits met in a momentous province-wide congregation to plan for their long-term future. At this meeting, they resolved to open new colleges in most of the major cities on the East Coast, specifically targeting Baltimore, Richmond, Philadelphia, and New York. To finance and to free up personnel for these efforts, Fathers Thomas Mulledy and William McSherry proposed selling off or at least renting most of the old plantations (including the slaves who worked on them).[185] The debate was heated, but the final vote came down six-to-four in favor of the Mulledy-McSherry plan.

The dissenters, including Father Francis Dzierozynski, offered two main reasons for their caution. First was the usual concern that selling the slaves would draw attention to the fact that Catholics were "different" from other Southerners, sparking further anti-Catholic bigotry among Protestants. The Maryland Jesuits were aware, no doubt, of the Protestant opposition that had recently prevented their French Jesuit colleagues from opening a college in Donaldsonville, Louisiana, and of mobs that had been harassing Catholics around the country with increasing violence. Second, Dzierozynski and the other conservative Jesuits worried about the spiritual well-being of the slaves and their access to the sacraments under different ownership. Under Jesuit ownership, the slaves could at least continue to live and worship with their families on the farms where they were born—the only homes many of them had ever known.[186]

---

184. Nalezyty, "History," 28. Beckett, "Listening," 25.
185. Beckett, "Listening," 37. Kuzniewski, "Our American Champions," 23.
186. Beckett, "Listening," 25, 37–38.

Regardless of the dissenters' logic, a decision had been made. The Maryland Jesuits wrote to Jan Roothaan in Rome requesting permission to sell the slaves as well as many of the plantations. In 1836, Roothaan sent his response. He was convinced that the sale of the slaves was necessary for the long-term financial health of the province, but "so that I may satisfy my own conscience," he attached a series of conditions to his approval. Slave families were not to be separated "as much as is possible." The eventual buyer must promise not only to keep the slaves together, but also to provide them with regular access to a priest and guarantee them freedom to continue practicing their religion. The Jesuits must continue to provide a home and care for any slave too old or infirm to be sold. Lastly, all funds raised from the sale must be invested for future growth of the province, not used to pay off debts or day-to-day expenses.[187]

William McSherry stepped down as provincial in 1837. He was replaced by Thomas Mulledy, who immediately used his new position of power to bring his long-desired sale to a conclusion. The buyer he identified was Henry Johnson, a former governor of Louisiana who was then serving in Washington as a member of the US House of Representatives. Johnson and his financial partner, Jess Batey, appeared to meet the conditions set out by Roothaan; they were Catholic and had the financial means to purchase virtually all of the Jesuit-owned slaves at once. They also promised in writing to arrange for a priest to visit their plantations every Sunday (and on holy days) to provide for the spiritual welfare of the slaves.[188]

The agreed-upon price was $115,000, of which $25,000 was to be paid up front. Of the initial proceeds, $8,000 was given to the Archdiocese of Baltimore, which had long claimed partial ownership of the slaves on the grounds that the Jesuit plantations had existed as Archdiocesan property before the Society of Jesus was restored in 1814. Another $17,000 was used to pay off debt that Georgetown University had accumulated under Mulledy's presidency (despite the fact that Roothaan had expressly forbidden using the proceeds for this purpose). The remaining $90,000 was collected over the next two dozen years, with the final payment coming in 1862. Those proceeds went into a general fund that, among other things, helped to finance the training of young Jesuits and supported various Maryland Province ministries during the province's period of expansion in the 1840s and 1850s.[189]

Several heroic Jesuits helped a number of the slaves escape to freedom before they could be sold. There is no way of knowing how many men and women succeeded in escaping, but the number was significant enough that Mulledy was apparently worried about its effect on the sale price. Knowing that he had subversive priests in his midst, Mulledy (with Johnson and local law enforcement) made unannounced visits to many plantations and rounded up the slaves before uncooperative Jesuits could give the

---

187. "Fr. Roothaan, SJ Lays Out the Conditions for the Sale of Enslaved Persons, 22 December 1836," Georgetown Slavery Archive, Georgetown University, https://slaveryarchive.georgetown.edu/items/show/94.

188. Beckett, "Listening," 42.

189. Ibid., 39–40. Kuzniewski, "Our American Champions," 25.

slaves proper warning. In total, more than 270 human souls were forced onto trans-
port ships and brought to Johnson's farms in Louisiana. In the aftermath of these
events, several Jesuits (and the Archbishop of Baltimore, Samuel Eccleston) wrote to
Roothaan to express their outrage at the way the slaves were treated, and accused
Mulledy of separating families in direct violation of Roothaan's orders.[190] Regardless
of where they stood on the morality of the sale, many of the Maryland Jesuits disap-
proved of Mulledy's handling of the situation.[191]

When Roothaan received these complaints, as well as reports that the original
conditions and stipulations attached to the sale had not been followed, he began
demanding Mulledy's resignation. In August of 1839, Roothaan sent an ultimatum:
Mulledy was to resign immediately or be dismissed. Ironically, Mulledy never received
the letter, because he had already resigned under pressure from his own colleagues
and embarked on a trip to Rome, where he hoped to tell his side of the story. When
the two men finally met face-to-face, Roothaan apparently gave Mulledy a cold reception, but stopped short of dismissing him from the Jesuit order.[192]

Mulledy paid a price for his actions, and ultimately expressed regret. Roothaan
refused to allow him to return to the United States (which must have pained the notoriously patriotic American) and instead assigned him to a minor post as chaplain to a
small group of English expatriates in France—a major demotion for a man who had
so recently been head of an entire province. In 1841, depressed and alone, the exiled
Mulledy wrote to his old friend, George Fenwick: "You all seem to have forgotten me,
but I must not complain of that—no doubt I deserve it."[193]

Mulledy might have remained in exile for the rest of his life if not for the intervention of his old foe, Father Francis Dzierozynski, who asked for his return in 1842.
The Maryland province was then in talks to open a new college in Massachusetts, and
badly needed a leader with Mulledy's executive experience. While the Maryland
Jesuits certainly disagreed with Mulledy's actions, they nonetheless admired their old
colleague's skills and stood ready to forgive him as an act of Christian mercy.[194]
Mulledy returned to the United States in 1842, and a year later, became the founding
president of the College of the Holy Cross.

The extent to which the slave sale fell short of Roothaan's original conditions did
not become fully apparent until years later. Mulledy had been criticized mainly for the
separation of families, but as it happened, other conditions of the sale also were not
met. Governor Johnson did not fulfill his promises to keep the slaves together or to
provide for their spiritual welfare. The Jesuits learned of his deceit through an informant from their own network: Father James Van de Velde, SJ—the same Father Van

---

190. Curran, *History of Georgetown Vol. I*, 128–129. Kuzniewski, "Our American Champions,"
25–26.

191. Beckett, "Listening" 41–42.

192. Kuzniewski, "Our American Champions," 25.

193. As quoted in Ibid., 26.

194. Ibid., 26–27.

de Velde who had accompanied Peter Kenney on his visit to St. Louis in 1831, and who eventually served as Saint Louis University's main recruiter in Louisiana.

Van de Velde rose to become president of Saint Louis University from 1840 to 1843. In 1848, he learned that one of his former students, William Thompson, was living on a plantation in Louisiana where more than a third of the slaves who had been sold to Governor Johnson were now laboring. Van de Velde visited the plantation and was outraged when some slave women came to him in tears, reporting "that they had not been to church in more than a year."[195] Apparently, Johnson had indeed separated large cohorts of the slaves from each other and had failed to build them a chapel or provide opportunities for them to worship, violating two of the major conditions of the sale contract. This was exactly what the conservative Jesuits like Dzierozynski had feared would happen when they opposed the sale in the 1830s. Van de Velde made efforts to build a chapel for the slaves in Louisiana and solicited funds from the Maryland Jesuits, arguing that the Jesuits had a moral obligation to step in and serve the spiritual needs of their neglected but still pious former slaves. In 1849, the slaves were sold yet again to a man named John Thompson, who assured the Jesuits in writing that he intended to fulfill Governor Johnson's original promises.[196]

Modern-Day Consequences and Reparations

In 2015, Georgetown University launched a Working Group on Slavery, Memory, and Reconciliation to explore the legacy of Jesuit slaveholding and its impact on the university. Among other recommendations, the working group proposed renaming two campus buildings originally named after Mulledy and McSherry—the architects of the sale. The former Mulledy Building was renamed for Isaac Hawkins, the first of the 272 slaves listed in the 1838 bill of sale. The former McSherry Building was renamed for Sister Anne Marie Becraft, OSP, a pioneering African-American Catholic nun who lived and worked in Georgetown. In an unprecedented move, the working group also recommended—and Georgetown adopted—a plan to recognize descendants of the slaves as children of alumni, giving them the same advantages in the admissions process usually given to legacy applicants.

In 2016, a similar working group at Holy Cross was divided over whether to rename Mulledy Hall, a dormitory. Some felt that erasing the founding president's name from a building would whitewash history and deny Holy Cross's past, including its connection to the 1838 slave sale.[197] President Philip Boroughs, SJ chose to rename the building Brooks-Mulledy Hall, keeping the Mulledy moniker, but adding the name of a transformative president and alumnus, John E. Brooks, SJ, under whose

---

195. Beckett, "Listening," 43.

196. Ibid., 43–44.

197. "Mulledy/Healy Legacy Committee. What We Know: Report to the President of The College of The Holy Cross, 18 March 2016," College of the Holy Cross, https://www.holycross.edu/sites/default/files/files/mulledy-healy/mulledycommitteereportfinal.pdf.

leadership the college racially integrated in the 1960s.[198] That solution proved temporary, and Mulledy's name was removed in 2020.

Today, descendants of the slaves sold by the Maryland Province in 1838 number in the thousands and live across the country, though a large concentration still exists in Maringouin, Louisiana, a town just 40 miles from the former campus of St. Charles College in Grand Coteau. Many of these descendants are still practicing Catholics. As of this writing, new discoveries about the slaves and their descendants are emerging almost daily, and our understanding of their history promises to improve in the future. In 2019, Georgetown University created and began raising money for an endowment to help support the descendants, which evolved into a foundation. This makes Georgetown the first mainstream undergraduate university to create such a fund in American history.[199] In 2021, the Jesuit Conference of the United States and Canada pledged to raise more than $100 million for the foundation.

While the 1838 sale was a momentous turning point, it did not signal the end of Jesuit slaveholding in the United States. Slaves continued to work at Saint Louis University, and as late as 1862, the Missouri Jesuits bought a new slave.[200] One Missouri enslaved family, consisting of George and Matilda (Hawkins) Tyler and their children, bought their own freedom by making hundreds of dollars in financial contributions to St. Francis Xavier College Church in St. Louis between 1848 and 1859.[201] In Kentucky, where the Jesuits operated St. Mary's College and eventually St. Joseph's College, slaves worked to support both institutions.[202] Slave labor was also present at St. Charles College in Grand Coteau and Spring Hill College in Mobile. In Maryland, the Jesuits continued to own some slaves, including those who were too old or infirm to be sold, and provided them a place to stay until their deaths. The formal end of Jesuit slaveholding in America did not come until slavery was finally outlawed nationwide.

In 2016, Saint Louis University partnered with the Central and Southern Province of the Society of Jesus to conduct more extensive research on the Missouri Jesuits' involvement with slavery, hoping to identify descendants of slaves who had played a role in their history. Records are incomplete, in part because there was never a single, documented sale of hundreds of slaves in Missouri as there was in Maryland. The project is ongoing and promises to shed new light on the role the Jesuits played in a tragic, terrible part of American history.

---

198. Philip L. Boroughs, SJ, "President's Response to Report of the Mulledy/Healy Legacy Committee," 16 June 2016, College of the Holy Cross, https://news.holycross.edu/blog/2016/06/16/presidents-response-to-report-of-the-mulledyhealy-legacy-committee/.

199. Rachel L. Swarns, "Is Georgetown's $400,000-a-Year Plan to Aid Slave Descendants Enough?" *New York Times*, 30 October 2019, https://www.nytimes.com/2019/10/30/us/georgetown-slavery-reparations.html.

200. Millett, "Memory," 333–334.

201. William Critchley-Menor, SJ, "Interview: How the Jesuits are Working to Confront their History of Slavery," *America*, 26 February 2021, https://www.americamagazine.org/politics-society/2021/02/26/black-history-slavery-jesuits-catholic-reconciliation-240100.

202. Shelley, *Fordham*, 39.

Nativism and Anti-Catholic Prejudice in Antebellum America

As slaveholders, the Jesuits contributed to the inherent inequality woven into early American culture; as Catholics, in different ways, they were also victims of it. Extensive anti-Catholic prejudice permeated the country at the time, and for most American Catholics, the mid-1800s were years of intense and open discrimination. The threats to their civil rights as US citizens, as well as to their physical safety and even their lives, were real.

The Jesuits and their colleges were major targets of the anti-Catholic sentiment that was, by then, coalescing into a national political movement known as Nativism. Nativism was a broadly anti-immigrant movement that took on a decisively anti-Catholic character, especially after the Irish potato famine of 1846–47 added waves of Irish Catholics to US immigrant rolls.

Jesuit colleges had been unusually diverse, tolerant places up to that time. Protestants typically made up a quarter or more of the students at Georgetown, Saint Louis, and the New York Literary Institute in the early 1800s. Georgetown enrolled its first Jewish student in the 1830s. The New York Literary Institute educated the son of New York's Protestant governor. Sons, nephews, and other relatives of US Presidents George Washington, Thomas Jefferson, Andrew Jackson, and John Tyler enrolled at Georgetown, where they mixed with the sons of prominent Catholics like St. Elizabeth Ann Seton. The sons of William Clark and other notable westerners (including, very likely, the son of Sacagawea) enrolled at Saint Louis. After visiting Missouri in 1830, journalist Anne Newport Royal was "deeply impressed by the liberality"[203] of Saint Louis University and described it as "'the most flourishing college at this time in the United States,'" with students of many faiths living and learning together.[204] Few of America's leading Protestant colleges at the time welcomed Catholic students to the same extent.

Particularly notable from a modern point of view is the extent to which antebellum Jesuit colleges embraced Hispanic students and faculty. Mexican, Cuban, and Central American students frequently enrolled at these schools in the early 1800s, and many Jesuit colleges published recruitment materials in Spanish through at least the Civil War. Spanish was one of the most common first languages for students at Saint Louis, Georgetown, and later Xavier, Santa Clara, and St. Joseph's (Kentucky) during their formative years. Those students would not have stood out as unusual next to the equally large numbers of French and German speakers on the campuses. Latin, of course, was the language of instruction in most classrooms, but conversations between students and faculty outside of class were decidedly polyglot.

Unfortunately, the tolerance Jesuits showed toward their adopted country was not long reciprocated. Across the United States, there was growing sentiment that the

---

203. Faherty, "Nativism," 449.
204. As quoted in Ibid., 449.

Catholic Church, with its hierarchical authority structure and strong ties to Europe, was fundamentally incompatible with American ideals such as individual liberty and representative democracy. Nativists viewed Catholics, at best, as unwelcome visitors who could never fit into American society, or, at worst, as devious intruders seeking to overthrow the United States government and replace it with a papal theocracy on American soil.

When Peter Kenney, SJ visited St. Louis in 1831, he found so much anti-Catholic sentiment in the city that he ordered the Jesuits not to wear their priestly cassocks outside the college grounds.[205] Similarly, the Jesuits of New York City in the 1840s so feared mob violence that they dressed in everyday street clothes whenever they went out in public. Unfortunately, for most Jesuits, any hope of blending into American society disappeared the minute they opened their mouths and started speaking their heavily accented English.[206]

The consequences of not blending in could be serious, even fatal. In 1844, violent anti-Catholic riots broke out in Philadelphia, during which Nativist mobs set fire to the Irish working-class suburb of Kensington, burning homes and reducing the local church, St. Michael's, to ashes. The attack stemmed from a request by Catholic students to be excused from reading a Protestant translation of the Bible, the King James Version, in Philadelphia's public schools.[207] In 1854, there were two separate incidents in which individual Jesuits were assaulted by Nativist mobs: in Maine, Father John Bapst, SJ (future co-founder of Boston College) was tarred and feathered, while in Alabama, a Jesuit missionary, Father Francis Nachon, was "ambushed . . . beat(en) and left for dead in the woods" while traveling to say Mass outside Mobile.[208] His attackers warned him that he could expect the same treatment if he ever dared to say Mass in their community again.[209]

Jesuit institutions were likewise targeted. Earlier chapters have already described how Jesuit attempts to open colleges in Donaldsonville and Baton Rouge, Louisiana, had to be abandoned due to local opposition. Even in places where the Jesuits successfully opened schools, however, those schools remained under constant threat. In Cincinnati, anti-Catholic street mobs rioted in response to an 1853 visit by Monsignor Gaetano Bedini, the first apostolic nuncio to the United States. Other Cincinnati rioters vandalized the young Xavier University and threw a brick through the window of the president's office.[210] In San Francisco, shortly after the Jesuits estab-

---

205. Garraghan, *Jesuits of the Middle U.S. Vol. I*, 319.

206. Gerald McKevitt, SJ, "Jesuit Higher Education in the United States," *Mid-America: An Historical Review* 73, no. 3 (October 1991): 213–214.

207. David R. Contosta, *Saint Joseph's: Philadelphia's Jesuit University: 150 Years* (Philadelphia: Saint Joseph's University Press, 2000), 22.

208. McKevitt, "Jesuit Higher Education," 214.

209. C. M. Widman, "Springhill College (1830–1898)," *Woodstock Letters* XXVII, no. 3 (1898): 272.

210. Bennish, *Continuity*, 58–59.

lished their first colleges in California, street marchers held up signs that read, "No more Jesuits wanted" and smeared the foreign priests in the local press.[211]

In Missouri, Saint Louis University's fledgling medical school was a casualty of Nativist violence. An anti-Catholic mob attacked the medical school in 1844, broke doors and windows, and destroyed its scientific equipment. The spark that ignited the riot seems to have been the discovery of some cadavers discarded next to the building. Though the bodies had obviously been used for classroom dissections, Nativists used them as evidence that the Jesuit priests were torturing and mutilating innocent people at the college. The irony was that all but one of the Saint Louis medical school professors were Protestant, and the Jesuits allowed both Methodists and Presbyterians to conduct religious services in the medical school facilities.[212] Faced with such prejudice, the medical faculty voted to dissociate from the university in 1848. At first, the Jesuits tried to ride out the crisis, but ultimately agreed to the separation in 1855 after yet another spurt of mob violence in the city.[213] It was an unfortunate example of genuine public service spirit on the part of the Jesuits crushed by anti-Catholic prejudice.

In Grand Coteau, the Jesuits at St. Charles College had to rely on local Catholic militia for security. As one Jesuit recalled,

> We were held up to the public as objects of hatred, unworthy to breathe the air of Louisiana. . . . Timely warnings were received in the shape of anonymous letters, containing among other compliments the following: that if after fifteen days we had not cleared the place, we should see ourselves stripped, whipped, and driven out.

> That these were not mere words, idle threats, became apparent; for real organizations were being set on foot in Lafayette, the next parish to ours, with the avowed purpose of expelling us. Meanwhile, in Opelousas, the newspaper was trying to excite a popular movement against us. It was owing to the devotedness of the members of Grand Coteau parish that things did not take a worse turn; for they too rose in arms and for many days made regular daily and nightly rounds for the security of the Fathers.[214]

Prejudice towards Catholics grew as their numbers swelled, and by the 1840s anti-Catholic sentiment was becoming commonplace in American life. Catholic immigrants were blamed for all sorts of social ills, from cholera outbreaks (to which working-class Irish immigrants were particularly susceptible due to their usually unsanitary job conditions) to public drunkenness.[215] Many Catholic immigrants came from European cultures that embraced alcohol, putting them on a collision course

---

211. McKevitt, *University of Santa Clara*, 105–106.

212. Faherty, "Nativism," 450–454.

213. Ibid., 456.

214. Maitrugues, "St. Charles' College," 20.

215. Warner, *At Peace*, 202.

with the largely Protestant-supported American temperance movement.[216] Reputable publications like *Harper's Weekly* fanned the flames and adopted a strong anti-Catholic editorial stance, while James Harper, a scion of the publishing family, pushed Nativist policies as mayor of New York.[217]

The Know-Nothing Party

By the 1850s, many Nativists were beginning to refocus their efforts away from mob violence and toward more legal means of achieving their ends. Thus was born what was formally known as the American Party, an anti-immigrant and anti-Catholic political party that brought together various factions dedicated to the preservation of Protestant America. The party's major goal was to win elections—first at the local level in 1853, then the federal elections of 1854—and once in power, to enact legislation that would stem the flow of Catholic immigrants.

The American Party was unconventional in the sense that it operated like a secret society; its members were obliged to deny their involvement in public. If asked, they would simply shrug and say that they "know nothing," leading some observers to give them the nickname by which they would be best known: the Know-Nothing Party.

The 1854 elections were a watershed for the Know-Nothing Party. Its candidates experienced remarkable electoral success, especially in places where Catholic immigrants were settling in large numbers. In the District of Columbia, they gained control of the city council.[218] In Massachusetts, they gained control of the state legislature and promptly used their power to create a "Joint Special Committee on the Inspection of Nunneries and Convents"—which legalized government inspection of facilities run by Catholic sisters who were suspected of anti-American insurrectionist activity.[219] In Ohio, the state legislature passed two bills expressly designed to weaken the Catholic Church: one new law made it difficult for Catholic immigrants to vote by establishing complicated voter eligibility requirements, while the other diluted the power of Catholic bishops, decreeing that Catholic churches were the legal property of their local congregations and not of the diocese as a whole.[220] Know-Nothings also achieved some measure of control over the state governments in Connecticut, Delaware, Kentucky, Maryland, New Hampshire, Pennsylvania, and Rhode Island.[221]

Where electoral victory proved difficult, the Know-Nothings were not above resorting to chicanery, violence, and deceit. In 1855, an angry mob destroyed ballot boxes in the Catholic neighborhoods of Cincinnati after it became clear that the

---

216. Bennish, *Continuity*, 59.
217. Warner, *At Peace*, 213.
218. Ibid., 216.
219. Kuzniewski, *Thy Honored Name*, 101.
220. Bennish, *Continuity*, 60.
221. Warner, *At Peace*, 216.

Catholic vote might unseat the Know-Nothing candidates for office.[222] Catholics, for their part, voted largely with the Democratic Party and struggled mightily to convince their fellow Americans that they were patriotic citizens who meant no harm.

In this environment, thirteen American colleges were founded by or taken over by the Jesuits in the 1840s and 1850s: Boston College (Massachusetts), Gonzaga (DC), Fordham (New York), Holy Cross (Massachusetts), Immaculate Conception (Louisiana), Loyola (Maryland), Santa Clara (California), St. Francis Xavier (New York), Saint Joseph's (Pennsylvania), St. Joseph's (Kentucky), St. Mary's (Kansas), Spring Hill (Alabama), and Xavier (Ohio). This second major wave of Jesuit colleges, emerging in the midst of strong anti-Catholic sentiment leading up to the Civil War, differed somewhat from the first wave that included such schools as Georgetown, Saint Louis, and the short-lived literary institutes in New York and Frederick. While the new Jesuit colleges still, for the most part, welcomed students of all faiths, their *raison d'etre* was increasingly to provide refuge for local Catholic populations and offer those recent immigrants educational opportunities that mainstream Protestant-controlled society denied them.

Jesuit colleges prior to the 1840s had embraced American culture and diversity, and had sought to contribute meaningfully to their adopted country. At first, their overtures were mutually embraced, and schools like Georgetown, Saint Louis, and the New York Literary Institute enjoyed high standing in American society. As American culture increasingly rejected and persecuted Catholics, however, Jesuit colleges were forced to become more insular.[223]

Benedict Fenwick, SJ, and the College of the Holy Cross (1843), Worcester, Massachusetts

One particularly egregious act of Nativist bigotry led indirectly to the founding of the College of the Holy Cross, the first Catholic college in New England. On August 11, 1834, a violent Nativist mob attacked the Ursuline convent in Charlestown, Massachusetts, across the river from downtown Boston. The Ursuline sisters had established a Catholic girls' school there, and it had enjoyed a good reputation for over a decade before antipathy toward the city's growing Irish immigration put it, and all Catholic institutions, in the crosshairs. After a biased trial, the perpetrators of the crime were acquitted of all charges, and cheers erupted as the Nativists left the courtroom as free men, never facing justice for the harm they caused to the sisters and their school.[224]

The incident helped to convince Benedict Joseph Fenwick, SJ, the second bishop of Boston, that Catholics in his diocese needed a safe place to be educated. Fenwick,

222. Bennish, *Continuity*, 59.
223. Curran, *History of Georgetown Vol. I*, 136–137.
224. Kuzniewski, *Thy Honored Name*, 18.

as mentioned previously, was a Georgetown alumnus who had served as both professor and president of his alma mater before a personality clash with Anthony Kohlmann led him to accept a post as a diocesan official in Charleston, South Carolina. He was one of the "first-generation" Jesuits who pledged their lives to each other at Holy Trinity Church in Georgetown that fateful day in October, 1806. By age 43, he was responsible for leading the Catholic Church in all of New England and was determined to establish the region's first Catholic boys' school.

Given the dangerous street gangs in and around Boston, Fenwick resolved to locate his school in a rural area—somewhere far enough outside the city to provide some measure of safety, while still close enough to be accessible within a few days' travel for working-class Bostonians. At first, he focused his efforts on an 11,000-acre property in northern Maine, which he purchased in 1835. There, in a small town named Benedicta near the Canadian border, Fenwick built a log cabin for the proposed college. However, he was unable to convince the Jesuits or any other order to send teachers to the remote location, and the project remained dormant for nearly a decade.[225]

A better opportunity (and location) presented itself a few years later. With fewer than thirty priests at his disposal to serve all six New England states, Fenwick had to be strategic with his personnel. In 1836, he made the fateful decision to assign Father James Fitton to the rapidly growing railroad city of Worcester, Massachusetts. Almost immediately, Fitton—who is today the namesake of Holy Cross's football stadium, Fitton Field—purchased a small farm for the purpose of building a Catholic academy (the equivalent of a modern-day elementary school). Fenwick saw the potential in the site and soon convinced Fitton to sell it to the Diocese. At first, Fenwick hoped to build a seminary on the property, but as time went on, it became clear that the Worcester location would work even better as the site of a college for lay boys.[226] It offered all of the advantages of the Maine location plus some extras; it was isolated from the Protestant gangs of Boston, but still within a day's travel for Boston Catholics. It also had a substantial (and growing) number of local students to serve.

All the while, Fenwick continued to negotiate with the Jesuits—namely, with Francis Dzierozynski as head of the Maryland Province and Jan Roothaan as superior general in Rome—about staffing the school. Reading between the lines of the correspondence among the three men, Holy Cross historian Anthony Kuzniewski concludes that the Jesuits had serious hesitations about both of the proposed locations. An urban school in Boston would fit nicely with the Jesuit ethos of education, but rural Maine? Worcester? Neither could hold a candle to Boston in long-term growth potential. But Fenwick could be a hard negotiator, and as Bishop of Boston, he held the upper hand. He tactfully implied to his fellow Jesuits that there would be no school in Boston unless they first agreed to open one on his terms in Worcester.[227]

---

225. Ibid., 20–22.
226. Ibid., 23–24.
227. Ibid., 25–27.

Location was not the only issue on which Fenwick was stubborn. He also insisted on modeling the Worcester school after his alma mater, Georgetown—which meant that it would be a boarding school. This was logical, because part of its mission was to give Catholic students a protected environment safe from the threats of Nativist mobs, and 24/7 supervision was one way to achieve that goal. However, a boarding school would also require a significant investment of personnel that the Jesuits were not yet prepared to make.

The third of Fenwick's non-negotiable points was even more controversial. He insisted that the college would be open to Catholic students only:

> I shall erect a College into which no Protestant shall ever set foot; for I cannot persuade myself that it is much to the advantage of Catholicity to have the mixture of boys of different creeds which prevails in all our Catholic establishments throughout the country.[228]

This flew in the face of Jesuit tradition, especially in the United States, where Georgetown and Saint Louis Universities had expressly made religious diversity part of their foundational missions. It is important to remember that the sociopolitical environment in Massachusetts was vastly different than that of Maryland or Missouri at the time. Catholics had been part of the Maryland establishment since colonial days, and they remained a majority in and around St. Louis for years after that city was incorporated into the United States. In Massachusetts, however, the government, culture, and public attitude still strongly reflected the state's Puritan Protestant roots. Catholics' status as unwelcome outsiders was even more apparent there than elsewhere in America. Fenwick's unconventional exclusionism, while both un-American and un-Jesuit, was arguably rational given his unique circumstances.

Lastly, Fenwick insisted that the best man to lead the college at Worcester was his old colleague, Thomas Mulledy, SJ, with whom his younger brother, George, had gone to Rome as a seminarian. Mulledy was then still in exile in France as punishment for his role in the 1838 slave sale. While his name was still toxic to many Jesuits, his leadership experience and skill were not in dispute. After learning that the Maryland Province and the Archbishop of Baltimore approved of the move, Roothaan ordered Mulledy back to America in 1843. After a brief stop in Georgetown, at which the students gave him a rousing welcome, he was sent to Worcester to lead the effort to get the new college off the ground.[229]

Had Fenwick not been a Jesuit and therefore close friends with the men with whom he was negotiating, it is possible that the Jesuits would have refused his repeated requests. At the time, they were preoccupied with long-term plans to open a college in every major East Coast city. At the 1835 province congregation, the Maryland Jesuits had resolved to prioritize Baltimore, Philadelphia, New York, and Richmond for their

228. Ibid., 22.
229. Ibid., 27. Kuzniewski, "Our American Champions," 27–28.

next college projects. Worcester was not even on the list, let alone the first priority. But Fenwick's reputation and experience within the Society of Jesus made all the difference. On June 21, 1843, Fenwick laid the cornerstone for the College of the Holy Cross, named after the Cathedral of the Holy Cross in Boston. The first building, known today as Fenwick Hall, was self-consciously modeled after Georgetown's Old North Building.[230] The keynote speaker in the ceremony was Father Charles Constantine Pise, who decades earlier had gone to Rome with Mulledy as a seminarian, and who had since become a well-known Catholic preacher.[231]

Holy Cross's Early Challenges

The new college struggled to fit in with its surroundings. Mulledy, and the other Jesuits who staffed the school, were mainly Southerners who practiced Southern customs—like smoking and chewing tobacco—that New Englanders considered unsanitary. They also spoke English with a distinctive Southern drawl that made them stick out like sore thumbs in their adopted home.[232]

There was also the issue of Holy Cross's legal right to grant degrees. Unlike the other colleges that the Jesuits had already built, Holy Cross was not the only school in its community. New England had plenty of chartered colleges, like Harvard, Brown, Dartmouth, and Amherst, to meet local demand. State legislators in Massachusetts questioned whether a new Jesuit school was necessary. That, combined with religious prejudice and concern over Holy Cross's "Catholic only" character, meant that the state government in Boston was reluctant to charter the school.

The Jesuits' solution to this impasse was simply to award Holy Cross degrees under Georgetown's charter. Students who completed the full course of study at Holy Cross technically received their degrees from Georgetown. They were, after all, completing the same *Ratio Studiorum* curriculum. Between 1849 and 1864, Georgetown granted bachelor's degrees to 68 Holy Cross students who had never set foot on the DC campus. In modern terminology, Holy Cross functioned as Georgetown's branch campus in Worcester.[233]

Holy Cross would not receive its own charter until 1865—ironically, two years after the Massachusetts legislature had already granted a charter to the Jesuits' second educational project in the state, Boston College. By the 1860s, some of the anti-Catholic prejudice in Massachusetts had started to wane, in part because northern Catholics had proven themselves to be patriotic Americans in the Civil War. Boston College's charter expressly stated that it was to be open to students of all religions; therefore, it was an easier sell to the state government. Holy Cross historian Anthony Kuzniewski concludes that the Jesuits' decision to prioritize Boston College's charter

---

230. Kuzniewski, *Thy Honored Name*, 24, 30.
231. Ibid., 32.
232. Ibid., 50.
233. Curran, *History of Georgetown Vol. I*, 36.

was "probably strategic," because obtaining approval for two Catholic colleges simultaneously would have been a tall order in the state legislature. While the negotiations were underway, Holy Cross could continue to offer degrees in Georgetown's name. Once Boston College was chartered, it would be much easier to argue for equal treatment for Holy Cross on the grounds that the two schools followed the same curriculum.[234] In the end, Holy Cross's exclusion of Protestants proved not to be the deal-breaker that many feared, and its 1865 charter signaled major progress in the level of religious tolerance in Massachusetts. Jesuits at the time celebrated the fact that "'Holy Cross is no longer a secondary branch of (Georgetown).'"[235]

Holy Cross's ties to Georgetown during its first two decades went far beyond the shared school name on diplomas. The two colleges frequently exchanged faculty and leadership. Father Mulledy's tenure as Holy Cross's first president did not last long, and he stepped down after just two years. Even though Bishop Fenwick respected Mulledy's executive experience, he soon came to loathe Mulledy's notorious temper, and the two men clashed intensely over whether the Boston Diocese or the Jesuit province should be financially responsible for the college.[236] In 1845, the conflict became so severe that Mulledy essentially switched offices with his old colleague, James Ryder, SJ. Ryder, who had been serving as Georgetown's president since 1840, moved north to become Holy Cross's second president, while Mulledy went south to lead Georgetown for the second time in his career.

Fire in Worcester Threatens Everything

The Jesuits' commitment to Holy Cross was tested early, when on July 14, 1852, a fire broke out in Fenwick Hall and destroyed everything but the building's east wing. All classes were cancelled, and students who lived in the building were sent home to their parents. Some faculty went temporarily to Baltimore, where the Jesuits were in the process of opening Loyola College.

In the immediate aftermath of the disaster, the Maryland Province expressed doubts about reopening Holy Cross. Worcester was too remote from the core of the Province's activities in Maryland and DC, and it was a drain on resources just at the time the Jesuits were actively expanding to more populous cities like Baltimore and Philadelphia.[237]

Fortunately for Holy Cross, the fire took place just as its most effective antebellum president was taking office. Antonio (Anthony) Ciampi, SJ, was an Italian-born missionary who had come to the United States to study at Georgetown. Newly ordained, he served three terms as president in Worcester: 1851–1854, 1857–1861, and 1869–1873. Ciampi quickly became Holy Cross's most vociferous advocate,

---

234. Kuzniewski, *Thy Honored Name*, 118.
235. Ibid., 119.
236. Kuzniewski, "Our American Champions," 26–28.
237. Kuzniewski, *Thy Honored Name*, 81.

arguing that the Jesuits had a moral obligation to live up to the commitment they had made to the Boston Diocese nine years earlier. Nothing less than the good name of the Society of Jesus was at stake. Moreover, Holy Cross had already established itself as a bedrock for the Catholic Church in New England; in its short life, it had produced many vocations to the priesthood.[238]

Ciampi's cause got a major boost when, a few months after the fire, Jan Roothaan appointed Charles Stonestreet, SJ as the new Maryland provincial. Stonestreet visited Worcester in person to inspect the damage, but was apparently unsure about the right course of action to take. To help make his decision, he sought the advice of the one Jesuit who knew Holy Cross well and whose opinion was still considered objective: Thomas Mulledy. Father Mulledy, who had by then completed his second term as president of Georgetown and was now serving as president of the St. John's Literary Institute in Frederick, advised Stonestreet to stay the course in Worcester. The Jesuits had made a legal and moral commitment to Holy Cross, and they had benefitted from it. Holy Cross boys were entering the Jesuit order at a higher rate than were Georgetown boys, so a second boarding school was a justifiable use of the province's resources. This time, Mulledy's notorious stubbornness worked out in Holy Cross's favor, and Stonestreet wrote to Roothaan in 1852, recommending that the Jesuits rebuild and keep the college open.[239]

The Healy Brothers: African-American Pioneers

Mulledy was correct when he argued that Holy Cross was a valuable source of vocations. Some of the most important Catholic and Jesuit leaders of the nineteenth century studied in Worcester during these early years. One family that stands out is the Healy family, from which four boys studied at Holy Cross and three entered the priesthood. James Healy (class of 1849) became a diocesan priest and, later, Bishop of Portland, Maine from 1875 to 1900. Sherwood Healy became a high-ranking official in the Diocese of Boston. Patrick Healy (class of 1850) joined the Jesuits and rose to become president of Georgetown—where he is still widely regarded as the university's greatest nineteenth-century leader. Georgetown's main building, Healy Hall, is named in his honor.[240]

The Healy brothers' professional accomplishments are even more notable because they were biracial. Their father, Michael Morris Healy, was an Irish-American plantation owner in Georgia; their mother, Mary Eliza Clark, was a slave who lived in a state of common-law marriage with her owner, whom she could not legally wed. This makes James Healy the first African-American US bishop, and Patrick Healy the first African-American president of a majority-white US university (Catholic or non-Catholic).

---

238. Ibid., 82–84.
239. Ibid., 86–87.
240. Ibid., 53, 93.

All of the Healy boys were light-skinned and could pass for white, but under Georgia law, the circumstances of their birth meant that they were considered slaves. If Michael Healy sought a college education for his sons, he had few options in America, and fewer still if he wanted a Catholic education. Georgetown, Saint Louis, and other Catholic schools in slave states like Louisiana, Kentucky, and Alabama were off-limits. Only Holy Cross, in the free state of Massachusetts, could give the boys opportunity commensurate with their abilities.

The Jesuits did not trumpet the fact that Patrick Healy was African-American as they promoted him through their ranks to the Georgetown presidency. However, his racial heritage was not exactly hidden, either. By 1853, three years after graduating from Holy Cross, Patrick Healy was back at his alma mater as a professor and a Jesuit scholastic. In a letter to his provincial, Father Charles Stonestreet, Patrick confessed to feeling some "anxiety" over the way his students whispered rumors about him behind his back. Though it was rarely spoken of in public, Healy's race was an open secret, and he confided that "hearsay . . . remarks are sometimes made (thought not in my hearing) which wound my very heart. You know—to what I refer." He also noted that his younger brother, Michael, still a student at the college, "is obliged to go through the same ordeal."[241]

As Patrick Healy progressed through the ranks, he encountered both kindness and discrimination from his fellow Jesuits. As a student at Holy Cross, he and his brothers were mentored and even baptized by their professor, George Fenwick, SJ (Benedict's brother). When he joined the Jesuit order after graduation, Patrick received a strong recommendation from Holy Cross President John Early, SJ, who urged Father Stonestreet to accept the promising young man despite his race and his status as the bastard child of parents who could not legally marry.[242] Given the sensitivities around Healy's race, the Jesuits initially assigned him to teach only in northern schools like Holy Cross and Saint Joseph's (Philadelphia).

However, in 1866, less than a year after the end of the Civil War and only three years after the Emancipation Proclamation, Patrick Healy became a professor at Georgetown. Two years later, he was promoted to prefect of studies (the number two position at the university) after the former prefect died in a storm while crossing the Atlantic from Rome.[243]

For a time, it seemed that the glass ceiling associated with his race would prevent Healy from rising any further. Even though he was almost universally admired for his teaching and administrative skill, in 1870 he was passed up for the position of Georgetown president, which went instead to his former mentor at Holy Cross, John Early, SJ. The provincial of the Maryland Jesuits, Joseph Keller, SJ, had urged Rome to appoint Healy over Early "despite the difficulty that perhaps can be brought up about him."[244] Nonetheless, Early was the safer choice, and Healy remained in the number two position.

241. As quoted in Ibid., 93.
242. Curran, *History of Georgetown Vol. I*, 274, 299.
243. Ibid., 273.
244. As quoted in Ibid., 298.

Although he had been overruled in 1870, Keller took matters into his own hands three years later. John Early died unexpectedly in 1873, and Keller seized the opportunity to appoint Healy to the Georgetown presidency on an emergency basis without immediate approval from Rome.[245] Thus began one of the most expansive and effective Georgetown presidencies of all time—resulting in significant growth for the university and the construction of the iconic building that now bears the name Healy Hall.

Holy Cross took a bit longer to commemorate the Healy brothers with a building, but in 1962, it built its own Healy Hall—a dorm—named after James Healy, now recognized as its first African-American graduate. During the 1960s and beyond, as the Civil Rights Movement shed a spotlight on America's racial history, the Jesuits became more cognizant of their own efforts to educate and promote these outstanding African-American boys—at a time when such integration was decades away in most mainstream school systems. The accomplishments of these men born into slavery in Georgia are something to be celebrated.

Meanwhile, in Cincinnati: The Origins of Xavier University (1831)

At the same time that Bishop Benedict Fenwick, SJ of Boston was laying the groundwork for Holy Cross, his cousin, Bishop Dominic Fenwick, OP of Cincinnati, was making even faster progress on what would become the second Jesuit college in the Midwest: Xavier University.

Edward Dominic Fenwick was, like the other prominent members of his extended family, a native Marylander. Educated in Europe, he joined the Dominican order and, after the upheaval of the French Revolution, returned to the United States in 1804 hoping to establish America's first Dominican school. Although he initially planned to build the school in Maryland, Archbishop John Carroll convinced him that the East Coast was already well-served by Georgetown and St. Mary's College in Baltimore. Dominic's services were needed even more desperately on the frontier, and in 1806, on Carroll's recommendation, he crossed the Appalachians to set up his ministry in Kentucky. There, just outside of Bardstown, he opened a small school named after St. Thomas Aquinas—the first Dominican school in the United States. One of its first students was a young Jefferson Davis, future president of the Confederate States of America.[246]

As time passed, Kentucky's population was gradually eclipsed by that of Ohio across the river. In particular, the city of Cincinnati (located about halfway between the growing manufacturing centers in Pittsburgh and Louisville) was developing into a frontier metropolis. Kentucky's agricultural, slave-based economy limited its population growth, while modern industry boomed in the free state of Ohio, drawing large

---

245. Ibid., 299.
246. Bennish, *Continuity*, 5–7.

numbers of Catholic immigrants from Ireland and Germany. As a result, Fenwick's attention increasingly focused on the north side of the Ohio River. When, in 1821, the new Diocese of Cincinnati was carved out of the Diocese of Bardstown, Fenwick was the logical choice as its first bishop.[247]

From the very beginning, Fenwick resolved to establish a college and seminary in Cincinnati. From 1823 to 1825, he travelled Europe raising money for the new diocese. Generous contributions allowed him to build St. Peter's Cathedral in 1826 and an attached seminary in 1829. By 1831, the cathedral complex came to include a lay boarding college for boys, originally named the Athenaeum. While the college was inspired by Fenwick's Dominican traditions, it was staffed by diocesan priests. Like most other Catholic colleges of the day, it opened its doors to students of all religions, and several Protestants enrolled.[248]

The Jesuits Come to Cincinnati (1840)

Dominic Fenwick was very familiar with the Society of Jesus; three of his cousins were prominent Jesuits in the Maryland Province, and as noted earlier, in 1831 he hosted Fathers Peter Kenney, William McSherry, and James Van de Velde in Cincinnati during their journey west to inspect Saint Louis University. However, he never explicitly sought the Jesuits' help in staffing his college. That request came from his successor. In 1832, Fenwick died of cholera and was replaced a year later by Bishop John Baptist Purcell, an Irish immigrant.

Under Purcell, the Athenaeum struggled and even closed temporarily in 1838–39. As was often the case in new dioceses, the Diocese of Cincinnati did not have enough priests to staff a school and simultaneously to minister to the faithful across its wide territory (which included the entire state of Ohio). During a visit to Rome, Purcell met with Jan Roothaan and begged him to send Jesuits to teach at the college.[249]

As fate would have it, Roothaan had just received a similar request from the first Catholic bishop of the newly established Diocese of Detroit, Frederick Rese. Faced with the two competing requests, Roothaan sought advice from the Jesuits who knew the American frontier best—those of the Missouri mission, led by Father Peter Verhaegen, SJ. Roothaan wrote to Verhaegen in 1839 asking whether the Missouri Jesuits could spare enough men to take control of two new colleges in Detroit and Cincinnati. Verhaegen replied that it would take at least eight Jesuits to staff both schools (more than Saint Louis University could afford to lose), but if Roothaan could spare at least four new Jesuits from Europe, the Missouri mission would offer up four of its own.[250]

Roothaan demurred. He could spare no more than two or three men. This meant that one of the two requests had to be refused, and he advised Verhaegen to prioritize

---

247. Ibid., 12.
248. Ibid., 17–19.
249. Ibid., 22.
250. Ibid., 22.

the Cincinnati college, since he judged (wrongly, in retrospect) that Cincinnati had more long-term growth potential than Detroit.[251] Even with the benefit of more than a century of hindsight, it is hard to second-guess Roothaan's reasoning; at the time, Cincinnati was by far the larger of the two cities.[252] It would be another four decades before Detroit grew large enough to attract the Jesuits' attention.

After receiving his orders, Verhaegen personally went to Cincinnati to inspect the Athenaeum building, and later dispatched a total of eight Jesuits from Missouri to staff it. To lead the effort, he appointed Father John Elet, SJ, a fellow Belgian immigrant who had been serving as president of Saint Louis University since 1836. In 1840, Elet became the first Jesuit president of the Athenaeum, which he promptly renamed St. Xavier College.[253]

The Missouri connection benefitted the college immediately. Its first student under Jesuit leadership was a native Missourian, Joseph Musick (aged thirteen). At least one of Mr. Musick's early classmates was Protestant.[254] Protestants were likewise represented on the early faculty; Prof. John Bernhard Stallo, a German immigrant, taught German at the college beginning in 1841. Three years later, he moved to New York and joined the faculty of what is today known as Fordham University (though it was not yet under Jesuit ownership).[255] As such, Stallo is likely the first lay and Protestant faculty member to jump from one of the twenty-seven Jesuit colleges to another.

Xavier Grows (and Shrinks)

Obtaining a charter for a Catholic college proved much easier in frontier Ohio than in pseudo-Puritan Massachusetts. The Jesuits were able to secure a charter from the Ohio legislature in 1842, a year before their colleagues in the east had even opened the doors at Holy Cross. As Cincinnati's population grew, it became clear that the Jesuits had made a good investment. Their college became a pillar of the city's Catholic community, enrolling 330 students by 1847.[256]

Although the Jesuits initially taught at both the college and the seminary divisions at St. Xavier, as the two divisions grew they eventually separated, leaving only the college under Jesuit control. By 1851, the seminary had moved to the city's Price Hill neighborhood (locally nicknamed "Pope's Hill" because of its large number of Catholic institutions). It is known today as the Athenaeum of Ohio-Mount St. Mary's Seminary and remains the main seminary for the Archdiocese of Cincinnati.[257]

---

251. Ibid., 22.
252. Muller, *University of Detroit*, 2.
253. Bennish, *Continuity*, 23, 29.
254. Ibid., 29.
255. Ibid., 36–37.
256. Ibid., 50.
257. Ibid., 46.

Soon, however, St. Xavier faced competition from within its own Jesuit family. In 1848, the Missouri Jesuits took control of St. Joseph's College in Bardstown, Kentucky. This meant that they now sponsored three boarding schools in relative proximity in Cincinnati, Bardstown, and St. Louis. The older, somewhat better-known Kentucky college began to siphon enrollment away from St. Xavier, and by 1853 there were only fifty-seven students boarding on the Cincinnati campus. Since the supervision necessary at boarding schools required a heavy investment of manpower, the Missouri Jesuits decided that year to transform St. Xavier into a day school and eliminate the dormitory. St. Xavier students who did not live in Cincinnati were forced to transfer to either St. Joseph's College or Saint Louis University to continue their Jesuit education.[258] As a result, as the Civil War loomed, St. Xavier was, like many Jesuit colleges, reducing its enrollment.

Fordham University (1846): From Rural Kentucky to the Big Apple

While the Missouri Jesuits were expanding to Cincinnati, French Jesuit missionaries were still operating St. Mary's College across the Ohio River in Kentucky, as they had since 1831. Their existence in the Bluegrass State, however, was becoming increasingly uncomfortable. Before the end of the 1840s, circumstances all but forced them to abandon Kentucky and relocate to New York.

Bishop Benedict Flaget, on whose invitation the French Jesuits first came to Kentucky, still nominally ran the Bardstown Diocese. But beginning in 1834, when Flaget was over seventy years old, the Vatican appointed another Frenchman, Guy Chabrat, as Flaget's coadjutor bishop. This meant that Chabrat was Flaget's administrative partner and designated successor, and that Chabrat held the real power in the diocese—a fact that became more apparent with each passing year. Chabrat held an unusual (and largely unexplained) antipathy toward the Jesuits, and seems to have been determined to make their lives difficult at every turn.[259]

As Chabrat's power increased, he insisted that the Jesuits spare some teachers from St. Mary's College to open a new school in Louisville, which was now clearly Kentucky's dominant city. The seat of the diocese relocated from Bardstown to Louisville in 1841. The Jesuits reluctantly agreed, and established the St. Ignatius Literary Institute in the city that same year.[260]

The St. Ignatius Literary Institute existed for only five years. It is debatable whether it counts as a "college" in American Jesuit history. It served students between the ages of ten and fourteen—and while those students were old enough to be educated at any Jesuit "college" in the country at that time, the upper age limit effectively marked

---

258. Ibid., 60.
259. Shelley, Fordham, 44.
260. Ibid., 43.

it as a prep school. At best, it could be considered a junior college, though it was never legally chartered to grant any sort of degree. It does, however, have the distinction of being the first of four American Jesuit schools to carry the name of the Jesuits' founder. (Three other schools—John Carroll University, Loyola University Chicago, and the University of San Francisco—were all originally named, "St. Ignatius College.")

Although the Literary Institute's enrollment crept as high as eighty, and the although the Jesuits purchased property in Louisville to build a proper campus in 1845, Bishops Flaget and Chabrat never backed the school financially. Bizarrely, they even thwarted some Jesuit efforts to fundraise for it. The diocese was rapidly building churches and a new cathedral in Louisville, and saw the Jesuit school as a competitor for donations. To complicate matters, Flaget was still pressuring the Jesuits to take control of his pet project, St. Joseph's College in Bardstown, which remained the school closest to his heart. The Jesuits increasingly found themselves in an untenable situation: responsible for virtually all education in the Louisville Diocese but cut off at the knees in their ability to fundraise.[261]

A Door Opens in New York

Meanwhile, more than 700 miles to the east, a forty-five-year-old Irish immigrant named John Hughes had just taken office as the fourth Bishop of New York City. Hughes had been an assistant bishop in New York since 1838, in which capacity, a year later, he purchased a large piece of property in what is today The Bronx hoping to build a college and seminary. Then as now, the property was located on an elevated site known colloquially as Rose Hill, in a village known as "Fordham."

As early as 1839, Hughes had offered this large parcel of land to the French Jesuits in the hope that they could build a college from scratch. They declined, being fully committed to St. Mary's College in Kentucky. Without Jesuit help, Hughes used his own resources to open a seminary (which he called St. Joseph's) in 1840 and a college (which he called St. John's) in 1841, initially staffing both with diocesan priests.[262]

New York had been without a Catholic men's college since Anthony Kohlmann, SJ, reluctantly shuttered the New York Literary Institute in 1813. Nearly three decades later, the city's booming Catholic (and particularly Irish) immigrant population made the need for a Catholic school even more pressing. St. John's College filled this need, but its growth would be hindered as long as it was in the hands of diocesan clergy who were also responsible for ministering to Catholics throughout New York State. During its five years under diocesan control, St. John's was led by four different presidents, none of whom could devote full-time attention to it. His personnel stretched thin, Hughes repeated his offer to the French Jesuits in 1843, a year after he became bishop.

---

261. Ibid., 43.
262. Ibid., 7.

This time, the French Jesuits' troubles with the Louisville bishops made them more receptive. Hughes's offer was attractive; not only would it give the Jesuits a foothold in America's largest city (something that Anthony Kohlmann had tried to achieve forty years earlier), but it would give them a reasonable excuse to escape the harassment of Bishop Chabrat in Kentucky. While they could not spare enough men to operate both St. Mary's and St. John's Colleges, abandoning St. Mary's now seemed to be on the table.

In Rome, Jan Roothaan was hesitant. He had approved the expansion to St. Mary's in 1831, and he did not want to renege on the commitment. In spite of the potential Kentucky once seemed to have as a center of Catholic culture, however, it was clear by the 1840s that New York held even greater promise. The final straw came in 1845 when Father Clement Boulanger, SJ visited the United States as an official representative of the French province. During the trip, Boulanger stopped in New York to meet with Bishop Hughes and negotiate possible terms for the transfer of St. John's College; he then traveled to Kentucky to inspect St. Mary's. What he saw confirmed the many complaints he had been hearing. Even the president of St. Mary's, the French-born Augustus Thébaud, SJ, described it as "a wretched little college."[263] The decision was obvious. Later that same year, Boulanger agreed on behalf of the Jesuits to buy St. John's College from the Diocese of New York for $40,000. In Rome, Roothaan reluctantly acquiesced.[264]

In 1846, a total of twenty-nine Jesuits packed up their books, lab equipment, and other supplies from St. Mary's College and the St. Ignatius Literary Institute, and made the more than 700-mile journey to New York. Father Augustus Thébaud, having just vacated the presidency of St. Mary's, became the first Jesuit president of St. John's.[265]

Back in Kentucky, the Literary Institute in Louisville closed immediately, but the Jesuit departure did not signal the end of St. Mary's. It limped along for several decades under diocesan control, briefly suspending operations after the Civil War. Priests from the Congregation of the Resurrection assumed control of the college in 1871, but discontinued its undergraduate programs in 1929, transforming the school strictly into a seminary. The seminary ultimately closed in 1976. The former campus is now the site of prison, and the small town in which it was located is called "St. Mary, Kentucky" to this day.

Was it a Snub?

Why did John Hughes offer St. John's College to the French Jesuit missionaries in Kentucky, but not to the Maryland Jesuits, who were much closer to New York and logically should have been invited? There is no evidence that Hughes ever

---

263. Ibid., 58.
264. Ibid., 3, 44–46.
265. Ibid., 46.

approached the Maryland Jesuits about running his school, even after the French Jesuits initially turned him down.

Historians have speculated that Hughes may have wanted to avoid a repeat of what happened thirty years earlier, when the Maryland Jesuits abandoned the New York Literary Institute. Knowing that the Maryland Province's first priority was— and would continue to be—Georgetown, Hughes probably did not want to entrust his school to a group of educators who would treat it as a side project. The Maryland Jesuits had already closed one school in New York; surely they were capable of doing so again if their resources were stretched too thin. For the French Jesuits, by contrast, a New York college would be the crown jewel of their ministry in the United States.[266]

It was a prescient move. For over twenty years, the Jesuits in New York City continued to operate as a branch of the French province of the Society of Jesus, and St. John's College was their top priority. Father Clement Boulanger, SJ, who had negotiated the original purchase, became the head of what the French Jesuits called their "New York-Canada Mission" and lived at the St. John's campus. St. John's was thus the home base for all French Jesuit activity on the east coast of North America, including Québec.[267] This New York branch of the Jesuits remained administratively separate from the Maryland Jesuits until 1879, when the two groups finally united to form the Maryland-New York Province.

Immediate Expansion: John Larkin, SJ, and St. Francis Xavier College, Manhattan (1847)

The Jesuits had been in New York for only a year when they undertook their first expansion. The area known today as The Bronx was then a bucolic, largely rural place well outside the population base of New York City. What is today a 30-minute train ride on the Metro North Railroad from Grand Central Station to the Fordham campus then required a day or more of travel. To make a Catholic education more accessible to the poor, mainly Irish immigrants who lived in the heart of the city, the Jesuits resolved to open a second college in Manhattan.

Leading the effort was Father John Larkin, SJ, a talented teacher who had served as the second and final president of the ill-fated St. Ignatius Literary Institute in Louisville. He was a competent leader; despite the challenges of fundraising in Kentucky, he had already managed to start construction on a new building for the Literary Institute when his superiors made the decision to relocate to New York.[268] Now, in Manhattan, he would create a school cast from the same mold as the one he never got the opportunity to finish in downtown Louisville. It would be

266. Arthur C. Bender, SJ, *A Brief History of the New York Province* (New York: New York Province of the Society of Jesus, undated), 3.

267. Shelley, *Fordham*, 59.

268. Garraghan, *Jesuits of the Middle U.S. Vol. III*, 256–257.

an urban day college, mainly designed to improve access to education for the urban working classes.

In a sense, the leaders of the two Jesuit schools in Kentucky—Father Augustus Thébaud of St. Mary's College and Father John Larkin of the St. Ignatius Literary Institute—simply reprised their roles in New York, with Thébaud assuming the presidency of the main boarding college (St. John's) and Larkin leading the downtown branch campus. Their New York ministry was largely a recreation of their Kentucky ministry, down to the details.

According to an often-told legend, Father Larkin left the St. John's campus in 1847 with fifty cents in his pocket. The train fare into Manhattan cost him forty-five cents, leaving him just five pennies with which to establish his college. With the help of some Catholic donors, he raised enough money to purchase a former Protestant church downtown, in the basement of which he opened a school that he called the College of the Holy Name of Jesus. Only a month later, that church was destroyed by fire, but classes continued when a better-established Catholic church across town, St. James, offered temporary quarters in its own basement.[269]

Father Larkin left the school he founded after only a year, and eventually succeeded Augustus Thébaud as the second Jesuit president of St. John's College. Soon after Larkin's departure from Manhattan, the College of the Holy Name changed its name to the College of St. Francis Xavier, which had a more distinctly Jesuit ring to it. The school eventually found a permanent home between West 15th and West 16th Streets in Manhattan on real estate that would become some of the most valuable in the city, if not the country.

St. Francis Xavier's convenient location was a major draw. Several students withdrew from the St. John's campus in Fordham to enroll at the downtown school—so many that the faculty at St. John's accused their colleagues of poaching valuable tuition dollars.[270] Because its lower costs made it attractive to first-generation immigrants, St. Francis Xavier actually had higher enrollment than St. John's for most of the 1800s, and was arguably the more influential of the two schools in New York society. By 1900, it was the third-largest Jesuit college in the United States by enrollment.[271]

Originally, graduates of St. Francis Xavier received their degrees from St. John's, since the Manhattan school lacked a charter.[272] That was rectified in 1861 when the New York state government empowered St. Francis Xavier to grant degrees in its own name. Without dorms, it had to draw its students almost exclusively from New York City, but that population alone was more than enough to fill its classrooms in the 1800s. Unfortunately, what was once its greatest asset—its downtown location— proved to be its greatest liability as the nature of higher education changed in the twentieth century. When a college education required nothing more than a classroom

---

269. Shelley, *Fordham,* 97–100.

270. Ibid., 104.

271. Ibid., 102, 117.

272. Ibid., 105.

and a chalkboard, Xavier thrived, but when laboratories, athletic facilities, and dorms became a crucial part of the undergraduate experience, Xavier had nowhere to expand and build such amenities.

By 1912, it was clear that Xavier's days as a college were over. Not only did it lack the proper facilities, but its neighborhood was becoming less residential and more commercial.[273] That year, it was absorbed into Fordham University by order of the Jesuit province. The original plan was to rename the undergraduate college of arts & sciences at Fordham "the College of St. Francis Xavier," but this led to protests from Fordham alumni.[274] In the end, the two institutions merged rather acrimoniously, and what was left of the old downtown school became Xavier High School. Today, Xavier is one of three Jesuit secondary schools in Manhattan—alongside the elite Loyola School and the tuition-free Regis High School.

Disputes at Fordham

When John Hughes originally sold the St. John's campus to the Jesuits, he retained diocesan ownership of the eight acres surrounding the neighboring St. Joseph's Seminary. The Jesuits of St. John's staffed the seminary but did not own it. This arrangement proved untenable in the long term. Hughes had a dictatorial management style and clashed with the Jesuits over issues as petty as the property line between the two institutions, even though they were meant to share resources. (It was only through the intervention of the Jesuits' trusted troubleshooter and future founder of Boston College, Father John McElroy, SJ, that the tensions with Hughes finally abated.) In 1860, Hughes blinked on the issue, discontinuing St. Joseph's Seminary and selling its property to the Jesuits to complete the Fordham campus.[275] (The modern-day seminary for the Archdiocese of New York, St. Joseph's Seminary in Yonkers, took its name in homage to that historic school but is an altogether different institution.)

Although Hughes often disagreed with the Jesuits who ran the college he founded, his influence over Fordham remained strong, and his legacy remains visible today (not least through his statue that stands prominently on campus). In an interesting quirk of history, while the college was still under diocesan control, Hughes sold a piece of campus property to the expanding New York railroads for one dollar—on the condition that the president of St. John's College would receive two rail passes "in perpetuity." To this day, the president of Fordham University still receives two free annual passes to the Metro North Railroad.[276]

Although St. John's College did not officially change its name to Fordham University until 1907, the term "Fordham" has always been associated with the school. It was a geographic reference to the village in which the campus was located; visitors would

---

273. Ibid., 118.
274. Ibid., 119–120.
275. Ibid., 84–88.
276. Ibid., 56.

have commonly called it "the Jesuit college at Fordham" long before the name change was official. Other colleges derive their names in similar ways; for example, Princeton University was originally "the College of New Jersey," but even before it changed its name in 1896, students often called it "Princeton" in reference to the local town.

Back, Briefly, to Bardstown: St. Joseph's College in Kentucky (1848)

While the French Jesuits thrived in New York, their departure from Kentucky was a serious blow to the frontier Catholics in that state. Many Kentuckians were descended from old Maryland families who had an affection for the Jesuits and who valued access to Jesuit education for their sons. Bishop Chabrat, widely seen as having forced the Jesuits out through his mismanagement, was the target of grumbles from parishioners and parents.

The loss of the Jesuits was particularly frustrating for Bishop Flaget, the one-time Georgetown faculty member who had led the Kentucky diocese for nearly forty years. During that time, he had offered his flagship school, St. Joseph's College in Bardstown, to the Jesuits more than a dozen times. Now that the French Jesuits were leaving his diocese seemingly for good, Flaget reached out in desperation to the Missouri Jesuits, all but begging them to come to Bardstown and fill the gap.

Just six years earlier, in 1840, the Missouri mission based at St. Louis had been elevated to the status of a vice province. This gave it some autonomy in its decision making. Father Peter Verhaegen, SJ, was in charge of the entire Missouri operation, while Fathers John Elet, SJ, and James Van de Velde, SJ, were serving as his top advisors. All three men were former presidents of Saint Louis University, and Elet was the sitting president of St. Xavier College in Cincinnati. The trio weighed Flaget's latest offer carefully, consulting with several fellow Jesuits before finally deciding to accept. In Rome, Jan Roothaan gave his consent immediately; no doubt he was happy that the Jesuit presence in Kentucky could be restored so quickly.[277] On July 20, 1848 (graduation day in Bardstown), the Missouri Jesuits announced that they would be taking control of St. Joseph's College the following academic year, and that Father Peter Verhaegen himself would serve as college's first Jesuit president.

Bishop Benedict Flaget died in 1850 at age 86, having led the Bardstown/ Louisville Diocese since its inception in 1808. His death came just two years after he finally achieved what he had spent most of his adult life trying to do—entrusting his beloved St. Joseph's College to the Jesuits. Hopefully, the accomplishment gave him peace in his final days and a genuine hope that St. Joseph's would survive in the long term. However, it was a pyrrhic victory at best, because built into the agreement between the diocese and the Jesuits were seeds of conflict that, long after Flaget's death, would destroy the arrangement he had brokered and lead to the death of the college itself.

---

277. Garraghan, *Jesuits of the Middle U.S. Vol. III*, 294–295.

As part of their contract with the diocese, the Missouri Jesuits agreed to assume responsibility for the college's $22,000 debt. However, unlike the situation in New York (where the Jesuits owned St. John's College outright), in Bardstown the diocese maintained ownership of all college property. The Jesuits were merely trustees.[278]

That financial arrangement proved untenable. St. Joseph's thirty-year-old, farmhouse-style classroom buildings began to decay, but the Jesuits were hesitant to build new facilities on property they did not own.[279] To make matters worse, the Civil War soon decimated tuition revenue. Only 67 students reported for classes on the opening day of the 1861 school year. The school was now operating at a deficit, and classes were suspended in December. Local students were sent home to their parents, but the college could not so easily dispense with seventeen boarding students (including some from Mexico) who were either too young, too poor, or too far from home to risk traveling through the war-torn South. Fifteen of those students were chaperoned up the Mississippi River where they enrolled at Saint Louis University. The other two attempted to leave Bardstown on their own, but were caught and imprisoned by Union soldiers in Louisville.[280]

St. Joseph's College never recovered from the Civil War, at least under Jesuit leadership. To save the historic institution, the Jesuits briefly considered transforming Saint Louis University into a day school so that all of its boarding students could enroll at St. Joseph's, but that would have inflicted serious injury on America's third-oldest Catholic college just to save its fourth-oldest. Reluctantly, in 1866, the Jesuits informed the Diocese of Louisville that they intended to withdraw.[281]

The new Bishop of Louisville, the French-born Pierre Lavialle, would have none of it. He was outraged at the prospect of losing the entire faculty and administration of his flagship college, and made it clear that if the Jesuits left St. Joseph's, they would be permanently banned from ever returning to his diocese in any capacity.[282] These protests succeeded in delaying the Jesuits' formal departure for two years, but by 1868, Bishop Lavialle had died and been replaced by Bishop William George McCluskey, a native New Yorker who took a more measured approach to the dispute. That year, with his acquiescence, the Jesuits finally left Bardstown for good.

St. Aloysius College (1849–1852), Louisville, Kentucky

The Jesuits' brief return to Kentucky resulted in St. Aloysius College, one of the shortest-lived Jesuit colleges in American history. Just as the French Jesuits at St. Mary's College had opened the St. Ignatius Literary Institute in downtown Louisville eight years earlier, the Missouri Jesuits at St. Joseph's College opened their own

---

278. Ibid., 296.
279. Ibid., 331.
280. Ibid., 324–325.
281. Ibid., 340.
282. Ibid., 341.

downtown branch, St. Aloysius College. The two downtown schools were similar in scope and in mission, serving urban students who could not travel to the rural boarding college. They were also similar in fate, and both closed within a few years.

In 1848, the same year the Missouri Jesuits arrived in Bardstown, the diocese asked them to assume responsibility for a free school (essentially an elementary school) attached to the cathedral in downtown Louisville. They agreed (against the wishes of Jan Roothaan in Rome, who had nixed the plan as an overstretch) and committed three teachers to the project. Their hope was to start a day college in Louisville, and use its tuition revenue to support the free elementary school.[283]

Leading the effort was Father John Emig, SJ, the only German Jesuit among the mostly Belgian missionaries who had come from Missouri. Emig purchased the lot next to the Cathedral school and constructed a single building for the college, which opened in 1849 and enrolled more than 100 students within a year. It was the first of three American Jesuit colleges to take the name of St. Aloysius Gonzaga, SJ. In 1851, the Kentucky legislature granted St. Aloysius a charter, authorizing it to grant college degrees.[284]

Despite this apparent success, attitudes within the Jesuit ranks soon soured against the college. Within two years, the decision to open it was seen almost universally as a mistake. In Rome, Jan Roothaan complained bitterly that the Missouri Jesuits had committed an act of insubordination by opening a college against his orders.[285] Closer to home, many Jesuits realized that they were shooting themselves in the foot by operating degree-granting schools in Cincinnati, Louisville, St. Louis, *and* Bardstown. The four colleges were cannibalizing each other's enrollment.[286] As Roothaan wrote to the Bishop of Louisville, "(I)n truth, the great plague of the Society in (the United States) is this, that we undertake too many things."[287]

The final nail in the coffin came in 1851, when Father Francis Xavier d'Hoop, SJ became the college's third president. Father d'Hoop, citing the college's debts, recommended its closure. Without any meaningful advocates within the Jesuit hierarchy, St. Aloysius College shut its doors in 1852 after only three years of existence.[288]

Reflecting on the Jesuit Experience in Kentucky

In total, the Jesuits staffed three colleges in Kentucky—or four, counting the St. Ignatius Literary Institute. This exceeds the number of colleges they established in any other state in the country except California, New York, and Louisiana. No other state in the early nineteenth century received more attention and investment from the Jesuits than Kentucky, and yet, by 1868, it all had come to nothing.

---

283. Ibid., 263.
284. Ibid., 269–271.
285. Ibid., 274.
286. Ibid., 276.
287. As quoted in Ibid., 274.
288. Ibid., 276.

As important as Kentucky once was to American Catholicism, by the latter half of the 1800s it was eclipsed by the new centers of Catholic population to the north and east. The Jesuits ably served the people of Kentucky for more than thirty years, but circumstances conspired against them. In the end, their major legacy was the hundreds of students whose lives they improved through education. After the Jesuits' departure, St. Joseph's College in Bardstown continued under diocesan control for about twenty years before finally closing its doors in 1889. It was resurrected in a different form in 1911, when the Xaverian Brothers reopened it as a high school; unfortunately, that iteration was to close in 1968. Today, the former campus is the site of the Bardstown Historical Museum and the Oscar Getz Museum of Whiskey History.

Spring Hill College (1847), Mobile, Alabama

When Jan Roothaan chastised the American Jesuits for "undertak(ing) too many things" by opening St. Aloysius College,[289] he surely had in mind another request that had recently come across his desk. In 1847, French Jesuits had taken control of Spring Hill College in Mobile, Alabama, adding yet another college to the ever-growing list of commitments on the Jesuits' plate in the United States.

Mobile, Alabama, is a fascinating city. Settled by French colonists in 1702, the small town on the west shore of Mobile Bay was held variously by the French, English, and Spanish prior to the American Revolution. Even after the Revolutionary War, it was unclear whether Mobile rightfully belonged to the United States or to Spanish Florida until the Americans seized the surrounding area in 1813. As American influence grew, Mobile (like Pensacola, Biloxi, and other Gulf Coast cities) became a pocket of Catholic culture in an otherwise passionately Protestant South. In some respects, it was like New Orleans in miniature. Indeed, Mobile even claims to be the home of America's oldest Mardi Gras celebration, one that began more than a decade before New Orleans even existed.

Few American cities that date back to the colonial era have prominent Catholic churches in the center of town. In East Coast cities originally settled by the English, the oldest Catholic churches are small, discreet buildings tucked unobtrusively into side streets away from public view. Old St. Joseph's Church, the Jesuit parish in Philadelphia, is an excellent example of this. By contrast, a handful of major American cities—including New Orleans, San Antonio, Albuquerque, and Mobile—were originally settled by Spanish or French Catholics. In these cities, Catholic churches and cathedrals were built to be seen, often in the heart of the main public squares and gathering places. Just as the magnificent St. Louis Cathedral stands above Jackson Square in the historic heart of New Orleans, so Mobile's beautiful Cathedral Basilica of the Immaculate Conception dominates one of the city's grandest open areas, Cathe-

---

289. Ibid., 274.

dral Square. Mobile is a rare example of an American city that has had a strong Catholic influence since colonial days—and in the heart of Protestant Dixie, no less.

In 1829, the Church hierarchy in Rome decided that the Catholic population of the Gulf Coast was large enough to warrant a diocese of its own. French-born Michael Portier was named its first bishop. It was left to his discretion where to build the seat of his diocese, which included modern-day Florida and most of the region between Pensacola and New Orleans. He settled on Mobile, largely due to its central location and easy accessibility by boat.

Portier had impeccable credentials for the job, and was as enmeshed as anyone in the tight network of frontier Catholicism. A graduate of St. Mary's Seminary in Baltimore, he had served in Missouri and New Orleans as an assistant to Bishop Guillaume DuBourg, the founder of Saint Louis University. One thing he did not have was a staff; when he assumed office, there were no priests working directly for him and a total of three missionaries in his territory, all of whom belonged to religious orders outside of his control.[290] To build up his resources, he toured Europe and the United States seeking volunteer missionaries. On his invitation, the Sisters of the Visitation, who operated America's oldest Catholic girls' school adjacent to Georgetown University, agreed to spare some teachers for the first girls' academy in Mobile.

Portier reportedly considered several locations for his boys' college, including Pensacola, St. Augustine, and even Tuscaloosa (which eventually became home to the University of Alabama).[291] In 1830, he settled on Mobile and bought property for a campus on the west side of the city. He envisioned the school as both a lay college and a seminary, both of which would be a first for the state. One of the college's early investors was the French Cardinal Joseph Fesch, an uncle of Napoleon Bonaparte, who had been Portier's schoolmate in Europe (and who also donated much of the art in Baltimore's Catholic cathedral). Fesch donated 30,000 francs to the college, a significant sum at the time.[292]

Portier named the school "Spring Hill College" because of natural spring water that bubbled up from the base of the hill on campus.[293] Later, some documents in the 1850s referred to it as "St. Joseph's College Spring Hill," but that name apparently never stuck.[294]

Like many frontier bishops, Portier initially did his best to staff the college with his own priests. Spring Hill's first president was Father Mathias Loras, a French missionary who later became the first bishop of the newly established Diocese of Dubuque in Iowa. (There, in 1839, he established the Catholic school now known as Loras College.)

---

290. Widman, "Springhill College," 268.

291. Joseph C. Mulhern, SJ, "Spring Hill Observes Centennial," *Woodstock Letters* LIX, no. 3 (1930): 336.

292. Platt, *Sacrifice*, 131.

293. Widman, "Springhill College," 268.

294. Platt, *Sacrifice*, 133.

Spring Hill enjoyed some early success and a strong local reputation. In 1836, it received a charter from the Alabama state legislature to grant degrees, making it the oldest college in the state and one of the oldest in the South. Still, Portier understood that he would eventually need to entrust the college to an established teaching order. There was no other way to secure its long-term growth and survival.

In 1839, Portier sold Spring Hill to a small French order, the Fathers of Mercy, who taught there for only two years before withdrawing. They were replaced by another French order, the Eudists, who ran the college from 1841 to 1846. Together, those two orders administered Spring Hill so poorly that its enrollment declined and its financial problems mounted. The situation became so dire that Portier assumed the college presidency himself, and sent Father John Bazin, a diocesan priest and former president of Spring Hill, to Europe in search of a replacement teaching corps. According-ing to several sources, none of which understood the reason for the stipulation, Portier explicitly told Bazin to offer Spring Hill to any religious order *except* the Jesuits.[295]

Unfortunately for Portier, the Jesuits were the only Europeans who expressed interest in the project. The French Jesuits based in Lyon (who at the time had just made the decision to move their American mission from Kentucky to New York) embraced the opportunity to expand further in the United States. Bazin's timing was fortuitous. Europe was on the verge of a series of upheavals, the Revolutions of 1848, and in this period of general instability, the French government forcibly closed most Jesuit schools in France. As a result, the French Jesuits had surplus teaching person-nel. Some of these excess teachers reinforced St. John's College (Fordham), but there were plenty left over for the college in Mobile. In Rome, Jan Roothaan approved the acquisition, and in 1847 a pioneering contingent of eight French Jesuits arrived in Alabama and purchased Spring Hill College from the diocese.[296]

Back to Grand Coteau

At about the same time, in 1848, the French Jesuits also agreed to resume control of St. Charles College in Grand Coteau, Louisiana. Frenchmen had founded the col-lege in 1837, but ceded it to the Missouri Jesuits a year later to focus on their ill-fated mission at St. Mary's College in Kentucky.[297] Ironically, after just ten years in Grand Coteau, the Missouri Jesuits were also looking to rid themselves of the isolated Louisiana school for the sake of sending reinforcements to Kentucky. In 1848, the Missouri Jesuits had agreed to take responsibility for St. Joseph's College in Bardstown and planned to free up faculty for the endeavor by withdrawing from St. Charles. The return of the French Jesuits to Grand Coteau benefitted both parties; it allowed the Missouri Jesuits to expand to Kentucky comfortably, while at the same time allowing the French Jesuits to set up a ministry in a state where French was still widely spoken.

295. Ibid., 131. Widman, "Springhill College," 271.
296. Mulhern, "Spring Hill," 339.
297. Widman, "Springhill College," 271.

For the rest of the nineteenth century, St. Charles College and its eventual New Orleans branch (the College of the Immaculate Conception), along with Spring Hill, were the core ministries of the Jesuits' New Orleans Mission. It was one of two French Jesuit missions in the United States (the other being the New York-Canada Mission, centered around Fordham).[298] None of this expansion would have been possible if not for the Revolutions of 1848, which produced an influx of refugee priests large enough to staff multiple American colleges. It was neither the first nor the last time that political change in Europe would produce immigrant college faculty that benefitted American Catholic education.

The Jesuit Experience in Mobile

The first Jesuit president of Spring Hill was Father Francis de Sales Gautrelet, SJ. By any measure, the Jesuits were more competent administrators than the two orders who preceded them, and the college's enrollment and financial situation improved. As the Civil War approached, however, the situation again became unstable. The war and subsequent Reconstruction period proved a challenging time in the college's history, and in 1869, tragedy struck directly when fire all but destroyed the building. Lost in the blaze were many of the priceless records and books donated by the college's European benefactors.[299]

The Jesuits moved quickly. The day after the fire, about ninety students and most of their professors packed up their belongings, left the devastated campus in Mobile, and relocated to St. Charles College in Grand Coteau. The sudden influx of students and faculty propped up the struggling Louisiana college, which had been teetering on the brink of closure.

Faced with the decision to close the college or rebuild, Spring Hill's president, Father Jean Montillot, SJ decided that Alabama's oldest college was worth saving. By the next academic year, the main building had been reconstructed and students had returned.[300] The little college in Mobile chugged along for generations—a small but steady pocket of Jesuit activity in the South. It was a pillar of the community in one of the few Southern cities where the Catholic Church has long had a strong civic influence.

The Four Sisters of the East: Saint Joseph's, Loyola, Gonzaga, and Boston College

While the French Jesuits were expanding to New York, Alabama, and Louisiana, and while the Missouri Jesuits were expanding to Ohio and Kentucky, the oldest American branch of the Jesuit family tree (Maryland) was planning a major expansion

---

298. Ibid., 271.
299. Mulhern, "Spring Hill," 340–341.
300. Ibid., 341.

of its own. In the 1850s, the Maryland Province finally followed through on plans that had been percolating for about twenty years, opening four new educational ventures up and down the East Coast.

At their province-wide leadership meeting in 1835, the Maryland Jesuits had resolved to open day colleges in most major northeastern cities, specifically targeting Philadelphia, Baltimore, New York, and Richmond. The hope was that the proximity of these proposed schools would enable them to share professors, such that a single Jesuit might be able to travel easily between, say, Baltimore and Washington to teach classes. Since all would follow the same *Ratio Studiorum* curriculum, teachers would be theoretically interchangeable.[301]

As it happened over the next fifteen years, the Maryland Jesuits were forced to delay most of their planned expansion when one of their own, Bishop Benedict Fenwick, SJ, strong-armed them into an unexpectedly heavy commitment at the College of the Holy Cross in Massachusetts. Any plans they may have had to expand to New York City were also rendered moot, as they were beaten to the finish line by their French colleagues. As the 1850s approached, however, the Maryland Jesuits were finally ready to spread their wings.

Because the Maryland Jesuits already operated boarding schools at Georgetown and Worcester, their focus for the immediate future would be on urban commuter colleges. Their strategy was to build downtown schools that offered a traditional Jesuit education for a reasonable price, mainly targeting local students who could not afford the heftier tuition at Georgetown or Holy Cross. This was both respectful of the past and decidedly forward-thinking. Traditional European Jesuit schools had operated on this model for centuries, situating themselves in the middle of densely populated cities to serve the maximum number of students. This "traditional" Jesuit day college served the needs of mid-nineteenth century America rather well. Underprivileged Catholic immigrants were packing densely into large cities, and in most cases, this type of college was exactly what the community needed. There was now a booming potential audience of first-generation Americans concentrated in the urban cores of the East Coast and starving for educational opportunity.

The four Jesuit colleges that emerged from this period in the 1850s were Saint Joseph's University in Philadelphia, Loyola University in Baltimore, Boston College in Massachusetts, and Gonzaga College (which is today a high school) in Washington, DC. The history of these four schools is so similar—and so intertwined—that they can reasonably be called the "four sisters" of eastern Jesuit education (or "three sisters," counting only those that remain colleges today). All four had the same mission: to bring Jesuit education to people (particularly disadvantaged Catholic immigrants) in America's biggest cities. All four were founded, staffed, and managed by a generation of Jesuits who had gained experience at Georgetown and Holy Cross. Collectively, the six colleges of the Maryland Province formed an educational network of

---

301. Curran, *History of Georgetown Vol. I*, 138.

remarkable scale for the time. Each was a link in a chain of urban schools that regularly exchanged faculty, presidents, and administrators, and collectively served hundreds of students at a time when most American colleges were miniscule operations.

Because they were founded at the height of the anti-Catholic Nativist movement, when mob violence against Catholics was a real threat and the intolerant Know-Nothing Party was gaining traction in American elections, the four sisters also served as refuges for young, urban Catholic men. As a result, they tended to attract a much more homogenous student body than did the Jesuit schools of the previous half-century. While the four sisters were open to students of any religion, in practice they enrolled a high percentage of Catholics—to an extent that made them noticeably different from more religiously diverse schools like Georgetown, Saint Louis, and St. Joseph's in Kentucky.[302]

Though it seems strange, by becoming more religiously homogenous than their predecessors, the new Jesuit colleges were becoming more "typically" American. Prior to the Civil War, the vast majority of American colleges were sponsored by churches or religious denominations, and their student bodies were largely limited to members of their own faith traditions.[303] The fact that most Jesuit colleges (excepting Holy Cross) expressly opened their doors to students of all religions marked them as unusually liberal for their day. Secular, public universities as we recognize them today were still rare, and their heyday would not arrive until the Morrill Act of 1862 established America's land-grant college system.

During this decade, an important transition took place in Rome. In 1853, Jan Roothaan died, and was replaced as superior general of the Society of Jesus by the Belgian-born Pieter Jan Beckx, SJ. Beckx would serve as the worldwide leader of the Jesuits from 1853 to 1887—another period of major expansion for Jesuit education in America. His American foot soldiers would eventually give him as many headaches as they had given his predecessor.

Beckx wanted to know more about the Americans under his supervision. At the time that the four sisters were coming into existence in the 1850s, Beckx appointed an official visitor to inspect the Jesuit schools in the United States: Father Felix Sopranis, SJ. Sopranis's role was similar to the role played by Peter Kenney, SJ, in the 1820s and 1830s. Acting as Beckx's eyes and ears, Sopranis had significant authority, and his decisions (timed as they were) greatly impacted the future of all Jesuit schools on the East Coast.

Saint Joseph's University (1851), Philadelphia, Pennsylvania

Jesuits had had a presence in the Keystone State for over a century before they established a college there. During the colonial era, they operated farmhouse-

---

302. Curran, *History of Georgetown Vol. I*, 136–139.

303. Nicholas Varga, *Baltimore's Loyola, Loyola's Baltimore, 1851–1986* (Baltimore: Maryland Historical Society, 1990), 28.

churches in Pennsylvania similar to those they ran in Maryland. In 1733, the Jesuits founded Philadelphia's oldest Catholic parish, known today as Old St. Joseph's Church, on Willings Alley, two blocks from the future site of Independence Hall.

As the name implies, Willings Alley is not a main thoroughfare. It was, and remains, a side street hidden from view of most of the city's commerce. Today, the humble little church is easy to miss. Its location is a reminder of the low status Catholics once had in Philadelphia, and reflects that antebellum Catholics had to worship almost secretively, even in relatively tolerant Pennsylvania. As mentioned earlier, the modest structure contrasts sharply with the prominent Catholic churches in French colonial cities like Mobile and New Orleans.

Shortly after the Jesuits were suppressed in 1773, they lost control of Old St. Joseph's Church. They would not return to it until 1833, when Father Peter Kenney negotiated it back from the Diocese of Philadelphia.[304] The Jesuits rebuilt the dilapidated old church on its original site in 1839, resulting in the building that still stands today.

By the late 1840s, the Maryland Jesuits were actively seeking to establish a Catholic college in Philadelphia. Embarrassingly, they were beaten to this goal by the Augustinians, who founded Villanova University in 1842.[305] In Rome, the aging Jan Roothaan was urging caution; not for the first time, he accused the American Jesuits of "the too hasty acceptance of colleges."[306] Nonetheless, the Maryland Province pressed forward, hoping that they could use their existing parish, Old St. Joseph's, as a base of operations for a new school.[307]

The pastor of Old St. Joseph's Church at the time was the French-born Father Felix Barbelin, SJ, a former Georgetown professor. While he supported the idea of a college in Philadelphia, his small church could not offer much in terms of facilities. Barbelin expanded the small rectory located catty-corner from the church; while the resulting building was still inadequate for the long-term, it was large enough to serve the roughly thirty students who enrolled in the inaugural class in 1851. A year later, the college secured a charter from the Pennsylvania legislature to grant degrees.[308]

From the start, Father Barbelin and his fellow Jesuits sought a larger building. An opportunity arose when Bishop John Neumann of Philadelphia (who is now recognized as a saint and is credited with establishing the first diocesan school system in the United States) offered the Jesuits control of a larger parish, St. John's, roughly ten blocks from Old St. Joseph's. Fortunately, St. John's Church already had a spacious school building attached to it. The Jesuits purchased the property from the diocese and assigned Father James Ryder, SJ to lead both the parish and the school. Father

---

304. Kuzniewski, "Our American Champions," 20.

305. Contosta, *Saint Joseph's*, 20.

306. As quoted in Ibid., 37.

307. Ibid., 20.

308. Ibid., 2, 21, 28.

Barbelin remained at Old St. Joseph's Church, now a full-time pastor without the duties of a college president.[309]

Ryder's name has appeared in these chapters before. He was part of the "second generation" of American Jesuits—one of the original eight young scholastics sent to Rome in 1820 to complete their seminary work. Between 1840 and 1851, Ryder had served continuously as a college president—twice as president of Georgetown, with a three-year term as president of Holy Cross in between. He was, ostensibly, the most experienced man available to lead the new venture in Philadelphia. But, by the time he assumed office in 1856, he was unwell and less than four years from death. The young Saint Joseph's College needed an energetic leader, not one who approached the assignment as a retirement post, and the Ryder presidency was not successful in terms of enrollment or financial security.[310]

In 1859, the official Roman visitor, Father Felix Sopranis, arrived in Philadelphia to inspect the school on behalf of Superior General Pieter Beckx. What Sopranis saw at Saint Joseph's College did not impress him—a small student body, an inadequate teaching staff, and a drain on financial resources that, he felt, could be put to better use elsewhere. Like his predecessor, Jan Roothaan, Beckx believed that the American Jesuits were overextending themselves, and after reading Sopranis's reports from the field he ordered his Maryland colleagues to pull the plug on Saint Joseph's College. In 1860, the Jesuits shuttered the school, vacated their newly acquired parish, and returned both the church and the school building to the diocese.

To add insult to injury, the diocese then asked the Christian Brothers to establish a downtown day college in Philadelphia—essentially as a replacement for the failed Jesuit school. Seven years after the Jesuits vacated it, the very same school building became the temporary home of LaSalle College (now LaSalle University).[311]

In the short term, many students displaced by the closure of Saint Joseph's College went back to the old facility on Willings Alley, where Father Felix Barbelin and a handful of other Jesuits continued sporadically to teach courses. Historian David Contosta has called that unofficial school "a thread of continuity" for the college. Still, what existed in that location was at best an underground high school, and no attempt was made to confer degrees or offer any sort of meaningful college-level plan of study. Saint Joseph's College thereafter was dormant for decades, only reopening well after the Civil War, in 1889.[312]

If not for the continued support of its founder, Father Barbelin, Saint Joseph's easily could have been relegated to the dustbin of history along with other failed colleges like St. Aloysius in Louisville and the New York Literary Institute. In 1866, however, Barbelin purchased a plot of land in the city's growing northern neighborhoods that the Jesuits would eventually develop into a new campus for a resurrected

---

309. Ibid., 32–33.
310. Ibid., 33–34.
311. Ibid., 35–36.
312. Ibid., 42.

Saint Joseph's College.[313] When that incarnation of the school opened in 1889, it inherited the original charter and legal persona of the first Saint Joseph's, renewing its mission at a time when Philadelphia's population was growing even faster than before. The booming city was, by then, large enough to support three Catholic men's colleges: Saint Joseph's, Villanova, and LaSalle.

Loyola University (1852), Baltimore, Maryland

The founding father of the American Church, John Carroll, originally envisioned a two-tiered Catholic education system in the United States. Georgetown College would be an undergraduate institution that trained lay boys, while in Baltimore, St. Mary's Seminary would train Georgetown's most promising alumni for the priesthood. Against his better judgment, Carroll allowed the Sulpician priests to open St. Mary's in 1791, before the first crop of Georgetown graduates was ready to enter the seminary. In what he saw as a temporary measure, Carroll gave the Sulpicians permission to open an undergraduate college in Baltimore, with the understanding that the tuition from that college could keep their operation afloat until St. Mary's one day enrolled enough seminarians to eliminate the lay undergraduates altogether.

Things did not work out according to plan. The "temporary" undergraduate division at St. Mary's remained open for more than fifty years and ultimately competed with Georgetown for students, enrolling many local Baltimore boys with no interest in the priesthood. America's two oldest Catholic colleges, located just 60 miles apart, spent much of the early 1800s standing in each other's way. The rivalry extended beyond the colleges themselves and soured relations between the Jesuits and Sulpicians. More than once before the 1850s, archbishops of Baltimore tried to broker a deal between the two orders, hoping to transfer the undergraduate division of St. Mary's College to the Jesuits. But, even with the archbishops' intervention, the two sides never were able to reach an agreement.[314]

This changed in the early 1850s, when after more than six decades, the Sulpicians resolved to close the undergraduate branch of St. Mary's College and transform the school exclusively into the seminary it was always intended to be. The Sulpician order's *raison d'être* is the training of priests, and their teaching obligations at the lay college had finally become seen as a distraction.

In 1851, Baltimore got a new archbishop—Francis Kenrick. Less than a year earlier, Kenrick had been serving as the Bishop of Philadelphia and had worked with the Jesuits to open Saint Joseph's College in that diocese. Having already built a relationship with the Jesuits during those negotiations, he began courting his old contacts in the Maryland Province about opening a Jesuit school in Baltimore. Kenrick's top priority as the head of America's oldest and most prestigious archdiocese was to fill the void created by the loss of St. Mary's College.

---

313. Ibid., 38.
314. Varga, *Baltimore's Loyola*, 4–6.

Plenty of obstacles stood in the way, most pressingly the need to find a campus and the need to assemble a faculty from the ranks of the overextended Maryland Jesuits. Fortunately, a wave of European Jesuits was coming to America at the time—mainly refugees from the political revolutions that rocked that continent around 1848. Spring Hill College and St. John's College (Fordham) had already benefitted from the sudden availability of French Jesuit refugees. The Maryland Province, too, was sheltering displaced Jesuits, many of whom were experienced teachers in their own countries. Although these men were incredible additions to the faculties of Georgetown and Holy Cross, there was always a fear that they would be recalled to Europe if circumstances improved. In the midst of that uncertainty, the Maryland Jesuits hesitated to commit resources to Baltimore.[315]

To free up faculty for a Baltimore school, the Jesuits considered—but decided against—closing the St. John's Literary Institute in Frederick.[316] A more expedient "solution" presented itself in 1852, when the College of the Holy Cross in Worcester nearly burned to the ground. While the Jesuits weighed whether to rebuild in Massachusetts, several of the displaced Holy Cross faculty were reassigned to the fledgling Baltimore college, and they proved to be the seed necessary to make it viable in the short term.[317] (As it happened, St. John's Literary Institute effectively closed its collegiate division by the end of the decade anyway, as the new Jesuit colleges in Baltimore and Boston took priority.)

To lead the project in Baltimore, the Jesuits assigned Father John Early, SJ. Early belongs to what might be called the "third generation" of American Jesuits trained by "first generation" priests like Father John McElroy and by "second generation" priests like Father James Ryder. An Irish immigrant, Early studied under McElroy at St. John's Literary Institute before transferring to Georgetown to finish his studies. As a young Jesuit in 1848, he succeeded Ryder as the third president of Holy Cross. Despite his relative youth (he was only 38 when he was asked to build a college from scratch in Baltimore), he was experienced. Whereas the aging Ryder failed to launch Saint Joseph's College successfully in Philadelphia, Early's energetic dedication made all the difference in the Charm City.

Early and his companions dubbed the new school Loyola College, making it the first American college to carry that name. For its first "campus," he leased two buildings on Holliday Street just north of what is today Baltimore's Inner Harbor. An ad he placed in the Baltimore *Sun* in 1852 promised that the new college had "secured the services of professors of known ability," and that "The course of studies will differ little from that heretofore pursued in St. Mary's, and will be essentially the same as that now followed in Georgetown College, D.C."[318]

---

315. Ibid., 8.
316. Ibid., 10–11.
317. Ibid., 13–14.
318. As quoted in Ibid., 21.

Under Early's leadership, Loyola wasted no time securing a charter, and it was officially empowered by the Maryland legislature in 1853 to grant degrees. The new college's association with a well-established Maryland institution like the Society of Jesus likely helped expedite that process.

Early served as president of the school for four years (a bit longer than the customary three-year term) after which he was promoted to the presidency of Georgetown. After completing his stint at his alma mater, he returned to Baltimore and led Loyola a second time, from 1866 to 1870. Then, it was back to Georgetown for another presidential term. (The Jesuits certainly made good use of their most talented personnel.) Early died in office at Georgetown, having led three different Jesuit colleges in his long career.

Loyola College's first "campus" in rented quarters on Holliday Street lasted only three years. Late in his first presidential term, Father Early moved the college to a more permanent home on Calvert Street in the city's rapidly growing Mount Vernon Place neighborhood. There it stayed for almost 70 years. The new "campus" was still decidedly urban and multi-purpose. A single building housed the college classrooms, a parish church (St. Ignatius), and apartments for the Jesuits themselves. Like many traditional Jesuit schools, Loyola was simultaneously a college, a parish, and a community center—a hub from which the priests not only taught but also ministered to the local flock. These men spent six days per week in the classroom and spent their evenings and weekends bringing the sacraments to prisons, hospitals, and family homes.

Though Loyola, like the other four sisters of the east, enrolled a high percentage of Catholic students, it welcomed others. The first class was approximately 25% non-Catholic, including Protestants, Jews, and others identified in official records as practicing "no religion."[319] In religiously diverse Maryland, where Catholics had long cooperated with people of other faiths and such toleration was much more ingrained in the local culture than elsewhere on the East Coast, it could be no other way.

Loyola got a major boost in prestige in 1859, when Father Felix Sopranis, SJ, acting as the official representative from Rome, recommended that the Maryland Province relocate its headquarters from Georgetown to Loyola.[320] This meant that the provincial resided in the Loyola College building—an arrangement that could be both a blessing and a curse, since it meant that the president of the college was always under the watchful eye of his boss. Since Father Sopranis also recommended the closure of Saint Joseph's College in Pennsylvania that same year, we can assume he felt that it was a higher priority to strengthen the Jesuit presence in Baltimore, America's oldest archdiocese, than in Philadelphia.

---

319. Ibid., 28.
320. Ibid., 19.

Boston College (1858), Boston, Massachusetts

While John Early was leading the Jesuit expansion into Baltimore, his former teacher and mentor at Frederick, John McElroy, was working on behalf of the Maryland Province in Boston. Opening a Jesuit school in America's emerging intellectual capital was both audacious and necessary. Unlike St. Louis, Mobile, Georgetown, Worcester, and most other cities in which the Jesuits had staffed colleges up to that point, Boston already had plenty of educational opportunity available to its citizens. Unfortunately, schools like Harvard limited their enrollment to a certain kind of citizen—namely the wealthy, white, upper-class Protestant boys from New England's ancient elite. Excluded were the thousands of mainly Irish Catholic immigrants who were resettling in the city as a result of the potato famine and other economic troubles of the nineteenth century. Since many of those boys were too poor even to afford the trip to Worcester, let alone pay Holy Cross tuition, Boston was crying out for a Catholic college.

Fortunately, the Jesuits did have a man in Boston—one with extensive experience in education. Father McElroy was stationed in the city as part of his enlistment as an Army chaplain during the Mexican War. In 1847, his connections in Massachusetts helped him become pastor of a Boston church (St. Mary's), where he began negotiating and strategizing with the diocese to open a Jesuit school. The Jesuits had long been interested in opening a college in Boston, but delayed that goal when Bishop Benedict Fenwick, SJ insisted on a "Worcester first" approach. After Fenwick died in 1846, his successor, Bishop John Fitzpatrick, proved more receptive to the idea of a Boston school.

As with Old St. Joseph's Church in Philadelphia, the Jesuits hoped to use McElroy's parish as a toehold from which to build up an academic presence in the city. McElroy explored several possible properties before buying a parcel in the city's South End in 1857. There, the following year, he oversaw the construction of the college campus. As was the case in Philadelphia and Baltimore, it was a "campus" only in the most basic sense; what McElroy actually built on the property was a church (named for the Immaculate Conception) and two schoolhouse buildings.

McElroy's expansionist activity had the fortune (or misfortune) of coinciding almost exactly with the visit of Father Felix Sopranis, SJ. Representing the Jesuit superior general in Rome, Sopranis recommended that the Boston school initially limit its enrollment to Jesuit scholastics (seminarians). The Maryland Province had, in fact, already considered this option. For several years, Jesuit seminarians had variously studied at St. John's in Frederick or at Georgetown, but St. John's was scaling back its ambitions in higher education and there was some feeling that Georgetown was not an ideal environment for the young priests-in-training. Its neighborhood offered many temptations and the college exploited the presence of the seminarians by recruiting them to teach courses, much like modern-day graduate students who are called to teach whenever full-time professors are unavailable. A Boston school, without any lay students to teach, could provide a distraction-free environment for the young scholastics. Thus, in 1860, just as McElroy was putting the finishing touches on his first school building, the Jesuits established what they initially called the Boston Seminary.[321]

Although McElroy laid the foundation for the school, he never served as its president. The first rector of the Boston Seminary was John Bapst, SJ, a Swiss missionary who had preached (and had been savagely assaulted by Nativists) in Maine. The outbreak of the Civil War disrupted what otherwise might have been a smooth introduction of classes, but the Jesuits never abandoned plans to develop the school into a full-fledged college. In the midst of the war in 1863 (a date still recognized by the school as its official founding) the Massachusetts legislature chartered "Boston College" to grant degrees to lay students. Father Bapst became (or perhaps more accurately, remained) its first president. The seminarians who had been staying on the campus left, and by 1869 they relocated to a purpose-built Jesuit seminary in Woodstock, Maryland. Boston College was now strictly an undergraduate school for lay students, as John McElroy had intended.[322]

The relative ease with which Boston College received its charter—two years before Holy Cross—was mainly because of its official openness to religious pluralism. Whereas Holy Cross prohibited non-Catholics from enrolling, Boston College's charter expressly stated, "no student in said college shall be refused admission...on account of the religious opinions he may entertain."[323] While Boston College's student body was overwhelmingly Catholic, the formal embrace of diversity made it more palatable to the heavily Protestant Massachusetts legislature.

"Boston College" was a typical Jesuit name, in the tradition of schools like Georgetown College, Saint Louis College, Santa Clara College, and others that came before it. Even in Europe, Jesuits frequently named their schools after the cities in which they were located, but in the United States, this tradition had the added benefit of helping the schools "blend in" to American society. The Jesuits selected this name before the rival Methodist school across town claimed the moniker "Boston University." When Boston College incorporated in 1863, the school that would become Boston University was not located in Boston but in Concord, New Hampshire; it would not relocate to New England's largest city until 1867. Two years later, it was chartered by the Massachusetts government under its present name.

The Fourth Sister: Gonzaga College (1858), Washington, DC

The Maryland Jesuits achieved most of the expansion they had planned at their 1835 congregation. They had originally targeted Baltimore, Philadelphia, Richmond, and New York for future Jesuit schools; by the end of the 1850s, virtually all of those

---

321. Edward I. Devitt, SJ, "History of the Maryland-New York Province XVI: Boston College and Church of the Immaculate Conception," *Woodstock Letters* LXIV, no. 3 (1935): 401–402.

322. Ibid. 403–405.

323. As quoted in Ibid., 406.

cities had a significant Jesuit presence—even if Philadelphia's was tenuous and New York's had been achieved through the efforts of French Jesuits from a different province. In addition, the Jesuits had become a force to be reckoned with in Massachusetts, where they sponsored two rapidly growing colleges.

The one project that never materialized was a Jesuit school in Richmond. This goal was modified when the Jesuits opened a day college in Washington, DC, supplementing their work at Georgetown. The Washington Seminary returned to the Jesuits' control in 1848, twenty-one years after they abandoned it. Originally founded by Anthony Kohlmann, SJ, the school had been operating sporadically under the tutelage of diocesan priests for two decades. By the 1850s, the Jesuits' growing resources meant that they were finally in a position to make a substantial investment in the venerable old day school. They obtained a charter to grant degrees in 1858 and changed its name to Gonzaga College to reflect its new scope. As when Georgetown obtained its charter more than forty years earlier, the only legislative authority with jurisdiction over the District of Columbia was the United States Congress itself, so Gonzaga's collegiate charter came via an act of the federal government and was signed into law by President James Buchanan.

Gonzaga became, in effect, what a Richmond school would have been—a day college for those who could not afford the boarding fees at Georgetown. With an urban campus built around a church, it functionally resembled Loyola, Saint Joseph's, and Boston College in character and mission. While those other schools all elevated themselves to university status over the next century and a half, Gonzaga's proximity to the Georgetown flagship meant that it could never do the same. Unlike its sisters to the north, it evolved strictly into a high school and abandoned its degree-granting programs by the early 1900s.

Meanwhile, Out West . . .

At the same time the Maryland Jesuits were peppering the eastern megalopolis with colleges, Jesuit missionaries were pushing west in pace with the American frontier. The Oregon Trail was expanding the limits of American settlement, and as pioneers pressed on in their covered wagons, the Jesuits established far-flung mission outposts to serve Catholic settlers and to seek out Native American converts.

The home base for most of this activity was St. Louis, from which dozens of Jesuit missionaries fanned out to the vast expanse of the Great Plains and Rocky Mountains—often a step ahead of the main waves of American settlement. Many of these men were the first Europeans to set foot in the regions they visited and the first to compile dictionaries of the local indigenous languages. Two of the most important explorers—not just in terms of Catholic history, but also in terms of American history as a whole—were Fathers Nicholas Point, SJ, and Pierre-Jean DeSmet, SJ.

Father Point left his thumbprint on the United States even before he set out for the west: in 1837, he founded St. Charles College in Grand Coteau, Louisiana. His greatest and most lasting contribution to American history, however, would come as a Rocky Mountain missionary. A talented artist, he was one of the first Europeans to sketch the native flora and fauna of the American west, and his detailed drawings were some of the first to depict day-to-day Native American life in the region. Today, his work is a historical treasure—among the earliest documentation we have of this part of America in its nineteenth-century state.

Father DeSmet left an equally varied legacy that influenced both higher education and western exploration. He was one of the original Belgian Jesuits who traveled to Missouri in the 1820s to assume control of Saint Louis University, where he served as treasurer. Later, he went on to explore much of the Rocky Mountains on both the American and Canadian sides of the border, preaching and building rudimentary chapels. In 1842, he founded a mission in modern-day Idaho among the Coeur d'Alene Indians; the original site is now a state park, and the mission church remains Idaho's oldest standing building.

Although DeSmet never served as president of any Jesuit college, he left a major mark on western Jesuit education. During his lifetime, he toured Europe frequently to raise money for Saint Louis University and to round up volunteers for the Indian missions. Two of the men he recruited to the Rockies were a pair of Italian Jesuits—John Nobili, SJ and Michael Accolti, SJ—whose missionary efforts ultimately led to the establishment of Santa Clara University in California.[324] Numerous small towns from South Dakota to Idaho are named after Father DeSmet, as is a small lake in Wyoming. The Jesuits have honored his memory by naming several of their ministries after him, including DeSmet Jesuit High School outside St. Louis and residence halls on the campuses of Gonzaga University in Spokane and Regis University in Denver.

St. Mary's College, Kansas (1848)

Many of the early Jesuit missions among the Plains Indians included elementary schools—often funded by the federal government through its Commissioner on Indian Affairs. Given the Jesuit propensity for expansion, some of these mission schools would inevitably develop into colleges. The first to emerge from this network was St. Mary's College of Kansas, which traced its roots to a log cabin schoolhouse built in 1848 as part of the Jesuit mission to the Potawatomi.

The original site of the St. Mary's Mission School is about thirty miles northwest of Topeka, a bit more than halfway between the University of Kansas in Lawrence and Kansas State University in Manhattan. More than a decade before either of those two universities existed (indeed, more than a decade before the State of Kansas existed), the Jesuits were among the few groups to open a European-style school in this remote area.

Many of the Jesuits who served in Kansas were former professors or students at Saint Louis University, and many were Belgian. The work was brutal and even dan-

---

324. McKevitt, *University of Santa Clara*, 14–17.

gerous. As the Civil War approached, St. Mary's was surrounded by the "Bleeding Kansas" violence that erupted between pro-slavery and anti-slavery factions in the disputed territory.[325] In the midst of the unrest, the Jesuit mission became a major community center and refuge for the local Potawatomi, and the Jesuits learned the native language well enough to preach in it on Sundays.[326]

Like many other Indian schools throughout the west, the St. Mary's Mission School educated both boys and girls, who all lived on campus (albeit in separate buildings). The Sisters of the Sacred Heart supplied the teachers for the girls' division.[327] Therefore, by some (extreme) stretches of logic, St. Mary's might be considered the first coeducational Jesuit college in the United States. Certainly, of all the Jesuit schools that eventually developed into full-fledged colleges, St. Mary's was the first to educate female students on its campus. However, the school that existed in the 1850s was hardly more than an elementary school, and the boys' and girls' divisions were not truly integrated. By the time a college actually emerged on the site, the Sisters had moved out and sold their remaining buildings to the Jesuits. All of the female students were gone by the time St. Mary's started to offer bachelor's degrees.[328]

St. Mary's Mission School would operate for more than twenty years before it received a collegiate charter from the Kansas government in 1869. Prior to that date, its students were almost exclusively Native Americans, though a handful of children of white settlers were attending by the early 1860s. In 1866, Father Pierre DeSmet, temporarily stationed at the mission, reported that there was an imbalance of supply and demand for education in the area; so many white students were seeking admission to the Mission School that the Jesuits had to turn them away in order to prioritize seats for the Native American boys, their original target audience.[329]

The Jesuits tried to keep their ministry focused on the Native Americans as long as possible, but as the 1860s drew to a close, the demographics of Kansas were changing. White settlers came to outnumber the natives, most of whom were being forcibly relocated to the Indian Territory (Oklahoma) by the federal government. The Jesuits considered closing St. Mary's Mission altogether, but with a relatively well-developed academic campus at their disposal, the provincial leadership in St. Louis decided to develop the Kansas site into a full-fledged college.[330]

Given its rural location, St. Mary's College could never be anything but a boarding school. This, however, meant that it would require a relatively large staff that the St. Louis Jesuits were not immediately prepared to devote to it. Progress in developing the college was slow—deliberately so. More than seven years after the school obtained its charter to grant degrees, the Jesuits continued to staff it much as they would an ele-

---

325. Garraghan, *Jesuits of the Middle U.S. Vol. III*, 2.

326. Ibid., 50.

327. Garraghan, *Jesuits of the Middle U.S. Vol. II*, 673.

328. Garraghan, *Jesuits of the Middle U.S. Vol. III*, 56.

329. Ibid., 44.

330. Ibid., 46.

mentary school, and their own internal records do not identify St. Mary's as a "college" until 1877.[331]

St. Mary's enrolled a small collegiate student body, and the heyday of its undergraduate division came in the early 1900s. As time passed, however, the isolated college could not survive competition from the state's public universities and from more conveniently located Jesuit schools like Rockhurst and Creighton. The Great Depression was the straw that finally broke its back. It closed in 1931, and the campus temporarily became home to Saint Louis University's school of theology. By the 1960s, however, the theology faculty and students had returned to Saint Louis and the Jesuits sold off the old St. Mary's campus. Today, the Society of St. Pius X operates an academy on the site.

Santa Clara University (1851): First on the West Coast

Even before the United States formally acquired the Oregon Territory by treaty in 1846, the Pacific Northwest was a major focus of the Missouri Jesuits' Indian mission work. To facilitate their outreach to the region's natives and Catholic pioneers, they established a headquarters in Oregon's Willamette Valley, from which they sent missionaries as far away as British Columbia and the borders of Alaska (then still controlled by Russia). They even staffed a school in the Willamette Valley that they called "St. Joseph's College," although it was in truth a high school. It operated briefly from 1843 to 1849 and was never chartered as a college, mainly because there was no functioning government to charter it. The United States did not organize the Oregon Territory until 1848, by which time the school was already in decline.

St. Joseph's College closed because the opportunistic settlers who built it were, by 1848, already packing up and relocating to America's next boom state, California. The American Jesuits as yet had no meaningful presence in California, which had just been incorporated into the United States after the Mexican War. Before it joined the United States, California and its Catholic churches were under the authority of Mexican bishops who never established any colleges to serve the region's sparse population. Catholic worship remained largely centered around a network of about twenty dilapidated coastal missions founded by St. Junipero Serra and California's other original Spanish explorers in the late 1700s. By the time California became an American state, most of these mission churches were still in the hands of Spanish-speaking Franciscan friars, as they had been for nearly 100 years.

When the Gold Rush broke out in 1848 and brought thousands of English-speaking Americans to California, church politics had to adapt to the changing demographics. Joseph Sadoc Alemany, OP, a Spanish-born American citizen, was appointed the first American bishop of Monterey in 1850. At about the same time,

---

331. Ibid., 53–54.

the booming population around San Francisco Bay caught the imagination of an Italian Jesuit, Michele (Michael) Accolti, SJ, who had been serving in the Oregon mission since 1844. Enamored with the stories of America's newest frontier, Accolti was convinced that California, not Oregon, would be the epicenter of US culture on the Pacific coast, and concluded that the Jesuits had to establish a presence there.[332]

In 1849, Accolti convinced his superiors to send him on a fact-finding expedition to San Francisco, where he explored possible sites for a new Jesuit mission. Assigned to accompany him on the trip was his old friend and fellow Italian, Giovanni (John) Nobili, SJ. Both Accolti and Nobili were seasoned missionaries—each with more than six years of experience preaching to the Native Americans of the northwest coast—and both originally came to the Oregon mission at the invitation of Father Pierre DeSmet. They had even shared the same boat on their initial journey from Europe to America.[333]

None of that prior missionary work prepared them, however, for what they found in California. San Francisco at the time was the epitome of the Wild West, populated by gamblers, tramps, prostitutes, squatters, and gun-slinging prospectors who lived in a state of near anarchy with only the most rudimentary law enforcement. Its people were a polyglot mix of American transients, Native Americans, and Spanish-speaking *Californios* (descendants of the early Mexican settlers). The two highly educated, refined Jesuits stood out like sore thumbs on its streets, but the city was crying out for the stabilizing influence of a college.[334]

Bishop Alemany recognized the need for Catholic education in his young diocese, and encouraged the two Jesuit visitors to establish a school. However, Accolti and Nobili were powerless to act without authorization from their Jesuit superiors, and communication between Europe and the West Coast of the United States was glacial. They wrote repeatedly to Jan Roothaan, then in his final years as superior general, seeking permission to expand the Jesuits' Oregon mission to California. The slowness of the nineteenth-century post office came into full view in 1850 when Accolti received a letter from Roothaan. No doubt hoping that it was a response to his repeated requests, he opened it only to discover that it was dated 1848—meaning that it had been mailed even before he first left Oregon for California. To his surprise, the letter informed him that he had been appointed the new head of the Oregon Mission. Reluctantly, Accolti packed up and returned to Oregon to accept the leadership position.[335]

Having discovered that Accolti was now his boss, Nobili followed orders to stay behind in California, where he continued to negotiate with Bishop Alemany about opening a college. For a campus, Alemany offered Nobili the old Spanish mission at Santa Clara. At the time, the ancient church was functioning as a parish under the leadership of a corrupt Franciscan friar named José Suárez del Real, who openly

---

332. McKevitt, *University of Santa Clara*, 15–17.

333. Ibid., 18–19.

334. Ibid., 18–19.

335. Ibid., 20.

housed mistresses on the property and sold church assets to finance his own vices, including gambling and gold prospecting.[336] Fortunately, when Alemany ordered the wayward priest off the property, he obeyed. Unfortunately, Suárez del Real left behind a large number of debts, legal entanglements, and squatters who lived in various buildings in the mission complex without clear title to them. It was not clear that Alemany, as bishop, even had the legal right to offer the old mission to the Jesuits; it would be years before the United States Land Commission settled all of the issues surrounding title deeds to the campus.[337]

Unwilling to wait years for authorization from Rome, Nobili accepted Bishop Alemany's offer and began to lay the groundwork for a school at Santa Clara. Meanwhile, Roothaan's reply to the original requests finally arrived. To the disappointment of Accolti in Oregon and Nobili in California, the superior general had decided not to authorize a Jesuit school in the San Francisco Bay Area. The two Italians were being denied permission to build a school that already existed. Fortunately, Roothaan's letter also authorized Nobili to stay in California and continue to explore possibilities for a future school, as long as he could drum up support and build a faculty from other Jesuit provinces around the world. Having obtained vague, conditional permission to do something he had already done, Nobili continued working on the college at Santa Clara.[338]

Roothaan's decision effectively meant that Nobili was now responsible for creating and managing a college entirely by himself. Fortunately, he proved up to the task. As the first president of Santa Clara College, he hired a handful of laymen as professors. From Oregon, Accolti supplemented that bare-bones faculty with some older Jesuits who were too sick or frail to continue serving in the harsh conditions of the Indian missions, and for whom teaching would be a retirement post.[339]

An even bigger issue than the lack of faculty was the condition of the campus. The land that constituted the old Spanish mission included a deteriorating church, several residences, ranches, an orchard, a vineyard, and other parcels claimed by various squatters. By stroke of luck, one of the wealthiest and most influential residents of the property was John Alexander Forbes, a British diplomat who happened to be Jesuit-educated. A Scotsman by birth, he was an alumnus of a Jesuit college in Uruguay, and continued his globe-trotting career when he moved to San Jose (then the capital of California) to represent British interests to the government. With a soft spot in his heart for Jesuit education, he agreed to give up his claim to the land (and even defended the Jesuits against other claimants in court) on the condition that his sons be allowed to attend Santa Clara College free of charge.[340]

---

336. Ibid., 11–12.
337. Ibid., 25, 32–33.
338. Ibid., 29–30.
339. Ibid., 25.
340. Ibid., 30–39.

First Degree on the West Coast

Santa Clara had no difficulty finding students; the small, but growing elite class of California landowners were practically starving for a place to send their sons. The opportunity appealed to Californians of all faiths; more than half of the boarding students in 1852 were Protestant.[341]

In 1857, Santa Clara became the first American college (of any kind) to award a bachelor's degree on the West Coast. Its first graduate, Thomas Bergin, became a San Francisco lawyer.[342] Although that milestone is not in dispute, it is debatable whether Santa Clara counts as the oldest college in California; it received its charter in 1855, four years after the Methodist-affiliated California Wesleyan College received a collegiate charter. While that institution (known today as the University of the Pacific) has some claim to being the oldest college on the West Coast, Santa Clara was irrefutably the first to grant a bachelor's degree.[343]

Santa Clara Loses a Founder, but Gains a Faculty

In spite of the challenges he faced, Father John Nobili did a remarkable job rehabilitating the old mission into something suitable for a college campus. The project ultimately cost him his life. While supervising the construction of a new chapel for the campus in 1856, he accidentally stepped on a nail and contracted a bacterial infection that led to tetanus. He died less than a month later, just shy of his 44th birthday.[344]

Santa Clara Historian Gerald McKevitt, SJ, observed that John Nobili was a reluctant founding father who had been somewhat roped into establishing a college in California. As he weathered the legal, administrative, and financial headaches of the project almost single-handedly, he was executing Michael Accolti's original vision. McKevitt writes, "In their joint effort, one man was the prime mover and the other the recruit."[345] Though he was not the man who first envisioned a Jesuit college in the Bay Area, Nobili devoted his sweat and ultimately sacrificed his life to the cause. Santa Clara University would not exist today if not for the outstanding leadership he provided during its tenuous first five years. While no statue of John Nobili stands on the Santa Clara campus (we do not even know what he looked like, because no image has survived),[346] his living monument is the old Spanish mission church that he saved from ruin and transformed into the campus centerpiece that it is today.

From Oregon, Father Michael Accolti continued to promote the interests of the school he helped to create. Knowing that its long-term survival depended on its abil-

---

341. Ibid., 40.
342. Ibid., 48.
343. Ibid., 28.
344. Ibid., 49.
345. Ibid., 22.
346. Ibid., 21.

ity to secure a large, stable supply of faculty, he went to Europe in 1853 seeking the help of his Italian Jesuit confreres. He managed to convince the Jesuit Province of Turin, Italy to take responsibility for Santa Clara and establish a formal mission in California. The following year, three Italian Jesuits arrived in San Francisco, the first of many who would reinforce the faculty and develop Santa Clara into a college worthy of the name.[347]

The University of San Francisco (1855), San Francisco, California

One of the original three Jesuits from the Turin Province who came to California in 1854 was Father Antonio (Anthony) Maraschi, SJ. Maraschi had already served in the United States for some time, having taught at Georgetown and Holy Cross and having served as one of the founding faculty members at Loyola College in Baltimore.[348] Logically he would have been an excellent addition to the Santa Clara faculty, but he and his superiors in Italy had other ideas.

Unlike his travel companions who continued south to Santa Clara to teach, Father Maraschi was under orders to remain in San Francisco, where he initially accepted an assignment as an assistant church pastor. Sensing that San Francisco would someday become one of the world's great cities, his Jesuit superiors urged him to acquire property for a permanent Jesuit presence in the downtown area. In 1855, only a year after his arrival in the United States, he built a church (named for St. Ignatius) on Market Street in the heart of what is today the city's bustling central business district. Next to the church, he built a schoolhouse for a small academy that soon enrolled a few dozen boys. Four years later, that school received a collegiate charter from the California government and renamed itself St. Ignatius College. (The relative ease with which it obtained the charter demonstrates the state's dire need for higher education at the time.) It was the first college of any kind in the City of San Francisco.

Whether Maraschi realized it or not, his actions reflected those of other Jesuits who had come before him to the United States. He had started a downtown day school in close proximity to a Jesuit boarding college. Over time, the relationship between St. Ignatius College and Santa Clara College became similar to that between Gonzaga and Georgetown in the nation's capital, Boston College and Holy Cross in Massachusetts, and St. Francis Xavier and St. John's (Fordham) in New York. Wherever they built schools, the American Jesuits seemed virtually incapable of leaving well enough alone; their almost insatiable drive to start new colleges, rather than just support existing ones, was a constant source of frustration for their superiors in Europe. Their actions were driven, altruistically, more by public need than by their own resources. Whenever a city showed growth potential, and wherever there was large

---

347. Ibid., 47.
348. Varga, *Baltimore's Loyola*, 23–24.

unmet demand for education, the Jesuits felt compelled to start a school whether they could afford it or not.

In 1861, Father Felix Sopranis visited the new California schools as part of his midcentury inspection tour. On the East Coast, Sopranis had ordered sweeping changes that, among other things, led to the closure of Saint Joseph's College in Philadelphia; his visit to the west was almost as injurious to the young St. Ignatius College. Alarmed that St. Ignatius was not yet requiring Latin and Greek for all students, the ever-conservative Sopranis made both subjects mandatory and insisted on a strict implementation of the *Ratio Studiorum*. The result was a sharp decrease in enrollment as many St. Ignatius students withdrew. Five years later, after much lobbying from the California Jesuits, Superior General Beckx rescinded Sopranis's order and gave the West Coast schools more leeway to adapt their offerings to local student demand.[349]

The presence of two Jesuit colleges in the Bay Area presented both problems and conveniences. On one hand, in this remote outpost (nearly 6,000 miles from the province headquarters in Turin and more than 2,000 miles from the nearest Jesuit university at St. Louis), the two schools could support each other by sharing resources and faculty. When a Jesuit professor became ill or unable to teach, his replacement could be "borrowed" from the school on the other end of the peninsula. Because Jesuit college presidents were limited to three-year terms, exceptionally talented leaders could stay in California with an appointment to the other school.[350] Between 1855 and 1900, about half of the men who served as president of Santa Clara College also served as president of St. Ignatius College. During that period, Santa Clara had ten unique presidents and St. Ignatius had eleven, but five of those Jesuits eventually served at both: Fathers Nicholas Congiato, Burchard Villiger, Aloysius Masnata, Giovanni Pinasco, and Robert Kenna.

On the other hand, the two schools competed for students. While ostensibly they served different audiences (with wealthier and more distant students boarding at Santa Clara and poorer local students commuting to St. Ignatius), inevitably St. Ignatius attracted some students who otherwise would have enrolled at the flagship college to the south. As in New York City, the downtown day college soon outpaced the boarding college in enrollment. By 1884, St. Ignatius enrolled about 700 students while Santa Clara enrolled only 160 (though both numbers include pre-collegians).[351]

To accommodate its growing enrollment, St. Ignatius moved to a new campus, abandoning its original Market Street location in favor of a more spacious building a few blocks away in what is today the dense Civic Center complex. That campus was destroyed by the devastating 1906 San Francisco earthquake, forcing the school to

---

349. Gerald McKevitt, SJ, *Brokers of Culture: Italian Jesuits in the American West, 1848–1919* (Palo Alto: Stanford University Press, 2007), 213–214.

350. McKevitt, *University of Santa Clara*, 128.

351. Henry Woods, SJ, "California Mission of the Society of Jesus," *Woodstock Letters* XIII, no. 2 (1884): 160.

relocate yet again to its present campus, northeast of Golden Gate Park. There, it thrived, renaming itself the University of San Francisco on its 75th anniversary in 1930. By the twenty-first century, what began as Father Maraschi's humble one-building academy had emerged as one of the premier Catholic research universities in the United States.

Jesuit Colleges and the Civil War (1861–1865)

When the Civil War broke out in 1861, the Jesuits were operating twelve colleges and universities in the United States, with two others in development. The largest network was that of the Maryland Jesuits, who sponsored two boarding schools at Georgetown and Worcester, along with two day schools in Baltimore and Washington. They had recently shuttered an unsuccessful day college in Philadelphia (not to reopen it for another three decades), but they were also in the process of opening a new college in Boston that would enroll its first students before the war came to an end.

In the center of the country, the Missouri Jesuits operated their flagship university in St. Louis, along with a boarding school in Bardstown, Kentucky and a day school in Cincinnati. They also sponsored a network of Indian mission schools across the west, one of which, in Kansas, was gingerly taking steps to transform itself into a college.

In the South, French Jesuits had taken control of boarding colleges in Mobile and Grand Coteau, along with a day college in New Orleans. The French Jesuits were also investing heavily in a pair of colleges in New York—Fordham, with an expansive campus north of the city, and St. Francis Xavier, which consisted of a few buildings in the heart of Manhattan.

Lastly, in the west, the Italian Jesuits sponsored two young schools in the San Francisco Bay Area.

A mere twenty years earlier, there had been only six Jesuit colleges in the United States, three of which—St. Charles (Louisiana), St. Mary's (Kentucky), and St. John's Literary Institute (Maryland)—were destined not to survive. In the span of one generation, the Jesuits had radiated out from their two permanent hubs at Georgetown and St. Louis and established a presence in most of the major American cities where large concentrations of Catholics lived. It was an incredible accomplishment at a time when communication and transportation were only as fast as the walking speed of a horse. This progress likely would have continued if not for the crippling effects of the Civil War. The conflict halted further Jesuit expansion for a decade—until the Missouri Jesuits opened their first postwar college in Chicago in 1870.

American Catholics were split in their loyalties during the Civil War, reflecting that the very nature of the Catholic Church in the United States was changing. Catholicism was still largely a Southern religion in 1861, although immigration was already in the process of transforming it into an overwhelmingly northern one. Long-established, landowning Catholic families in Louisiana, Maryland, and Kentucky tended to support the Confederacy. More-recent Catholic immigrants of Irish, German, and Italian extraction were settling mainly in northern states. Even though these newcomers had no economic or historic sympathies toward slavery, their commitment to the abolitionist cause was often lukewarm. In the north, the anti-Catholic Know-Nothing Party essentially folded into the Republican Party by the late 1850s, leaving some Catholics deeply skeptical of the 1860 Republican presidential candidate, Abraham Lincoln. Many former Know-Nothing Party members supported and campaigned for Lincoln, and the anti-slavery abolitionist movement tended to include large numbers of anti-Catholic Nativists, making it hard for Catholic immigrants to find a political home.[352]

On Jesuit college campuses, for the most part, geography determined prevailing opinions. Nearly all schools had a mix of northern and Southern students, which made for interesting classroom debates. When the country split in two, three Jesuit schools—at Mobile, Grand Coteau, and New Orleans—were geographically and politically in the grip of the Confederacy. Seven schools (one in Ohio, and two each in Massachusetts, New York, and California) were solidly in the Union. The remaining schools were in border states—Maryland, Kentucky, Missouri, and the District of Columbia—which practiced slavery but chose not to secede. It was in these schools that the debate over slavery was most toxic, causing classmates to take sides against each other in the debate halls and eventually on the battlefield.

The Maryland Jesuits collectively chose not to vote in the 1860 presidential election, lest their sharply divided students accuse them of showing favoritism to one candidate over another. The Missouri Jesuits also attempted neutrality, urging faculty at Saint Louis and St. Joseph's to keep their opinions to themselves and to recognize the authority of the Union government so long as Missouri and Kentucky remained in the United States.[353] From Rome, Superior General Pieter Beckx warned American Jesuits not to take sides in the country's contentious politics, but "'to keep themselves free from all party spirit.'"[354] As Catholics themselves were deeply divided in their opinions, the Church hierarchy chose to walk a fine line.

The most immediate, dramatic effect of the war on the colleges was a rapid reduction in enrollment, as young men of college age enlisted to fight. One exception was Spring Hill College in Mobile, where enrollment actually increased near the end of the war as wealthy Southern parents sought to enroll their sons as insurance against a Confederate draft.[355] The draft even affected faculty and staff. Although clergy were generally exempt from military service, the Confederate Army tried to conscript the Jesuit brothers (who were technically laypeople) and scholastics who had not yet taken final vows as priests. Spring Hill president Francis de Sales Gautrelet, SJ, personally visited Jefferson Davis in Richmond to lobby against this policy. Davis, who was himself a product of Catholic education and had studied under future Cincinnati Bishop Dominic Fenwick as a boy in Kentucky, intervened to exempt the

---

352. Varga, *Baltimore's Loyola*, 67. Shelley, *Fordham*, 90.
353. Bennish, *Continuity*, 67.
354. As quoted in Varga, *Baltimore's Loyola*, 67.
355. Mulhern, "Spring Hill," 340.

Jesuits.[356] In Louisiana, the staff of St. Charles College were excused from the draft because theirs was the state's only functioning college west of the Mississippi.[357]

In the north, Father Pierre DeSmet, representing Saint Louis University, negotiated a similar draft exemption in an 1863 meeting with the US Secretary of War, Edwin Stanton.[358] Word of the exemption travelled slowly in the west, however, and in 1864 four Jesuit professors and administrators at St. Xavier College in Cincinnati learned that they were being drafted into the Union Army—among them John DeBlieck, SJ, a former president of St. Xavier and a future president of what is now Loyola University (Chicago). Knowing that this loss would be a serious blow to the local Catholic community and potentially a fatal blow to St. Xavier College, parishioners at the college church raised $1,200 to pay the priests' exemption fees.[359] The Jesuits would not be forced to take up arms on either side.

Nonetheless, with few students to teach, many Jesuits enlisted voluntarily as military chaplains in both armies. Four Spring Hill faculty members served as chaplains in the Confederacy.[360] Three Fordham professors, one Santa Clara professor, and one Holy Cross professor served the Union in a similar capacity.[361] One particularly notable figure was Joseph O'Hagan, SJ, a former Georgetown professor and future president of Holy Cross, who served the Union as chaplain to the Army of the Potomac. O'Hagan was briefly taken prisoner by the rebels in Richmond, underscoring the fact that military chaplains, though non-combatants, were still frequently in serious danger on the battlefield. They willingly risked their lives to hear soldiers' confessions before battle and bring the sacraments to the dying and wounded.[362]

Even some Jesuits who did not volunteer for service found themselves pressed into duty through other circumstances. A priest from St. Charles College in Louisiana, Father Francis Abbadie, once tried to cross a Confederate checkpoint during routine travel. Arrested on the spot, he was taken into the soldiers' camp, where several of his former students serving in the Confederate Army recognized him. Before long, dozens of St. Charles alumni and their brothers-in-arms were flocking to Father Abbadie for a blessing and confession, making him briefly the most popular prisoner at camp.[363]

Early in the war, the Union Navy blockaded Mobile Bay and captured New Orleans, depriving the South of two of its major ports and isolating the Jesuit colleges in those cities. Jesuits at Spring Hill, living in quarantine and without access to neces-

---

356. Widman, "Springhill College," 271.

357. Platt, *Sacrifice*, 67.

358. Faherty, *Better*, 142–143.

359. Bennish, *Continuity*, 73.

360. Widman, "Springhill College," 273.

361. Shelley, *Fordham*, 94. Kuzniewski, *Thy Honored Name*, 115. McKevitt, *University of Santa Clara*, 74.

362. Curran, *History of Georgetown Vol. I*, 250–252.

363. Maitrugues, "St. Charles College," 22.

sities, made their own wine on campus for use during Mass.[364] In Louisiana, the Confederate Army occupied St. Charles College in Grand Coteau, but ceased to defend it after the battle of Vicksburg left the western half of the Confederacy under Union control.[365] The College of the Immaculate Conception in New Orleans was relatively unaffected by the fighting, although one Union officer (acting on his own authority) confiscated the valuable candelabras from Immaculate Conception Church. The French Jesuits eventually got the candelabras back after the French consulate intervened.[366]

Among the colleges located in border states, enlistment tilted in favor of the Confederacy. More than three-quarters of Georgetown alumni who fought in the war did so on behalf of the South. (Many of these men were also alumni of Loyola College in Baltimore; they had transferred to Georgetown to complete their studies. Loyola historian Nicholas Varga counts at least nine Loyola-Georgetown students who fought in Confederate gray and only one who fought in Union blue.)[367]

With the possible exception of St. Joseph's College in Kentucky (which closed), no Jesuit school was more directly affected by the war than Georgetown. With a campus situated on the border of the two warring countries, directly in view of Confederate territory across the Potomac River, it was not an attractive place for parents to send their sons. During the war, Georgetown's enrollment fell to its all-time low: seventeen students. Virtually empty, the hilltop campus presented a strategic defensive opportunity for the Union Army, which commandeered the buildings and used them as a base from which to defend the narrow strait separating Virginia from the nation's capital. The Sixty-Ninth New York Regiment—also known as the "Irish Regiment" due to its large number of Catholic soldiers from the slums of New York—was stationed on campus; Abraham Lincoln personally visited Georgetown in 1861 to inspect them. A year later, after the First Battle of Bull Run in nearby Manassas, Virginia, the wounded were taken to Georgetown, where the spacious Holy Trinity Church became a makeshift hospital. Shortly after the battle, at least four Jesuits from Georgetown and Gonzaga College left DC for Manassas, where they tended to the wounded and heard confessions of the dying.[368]

With faculty and student rolls depleted, the future of every Jesuit college in the Union and the Confederacy was in doubt. Inter-school squabbles occasionally broke out over the limited monetary and human resources that remained. James Clark, SJ, the wartime president of Holy Cross and former Georgetown faculty member, argued to his Maryland superiors that "'Georgetown College . . . certainly does not need all the teachers they had.'"[369] Clark, a West Point graduate and a military man before he became a Jesuit, did not succeed in permanently poaching Georgetown's faculty, but

---

364. Mulhern, "Spring Hill," 340.
365. Platt, *Sacrifice*, 67.
366. Cook, *Founded on Faith*, 30–31.
367. Varga, *Baltimore's Loyola*, 66–67.
368. Curran, *History of Georgetown Vol. I*, 243–246.
369. As quoted in Ibid., 246–247.

his loyalty to the United States did help Holy Cross to become perhaps the most staunchly pro-Union Jesuit college during and after the war.[370]

Remarkably, in spite of all of this uncertainty, the only casualty of the Civil War among Jesuit colleges was St. Joseph's College in Kentucky. It cancelled classes altogether and sent students home, transferring all remaining boarders to Saint Louis University. It never truly recovered before the Jesuits withdrew in 1868. All other Jesuit schools, while weakened, persevered. St. Charles College in Louisiana very nearly closed, but caught a lifeline when it was asked to house displaced Spring Hill students after the 1869 fire in Mobile. Boston College began offering its first classes before the war's end, and Santa Clara, in splendid isolation on the West Coast, actually benefitted from the Jesuits' excess teaching staff. With a surplus of men in the east, the Jesuit hierarchy assigned an experienced educator, the Swiss-born Father Burchard Villiger, SJ, to become president at Santa Clara. Villiger was an accomplished leader, having served as president of Gonzaga College in DC and as prefect at Georgetown. En route to New York, where he planned to catch a steamer to his next assignment in California, he barely escaped Maryland with his life; his was the last train north from Baltimore before many of the tracks and bridges were destroyed in the war.[371] After arriving at Santa Clara, he became "the most progressive and imaginative of its early presidents."[372] Villiger would also serve as president of St. Ignatius College in San Francisco before returning east to lead Saint Joseph's College in Philadelphia.

One effect of the Civil War is visible on the athletic fields. When its students returned to campus after the conflict, Georgetown adopted its official school colors—blue and gray—to symbolize healing and the reunification of the North and South. That decision directly or indirectly influenced other schools in the Maryland Province, many of which incorporated Georgetown's distinctive gray into their uniforms as well. Loyola College in Baltimore paired gray with green, while Saint Joseph's in Philadelphia selected gray and scarlet. Even Fordham began to use silver or gray accents on its maroon and white uniforms. In the Midwest, Xavier University today uses blue and silver as its colors. Loyola Marymount University in California likewise uses blue and gray (along with red). The color scheme is a sign of solidarity among Jesuit schools and the unexpected legacy of a student-led act of reconciliation after America's worst civil conflict.[373]

Student Life at Early Jesuit Colleges

Student life at Jesuit colleges in the nineteenth century was remarkably consistent from school to school. There were naturally some differences between boarding and

---

370. Kuzniewski, *Thy Honored Name*, 115.

371. Burchard Villiger, SJ, "Autobiography of Father Burchard Villiger," *Woodstock Letters* XXXII, no. 1 (1903): 75.

372. McKevitt, *University of Santa Clara*, 66.

373. Varga, *Baltimore's Loyola*, 240.

day colleges, but even then, the day colleges faithfully reproduced the educational experience of a Jesuit boarding school as best they could. The similarities went beyond the shared curriculum, the *Ratio Studiorum*. The daily schedules and even the extracurricular offerings at Jesuit colleges were largely uniform. In addition to being a common lesson plan, the *Ratio* was also a teacher's handbook that prescribed standard behavior for everything from student discipline to awards ceremonies.[374]

Schedule

Classes met six days per week, Monday through Saturday, with half-days on Saturday and one other day at midweek (usually Wednesday or Thursday). Catholic students were expected to attend Mass in the college chapel on Sundays, but this would have been routine for most of them; they also attended Mass every weekday to start the school day. Non-Catholic boarding students, at least in some schools, attended daily Mass along with their Catholic classmates, but on Sundays they were free to attend whatever church their parents requested. Rules about Mass attendance for non-Catholics generally became more liberal over time, and by the mid-1800s, most non-Catholics were exempt from daily Mass. However, some non-Catholic students still chose to join their friends in church every morning.

In boarding colleges, the day typically began around 6 a.m. (mercifully pushed back to 7 or 8 a.m. during the dark, cold winter months). Boarding students were expected to rise around 5 or 5:30 a.m. and wash their faces. At Georgetown, the main source of fresh water was a pump outside the building, and at Holy Cross, it was a washroom in the basement—both of which must have been absolutely frigid in the wintertime.[375] (The site of Georgetown's old pump is memorialized by a small gazebo in its main quadrangle.)

After morning Mass, there was usually a solid three- or four-hour block of classroom time, followed by a long lunch, when students ate as a group and then enjoyed a few hours of extracurricular activities or recess outdoors. While outside of class, they were always under the supervision of a Jesuit (usually a scholastic or a newly ordained young priest). Four days per week, classes resumed in mid-afternoon and finished around 5 p.m., after which the students ate dinner together and had enforced study time in the dorms or classrooms. Lights went out between 8 and 9 p.m. It was a grueling daily schedule, all the more so when we remember that most of the students were in their mid-teens or younger.

---

374. In describing these generalities, I am summarizing the accounts of student life as related in Bennish, *Continuity*, 69; Curran, *History of Georgetown Vol. I*, 182–190; Kuzniewski, *Thy Honored Name*, 57–70); McKevitt, *University of Santa Clara*, 45; Varga, *Baltimore's Loyola*, 56–57; and William C. McFadden, SJ, "'Catechism at 4 for All the Schools': Religious Instruction at Georgetown," in *Georgetown at Two Hundred: Faculty Reflections on the University's Future*, ed. William C. McFadden (Washington: Georgetown University Press, 1990), 143–168.

375. Kuzniewski, *Thy Honored Name*, 63.

In day colleges, Catholic students were also expected to arrive on campus around 7 or 8 a.m. for Mass; non-Catholics were allowed to arrive an hour later when classes actually began. Students went home after 5 p.m. without needing to be fed dinner, reducing the college budget dramatically.

Classes were in session from September through July, with the only extended vacation during the month of August. Holidays (when classes were cancelled and the food was slightly better than normal) were common, including secular celebrations like Washington's Birthday and religious ones like All Saints' Day and Easter. The college president could also declare holidays unexpectedly as a reward for good behavior, or to celebrate the arrival of an important visitor or speaker.

Curriculum and Classroom Structure

Whenever possible, a single Jesuit professor taught the same group of students from enrollment to graduation. Faculty specialized in a cohort of students, not in individual subjects. The Jesuit assigned to teach a specific cohort of students was expected to teach the entire core curriculum to his group, including Latin and Greek as well as philosophy and "natural philosophy" ("science" in modern terminology). There were exceptions, since professors frequently came and went from campus, but the *Ratio Studiorum* curriculum put a great deal of emphasis on a single professor's ability to teach the entire catalogue of courses to the same group year after year, following the same students through their entire academic career. Jesuit professors had to be true "renaissance men" capable of teaching multiple subjects over the course of a day, and they were expected to get to know their students' abilities and learning styles, adapting the pace and content of the lessons to their assigned group's particular needs. The only normal exceptions to this rule were electives like music, foreign languages, bookkeeping, and similar subjects that were taught by specialized faculty.

One subject that was surprisingly absent from Jesuit classrooms was theology, at least as we recognize it today. In the nineteenth century, theology—the scientific study of God and scripture—was seen as a kind of professional education for priests and was only appropriate for those entering that profession, in the same way that law or medicine were only taught at specialized schools. Aspiring clergymen studied theology in the seminaries, but the subject was not incorporated into the standard college curriculum any more than classes on surgery or legal writing. For students at early Jesuit colleges, religion was something that was experienced, not studied. They heard sermons from their professors every day at Mass and they prayed with each other at assemblies, but they never explored theology in any formal academic way in the classroom.

Apart from religious services on campus, the only uniquely "Catholic" aspect of a Jesuit college curriculum was a weekend catechism lesson, which usually took place on Saturdays. At Georgetown, the catechism lesson took the form of an hour-long lecture beginning at 4 p.m. In day schools, Catholic students stayed on campus for an extra hour on Saturday afternoons to hear the equivalent of what we, today, would call a "Sunday school" lesson. These short, rote lessons on the Catechism of the

Catholic Church were not comparable to the kind of theology courses available on Jesuit campuses today, or the kinds of theology courses the Jesuits themselves would have taken during their seminary formation at the time. It was not until the late 1800s that catechism lessons became integrated into the daily schedule at some colleges,[376] and not until the mid-1900s, mainly after World War II, that many Jesuit colleges organized theology departments and started offering undergraduate degrees in that subject. Jesuits were not unique in this regard; the same was true at virtually all American Catholic colleges sponsored by all religious orders.

The Reading of the Marks

One tradition that invariably made its way into every Jesuit school was the monthly ceremony known as the "reading of the marks." Prescribed by the *Ratio Studiorum*, the ceremony was designed to incentivize hard work by rewarding students who did well and publicly shaming those who failed. Roughly once per month, the student body would assemble and listen while the president identified them, by name, in order of the grades they had achieved over the past thirty days. Those at the top of the list were lauded with medals and formal prizes, especially at the end of the school year. Those at the bottom were humiliated into working harder, and if they did not improve by the end of the year, they might be required to repeat the grade level. Advancement from one grade to another was not automatic; only those deemed to have mastered the year's material were allowed to continue.

Exams to advance from one grade level to another, given in June and July, could be brutal for faculty as well as students. Each student took a series of oral and written tests in every subject over a two-week period. In a kind of peer-review quality control, the Jesuit who gave the year-end exam was usually not the Jesuit who had been the students' primary instructor all year. This allowed the Jesuits to check up on each other's classes, since the performance of the students reflected, to some degree, the competence of the teacher.[377]

With this kind of rigor, it should not be surprising that few students actually completed the six- or seven-year curriculum. The overwhelming majority of students at Jesuit colleges attended for only a year or two and left without earning a degree. Even though they enrolled hundreds of students, most early Jesuit colleges awarded fewer than ten degrees per year. The A.B. degree was a mark of endurance as much as a mark of academic accomplishment. In modern terminology, we would say that Jesuit colleges' graduation rates were abysmally low, but such rates were not seen internally or externally as a measure of a school's academic quality at the time. For most nineteenth-century students, a Jesuit education was a temporary experience and did not result in a permanent credential or diploma. Even students who spent only a year or two in the system still thought of themselves as proud alumni of the school.

---

376. McFadden, "Catechism," 147.
377. Kuzniewski, *Thy Honored Name*, 58.

Exhibitions

An important part of the graduation ceremonies at the end of each year was a public exhibition of student work. Students who performed extremely well during the year were invited to give orations in Latin, to demonstrate chemistry experiments in front of an audience, or otherwise showcase their knowledge. These exhibitions were public affairs, and dignitaries from the local community attended along with towns-people and underclassmen, all seeking to be dazzled by cutting-edge student work. In an age before such things were common, these events were like science fairs, museums, and debate competitions rolled into one, and they were a welcome form of entertainment for nineteenth-century audiences.[378]

Being selected to speak at these exhibitions was a high honor and was part of the competition that characterized the classroom experience. Not only did the best-performing students get to display their skills to great acclaim to the community, but they also received prizes (like medals) or financial awards (like scholarships or even cash). There were competitions within individual colleges and even across the Jesuit college network. In 1886, the Jesuit province on the East Coast sponsored a contest, offering $100 (almost enough to pay for an entire semester of tuition at most colleges) for the best student paper on Christian doctrine.[379] That same year, the Midwestern Jesuit province sponsored an intercollegiate contest for Latin writing, the winner of which received a gold medal.[380]

Exhibitions were also high-profile affairs that allowed the colleges to highlight their role as community assets to well-placed friends. At Holy Cross's first exhibition in 1844, attendees included former Massachusetts Governor Levi Lincoln, founding father Bishop Benedict Fenwick, and noted New England Catholic writer Orestes Brownson (whose sons would go on to become Holy Cross alumni). At Georgetown, John Quincy Adams and other US presidents sometimes officiated the graduation ceremonies and handed out the prizes.[381]

The Commercial Track

The *Ratio Studiorum* emphasized the classics, and that was the standard path to a bachelor's degree. An education based heavily on Latin, Greek, and the poets of ancient Rome, however, was not always in high demand among the farmers and merchants of the rough-and-tumble American frontier. Partly out of a need to serve their communities and partly as a practical necessity, most Jesuit colleges made an important concession to modernity by offering two different tracks for students—one, the traditional *Ratio Studiorum* leading to a six-year A.B. degree, and the other, a "commercial" track leading to a two-year or four-year diploma.

---

378. See Varga, *Baltimore's Loyola*, 84.

379. McFadden, "Catechism," 46.

380. Muller, *University of Detroit*, 68.

381. Curran, *History of Georgetown Vol. I*, 219–222. Kuzniewski, *Thy Honored Name*, 67.

In modern terminology, these "commercial" tracks resembled business schools, emphasizing practical skills like bookkeeping, accounting, and management. These skills appealed to first-generation American immigrants who cared more about their economic prospects in the United States than about Ovid and Cicero. Although many Jesuit schools loathed to admit this, enrollment in the commercial track often exceeded enrollment in the standard classical track. This is also partly why graduation rates were so low; "commercial" students were never eligible to earn a degree. Santa Clara College devoted an entire building to its commercial division, complete with mock bank and telegraph offices.[382]

By 1862, the commercial track had become so common at Jesuit schools that the Jesuits issued a policy statement establishing standardized practices for it. It was a begrudging recognition that the commercial track had become essential to the schools' survival, and had to coexist with the traditional *Ratio Studiorum* without diluting it drastically.[383] Another concession to the realities of American education were evening schools, which the Jesuits operated in St. Louis, Cincinnati, and elsewhere, giving local townspeople an opportunity to attend after-hours lectures, mainly for enrichment. As some of the only educational institutions in town, the Jesuit colleges felt a responsibility to make education accessible to working-class students who labored long hours in the city during the day.

Residence Life

Sleeping arrangements at the early Jesuit boarding colleges were nothing like those in modern-day colleges. Even the most Spartan dorms today are luxurious compared to what passed for living quarters then. Private rooms (and privacy in general) were unheard of. Most student dormitories were barracks-style, with beds arranged in rows in large, open rooms. The all-male students slept close enough to hear each other breathe in conditions similar to those of a modern-day summer camp, and the only barrier between one bed and another (if any at all) was a thin curtain. Monitoring the large communal bedrooms at all hours of the night were hawkish young Jesuit scholastics, ready to put a stop to any chicanery.

Daily bathing was not yet a standard part of personal hygiene, so students and faculty sometimes went days without washing anything more than their faces. The college washrooms had only a handful of bathtubs shared by all students. We can only imagine how this affected the learning environment. Some evidence comes from the diary of a Holy Cross student, who wrote home to his parents about a classmate, "O'Neil took a bath today to our great joy."[384]

Living conditions for Jesuit faculty were scarcely better. Older Jesuits sometimes had the privilege of a private room, but young scholastics often slept with the students

---

382. McKevitt, *University of Santa Clara*, 109.
383. Ibid., 108.
384. As quoted in Kuzniewski, *Thy Honored Name*, 63–64.

or shared quarters with each other. At Santa Clara, while proper facilities were being constructed, the early Italian Jesuits sometimes slept outdoors and set up mattresses wherever they could find space.[385]

Boarding students were normally prohibited from leaving campus without supervision. On the rare occasions when they did venture out, the excursions usually took the form of a brisk walk into town chaperoned by a Jesuit scholastic. Georgetown students could walk to the White House, while Holy Cross students regularly toured downtown Worcester. The boys were easy to spot in their school uniforms, which normally consisted of a blazer, slacks, and (for underclassmen) a beanie.

Discipline

Students who broke the rules could expect to be punished. The most common sentence for minor offenses was memorizing lines of Latin. This was similar to what many students did in the classroom on a daily basis, so it amounted to an extra homework assignment. Students could lose recess privileges or otherwise face isolation from their friends. At Georgetown, misbehaving boys could be forced to stand in the stairwell for hours or, worse, live for extended periods of time on the top floor of the twin towers of the Old North Building. In the days before air conditioning and in the humidity of Washington, DC, those hours must have been unbearable.[386]

For more serious infractions, corporal punishment was practiced, as was expulsion from the school. The rules tended to be strict, although some individual Jesuits could be more lax than others in enforcing them. Just as today, students usually learned what they could get away with, and with whom.

Extra-curricular Activities

There were three staple student clubs at virtually every Jesuit college: a religious sodality, a debating society, and a drama troupe, the nature and character of which were similar from school to school.

Sodalities

The religious sodality was usually the first club the Jesuits organized on any campus. In Catholic parlance, a "sodality" (from the Latin *sodalis*, meaning "member" or "comrade") is essentially a club that exists for the purpose of promoting religious observance among its members. Naturally, every student at a Jesuit college was expected to be reverent at religious ceremonies and to attend daily Mass if he was Catholic, but students who joined the sodality were held to an even higher standard, committing themselves to additional prayer, daily recitation of the rosary, and other

---

385. McKevitt, *University of Santa Clara*, 45.
386. Curran, *History of Georgetown Vol. I*, 192–193.

religious activities during recess. It was a prestigious and selective group, limited only to the most pious boys on campus.

The first to be organized was at Georgetown, which established the Sodality of Our Lady Immaculate in 1810. Saint Louis University established its Sodality of the Blessed Virgin Mary in 1835.[387] Loyola College (Baltimore) founded its Sodality of the Immaculate Conception in 1852, mere months after it opened its doors.[388] Similar sodalities popped up wherever the Jesuits taught. At St. Mary's College in Kentucky, the French Jesuits established the Parthenian Sodality in 1837; along with the drama club, it was one of two student clubs they maintained when they relocated to St. John's College (Fordham) in New York.[389]

The religious practices of the Jesuit college sodalities influenced American Catholic religious practice as a whole. In 1830, at Georgetown, members of the Sodality of Our Lady Immaculate began a tradition of holding special devotionals to the Virgin Mary during the month of May. It was the first time this particular devotion was practiced in the United States. George Fenwick, SJ (who spent most of his career as a beloved faculty member at Holy Cross) was at the time a Georgetown professor and introduced the tradition after learning about it during a trip to Rome.[390] The May devotional soon extended beyond Georgetown and became a staple practice among American Catholics. Today, Catholic churches and schools around the country venerate the Virgin Mary during May—an enduring legacy for a tradition first introduced by a Georgetown extra-curricular club.

Debating Societies

The first non-religious club at virtually every nineteenth-century Jesuit college was the debating society. A key goal of the *Ratio Studiorum* curriculum was *eloquentia perfecta*—the development of a student's oral communication skills through persuasive and beautiful public speaking. In the classroom, all students were expected to recite Latin poetry, perform memorized and extemporaneous orations, and debate. Students who were especially keen to develop those skills outside of class joined the debating club.

In 1830, Georgetown (under the leadership of Father James Ryder, SJ) organized the Philodemic Debating Society for intramural debate. Other Georgetown faculty members who helped to support the club early in its existence include George Fenwick, SJ (who would play a similar role at Holy Cross), and Felix Barbelin, SJ (the future founder of Saint Joseph's University in Philadelphia).[391] The student group

---

387. "Catalog—1898," Saint Louis University Digital Archives, 42, http://digitalcollections.slu.edu/digital/collection/catalogs/id/3551/.

388. Varga, *Baltimore's Loyola*, 24–25.

389. Shelley, *Fordham*, 137.

390. Daley, *Georgetown University*, 164.

391. Curran, *History of Georgetown Vol. I*, 213.

met regularly to argue whatever topic they chose for that week, often touching on politics, slavery, and other contemporary issues. (In their first-ever debate, Philodemic students argued whether George Washington or Napoleon Bonaparte was a better leader. The final decision came down in favor of Washington.)

Over time, Georgetown's Philodemic Society became a model for other debate clubs around the country. The clubs were similar in purpose and scope; even the names were sometimes identical. Holy Cross's debate club was also originally called the Philodemic Society, but was renamed the BJF Debating Society after the 1846 death of the college's founding father, Benedict Joseph Fenwick.[392] At St. Xavier College in Cincinnati, the club was called the Philopedian Society, and it held its first debate in 1841.[393] Both Santa Clara College and Saint Louis University used the name "Philalethic Debating Society." The only school to break this alliterative pattern was St. John's College, (Fordham), which founded the rather prosaically named "St. John's Debating Society" in 1854.[394] Jesuit colleges founded later in the century kept up the tradition, as with the University of Detroit's Philomathic Debating Society.[395]

These clubs almost always had their own dedicated space on otherwise cramped campuses, reflecting their importance. When Georgetown built its impressive main building, Healy Hall, in the 1870s, the Philodemic Society was the only student club to receive its own room—an ornate space located directly atop the main stairway. At Santa Clara, the Philalethic Society began meeting in 1856 in a spacious classroom in the old California Hotel, an adobe building that the college had acquired two years earlier.[396] At Saint Louis University, the Philalethic Society had its own eponymous building on campus. When Boston College constructed its majestic main building, Gasson Hall, in 1913, its Fulton Debating Society received its own dedicated room.

Despite their similarities, each of the debating clubs had some unique local flair. The topics that students debated often reflected issues of local concern. At Santa Clara, one of the earliest debate topics was whether gold mining or agriculture would be better for California's long-term economic development.[397] In 1859, Georgetown students debated whether the South should secede from the United States.[398] In 1870, Saint Louis University students debated whether the federal government should be relocated to Missouri.[399]

Debate was so popular that some colleges started secondary clubs for less experience students—a kind of "junior varsity" team. Georgetown had its Philonomosian

---

392. Kuzniewski, *Thy Honored Name*, 67.

393. Bennish, *Continuity*, 33.

394. Shelley, *Fordham*, 140–141.

395. Muller, *University of Detroit*, 30.

396. McKevitt, *University of Santa Clara*, 99.

397. Ibid., 99.

398. Curran, *History of Georgetown Vol. I*, 233.

399. St. Louis University, *A Debate by the Philalethic Society of Saint Louis University on Monday, February 21, 1870* (St. Louis: George Knapp & Co. 1870), https://catalog.hathitrust.org/Record/000195006.

Society; at Santa Clara, it was the Philhistoric Society; at Holy Cross, it was the Philomathian Society; at Xavier, it was the Philhermenian Society. In each case, these "junior varsity" clubs folded and only the original debate clubs survive on campus today.

Drama Troupes

Drama was closely related to the Jesuits' emphasis on public speaking, so it is no surprise that Jesuit schools were generally ahead of other American colleges in emphasizing theater. In fact, the first Jesuit college at Messina in Sicily is known to have staged theatrical productions.[400] Student performances of Shakespeare and contemporary plays were major community events, drawing spectators from around the neighborhood.

Georgetown's Mask and Bauble Dramatic Society, founded in 1852, claims to be the oldest continuously performing college drama troupe in the United States. Holy Cross opened a Dramatic Club a year earlier in 1851, but Georgetown's group has performed without interruption and can trace its legacy to an even earlier club, the Shakespearian Club, founded in 1850. Harvard University's Hasty Pudding Society is technically older than both, dating to the 1790s, but it has not staged a performance every year.[401]

St. John's College (Fordham) first sponsored a drama troupe in 1855, and Loyola (Baltimore) did the same in 1865.[402] Santa Clara built its first dedicated theater (which doubled as a gym) in 1857—just six years after the college's founding.[403]

Although they were pioneers in college theater, Jesuit schools never considered it to be anything more than an extra-curricular activity. They did not offer specialized degrees in theater, since the *Ratio Studiorum* curriculum did not allow for what we call "majors" today. The first American university to offer an undergraduate degree in drama was Pittsburgh's Carnegie Tech (now known as Carnegie Mellon University) in 1914.

Languages

Jesuit schools emphasized modern foreign languages, and this curricular feature set them apart from other American colleges and universities. At a time when mainstream colleges like Harvard and Yale largely ignored foreign languages, Jesuit colleges offered such courses as electives—partly due to their built-in availability of European faculty and partly to help their immigrant students maintain distinct ethnic identities. Georgetown offered French and Spanish as early as the 1790s, making it one of the first American colleges to do so; by the 1830s, it was offering German and Italian,

---

400. Curran, *History of Georgetown Vol. I*, 217.
401. Ibid., 216. Kuzniewski, *Thy Honored Name*, 141.
402. Varga, *Baltimore's Loyola*, 72–73. Kuzniewski, *Thy Honored Name*, 67.
403. McKevitt, *University of Santa Clara*, 61.

both of which were at the time highly unusual additions to an American college curriculum.[404] Loyola (Baltimore) and Xavier also offered German well before that language was standard on American campuses. At Xavier, the public exhibition at graduation in 1841 included student orations in Latin, Greek, French, and German.[405] When Santa Clara opened its doors in 1851, a local newspaper boasted that the new school would offer Spanish, French, Latin, German, and Greek.[406]

Jesuits were, in general, accomplished linguists—and the vast majority of Jesuit faculty in America spoke English only as a second language. Students, too, were overwhelmingly multilingual; most were either foreign-born (including large numbers of Spanish-speakers from Latin America) or were first-generation American citizens who spoke another language, like German, at home. Even students whose families had lived in North America for generations often spoke a first language other than English; those who hailed from Louisiana and Missouri overwhelmingly spoke French. At St. Xavier College in Cincinnati, "school rules stated that 'French and English are spoken indiscriminately during the hours of recreation.'"[407] Spanish was prevalent at the California schools, French at the Southern schools, and French and German at the Midwestern schools.

Intriguingly, this curricular strength has persisted. Georgetown sponsored a School of Languages and Linguistics between 1949 and 1995, and still has some of the strongest and most comprehensive language programs of any university the country.

Administrative Structure

As uniform as the Jesuit education experience was from a student perspective, it was even more so from the perspective of the faculty and staff.

As a rule, nineteenth-century Jesuit colleges were organized in the way prescribed by the *Ratio Studiorum*. There was a *rector*, who served as both the president of the college and the superior of the Jesuit community. He was responsible not only for managing the school but also any other ministries the priests might pursue, including parish work, prison and hospital chaplaincies, etc. Second in command at the college was the *prefect of studies*, roughly the equivalent of a modern-day dean, who oversaw student discipline, student life, and the school's day-to-day operation. Both the rector and the prefect of studies typically taught and examined students in the classroom just like other professors.

Rectors were appointed by the provincial, and they served a standard term of three years. Exceptionally talented leaders could have their positions renewed for a second consecutive three-year term. The frequent shifting of college presidents in Jesuit institutions had positive as well as negative effects. As Loyola historian

---

404. Curran, *History of Georgetown Vol. I*, 208.
405. Bennish, *Continuity*, 35. Varga, *Baltimore's Loyola*, 57.
406. McKevitt, *University of Santa Clara*, 27.
407. Bennish, *Continuity*, 37.

Nicholas Varga has observed, it promoted good relations among individual Jesuits, since "today's subordinate might be tomorrow's superior."[408] Although it made long-term planning difficult, it also mitigated the damage any one incompetent president could do to an institution. It forced the colleges to establish a standard "Jesuit" way of doing things that superseded the whims of any particular individual.[409]

A nineteenth-century Jesuit college president was more a caretaker than a strategic leader. His role was not necessarily to innovate, but to preserve the institution until he could hand it off to one of his colleagues. It was a good strategy for stability, but not for innovation. In time, this emphasis on tradition would make Jesuits schools relatively conservative, but in the nineteenth century, when over 70% of Catholic colleges failed, it was mainly a virtue.[410] St. Ignatius had advised his followers not to develop strong ties to any one place, but to stay focused on the big picture. They were to make decisions based on the best interests of the Church and the world as a whole, not necessarily on the best interests of any individual college.

Nonetheless, when the Jesuits had a truly talented leader in their ranks, his skills were not wasted. Some presidents were shuttled from one college to another so that many different institutions could benefit from their leadership. Burchard Villiger, SJ, served as president of Gonzaga College (DC), Santa Clara College, St. Ignatius College (San Francisco), and Saint Joseph's College (Philadelphia). When they did develop a strong passion for one institution, Jesuits could serve as president more than once. Anthony Ciampi, SJ, was president of Holy Cross on three non-consecutive occasions. At Georgetown, John Early, SJ, and Bernard Maguire, SJ, alternated as president four times between 1852 and 1873.

In addition to the rector and the prefect of studies, there was the corps of Jesuit priests who served on the faculty. A handful of Jesuit brothers often lived on campus as well. Although some brothers did teach (particularly later in the century), more often they provided for the physical maintenance of the school—working the farms, managing the livestock, painting the hallways, and constructing and maintaining the buildings. Some also served as cooks. This is not to say that all brothers did low-level manual labor; some were talented artists and architects who transformed the campuses into beautiful learning environments. Georgetown University's ornate Gaston Hall features exquisite murals painted freehand by Brother Francis Schroen, SJ, who also used his artistic talents to decorate Holy Name of Jesus Church at Loyola University (New Orleans), Boston College's Fulton Debate Room, and the beautiful original chapel, parlor, and assembly hall at the Loyola School in New York City.[411] Another brother, Bartholomew Tortore, SJ, painted the beautiful Adobe Lodge at Santa

---

408. Varga, *Baltimore's Loyola*, 19.

409. Ibid., 23.

410. Power, *Catholic Higher Education*, 61.

411. James P. Fagan, SJ, "The Loyola School, New York," *Woodstock Letters* XXXIII, no. 1 (1904): 78. Georgetown University Library, "Highly Decorated: The Work of Brother Francis Schroen, SJ," 2006., https://library.georgetown.edu/exhibition/highly-decorated-work-brother-francis-c-schroen-sj.

Clara.[412] Brothers were essential contributors to the colleges and they maintained physical environments to match the intellectual environments cultivated by the priests.

Scholastics (Jesuits in training) were, like modern-day graduate students, often assigned to teach while they were completing their seminary studies. In boarding schools, it was often the scholastics who watched the boys 24/7, chaperoned off-campus excursions, broke up fights, and performed other tasks inherent in supervising a group of live-in teenagers. Since many scholastics were themselves in their early twenties, they could relate to the boys best and still had the energy to stay up late, keeping watch over the dorms well into the night.[413]

Some scholastics could be a tad rebellious themselves. In his history of Saint Louis University, historian William Barnaby Faherty, SJ, retells a famous campus legend:

> An anecdote in Saint Louis University folk-lore concerns the final exam of a harassed scholastic, later to be president of the University. This young man rushed into a theology examination from the recreation yard, where he had momentarily left the students to fend for themselves. He heard the first questions. Caught completely unprepared, he pointed to the school yard, "There is just one thing I have to check before this examination."

> While the reverend examiners presumed he had gone back to the recreation field to give some directive to the students, he hurried to his room. Checking up on the matter of the question, he rushed back to pass his test with honors.[414]

Last in both numbers and influence were the laypeople on campus. All Jesuit colleges employed a handful of lay teachers, but these men were typically only hired as a last resort, when it was impossible to find a Jesuit capable of filling the position. Often, they taught music, art, bookkeeping, foreign languages, or other specific electives that Jesuits lacked the expertise to teach. Although some laymen did teach for more than one year, they had virtually no job security and worked with the full knowledge that their positions would be the first to be cut in the event of a budget crisis—or simply in the event that a qualified Jesuit became available to replace them. Few records are available about their pay, but it is widely assumed to have been low. Simply put, it was almost impossible for a layman to have a long-term career as a Catholic college professor during the early 1800s. Anyone who sought such a career had virtually no option but to become a Jesuit himself.

Laypeople also occupied service jobs on campus, serving as cooks and maintenance workers—when those roles were not filled by Jesuit brothers. At the Southern schools, the laypeople on campus also included slaves, who served as laborers, cooks, custodians, and messengers, to name a few examples. While the vast majority of the people on Jesuit campuses were men, some women—including nuns, laywomen, and slaves—

---

412. McKevitt, *University of Santa Clara*, 99.
413. Kuzniewski, *Thy Honored Name*, 122.
414. Faherty, *Better*, 56.

served as laundresses, cooks, or caretakers. In the 1700s, Georgetown advertised that it had arranged an off-campus housing option for non-Catholic students who preferred not to attend Catholic Mass in the dorm; those students would live in a neighborhood home, where they would be "put under the care of a 'widow-lady of most reputable character.'"[415] The first classes at Saint Louis University were held on the property of a generous widow, a Mrs. Alvarez, who offered her own home for the purpose.[416] In discussing the role of women, it must also be noted that many early Jesuit schools were located near girls' schools run by various orders of Catholic sisters. Most of these girls' schools were founded around the same time as the Jesuit college, and in some cases (like Grand Coteau) predated the Jesuit college and influenced its location.

In sum, the administrative structure at most Jesuit schools in antebellum America was hierarchical, starting with the rector and prefect of studies, down through the priests, brothers, scholastics, and laypeople (faculty, staff, and slave). Despite this clear pecking order, the campus communities were not large. The combined number of Jesuit priests, brothers, and scholastics on campus was often less than twenty. A handful of Jesuits could operate an entire school, especially considering that the total enrollment at most schools was under 200, and rarely exceeded that level until after the Civil War.

Lastly, it is important to remember that ultimate authority over all Jesuit colleges rested not in the president's office, not even in the provincial's office, but in Rome. The Jesuit hierarchy had final say over all matters, even, to some extent, day-to-day budgetary issues. As late as the 1880s, the president of Santa Clara University was informed by his superiors that he could not spend more than $30 without consulting with his advisors, or spend more than $100 without express permission from his provincial—who lived nearly 6,000 miles away in Italy.[417]

Today, state colleges and universities often complain about the bureaucracy of state government and the challenges of making decisions when all matters of college life—from tuition rates to campus construction—are ultimately under the jurisdiction of the governor and state legislature. Imagine, then, the challenges of operating a college when all of those decisions were subject to approval by a superior on another *continent*, especially at a time when communication was only as fast and reliable as transatlantic ships.

---

415. McFadden," Catechism," 145.
416. Faherty, *Better*, 8.
417. McKevitt, *University of Santa Clara*, 124–125.

Part IV:

The Great Expansion (1865–1918)

Overview, 1865–1918

Between the Civil War and the First World War, the character of the Catholic Church in America changed. Immigration transformed Catholicism from a predominantly rural, Southern religion into a mainly urban, northern one. The center of gravity of the country's Catholic population—which had long been the former French colonies along the Gulf Coast, the Mississippi River, and the Ohio River—shifted to the booming industrial cities of the northeast and the Great Lakes. The old hubs of the Church in places like Maryland, Louisiana, Kentucky, and Missouri were eclipsed in size and importance by younger, faster-growing dioceses in Illinois, Massachusetts, Michigan, New York, New Jersey, Ohio, Pennsylvania, and Wisconsin. Catholic immigration, which had been mainly Irish and German in the early nineteenth century, took on a more Italian and Eastern European flair. Drawn by the economic opportunities of the industrial revolution, this new wave of Catholic immigrants quickly outnumbered the Southern Catholics who traced their American roots to the era of British, Spanish, and French colonization.

The Jesuits, nearly always first on the scene wherever Catholics settled, were characteristically quick to respond to these developments. They began by reducing their Southern presence, withdrawing from their last remaining college in Kentucky in 1868. Shortly after, they went on a building spree that resulted in twenty-three new Jesuit colleges and universities. Across the country, the pattern repeated. As cities grew, new dioceses sprung up and new bishops took office. Seeking to fortify the local Church with a Catholic college, those new bishops called in the Jesuits. The Jesuits' reputation as educators put them at the top of almost any young diocese's wish list. By the first decade of the 1900s, there were slightly more than sixty Catholic colleges and universities in the United States, and almost half of those were Jesuit.[1]

The Midwest

If the pre-Civil War era belonged to the Maryland Jesuits of the East Coast, the post-Civil War era was now the Missouri Jesuits' time to shine. From their base in St. Louis, the Missouri Jesuits responded to the rapid demographic changes taking place on their doorstep—reorienting themselves toward the Great Lakes region even as they continued their traditional missionary work among the Native Americans of the Plains and Rockies. Between 1870 and 1910, the Missouri Jesuits established colleges

---

1. Cook, *Founded on Faith*, 35.

in Chicago, Detroit, Milwaukee, Omaha, and Kansas City, while maintaining their existing commitments in Cincinnati, St. Louis, and central Kansas. They even toyed with additional colleges in eastern Kansas, southern Illinois, and northern Wisconsin, all of which they eventually had to abandon.

As impressive as this expansion was, the Missouri Jesuits alone could not meet the booming demand for Catholic education in the Midwest. Fortunately, an entirely new branch of the Jesuit family tree arrived in the region at the same time. A wave of German Jesuits—fleeing Otto von Bismarck's *Kulturkampf* persecutions of the 1870s—made a home in Buffalo and soon built an ambitious education ministry in the Great Lakes region. Drawn to the Midwest's large population of German immigrants, they supplemented the work of the Missouri Jesuits by establishing colleges in Buffalo, Cleveland, Toledo, and rural western Wisconsin.

Although the Midwestern Jesuits opened a remarkable number of colleges, they had no choice but to turn down some bishops' invitations due to lack of manpower. Among the opportunities they declined during this period were offers to establish colleges in Grand Rapids, Indianapolis, Lincoln, Minneapolis/St. Paul, Nashville, Oklahoma City, and Sioux Falls.[2]

The East

In the east, the Jesuits of the Maryland Province also expanded, but more indirectly than their Midwestern colleagues. Despite the hardships of the Civil War, they kept their five prewar colleges open, maintaining a presence in almost every major city in the Boston-Washington corridor. Two exceptions were Philadelphia, where they had shuttered Saint Joseph's College just before the war broke out, and New York City, which was still rather awkwardly in the hands of the French Jesuit missionaries who controlled St. John's College (Fordham) and the College of St. Francis Xavier in Manhattan. Those French Jesuits branched out across the Hudson River to open a third college, Saint Peter's, in Jersey City.

In 1879, logic and geography prevailed over history, and the French mission in New York merged with the Maryland Province, filling the gaping doughnut hole in the middle of the Province's footprint. The combined operation, known as the Maryland-New York Province, finally brought the three New York-area colleges into the same network as the other Jesuit schools on the East Coast. In 1889, the eastern Jesuits forged the last link in the chain when they resurrected the long-dormant Saint Joseph's College in Philadelphia after a slumber of thirty years. Nearly every Catholic family in the megalopolis now had access to a Jesuit education for their sons.

The Maryland-New York Province was poorly named; the two states should have been listed in reverse order. New York quickly became the combined Province's headquarters and major focus. By the early 1900s, there were four Jesuit colleges in

---

2. Garraghan, *Jesuits of the Middle U.S. Vol. III*, 502–504.

the New York City area, including a new proto-college in Brooklyn. Not for the first time in the Province's long history, rivalries broke out among the Jesuits themselves, pitting the old guard in Maryland against an entrenched New York faction accustomed to handling its own affairs. The two sides disagreed on multiple issues, including whether to develop Fordham or Georgetown into the Jesuits' flagship university in the east.

The West

In the west, the Italian Jesuits based in the San Francisco Bay Area expanded in both directions along the Pacific coast. Building from a foundation that included the Jesuits' deep mission roots in the Pacific Northwest, they opened Gonzaga University in Spokane, followed by Seattle University. Unwilling to pass up a good opportunity, they also expanded south to the rapidly growing city of Los Angeles, laying the groundwork for today's Loyola Marymount University even though the project stretched their resources to their limits. A short-lived college in San Jose, California sprung up in the late nineteenth century, but with two other Jesuit schools already serving the Bay Area, it was redundant and folded after fourteen years.

The Jesuits in California were originally from northern Italy, and they operated as a mission of the Turin Province of the Society of Jesus. In the 1870s, Jesuits from the opposite end of Italy (the Naples Province) also sent missionaries to the American west. The Naples Jesuits focused their work on the Rocky Mountains and established their first college just outside Santa Fe in what is today New Mexico. A second college in Morrison, Colorado soon followed. In 1888, seeking to establish a presence in Denver, the Naples Jesuits closed both of their existing colleges and merged them into a single institution, known today as Regis University.

The South

In the South, the New Orleans Jesuits ambitiously tried to match the expansionism of their colleagues around the country, but circumstances and demographics conspired against them. They built a new college in Augusta, Georgia and took control of an existing college in Galveston, Texas—neither of which survived beyond the 1920s. They also built schools in Tampa, Florida and Shreveport, Louisiana, intending to develop both into full-fledged colleges. However, neither one ever became anything more than a high school in practice.

With its overwhelmingly Protestant population, its Reconstruction-era hostility to foreign influence, and its still-agrarian economy, the nineteenth-century South lacked a hospitable climate for a Jesuit-style classical education. In the long term, Jesuit universities in places like Texas and Florida likely would have succeeded and would have been major assets to Southern Catholics. Unfortunately, it would be more than 100 years before immigration from Latin America and domestic migration from the northern United States made the region's Catholic population large enough to support strong Catholic colleges. Although the Jesuits had a knack for identifying cities with long-term growth potential, in this case, they were simply too far ahead of their time.

In spite of the Jesuits' best efforts, only two Southern colleges (in New Orleans and Mobile) would survive in the long term. All others—including the grandfather of them all, historic St. Charles College in Grand Coteau—would either close their doors for good or downgrade their ambitions and become high schools.

Changing Expectations

The late 1800s were a time of significant change for American higher education. Nothing represented—or fueled—this change more than the Morrill Act of 1862, which established America's land-grant college system. The Act was a game-changer in the way American students viewed the nature and purpose of a college degree, and it enabled science and engineering to become the centerpieces of American public college education. More than ever before, undergraduate education came to be seen as a practical endeavor—an experience meant to provide students with concrete skills for their future careers. Governments began to think of education as an economic engine that could fuel the country's growth.[3]

Under the Morrill Act, the federal government granted large tracts of unsettled western land to the states, with the expectation that state governments would sell it and use the proceeds to build public universities. As a condition of the grant, the resulting universities were expected to emphasize practical sciences like agriculture, engineering, military science, and other fields that would contribute tangibly to the economic needs of the growing country.

Prior to the Morrill Act, all college education—even at public and Protestant universities—tended to focus on the classics, Latin, and the ancient philosophy that had long formed the basis of Western culture. In other words, Jesuit colleges and their centuries-old *Ratio Studiorum* curriculum were in the American mainstream. As attitudes changed, however, and the American public began to define a college education mainly in utilitarian terms, even private universities like Harvard and Yale began to reorient themselves toward the hard sciences in imitation of the public land-grant schools. The traditional Jesuit curriculum came to be seen as old-fashioned, and Jesuit schools rapidly fell behind the trends. As American science gradually moved ahead of European science, Jesuit schools—which more or less replicated a European college environment—saw their reputations suffer. Their largely European faculty became viewed as conservative and out-of-touch with American students' needs.

Bigger Campuses, More Courses

Land-grant colleges set the standards for higher education nationwide, but their influence was particularly strong in the west and Midwest—the very regions where the

---

3. Rizzi, "We've Been Here Before," 158.

Jesuits were expanding the fastest. Schools like Ohio State, Michigan State, and the University of California quickly dominated their local markets and came to define what the American public viewed as a "normal" college experience: sprawling, residential campuses, private offices for faculty, fields and gyms for recreation, and an overall emphasis on research as well as teaching. In other words, they offered the exact opposite of the educational experience at many Jesuit colleges, most of which were still downtown commuter schools whose "campuses" consisted of a single building next to a church.

In the long term, this shift in American attitudes forced two major changes on Jesuit education. First, to compete in the American market, Jesuit colleges had to offer dorms, athletic facilities, and other accoutrements that undergraduate students had come to expect. The days of the downtown commuter college were numbered. Between the 1880s and 1920s, as their original buildings fell into disrepair and the urban neighborhoods around them began to decay, virtually all Jesuit colleges built proper campuses in the suburbs or less-developed parts of town. The only Jesuit colleges that stayed on their original campuses were the few that already owned large tracts of property: Georgetown, Gonzaga, Fordham, Holy Cross, Santa Clara, Spring Hill, St. Charles (Louisiana), and St. Mary's (Kansas).

The second change came in the curriculum. Although they continued to offer traditional liberal arts degrees and remained convinced of their value, Jesuit colleges also began to expand their graduate and professional programs.

Graduate and Professional Education

All nineteenth-century American Jesuit colleges originated as undergraduate liberal arts schools, and at least initially, there was little expectation that they would become anything different. Graduate and professional education was not on the table. The Jesuits did not originally set out to build comprehensive universities that offered a wide range of degrees, and the modest school buildings they constructed reflected those modest ambitions. Indeed, the Jesuits' main motivation in founding most of their colleges was simply to expand access to education. The original mission of most Jesuit colleges was more akin to that of a modern-day community college than that of a modern-day research university.

By the late 1800s, however, the worlds of educational access and educational prestige were converging. It was becoming obvious that professional education—especially in law, engineering, and medicine—was one of the best ways for a first-generation immigrant to advance economically in American society. If the Jesuit schools wanted to give poor, underprivileged students access to a life-changing education, they would have to offer more than liberal arts degrees. Since Catholics and other first-generation Americans were often unwelcome at the country's better-established law and medical schools, it was up to the Jesuits to build their own.[4]

---

4. Ibid., 158–159.

In the era leading up to the First World War and slightly afterward, Jesuit universities added to their repertoire fifteen schools of law, six schools of medicine, five schools of engineering, seven schools of dentistry, three schools of social work, three schools of pharmacy, and two schools of journalism. Virtually all Jesuit universities likewise came to include a school of business administration or its equivalent, and a few began offering extension programs or diploma programs that, in time, grew into schools of nursing and education.

The First Women Students

Professional schools also paved the way for another milestone: coeducation. Schools of nursing allowed women to enroll at the universities in a technical sense, though their classes were held in separate buildings and the diplomas they received were not, at first, bachelor's degrees. Schools of law, medicine, education, and other specialized programs began to accept women on a piecemeal basis in the early 1900s. Even while the core undergraduate liberal arts programs remained all-male, the professional schools began to produce the first female graduates in American Jesuit higher education. Although it would take another three generations before most Jesuit universities became fully co-ed, the presence of women in some degree programs increasingly made their exclusion from others seem indefensible.

Research

The late 1800s also saw the rise of the research university. In 1876, Baltimore's Johns Hopkins University opened its doors as the first American university expressly dedicated to graduate study and research, rather than to traditional undergraduate education. This radical new idea—that a university existed primarily to create new knowledge rather than to transmit old knowledge—soon took hold throughout the country and transformed the way many universities defined their missions. Faculty at the turn of the twentieth century began to see themselves more as researchers than as teachers, and they established national organizations like the Association of American University Professors to defend their professional autonomy. American universities encouraged specialization, hiring professors to teach in a single discipline. The standards of the discipline, not the standards of the university, began to govern faculty members' work.[5]

This flew in the face of centuries of Jesuit tradition. Under the *Ratio Studiorum*, a single Jesuit taught multiple subjects throughout the day. Jesuit teachers were valued for their versatility and flexibility, not for their narrow expertise. Jesuit colleges were designed so that a small corps of priests could run the entire institution on

---

5. For a good general description of this phenomenon, see George M. Marsden, *The Soul of the American University: From Protestant Establishment to Established Nonbelief* (New York: Oxford University Press, 1996).

a cheap budget; the faculty were a flexible crew, with every professor capable of teaching almost everything that needed to be taught. But, as American academia began to favor specialists over Renaissance men, the traditional Jesuit model increasingly became an aberration.

The rise of the research university most directly affected Jesuit education in 1887, when the Catholic bishops of the United States created a graduate-only institution, the Catholic University of America, in Washington, DC. The new university competed directly with the Jesuits' flagship school at Georgetown and briefly retarded its growth. Moreover, the Church hierarchy pressured Catholic colleges around the country to send their best undergraduates to Catholic University's graduate and professional programs to ensure the new university's viability. This set up a number of conflicts between the Jesuits and the bishops that did not fully resolve until the twentieth century.

Anti-Catholic Resistance and Other Developments

There were changes taking place in the Catholic Church as well. In 1884, meeting at the Third Plenary Council of Baltimore, the US bishops essentially decreed that every Catholic parish in the United States had to sponsor its own school and that every Catholic child had to enroll. Over the next few generations, American Catholics built what Sister Patricia Byrne described as "the largest private school system in the history of the world."[6] While this rapid expansion carried many benefits, it created more competition for the Jesuits from within their own Church. In many cities, the Jesuit college had been the only Catholic school in town. With an associated high school and sometimes elementary school, it had served the community at all levels. By the late nineteenth century, there were often multiple Catholic schools within a single neighborhood. Although the vast majority of these schools were never chartered to grant degrees like the Jesuit college, the wide availability of Catholic education siphoned enrollment from the colleges' lower divisions, historically a major source of their revenue.

Perhaps inevitably, this explosion of Catholic influence in the country brought out anti-Catholic bias. Anti-Catholic resistance in the United States overall became less violent but more sophisticated. The Know-Nothing Party had officially disbanded, but its former members worked within the Republican Party to enact a series of laws, known as the Blaine Amendments, which targeted America's growing Catholic school system. Many of these laws, without mentioning Catholics by name, prohibited the use of taxpayer money in all religious schools. Behind closed doors, the laws' advocates and detractors equally acknowledged that their main purpose was to weaken the country's exploding Catholic school system. Jesuit schools like Georgetown and Saint Louis had previously benefitted from government support, but that state investment largely dried up until World War I brought the military to Jesuit campuses for recruitment and training.

---

6. Thomas Shelley, citing Byrne's original idea, in Shelley, *Fordham*, 362, 431.

Athletics

The late nineteenth century also saw the beginnings of what we today call intercollegiate athletics. Sports had always been popular in the testosterone-fueled, teenage atmosphere at most Jesuit colleges, but through the mid-1800s they usually took the form of intramurals—particularly baseball, since football and basketball had yet to be invented. A (literal) game-changer took place in 1869, when Rutgers defeated the College of New Jersey (Princeton) 6–4 in the country's first intercollegiate football game. Intercollegiate basketball made its debut in the 1890s. For the first time, Jesuit schools began to field traveling teams—often with mixed reaction from Jesuit leaders. Many Jesuits were enthusiastic about the benefits of athletics and their contribution to the Jesuit ideal of *mens sana in corpore sano* (healthy mind in a healthy body). Others objected to the emphasis the schools were placing on athletics at the expense of academics. In the end, Jesuit authorities set strict rules about when games could be scheduled, how far teams could travel, and other details.

To the Future

With the possible exception of athletics, the Jesuits were slow to respond to the educational trends in the late nineteenth century, but change was inevitable and reforms picked up speed after 1900. Like it or not, the American academy was changing, and the Jesuits would change with it. But first, they had a lot of building to do.

The Five Sisters of the Midwest: Loyola, Detroit, Creighton, Marquette, and Rockhurst

In a span of less than twenty years in the 1870s and '80s, the Missouri Jesuits founded four colleges, known today as Loyola University (Chicago), the University of Detroit Mercy, Creighton University, and Marquette University. In 1910, they also founded Rockhurst University in Kansas City—a late addition cut from the same rock as the others. Almost like a public university system that builds branch campuses in every corner of its state, the Missouri Jesuits built a network of Midwestern colleges, serving as many people, in as many places, as they reasonably could.

The Missouri Jesuits' postwar building spree resembled the Maryland Jesuits' prewar expansion of the 1840s and '50s. In both cases, the Jesuits sought to build a college in almost every major city under their jurisdiction. However, the Missouri Jesuits were even more ambitious in the scope and scale of their projects. Since they were building their network just as the nature of American higher education was changing, they pushed most of their new universities to adhere to the emerging American norms. Whereas the Maryland Jesuits had built a network of modest undergraduate colleges, the Missouri Jesuits developed virtually all of their new schools into comprehensive universities. The Maryland Jesuits had developed only one true university (Georgetown) orbited by a handful of satellite liberal arts colleges. For the Missouri Jesuits,

Saint Louis University remained the flagship, but over time it became first among equals—*primus inter pares*, as their Latin professors would have said—as some of its daughter universities like Marquette and Loyola surpassed it in size.

Much like Boston College, Saint Joseph's, and Loyola (Baltimore) in the east, the five new Midwestern colleges could be called "sister schools" in that that they almost all share a similar origin story. With one exception (Creighton), the new Midwestern colleges and universities traced their roots to a Jesuit church. In the same way that Father John McElroy used his parish ministry in Boston to lay the groundwork for Boston College, the Midwestern Jesuits often began their work in each city by taking control of a Catholic parish. This foothold enabled them to begin fundraising and networking in the local community, building an audience for a future college. In every instance, even as they busied themselves with pastoral ministry, a permanent college was the Jesuits' ultimate goal.

In part, the Missouri Jesuits were able to pursue this aggressive expansion plan because of an administrative change. In 1863, the Missouri Vice Province based in St. Louis was elevated to a full-fledged province, giving it a new level of prestige and decision-making authority. Although all decisions were still ultimately controlled from Rome, the Missouri Jesuits were now on equal footing with their Maryland colleagues. Earlier in the century, the Maryland Jesuits began their biggest building spree about a decade after they had been elevated from a mission to a province, and the same pattern of behavior held true in the Midwest. Recognition from Rome empowered ambition at home.

Like their colleagues around the country, the Missouri Jesuits sometimes opened colleges even before they could spare enough teachers to do so. Their general attitude was that, if a city was large enough, and important enough, it simply had to have a Jesuit college. Student demand, not teacher supply, sometimes shaped their decisions more than it reasonably should have. Wherever there was a need for a school, especially in cities that seemed destined to grow, the Jesuits found it hard to turn down a good investment.

Loyola University (1870), Chicago, Illinois

No city reflected the new face of American Catholicism better than Chicago. It was an industrial town, where the meatpacking, manufacturing, and railroad industries enticed thousands of immigrants in the late 1800s. Along with Catholics of Irish and German stock, it also attracted throngs of Poles, Slovaks, Lithuanians, Italians, and other nationalities that were beginning to arrive in America in large numbers. The hard-nosed, working-class Catholic culture that emerged from this melting pot, for generations, defined the American church. Ethnic neighborhoods peppered the city, each with its own Catholic parish operating in its own immigrant language. Congested business districts sometimes had multiple Catholic churches within a few blocks of each other, each serving a different immigrant group. Chicago was far from alone; a similarly patchwork Catholic culture emerged in other industrial cities like

Detroit, Pittsburgh, Buffalo, and Cleveland. But Chicago was the largest such city—the dominant center of gravity in a new Great Lakes megalopolis that stretched from Upstate New York to northern Minnesota.

Despite its large Catholic population, Chicago lacked a Catholic college in the late 1860s. Its first Catholic bishop, William Quarter, founded a school in 1844 that became known as the University of St. Mary of the Lake. Unfortunately, that school succumbed to the fate of many early diocesan universities and closed in 1866. As immigration surged, the city was in desperate need of a replacement college—one affiliated with a stable teaching order.

The Jesuits were no strangers to the Windy City. Father James Van de Velde, SJ (whose long career included memorable stints as a professor at Georgetown and Saint Louis Universities and as a preacher in Louisiana) served as Chicago's second bishop from 1849 to 1853. Van de Velde wanted to offer the University of St. Mary of the Lake to his fellow Jesuits,[7] but unlike another early Jesuit bishop, Benedict Fenwick in Boston, he was not unreasonably pushy. He intended to staff his city's fledgling Catholic college as best he could with his own diocesan priests until the Jesuits had the resources to take it off his hands. Unfortunately, the university folded before that day came. Had it survived a few years longer, its fate might have been different; as it was, the Jesuits had to build a college from scratch.

The Missouri Jesuits' first official toehold in Chicago came in 1857, when they founded Holy Family Church at the invitation of the city's third bishop, Anthony O'Regan. Located close to the city center near what is today the campus of the University of Illinois-Chicago, the new parish flourished, and its impressive building (completed in 1860) still stands. Leading the project was Holy Family's first pastor, Father Arnold Damen, SJ, who had previously served as pastor of St. Francis Xavier College Church on the campus of Saint Louis University. When the Great Chicago Fire of 1871 reduced most of the city to ashes, Holy Family Church miraculously survived, making it one of the oldest standing structures—and the second-oldest Catholic church—in the city.

Even before construction began on Holy Family Church, it was widely expected—even among the general public—that the Jesuit parish would be the first step toward a Jesuit college in Chicago. When the cornerstone of the church building was laid in 1857, a local newspaper reported, "'The Reverend gentlemen . . . propose . . . the erection of a temple of worship which will surpass in size any other in Chicago . . . and also, it is understood, to found a collegiate institution . . . which it is anticipated will eventually rival that of Georgetown, District of Columbia.'"[8]

Under Father Damen's leadership, a school building went up next to Holy Family Church and opened its doors in 1870. As was often the case in Jesuit higher education, the new school was always marketed as a "college" even though its first students were

---

7. Garraghan, *Jesuits of the Middle U.S. Vol. III*, 356.
8. As quoted in Ibid., 403.

really of high school age or younger. The intention was to add college-level courses as the students moved up to higher grade levels. The Jesuits dubbed the new school St. Ignatius College, making it the third American college to claim that name (after St. Ignatius College in San Francisco and St. Ignatius Literary Institute in Louisville).

Father Damen served as the school's inaugural pastor/president for two years. In 1872, he bequeathed the office to Father Ferdinand Coosemans, SJ, who had already served a term as president of Saint Louis University in the early 1860s. Of St. Ignatius College's first six presidents, three (Ferdinand Coosemans, Thomas O'Neil, and Joseph Zealand) previously served a term as president of Saint Louis. Their executive experience shepherded the Chicago school through the growing pains associated with any new academic institution. With its ninth president, St. Ignatius College returned the favor; James Hoeffer, SJ led St. Ignatius for four years in the 1890s before becoming president of Saint Louis.

As the Jesuits' first post-Civil War expansion project, St. Ignatius College was more acutely aware than the schools that preceded it of its place in the Jesuit *network*. It was, arguably, the first Jesuit college built at a time when the Jesuits themselves were already a national brand in American education. Throughout its early history, St. Ignatius emphasized its connections to other Jesuit schools around the country, consciously linking itself to those institutions in its marketing materials. In 1895, the Chicago Jesuits began requiring all St. Ignatius students to wear a distinctive lapel pin and urged other Jesuit schools to do the same, hoping that the pin would become a universal "emblem for the colleges of the society." Within four years, all of the colleges in the Missouri Province had followed suit—although they usually modified the original design, using their own school colors rather than the maroon and gold of St. Ignatius College. The hope was that alumni would continue to wear the pins throughout their lives, making it easy for Jesuit-educated men to identify each other wherever they traveled.[9] Outside of the Missouri Province, however, the initiative never universally caught on. Moreover, there were so many variations in the pins from school to school that they never quite worked as a common identifier.

St. Ignatius College's location presented problems almost immediately. A few decades after Holy Family Church opened, the Catholic population of the surrounding neighborhood sharply declined, and it became one of the city's first urban slums. To attract more students, the Jesuits experimented with a satellite site in a more desirable northern part of town between 1888 and 1890. Even though it was essentially a branch campus of St. Ignatius College, that school went by the name St. Aloysius College, implying that it was a different institution altogether.[10]

Although the branch campus closed after just two years, it remained clear that St. Ignatius College needed a larger campus in a better location to survive.[11] An ideal

---

9. F.J.K., SJ, "The Badge of Loyola: An Emblem for the Colleges of the Society," *Woodstock Letters* XXIX, no. 1 (1900): 1–5.

10. Garraghan, *Jesuits of the Middle U.S. Vol. III*, 458–459.

11. Ibid., 458–459.

opportunity arose in 1906, when President Henry Dumbach, SJ, purchased undeveloped lakefront property from the Chicago, Milwaukee, and St. Paul Railroad near the northern city limits. Although it was under thirty acres in size, the parcel was spacious compared to the college's existing facilities, and the neighborhood surrounding the new property, Rogers Park, was about to experience a building boom.[12] The beautiful lakefront campus opened to students in 1912 and remains the university's home to this day.

Father Dumbach was a visionary who laid much of the groundwork for the college's growth, but his successor, Alexander Burrowes, SJ, transformed St. Ignatius College into Loyola University in 1909. It was the third American Jesuit school to claim that name, after Loyola College in Baltimore and Loyola University in New Orleans, edging out the fourth, Loyola College in Los Angeles (now Loyola Marymount University), by eight years. All four of the major Jesuit provinces in the United States named one of their colleges "Loyola," which explains why there are four "Loyolas" in the country today—one each on the East Coast, in the South, in the Midwest, and on the West Coast, coinciding with old provincial boundaries.

Part of the motivation for Loyola's upgrade to university status was a local academic arms race. Chicago's other major Catholic men's college, the much-younger St. Vincent's College (opened by the Vincentian priests in 1898), re-chartered itself as DePaul University in 1907. Although Chicago was large enough to support both schools, the Jesuits naturally had to keep up. (And no self-respecting Jesuit school could play second fiddle in its own city to the Vincentians!)

Loyola's new name and facilities, along with Chicago's booming Catholic population, enabled the university to realize its potential. It transformed itself rapidly into a comprehensive Catholic university befitting one of America's most Catholic cities. Within a few years of the name change, it added schools of law (1908), medicine (1909), engineering (1911), social work (1914), and dentistry (1924).[13] The progress was impressive for what had been a small, commuter liberal arts college just a generation earlier.

Still, it took some time for the Chicago Jesuits to transition all of their college-level programs to the new Rogers Park campus. Until the early 1920s, they continued to offer some undergraduate courses on the old St. Ignatius campus, which essentially meant that there were two Jesuit colleges in the city (or, perhaps more accurately, one college with two locations). When the United States government established Students Army Training Corps (SATC) units at various colleges throughout the country during World War I, it put separate units at Loyola University and St. Ignatius College, treating them as different institutions.[14] A formal separation of the schools

---

12. Ibid., 459.

13. Ibid., 461.

14. "The Students Army Training Corps: Second Edition. Descriptive Circular," October 14, 1918, University of Colorado Archives, https://cudl.colorado.edu/MediaManager/srvr?mediafile=MISC/UCBOULDERCB1-58-NA/1511/i7375352x.pdf.

finally took place in 1922, at about the same time that most Jesuit colleges around the country were spinning off their prep divisions into separate high schools. In Chicago, St. Ignatius discontinued its degree programs and is known today as St. Ignatius College Prep. The collegiate students all concentrated in Rogers Park.

Loyola University's spacious new Lake Shore Campus also allowed it to become a residential university, and provided it with a new opportunity to draw attention to its place in the Jesuit education network. As it constructed residence halls over the course of the next hundred years, Loyola named most of those buildings after other Jesuit colleges and universities. Although many Jesuit schools name their dorms after Jesuit saints and historical figures, Loyola, uniquely, pays tribute to other *schools* within the family network. Visitors to the Loyola campus today will see buildings named Canisius Hall, Fairfield Hall, Fordham Hall, Georgetown Hall, Gonzaga Hall, St. Louis Hall, LeMoyne Hall, Marquette Hall, Regis Hall, San Francisco Hall, Santa Clara Hall, Seattle Hall, St. Joseph's Hall, Spring Hill Hall, and Xavier Hall. It is a unique and special monument to the identity that all of these colleges and universities share. While all Jesuit schools to some extent emphasize these relationships, that pattern of behavior has been especially pronounced at Loyola from the very beginning.

The University of Detroit Mercy (1877), Detroit, Michigan

If Chicago emerged as America's second city in the late 1800s, then Detroit emerged as the Midwest's second city at the same time. Located at a strategic chokepoint on the series of small waterways that connect Lake Erie and Lake Huron, Detroit has a long Catholic history, tracing its roots to one of the original French forts on the Great Lakes. Dubbed "Detroit" (meaning "strait") by its early French explorers, it was originally no more or less important than other chokepoint settlements like Sault Ste. Marie or St. Ignace, which guard the entrances to Lake Superior and Lake Michigan several hundred miles to the north. But as industrialization took hold on Michigan's Lower Peninsula, it was Detroit that became the center of the state's population and economy.

The University of Michigan, now a public institution, was arguably the first Catholic university to operate within the state's modern-day borders. At the very least, it was heavily influenced by the Catholic educational tradition. A French missionary, Father Gabriel Richard, co-founded the university in 1817 and served as its first vice president. Although the school was then located in Detroit and went by the unwieldy name "Catholepistemiad of Michigania," it led directly to the large public institution located in Ann Arbor today.

Early attempts to found a true Catholic college in Detroit were less successful, and the goal remained elusive in the mid-1800s. The Jesuits seriously considered an offer from Detroit's first bishop, Frederick Rese, to come to the city in 1839. Three years earlier, Rese had opened a school that he called the College of St. Philip Neri, which he hoped the Jesuits could staff permanently. But without enough personnel to accept both opportunities, the Missouri Jesuits decided instead to accept a better offer in Cincinnati, taking control of what is today Xavier University. Without Jesuit help, the College of St. Philip Neri literally and figuratively collapsed when it burned to the ground after being struck by lightning in 1842, leaving Detroit without a permanent Catholic college for a generation.[15]

Detroit's next bishop, the German-born Caspar Henry Borgess, did not give up on his predecessor's dream. When German Jesuits settled in Buffalo in the 1870s, he tried to entice them to open a college in his diocese, to no avail. He then found a more receptive audience in the Missouri Jesuits, who had turned down the offer thirty years earlier.

This time, three decades of growth and experience made all the difference. In the years between the two offers, the Missouri Jesuits had recruited more men and had been elevated to the status of a full province, giving them much more flexibility to respond favorably. The head of the Missouri Province at the time, Thomas O'Neil, SJ, was a former president of Saint Louis University and a future president of St. Ignatius College in Chicago. No stranger to higher education, he accepted Bishop Borgess's offer and assigned a pioneer contingent of four Jesuits to lead the project in 1877. As a base of operations, Bishop Borgess gave them control of Ss. Peter and Paul Parish in Detroit.[16]

The head of the small band of Jesuits was 62-year-old John Baptist Miège, SJ. A Frenchman by birth, Father Miège was at the end of a long and distinguished career as a frontier missionary and educator. He had previously taught at Saint Louis University and was closely associated with the Jesuit Indian mission in Kansas that grew into St. Mary's College. Between 1850 and 1857, he served as the Vatican's Vicar Apostolic (essentially, a bishop) to the Indian Territory—which meant that he was responsible for all Catholic missionary activity throughout the vast Great Plains region. Though he made his home base at Leavenworth, he traveled extensively, worked with innumerable Native American groups, and lived in the roughest of frontier conditions. By comparison, a post to Detroit at the end of his career must have seemed comfortable.

In 1877, Father Miège and his three companions purchased a large mansion, which served both as a residence for themselves and as the first "campus" of what they called Detroit College. As was often the case, the original building was meant only as a temporary home. As enrollment grew in the education-starved city, the Jesuits had to upgrade their facilities twice in the 1880s.[17] In keeping with standard Jesuit practice, early advertisements for the school promised that Catholic students would be expected to attend Mass daily, but that non-Catholic students were welcome to enroll and "no undue influence will be used to make a student change his religious belief."[18]

---

15. Muller, *University of Detroit*, ix, 2.
16. Garraghan, *Jesuits of the Middle U.S. Vol. III*, 482–483.
17. Ibid., 483–484.
18. Muller, *University of Detroit*, 21.

Despite the college's openness and ecumenism, there was some opposition to the Jesuits' arrival from anti-Catholic bigots in Detroit, and the legacy of Nativism was still on display. The June 8, 1877 edition of the *Detroit Evening News* reported:

> The average American . . . must have experienced a small thrill of horror when he read the recent announcement in *The News* that this dreaded order had actually established a branch in Detroit. . . . (T)hose who look on the jesuit (sic) as the embodiment of pride, arrogance, ambition, craft and cruelty, would no doubt be astonished to meet the four quiet, unostentatious, courteous, learned and gentlemanly persons, who, with so little display or advertisement installed themselves at the cathedral last week as the representatives of the Society of Jesus in Detroit.[19]

Detroit's population was already growing at the time of the college's founding, and that growth was about to hit the gas pedal and accelerate. Shortly after the Ford Motor Company began operations in 1903 (soon to be followed by General Motors, Chrysler, and others), the city's population exploded—growing by more than 60% between 1900 and 1910 and more than doubling between 1910 and 1920. The auto industry and its associated manufacturing jobs drew particularly large numbers of Polish and other Eastern European immigrants, who filled the city's Catholic churches to overflowing and pushed the local clergy to their limits. As proprietors of the city's only Catholic men's college, the Jesuits were uniquely positioned to take advantage of this growth. While the city built up rapidly around them, their presence in Detroit became a valuable asset, and they invested heavily in the school's physical and academic footprint.

Detroit College's original 1881 charter from the State of Michigan was due to be renewed in 1911, just as the city's population boom was picking up steam. The college president at the time, Father William Hornsby, SJ, shrewdly used the renewal as an opportunity to re-incorporate the college as a full-fledged university, and it became known thereafter as the University of Detroit.[20]

As was the case in Chicago, the Detroit Jesuits were determined to justify their school's new status by rapidly expanding its offerings. The early 1900s brought schools of engineering (1911), law (1912), pedagogy (1912), business (1916), and aeronautical engineering (1916).[21] These moves were strategic, but also necessary; the city's residents needed a comprehensive Catholic university, and the local industrial economy demanded workers with expertise in business and science. The university negotiated official co-op partnerships with General Motors and dozens of other machinery companies in the city, which provided practical experience to engineering students and helped cover their tuition.[22]

---

19. As quoted in Ibid., 6–7.
20. Garraghan, *Jesuits of the Middle U.S. Vol. III*, 484.
21. Ibid., 485. Muller, *University of Detroit*, 88.
22. Muller, *University of Detroit*, 85–86.

This expansion resulted in a space crunch on the original campus, and in 1922 the Jesuits bought property northwest of downtown that still serves as the university's main campus today. Unlike some other Jesuit schools, however, the University of Detroit did not completely discard its original downtown property, and some of those strategically located buildings continued to house its law school and other professional programs.

As the city of Detroit's fortunes rose and fell in the twentieth century, it brought the university's fortunes with it, leading in part to a 1990 merger between the Jesuit school and Mercy College of Detroit. Although there was temptation to relocate out of the deteriorating inner city to the wealthier suburbs, the university remained a relatively stable employer in a city that sorely needed one. Today, the university is, along with the state-sponsored Wayne State University, one of only two research universities within the Detroit city limits, contributing to a long-term solution to Detroit's post-industrial economic problems.

Creighton University (1878), Omaha, Nebraska

Omaha, Nebraska in the 1870s was reminiscent of St. Louis at the time of the Jesuits' arrival almost 50 years earlier: it was a frontier town, with dirt roads, a small but hearty population, and a dire need for modern schools. Nebraska entered the Union as the 37th state in 1867, and as its largest city and gateway to the outside world, Omaha seemed poised to become a center of commerce for the mid-Plains. It was also squarely in the middle of a region that the Jesuits, because of their missionary work among the Plains Indians, knew better than most religious orders. The Jesuits had lived and worked in the vicinity of Omaha even before there were many Catholic settlers to serve. After the Homestead Act of 1862 drew new settlers with the promise of free land, the Jesuits' focus naturally shifted from missionary work to education.

700 miles separate Detroit from Omaha, but only one year separates the founding of the Jesuit colleges in those two cities. Moreover, both colleges, near the easternmost and westernmost edges of the Missouri Jesuits' territory, ultimately traced their roots to John Baptist Miège, SJ. Twenty years before Father Miège became the founding president of the University of Detroit, he was serving as the bishop to the entire Great Plains region. During an 1857 visit to the Nebraska Territory, he met a well-to-do Catholic pioneer family, the Creightons, who had settled in Omaha and lobbied him to send priests to the fledgling city. That meeting began a long friendship between the Jesuit order and the Creighton family, who continued to advocate for their adopted hometown. Twenty years later, the relationship that Father Miège had cultivated during his time as bishop provided the means by which the Jesuits opened Nebraska's first Catholic college.[23]

---

23. Garraghan, *Jesuits of the Middle U.S. Vol. III*, 463.

John and Edward Creighton were brothers and business partners who married a pair of sisters, Sarah and Mary Wareham. All four were originally from Ohio, but made a small fortune in the west by laying telegraph wire in territories that later became Utah and Montana. Their various business interests also came to include oil speculation in Wyoming and banking in Nebraska. As their wealth grew, their commitment to the civic interests of Omaha grew with it, leading them to speculate about endowing a college in the city.[24]

In the Gilded Age of the late 1800s, it was not unusual for wealthy business tycoons and robber barons to become philanthropists late in life. Steel magnate Andrew Carnegie published his famous essay, "The Gospel of Wealth," in 1889, arguing that the rich have a special obligation to use their wealth for the benefit of society. Schools were a favorite target of such largesse, and many great private universities trace their origins to this era. The Rockefeller family of Standard Oil fame founded the University of Chicago in 1890, originally as a Baptist institution. Many Methodist universities received transformative gifts from wealthy business leaders around this time: the Vanderbilt railroad family endowed their eponymous university in Nashville in 1873, while Asa Candler, founder of the Coca-Cola Company, helped to finance Emory University's new campus in Atlanta in 1915. The generosity of tobacco magnate Washington Duke enabled the former Trinity College to relocate to Durham, North Carolina in 1892, after which it changed its name to Duke University. In central Pennsylvania, Chocolate tycoon Milton Hershey built the Milton S. Hershey School—still one of the country's only tuition-free private schools—in 1909. And of course, the intellectual father of the movement, Andrew Carnegie himself, founded a Pittsburgh technical school known today as Carnegie Mellon University in 1900.

This kind of philanthropy was almost unheard of among Catholics. Protestant universities were almost exclusively the beneficiaries of such gifts. At a time when most American Catholics were working-class, first-generation immigrants, the Creighton family was one of the few Catholic families with the means to endow a university.

Edward Creighton died unexpectedly in 1874 at age fifty-four, and his widow died less than two years later. In her will, Mary Lucretia Wareham Creighton left an initial endowment of $100,000 to found a Catholic college in Omaha, with the gift to be administered by whatever Catholic bishop had jurisdiction over the city. (The Diocese of Omaha was not formally established until 1885.)[25]

The local bishop, James O'Connor, wisely hesitated to accept the gift until he could secure a commitment from an established teaching order to staff the college. The Jesuits were a logical choice, given their experience in the region. From their St. Louis headquarters, the Missouri Jesuits could only be cautiously optimistic about Bishop O'Connor's offer. On one hand, Omaha was a small city, and it would be years

---

24. Ibid., 463–464, 471.
25. Ibid., 463–464.

before its Catholic population was large enough to support a college comfortably. On the other hand, the huge endowment, worth many millions of dollars in today's currency, was too attractive to pass up. Rarely did the Jesuits have an opportunity to establish a new college without taking on significant debt. Here was a ready-made opportunity that would cost the province little except manpower.[26]

In 1877, Provincial Thomas O'Neil, SJ accepted the offer, and the following year Father Roman Shaffel, SJ arrived in Omaha with three Jesuit companions to serve as the college's first president. Like many of the Missouri Jesuits, Father Shaffel was Belgian by birth, and he had been teaching at St. Ignatius College in Chicago when the call came to move west. In addition to a skeleton staff, the Missouri Province also supplied the college with a generous library of books that it had salvaged when it withdrew from St. Joseph's College in Kentucky nine years earlier. A healthy inaugural class of 120 boys enrolled, and within two years, Creighton College was incorporated as Creighton University.

Although it started strong, the college faced significant early challenges. The Jesuits' classical curriculum proved to be a hard sell for the farmers and homesteaders of Nebraska, who had little interest in keeping their sons away from the plow for six years to study Latin and Greek. Like most Jesuit colleges, Creighton initially offered a commercial track along with its standard classical track, but demand for the classical track was so low that it was discontinued from 1884 to 1887, making Creighton essentially a business school. The Jesuit authorities in Europe were unhappy with this development, but they accepted it as a temporary concession to local demand.[27]

Fortunately for Creighton, its leaders and advocates during this period were respected Jesuit educators who ensured that the college never lost the trust or support of those higher authorities. Its second president, Thomas Miles, SJ, (a native of Bardstown, Kentucky and an alumnus of St. Joseph's College) took office in Omaha soon after stepping down from the presidency of St. Ignatius College in Chicago. Creighton's third president, Joseph Zealand, SJ, went on to lead St. Ignatius after leaving Omaha. Their educational credentials were impeccable and their commitment to the Jesuit tradition was never in doubt, which made the college's temporary concessions to modernity more palatable.

The Creighton family's endowment, generous as it was, could not supply vocations to the Jesuit order. The Missouri Jesuits' academic personnel were stretched so thinly across Detroit, Chicago, Cincinnati, Milwaukee, St. Louis, eastern Kansas, and Omaha that, in 1882, they seriously considered withdrawing from at least one of their college commitments. As one of the youngest colleges on the roster, Creighton was a key candidate to be cut. The Missouri Jesuits even offered Creighton to the German Jesuits in Buffalo, who declined to take it off their hands. Ironically, the fact that most

---

26. Ibid., 465, 469.
27. Ibid., 470–471.

Creighton students were enrolled in the commercial track, rather than the classical track, worked to its advantage during these lean years. With so little demand for Latin and Greek, the Jesuits could keep their clerical teaching staff to a minimum and hire lay professors, whose salaries could be partially covered by the endowment and who were perfectly suited to teach bookkeeping and accounting. This meant that Creighton's development as a true university was delayed, but it also ensured the school's long-term survival as a Jesuit institution.[28]

After surviving those growing pains, Creighton began to flourish. It was the only respectable institution of higher education in Omaha, and as the city's population grew, it met the region's need for doctors, dentists, lawyers, and scientists. Its growth benefitted from the continued generosity of the Creighton family, who had a keen interest in ensuring the success of their namesake school. Edward Creighton's surviving brother, John, was a science enthusiast who donated state-of-the-art lab equipment and an astronomical observatory to the university, giving it unusually strong science programs for a Catholic school at the time. In 1899, John Creighton's continued donations helped to save the school from a budget crisis, and upon his death in 1907, he bequeathed it almost $3 million.[29]

This ongoing generosity provided the seed money for many of the university's professional programs. The first was a medical school, badly needed in a state where many settlers lived a day or more from the nearest doctor. During the 1880s, John Creighton and his wife Sarah donated $50,000 to Omaha's struggling St. Joseph's Hospital, which renamed itself Creighton Memorial Hospital in gratitude. Although this gift initially had nothing to do with the university, the Creightons' desire to support the hospital eventually led John to approach the Jesuits about starting an affiliated medical school. Opened in 1892, it was one of the first medical schools in the region and it helped the Creighton family's two biggest charitable interests—the university and the hospital—to forge an affiliation that continues to this day.[30]

Seed gifts from the Creighton family also helped to support new schools of law (1904) and dentistry (1905), both of which opened in the purpose-built Edward Creighton Institute that John Creighton erected as a memorial to his brother in downtown Omaha. Creighton Memorial Hospital got an additional boost when the university acquired a school of pharmacy in 1905, absorbing the previously independent Omaha College of Pharmacy.[31]

Although Creighton University's expansion never would have been possible without the seemingly bottomless pockets of its biggest donors, much credit also goes to its president at the time, Michael Dowling, SJ, who skillfully shepherded it through

---

28. Ibid., 470.
29. Ibid., 475–477.
30. Ibid., 473.
31. Ibid., 480.

this period of growth. Father Dowling's entire career was defined by the Missouri Jesuits and their various educational projects. A graduate of St. Xavier College in Cincinnati, he taught as a young faculty member in both Cincinnati and St. Louis. He served as Creighton's president twice (1885–1889 and 1898–1908); in between, he was president of Detroit College. The unusually long tenure of his second term, one of the most transformative in the university's history, provides tacit acknowledgement of his skill and his value in securing the ongoing donations that kept the institution viable. Father Dowling and John Creighton had a close personal rapport, and the Jesuit officials in Saint Louis certainly did not want to jeopardize that relationship simply because Father Dowling had reached the end of the usual three-year presidential term. When he finally stepped down from the president's office at Creighton, Father Dowling went on to co-found Rockhurst University in Kansas City and serve as its inaugural president.

For all of his work with the Catholic Church in Omaha, John Creighton received a noble title, Count of the Holy Roman Empire, from Pope Leo XIII in 1898, after which he went by the name "Count" John Creighton. The most transformative donor in the history of nineteenth-century Jesuit higher education is buried at Holy Sepulchre Cemetery in Omaha, where his mortal remains rest next to those of his friend, Father John Dowling, SJ.

Marquette University (1881), Milwaukee, Wisconsin

Milwaukee, Wisconsin is one of the few American cities where the number of "Schmidts" in the census has long exceeded the number of "Smiths." German immigrants flocked to the city in large numbers in the mid-1800s and brought Bavarian Catholicism to the shores of Lake Michigan.

Previously part of the Diocese of Detroit, Milwaukee was erected a diocese in 1843, five years before Wisconsin achieved statehood. John Martin Henni, a Swiss immigrant who entered the priesthood under the mentorship of Bishop Dominic Fenwick in Cincinnati, was its first bishop. He held the position for nearly forty years until his death in 1881.

While in Cincinnati, Henni had taught at the Athenaeum (the forerunner of Xavier University before it fell into Jesuit hands), and he understood the importance of education. Like many Catholic bishops of the frontier era, he put a Catholic school at the top of his wish list for the fledgling diocese, and almost immediately set out on a European tour to raise funds. After crossing the Atlantic in 1848, he courted Jesuits from his country of birth, Switzerland, tempting them with the intriguing opportunity to serve one of America's largest communities of German-speaking immigrants. Unfortunately, the Swiss Jesuits declined Henni's offer due to a lack of funds. Shortly thereafter, Henni met a Belgian businessman, Baron Guillaume Joseph de Boey, who pledged 75,000 francs (roughly the equivalent of $16,000 in nineteenth-century money) to the cause. With news of the donation in hand, Henni returned to the Swiss Jesuits, who were suddenly much more interested.[32]

Since Wisconsin fell under the jurisdiction of the Missouri Province of the Society of Jesus, the Swiss Jesuits would have to seek permission from St. Louis as well as Rome before opening a college in Milwaukee. In Rome, the usually cautious Jan Roothaan was uncharacteristically bullish on the opportunity. It was a natural fit if ever there was one; here were German-speaking Jesuits ready and willing to serve a German-speaking American audience, with financing ready for the taking.

In St. Louis, however, the Missouri Jesuits (then under the leadership of former Saint Louis University and St. Xavier College president John Elet, SJ) were just as uncharacteristically reluctant. Elet wrote to his Swiss colleagues, advising them that the $16,000 donation fell well short of what they would need to open a successful college in America, and further warning (somewhat bizarrely) that they should be wary of working with Bishop Henni. Exactly what Henni had done to cross Elet is unclear, but historian Thomas Jablonsky speculates that the two men must have met in Cincinnati around 1840, when Elet was president of St. Xavier College and Henni was a diocesan official.[33] Clearly they had worked together, and for some reason bad blood lingered between them. In lieu of the Milwaukee project, Elet suggested that the Swiss Jesuits take over the already-established St. Joseph's College in Bardstown and St. Aloysius College in Louisville, both of which would have lower start-up costs.[34]

Roothaan could scarcely believe his ears. For his entire career as superior general, the American Jesuits had worn him down with requests to open new colleges all across the country, many of which he had been forced to decline for lack of resources. He had never even approved the creation of the Louisville college that Elet was putting on the table. Now, when he was ready and willing to greenlight a project in Milwaukee that had *both* teachers *and* financing in place, the Americans were the ones urging caution? Roothaan wrote to Elet in 1849, urging him to "put no obstacle in the way of the aforesaid acquisition . . . it must be borne in mind that almost the entire diocese of Bishop Henni is settled by Germans. Where will you find among your own subjects German workers for this business?"[35]

Elet, trying to keep the open mind that his boss was ordering him to keep, visited Milwaukee in 1849 to inspect the city for himself. What he saw convinced him that a college was needed, and that Bishop Henni was a trustworthy partner, regardless of whatever grudge he once held against the man. With Elet's permission, a pair of Swiss Jesuits came to Milwaukee with orders to lay the groundwork for a new college: Fathers Anthony Anderly, SJ, and Friedrich Hubner, SJ. They established a temporary base of operations at a mission church in nearby Green Bay, from which they

---

32. Ibid., 353–355. Thomas J. Jablonsky, *Milwaukee's Jesuit University: Marquette, 1881–1981* (Milwaukee: Marquette University Press, 2007), 17.

33. Jablonsky, *Milwaukee's Jesuit University*, 17.

34. Garraghan, *Jesuits of the Middle U.S. Vol. III*, 355–357.

35. As quoted in Ibid., 356–357.

negotiated real estate purchases and other details with the anxious Bishop Henni while ministering to local German immigrants.[36]

Unfortunately, the effort seemed to have been doomed from the start. Father Hubner fell ill and died shortly after arriving, and Father Anderly suffered a painful rib injury after falling off a chair, forcing him to return to Switzerland after just eleven months in Wisconsin. A third Swiss Jesuit, Father Joseph Brunner, attempted to continue their work from Green Bay but became distracted from his original mission. Having discovered that there were large numbers of rural German-American Catholics throughout the state without access to a priest, he busied himself ministering to the settlers in and around northern Wisconsin. He became widely known for his pastoral work on the shores of Lake Michigan, but those efforts took up so much of his time that the college project went on the back burner. Sensing that the harsh conditions of the American frontier were detrimental to their men's health—and that Brunner was no longer committed to his original assignment—the Swiss Jesuits recalled Brunner from the United States and abandoned all plans to start a school in Milwaukee.[37]

This hiccup ultimately delayed the opening of a Jesuit college in Milwaukee by some thirty years. Still, the Missouri Jesuits never gave up. Individual Jesuits, among them Father Pierre DeSmet, continued to push for the college at every opportunity. As usual, scarcity of funding and paucity of personnel were the main obstacles, but in 1855, the Missouri Jesuits agreed to take control of a parish in Milwaukee, St. Gall's, with the express purpose of using it to lay the foundations for a college. Two years later, the parish opened St. Aloysius Academy, renamed St. Gall's Academy in 1864. Unfortunately, the school closed in 1872, mainly due to lack of faculty. The Missouri Jesuits at the time were prioritizing St. Ignatius College and concentrating their available teachers in Chicago, though they continued their parish ministry in Milwaukee.[38]

By 1881, the time was ripe. After almost three decades, the Jesuits at St. Gall's Church had become a fixture in the local Catholic community, and the city's population had ballooned to 115,000—more than five times what it was when the Jesuits arrived. Despite this growth, Milwaukee still was not a college town; there was no university—public or private—within the city limits, and its citizens had to travel to the University of Wisconsin in Madison for higher education. The school that is today the University of Wisconsin-Milwaukee was not founded until 1885, and even then, it remained little more than a state teachers' college until the 1950s. Milwaukee needed a university, and the Jesuits were finally able to give it one.

The name of the school was never in doubt. As early as 1850, the Jesuits started referring to their nascent educational project in Milwaukee as "Marquette College"—after the seventeenth-century missionary, Jacques Marquette, SJ, who explored the Great Lakes and Mississippi River for France.[39] Father Marquette was

---

36. Ibid., 360–365. Jablonsky, *Milwaukee's Jesuit University*, 17–18.
37. Garraghan, *Jesuits of the Middle U.S. Vol. III*, 365–371.
38. Ibid., 376, 379–385.
39. Ibid., 373.

among the first Europeans to lay eyes on the land that became Wisconsin. Associating their efforts with his name was the Jesuits' way of reminding their fellow Wisconsinites that Catholics—and Jesuits—had been a part of the region's history since the colonial era.

The college opened its doors in 1881, just two days before the death of now-Archbishop Henni. Hopefully, the news that his dreamed-of college was finally underway, after a delay of almost forty years since his first fundraising trip to Europe, gave him a sense of accomplishment in his final hours.

The first president of Marquette College was Father Joseph Rigge, SJ. A noted scientist with interests in chemistry, astronomy, and physics, he left the post after just one year to join the faculty at Creighton College. The generous donations of the Creighton family allowed the Jesuits to operate one of the country's best science programs at Omaha, and the state-of-the-art lab equipment needed the Jesuits' best scientific minds to operate it. Succeeding Rigge at Marquette were Isidore Boudreaux, SJ and then Joseph Keller, SJ; the latter had recently served as president of Saint Louis University from 1877 to 1881. Keller would emerge as one of the strongest advocates for the college within the Missouri Province, pushing the Jesuits to maintain their commitment to it even as Marquette was losing money in the 1880s.[40]

Like almost every other Jesuit college, Marquette soon outgrew its original building. The generosity of a Catholic donor, Robert Johnston, enabled it to move to its present campus between 1905 and 1907. The beautiful Johnston Hall, the oldest standing classroom building on the campus today, memorializes the donation.

With its new location came new growth opportunity. When the Jesuits first explored the possibility of building a school in Milwaukee, they had no intention of developing it into anything more than a traditional Jesuit liberal arts college, but circumstances demanded that it expand its scope fairly quickly. The large, education-starved city was crying out for a university with specialized schools that could meet the growing need for doctors, lawyers, engineers, and other learned professionals. In 1907, the Milwaukee school was re-chartered as Marquette University, which empowered it to add professional schools.

The first professional programs at the university were medical in nature. In 1907, Marquette acquired the twelve-year-old Milwaukee School of Medicine, which also included programs in pharmacy and dentistry. The dental program proved to be a permanent addition to the university; Marquette's School of Dentistry is, today, the only dental school in the State of Wisconsin. The schools of pharmacy and medicine proved to be fleeting. Administrative issues forced Marquette to sever ties with the Milwaukee School of Medicine in 1912 and affiliate instead with another private school, the Wisconsin College of Physicians and Surgeons. That revamped medical school enabled Marquette to affiliate with Milwaukee's Trinity Hospital and incorporate its training program for nurses, the forerunner of today's Marquette School of

---

40. Ibid., 453.

Nursing.[41] In the long term, however, even the reconstituted medical school proved to be too expensive for the university to operate, and it separated from the university in 1967 after fifty years under the Marquette umbrella. It is known today as the Medical College of Wisconsin, an independent, private institution.

After securing its first medical school in 1907, Marquette turned its attention to a law school in 1908. Without a major university in the city, two independent law schools had sprung up, neither of which was financially stable. Milwaukee Law School traced its roots to 1892 when a group of local lawyers informally started teaching. The operation was so rudimentary that the students referred to it as the "Milwaukee Law Class" for its first four years, because "school" was too generous a term. A second school, the Milwaukee University Law School, opened in 1906. Marquette University purchased both institutions in 1908, merging them into a single law school under the university's auspices.

Marquette also established a School of Engineering—an absolute necessity if it hoped to compete with the University of Wisconsin in Madison—in 1908. Two years later, it added a School of Journalism and a College of Business Administration named for donor Robert A. Johnston. It also attempted (ultimately unsuccessfully) to establish a music conservatory between 1910 and 1911.[42] Thus, by the onset of World War I, Marquette had established itself as one of the largest and most comprehensive Catholic universities in the United States, and the almost unchallenged leader of higher education in Milwaukee.

Elsewhere in the Missouri Province . . .

In sum, by the early 1900s, the Missouri Jesuits were under immense pressure to respond to the changing demographics of the Great Lakes region by building up their universities in Chicago, Detroit, and Milwaukee, while at the same time cultivating the generosity of their loyal donors in Omaha. They did not neglect their flagship institution in St. Louis, where they added schools of medicine (1903), business (1910), and law (opened as a department in 1843 but expanded into a school at the turn of the century). The Missouri Jesuits' other historic institution, St. Xavier College in Cincinnati, was also taking steps toward university status by adding schools of business (1910), journalism (1914), education (1914), sociology—that is, social work (1918), and law (1919). St. Xavier College ultimately became Xavier University in 1930.

By the onset of World War I, the Missouri Jesuits found themselves responsible for the upkeep of six universities, all of them large by the standards of the early 1900s. This massive network stretched their resources, but as so often in Jesuit history, student need, not faculty availability, shaped the decisions. Only one of the Missouri Province's schools was still operating as traditional liberal arts colleges: St. Mary's College in rural Kansas.

---

41. Ibid., 456.
42. Ibid., 455.

The network, in the end, was too ambitious. One of the universities in the province would have to give way, and ultimately, that school was Xavier. Always relatively small and underdeveloped compared to the others, Xavier discontinued most of its professional schools by the mid-1900s, ultimately closing all but its business school. It reverted to being primarily a liberal arts college, albeit with a diverse collection of departments and a popular evening division. The Missouri Jesuits simply could not afford to develop Xavier at the same pace and level as their other universities, though they certainly tried. Likewise, St. Mary's College of Kansas fell behind the province's other priorities, and it closed its undergraduate program in 1931, becoming the theological school of Saint Louis University.

False Starts in the Midwest

The Missouri Jesuits made three additional attempts to open colleges in the late nineteenth and early twentieth centuries. Although they varied in their level of success, all three projects had to be abandoned so that the province could concentrate its resources on its six high-demand universities.

The first was the St. Francis Institute, a school that operated between 1871 and 1891 in rural southeastern Kansas. Like nearby St. Mary's College, it grew out of a Native American mission school that the Jesuits had previously operated—in this case, as part of a mission to the Osage Nation that began in 1847. Enrollment patterns at the former Osage Manual Labor School began to change as the United States government forcibly relocated the Osage people out of Kansas to make room for white settlers, and those settlers, lacking any other local option, began to enroll their sons at the Jesuit school. As it grew, it gradually added courses in Latin and other staples of a Jesuit college curriculum, but the primary focus remained business and trades. In effect, it was the only nineteenth-century Jesuit college that offered only the commercial track without developing a full-fledged *Ratio Studiorum* curriculum. Most of the faculty and administration were Jesuit brothers or scholastics.[43]

After twenty years, the Institute closed its doors. The Jesuits were operating two schools in rural Kansas and could not afford to develop both into proper colleges. St. Mary's College was the better established of the two, so the St. Francis Institute had to be cut. Its final president was Father Roman A. Shaffel, SJ, who had previously served as the founding president of Creighton University. The property was sold to the Passionist Fathers, and today, the approximate location (in the small town of Osage Mission, Kansas) is home to St. Francis Catholic Church and the Osage Mission-Neosho County Museum.

Does the St. Francis Institute count as a Jesuit "college"? I would argue that it deserves to be included on the list of Jesuit higher education projects because its 1871 state charter classifies it as something more than the Native American industrial

---

43. Ibid., 450–451.

school that it was founded to be more than twenty years earlier. After abandoning its original mission, it became, in effect, a specialty business school. Although it was more like a modern-day high school than a college, it was in step with "higher education" in its day. Using modern terminology, it might be called the equivalent of a two-year technical school, much like a culinary institute or a business college. Schools of that sort qualify for federal higher education funding today, so it is defensible to include the St. Francis Institute as part of the Jesuit higher education network in America.

Regis College (1910–1913), East St. Louis, Illinois

The second failed college was truly bizarre. Just across the Mississippi River from St. Louis, in Illinois, is the suburb of East St. Louis. Today, East St. Louis is known mainly for its poverty, but during a period of growth in the early 1900s, the Bishop of Belleville, Illinois invited the Jesuits to open a school there. As usual, the Jesuits began by accepting responsibility for a local church, and by 1910 they opened Regis College. It was never more than a high school in practice, but it received a charter to grant college degrees from the Illinois legislature. Though it was a college in name and in law, it never functioned as such, and after three years of enrollment struggles the Jesuits withdrew in 1913.[44]

The Jesuits were certainly known for operating multiple colleges within short distances of each other, but Regis College, less than four miles from Saint Louis University, was a particularly egregious example. It never could have pursued any ambitions in higher education without competing with its sister university on the other side of the river. Perhaps under different circumstances the relationship between the two schools could have evolved into something similar to that between Georgetown and Gonzaga College in Washington, DC, but the Jesuits never assigned more than a handful of teachers to Regis and quite logically pulled the plug. With a lifespan of just three years, Regis College (along with St. Aloysius College in Louisville) has the distinction of being one of the two shortest-lived Jesuit colleges ever to operate in the United States.

Allouez College, Superior, Wisconsin

Perhaps the strangest Jesuit college project of all took place in the small town of Superior, Wisconsin, located on the far western tip of Lake Superior. This college had a name, a president, and a charter, but no students.

Superior, Wisconsin is effectively a suburb of Duluth, Minnesota, the nearby and much larger mining town that provided many of the raw materials for America's steel industry. As the region's population grew through industrialization, it took on an ethnic, heavily Eastern European character similar to that of Detroit, Pittsburgh, and Chicago. The bishop of Superior invited the Jesuits to open a college in his diocese,

---

44. Ibid., 499–500.

and they, according to pattern, accepted control of a local church to begin the planning. A trio of Jesuits arrived in 1909, but one drowned in 1912 and the other died unexpectedly in 1914. With only one remaining Jesuit in the city, the Missouri Province canceled the project.[45]

If they had opened the school, the Jesuits had planned to name it Allouez College after Claude-Jean Allouez, SJ, a seventeenth-century French Jesuit missionary (and contemporary of Father Jacques Marquette) who is best known for exploring Lake Superior and preaching to the local natives. At the time the project came to a halt, the Jesuits had acquired property for a campus and secured a charter to grant degrees from the Wisconsin state legislature, but no students ever enrolled.[46]

Even though the Missouri Jesuits cut their losses in all three of these cases, the failures were still costly. The money used to develop the campus in Kansas and acquire property in East St. Louis and Superior could have been invested in other colleges in the province, where it was certainly needed. By emphasizing breadth over depth, the Jesuits extended the scope of their reach but prevented individual colleges and universities from becoming as stable and well-resourced as they otherwise might have been.

Rockhurst University (1910), Kansas City, Missouri

The only lasting institution that came out of the Missouri Province's mini-burst of expansionist energy in 1910 was Rockhurst University in Kansas City, Missouri. Rockhurst was initially a commuter school and was one of the last day colleges founded according to the standard nineteenth-century Jesuit *modus operandi*. Located ninety miles east of St. Mary's College in Kansas, it was, in many ways, designed to serve city boys who could not afford the travel and lodging necessary to attend the rural boarding college. Chronologically, Rockhurst is the last Jesuit institution cast in the mold of Boston College, Saint Joseph's (Philadelphia), Loyola (Baltimore), Loyola (Chicago), and the many others that originated as downtown commuter colleges. It was a nineteenth-century educational model squeezed into the twentieth century, at a time when modern tastes and regulations were already making the old model anachronistic.

Jesuit missionaries had been active in Kansas and Missouri long before Kansas City became a metropolis. The city emerged as a regional hub around the 1850s. Located at the confluence of the Missouri and Kansas Rivers, it was a natural location for meat and grain processing as well as the rail commerce that brought those products to the rest of the country. In keeping with their strong missionary tradition in the area, the Jesuits established a parish, St. Aloysius, in the growing city in 1891.[47]

---

45. Ibid., 501–502.
46. Ibid., 501–502.
47. Ibid., 497.

The parish once again proved to be a foothold for a college ministry. In 1908, fresh from his second term as president of Creighton University, Father Michael Dowling, SJ, was assigned to St. Aloysius Church. There could be no mistaking the purpose of the assignment; Father Dowling was a respected educator with two decades of experience leading the Jesuit colleges in Omaha and Detroit, during which he was the most prolific fundraiser in the province. He was not being sent to a church in Kansas City because of his pastoral skills. The Jesuits wanted a new college for Missouri's second-largest city, and Dowling knew how to build one.

Like Milwaukee, Kansas City was underserved by existing colleges and universities at the turn of the century. Educational opportunity in the city had not kept pace with its booming population. The only research university in the city today (the University of Missouri-Kansas City) did not open in its current form until the 1930s. Local residents had to travel to Lawrence in the west or Columbia in the east to attend major public universities on either side of the state line. The Jesuits saw a strategic opportunity to build what could become the city's leading urban college, just as they had done in Milwaukee.

In 1910, Father Dowling secured a charter from the Missouri legislature allowing the proposed Jesuit college to grant degrees, although it would be four years before students actually enrolled. He named the school "Rockhurst College." The suffix "-hurst" comes from an Old English word referring to forests and wooded areas, much like the Latin suffix, "-sylvania." It is fairly common in Catholic colleges; among the schools that have used it are Mercyhurst University (literally, "woods of mercy") in Erie, Pennsylvania and the now-defunct Marylhurst University ("woods of Mary") in Oregon. Dowling chose the name in reference to the rocky soil and forests of the area,[48] and he may have been inspired by the Jesuit school in England, Stonyhurst College, whose name has essentially the same meaning.

Dowling died in 1915, having lived long enough to see the first class of boys enter Rockhurst College seven months earlier. Although Dowling is credited with being the first president of Rockhurst, he never truly led the school while it was in operation. He merely provided the administrative muscle that made the project a reality, and kept it afloat during the four uncertain years between its charter in 1910 and its first entering class in 1914. When the first students enrolled, Father Aloysius Breen, SJ, was serving as principal, and Rockhurst's official records recognize him as the school president after Dowling's death the following year. Breen had previously served as president of St. Mary's College in Kansas, and would go on to lead Regis University in Denver in the late 1920s and early 1930s before the end of his career.

Like many Jesuit colleges, Rockhurst was effectively a high school for the first few years of its existence, but some generous donations from local benefactors enabled it to offer its first college-level courses in 1917 and award its first degrees in 1921.[49]

---

48. Ibid., 498.
49. Ibid., 499.

Since it was born during World War I and came of age in the inter-war period, most of its history properly belongs in that era. During the 1920s, the delineation between college and high school sharpened, which meant that Rockhurst almost immediately had to draw a line between its older and younger students.

Ultimately, Rockhurst was slow to develop into a comprehensive university. Even though Kansas City certainly needed an institution of larger scope and scale, the Missouri Jesuits did not have the financial resources to develop it into the province's seventh research institution. As will be discussed in detail later, Jesuit planners in the 1930s deliberately kept the college small, knowing that they could not afford to maintain it if it grew as rapidly as other Midwestern Jesuit schools. It did not achieve university status until 1999, generally leaving the professional education to nearby Creighton and Saint Louis Universities. Still, it was a necessary addition to what remains a generally underserved metro region.

The "Other" Midwestern Jesuits: German Refugees Arrive

Even though the Missouri Jesuits were remarkably successful in opening colleges to serve the industrializing Midwest, they could not meet all of the region's demand for Catholic education on their own. Fortunately, a new branch of the Jesuit family tree—consisting of German refugees who settled initially in Upstate New York—helped to fill gaps. The efforts of the German Jesuits resulted in two successful additions to the Jesuit higher education network: Canisius College in Buffalo and John Carroll University in Cleveland. They also brought about new colleges in Toledo, Ohio and in rural western Wisconsin, both of which had long lifespans but ultimately shut their doors.

Like the English Jesuits of the East Coast, the Belgian Jesuits of the Midwest, the French Jesuits of the South, and the Italian Jesuits of the far west, the German Jesuits of the Great Lakes mainly saw themselves as missionaries—importing European-style education for the Catholic community in America. They sought to help first-generation immigrants maintain their cultural heritage while also preparing themselves for economic success in their adopted country. However, much like the French and Italian Jesuits who preceded them in the 1840s and 1850s, the Germans of the 1870s and 1880s were not entirely in control of the circumstances that brought them across the Atlantic.

The term "Germany" was simply a cultural or regional reference prior to the late nineteenth century. Politically, the German-speaking regions of Europe were fractured into dozens of tiny microstates, kingdoms, principalities, and other autonomous units. This changed in the 1870s and 1880s, as the northern kingdom of Prussia absorbed its weaker neighbors to become the dominant political and military force in the region. Prussia's Iron Chancellor, the ruthless Otto von Bismarck, sought to unify the new German state culturally as well as politically. To ensure that Prussian-style Protestantism would dominate the country, Bismarck expelled prominent Catholic missionary organizations. Because the borders of modern Germany came to include predominantly Catholic areas like Bavaria and other Alpine regions, Bismarck and his coterie took extreme measures to limit Catholic influence in the unified country. Collectively, this series of discriminatory policies became known as the *Kulturkampf* (cultural struggle).

Although all Catholic organizations in Germany were in some way affected by the *Kulturkampf*, the Jesuits were among those specifically targeted. In 1872, the Reichstag passed the "Jesuits Law" (*Jesuitengesetz*), which forced all Jesuit-affiliated schools throughout the German empire to close. As they fled their homeland, the German Jesuits sought refuge in the United States, where they already had a small missionary presence in Buffalo, New York.

The Jesuit presence in Buffalo was then only about twenty years old. In the 1850s, the French Jesuits based at St. John's College (Fordham), had started a small parish ministry in Buffalo with two churches, St. Michael the Archangel and St. Ann. Because the congregations were mainly German-speaking and the Fordham Jesuits were mainly Francophone, they quickly called in reinforcements from their German colleagues. In 1869, a pioneer contingent of German Jesuits arrived at Buffalo to take control of the two parishes, which together became an official mission of the German provinces. It was a fortuitous move, coming just three years before the *Kulturkampf* crisis. Suddenly, what began as a minor outreach to German-American immigrants on the shores of Lake Erie became a last-minute refuge; dozens of persecuted priests fled Europe for Buffalo, where the two churches dutifully took them in.[50]

The Jesuits were not alone. Other orders of German priests resettled in the United States at the same time, and American higher education benefitted as a result. Refugee priests from the Congregation of the Holy Ghost (known today as the Spiritans) settled in Pittsburgh and opened what is now Duquesne University in 1878. Others, like the Franciscans and Benedictines, sent priests to reinforce their existing American schools.

Canisius College (1870), Buffalo, New York

A year after taking control of St. Michael the Archangel parish in Buffalo, the German Jesuits—led by Father William Becker, SJ—opened Canisius College. It took its name from St. Peter Canisius, SJ, a sixteenth-century Jesuit who preached in central Europe and helped large regions of Germany remain Catholic during the Protestant Reformation. The Buffalo school was initially housed in a single building adjacent to the church and it enrolled a small number of students, almost all of high school age or younger.

Although most students came from the local area, Canisius also built a small dormitory for boarding students who traveled from outside the city. For many such stu-

---

50. Bender, *Brief History of the New York Province*, 29.

dents, the attraction to Canisius lay in its German identity. The school was decisively and unapologetically German in its character, organized along the lines of a German *progymnasium* and staffed by Jesuits who, in general, spoke only German outside of the classroom and only German and Latin inside of it.[51] The college's code of discipline was even stricter than that of most Jesuit schools. From as far away as Ohio, immigrant families seeking an authentically German education for their sons were willing to send them off to Canisius. As more Jesuit refugees from the *Kulturkampf* arrived in the United States during the 1870s, they became effective recruiters for Canisius College whenever they preached to German-speaking communities throughout the industrial Midwest.[52]

The presence of a Jesuit college in Buffalo (even one with such a focused ethnic identity) was cause for celebration in the local Catholic community. The first bishop of the newly established Diocese of Buffalo, John Timon, had for years pressured the French Jesuits at Fordham to open a college attached to St. Michael and St. Ann parishes. Although the French Jesuits were unable to fulfill those requests, after the German takeover there were finally enough teachers to make the dream a reality.[53]

The German *progymnasium* model was not terribly different from that of other American Jesuit colleges at the time; it featured a six-year plan of study and followed the classical *Ratio Studiorum*, albeit with a strong emphasis on German language, culture, and history. In a relatively short time, Canisius added many of the trappings of a typical American Jesuit college, including a commercial division for those who wanted a business education without Latin and Greek (which existed until 1894). English began to supplant German as the main language of instruction by the end of the 1870s, and by the 1890s, the six-year *progymnasium* model had started to evolve into the familiar four-year high school/four-year college model that was becoming the standard in America.[54] Canisius was somewhat ahead of other nineteenth-century Jesuit colleges in adopting this format.

The main impetus for Americanizing the college was recruitment. What had once been a major virtue of the college—its German character—became a liability as German immigrants began to assimilate into American culture and the ethnic makeup of Buffalo became more diverse. So few of the Canisius faculty spoke English that it was becoming impossible to attract students from outside the German community, and occasionally even within it. Buffalo's booming manufacturing economy was attracting large numbers of Irish, Polish, and other Eastern European immigrants, all of whom needed an education just as desperately as their German neighbors. Some were choosing to attend the region's other Catholic school, Niagara University, which was operated by the Vincentian priests and was growing rapidly. In 1883, Canisius

---

51. Edward Dunn, SJ, "A Gymnasium in Buffalo: The Early Years of Canisius College," *Urban Education* 18, no. 4 (January 1984): 428.

52. Ibid., 431, 433.

53. Ibid., 426.

54. Ibid., 429, 434–435.

began to compete directly with Niagara after the New York State Board of Regents granted the Jesuit college a charter to confer degrees.[55]

Although it began life as a boarding school, Canisius's dorm facilities were never satisfactory and by 1901, they were in such disrepair that the Jesuits were planning to convert the school to a commuter college.[56] The final boarders left the original campus in 1908. Four years later, Canisius underwent the rite of passage common to almost all urban Jesuit schools when it outgrew its original building and moved to a larger campus. The move had been planned for some time. Canisius President Henry Behrens, SJ, had purchased the property for the new campus almost forty years earlier, in 1874, knowing that the little college next to St. Michael Church would one day need more than a single classroom building. It took two generations before Canisius improved its enrollment and its balance sheets to such a degree that it actually needed the space, but Father Behrens's purchase proved to be a good investment.

The new location, still in use today, was slightly north of downtown in the growing residential neighborhood of Hamlin Park. The spacious property had been owned by the Sisters of St. Joseph, who used it for retreats. Even in its new home, Canisius was initially a commuter school, with no dorms and only one large building (Old Main) housing all classes and administrative activity. Fortunately, as American attitudes toward college life changed in the twentieth century and dorms became an expected part of the undergraduate experience, the larger campus provided room to expand and build new student residences.

John Carroll University (1886), Cleveland, Ohio

As more of their European colleagues fled persecution in Bismarck's Germany, the Buffalo Jesuits saw their numbers increase, giving them the ability to expand beyond their home base in western New York. Although they still struggled to staff Canisius College with competent, English-speaking teachers,[57] they never forgot their original plan to minister to the German diaspora in the United States, and went far and wide to achieve that goal.

Three of the cities with the largest German-American populations—Milwaukee, St. Louis, and Cincinnati—were already well served by the Missouri Jesuits. But there were plenty of other Midwestern cities where the Buffalo Jesuits could be of use. By the 1880s, the Buffalo Mission had taken a particular interest in another city on Lake Erie—Cleveland, located less than 200 miles away. Demographically, economically, and culturally, Cleveland resembled Buffalo, Detroit, Chicago, and other cities where Jesuit schools had successfully taken root. Yet it still lacked a Catholic college, even as its population boomed in the late nineteenth century.

55. Ibid., 431.
56. Ibid., 432.
57. Ibid., 431.

The Jesuit experience in Cleveland followed the familiar pattern. In 1880, Father Michael Zoeller, SJ, became pastor of St. Mary of the Assumption Parish, a predominantly German-speaking congregation near the city center. Richard Gilmour, a Scottish-born convert to Catholicism and second bishop of Cleveland, offered the parish to the Buffalo Jesuits with the usual stipulation that they use it as a base from which to build a college as quickly as possible. Gilmour was a protégé of Cincinnati Bishop John Baptist Purcell—the same man responsible for bringing the Jesuits to Xavier University in southwestern Ohio forty years earlier—and he had a comparable respect for both the Jesuits and for Catholic education.

Six years after the Jesuits arrived at the parish, they opened St. Ignatius College—the fourth American college to bear that name. Although Father Zoeller did much of the preparatory work, he never served as president of the college; the first man to hold that job was Father John Neustich, SJ, a German refugee who had served on the Canisius faculty and who brought three of his Canisius colleagues with him for the new venture.[58]

In 1890, during the presidency of Henry Knappmeyer, SJ, St. Ignatius College received its charter to grant degrees from the State of Ohio. Nonetheless, the little school on Cleveland's West Side operated essentially as a German *progymnasium* like its elder sister in Buffalo, never becoming much more than a high school during the nineteenth century. By the early 1900s, the development trends in Cleveland had changed, and the Jesuits began to fear that they were literally on the wrong side of town. St. Ignatius College was landlocked in an urban neighborhood on Cleveland's West Side, but much of the city's growth was actually taking place in the more affluent eastern suburbs. To serve the other end of town, the Jesuits opened a second school—Loyola High School—on the East Side in 1907.[59]

Both Cleveland schools continued to operate through World War I and its aftermath. St. Ignatius in the west was both a college and a high school, while Loyola in the east was merely a high school. In 1922–23, the Jesuits made the strategic decision effectively to swap the two. Believing that their college would be better positioned to succeed if it were in the east, they closed Loyola High School and purchased land for a new college campus in the affluent eastern suburb of Shaker Heights. The two high school programs consolidated on the original St. Ignatius campus in the west, while the college programs began a decade-long process of relocating to the new campus.[60]

In 1923, when the Jesuits announced that the undergraduate division of St. Ignatius College would relocate to the suburbs, they also announced that it would change its name to "Cleveland University." The new name proved controversial, because unbeknownst to the Jesuits, a coalition of local schools was, at the time, also making plans to create a "Cleveland University" that would be secular in nature. Even

58. Garraghan, *Jesuits of the Middle U.S. Vol. III*, 491.

59. Ibid., 492.

60. Ibid., 493.

though the Jesuits had a legal preemptory right to the name, they acquiesced, and chose instead to name the relocated school "John Carroll University" after the founding father of the American Catholic Church.[61] The controversy took place over four months in 1923, meaning that St. Ignatius College had three different names in one year. In the end, it was all for naught, because efforts to establish the other "Cleveland University" fell through and neither side ultimately used the name.

The college division of John Carroll University finally moved to Shaker Heights (to a neighborhood that eventually named itself University Heights) in 1936. The original West Side campus of St. Ignatius College, including its ornate main building constructed in 1891, remains the home of St. Ignatius High School today.

Campion College (1880–1925), Prairie du Chien, Wisconsin

The Buffalo Jesuits built two colleges that were destined not to survive. The first of these came in 1880 in the small city of Prairie du Chien, Wisconsin. Prairie du Chien (which translates from French as "Prairie of the Dog") is located in the far western part of the state on the Mississippi River, just across the Iowa border. It is roughly halfway between Dubuque, Iowa to the south and La Crosse, Wisconsin to the north. Although the region has never had a large population, it did have some significance in early American Catholic history. Prairie du Chien dates to the French colonial era, and nearby Dubuque was one of the earliest Catholic dioceses erected west of the Mississippi in 1837. In the early nineteenth century, this section of the Mississippi valley had one of the larger concentrations of Catholics in the United States.

Shortly after the Civil War, the city was home to a small school called Prairie du Chien College. When that college failed, a local resident named John Lawler purchased its building in 1869 and offered it to the Missouri Jesuits in St. Louis, who declined. He then offered it to the Christian Brothers, who ran a small school on the site for five years before withdrawing. Finally, in 1880, Lawler offered the property to the German Jesuits in Buffalo, who found it an attractive proposition. They had plenty of refugee teachers, but little money, so the prospect of a ready-made college to which they could send surplus faculty seemed to be a good fit. Father William Becker, SJ, who had served as founding president of Canisius College a decade earlier, took the helm at Prairie du Chien and named the revived school Sacred Heart College.[62] In 1881, it received a state charter.

After just eight years, the Buffalo Jesuits concluded that Sacred Heart was too small to justify even the minimal investment they were putting into it, and they converted it into a Jesuit seminary. Ten years later, however, in 1898, they reopened the college to lay students. While the large majority of those students were, as usual, of high school age, Sacred Heart enrolled a small number of undergraduates and continued to award bachelor's degrees. In 1913, it changed its name to Campion College of

61. Ibid., 493.
62. Ibid., 489.

the Sacred Heart, honoring St. Edmund Campion, SJ, a sixteenth-century English Jesuit and martyr associated with Oxford University.[63]

After World War I, however, it was clear that Campion College had run its course as an undergraduate institution, and the Jesuits downgraded it to a high school in 1925. It continued to operate for another fifty years, producing several notable alumni (including a future president of Mexico, Vicente Fox) before closing its doors for good in 1975. The campus briefly served as a Lutheran boarding school, but is today the site of a Wisconsin state prison.

St. John's University (1898–1936), Toledo, Ohio

The second failed project of the Buffalo Jesuits was in Toledo, Ohio. It is easy to see why Toledo was an attractive location; though much smaller than nearby Detroit and Cleveland, it was demographically similar and lacked a Catholic college. By building a school there, the Buffalo Jesuits would have a presence on the eastern tip, western tip, and the center of Lake Erie, and all three schools would be within a day's journey of each other by rail. Toledo was, at the time, part of the Diocese of Cleveland, but its Catholic population was growing and within twelve years it would be carved out as a diocese unto itself.

The German Jesuits took control of a parish church in Toledo in 1869—the same year they arrived in Buffalo—but it was not until almost thirty years later that they established a college there. The school opened its doors in 1898 and received a legal charter as St. John's College in 1900. The "St. John" after whom it was named was St. John Berchmans, SJ, a Belgian Jesuit of the early 1600s who died at age 22 before he could make his final vows. In 1903, the college received university status, but the move was premature: it did not open its first professional school, a law school, until six years later. Like the short-lived law school at Xavier University in Cincinnati, the St. John's University Law School was exclusively an evening program and failed to achieve accreditation from the American Bar Association for that reason. It closed in 1924, leaving only the undergraduate college.[64]

Despite the issues with the law school, the Jesuits had high hopes for St. John's University and even purchased land for an expanded campus in 1921. Unfortunately, nothing was done with the new property. The school remained in its original location until 1936, when the financial difficulties of the Great Depression forced it to close. It had been a small, but important pillar of the local civic and church community for nearly four decades.

About thirty years later, then-Bishop George Rehring of Toledo invited the Jesuits back into his diocese to establish a boys' high school. Father Nicholas Gelin, SJ, an alumnus of the "old" St. John's, led the effort, and in 1965 an entirely new school—called St. John's Jesuit High School—opened its doors. Other than its

---

63. Ibid., 490.
64. Ibid., 494–495.

shared name and its shared Jesuit identity, there was no connection between the high school and the old college. For many St. John's alumni in and around Toledo, however, it was gratifying to see the Jesuits return to northwest Ohio and to know that the spirit, at least, of the old college lived on.

The End of the Buffalo Mission

Geographically, the Buffalo Mission was always an awkward addition to the American Jesuit map. It had responsibility for portions of Upstate New York, northern Ohio, and parts of Michigan and Wisconsin, and its activities overlapped with the territory of the Missouri Jesuits based in St. Louis. At its peak, it controlled four colleges as well as parishes in Iowa and Minnesota. It also sponsored a large missionary network among the Sioux of South Dakota.[65]

By the early 1900s, the German character of the mission had begun to fade and its reason for existing became less clear. In 1907, it was dissolved and its assets were divided among the logical Jesuit provinces. Canisius College, being located in New York State, became part of the Maryland-New York Province. The Midwestern schools—St. Ignatius College (Cleveland), St. John's University (Toledo), and Sacred Heart College (Prairie du Chien)—were absorbed by the Missouri Province. This made Missouri by far the largest Jesuit province in the United States, both in its number of colleges and in the breadth of its geography, which stretched from Ohio to the Rocky Mountains.

For the colleges of the former Buffalo Mission, the transition provided some stability, but it also meant that they were now part of much larger networks of Jesuit universities, most of which were older and bigger than they were. As the newcomers, they were relatively low on their new provinces' lists of priorities. Neither the Maryland-New York Province nor the Missouri Province was able to invest the money and personnel necessary to develop these late additions into anything more than they already were. As a result, Canisius and John Carroll remained small, while the other two schools closed.

For the German Jesuits, the dissolution of the mission was a source of "frustration and disappointment. They had been buoyed up by a great hope for a new Germany in the new world."[66] No doubt it was difficult to accept the end of their dream, but the legacy of that dream includes two American colleges that continue to improve students' lives to this day.

Eastern Jesuit Colleges, 1865–1918

While the Midwestern Jesuits were in the midst of their late nineteenth-century building spree, their colleagues on the East Coast were expanding more modestly.

---

65. "The Buffalo Mission: 1869–1969," *Woodstock Letters* 98, no. 4 (1969): 465–466.
66. As quoted in Dunn, "Gymnasium," 435–436.

During the decades between the Civil War and World War I, the East Coast Jesuits only established three new colleges, one of which resurrected an old project. They reopened Saint Joseph's College in Philadelphia after a slumber of almost thirty years, and founded new colleges in Jersey City, New Jersey and Brooklyn, New York.

Not that all was quiet on the eastern front. The Maryland Province—which controlled Georgetown, Boston College, Holy Cross, Loyola (Baltimore), and Gonzaga (DC)—merged in 1879 with the French Jesuit mission in New York, which controlled St. John's College (Fordham) as well as two rapidly growing commuter colleges in the greater New York City area. The combined Maryland-New York Province was an academic behemoth, but as often occurs with corporate mergers, the newly united Jesuits bickered among themselves and fought over competing priorities. The most divisive issue was whether to develop Georgetown or Fordham into the province's premiere university.

With the heart of their work concentrated in America's oldest and largest cities, the eastern Jesuits also became heavily involved in the growing labor movement, ministering to and advocating for the working-class poor. Urban Catholic immigrants often worked in hellish industrial conditions a stone's throw away from Jesuit colleges. Over time, in a pattern that would continue well beyond World War I, the eastern Jesuits developed a reputation for radical social activism that paired awkwardly with their conservative educational traditions. They pushed for workers' rights and promoted the principles of Catholic social teaching at a time when Catholicism was largely seen as a working man's religion, and the inequalities between America's ruling class and its recent arrivals were growing. Pope Leo XIII's 1891 encyclical, "*Rerum Novarum*: Rights and Duties of Capital and Labor," brought workers' rights to the forefront of Catholic social thought, and the New York Jesuits in particular sought to empower urban workers to improve their condition.

Even as they took steps to develop Georgetown and Fordham into nationally prominent research universities, the eastern Jesuits continued to see education fundamentally as a human right. All three of the schools they opened in this period—Saint Joseph's College, Saint Peter's College, and Brooklyn College—existed primarily to provide the urban poor with access to education. Tuition was free, or reasonably low, and they sprang up in dense urban areas. The Jesuits spent enormous sums of money on these projects that otherwise could have been invested into their flagship schools, but their commitment to social justice demanded that they prioritize accessibility over prestige (and at times, even over quality).

Catholic education as a whole was proliferating at this time, particularly in the industrial cities of the East Coast and the Midwest. At the Third Plenary Council of Baltimore in 1884, the US bishops effectively mandated that every Catholic parish have its own elementary school. This was the origin of the "Catholic grade school" that became iconic in American history. A typical Catholic grade school consisted of a small building, attached to a church, where a team of resident nuns taught children from the neighborhood. Like the parishes themselves, these schools often took on an ethnic flavor; Polish-American immigrants, for example, often built neighborhood schools in which the nuns taught in English in the mornings and Polish in the afternoons.[67]

Despite this progress, however, for most urban Catholic immigrants, education ended at roughly the equivalent of eighth grade before children went off to careers in mining, manufacturing, and domestic work. Hardly any of the tiny parish elementary schools had the means or the ambition to become respectable American colleges. While the Jesuits were not the only branch of the Catholic Church establishing schools at this time, they were by far the largest religious order building actual colleges and universities in an attempt to break the cycle of immigrant poverty. Even though the Jesuit commuter colleges in places like Baltimore, Philadelphia, and Jersey City looked much like any other Catholic school going up in those cities, they had one thing the others didn't—accreditation to grant degrees.

Saint Peter's University (1873), Jersey City, New Jersey

Even at a time when immigrants were flocking to the United States in droves, few parts of the country were growing as rapidly as northern New Jersey. Newark and its environs had a substantial industrial base of its own, and combined with spillover settlement from New York City, the area attracted new residents at a breakneck pace. As one of the two states in eyesight of any immigrant disembarking on Ellis Island, New Jersey ballooned in population from less than a million in 1870 to more than 2.5 million by 1910.

Saint Peter's traces its origins to a familiar individual. In the early 1870s, Father John Bapst, the founding president of Boston College, was serving as superior of the Jesuits' New York Mission based at Fordham. In his new position, he made the acquaintance of James Roosevelt Bayley, the first bishop of nearby Newark and a nephew of St. Elizabeth Ann Seton, the first American-born Catholic saint. Bishop Bayley was badgering the New York Jesuits to open a college somewhere in his diocese to serve the poor and to take some enrollment pressure off Seton Hall—the diocesan college he had founded fourteen years earlier and named in honor of his aunt. Bayley seems never to have considered offering Seton Hall to the Jesuits; he simply wanted them to bring a second college to the diocese. To facilitate the expansion, he offered the Jesuits St. Peter's Parish in Jersey City. Father Bapst accepted the offer in 1870, and two years later, the proposed college received a charter from the New Jersey legislature. Eight years later, it opened its doors to its first class.[68]

Saint Peter's College (which simply took its name from its host parish) was functionally similar to St. Francis Xavier College across the Hudson in Manhattan. It was

---

67. Thomas I. Monzell, "The Catholic Church and the Americanization of the Polish Immigrant," *Polish American Studies* 26, no. 1 (1969): 1–15.

68. Bender, *Brief History of the New York Province*, 6.

intended from the start to be a commuter school, mainly serving those who could not afford the tuition and travel costs necessary to attend St. John's College (Fordham) or Seton Hall. As it turned out, that audience was rather large. By 1895, the enrollment at both St. Francis Xavier and Saint Peter's exceeded that at Fordham—although Fordham enrolled slightly more students in its college-level program than Saint Peter's. The imbalance was only temporary, however, and after a generation Fordham clearly emerged as the dominant institution.[69] As it grew into a comprehensive university, Fordham would surpass Saint Peter's in total enrollment before 1900 and St. Francis Xavier before 1910.

Still, the growth of Saint Peter's was respectable, and on the cusp of World War I it enrolled more than 550 students, of whom 84 were in the college division.[70] The war, however, proved disastrous for the school, forcing Saint Peter's to suspend operations as a college for eleven years.

Back to Philadelphia: Saint Joseph's University (1889)

Since closing the first iteration of Saint Joseph's College in 1860, the Jesuits had maintained only a bare-bones presence in Philadelphia, but it was enough to keep the college alive from a purely legal standpoint. Between 1860 and 1889, the non-functioning college officially had two presidents—Father Felix Barbelin, SJ (who served until shortly before his death in 1869) and Father Burchard Villiger, SJ. Father Villiger was a longtime fixture in the Maryland Province who also served as president of both Santa Clara College and St. Ignatius College (the University of San Francisco) in California during and after the Civil War. After his return from California, the Maryland Jesuits stationed Villiger in Philadelphia in 1868. Although Villiger's assignment was technically to serve as pastor of Old St. Joseph's Church, the Jesuits obviously expected something more than pastoral work from a man of his status and experience. The task of resurrecting Saint Joseph's College fell squarely on his shoulders. These two "presidents," along with a "board of trustees" consisting of other Jesuits who met annually as a technicality, allowed Saint Joseph's College to continue to exist in the eyes of the state even though it did not graduate any students for three decades.[71]

Before his death, Father Barbelin had purchased property in North Philadelphia for the purpose of building a new school. Father Villiger developed it, starting with the impressive Church of the Gesù, completed in 1888. As Saint Joseph's historian David Contosta speculates, "It is . . . probable that his successful gamble at Santa Clara, where attractive new buildings had served as a self-advertisement for the col-

---

69. "Students in Our Colleges in the U. States and Canada," *Woodstock Letters* XXIV, no. 3 (1895): unnumbered page.

70. "Students in Our Colleges in the United States and Canada, October 1, 1915," *Woodstock Letters* XLIV, no. 3 (1915): unnumbered page.

71. Contosta, *Saint Joseph's*, 36–41.

lege, influenced Villiger's decision to put up an imposing new church."[72] The college reopened the following year as a tuition-free institution, with both a commercial and a classical track to serve the working-class boys.

Saint Joseph's was able to avoid charging tuition in part because of a generous bequest of $72,000 from a local businessman, Francis Drexel, one of the wealthiest Catholics in the United States.[73] Few families have done as much for American higher education as the Drexels of Philadelphia. Francis's daughter, known today as St. Katharine Drexel, established the Sisters of the Blessed Sacrament to minister to Black Catholics in the South. In 1925, she became the founding mother of America's only Catholic, historically Black college: Xavier University of Louisiana (located in New Orleans). Francis's brother, Anthony Drexel, founded the (secular) school now known as Drexel University in Philadelphia in 1891. Today, the main library at Saint Joseph's University is named in Francis Drexel's honor.

Saint Joseph's would remain on its new campus in North Philadelphia until the 1920s, when it relocated to its current campus in the Overbrook/Wynnefield area of town straddling the city limits. The "original" campus in North Philadelphia—actually the third campus in the extended history of the school—remains home to Saint Joseph's Preparatory School and the Church of the Gesù.

Brooklyn College (1906–1921), Brooklyn, New York

The circumstances that brought the New York Jesuits across the Hudson River to Jersey City were similar to those that brought them across the East River to Brooklyn. By the turn of the century, the Brooklyn Diocese already had two major Catholic men's colleges: St. Francis College (operated by the Franciscan Brothers near downtown) and the College of St. John the Baptist (operated by the Vincentians in Bedford-Stuyvesant.) Today, the latter school is known as St. John's University and its main campus is located in Queens.

With other options available, a Jesuit school in the borough had never been a high priority. However, Brooklyn's second bishop, Charles McDonnell, was a graduate of St. Francis Xavier College in Manhattan and an enthusiast for the Jesuit style of education. He was convinced that a Jesuit college was necessary in his rapidly growing diocese and lobbied his former professors in Manhattan to expand.[74]

In 1906, the Maryland-New York Province decided that it could justify a college in Brooklyn given its finances and its personnel. This proved to be a rather costly misjudgment. For a campus, the Jesuits purchased land that once housed the Kings County Penitentiary at an exorbitant cost of over $200,000, which cursed the school

---

72. Ibid., 41.
73. Ibid., 43, 51–52.
74. Bender, *Brief History of the New York Province*, 22.

with an immense debt from which it was never able to recover. Brooklyn College opened its doors to students in 1908 and received a temporary charter from the state the same year, but its debt was so enormous that it was having trouble meeting day-to-day operating expenses.[75] Almost immediately, it was obvious throughout the province that Brooklyn College would have to close, but through some legal sleight of hand and emotional decision making, the Jesuits were able to preserve it a few more years.

A Reckoning in the East: World War I Closes Saint Peter's and Brooklyn Colleges

World War I damaged eastern Jesuit education in more ways than one. In 1916, German spies planted explosives on a train carrying a shipment of weaponry through Jersey City en route to Europe; the explosion, which became known as the Black Tom Incident, was only a mile from Saint Peter's College and caused $12,000 in damage to the church and school.[76] Even more significant was the war's effect on enrollment. The fighting, combined with the resulting Spanish Flu epidemic of 1918, greatly reduced the population of college-age males through death and dislocation. No Jesuit colleges were more vulnerable to these changes than the commuter schools, which relied on local students to survive.

When the war broke out, the Maryland-New York Province was already in the process of reconfiguring its New York colleges. At a 1912 meeting on the Fordham campus, the Jesuits concluded that they were sponsoring too many schools in the New York City area, and decided to consolidate the undergraduate divisions of St. Francis Xavier College, Brooklyn College, and Saint Peter's College into Fordham. This meant that Fordham would become the Province's largest university and the other three colleges would be downgraded to feeder high schools.[77]

St. Francis Xavier College, the oldest of the trio, was the first casualty. It sent its college-level students and faculty to Fordham almost immediately in 1912, permanently redefining itself as Xavier High School. The other colleges proved more durable. Saint Peter's College and Brooklyn College were both located outside of the Archdiocese of New York, so other bishops had to be consulted and the political considerations associated with closing the schools were more complicated. The situation in the Brooklyn Diocese was particularly sensitive, since the Jesuits had made a commitment to Bishop McDonnell, a loyal supporter of Jesuit education, just six years earlier. To complicate matters further, the president of Brooklyn College, John O'Rourke, SJ, proved to be less compliant than his colleagues at St. Francis Xavier, vigorously defending the interests of the six-year-old school to his superiors, even as it hemorrhaged money.[78]

---

75. Ibid., 22.
76. Ibid., 26.
77. Shelley, *Fordham*, 118.
78. Ibid., 119.

World War I rendered these concerns moot. In 1919, Father Joseph Rockwell, SJ, the head of the Maryland-New York Province, reported to Rome that nearly all of the province's commuter colleges (including Saint Joseph's, Loyola-Baltimore, Saint Peter's, and Brooklyn) were on the chopping block due to the shortage of professors and students. In the latter three schools, there were no longer any college-age students registered at all. The only remaining students were all in the high school divisions.[79]

Ultimately, Saint Joseph's survived the war because it landed a Students Army Training Corps (SATC) contract from the federal government that helped to pay for operating expenses and fill otherwise idle classrooms. Loyola did not even attempt to secure an SATC unit; its building was too small, and the Jesuits did not want it to compete with Georgetown's bid. Instead, they chose to suspend Loyola's college-level classes and temporarily relocate its undergraduate faculty to Georgetown. Loyola was spared total closure, however, because it was the only Catholic men's college in Baltimore.[80] Boston College, which until very recently had been a commuter school, was apparently never in danger; it had just moved to a spacious new campus in Chestnut Hill in 1913, anticipating future growth.

For Saint Peter's and Brooklyn Colleges, the war signaled the end of the struggle to survive. Saint Peter's formally suspended its collegiate division (which had been empty for a year anyway) in 1919. Thereafter, it continued to operate as a high school until a small group of determined Jesuits reopened the college division in 1930. Thus, Saint Peter's as we know it today is more properly understood as a college that began its life in the twentieth century.

Brooklyn College, which was practically on life support when the war began, went down kicking and screaming. Beset by debt, the school was in danger of losing its provisional charter, which was due to expire in 1913. President John O'Rourke, SJ creatively worked around this issue by legally redefining Brooklyn College as a high school, but continuing to award bachelor's degrees under the charter of St. Francis Xavier College, which by then was no longer operating as an undergraduate institution. Thus, at the same time St. Francis Xavier's college-level students and faculty were relocating to Fordham, its charter to grant degrees was being appropriated in Brooklyn. Students who graduated from Brooklyn College technically received their degrees from St. Francis Xavier, a college that no longer existed, except in the eyes of the law.[81]

It was an unworkable arrangement. After operating in this legal limbo through the end of the war, the Jesuits finally gave up, and in 1921, put an end to any pretense that the school they were operating in Brooklyn was anything but a high school. The undergraduate division of Brooklyn College shut its doors for good. It was perhaps more than a coincidence that Bishop Charles McDonnell, who had pushed so hard to

79. Varga, *Baltimore's Loyola*, 208. Contosta, *Saint Joseph's*, 76–77. Bender, *Brief History of the New York Province*, 32–33.

80. Varga, *Baltimore's Loyola*, 208. Contosta, *Saint Joseph's*, 76–77.

81. Shelley, *Fordham*, 120. Bender, *Brief History of the New York Province*, 22–23.

establish a Jesuit college in Brooklyn, died that same year, removing the last political barrier to the college's closure.

The high school division in Brooklyn, however, survived. Brooklyn Preparatory School (as it became known after 1927) continued to operate as an all-male Jesuit high school until its closure in 1972. The campus is now the site of the City University of New York's Medgar Evers College. CUNY's modern-day Brooklyn College, founded in 1930, is an unrelated institution.

Making Universities out of Georgetown and Fordham

Like their colleagues in the Midwest, the East Coast Jesuits sought to respond to trends in education and develop at least some of their colleges into proper universities, with multiple professional schools and a variety of undergraduate and graduate degrees.

The Missouri Jesuits technically had a flagship university at St. Louis, but as they liberally built up Marquette, Creighton, Detroit, and Loyola (Chicago) to university status, those schools all challenged Saint Louis University in size and prestige. The East Coast Jesuits were in a slightly different situation. For generations, Georgetown had been the marquee university of the old Maryland Province, while St. John's College at Fordham was the centerpiece of the old New York Mission. When this province and mission combined in 1879, the two factions naturally promoted the interests of their own schools. This led to controversy over which university—Georgetown or Fordham—deserved to get the bulk of the province's money and attention.

Arguments could be made on both sides. Georgetown was older, was better established in the American academic community, and was the only eastern Jesuit school that could boast a clientele of some means and status in American society. It already had a medical school that predated the Civil War (1851), and in the postwar era, it opened or affiliated with schools of law (1870) and dentistry (1901). It had been a "university" officially since its charter in 1815, and by the 1890s, it was enrolling a few dozen graduate students in the arts and sciences.

St. John's College (Fordham) had the advantage of location. New York City was a significantly larger commercial center than Washington, DC. Washington's biggest economic engine, the federal government, was still relatively small and provided fewer prospects for fundraising and employment than New York. New York was home to the Maryland-New York Province's headquarters, and after 1909, was the home of the Jesuits' flagship publication, *America* magazine.

In 1907, St. John's College officially changed its name to Fordham University. It established its own schools of medicine and law (both in 1905), a school of pharmacy (1912), and a Teachers' College (1916). Stemming from the New York Jesuits' interest in human rights and urban poverty, it also opened a School of Sociology and Social Service (comparable to a modern-day school of social work) in 1916. Finally, between 1912 and 1921, the Jesuits folded their three smaller New York-area colleges into

Fordham, greatly increasing its undergraduate population. Fordham seemed poised for immense growth and was, to all appearances, a good investment for the Jesuit province.

Another issue that exposed the cleavages in the new province was the location of its main seminary. In 1869, the Maryland Jesuits built a seminary at rural Woodstock, Maryland, dubbing it the College of the Sacred Heart. More commonly known as Woodstock College, its student body consisted entirely of Jesuits-in-training. Prior to that time, the Maryland Province had struggled with where to educate its seminarians, who completed various stages of their education at the old St. John's Literary Institute in Frederick, at Georgetown, and briefly at the Boston Seminary before it became Boston College.

When Woodstock opened its doors, all of the faculty and students who were at the time engaged in theological studies at Georgetown relocated. Even though Jesuit colleges were not organized into "departments" during this era, it might be said that the rough equivalent of Georgetown's "theology department" moved to Woodstock. The move was meant to provide a more reflective atmosphere and fewer distractions for the seminarians, but the construction costs for the new seminary were high—more than a quarter-million dollars.[82]

Woodstock became a bedrock institution in American Jesuit life and trained many of the priests who went on to lead Jesuit universities from coast to coast for the next century. It may have been best known for its newsletter, *The Woodstock Letters*, which chronicled Jesuit news and history for a national audience. As a school of theology, it developed a strong academic reputation and its faculty were respected scholars. However, the isolated location was inconvenient, and in the newly united Maryland-New York Province there was strong sentiment that the seminary should be relocated to Fordham or back to Georgetown so that it could benefit from the resources and facilities of an actual Jesuit university. The Jesuit superior general in Rome, Franz Xavier Wernz, SJ, preferred Fordham "because he regarded New York City rather than Washington, DC as the intellectual and cultural capital of the United States."[83] The old Maryland guard within the province found this suggestion offensive, and vigorously defended the need for strong Jesuit institutions south of the Mason-Dixon Line. Since the province headquarters was now in New York, the center of gravity for Jesuit activity was shifting northward, and the older Maryland Jesuits jealously guarded whatever provincial assets they had left in their traditional home base.

After considering multiple locations in New York City and in the Hudson Valley, the Jesuits simply kept Woodstock where it was. The epilogue of the controversy is doubly ironic. Woodstock continued to educate priests in rural Maryland until its 100th anniversary in 1969, when it finally relocated to New York City. By then, however, fewer men were entering the Jesuit order and Woodstock became a casualty of declining vocations in 1974. Many of its assets, including its library, relo-

---

82. Curran, *History of Georgetown Vol. I*, 277.
83. Shelley, *Fordham*, 194.

cated to Georgetown. Thus, after all the controversy over whether Woodstock rightfully belonged at Fordham or Georgetown, parts of it ultimately went to both, but it never truly functioned as a seminary at either.

Competition with the Catholic University of America

During the late 1800s, Fordham had one other advantage over Georgetown in the race to become the province's leading university: ecclesial politics. In 1887, the Catholic bishops of the United States founded the Catholic University of America in Washington, DC less than five miles from Georgetown. As the school's name implies, the bishops' original intent and expectation was that it would indeed be "the" Catholic University of the United States—the most comprehensive and prestigious research institution within the American Catholic education system. It would operate strictly as a graduate school, and would offer master's, doctoral, and professional programs of interest to the Catholic Church. The country's many Catholic undergraduate colleges and universities would feed their alumni into it, making it the leading intellectual center of the Church in America.

It was an unusually top-down approach to education from bishops, who typically left the business of running colleges and universities to religious orders. However, it was also a genuine attempt on the bishops' part to keep up with educational trends. In the late 1800s, the German model of higher education—wherein a university exists primarily to conduct research and create new knowledge, rather than to teach students—was coming to America. The Johns Hopkins University in Baltimore was the first American university founded on this graduate-only model, and it was destined to change the way American higher education worked. The Catholic Church had to participate in this trend in order for its education system to remain relevant, but there was serious doubt that the American Catholic community had the resources to create any university with a scope and mission on par with that of Johns Hopkins. The bishops stepped in because no one else could.

There was only one problem: several other Catholic colleges around the country were taking baby steps toward becoming universities themselves. The biggest obstacle to Catholic University's success was Georgetown and its competing programs. Not wanting to provoke the ire of the US bishops, the Jesuit hierarchy ordered Georgetown to de-emphasize its burgeoning graduate programs. Although Georgetown had enrolled a few dozen graduate students per year in the 1890s, the number fell to zero from 1907 to 1914 and did not return to double-digits until 1920.[84] In this environment, Fordham, not Georgetown, certainly seemed like a safer political option to develop into the flagship Jesuit university in the East.

An even bigger issue was Georgetown's well-established law and medical schools, both of which had excellent reputations in Washington, DC. In 1894, Archbishop

---

84. Curran, *History of Georgetown Vol. II*, 395–396. Power, *Catholic Higher Education*, 217–218.

Francisco Satolli, the Apostolic Nuncio to the United States, ordered the Jesuits to transfer control of both schools to the Catholic University of America, framing the request as the desire of the pope himself. This was probably an exaggeration; by all accounts, the request was Satolli's, but he did speak for the pope in such matters. Although the Jesuits at Georgetown were unhappy with the prospect of losing the two professional schools, there was very little they could do to prevent it without breaking their vows of obedience.[85]

The saving grace for Georgetown's law and medical schools came not from the university's Jesuit leadership, but from its law and medical faculty, most of whom were laymen and non-Catholic. Virtually all of the professors at both schools protested that they would walk away from their jobs rather than accept the reassignment. The dean of Georgetown Medical School wrote to Archbishop Satolli refusing to cooperate, pointing out that most of his faculty were not Catholic and therefore were not persuaded by the wishes of the pope. The Jesuits sided with their faculty, explaining that Georgetown's long history of diversity and tolerance made it an attractive place for non-Catholics to work, whereas Catholic University's expressly religious name and mandate would make it toxic to many in the American academic community. Archbishop Satolli backed down, and both Georgetown's law and medical schools stayed put.[86]

In the end, the eastern Jesuits did not have to choose between Georgetown and Fordham, and they developed both schools into large and comprehensive research institutions. Beginning in the 1920s, they did the same at Boston College, which rapidly added professional schools of its own to carve out a place in the crowded Boston education scene. Still, some rivalry between Georgetown, Fordham, and Boston College persisted. Fordham aggressively expanded through the 1920s and 1930s until, in 1935, it briefly lost accreditation from the Association of American Universities. Although (as will be described later) the rationale for the decision was suspect, it devastated Fordham's reputation and essentially allowed Georgetown to move forward unopposed as the leading Catholic university in the East.[87]

In understanding the Jesuits' motivations during this time period, it is important to remember that they always sought to do what was best for the full network of schools that they operated, not necessarily what was best for any one institution. Unlike other teaching orders who operated only one college, like the Augustinians (Villanova) or Spiritans (Duquesne), the Jesuits' goal was often to serve the greatest number of students and spread their influence as widely as possible, not to concentrate their resources on one school to develop it into the best university possible. As historian Philip Gleason observed, this meant that the "needs of any single institution had to be evaluated in terms of the overall welfare of the Society. Sometimes this involved

---

85. Power, *Catholic Higher Education*, 217–218.

86. Ibid., 217–218. Curran, *History of Georgetown Vol. II*, 14–15.

87. Shelley, *Fordham*, 267–268.

decisions injurious to a college. . . . But such decisions, though sometimes mistaken, were quite rational when considered in the light of the Society's larger needs."[88]

Western Jesuit Colleges, 1865–1918

Half a continent away from New York were the still-thriving Jesuit missions to the Native Americans west of the Mississippi. While the East Coast Jesuits worked to combat the problems associated with overpopulation in America's largest urban areas, their colleagues in the far west were still working as missionaries in regions that had few urban areas at all.

For an order that prided itself on being first on the scene wherever a college was needed—and that tended to stake out land claims in promising cities before the outside world fully recognized those cities' potential—the west was a tantalizing region. It was inevitable that the Jesuits would expand there. At the end of the Civil War, there were only two Jesuit colleges west of Kansas, both located in the San Francisco Bay Area and both managed by Italian missionaries from the Turin Province. But the Jesuits also had a significant, longstanding presence in the Native American communities throughout the Rocky Mountains and the Pacific Northwest, where they were respected preachers, church-builders, and translators. Before World War I, those missions would coalesce to form new Jesuit colleges in New Mexico, Colorado, and Washington State. The California Jesuits would expand south to Los Angeles and San Jose. Although much of this activity was overseen by the Turin Province, the Turin Jesuits received ample help from an entirely new wave of Italian missionaries from Naples.

Las Vegas College (1877–1888), Las Vegas, New Mexico

The twin cities of Albuquerque and Santa Fe date to Spanish colonial days. By the nineteenth century, they were the only major urban settlements in the New Mexico Territory and were among the most isolated pockets of population anywhere in the United States. Like New Orleans, Mobile, and other cities founded by Catholics during the colonial era, Albuquerque was built around a church—in this case, the adobe Church of San Felipe de Neri, built by the region's original Franciscan missionaries in 1706 and located in the heart of the city's Old Town. In 1867, Italian Jesuits from Naples took control of the more than 150-year-old parish and made it their base of operations for a new mission to the southern Rocky Mountains. At the time, Albuquerque had only been part of the United States for about twenty years; its population included primarily Spanish-speaking Catholics who traced their roots to the Mexican era, Native Americans, and a trickle of English-speaking ranchers and frontiersmen migrating from the East.

---

88. Gleason, "First Century," 50.

The Naples Jesuits who came to Albuquerque in the 1860s represent the last and smallest branch of the American Jesuit family tree. Although they were Italian like their colleagues in California, they belonged to a different province and made the decision to come to the United States independently. The circumstances that brought them across the Atlantic were similar to those that brought the German Jesuits to Buffalo at roughly the same time. Southern Italy was in the process of unifying under Giuseppe Garibaldi, who forced the Jesuits out of Naples by confiscating their property.[89] Once again, Europe's instability was America's gain, resulting in a surplus of Jesuit teachers suddenly available to serve in the United States. The Naples Jesuits built two colleges in New Mexico and Colorado that quickly merged into a third, known today as Regis University in Denver. Their leader was an energetic Italian in his thirties, Donato Gasparri, SJ, and his vision shaped the entire mission.

Father Gasparri's first educational project was a school in Albuquerque that he called Holy Family College. Although he began advertising the school in 1872 and apparently secured a building for it, it is not clear whether any students enrolled or any instruction took place. What we do know is that the Jesuits abandoned the project by 1875, having failed to obtain a charter from the territorial government despite Gasparri's intense lobbying.[90]

Two years later, the Jesuits received a $3,000 donation from the Sisters of Loretto that revitalized their ambitions. Gasparri and his colleagues began planning for a new college in Las Vegas, a town sixty miles east of Santa Fe (and not to be confused with the more famous gambling city in Nevada, which would not even exist for another three decades). The Jesuits originally intended to name the school St. Mary's College, but the Christian Brothers (who had beaten the Jesuits to the New Mexico Territory) were already operating an elementary school with a similar name nearby. To avoid confusion, the Jesuits quickly renamed their school Las Vegas College.[91]

In 1877, the Jesuits opened Las Vegas College in the private home of a local resident, Dom Francisco Lopez. Once again, they sought to incorporate the institution legally, and this time the territorial legislature in Santa Fe approved the bill. However, the unelected territorial governor, Samuel Beach Axtell, vetoed it when it reached his desk—most likely under pressure from greedy American land speculators who viewed the lingering Mexican/Catholic influence in New Mexico as a threat to their business interests.[92]

The Jesuits objected to the veto, pointing out that their proposal was identical to the charter that had been approved for St. Michael's College, the Christian Brothers' college in Santa Fe, just four years earlier. Responding to the controversy, Governor Axtell addressed the legislative chamber in person, where he shared his unabashedly

---

89. Harold L. Stansell, SJ, *Regis: On the Crest of the West* (Denver: Regis University, 1977), 2.

90. Ibid., 5–6. "Varia," *Woodstock Letters* VII, no. 2 (1878): 132–133. "Las Vegas College, New Mexico," *Woodstock Letters* VII, no. 1 (1878): 40–43.

91. Stansell, *Regis*, 8–9.

92. Ibid., 14–15. "Varia." *Woodstock Letters* VII no. 2. (1878): 132–133. "Las Vegas College, New Mexico," 40–43.

prejudiced rationale. Although he objected to a few legal technicalities in the bill—including the fact that the proprietors of the college were not US citizens—he made it clear that his real issue with the Jesuit college was that it was *Jesuit*:

> It is difficult to decide whether the man (Father Gasparri) who seeks to establish the Society or the Society which he seeks to establish is worse. Both are so bad that you cannot decide between them. This Neapolitan adventurer, Gasparri, teaches the public that his dogmas and assertions are superior to the statutes of the United States and the laws of the Territory. No doctrine or teaching can be more dangerous to good government than this; especially in New Mexico where the mass of the people are ignorant. . . . The Society which he seeks to establish in New Mexico is worthy of just such a leader. It has been denounced time and again by the head of the Catholic Church, and justly expelled from the most enlightened countries of Europe.[93]

The territorial legislature nevertheless overrode the governor's veto, and Las Vegas College received its charter in 1878. However, Governor Axtell was so vehemently opposed to the Jesuits that he appealed to the United States Congress, which still held ultimate authority over territories that had not yet achieved statehood. In Washington, Axtell's appeal fell on the sympathetic ears of Senator James Blaine, Congressman William Frye, and others who opposed the growing influence of Catholic schools in America; by a two-thirds vote in Washington, the House and the Senate sided with Axtell in 1879, effectively revoking Las Vegas College's charter after it had been in effect for a full year.[94]

Nonetheless, by 1880, the college had moved into a two-story adobe building that became the "chief attraction in town," though there was admittedly little competition for that honor.[95] A Jesuit serving on the faculty reported that the Mexican-American students were shockingly poor, but that the school was slowly improving their economic prospects. The priests were working night and day in the community, even though, "Oftentimes there is not sufficient money in the house to pay for the next meal. Truly, the love of God alone could make men waste away their lives in such a desert."[96] The same Jesuit professor commented on the local cuisine: "The 'chile,' a species of red pepper, I cannot eat; but if you could only see how the boys take it,—it is a sort of ice cream and strawberries for them."[97]

Las Vegas College became a cultural pillar of the community in a region that severely lacked modern education. It introduced students to theater, debate, and books for the first time in their lives. It staged theatrical performances that were unlike anything the isolated locals had ever seen. Over the course of its eleven-year

---

93. As quoted in "Las Vegas College, New Mexico," 42–43.
94. Stansell, *Regis*, 15–16.
95. M. T. Hughes, SJ, "New Mexico," *Woodstock Letters*, IX, no. 2 (1880): 134.
96. Ibid., 135.
97. Ibid., 139.

lifespan, it exerted an important influence on the community, but because so few students were capable of paying tuition, it was almost entirely a charity and became unsustainable. Greener pastures (literally and figuratively) soon beckoned a few hundred miles to the north.

Regis University (1888), Denver, Colorado

In 1883, the first bishop of Denver, French-born Joseph Machebeuf, attended the year-end awards ceremony at Las Vegas College. He was friendly with the New Mexico Jesuits, having served previously as a diocesan official in Santa Fe, and he used the opportunity to invite them to establish a second college in Colorado. The president of Las Vegas College, the Italian-born Father Dominic Pantanella, SJ, readily agreed in principle. The following year, Bishop Machebeuf purchased a former hotel in the mountain town of Morrison, located southwest of Denver at the very base of the Rockies, and offered it to the Jesuits as a potential school building. Although Morrison was farther from the urban core than the Jesuits would have liked, they seized the opportunity and opened Sacred Heart College on the site. Father Pantanella moved north to serve as the new college's first president. Both sides agreed that the building would be only temporary; eventually the bishop and the Jesuits both expected that the school would relocate to Denver.[98]

Sacred Heart College operated in Morrison for four years. It was so remote that it could not attract commuter students, but fortunately, the old hotel was ready-made to house boarding students and their live-in Jesuit teachers. By 1887, the Jesuits were actively seeking a more permanent campus. Father Pantanella seriously considered relocating the school to Colorado Springs, more than eighty miles to the south, and even bought property in that city—but Bishop Machebeuf was adamant that Denver take priority.[99] Fortunately, a perfect solution to the problem soon arose when a wealthy Denver landowner, John Brisben Walker, made a generous donation.

Walker was a native of the Pittsburgh region who had attended both Gonzaga College in Washington, DC, and Georgetown. His career took many different paths, but he was best known as a writer and publisher, having worked at newspapers in both the nation's capital and Cincinnati. By the 1880s, he was living in Denver, where he owned a large alfalfa ranch and sent two sons to the Jesuit college in Morrison. Grateful for his own Jesuit education and that of his children, he offered the Italian missionaries any forty acres of his undeveloped property. The plot that Pantanella chose remains the campus of Regis University to this day. A few years later, the entrepreneurial Walker sold the rest of his ranch and eventually became the owner and publisher of *Cosmopolitan* magazine in New York.[100]

---

98. Stansell, *Regis*, 20–21, 25, 37.

99. Ibid., 36–37.

100. Ibid., 28, 43–45.

The Jesuits relocated Sacred Heart College to the new site in 1888, and simultaneously decided to close their college in New Mexico, merging the two institutions into one. Although Las Vegas College had started with great potential, it was becoming increasingly untenable after eleven years of existence. A high percentage of its Mexican and Mexican-American students paid their tuition bills in livestock or grain rather than cash. Railroads first came to the city in 1879, and while they brought some Jesuit reinforcements from the east, they also brought settlers and criminals attracted by the town's semi-lawless atmosphere. Las Vegas was developing a reputation as an unsafe pocket of the Wild West, beset by drunkards and gunslinger violence. (One Jesuit observed that it was actually the rough-and-tumble transients, not the long-established Mexican-American residents, who were most responsible for the town's high murder rate.) At the same time, the Jesuits were increasingly at loggerheads with the new bishop of Santa Fe, who sought to limit the pastoral and sacramental work they could perform in the diocese.[101]

The Denver campus had far more promise. Although Father Pantanella supervised most of the construction in Denver, it was actually his colleague, Father Salvatore Personè, SJ, who became the first president of the unified school in 1888. Personè was the sitting president of Las Vegas College, so his leadership would give the old college continuity even as it abandoned its campus. There were 152 students in the first combined class in Denver, including 29 from Las Vegas and 27 from Morrison.[102] In 1893, Sacred Heart received its collegiate charter from the young Colorado government.

Sacred Heart College operated primarily as a classical liberal arts school for the remainder of its life under the Italians missionaries. In 1910, the Naples mission to the Rockies was dissolved and responsibility for the college fell to the Missouri Province, giving the Missouri Jesuits a mammoth footprint that stretched from Cleveland in the east to Denver in the west, including ten colleges and universities.[103] Thereafter, Sacred Heart benefitted from an influx of experienced administrators from the Missouri Province who had honed their skills at schools like Loyola (Chicago), Marquette, and Creighton. Even though the Denver college faced serious debt and accreditation issues that threatened its very existence in the twentieth century, the Missouri Jesuits were experienced enough to guide it through those challenges.

Shortly after the Missouri Jesuits took over, in 1921, Sacred Heart College changed its name to Regis College in honor of St. John Francis Regis, SJ, a seventeenth-century French Jesuit who had spent part of his career preaching in the mountainous regions of Europe. There were several reasons for the name change. The college's original initials, S.H.C., led some students to refer to it as "The Shack," which was thought to be undignified. Cheers from rival colleges on the athletic fields, where

101. Ibid., 11. Hughes, "New Mexico," 135–138. "New Mexico," *Woodstock Letters* XIII, no. 1 (1884): 42–43. Frank Morris, "Regis . . . The College the Pioneers Built," *Roundup Magazine* (Spring 1958): 12–14, https://epublications.regis.edu/cgi/viewcontent.cgi?article=1018&context=roundup.

102. Stansell, *Regis*, 48–50.

103. Morris, "Regis," 14.

opposing teams threatened to do unspeakable things to "Sacred Heart," were beginning to sound religiously offensive. [104] The name change was also an opportunity to honor a Jesuit saint—one whom the original Belgian pioneers of the Missouri Province were known to have venerated. [105] Left unsaid was the fact that the less overtly religious moniker could help to attract students in a state where Catholics were a relatively small minority. Moreover, the name, "University of Denver" had already been claimed by the Methodist institution across town.

The Naples Jesuits never developed any graduate or professional schools at the college, and once the Missouri Jesuits took over, it remained small compared to the other universities in the province. Overall, the Missouri Jesuits did relatively little to develop graduate or professional schools at any of the colleges that they inherited from the Germans (John Carroll, St. John's, and Campion) or from the Italians (Regis) at the turn of the century. All four of these schools remained small liberal arts institutions and, moreover, St. John's and Campion both closed. (To be fair, the Missouri Province had its hands full with more fundamental concerns, like keeping the schools alive. It gave Regis $100,000 in 1945 to help pay off the college's debt, and helped John Carroll relocate to its new suburban campus in the 1930s.) In terms of its enrollment, Regis remained primarily a high school and was technically only accredited as a junior college through the 1930s. It was not fully accredited to grant bachelor's degrees until 1952, and did not achieve university status until 1991. [106]

Although the American Jesuits built a total of four colleges (and one seminary) that they originally dubbed "Sacred Heart College," none survived under that name. Those in Colorado, Wisconsin, and Florida all changed their names, while the college in Georgia and the seminary in Woodstock, Maryland closed permanently. The popularity of the name reflects the fact that Jesuits have a special devotion to the Sacred Heart of Jesus; the image is associated with a seventeenth-century French Jesuit, St. Claude La Colombière, SJ. Sacred Heart Basilica in Conewago, Pennsylvania, founded by the Jesuits in the 1700s, is believed to be the oldest church in the western hemisphere with that name.

Gonzaga University (1887), Spokane, Washington

The Jesuits were among the first Europeans to live and work permanently among the Native Americans of the Pacific Northwest, and in 1833, they received a formal mandate from Pope Gregory XVI to evangelize the indigenous people of the United States. Like most Jesuit activities west of the Mississippi, the missions in the northern Rockies were originally a project of the Belgian Jesuits who operated Saint Louis University. Many times, the Jesuits sent missionaries at the invitation of the natives themselves, who "did not view (the European priests) as Americans" and therefore did not

---

104. Stansell, *Regis*, 80–81.
105. Garraghan, *Jesuits of the Middle U.S. Vol. III*, 500.
106. Stansell, *Regis*, 153, 166.

hold them "accountable for repressive United States policy."[107] On three separate occasions between 1831 and 1839, representatives from the Salish (also known as the Flathead) tribe traveled more than 1,600 miles from their home in what is today Montana to visit Saint Louis University, where they hoped to request missionaries to come and live with them. The Salish had heard of the Jesuits through their trading contact with Iroquois and Canadian fur trappers, and were intrigued by stories of the "book of heaven" that the Jesuits reportedly used to preach and redeem souls.[108] As the Jesuits' reputation grew, other native tribes like the Coeur d'Alene of Idaho invited them onto their lands to establish schools.

Although he was by no means alone in his efforts, the Jesuit most associated with the western Indian missions was, once again, Saint Louis University professor and treasurer Pierre DeSmet, SJ. When he was not preaching and building churches in the west, DeSmet was touring Europe and the United States to raise money for the missions, dazzling audiences with stories that blended the romanticism of the Wild West with the pietism of the Jesuit missionary impulse. His fundraising tours made him something of a celebrity in Europe. He developed a reputation (which he did nothing to discourage) as a pioneer adventurer fighting to bring the trappings of the Catholic faith to eager western audiences—a kind of Catholic version of Buffalo Bill Cody and Wyatt Earp rolled into one.

So persuasive were DeSmet's abilities as a raconteur that he convinced dozens of young European Jesuits to volunteer for the western missions, among them the Italian co-founders of Santa Clara University, Michael Accolti, SJ, and John Nobili, SJ. By 1854, there were so many Italian missionaries on the American frontier that the Turin Province of the Society of Jesus formally assumed control of the mission network—which included Santa Clara as well as a growing number of mission outposts across what is today Montana, Idaho, Oregon, and Washington State.

In 1862, the Turin Jesuits sent a twenty-five-year-old recruit from Sicily off to the American missions, Giuseppe Cataldo, SJ. After briefly serving on the faculty at Santa Clara, Cataldo (who Anglicized his first name to Joseph after his arrival) found his true calling in the Rockies. His commitment to the region was so strong that, in 1877, he was named head of the entire mission. Unfortunately, the operation that Cataldo inherited was not healthy, literally or figuratively. The harsh conditions on the frontier were taking a toll on the Jesuit personnel, and most of the men Pierre DeSmet had originally recruited "were then either dead or disabled by old age," leaving the mission in dire need of reinforcements.[109]

Although he lacked DeSmet's charisma, the diminutive Father Cataldo proved to be an effective recruiter and manager. On tours of Europe and the eastern United

---

107. McKevitt, *Brokers*, 121.

108. Walt Crowley, *Seattle University: A Century of Jesuit Education* (Seattle: Seattle University, 1991), 19.

109. Gerald McKevitt, SJ, "The Jump that Saved the Rocky Mountain Mission: Jesuit Recruitment and the Pacific Northwest," *Pacific Historical Review* 55, no. 3 (1986): 431.

States, he netted more than thirty new Jesuit recruits, which enabled him and his successors to expand the mission's footprint. By the 1890s, that footprint included more than thirty churches and fifteen Indian schools with a combined enrollment of over 1,000. The financing for all of these activities came from private donations (including one from the Drexel family of Philadelphia, who also gave transformative gifts to Saint Joseph's College in that city), and from the federal government, which funded religious missions to the west until 1900.[110]

It was perhaps inevitable that at least one Jesuit college would emerge from this large network of missionary activity. Less than three years after he became head of the operation, Cataldo began to explore the possibility of opening a mission college in the young city of Spokane Falls, located in the eastern part of the Washington Territory. The city, which incorporated in 1881 and dropped the word "Falls" from its name in 1891, then had barely over a thousand residents, most of whom were employed in mining and timber. Cataldo liked the location mainly because it was central to the existing Jesuit missions. It had access to the region's original highway—the Spokane River— and to its newest form of transportation, the Northern Pacific Railroad (completed in 1883). All of this made it a relatively easy journey—or at least, what passed for an easy journey at the time—from the Indian schools that would presumably feed into it.

But even as the arrival of Northern Pacific Railroad made the Jesuits' work easier, it also changed the nature of that work in profound ways. The railroad was bringing settlers from the east, including some who were Catholic. Whereas the Jesuits had once worked strictly with the region's indigenous population, now they were under intense pressure to serve the growing roster of Catholic pioneers eking out a living in the northwestern forests. A college, Cataldo thought, could provide a necessary service to both groups.[111] He bought property for a campus in 1881, but had no immediate means to develop it.

In a fairly unusual development in American Jesuit history, the final push to establish a college in Spokane Falls came from civic, not ecclesial, authorities. As settlers poured in to the region straddling Washington and Idaho, and as those two territories moved toward statehood in the 1880s, local cities were competing to become the area's economic hub. In this arms race, higher education emerged as a priority. At the time, citizens of nearby towns like Cheney, Moscow, and Pullman were laying the groundwork for schools that would evolve, respectively, into Eastern Washington University (1882), the University of Idaho (1889), and Washington State University (1890). Western towns rose and fell on the whims of fickle industries, and many cities understood that they had to diversify their economies beyond mining and lumber to avoid becoming ghost towns after those resources were depleted.

Wisely, the citizens of Spokane Falls also identified higher education as an anchor industry that would ensure the city's future. Seeking a college of their own, a

---

110. Ibid., 428, 430, 438, 442, 450. McKevitt, *Brokers*, 122, 150.
111. McKevitt, "Jump," 434.

group of local settlers led by the city's future mayor and largest landowner, James Glover, wrote to Father Cataldo pledging $2,650 to support the proposed Jesuit institution. Since Cataldo had already bought undeveloped property for a campus along the Spokane River, the money was a welcome development.

There was only one issue with the donation: the civic leaders of Spokane insisted that the new school be open to white students only, not to Native Americans. This flew in the face of Cataldo's original vision; he had specifically wanted the college to be a place for Indian education, with white settlers almost as an afterthought. Still, disappointingly, he accepted the terms of the donation. The new college excluded Native Americans, at least at first. Given Cataldo's record, we can be certain that his decision was not motivated by racism toward the local indigenous people. He had spent virtually his entire career ministering to them, learning their languages, championing their rights, and fervently opposing, in his words, "'the universal neglect of the Indian Race in the American Republic.'"[112] He likely justified the decision on the grounds that Jesuit missionaries were already operating multiple schools and missions for the indigenous people—including one mission to the Spokane Indians just north of town—but no school for white students. Even if the two races could not be educated together, he had to acknowledge that the growing population of white settlers desperately needed an education, too. He also hoped that a successful all-white institution might someday become an attractive option for local Native Americans.[113] In that respect, at least, he was correct; in the long term, the college endured, but its racist admissions policies did not.

Cataldo named the new school Gonzaga College in honor of his fellow Jesuit and fellow Italian, St. Aloysius Gonzaga, SJ. In its inaugural school year (1887), Gonzaga had a problem virtually unheard of in Jesuit history—more faculty than it needed. A total of seventeen Jesuits were stationed at the school, which enrolled just seven boys. Certainly, the faculty-student ratio would have been more balanced if not for the whites-only admission policy; the Jesuits had a ready-made audience of Native American students within their own mission network who could have enrolled at the college that year. One Jesuit from out in the mission field, Father Joseph Joset, SJ, arrived on the college doorstep in 1887 with two Native American boys and attempted to register them for classes. When he was turned away, he became incredulous and chastised his colleagues for their closed-mindedness. After all, had they not all come to America to risk their lives in service to the very native people they were now excluding from the college? And didn't the natives have a better claim to being "American" than most of the Jesuits themselves, who were European?[114]

112. As quoted in Crowley, *Seattle University*, 21.

113. Jim Kersher, "Zag History 101," *The Spokesman Review* (July 8, 2007), https://www.spokesman.com/stories/2007/jul/08/zag-history-101/.

114. Michael M. Canaris, "*Alma Mater, Mater Exulum.* Jesuit Education and Immigration in America: A Moral Framework Rooted in History and Mission," in *Undocumented and in College: Students and Institutions in a Climate of National Hostility*, ed. Terry-Ann Jones and Laura Nichols (New York: Fordham University Press, 2017), 86.

Although Father Cataldo founded Gonzaga College, he never led the institution directly as president. His influence ran deep in the college's early leadership, however, and Gonzaga's surplus of faculty reflected his early successes in recruiting priests for the Rocky Mountain Mission. Seven of the thirty-one Jesuits he brought to the American west eventually served as Gonzaga's president.[115] The unusually robust faculty also reflected that the Rocky Mountain Mission was developing a reputation for lax recruitment standards in its own ranks. So desperate were the Rocky Mountain Jesuits to staff their dozens of projects that they accepted many prospective priests who had been turned away by Jesuit provinces farther east. These recruits often had passion for the work but lacked the skill to do it well, and, "In 1898 James Rebmann, then president of Gonzaga College, complained to the Jesuit superior general in Rome that many of these young men were 'good religious,' but few of them were intellectually gifted or sufficiently educated to be good teachers."[116]

Fortunately, the quality of the education at Gonzaga improved, and it soon became a college in law as well as in name. When Gonzaga opened its doors in 1887, a state charter was hard to come by, because the Washington Territory was itself still two years away from statehood and was busy making preparations for entering the union. In 1894, the young state legislature empowered Gonzaga to grant degrees, and in 1912, that charter was amended to elevate the college to university status. A law school opened that same year, and schools of education and engineering followed in the post–World War I era. While an education school was still uncommon in Jesuit circles, the engineering school was no surprise. In the shadow of two land-grant colleges, Washington State University and the University of Idaho, Gonzaga had little choice but to offer strong engineering and science programs.

Seattle University (1891), Seattle, Washington

By the 1890s, the influx of settlers from the east was fundamentally reshaping the demographics of the Pacific Northwest and redefining the nature of the Jesuits' work. Nowhere was this truer than in the region's emerging urban hub, Seattle. Because of a surge in Irish and German immigration in the 1870s and 1880s, Seattle now had the largest concentration of Catholics north of California. As the home of the University of Washington, it was overtaking other cities on Puget Sound—including Tacoma and the state capital, Olympia—as the region's dominant commercial and educational center. Yet no Jesuit had ever visited it. Joseph Cataldo had placed a big bet on Spokane's future and he remained committed to that city, but he could not ignore the pleas for help coming from Seattle almost 300 miles to the west. In 1890, Cataldo asked one of the Rocky Mountain Mission's young priests, French-born Father Augustine Laure, SJ, to visit Seattle on a fact-finding mission.[117]

---

115. McKevitt, "Jump," 444.

116. Ibid., 449.

117. Crowley, *Seattle University*, 22.

At the time, the local diocese was based in Vancouver, Washington, about 160 miles south of Seattle on the outskirts of Portland, Oregon. German-born Bishop Egidius Jünger had been badgering the Jesuits to open a school in Seattle, probably realizing that the diocese itself would eventually move there (which it did in 1907). As usual, the Jesuits did not have the resources take on such a commitment at the time, but as the largest order of priests in the Pacific Northwest, they were at least better positioned than any others to supply what the growing city needed. Bishop Jünger's offer became even harder to refuse when Father Laure, after arriving in Seattle, wrote back to Cataldo with glowing reviews. Compared to the remote Indian missions where Laure had spent most of his career, Seattle, with its 42,000 inhabitants, must have seemed like a metropolis.[118]

Cataldo was convinced. He dispatched a former Gonzaga faculty member, Leopold Van Gorp, SJ, to purchase land in the "big" city for a Catholic boys' school. Van Gorp bought a parcel from Arthur Denny, who just three decades earlier had donated the land for the University of Washington's original campus, but who now charged the Jesuits a king's ransom of more than $18,000.[119] Van Gorp's original purchase remains the site of Seattle University's main campus today, although it has not been in continuous use throughout the school's history.

Even though the Jesuits now had land for a campus, an impatient local priest, Francis Xavier Prefontaine, took it upon himself to open a Catholic school in Seattle in February, 1891, hoping both that it would pressure the Jesuits to expedite their own project and that it could fill the gap until the Jesuit school was up and running. Father Prefontaine named the school after his own patron saint, calling it St. Francis Hall. This slightly devious act had the desired effect; with a class of students already assembled, the Jesuit plans for Seattle leapt forward by a few months, and Cataldo agreed to send teachers to staff St. Francis Hall while a more permanent campus could be built on the property Father Van Gorp had purchased. In September, 1891, a pair of Jesuits from the Rocky Mountain Mission—the French-born Victor Garrand, SJ and the Dutch-born Adrian Sweere, SJ—assumed control of the school with a five-year lease from Father Prefontaine. They promptly renamed the church and school complex after the Immaculate Conception.[120]

At first, Immaculate Conception School was not substantially different in scope from some of the Indian schools that the Rocky Mountain Jesuits had been operating. It mainly enrolled young children in primary grades. The only major differences were its location (urban) and its immigrant student body. It soon became apparent that the school was meeting a sizable pent-up demand, as a large class of 90 boys enrolled. Assisting Fathers Garrand and Sweere on the faculty were three Catholic nuns from the order of the Holy Names of Jesus and Mary. Although the sisters taught mainly

---

118. Ibid., 22–23.
119. Ibid., 23.
120. Ibid., 23–25.

the youngest students, they were, in some sense, among the first female faculty members at an American Jesuit college. Like the Jesuits, the Sisters of the Holy Names were known for their work in the Pacific Northwest and had been operating a Catholic girls' school in Seattle since 1880. Historic Holy Names University in Oakland, California is the only surviving college that grew out of their many educational projects.[121]

For three years, Immaculate Conception School operated at the old St. Francis Hall location until, in 1894, Father Garrand succeeded in constructing a larger and more impressive building—known today as Garrand Hall—on the permanent campus. Despite an economic downturn in the United States, the Jesuits finished the building in just three years because of European bank loans they were able to obtain through their European contacts, and because most of the construction workers were either Jesuits or local parishioners who volunteered their labor.[122]

Timing was on the Jesuits' side. Seattle's best days of the nineteenth century began in 1896, when gold was discovered in the Canadian Klondike, and Seattle became the last stopping point for prospectors seeking to strike it rich in the Arctic. The Klondike Gold Rush seldom turned prospectors into millionaires, but it made extremely rich men out of any Seattle business owners with the foresight to invest in railroads, clothing, bacon, sugar, or the transportation networks that connected Seattle to Alaska and California. The Yukon's mineral wealth was fuel for Seattle's economic engine, and as the city boomed, the timing was right to expand Immaculate Conception School. In 1898, it received a collegiate charter from the state government, and changed its name to Seattle College. The name honored both the city itself and its namesake, Chief Seattle (or "Sealth") a nineteenth-century local indigenous leader who was baptized Catholic late in life.[123]

In its early days, Seattle College is best understood as a typical Jesuit downtown day school in the mold of St. Francis Xavier College of New York or St. Ignatius College in San Francisco. Jesuit behavior in Washington State followed the usual pattern, whereby the Jesuits built a "main" boarding college in a relatively small city (in this case, Gonzaga in Spokane) followed shortly thereafter by a downtown commuter college in a nearby large city. What other groups of Jesuits had already done in New York, Boston, New Orleans, Washington (DC), and San Francisco, the Rocky Mountain Jesuits did in Seattle. Nowhere was there a secret handbook that prescribed the Jesuits to do any of this, but the Jesuit ethos of education led different groups of Jesuits in different parts of the country to follow the same pattern of behavior independently.

Seattle College's early fortunes were tied to those of its sister school to the east—not only because Spokane was the headquarters of the entire Rocky Mountain Mission, but because most of Seattle College's early faculty and presidents had served pre-

---

121. Ibid., 23–25.
122. Ibid., 27.
123. Ibid., 31.

viously at Gonzaga. Much like the "other" pair of western Jesuit colleges in San Francisco and Santa Clara, the two Jesuit colleges in Washington State exchanged faculty and leadership regularly.

That web of connection soon expanded. Between 1907 and 1909, the Jesuit superior general in Rome united the old California and Rocky Mountain Missions to create the California Province. Gonzaga and Seattle were no longer under the supervision of their Italian bosses in Turin, and were now part of a single western Jesuit network that included Santa Clara and St. Ignatius (San Francisco). Seattle thereafter exchanged faculty with all four western Jesuit colleges. Its seventh and ninth presidents—Fathers Joseph Tomkin and William Boland—were experienced educators in California, while its eighth and tenth presidents—Fathers Jeffrey O'Shea and Walter Fitzgerald—had worked previously at Gonzaga.

A 1907 fire severely damaged the Garrand building, but unlike their reaction to previous college fires in Mobile, Grand Coteau, and Worcester, the Jesuits never seem to have seriously considered relocating Seattle College's students to a different Jesuit campus. Logically, the displaced students and faculty could have been sent to Gonzaga, but there was never any real doubt that the Jesuits would rebuild on Puget Sound. Seattle's Catholic population was growing quickly and the downtown college looked like an excellent long-term investment.[124]

A decade later, however, the combined effects of World War I and the 1918 Spanish Flu epidemic decimated Seattle College's enrollment, and Gonzaga came calling anyway. Because Seattle lacked a Student Army Training Corps program, most of its students transferred to Gonzaga to take advantage of the SATC unit in Spokane. Seattle College thereafter did not award any bachelor's degrees until 1925, when it granted three to a trio of young men who had transferred from Gonzaga to finish their studies.[125]

After essentially suspending its undergraduate program in 1918, Seattle College became a high school in everything but name. Apart from its accreditation, it was not much different from the two other high schools that were emerging from the Jesuits' old Indian mission network at the time: Loyola High School (1912) in Missoula, Montana and Marquette High School (1918) in Yakima, Washington. Seattle College's fortunes looked so bleak that in 1919 it abandoned its campus and relocated to a smaller property at the northern end of town—a location that unfortunately put it almost directly in the shadow of the University of Washington. There it remained until the Great Depression put a stop to further expansion plans. In desperation, the tiny college returned to its original campus, which fortunately had never been sold.[126]

Because of this long pause in its collegiate ambitions, Seattle University today is probably best understood as a college that emerged in the 1930s and 1940s, albeit with a substantial foundation from the generations that came earlier. The high school

---

124. Ibid., 34.
125. Ibid., 34–40.
126. Ibid., 42–43.

kept the germ of a college alive until the enrollment boom of the post-World War II era finally allowed the undergraduate and graduate programs to blossom.

Father Joseph Cataldo, whose vision had brought Gonzaga and Seattle Colleges into existence, lived to 91 years of age, and in the twilight of his life both colleges revered him as a founder. Tragically, he died in a car accident in 1928. As historian Walt Crowley wrote, "Cataldo, who had traversed the Pacific Northwest by horse, wagon, river raft, steamboat, locomotive, and most of all, on foot, was brought down by a missed curve on the road to Pendleton."[127] The City of Spokane "buried him with the honors due a founding father."[128]

California Colleges, 1865–1918

Prior to their 1909 merger, the California Mission and the Rocky Mountain Mission mainly focused on their own interests and projects. Ultimately, both groups answered to the same provincial in Turin, Italy, but the Jesuits of California and of the Pacific Northwest functioned as separate units.

The California Jesuits, who were even more homogenously Italian than their colleagues to the north, spent most of the late 1800s maintaining their two Bay Area colleges. A significant portion of their faculty were academically conservative, and as the University of California-Berkeley (1868) and Stanford University (1885) sprung up in their own backyard, the Jesuits doubled down on the classical *Ratio Studiorum* curriculum as a way to distinguish themselves from their competition.[129] Santa Clara still enjoyed a strong reputation as one of the two oldest colleges in California, but it was small compared to its neighbors, enrolling just 171 students (more than half of whom were in the high school division) in 1900. It remained healthy by Jesuit standards, but it was no longer the college of choice for California's ruling elite, as it had been when it first opened. St. Ignatius College (the future University of San Francisco) was larger, with 239 students, but only 59 of those were undergraduates.[130]

In 1883, the American-born Robert Kenna, SJ, became Santa Clara's first non-European (and only its second non-Italian) president. He attempted some modernization of the curriculum, but his superiors overruled him and pushed both Santa Clara and St. Ignatius Colleges deeper into the classical mold (hurting enrollment at both institutions).[131] Had Kenna been allowed to follow through on his visionary plans for the school, Santa Clara College might have developed into a university much sooner than it did.

---

127. Ibid., 42.

128. McKevitt, "Jump," 431.

129. McKevitt, *University of Santa Clara*, 124.

130. "Students in Our Colleges in the United States and Canada, Oct. 1, 1901," *Woodstock Letters* XXIX, no. 3 (1901): 550.

131. McKevitt, *University of Santa Clara*, 122–123.

In the end, a natural disaster sparked reform at both colleges. The devastating 1906 San Francisco earthquake destroyed St. Ignatius College, along with most of the surrounding neighborhood. Since the quake happened on April 18, with only two months to go in the school year, the graduating seniors from St. Ignatius relocated to Santa Clara to finish their studies.[132]

Because St. Ignatius had been the larger of the two schools—indeed, it was one of the largest Jesuit schools in the country at the time—there was never any doubt that it would be rebuilt. After a brief hiatus, it resumed classes in rented quarters west of downtown and, by the 1920s, came back stronger than ever on a much larger campus northeast of Golden Gate Park that remains the home of the University of San Francisco today. Unfortunately, the money the Jesuits sank into that location dashed plans already in the works to relocate and expand Santa Clara.

Since 1901, Santa Clara had been looking to abandon its historic mission campus for more spacious quarters in preparation for its expected future development as a university. It even acquired a 600-acre tract of property for that purpose near Mountain View, California—the future headquarters of Google in the heart of what would become Silicon Valley. Although Santa Clara itself was relatively undamaged by the 1906 earthquake, the total destruction of St. Ignatius College meant that virtually all of the Jesuits' resources would have to go to the rebuilding efforts there. Santa Clara abandoned plans to develop the Mountain View campus and, in 1926, sold the large property for $250,000.[133] To this day, the neighborhood—which now includes a country club and some extremely valuable residential homes—is known by the name the Jesuits gave it: Loyola Corners. Even though a quarter-million dollars was a sizeable sum in the 1920s, we can only imagine what that 600-acre parcel in Silicon Valley would have been worth if the Santa Clara Jesuits had held onto it for another eighty years!

With St. Ignatius College on a new, bigger campus and with Santa Clara recommitted to its old, existing one, the Jesuits decided to invest in the human capital of both schools and develop both into universities. Not coincidentally, the expansion began shortly after the creation of the California Province in 1909. By then, the changing nature of American higher education had made it clear—even to the conservative wing of the province—that Santa Clara and St. Ignatius had to offer more than a traditional liberal arts education to remain relevant.

At Santa Clara, the task of leading this expansion fell to an alumnus of the school (and protégé of Father Kenna), James Morrissey, SJ, who assumed the president's office in 1910. At St. Ignatius, it fell to Alberto Trivelli, SJ, a visionary leader who came to office in 1911 and also oversaw the school's relocation to its new campus after the earthquake. Once the decision was made, both colleges expanded rapidly. Santa Clara opened a law school in 1911, followed by a school of engineering in 1912. St.

132. Ibid., 155.
133. Ibid., 134, 202.

Ignatius College likewise opened a law school in 1912. Shortly after the First World War, Santa Clara (1923) and St. Ignatius (1925) both opened schools of business.

St. Joseph's College (1884–1898), San Jose, California

The California Jesuits' only failed project was a day college in San Jose, a mere five miles from Santa Clara. From the beginning, the faculty at Santa Clara College had done pastoral work among the people of San Jose, the nearest city to their campus. When Bishop Joseph Sadoc Alemany entrusted the Santa Clara Mission to the Jesuits for the purpose of building a college in 1851, he also entrusted to them San Jose's main Catholic parish—which was, like the city itself, named after St. Joseph. Like most of California's Catholic houses of worship at the time, St. Joseph's Church was a humble adobe structure. The Santa Clara Jesuits visited it whenever they could to bring the sacraments to the congregation.

In 1868, an earthquake destroyed the church and in 1875, a fire consumed its replacement. Rather than abandon the historic site in the heart of the growing city, the Jesuits opted to rebuild a larger and stronger structure. Between 1876 and 1886, they constructed the impressive building that stands today, with a soaring dome that has become a landmark in San Jose's central business district. As they footed the bill for this intense project, the Jesuits decided to make the most of the investment and opened a downtown day college on the site. In the lot next door to the church, they built a state-of-the-art brick and terra-cotta school building that featured San Jose's first elevator.[134] Apart from that modern marvel, the building had all of the trappings of a Jesuit college—a debating hall for the debate club, a chapel for the sodality, and an auditorium for exhibitions and the monthly reading of the marks. The school's prospectus described it as "located in the most central and elegant part of town" and boasted that the building's basement was paved with asphalt, which "affords the students very ample room for playing in all seasons of the year."[135]

Like most Jesuit colleges, St. Joseph's had a prep division, a commercial division leading to a certificate, and a classical undergraduate division leading to a degree. Tuition for the prep and collegiate programs was free, but students interested in the high-demand commercial program paid $4 per month. The lower divisions opened in 1882, while the first collegiate class entered two years later. The school's prospectus promised that "Those students who shall have completed in a satisfactory manner the classical course . . . will be admitted without further examination into the scientific course either in Santa Clara College, Santa Clara, or St. Ignatius College, San Fran-

---

134. Agnes Solari and Margaret Zero, "St. Joseph's College and Rectory Building, 1892–1977," Jesuit Archives and Research Center, St. Louis, Missouri, 5.

135. "Prospectus, St. Joseph's College, San Jose, California, For the Scholastic Year 1892–3," Jesuit Archives and Research Center, St. Louis, Missouri.

cisco."[136] As such, St. Joseph's was essentially the equivalent of a community college. It offered, for free, the first few years of a Jesuit college experience to poor urban boys who could not afford Santa Clara.

Despite the incentives of free tuition and guaranteed admission to one of the Bay Area's two senior Jesuit colleges, very few students took advantage of the classical course. In 1891, St. Joseph's College enrolled just 86 students, only six of whom were in the collegiate division (as compared to 62 in the commercial division). Even counting the prep students, it was the third smallest Jesuit college in the United States, behind only three-year-old Gonzaga College in Spokane (with 62 students) and Saint Peter's College in Jersey City (with 85).[137] In some years, enrollment in the undergraduate program at St. Joseph's was zero.

The California Jesuits clearly believed in St. Joseph's potential, at least at first. At the 1893 World's Fair in Chicago, the Catholic Church set up a grand exhibition highlighting the contributions of Catholic education in the United States, and St. Joseph's College was featured prominently in the booth representing the Archdiocese of San Francisco.[138] However, it was simply too close to Santa Clara College and at the time, local demand could not support three Jesuit schools in in the Bay Area. By the end of the century, the Jesuits had to acknowledge that what they were operating in San Jose was really just a high school and an elementary school, and they decided to cut their losses by reassigning St. Joseph's Jesuit faculty to the two other California colleges. That year, in addition to shuttering St. Joseph's college division, they invited another teaching order, the Marist Brothers, to take control of the elementary division. Dropping any pretense of higher education, the school renamed itself St. Joseph's Academy.[139]

The same 1906 earthquake that destroyed St. Ignatius College in San Francisco also damaged the St. Joseph's Academy building so severely that the Academy relocated to a new site in the western part of town. Thereafter, the original building was used as a rectory for St. Joseph's Church and for street level retail before being condemned and razed in 1977.[140]

In 1981, San Jose became a diocese of its own, and the new bishop needed a church to serve as its Cathedral. Because St. Joseph's was one of the largest and most beautiful church buildings in the city, not to mention conveniently located in the heart of downtown, it was the obvious choice. The Jesuits surrendered it to the

---

136. Ibid.

137. "Students in Our Colleges in the U. States and Canada, 1890–'91," *Woodstock Letters* XX, no. 3 (1891): unnumbered page.

138. *The Catholic Educational Exhibit at the World's Columbian Exposition, Chicago, 1893*, edited by a well known Catholic writer, under the special supervision of the Rev. Brother Maurelian (Chicago: JS Highland and Company, 1896), 59, https://luc.access.preservica.com/uncategorized/digitalFile_ 1c1d59f7-4c74-4d85-9463-8db53035ecf0/.

139. Solari and Zero, "St. Joseph's College," 3.

140. Ibid., 4–5.

Diocese of San Jose in 1991 and, in a trade deal, the Diocese granted the Jesuits control of Most Holy Trinity Church—a much humbler immigrant parish serving mainly Hispanic and Asian Catholics—on San Jose's east side. Today, the old church is known as the Cathedral Basilica of St. Joseph, and the neighboring lot on which the old college building once stood is occupied by a parking lot and a few bars and restaurants.

Loyola Marymount University (1911), Los Angeles, California

The Jesuits can be forgiven for overlooking Los Angeles when they first arrived in California. When Fathers Michael Accolti and John Nobili initially scouted locations for a Jesuit college in the Golden State in 1849, California's population and economic activity were overwhelmingly concentrated in the San Francisco Bay Area. Southern California was still an undeveloped desert, largely unsuitable for agriculture, and Los Angeles itself had fewer than 2,000 residents. Even the Franciscan missionaries and Spanish colonists who founded the small settlements at Los Angeles, San Diego, and the surrounding areas had treated them as little more than ranching outposts.

As time passed, however, southern California's near-perfect climate and access to the Pacific Ocean brought more settlers, and irrigation projects solved the region's water problems. The growth caught the attention of the California Jesuits, who opened a parish in Santa Barbara in 1908. As always, their ultimate goal was a Jesuit college for southern part of the state, but in the short term they were too preoccupied with the aftermath of the 1906 earthquake to act on those plans.

Los Angeles already had a Catholic college at the time—one that was old and well-established. In 1865, while the Civil War was ending and Los Angeles was still under the jurisdiction of a diocese based 300 miles north in Monterey, Bishop Thaddeus Amat invited priests from his own religious order (the Vincentians) to establish a college in the small but largely Catholic city. The school they built, St. Vincent College, was the first college of any kind in southern California.

For nearly fifty years, St. Vincent College enjoyed a strong reputation in the local community, but the early 1900s it was facing some serious issues. Construction projects had left it heavily in debt, and a new bishop, the Irish-born James Conaty, was increasingly clashing with the college leadership. Just prior to becoming the head of the Monterey-Los Angeles Diocese, Bishop Conaty had served as the second president of the Catholic University of America from 1896 to 1903. Despite some notable accomplishments in Washington, DC, he had gotten caught up in faculty politics and ultimately fell victim to behind-the-scenes campaigns to replace him. When he left the university presidency, it was not under the best of circumstances.[141]

---

141. C. Joseph Nuesse, *The Catholic University of America: A Centennial History* (Washington; Catholic University of America Press, 1990), 125–126.

After arriving on the West Coast, Conaty resolved to establish a Catholic research university that would be equal in scope and prestige to the struggling school he left behind in Washington, DC. Historians have suggested that he may have been motivated at least in part by a desire for redemption.[142] He began pressuring St. Vincent College to expand and introduce a full array of graduate and professional programs, transforming itself into the leading Catholic university in the West. Unfortunately for Conaty, the college's Vincentian leadership had neither the resources nor the patience to live up to those grand ambitions.

Conaty played his cards well. With the Vincentians resisting his overtures, he began to negotiate with the Jesuits about opening a competing college, potentially in San Diego or Pasadena. Arguably, either city would have been distant enough from St. Vincent College to serve a different market, but the Vincentians resented the idea that Conaty would sanction a second Catholic school anywhere in the still-small diocese. Seeing the writing on the wall, the Vincentians withdrew from Los Angeles in 1910, abandoning historic St. Vincent College and reallocating their personnel to their four other American schools: DePaul University in Chicago, St. John's College (now University) in New York City, Niagara University near Buffalo, and the University of Dallas (now a diocesan institution) in Texas.[143]

Conaty then began pressuring the Jesuits, not simply to take control of St. Vincent College, but to transform it into a research university akin to a western version of the Catholic University of America. This was obviously far beyond their means at the time, but the first provincial of the new California Province, Herman Goller, SJ, was so entranced by Los Angeles's potential that he gave Conaty a verbal commitment. Just three months later, Father Goller died. The new provincial, James Rockliff, SJ, was less enthusiastic about the project but felt morally obligated to follow through on Goller's promise.[144]

As the California Jesuits tried to work out how to staff a college in Los Angeles on top of their existing obligations, a faction of the province began to push for something that would have seemed unthinkable under any other circumstance: abandoning Santa Clara. There were some strong arguments to be made. Relocating the historic college to Los Angeles would get it out of the shadow of Stanford and Berkeley, and potentially allow it to become the dominant university in southern California. (The school that would become UCLA was just a state teachers' college at the time, and would not affiliate with the University of California for another nine years, in 1919.) Moving Santa Clara south would also clear a path for the rebuilt St. Ignatius College (University of San Francisco) to attract more students and serve the Bay Area on its own. From a resource point of view, it made sense for the Jesuits to have one university each in northern and southern California. No less

---

142. McKevitt, *University of Santa Clara*, 158.
143. Ibid., 158–159.
144. Ibid., 159–160.

a figure than Father Robert Kenna, a Santa Clara alumnus and two-time president, supported the proposal.[145]

For others, the thought of abandoning the college that had conferred California's first bachelor's degrees—a college whose very campus, built on the ruins of an old Spanish mission, served as a tangible reminder of the state's Catholic roots—seemed a mistake. Santa Clara's defenders acknowledged that it was small, but it had a strong reputation and the best brand recognition of any western Jesuit school. Surely there was a way to accept the Los Angeles opportunity without destroying what generations of Jesuits had already built. As it turned out, there was—but the compromises necessary left all sides feeling somewhat disappointed. After weeks of deliberation, the Jesuits committed only to establish a commuter college in Los Angeles, starting with a high school and adding college-level courses someday in the future. This meant that Santa Clara would have to relinquish only a few precious teachers, but it meant that the new school would be a far cry from what Bishop Conaty had envisioned as the greatest Catholic research university west of the Mississippi.[146]

Conaty was also disappointed when the Jesuits announced, shrewdly, that they planned to create an altogether new institution rather than simply assume control of St. Vincent College. This was wise, because it allowed the Jesuits to start from scratch without assuming the old college's significant debt. However, it angered the alumni and students of St. Vincent, who had been promised continuity for the venerable old college and hated to watch it die. In the end, when the Jesuits opened what they initially called Los Angeles College in 1911, it was a spiritual, but not legal, successor to the former school.[147] To help soften the blow, Los Angeles College renamed itself St. Vincent College in 1915, claiming the identity of the old school but not its debts. Two years later, it changed its name yet again, becoming Loyola College of Los Angeles. This meant that every major Jesuit province in the United States now had a college or university named "Loyola" in one of the cities it served (Baltimore in the East, Chicago in the Midwest, New Orleans in the South, and Los Angeles in the West).

The first Jesuit president of Los Angeles College in 1911 was Richard Gleeson, SJ, who had just stepped down from the presidency at Santa Clara a year earlier. In addition to the Jesuit transplants from northern California, the school consisted mainly of students and lay teachers left behind by the closing of St. Vincent. Despite the challenges of operating three colleges at once, the California Jesuits successfully added both an undergraduate program and a law school to their Los Angeles operation by 1920. Loyola Law School quickly became—and remains—a school of choice for Angelinos who seek to make an impact in the local legal market. Many of its graduates have gone on to play high-profile roles in the entertainment industry in Hollywood.

---

145. Ibid., 160–161.
146. Ibid., 161–165.
147. Ibid., 165.

Although the decision to open it was among the most divisive issues the California Jesuits ever faced, the college in Los Angeles proved to be extremely successful. It became the dominant—indeed, the only—Catholic men's college in America's second largest city. In 1926, local real estate developer Harry Culver (from whom Culver City, California takes its name) donated 99 acres in the beautiful hilltop neighborhood of Del Rey Hills, now known as Westchester. Considering the skyrocketing property values in southern California over the next few decades, this may well have been the most generous property donation ever given to a Jesuit school. It enabled the college (with the exception of the law school, which purchased its own new campus near the city center) to relocate from downtown and resettle on one of the most strikingly beautiful campuses of any Jesuit institution in the country. Only the preparatory school remained on the original Venice Boulevard building. As the film industry boomed in southern California, Loyola College became an important creative center for Jesuits involved in media production, and eventually became the first American Jesuit university to establish a School of Film and Television.

In 1953, Loyola paid a moving tribute to its place in the Jesuit education network when it built the mission-style Chapel of the Sacred Heart on the edge of its hilltop campus. The chapel, which overlooks nearby Marina Del Rey with an exquisite view, features thirty beautiful stained glass windows. Each window depicts a Catholic saint (mainly, although not entirely, Jesuits) and twenty-seven of the windows feature the name and crest of one of the twenty-seven Jesuit colleges that existed in the United States at the time. The windows representing Georgetown and Santa Clara are given pride of place behind the chapel's altar, and the window representing Loyola features the image of Christ the King. The striking chapel has become the centerpiece of the campus—a symbol both of the university and of the connections it shares with its sister schools from the East Coast to the West.

Loyola later merged with the all-female Marymount College in 1973, resulting in its present name: Loyola Marymount University. It remains the only Catholic research university in Los Angeles, and one of only three institutions of Catholic higher education in the city. Whereas there are more than fifteen Catholic colleges and universities in the greater New York City area and more than eight in greater Chicago, Loyola Marymount almost single-handedly dominates the Catholic university scene in Los Angeles. It is an impressive outcome for a school the Jesuits almost refused to accept.

Southern Jesuit Colleges, 1865–1918

Although they lived in some of the oldest Catholic communities in the country, Southern Catholics became something of an afterthought in the late nineteenth century, largely overshadowed by the Church's efforts to respond to the demographic surge in the industrial north and to evangelize the newly opened west. The Jesuits, however, still had a significant Southern presence in the form of the New Orleans Mission overseen by the French Province of Lyon.

While their colleagues around the country were building a brand-new infrastructure in places where the Catholic Church was growing, the Jesuits of the American South also attempted to expand. But because Catholics remained a relatively small demographic group in the region, the Jesuits' Southern educational network was overall less successful. At the end of the Civil War, the New Orleans Mission was operating three schools: the College of the Immaculate Conception in New Orleans, Spring Hill College in Mobile, and historic but isolated St. Charles College in Grand Coteau. By the middle of the 1920s, there were only two Southern Jesuit schools left: Spring Hill in Mobile, and a new university in New Orleans (Loyola) that had only indirect ties to Immaculate Conception. Although the Southern Jesuits founded or took control of six new colleges in the intervening years, few survived, and there was ultimately a net loss in the number of Jesuit colleges in the South.

The New Orleans Mission operated as a branch of the French Province until 1907, when it grew large enough to become a province of its own. Unfortunately, unlike the situation elsewhere in the United States, the decision to erect an independent province arguably hurt Jesuit activities in the South. Severing ties to their European supervisors cut off the supply of French missionaries who, until then, had crossed the Atlantic regularly to staff schools and parishes. Without those constant reinforcements from France, the New Orleans Jesuits had to recruit their own priests from the small Catholic communities in the South, and it became difficult to sustain all of their new ministries. It was the rare case in American history where the erection of a Jesuit province ultimately resulted in a reduction of Jesuit activity.

St. Mary's University (1884–1922), Galveston, Texas

The New Orleans Jesuits' first and longest-lasting expansion project was St. Mary's University, the only Jesuit college ever to operate in Texas. Located in Galveston, St. Mary's had a long history before the Jesuits assumed control in 1884.

Galveston today is best known as the port city for Houston—the part of the greater Houston metro area that faces outward toward the Gulf of Mexico and connects the region to the wider world. Although it is today essentially a suburb, Galveston's population exceeded Houston's until the 1880 census. When settlers arrived in the 1820s, the Galveston area was already a longtime staging ground for French pirates from Louisiana—including the legendary New Orleans privateer, Jean Lafitte—as they sought to intercept Mexican gold en route to Europe. In 1847, two years after Texas achieved statehood, Galveston became the seat of Texas's first non-Mexican Catholic diocese. To this day, the local archdiocese is officially named the Archdiocese of Galveston-Houston.

The first Catholic bishop of Galveston, the French-born Vincentian Jean Marie Odin, CM, established St. Mary's University as a college and seminary between 1852 and 1855, and it received a state charter in 1856. Finding an order of priests willing to staff the school proved to be a major challenge. At various points in its 23-year history before the arrival of the Jesuits, St. Mary's was managed and/or staffed by diocesan clergy and by multiple religious orders, none of which spent more than a few years at the school. Some of the orders who taught at St. Mary's, like the Oblates of Mary Immaculate and Congregation of Holy Cross, eventually left Galveston to focus their ministry in San Antonio, Austin, and other Texas cities with even larger Catholic populations.

When Galveston's third bishop, Nicolaus Gallagher, turned to the Jesuits, it was almost an act of desperation to save the beleaguered university. A Jesuit presence, he hoped, would finally bring some stability to a school that had become something of a hot potato. For the Jesuits, St. Mary's was a natural fit both geographically and culturally; Galveston was a short sea voyage away from mission headquarters in Louisiana, and like many cities along the Gulf Coast, it had close historic and economic ties to New Orleans.

The Jesuits assumed control of the university and its attached parish in 1884. As usual, in addition to teaching, they had a full slate of pastoral responsibilities, serving as chaplains to the local hospital and spiritual leaders to the city's racially diverse population, including its African-Americans.[148] The Jesuits who settled in Galveston were reportedly entranced by the natural beauty of the surrounding island, its swashbuckling history, and its long term growth potential—but they found the academic standards at the struggling university to be sub-par and judged the attached church building to be inadequate for the size of the congregation.[149]

The enrollment at St. Mary's was healthy and hovered around 100 (though the vast majority of those students were in the pre-college programs), and by the 1890s the Jesuits had put the finishing touches on a new church. But on September 8, 1900, tragedy struck when a devastating hurricane hit Galveston. Local fishermen and other residents fled to the college for safety, but within a few hours the building in which they were sheltering was flooded; strong winds blew the roof off of the school auditorium and about 400 desperate survivors ran to the last remaining classroom building on campus. Fortunately, that structure withstood the chaos outside because the broad walls of the church next to it acted like a shield, deflecting the tidal waves. The Jesuits did everything they could to pray with the stranded townspeople and keep them calm as the water levels rose. After the winds died and the seas retreated, what was left of the college became a makeshift hospital for three weeks. The new church, into which the Jesuits had poured so much money and sweat, was almost completely destroyed.[150]

The Jesuits resolved to rebuild, and within five years enrollment at St. Mary's was back above 90, where it remained even through the First World War. Still, virtually all of those students were enrolled in the high school division and the number of students pursuing bachelor's degrees was typically less than ten. The undergradu-

---

148. "Galveston, St. Mary's University," *Woodstock Letters* XIX, no. 1 (1890): 79.

149. Ibid., 78–80.

150. J.A. Hogan, SJ, "Reminisces of the Galveston Storm," *Woodstock Letters* XXIX, no. 3 (1901): 429–432.

ate program never truly recovered from the hurricane, and when the New Orleans Province restructured itself in 1922, St. Mary's University was one of the casualties. That year, the school closed for good. Its younger students had the option to transfer to the city's other Catholic high school, St. Thomas, which was run by the Basilian Fathers. But St. Thomas was not chartered to grant degrees, and Houston was left without a true Catholic university for a generation, until the Basilians expanded their operation and established the University of St. Thomas in 1947. The approximate site of the original St. Mary's University is today the parking lot of Galveston's Sacred Heart Catholic Church.

Sacred Heart College (1900–1917), Augusta, Georgia

The next expansion project of the New Orleans Jesuits was, at first glance, an odd choice. It took place in the small city of Augusta, Georgia, located on the Savannah River just across the South Carolina border. Augusta had a relatively strong economy thanks to its role as a depot in the cotton industry, but its Catholic population was miniscule. The only Catholic residents to speak of were a handful of first and second-generation Irish immigrants who came to the city to work for the cotton companies; most of them occupied low-level clerical jobs and had little interest in higher education. Meanwhile, the city's overwhelmingly Protestant governing class often viewed the work of Catholic teaching orders with suspicion. When the Sisters of Mercy sent teachers to work in the local public school system in 1904, the city voted to close the schools rather than accept the sisters' free labor.[151]

On closer examination, however, Augusta was not as strange a choice for a Jesuit school as it might seem. The working-class Irish population, though small, was exactly the kind of audience the Jesuits typically targeted. What they lacked in numbers, they made up for in need, and the opportunity to help a disadvantaged community of immigrants always fit well into the Jesuit ethos. Since 1874, the Jesuits had operated Sacred Heart Church in Augusta with a long-term plan of establishing a college whenever circumstances allowed. Between 1897 and 1900, they built a grandiose new church building (which still stands) along with a small school next door. They began teaching students in 1900 and obtained a state charter to grant degrees in 1902.

The opportunity for social mobility in the local Irish population was great, but the Jesuits struggled to convince parents that a college education was a good investment. Complaining that many of these first- and second-generation Americans had low professional aspirations for their children, the Jesuit founders of Sacred Heart College wrote:

---

151. J. M. Salter, SJ, "Our College at Augusta, Georgia," *Woodstock Letters* XXXIV, no. 3 (1905): 383.

We have therefore a threefold end to accomplish: in the first place to raise the ambition of many whose talents warrant them to aim higher than a clerkship or bookkeepers desk; secondly, to make those desiring to be engineers &c., realize that a liberal education is the very best foundation for their specialty; thirdly, to make non-Catholics especially, appreciate the fact that our diploma is of as much intrinsic worth as that of one of our State Universities.[152]

In other words, the college that the Jesuits opened in 1900 had a typical Jesuit mission in a slightly unusual place. The working-class Catholic students who filled its classrooms were few in number, but they had more room than other Southern Catholics (descended from the colonial-era landed gentry) to move up in American society. The Jesuits came to Augusta because their services were needed, not because they were in demand. At the same time, the college could contribute to inter-religious dialogue. The annual exhibition of student work, along with the annual theater performances, drew the attention of many local Protestants who had never seen such cultural resources before in Augusta. Protestant students, who came to represent as much as half the student body, were being introduced to the Catholic educational tradition in a state where all things Catholic were routinely viewed with suspicion.[153]

In the end, however, bigotry (combined with a natural disaster) proved too much for Sacred Heart College. The school building and its neighboring church were located about a block away from the Savannah River on one side and a canal used for shipping cotton on the other. On August 26, 1908, a flood caught the Jesuits (and the city) by surprise, and within a few hours, the rising river waters had submerged the ground floor of the college building. The Jesuits who lived upstairs were stuck in the upper floors for a day, without much food, before the water levels started to recede. Fortunately, there was no loss of life because the school year had not yet started. Unfortunately, the citywide destruction combined with the unhealthy conditions of the sludge-coated downtown area left many parents unwilling or unable to enroll their sons at Sacred Heart. Enrollment fell by half compared to the previous academic year.[154]

Although the Jesuits reported that "the better class" of Protestants in the city supported Sacred Heart College and wished to see it succeed after the flood, there was also a strong strain of anti-Catholic sentiment within the local and state governments.[155] Local lawmaker Thomas Watson, who represented Georgia in both the United States House of Representatives and Senate during his career, publicly accused the Jesuits of organizing an insurrectionist Catholic militia at the college. He based this absurd charge on the fact that the school sponsored a cadet drill team—a common extracurricular activity in Southern colleges at the time. The sight of Catholic students march-

---

152. Ibid., 382–383.

153. Ibid., 383–384.

154. L. G. Bashnal, SJ, "The Flood at Augusta, Georgia," *Woodstock Letters* XXXVIII, no. 1 (1909).

155. Ibid., 72.

ing, holding fake weapons, and learning paramilitary tactics during recess proved too much for some of the city's more prejudiced Protestant Brahmins.[156]

The final straw came when a competing local private school, Richmond Academy, affiliated with the state and became tuition-free. Although the Jesuits had successfully recruited students away from the Academy for about a decade, they could no longer compete. Facing the double blow of a hostile local government and a poor Catholic population unwilling to pay tuition for an education available elsewhere for free, the Jesuits begrudgingly decided to shut down Sacred Heart College, including its high school division. By 1917, its last year of existence, the school enrolled just 14 students.[157] Richmond Academy went on to thrive, and it still exists today as one of the oldest operating public high schools in the United States.

After Sacred Heart College closed, the Jesuits did not immediately leave Augusta. They continued to minister at Sacred Heart Church until 1971, when urban decay greatly reduced the downtown Catholic population and diminished the need for a church. After the Jesuits withdrew, the buildings sat vacant for several years, but were eventually salvaged and repurposed as a local arts venue. The complex is today known as the Sacred Heart Cultural Center, and hosts weddings, community events, and office space for nonprofit organizations. It is listed on the National Register of Historic Places.

Loyola University (1904), New Orleans, Louisiana

The Jesuits had operated a college in New Orleans since 1849, when they opened the College of the Immaculate Conception as a downtown commuter school for students who lacked the means or the patience to make the five-day journey to isolated St. Charles College. Whereas location was St. Charles's biggest drawback, it was Immaculate Conception's greatest asset. Situated just a block west of the famous French Quarter and a short walk from the iconic St. Louis Cathedral in Jackson Square, the New Orleans college was central to the city's population. It survived the Civil War unscathed, and in a largely Catholic city where the Jesuits and their brand of education were held in high regard, it became a respected civic institution. By 1900, Immaculate Conception enrolled almost 330 students, making it the sixth-largest Jesuit school in the country (behind St. Francis Xavier in New York, St. Xavier in Cincinnati, Boston College, St. Ignatius in Chicago, and Holy Cross).[158]

Unfortunately, as a commuter college, Immaculate Conception was at the whim of the frequent yellow fever epidemics that had made the Jesuits so wary of opening a college in New Orleans in the first place. Its cramped urban location left little room for growth, so the Jesuits began to strategize early about relocating. By the late 1800s,

---

156. Platt, *Sacrifice*, 94–97.

157. Ibid., 92–93, 96–97. Salter, "Our College," 383. "Students in Our Colleges in the United States and Canada, October 10, 1917," *Woodstock Letters* XLVI, no. 3 (1917): unnumbered page.

158. "Students in Our Colleges in the United States and Canada. October 1, 1900," *Woodstock Letters* XXIX, no. 3 (1901): 550.

the city was spilling out of its original colonial boundaries, with most of the residential development taking place in the booming uptown neighborhoods to the west. One of the catalysts for this growth was the 1884 World Cotton Centennial celebration, a World's Fair that took place on land that is today Audubon Park. After the exhibition drew attention to the area, the surrounding neighborhood started to sprout Gilded Age mansions, including some of the most beautiful Victorian and Edwardian homes in New Orleans. Connecting the city's old and new neighborhoods were its famous streetcars, which Catholic priests and nuns traditionally rode free of charge, and which continue to operate along St. Charles Avenue today.

Shortly after the cotton exhibition, the head of the New Orleans Mission, Father John O'Shanahan, SJ, sought to buy a large estate just north of St. Charles Avenue near the site of the fair. The owner of the property, Pierre Fouchet, offered the entire estate to Father O'Shanahan at the relatively bargain price of $75,000, but in a move he would later regret, the humble priest declined the offer after his fellow Jesuits cautioned that such extensive real estate speculation was unbecoming of a not-for-profit organization like the Society of Jesus. In 1889, O'Shanahan paid $22,500 for just a small portion of the Fouchet property—about 15 acres—that is today the heart of the Loyola University campus. Two years later, the remainder of the estate that Father O'Shanahan turned down was sold to Tulane University, another downtown college that was seeking to expand into the booming neighborhood.[159]

One of the brokers of the Jesuits' real estate deal was New Orleans lawyer (and future Supreme Court justice) Edward Douglass White, a Louisiana native who had attended both the College of the Immaculate Conception and Georgetown University. He would later serve as a US Senator from Louisiana before becoming only the second Catholic (after Roger Taney) to sit on the country's highest court, where he served as chief justice from 1910 to 1921. Although he did not negotiate the best possible financial deal for the New Orleans Jesuits, in the long term he still helped them acquire some of the most desirable real estate in the city.

For years, however, the Jesuits lacked the means to do anything with the valuable property. They obtained permission from the local bishop to build a church on the site in 1892, but that was all the progress they had made by the time Tulane began to move into its new campus next door in 1894. After more than a decade of preparation and fundraising, the Jesuits opened a small school—which they dubbed Loyola College—next to their new church, under the direction of Albert Biever, SJ.

Born in Luxembourg, Father Biever was an experienced missionary known for his energy and his selfless work in caring for yellow fever victims. According to legend, when Father O'Shanahan assigned Biever to start the new college, he offered the younger priest just one nickel to cover his taxi fare to the site.[160] If true, Biever's

---

159. Cook, *Founded on Faith*, 32–34. Bernard Cook, "Jesuit Priest Advised not to Purchase Tulane's Land," *The Maroon*, September 8, 2011, https://loyolamaroon.com/100992/features/jesuit-priest-advised-not-to-puchase-tulanes-land/.

160. Cook, *Founded on Faith*, 35.

accomplishment was even more impressive than that of Father John Larkin in New York City six decades earlier. Larkin at least claimed to have had 45 cents in his pocket when he started the College of St. Francis Xavier in Manhattan; accounting for inflation, it was a princely sum compared to what Biever had to work with!

The expectation initially was that the two Jesuit colleges in New Orleans could coexist. The demand for a Jesuit education in the heavily Catholic city was so robust that two neighborhood colleges—one for downtown and one for the rapidly growing residential areas to the west—made sense. In the long term, the Jesuits realized that landlocked Immaculate Conception could not survive without room to grow, but for the time being, both colleges were at least financially justifiable. As a sign of their need for money as well as their modest short-term hopes for Loyola, the Jesuits sold part of the Loyola campus to Newcomb College (the women's college of Tulane University) in 1904.[161] This brought Tulane's campus into even closer proximity to the smaller Jesuit school.

Like virtually all Jesuit colleges at the time, Loyola had both a prep division and a college division, but that model was already becoming anachronistic by the early 1900s. The college division initially had no charter of its own; it granted degrees under the authority of the charter granted decades earlier to St. Charles College in Grand Coteau. This was defensible from a legal point of view, since most Jesuit schools, houses, and churches in Louisiana were civilly incorporated as a single entity. Loyola could claim to be part of the same corporate body as St. Charles. However, the behavior raised regulatory eyebrows in the state government in Baton Rouge, and some government officials began to argue that Loyola and the College of the Immaculate Conception had been awarding degrees illegally. This led Father Biever to push for an independent charter for Loyola, which he finally obtained in 1912 after some difficulty. Tulane University lobbied hard against it, but Loyola had friends in the form of state Senator William Byrnes and US Senator Robert Broussard (both Georgetown alumni) who helped to push the bill through. Biever originally hoped to name the newly chartered school "Marquette University," but after objections from the Jesuits in Milwaukee, he settled on "Loyola University of the South."[162]

With Loyola's ambitions to transform itself into a university gaining steam, the Jesuits moved to draw a clear distinction between their two New Orleans schools. Loyola, having the larger campus and the most growth potential, was designated as the sole Jesuit university in the city and absorbed Immaculate Conception's college-level students and faculty in 1911. Concurrently, Loyola's prep division transferred entirely to Immaculate Conception, which became strictly a high school. To accommodate the increased enrollment, in 1926, Immaculate Conception moved to its present location about thirty blocks north of the original campus, renaming itself Jesuit High School. The old school building was razed, and the site is now home to a hotel

---

161. Platt, *Sacrifice*, 120.

162. Ibid., 123. Cook, *Founded on Faith*, 45–47.

catering to French Quarter tourists. The church that stood next to the original school—also called Immaculate Conception—remains operational and in Jesuit hands today.

As it became the flagship university of the New Orleans Province, Loyola added professional schools on pace with the other Jesuit universities in the country at the time. In 1914, it opened schools of law and dentistry, and five years later it absorbed the previously independent New Orleans College of Pharmacy. Although the dental and pharmacy programs would not survive in the long term, Loyola would eventually add a successful College of Music in 1932—making it only the second American Jesuit university, after Marquette, to sponsor such a college.

As neighboring Tulane University expanded and the grounds of the old cotton exhibition became Audubon Park, Loyola's immediate neighborhood became a hub for the city's cultural and educational activity. Although Loyola today is tucked into what appears to be a small corner of the Tulane campus, behind the façade of its small geographic footprint is the fact that the Jesuits, in effect, started all of that development when they first recognized the neighborhood's potential for academic use. Although the acreage it occupies is small compared to that of Tulane or Audubon Park, Loyola sits squarely between those two institutions, facing the bustling traffic and streetcars along St. Charles Avenue. Its central location on the city's grandest boulevard reflects its keystone role in the Fourteenth Ward's history.

False Starts in Shreveport and Tampa

The New Orleans Jesuits also opened two high schools that they intended to develop into colleges. As was the standard Jesuit practice, both schools at first enrolled students only in the lower, prep divisions, with the expectation that college-level courses would be added as those students progressed. As it happened, neither of the two schools ever developed college courses or granted degrees, although the Jesuits typically referred to both as "colleges" and included them on published lists of the colleges they sponsored.

The first was Sacred Heart College in Tampa, Florida, which opened in 1899. As early as 1914, Sacred Heart was planning to apply for a collegiate charter from the Florida legislature.[163] That charter was awarded in 1929, and the school adopted the name Tampa College. However, its bachelor's degree programs never fully developed and the school changed its name again to Jesuit High School in 1940.

In Shreveport, at the northwest corner of Louisiana, the New Orleans Jesuits opened St. John Berchmans College in 1902. Officially, it was named after the Cathedral of the same name in Shreveport, but it was also the second American school (after St. John's University in Toledo, Ohio) to bear the name of the seventeenth-century Jesuit saint. The Shreveport school continued to use the term "college" to describe itself until 1941, when amid the lean years of World War II, the Jesuits

---

163. Platt, *Sacrifice*, 128.

finally dropped any pretense of higher education and renamed it St. John's High School.[164] In 1982, facing a shortage of personnel, the Jesuits withdrew permanently and handed the school over to the Diocese of Shreveport. It is now known as Loyola College Prep, and is the only Catholic high school in the city.

Norbert de Boynes, SJ: The Hatchet Man Arrives

Quite some time had passed since the Jesuit general in Rome had sent an official visitor to serve as his eyes and ears in the United States. Just as his predecessors had sent Father Peter Kenney in the 1820s and '30s and Father Felix Sopranis in the 1860s, the new Superior General, Polish-born Wlodimir Ledóchowski, SJ, sent an official emissary to inspect the American provinces in 1919.

This time, the visitor was a Frenchman, Norbert de Boynes, SJ, who had most recently served as head of the Jesuit province in Paris. His first stop in the United States was Boston. Between late 1919 and 1921, de Boynes inspected the Maryland-New York Province, traveling down the megalopolis to meet with the various Jesuits, examine students, and inspect the facilities. Given the size of the province (more than 1,000 Jesuits), there was serious discussion about whether it should be split in two. De Boynes considered several proposals but ultimately decided against a formal split. All in all, his visit to the East Coast was relatively inconsequential.[165]

The same could not be said about his visit to the New Orleans Province. After completing his work in the east, de Boynes arrived in Louisiana in 1921 to begin an inspection of the Southern Jesuit churches and colleges. The contrast between the gritty industrial cities of the north and the slow pace of life in the still-agrarian South could not have been sharper. There was an even greater contrast in the size of the two provinces. Whereas the Maryland-New York Jesuits were over 1,000 strong, the New Orleans Jesuits had just over 300 men to serve a geographic area many times the size of the Boston-Washington corridor.[166]

There was a sense among some Southern Jesuits that the New Orleans Province was overextended. One influential Jesuit who held this view was Father Edward Cummings, SJ, a former president of Spring Hill College who was serving as president of Loyola University in New Orleans at the time. De Boynes's interviews with Cummings and others convinced him that contraction, not expansion, was necessary for the province's health.[167]

De Boynes made sweeping recommendations. To shore up personnel for the projects that mattered most, he advised the New Orleans Jesuits to close two of

---

164. Ibid., 128.

165. James L. Burke, SJ, *Jesuit Province of New England: The Formative Years* (Boston: Society of Jesus of New England, 1973), ch. 2, p. 8, https://crossworks.holycross.edu/nenprovhistory/1/.

166. Thomas H. Clancy, SJ, "After the Suppression," Loyola University New Orleans University Chaplain, Loyola University New Orleans, 1996–2022, http://president.loyno.edu/after-suppression.

167. Platt, *Sacrifice*, 50–51.

their institutions: St. Mary's University in Galveston, and St. Charles College in Grand Coteau. St. Mary's had never truly recovered from the hurricane of 1900, and at the time of de Boynes's visit, it enrolled just 98 students, all of whom were in the pre-college programs. Venerable old St. Charles College was a harder pill to swallow; it was the oldest college in the South—and the third-oldest in the entire country—founded and continuously operated by Jesuits. Still, the decision was long overdue. The Jesuits had made multiple attempts to close St. Charles throughout its troubled existence, but circumstances—like the 1856 failure of the Jesuit college in Baton Rouge or the 1869 fire at Spring Hill College—had always forced them back to the relative safety of Grand Coteau. When de Boynes arrived, St. Charles enrolled just 157 students, only thirteen of whom were actually pursuing bachelor's degrees. Clearly, the Jesuits' teaching personnel could be put to better use at the schools in Mobile and New Orleans, where enrollments were surging past 300. Although the de Boynes report finally put an end to St. Charles's undergraduate programs, the secluded, reflective atmosphere of the old campus proved to be perfect for retreats and for educating seminarians. The Jesuits continue to use it for both of those purposes to this day.[168]

Father Edward Cummings's influence over the de Boynes report is evident in the fact that the two colleges he had personally led during his career—Loyola and Spring Hill—escaped the axe. Also spared were the two proto-colleges at Shreveport and Tampa. Both logically should have been candidates for closure since they had never developed into the colleges they advertised themselves to be. Scholar Eric Platt speculates that de Boynes may have simply given the schools a pass because they were, in fact, just high schools and did not require the level of financial or human investment necessary to run a true college.[169] Without question, had Sacred Heart College in Augusta not closed on its own five years earlier, it, too, would have been pushed into its grave by the de Boynes report.

1922 was therefore a watershed year for the Southern Jesuits. Although they had tried to build an educational network comparable in scope to those of their colleagues around the country, only two of their colleges survived. Both Loyola and Spring Hill benefitted from the influx of faculty made possible by the pruning of the other institutions. It was a rare instance in which the American Jesuits emphasized quality over quantity and stability over accessibility. Nonetheless, with their college-building days finished, the New Orleans Jesuits did develop a renewed interest in high schools. In addition to reinforcing their existing high schools, they eventually returned to Texas, where they opened what is today Jesuit College Prep in Dallas in 1942. In 1960, they returned to the Houston metro area with the opening of Strake Jesuit College Prep.

---

168. "Students in Our Colleges in the United States and Canada, October 10, 1920," *Woodstock Letters* XLIX, no. 3 (1920): unnumbered page.

169. Platt, *Sacrifice*, 127–128.

Education and the Anti-Catholic Environment in the late 1800s

The Jesuit schools that came into the world during the second half of the nineteenth century found themselves in a very different environment than those founded in the first half. Education in America, including higher education, was no longer exclusively the domain of the wealthy elite. Free public schools were becoming more common, and teachers who stood in front of large, open classrooms were fast replacing private tutors who made house calls to the rich. For the first time, a formal education (beyond self-study through books and apprenticeships) became a realistic goal for most Americans. Students who wanted to attend an actual, functioning school no longer had to travel hundreds of miles for the privilege.

This democratization of educational opportunity, and the associated expectation that the government was now a provider of education, began to affect colleges and universities. Government investment in higher education, which had been limited throughout most of American history, crossed a threshold when Congress passed the Morrill Act in 1862. The creation of public land-grant universities meant that bachelor's degrees were more widely available than ever before, and Jesuit institutions, many of which had been the first and only colleges in their communities, were quickly thrust into a crowded, competitive space. Although most Jesuit schools were established to provide access to education, by the late 1800s they were no longer the cheapest or most accessible option for local students—including Catholic students who could attend nearby public institutions for more reasonable tuition.

Catholic immigrants were beneficiaries of this great expansion in education, but they were also agents of it. They built Catholic elementary schools at a breakneck pace. More than any other immigrant group, Catholics were creating a parallel society within the United States. They built their own schools, hospitals, senior centers, and cemeteries. At a time when there were hardly any government social services, Catholic priests, sisters, and brothers were often the only social safety net. They served as social workers, health care professionals, and caregivers to those who could not rely on their own families for help.

American Protestants had taken advantage of government financing for their schools and social service institutions since the colonial era. Even in the 1800s, it was common for taxpayer-funded public schools to include lessons on (the Protestant version of) the Bible. American Protestants never built a network of private schools comparable to that of their Catholic neighbors in part because they viewed the public school system as their own. As a result, many Catholic educators (including the Jesuits) were downright vitriolic toward the American public school system and viewed it as inherently anti-Catholic.[170]

---

170. McKevitt, *University of Santa Clara*, 106.

At first, Catholics received some public funding for their educational activities, just like their Protestant counterparts. As noted earlier, the first Jesuit missionaries who settled in St. Louis and built a network of Indian schools in the Plains and Rockies were largely supported by federal tax money. Georgetown's first government financial support came as early as the 1830s. However, as Catholics grew in number and their institutions became more visible in American society, some influential factions in America's Protestant ruling class discovered a renewed enthusiasm for the separation of church and state. Even though street mob violence against Catholics was becoming rarer and formal anti-Catholic political parties like the Know-Nothings had officially disbanded by the late 1800s, there were still plenty of opportunities for anti-Catholic bigots to weaken the Church's influence through stealth.

The Blaine Amendments

One way in which the anti-Catholic factions accomplished this goal was through a series of legislative maneuvers known as the Blaine Amendments. In 1876, Congressman (later Senator) James Blaine of Maine proposed a federal constitutional amendment banning government funding for schools controlled by religious groups. The proposal passed in the House but failed to clear the Senate, so proponents of the measure turned their attention to the various state constitutions.

This was a particularly fruitful era for such efforts, because many new western states were entering the Union and writing their state constitutions. Dozens of states, new and old, adopted constitutional amendments prohibiting state funding for religiously affiliated schools. Although the laws did not single out the Catholic Church by name, they were clearly targeting the country's booming Catholic school system, something supporters of the amendments readily admitted. (As of 2020, some version of the Blaine Amendments remained on the books in thirty-seven states.)[171] The result was that Catholics were largely on their own in building their civic infrastructure. Catholics built the country's biggest network of private schools, hospitals, and charities, largely on the backs of volunteers (along with significant debt). Despite the fact that their own government denied them support as a matter of policy, they nonetheless opened these institutions to Catholics and non-Catholics alike.

At the same time Catholic schools were under legal fire from the Blaine Amendments, they faced cultural opposition from the American academy. As a college education became more accessible to the poor and a degree came to be seen more as a right than a privilege for the elite, America's Protestant ruling classes pushed back by creating artificial barriers to admission in the country's most prestigious private universities.

Throughout American history, education has been seen, paradoxically, as both a human right and as a status symbol. The rich have used it as a way to differentiate

---

171. Nick Sibila, "The Court Case that Could Finally Take Down Antiquated Anti-Catholic Laws," *The Atlantic* (January 12, 2020), https://www.theatlantic.com/ideas/archive/2020/01/espinoza-montana-bigoted-laws/604756/.

themselves from the poor and restrict access to the upper class. Now that education was becoming widely available, the wealthiest Americans had to devise new ways to maintain their elitism. If public schools were opening their doors to anyone who wanted to learn, the rich would simply set up private schools where high tuition would limit enrollment to the privileged few. As more and more Americans sought to enter the learned professions like law and medicine, those professions kept their ranks small by mandating long and expensive entrance requirements—like a degree from an expensive university. Law schools, which previously required only a high school diploma or less for admission, began requiring a college degree; they also added a third year to their own degree programs, which made a legal education more expensive and out of reach for many.

With immigrants—Catholic and otherwise—flooding American society and gaining access to college degrees in record numbers, it was inevitable that there would be clashes between the upper-class establishment and activist groups—like the Jesuits—who sought to improve the status of the poor through education. One of the biggest controversies that erupted during this time pitted the Jesuits against an institution that represented the very pinnacle of the American establishment: Harvard University.

Harvard v. the Jesuits

No single individual represented the changing values in American higher education better than Harvard's longest-serving president, Charles W. Eliot. Eliot led the country's oldest university for four decades, from 1869 to 1909, and his time in office perfectly coincided with the rise of the American research university. Convinced that students should be free to choose their own path of study, Eliot replaced what was left of Harvard's traditional classical curriculum with a more laissez-faire elective system. In effect, he reconceptualized the university, not as an intellectual feast where students were served one prepared course after another, but as a buffet in which students could select from dozens of different offerings. The new approach fit nicely with the emerging model of a research university, where faculty specialized in narrow fields and demanded the academic freedom to teach whatever courses they wanted. Students selected courses as they would select any goods in a supermarket, with no inherent cohesion to the curriculum.

Eliot's concept of a college education could not have been more different from the Jesuit model. With their rigidly sequential, 300-year-old curriculum and emphasis on the classics, the Jesuits represented everything that Eliot considered broken about the traditional American education system. His bias had real effects. In the 1890s, Harvard Law School began publishing a list of approved colleges and universities around the country whose graduates it deemed "qualified" for admission without special examination. There were only three Catholic colleges included on the original 1893 list: Boston College, Georgetown, and Holy Cross. This came as a disappointment to graduates of St. John's College (Fordham) as well as the dozens of other Catholic colleges from coast to coast. A year later, Notre Dame was added to the list, making it the only non-Jesuit Catholic school to qualify.[172]

The ultimate insult came in 1897, when Boston College and Holy Cross both were removed from the list, leaving Georgetown as the sole representative of America's more than two dozen Jesuit colleges. The dean of Harvard Law notified the presidents of the two jilted Massachusetts schools that the decision had been made by a faculty committee. Harvard faculty had observed that alumni of Holy Cross and Boston College performed poorly in law school; only one Holy Cross graduate had come close to graduating with honors at Harvard Law, and the others were, on average, judged to be at least two years behind Harvard College alumni academically.[173]

Holy Cross and Boston College both argued that, since they followed the same *Ratio Studiorum* curriculum as Georgetown, it was illogical to exclude their alumni when Georgetown's were somehow deemed qualified for admission. Harvard briefly seemed willing to acquiesce to this request, but after St. John's College (Fordham) added its voice to the mix and made the same argument, Eliot balked. Holy Cross and Boston College would, like Fordham, remain off the list.[174]

There was some logic behind Harvard's decision to include Georgetown while excluding all other Jesuit schools, and it shows that the decision was not entirely motivated by academic concerns. Harvard at the time still drew most of its students from New England, so Holy Cross and Boston College were the only Jesuit schools reasonably likely to send large numbers of graduates to Harvard Law. Georgetown was still mainly a Southern school, and the number of its alumni who applied to Harvard was negligible. In a letter explaining himself to the president of Boston College, Eliot wrote, "Georgetown is the best of the Jesuit colleges, and is entitled to stand in the Law School list if any Jesuit college is to be admitted to the list." He even went so far as to admit that Harvard had kept Georgetown on the list in part to avoid the perception that all "Catholic colleges had been excluded on religious grounds."[175]

In other words, including Georgetown on the list was a relatively easy way for Harvard to show openness to Catholics on paper without actually admitting many. Although the curriculum at all Jesuit schools was virtually identical, Georgetown stood apart because its students were, in general, wealthier and more likely to come from the upper Protestant classes. Regardless of the educational similarities among the institutions, schools like Boston College, Holy Cross, and Fordham enrolled a high percentage of working-class Irish immigrants, precisely the kind of upwardly mobile urban poor who were not welcome at an elite institution like Harvard. Eliot's decision smacked of the kind of academic snobbery that would rattle Catholic univer-

---

172. Shelley, *Fordham*, 150. For a detailed look at the events described in this section, see also Kathleen A. Mahoney, *Catholic Higher Education in Protestant America: The Jesuits and Harvard in the Age of the University* (Baltimore: Johns Hopkins University Press, 2003).

173. Kuzniewski, *Thy Honored Name*, 178–179.

174. Ibid., 179.

175. As quoted in Ibid., 180.

sities for the next century, and it seems to have been motivated more by concerns about class than about classrooms.

The uproar over Harvard's decision in Catholic circles was so great that Eliot felt compelled to address it in an 1899 speech, which was adapted and published as an article in the *Atlantic Monthly* later that same year. Although the speech and the article mainly defended Harvard's elective system, Eliot used the opportunity to attack the *Ratio Studiorum*, describing it as an obsolete relic of the past comparable to the curriculum a Muslim student might encounter at a Middle Eastern madrassa. For Eliot, there was no way to justify a uniform school curriculum, particularly one that had been stale for centuries. He criticized the Jesuits for following a plan of study that "has remained almost unchanged for four hundred years, (sic) disregarding some trifling concessions made to natural science."[176]

Many Jesuits vociferously pushed back against these charges. Former Fordham president Thomas Campbell, SJ, took a scorched-earth approach, describing Eliot's ideas as academic fads that were doomed to fail. Campbell criticized any Catholic family foolish enough to buy into the nonsense of electivism and enroll their sons at a school like Harvard.[177] Fordham could afford to be harsh in its response because, realistically, it knew that its future dealings with Harvard would be minimal. Boston College, on the other hand, had to be more diplomatic in its approach. Hoping to express his concern without roiling the Boston educational establishment, Boston College president Read Mullen, SJ wrote a number of polite but firm rebuttal letters to Eliot that were later published in the *Boston Globe*.[178]

The most famous response to Eliot, however, came from former Boston College president Timothy Brosnahan, SJ, who was then on the seminary faculty at Woodstock College in Maryland. Brosnahan wrote a thoughtful and eloquent rebuttal to Eliot's article that he attempted to publish in the *Atlantic Monthly*, but the editors rejected it, refusing the print the Catholic counterpoint to Eliot's original piece. Brosnahan had no choice but to publish his response in a Catholic periodical, the *Sacred Heart Review*, in 1900. Among other things, he pointed out that Eliot's understanding of the *Ratio Studiorum* was factually incorrect in at least one detail: the Jesuit curriculum was 300 years old, not 400 as Eliot had claimed. Brosnahan also made a cogent defense of the role of the humanities in education, and pointed out that the Jesuits' concessions to natural science were more than "trifling." He argued, furthermore, that a student at a Jesuit college could potentially have more exposure to modern science than a student at Harvard, where Eliot's elective system made it possible to graduate without taking any science courses at all.[179]

By itself, Harvard's dismissal of the Jesuit education system would have been damaging enough, but the snubs were not limited to Harvard Law. A similar contro-

---

176. As quoted in Ibid., 181. See also Shelley, *Fordham*, 150–151.
177. Shelley, *Fordham*, 151–152.
178. Kuzniewski, *Thy Honored Name*, 181.
179. Shelley, *Fordham*, 151.

versy took place in New Orleans in 1910, when Tulane Law School refused admission to three Loyola University alumni. Ostensibly, this was because Loyola students graduated from the *Ratio Studiorum* curriculum after six years without a transcript. They had spent their college years enrolled in what amounted to an experience, not in specific courses. The Tulane admissions committee, therefore, felt that it was unable to judge what Loyola students had studied or how well they had performed. When Tulane asked Loyola for a course catalogue, the Jesuits could not provide one, because they had never even printed one for Loyola; they simply provided a copy of the catalogue from Spring Hill College, explaining that the curriculum in every Jesuit school was the same.[180]

Tulane's president, Edwin Craighead, eventually learned about the controversy and, to his credit, berated his faculty on the law admissions committee for discriminating against Catholic college graduates. After all, Tulane's law, medical, and engineering schools at the time routinely admitted students with *no* college degree at all. Why deny admission to Loyola graduates who exceeded those standards? Ultimately, the Tulane faculty blinked and agreed to recognize Loyola degrees as legitimate. As a side effect, Tulane also began to recognize degrees from Spring Hill.[181] Four years later, Loyola opened a law school of its own.

Culture Clash and Growing Pains in Academia

The clashes between Harvard, Tulane, and the Jesuits were visible symptoms of a broader shift taking place in American higher education. Many leading American universities were, like Harvard, transitioning from the small, faith-based liberal arts colleges they had always been into large, modern institutions that emphasized research over undergraduate education. University faculty were beginning to think of themselves as a distinct profession comparable to lawyers or doctors, and they created new professional organizations to advocate for their interests. The American Association of University Professors (AAUP), founded in 1915, promoted national standards for tenure and academic freedom—the notion that professors had a right to teach and study whatever they chose without fear of losing their jobs.

As the industrial revolution swept across the United States, innovation in science and technology became a top priority for American corporations, and they used their considerable wealth to invest in research institutes that advanced their business prospects. In Pittsburgh, steel magnate Andrew Carnegie established Carnegie Technical Schools, and aluminum magnate Andrew Mellon established the business-friendly Mellon Institute for Industrial Research (the two forerunners of modern-day Carnegie Mellon University) in 1900 and 1913, respectively. Such institutions pushed American academia even further toward practical, applied research—continuing a trend that began with the land-grant universities in the 1860s. Andrew

---

180. Platt, *Sacrifice*, 123. Cook, *Founded on Faith*, 43–44.
181. Platt, *Sacrifice*, 123. Cook, *Founded on Faith*, 43–44.

Carnegie also invested in the Carnegie Teachers Pension Fund, forerunner of the Carnegie Foundation for the Advancement of Teaching, in 1905 to provide pensions to university employees. Along with the AAUP and the newly formed accreditation agencies, these organizations pushed all American universities to fall in line with the emerging national standards for tenure, faculty governance, and academic freedom.[182] A national academic culture began to take shape, one that was defined by secular scientific standards of excellence much more than by local tradition. In the process, American higher education was becoming homogenized.

In this environment, faculty members who had once been loyal to their institutions were now becoming loyal primarily to their disciplines.[183] The need to conduct research efficiently meant that all economists, all engineers, all chemists had to speak the same professional languages and operate their labs according to standard practices. As a result, scientists increasingly expected that their work habits and responsibilities would be no different whether they taught at a Jesuit school or a land grant school.[184]

The concept of academic freedom was slow to take hold at Catholic institutions, because most faculty were priests bound by vows of obedience to their superior, the college president. In public and Protestant institutions, however, academic freedom quickly redefined the college experience and shifted the role of a faculty member from knowledge transmission to knowledge creation.

The Catholic approach to education was so radically different from the emerging research university model that many academic elites began to think of the term "Catholic university" as an oxymoron.[185] Catholic colleges were designed to preserve ancient wisdom passed down through the centuries, not to innovate. As mainstream academia left traditional liberal education in the rear-view mirror, the Jesuits and their *Ratio Studiorum* increasingly seemed out of touch and old-fashioned. The Catholic intellectual tradition emphasized philosophy and the classics, which served to reinforce existing anti-Catholic prejudices among academics who saw those fields as irrelevant to "true" science.

Those Catholic and Jesuit universities that attempted to follow their cherished traditions were essentially left out of the academic arms race. The one Catholic institution designed to meet the new standards, the Catholic University of America, was struggling financially. Meanwhile, the only Catholic university that had a history and reputation strong enough to develop into a university of national scope—Georgetown—was self-consciously limiting its growth to avoid competing with its crosstown rival and angering the American bishops.

182. Marsden, *Soul*, 281–282, 306.

183. Stephen M. Fields, "Newman's Challenge to the Contemporary Academy," *Christian Higher Education* 2, no. 3 (2003): 251–267.

184. Michael Rizzi, "Newman's *Idea of a University* in Dialogue with the Land O'Lakes Statement of 1967," *Newman Studies Journal* 16, no. 2 (2019): 40.

185. Paul A. Fitzgerald, SJ, *The Governance of Jesuit Colleges in the United States, 1920–1970* (Notre Dame: University of Notre Dame Press, 1984), 24. Marsden, *Soul*, 246.

The Jesuits Become a Bastion of Conservatism

As these winds of change were blowing, the Jesuits' initial reaction in the late nineteenth century was to dig in their heels and recommit firmly to the classical curriculum. In 1887, the Missouri Jesuits published a guidebook for their seven colleges and universities that reaffirmed the value of the *Ratio Studiorum* and even encouraged colleges to discontinue their commercial courses whenever feasible. As historian Philip Gleason explains, "the Jesuits believed that by adamantly opposing everything that smacked of utilitarianism they were standing foursquare in their tradition."[186] Many Jesuit colleges still relied on the students in the popular commercial track for tuition income, however, so eliminating those programs was out of the question for all but the wealthiest and best-established Jesuit institutions. Nonetheless, the Jesuits continued to give lip service to the idea that their schools were first and foremost classical colleges, even though enrollment statistics suggested that many were primarily high schools with attached commercial programs.

In the east, the Maryland-New York Province released a similar document in 1889 that urged its nine colleges and universities to stand firm in their tradition, no matter the market conditions. St. John's College (Fordham) briefly discontinued its commercial division in the 1890s but saw a dramatic decrease in enrollment as a result.[187] The western Jesuits were equally committed to the old ways—to such an extent that Santa Clara and its sister schools were soon dwarfed by emerging research giants like Stanford and Berkeley. Even the incentive of free tuition could not entice students at St. Joseph's College in San Jose to enroll in the empty classical division over the popular commercial track.

It became increasingly difficult to sustain these conservative positions. Gradually, the Jesuits softened their opposition to all things modern. There were two main reasons. First was a decision by the Jesuit leadership in Rome. Meeting in a worldwide congregation in 1906, the Jesuits considered revising and modernizing the *Ratio Studiorum*, but ultimately decided that they could not come up with a single curriculum that met the "special needs of (all of the) different countries" in which they operated schools. They chose instead to empower each individual Jesuit province to adapt the *Ratio* to local customs.[188] This development was significant, because it officially acknowledged the reality that there were (and should be) regional variations in the universal Jesuit curriculum. In the United States, Missouri Provincial Henry Moeller, SJ, responded rapidly by reorganizing the traditional six-year curriculum at all of the province's schools into an eight-year curriculum—four years of high school, and four years of college. The Midwestern Jesuit schools were finally operating on the same timetable as their secular counterparts.[189]

---

186. Gleason, *Contending*, 53.
187. Ibid., 54.
188. As quoted in Garraghan, *Jesuits of the Middle U.S. Vol. III*, 508.
189. Ibid., 508.

The second reason for the change was the generational shift that took place in the early 1900s, as Jesuits who had served as college presidents and professors at the turn of the century rose to higher office in the provinces, replacing their more conservative predecessors who had come of age around the time of the Civil War. This new generation of leaders was less nostalgic for the old ways and understood from experience that Jesuit colleges would have to adapt if they hoped to survive. By the early 1910s, many Jesuit provincials were ready to approve aggressive steps toward modernization, including graduate and professional programs.

The First Jesuit Graduate Schools

Graduate education was the first concession that many Jesuit universities made to the new trends. Universities like Georgetown and Saint Louis had awarded master's degrees since the mid-1800s, but as was standard practice at that time, those degrees were essentially honorary and were given to those who could demonstrate independent study of a subject over a one- or two-year period. The notion that a graduate degree could be taught and awarded on the basis of classroom work was new to the late 1800s, and it roughly coincided with the rise of the research university. Saint Louis University was the first Jesuit institution to modernize its criteria for graduate degrees: beginning in 1861, it gave master's candidates the option *either* to spend a year studying philosophy on campus *or* to demonstrate two years of work "in a learned profession." This was likely an attempt to boost enrollment during the Civil War, but it did not work; no students chose the first option for many years. The first American universities to confer master's degrees based on an actual in-class curriculum were Harvard (1874), Yale (1876), and Princeton (1879).[190]

Now that master's degrees were beginning to recognize something more than general intelligence, they presented a problem for Jesuit schools. Because it was a specialized academic credential, a master's degree implied that a student had studied a single topic intensely. The Jesuits so far had resisted that kind of specialization among their faculty and their students. Academically, the move to graduate education meant that the Jesuits would have to think beyond their broad, undergraduate liberal arts curriculum and devise a narrower program of study for graduate students. Administratively, it implied that Jesuit colleges would have to organize themselves into specialized departments. For the first time, Jesuit colleges would have to operate as something other than a single academic unit where all priest-professors taught all subjects.

There was some precedent for this, since Jesuit schools had occasionally hired lay faculty who specialized in teaching music, bookkeeping, or other subjects, and some law and medical departments had operated more or less autonomously from the main university. But change came slowly, and the push to organize departments of English, chemistry, history, etc. did not truly pick up steam until the 1920s.[191]

---

190. Power, *Catholic Higher Education*, 338–339.
191. Gleason, *Contending*, 57.

Some of the largest Jesuit universities, like Georgetown, Saint Louis, and Fordham, experimented in the meantime with offering what amounted to "general" master's degrees in philosophy. Georgetown published a catalogue listing the requirements for its A.M. degree in 1877. If that milestone represents the origins of Georgetown's graduate school, then it qualifies as the first Catholic graduate school in the United States. In truth, however, what Georgetown developed that year was more a set of curriculum requirements than a graduate school, and it did not organize a formal graduate department until 1891. Whatever its true origin, Georgetown's place in the vanguard of this movement was cut short. Facing pressure to let the Catholic University of America handle all graduate education in the nation's capital, Georgetown's graduate programs went on hiatus from 1907 to 1914. The Jesuit superior general in Rome, Franz Wernz, SJ, directed the Maryland-New York Province to invest in Fordham as its flagship research university over Georgetown. Only Wernz's death in 1914 finally stemmed the flow of resources from Washington to New York and enabled Georgetown to revive its dormant graduate school.[192]

Saint Louis University, which had both a long tradition of awarding master's degrees and a well-known evening lecture series open to the community, decided to combine the two initiatives in the early 1880s and offer a master's degree to any student who attended the lecture series consistently. Meanwhile, many other Jesuit institutions continued to offer the old-fashioned master's degree based essentially on a student's reputation. Although the requirements were often minimal and were inconsistent from school to school, the number of students who received master's degrees from Jesuit institutions in the late 1800s remained small. The only colleges that awarded them on a semi-regular basis were Georgetown, Holy Cross, Saint Louis, Spring Hill, St. Ignatius (San Francisco), St. John's (Fordham), St. Francis Xavier (New York), Santa Clara, and Xavier (Cincinnati). Most of these institutions awarded only one or two master's degrees per year, and even the best-established programs rarely awarded more than fifteen in a year.[193]

Doctoral degrees were largely beyond the pale at this time. Historian Philip Gleason identifies Saint Louis University as the first American Catholic university to confer a PhD for anything other than honorary causes; in 1883, it awarded a doctorate to a Protestant minister, Rev. Martin Willis, apparently after actual classroom work. Georgetown was experimenting with an institutionalized PhD program by the 1890s, but that program, like the rest of Georgetown's graduate programs, was suppressed shortly thereafter in deference to the Catholic University of America. It would not be until well into the 1900s, mostly in the 1920s and 1930s, that Jesuit institutions would begin to offer PhDs in step with their secular counterparts.[194]

---

192. Ibid., 170. Curran, *History of Georgetown Vol. II*, 11, 56. Power, *Catholic Higher Education*, 339–340.

193. Power, *Catholic Higher Education*, 339–342.

194. Gleason, *Contending*, 170.

Professional Schools

Although graduate school was slow to come to Jesuit universities, schools of law, medicine, and other professions thrived—especially after the turn of the twentieth century, when the Jesuits deliberately developed many of their colleges into comprehensive universities. The best way to do so was often to add new degree programs, either by incorporating already-existing schools of pharmacy, dentistry, etc. into the college, or by building such schools from scratch.

By the early 1900s, it was obvious that Catholic immigrants and their children could acquire wealth, prestige, and status in American society relatively quickly through professions like law and medicine. If America's best law schools (like Harvard and Tulane) were deliberately stacking the deck against Catholic applicants and denying admission to alumni of Jesuit colleges, then the most obvious solution was for the Jesuits to start law schools of their own.[195]

Enrollment in the high-demand professional schools often exceeded that in the core classical colleges. Many Jesuits remained steadfast in their commitment to the *Ratio Studiorum,* but as tuition revenue from the surging law and engineering programs began to prop up the struggling classical divisions, professional schools became essential to the survival of some Jesuit institutions. By the onset of World War I, the enrollment patterns at many Jesuit universities had evolved into an awkward barbell shape. On one extreme were the large high school divisions; on the other were the professional schools, and in the middle were the classical bachelor's degree programs—still taught by Jesuit faculty, but relatively small compared to the rest of the university.

Often these professional schools were located on separate campuses, usually in downtown areas convenient to transportation. Georgetown's law and medical schools were originally located in their own buildings in downtown Washington. Fordham concentrated most of its professional schools, including law, education, social service, and business, in rented space in the Woolworth Building in Manhattan starting in 1916. Even when the Woolworth lease expired, the advantages of a downtown location were too great to ignore, and Fordham relocated the schools to a building near New York's City Hall and ultimately to Lincoln Center.[196] In Chicago, Loyola University maintained a downtown campus for its schools of law, business, and social work. In Detroit and Los Angeles, the Jesuit universities kept their law schools downtown even when their undergraduate programs relocated to green suburban campuses.

Another common thread uniting the professional schools was their predominantly lay faculty. Because only a handful of Jesuits were trained as lawyers, medical doctors, or engineers, adding professional schools inevitably meant hiring lay professors. For the first time, non-Jesuit and even non-Catholic professors could make a living by teaching full-time at Jesuit universities. Professional schools in the nine-

---

195. Rizzi, "We've Been Here Before," 158–159.
196. Shelley, *Fordham,* 281, 287.

teenth century began a phenomenon that continued into the twentieth century and beyond, as the faculty became predominantly lay and more diverse.

Their separate campuses, lay leadership, and academic autonomy helped to give the professional schools a sense of separation from the main university. The Jesuits nominally held control, but the lay deans and faculty sometimes ran the schools with minimal supervision. Over time, the Jesuits sought to rectify this issue by creating the position of "regent"—a Jesuit priest appointed as titular head of the professional school. Regents had final authority over decisions and represented the central university and its Jesuit administration at school-level meetings. Underneath the regent was the dean, who actually managed the school's day-to-day operations. In practice, some regents were little more than figureheads, while others could and did micromanage their subordinates. To the extent possible, the Jesuits also tried to keep physical reminders of the university's Jesuit identity visible in the professional schools. At Fordham's City Hall campus, for example, an inscription above the door read "Magnas Ignatius Urbes," which historian John Daley, SJ translates loosely to mean, "St. Bernard loved the valleys, Benedict the hills, Francis the little towns, but Ignatius sought the great cities."[197]

Seminaries

Technically, the first professional schools at Jesuit colleges were theology programs for seminarians. Many of the schools that began life as diocesan colleges—including Fordham, Saint Louis, Spring Hill, and Xavier—housed seminary divisions in the early 1800s. Smaller Jesuit schools like St. Charles (Louisiana), Gonzaga (DC), and St. John's (Maryland) were used to train Jesuit priests, as was Georgetown, sporadically. Boston College even began its life as a seminary. However, these were marriages of convenience, and in keeping with Catholic tradition, most theology programs moved off campus in the mid-1800s or as soon as separate seminaries could be built. It would not be until the late 1900s that most of these seminaries closed or re-incorporated into the colleges as a cost-saving measure.

Medical Schools

The first non-seminary professional programs at Jesuit colleges were in medicine. Jesuit authorities in Rome proposed a medical school for Georgetown as early as the 1830s, but nothing came from those discussions. Saint Louis University established the nation's first Jesuit medical school in 1842 after recruiting a group of local doctors and promising them near-full autonomy in managing it. However, as already mentioned, violent anti-Catholic street mobs repeatedly attacked the school, forcing it to separate from the university in 1855. For the next few decades, the former Saint Louis University Medical School operated independently, without Catholic supervision, as

---

197. Daley, *Georgetown University*, 178 (n. 39).

the St. Louis Medical College. In 1891, it affiliated with Washington University in St. Louis, and still exists today as that institution's highly acclaimed School of Medicine. Since Washington University's reputation today is built largely around its outstanding medical programs, it is no stretch to say that Saint Louis University's loss was Washington University's gain.

The first permanent Jesuit medical school emerged at Georgetown, mostly by serendipity. In 1849, an ecumenical group of four Catholic, Protestant, and Jewish doctors in Washington petitioned Georgetown President James Ryder, SJ, to put the university's weight behind a medical school that they hoped to establish. The school was to be financially independent of the university, and as was the case at all such "proprietary" schools at the time, its faculty planned to split the tuition profits among themselves at the end of the academic year. Georgetown invested very little in the project, but the university's endorsement was important because it enabled the medical school to award degrees under Georgetown's charter. Considering its downtown location and its minimal Jesuit involvement, the school was part of Georgetown University in name only until the late 1800s. By then, the original proprietary faculty members had retired or resigned, opening the door for Georgetown presidents Patrick Healy, SJ (in the 1870s) and J. Havens Richards, SJ (in the 1890s) to take steps that brought the medical school more fully into the Georgetown fold.[198]

Almost forty years after the debacle in St. Louis, the Missouri Province Jesuits returned to medical education in 1892, when the Creighton family's largesse enabled them to open a new medical school in Omaha. Creighton University Medical School worked hand in hand with the family's other benefaction, Creighton Memorial Hospital, and was among the best schools of its kind west of the Mississippi. Its donors' deep pockets enabled it to buy state-of-the-art scientific equipment never before seen in Nebraska.[199] Unfortunately, because of the high start-up costs for medical schools, few other Jesuit universities could follow Creighton's example and build a new school from the ground up. Far more often, they simply acquired existing medical schools.

The issue of start-up costs became particularly apparent in St. Louis over the next decade. Saint Louis University had the opportunity to revive medical education on its campus in the 1890s, but President Joseph Grimmelsman, SJ declined a petition by local Catholic doctors to open a medical school at the university. The idea did not become feasible until 1903, when a new president, William Banks Rogers, SJ, approved an offer to affiliate with the existing Marion Sims-Beaumont College of Medicine.[200]

Once the Missouri Province Jesuits reacquired a taste for medical education in Omaha and St. Louis, they charged forward elsewhere. Marquette University acquired the independent Milwaukee Medical College in 1907, and between 1909 and 1910, Loyola University (Chicago) acquired both the Illinois Medical School and the Bennet School of Medicine. Seven years later, Loyola also purchased the assets of the

---

198. Curran, *History of Georgetown Vol. I*, 156–160, 329–330. *Vol. II*, 25.
199. Garraghan, *Jesuits of the Middle U.S. Vol. III*, 473.
200. Faherty, *Saint Louis University*, 15–16.

Chicago College of Medicine and Surgery.[201] With four medical schools now under the supervision of the Missouri Province, medicine became a key ministry for the Midwestern Jesuits.

Marquette's medical school proved problematic from the start, and once again, Father Grimmelsman was involved. After stepping down from the Saint Louis presidency, Grimmelsman served a second term as president of Marquette, where he clashed with the medical faculty. Marquette's new medical school was a proprietary institution like Georgetown's, and Grimmelsman accused it of prioritizing profit over quality education. The university and the medical school parted ways in 1912, a year after Grimmelsman took office. Despite his pugnacious track record, Grimmelsman had no animus toward medical education; under his leadership, Marquette soon entered into another affiliation agreement with the Wisconsin College of Physicians and Surgeons.[202] That marriage lasted more than fifty years, but ultimately the school spun off and became the independent Medical College of Wisconsin in 1967. Even after separating, the university and the medical college continued to collaborate; today, they sponsor a joint department of biomedical engineering.

In the Maryland-New York Province, a medical school was an important part of the brief effort to transform Fordham into the flagship Jesuit research university in the East. The Fordham Medical School opened in 1905 and existed for just sixteen years. Despite grand ambitions and the strong support of the Jesuit superiors, the project faced serious problems. City regulators hesitated to allow Fordham to open a hospital on its campus because there was already a brand-new public municipal hospital in the neighborhood—located on property that Fordham itself had sold to the city in 1904. A succession of embattled deans struggled to raise funds for the school, which began hemorrhaging money and operating on unsustainable deficits. Pressuring Fordham to build better facilities, the American Medical Association briefly downgraded the school to its list of second-tier institutions from 1913 to 1914.[203]

For all of its problems, Fordham Medical School did develop a decent reputation and played an important role in the New York City healthcare scene. Unlike other medical schools in the United States, it did not place restrictions on the religion of the students who enrolled and opened its doors widely to New York's Jewish residents, who were frequently at the mercy of discriminatory admissions quotas elsewhere. As a result, most of the Catholic medical school's students were Jewish.[204] By 1921, however, the financial losses became unsustainable and the Jesuits closed Fordham Medical School for good, leaving Georgetown as the sole Jesuit medical school in the East.

Loyola University (New Orleans) briefly toyed with medical education starting in 1915, but not much came of the effort. Some Loyola medical and dental faculty received international attention during World War I when they helped to staff a US

---

201. Garraghan, *Jesuits of the Middle U.S. Vol. III*, 461.

202. Ibid., 455.

203. Shelley, *Fordham*, 181–189.

204. Ibid., 190.

Army base hospital in Italy, and along with the Sisters of Charity from New Orleans who served as nurses, they would go down in military history as the "Loyola Unit." But by 1922 Loyola had closed its medical division.[205]

Lastly, the University of Detroit attempted to acquire the Detroit Medical College between 1909 and 1911, but the asking price ($225,000) was seen as too high.[206] Rebuffed, Detroit Medical College eventually merged with several other local schools in 1933 to form what is now known as Wayne State University.

One snapshot of American (and Jesuit) medical education at this time comes from the Flexner Report. In 1910, the Carnegie Foundation for the Advancement of Teaching published the results of a two-year nationwide inspection tour of all 155 medical schools in the United States and Canada, with the goal of reforming and standardizing medical education. The Flexner Report was critical of most medical schools around the country and recommended closing more than 75% of them. It was particularly disparaging toward proprietary schools, which often admitted students who lacked even a high-school level of education and used their tuition profits to enrich faculty rather than invest in lab equipment. It pushed all schools to adhere to the model emerging at Johns Hopkins, where the medical school was first and foremost dedicated to scientific research. In the decades following the report, across the country, the majority of the medical schools that had been labeled as inadequate closed—including virtually all historically Black institutions. The five Jesuit-affiliated medical schools were subject to many of the same criticisms as their secular counterparts, but four avoided closure. The only casualty was Fordham, which shuttered in 1922 despite a fairly average review in the report. Ironically, Fordham, along with Marquette, was one of the two Jesuit schools with the highest admissions standards at the time; both required applicants to have at least a high-school level of education. The report notes the following statistics for the Jesuit-affiliated schools: 89 students and 74 instructors at Georgetown; 168 students and 67 instructors at Marquette; 175 students and 49 instructors at Creighton; 42 students and 72 instructors at Fordham; 243 students and 121 instructors at Saint Louis. (Loyola in Chicago was still in the process of acquiring its medical school.) Most faculty were part-time; the report criticized Creighton because it relied on the Omaha city gas inspector to teach chemistry. It also noted that Georgetown and Marquette Medical Schools were part of their parent universities in name only, whereas the schools at Fordham, Creighton, and Saint Louis were more closely integrated with the rest of their institutions. In a rare instance of praise, it singled out Saint Louis University as "an excellent example" of an up-and-coming school that was achieving good results with a limited budget.[207]

205. Cook, *Founded on Faith*, 62, 77.

206. Muller, *University of Detroit*, 157–159.

207. Flexner, Abraham, *Medical Education in the United States and Canada* (New York: Carnegie Foundation for the Advancement of Teaching, 1910), 79, 81, 201, 255, 259, 260–61, 270, 318, http://archive.carnegiefoundation.org/publications/pdfs/elibrary/Carnegie_Flexner_Report.pdf .

Outside of the Jesuit network, no other Catholic university successfully developed an allopathic medical school—that is, a medical school that awards the M.D. degree. Niagara University and Seton Hall University abandoned their short-lived medical schools, the latter of which became independent and ultimately incorporated into Rutgers. More recently, a handful of Catholic institutions like Marian University in Indianapolis, the University of the Incarnate Word in Texas, and Duquesne University in Pittsburgh have taken steps to open osteopathic medical schools, which award the D.O. degree rather than the M.D. There are also some Catholic universities, like Notre Dame in Indiana and Seton Hill in Pennsylvania, that allow third-party medical schools to hold classes on their campuses. One Jesuit institution, Gonzaga University, entered into such an arrangement with the University of Washington School of Medicine in 2016. But across the country, there remain only four Catholic universities that grant a traditional medical degree in their own names: Georgetown, Saint Louis, Creighton, and Loyola (Chicago).

At the four Jesuit universities where they existed and thrived in the long term, medical schools were transformative. They required massive financial investments and brought ancillary institutions to campus, including hospitals, pharmacy and dental schools, and even nursing schools, which were a precursor to full coeducation. In the long term, they also did more than any other professional schools to contribute to the Jesuit universities' research capacity, which would become critically important in the twentieth century as they applied for federal research dollars.

Dental Schools

The prevalence of dental schools at Jesuit universities is something of a curiosity. Very few private universities in American history have ever established dental schools. There is nothing unusual about the dental profession that makes it particularly suited to the Jesuit brand of education, but dental schools emerged at Georgetown, Saint Louis, Marquette, Detroit, Loyola (Chicago), Loyola (New Orleans), and Creighton. One explanation is that Jesuit universities with medical schools saw value in rounding out their healthcare programs by adding programs in dentistry. Six of the seven Jesuit universities with a dental school also had some form of medical school.

More than half of the Jesuit dental schools were obtained by acquisition. Georgetown acquired the independent Washington Dental College in 1901. Perhaps in emulation of Georgetown, others followed suit. The dental schools at Saint Louis and Marquette came packaged together with the medical schools that they acquired in 1903 and 1907, respectively. Loyola University (Chicago) affiliated with the Chicago College of Dentistry in 1923. The exceptions were Creighton University, which built its own dental school in 1905 through the generosity of the Creighton family, and Loyola University (New Orleans), which built its own dental school in 1914. In New Orleans, the new school was a strategic move by Loyola's founding president, Father Albert Biever, to take advantage of deteriorating conditions at neighboring Tulane University. Tulane Dental School was facing serious financial trouble, and when it closed permanently, several of its best faculty moved across the street to form the core of a new school at Loyola. In effect, Loyola stole the school from its secular rival.[208] Much later, in 1932, the University of Detroit built its own dental program; it originally hoped to revive its old plans for a medical school at the same time, but the Great Depression forced it to scale back those ambitions.[209]

The dental education at Jesuit universities was, overall, reputable. Georgetown's dental school boasted Alexander Graham Bell as an early faculty member, and by the late 1900s, it had grown into the biggest dental school in the country. However, as prevalent as they once were, several Jesuit dental schools closed from the 1960s to the 1990s. This was not a phenomenon unique to Jesuit universities; the dental profession was changing rapidly and the American education system was graduating far more dentists than the employment market could support. It was also virtually impossible for a dental school to turn a profit or break even on its finances; the high cost of educating a dentist meant that only taxpayer-subsidized public universities could generally afford to do so. Emory University and Northwestern University were among the private universities that discontinued their dental schools, and since both of those prestigious institutions had much bigger endowments than any Jesuit university, it is hard to imagine how the Jesuit schools could have avoided a similar fate.

Saint Louis University discontinued its dental school in 1967 and replaced it with a much smaller graduate program in orthodontics, which still exists today as the Center for Advanced Dental Education. Loyola University (New Orleans) closed its dental school in 1971; the State of Louisiana stepped in to build a publicly funded dental school in New Orleans that same year. Georgetown and Loyola (Chicago) closed their schools in 1990 and 1993, respectively.

This left only Marquette, Creighton, and Detroit. Marquette's program, being the only dental school in the State of Wisconsin, receives taxpayer support and offers reduced tuition for Wisconsin residents; it functions essentially as a public school under the auspices of a private university. The survival of the programs at Creighton and the University of Detroit Mercy is a testament to their leadership, faculty, and community support. The Detroit dental school teetered on the brink of closure after accreditors from the American Dental Association visited in 1993 and identified serious problems with its facilities. Recognizing how important the school was to the dental profession in Michigan, the university met the challenge and built a new facility in 1996.[210]

---

208. Cook, *Founded on Faith*, 59.

209. Muller, *University of Detroit*, 186–187.

210. Shari S. Cohen, "University of Detroit Mercy—Renewal and Change for a New Century," in *Legacy of Excellence: A Continuing History of Jesuit and Mercy Higher Education in Detroit*, ed. Herman J. Muller, SJ, Mary Justine Sabourin, RSM, and Shari S. Cohen (Detroit: University of Detroit Mercy Press, 2003), 268–269.

Hospitals, Nursing Schools, and Pharmacy Schools

Jesuit universities with medical and dental schools inevitably opened clinics. At the turn of the twentieth century, hospitals were much less complex institutions than they are today. They were essentially charities—places where the poor could go for healthcare if they could not afford the luxury of a doctor's house call. Many hospitals consisted of a single building with beds, often arranged in an open floor plan. Although there were plenty of Catholic hospitals operating in the United States, most were run by women's religious orders; the Jesuits were not particularly known for their expertise in healthcare. Therefore, when the Jesuits affiliated with a hospital or built one from the ground up, they generally entrusted its day-to-day management to an order of Catholic nuns who also provided most of the patient care.

The first hospital to affiliate with a Jesuit university was in Omaha, although the Jesuits had relatively little to do with it. The Franciscan Sisters had run a small hospital there for eight years when, in 1888, the Creighton family took an interest in the operation and donated a sizeable endowment; it renamed itself Creighton Memorial Hospital in gratitude. Four years later, the Creighton family, perceiving that a medical school could support their interest in the hospital, reached out to the Jesuits and endowed Creighton Medical School at their eponymous university. The two institutions entered into a lasting and mutually supportive affiliation.[211]

Georgetown was the first Jesuit university to build a hospital from scratch. Georgetown University Hospital opened in 1898, two blocks from the university's main campus, in what is known today as Nevils, a residence hall. Once again, the Franciscan Sisters provided the clinical staff.[212] In Milwaukee, Marquette, between 1912 and 1923, affiliated with Trinity Hospital to support its ill-fated medical school. In Missouri, Saint Louis University Medical School cooperated with several independent Catholic hospitals in the city, but eventually built its own medical center through a bequest in the 1930s.[213]

The healthcare snowball kept rolling and growing. Because hospitals needed a supply of clinical workers to keep them afloat, many established their own training schools for nurses. The Franciscan Sisters who operated Georgetown University Hospital began teaching young nurses in 1903. At the time, the program was not a fully incorporated school of Georgetown University, nor did it offer bachelor's degrees; it simply awarded diplomas. Nonetheless, it was affiliated with the broader Georgetown enterprise, and the young women who enrolled technically became Georgetown students. When Marquette acquired Trinity Hospital, the hospital's nursing school came along as part of the package. By the 1930s, Marquette had also affiliated with Milwaukee's St. Joseph's Hospital, which had its own nurses' training division.

---

211. Garraghan, *Jesuits of the Middle U.S. Vol. III*, 473. Dennis N. Mihelich, *The History of Creighton University: 1878–2003* (Omaha: Creighton University Press, 2006), 74.

212. Curran, *History of Georgetown Vol. II*, 27.

213. Garraghan, *Jesuits of the Middle U.S. Vol. III*, 445, 456.

Over time, because these nurses' training programs were associated with Jesuit universities, they began to offer nursing degrees under the universities' charters. In 1936, the St. Joseph's Hospital nursing program in Milwaukee fully incorporated into Marquette University as the Marquette College of Nursing. In Omaha, between 1928 and 1929, Creighton University affiliated with two local nursing diploma programs run by the Franciscan Sisters at St. Joseph's Hospital and the Sisters of Mercy at St. Catherine's Hospital, opening the door for ambitious students at either school to continue their education beyond the nursing certificate and toward a bachelor of science degree.[214] In 1935, Loyola University (Chicago) entered into an agreement with five different Chicago-area hospitals and combined their nurses' training schools into a single entity, the Loyola University School of Nursing.[215] Saint Louis University opened its nursing school in 1928 and began offering bachelor's degrees almost immediately.[216] By the end of the 1930s, every Jesuit medical school had a nursing school associated with it.

Today, thirteen of the twenty-seven Jesuit colleges and universities sponsor schools of nursing. While most of these schools emerged independently during the 1930s or later, it was the medical centers and hospitals that first introduced nursing— and in most cases, female undergraduate students—to Jesuit higher education.

Creighton also expanded its healthcare programs by acquiring the Omaha School of Pharmacy in 1905. Marquette briefly acquired a pharmacy school as part of its original merger with the Milwaukee School of Medicine, and Loyola (New Orleans) acquired the New Orleans College of Pharmacy in 1919. Neither Marquette's nor Loyola's programs would survive, however, leaving Creighton as the sole Jesuit pharmacy school in the United States.

The four principal Jesuit hospitals at Georgetown, Saint Louis, Creighton, and Loyola (Chicago) built vast clinical networks throughout their respective regions, opening dozens of outpatient centers, cancer centers, nursing homes, and other facilities under the university's brand. By the late 1900s, though, the economics of healthcare in the United States were changing and independent, private hospital systems found it difficult to operate without heavy financial losses. By the early twenty-first century, all four Jesuit university hospital systems had affiliated with much larger healthcare networks to share costs and minimize risk. Today, as is typical among many university health systems, none of the four Jesuit hospitals is managed directly by its affiliated university. The hospitals and universities operate as separate but cooperative institutions, with the hospitals managing all clinical activities and the universi-

214. Mihelich, *History of Creighton*, 171–174.

215. "Niehoff School of Nursing Golden Jubilee Celebration," Loyola University Chicago, Archives and Special Collections, NSON–Golden Jubilee records UA1985.16, updated Oct. 2010, https://www.luc.edu/media/lucedu/archives/pdfs/nson_jubilee.pdf.

216. Saint Louis University School of Nursing, "Carrying Commitment Forward: School of Nursing Celebrates 90 Years," *Cura Personalis* (Spring 2018): passim, esp. 5–7, https://www.slu.edu/nursing/about/cura-pdfs-jpgs/curapersonalis2018.pdf.

ties generally managing research and residency programs. The Jesuits on the university campus typically also provide pastoral care to the hospital patients.

Law Schools

By the early 1900s, law schools had become the most common professional schools at Jesuit universities. With secular American law schools like Harvard and Tulane discriminating against Catholics in general and against the Jesuit educational system in particular, it was inevitable that the Jesuits would find themselves drawn into legal education. It was, in many respects, a perfect match. Thousands of first-generation Americans were seeking to become lawyers as a way to improve their economic prospects, especially in the densely populated cities home to Jesuit universities. Unlike medical schools, law schools were inexpensive to operate; they required no labs or scientific equipment—just books and classroom space. The means of legal education (Socratic teaching, with an emphasis on reason, persuasive public speaking, and elocution) as well as the ends of legal education (social justice) fit nicely into the Jesuit ethos. If any professional school fit the ideals of the traditional Jesuit curriculum, it was a law school.

Like Abraham Lincoln, many early nineteenth-century lawyers were self-trained through private study or apprenticeships. At the time of the Civil War, law schools were still rare among public universities, and virtually unheard of at Catholic universities. Gradually, as a formal degree became necessary to practice law, the Jesuits built one of the largest networks for legal education that the country had ever seen. Sixteen Jesuit universities developed their own law schools, often serving primarily evening and weekend students.

Saint Louis University began offering legal education in 1843, when a local judge and former US Congressman from Kentucky, Richard Aylett Buckner, was hired as a professor. Long before its formal law school existed, Santa Clara's campus included a mock courtroom where students in the commercial division practiced arguments. Georgetown, however, became the first Jesuit university to establish a permanent law school in 1870. In the years leading up to World War I, a law school was typically the first priority for any Jesuit college that made the decision to become a university. After Georgetown, the first to add a law school was the well-financed Creighton University, in 1904. Fordham followed in 1905, as part of the Maryland-New York Province's efforts to develop it into the premiere Jesuit university in the East.

1908 was a busy year for the Missouri Province, which added law schools at Saint Louis, Loyola (Chicago), and Marquette simultaneously. In the west, Santa Clara opened its law school in 1911, and the California Jesuits, recognizing a good thing when they saw one, added law schools at Gonzaga and St. Ignatius (San Francisco) a year later. 1912 saw the establishment of law schools at the University of Detroit and Loyola (New Orleans). The California Jesuits added a law school at Loyola (Los Angeles) in 1920, and the eastern Jesuits did the same at Boston College in 1929. Significantly later, in 1994, Seattle University rounded out the list of Jesuit law schools when it acquired a beleaguered, 22-year-old law school that previously had been affiliated with the University of Puget Sound.

With the exception of Marquette and Seattle Universities, which merged with pre-existing law schools, all Jesuit law schools were developed in-house. Their faculty were overwhelmingly laymen, and their students were religiously diverse, consisting mainly of urban, working-class men who took classes at night and were often shut out of more prestigious law schools due to discrimination, financial hardships, or simply an inability to take classes during the day.

Two Jesuit universities—both in Ohio—started law schools that did not survive. The now-defunct St. John's University in Toledo opened a law school in 1909, and Xavier University in Cincinnati did the same in 1919.[217] Both Ohio law schools were strictly evening programs, a characteristic that ultimately led to their downfall. As law schools proliferated, members of the legal profession became concerned about the glut of attorneys flooding the job market, particularly those from the lower classes of society who had gotten their degrees at less prestigious evening colleges. Gradually after the turn of the century, the American Bar Association and other regulatory agencies began to add barriers to legal education. Even though most law schools had traditionally admitted students with no more than a high school education, they now began to require a bachelor's degree. Law school became effectively a graduate school, and to emphasize their graduate nature, many law schools began to refer to their degrees as JD, or "Juris Doctor," rather than the traditional LLB, or "Bachelor of Laws." Regulators added a third year of study to the law school curriculum, and denied accreditation to law schools that offered only evening classes.

The effect—arguably, the intention—of these reforms was to restrict access to the legal profession. A mandatory third year of study made a law degree more expensive, and put it further out of the reach of students who were not already part of America's established Protestant classes. By denying accreditation to law schools that lacked full-time day programs, the regulators may as well have put a target on the backs of the Jesuit schools and other universities whose law programs were designed around the needs of part-time evening students. When the American Bar Association published its first list of approved law schools in 1923, there was not a single Jesuit (or even Catholic) institution included. The following year, only three Catholic institutions made the cut—Georgetown, Saint Louis, and Creighton. A year later, Loyola (Chicago), and Marquette were added, along with fellow Catholic schools DePaul, Notre Dame, and the Catholic University of America. While most Jesuit law schools eventually adapted to the new rules, those in Toledo and Cincinnati proved unable to do so and closed in 1924 and 1934, respectively.[218]

Saint Joseph's College in Philadelphia explored the possibility of adding a law school on several occasions, but nothing came from the discussions. In 1927, it asked

---

217. Bennish, *Continuity*, 129.
218. Bennish, *Continuity*, 152. Garraghan, *Jesuits of the Middle U.S. Vol. III*, 495–496.

the Jesuit general in Rome for permission to open a law school, but the general declined after learning that the Archbishop of Philadelphia, Dennis Cardinal Dougherty, opposed the idea. Dougherty's principal objection was that he did not want Saint Joseph's to compete with the law school at the Catholic University of America. After Dougherty's death in 1951, Saint Joseph's briefly revived the idea, but dropped it again after rival Villanova won approval from state regulators to open Philadelphia's first Catholic law school in 1953.[219] Also during the 1950s, Regis College considered acquiring Westminster School of Law in Denver, but had to pass on the opportunity due to insufficient funds.[220] Westminster instead merged with the University of Denver.

Business Schools

Jesuits had a love-hate relationship with business education during the late nineteenth century and beyond. On one hand, business education had a long history on Jesuit campuses. The "commercial track," which allowed students to study bookkeeping and other business skills, was present at virtually every Jesuit college and generated much-needed tuition revenue. It was arguably the oldest form of professional education available at Jesuit colleges, even though it was seen at the time as a track for students of lower academic ability.

On the other hand, the nineteenth-century Jesuits never viewed the commercial track as much more than a necessary evil. They discriminated against the commercial students by awarding them only a certificate or diploma, while reserving bachelor's degrees for the students who completed the classical *Ratio Studiorum* curriculum. This practice continued even at colleges where enrollment in the commercial track far outpaced enrollment in the classical track. At St. Joseph's College in San Jose, the entire student body was enrolled in the commercial course, but the Jesuits stubbornly held onto the fiction that it was also a classical liberal arts college.

Gradually, these attitudes changed, and some Jesuit universities organized formal schools of commerce and finance. The Missouri Province Jesuits were light years ahead of their colleagues in this regard, no doubt in part because of the unique environment of the Midwest. Midwestern farmers and factory workers were nothing if not pragmatic, and as the industrial revolution brought some of America's biggest companies to the region, business became as lucrative a career path as law. The Missouri Jesuits also had a long history of offering commercial education through their Indian mission schools.

Accordingly, the Missouri Jesuits' flagship institution, Saint Louis University, set a precedent in 1908 when it opened its School of Commerce and Finance—the first business school west of the Mississippi.[221] Similar schools followed at Marquette

---

219. Contosta, *Saint Joseph's*, 114–113, 205–206.
220. Stansell, *Regis*, 198.
221. Garraghan, *Jesuits of the Middle U.S. Vol. III*, 441.

(which opened the Robert A. Johnston College of Business Administration in 1910), Xavier (which opened the St. Xavier School of Commerce, Accounts, and Finance in 1911) and Detroit (which opened a School of Commerce and Finance in 1916).

Most other Jesuit business schools came after the First World War, but once again, the Midwestern Jesuits led the way at Creighton (1920) and Loyola Chicago (1924). The West Coast Jesuits were similarly open minded, starting a College of Commerce and Finance at their flagship Santa Clara University in 1923 and at St. Ignatius College (the University of San Francisco) two years later.

The eastern Jesuits lagged behind their colleagues. Fordham was an early pioneer, operating a School of Accounting at its downtown campus in 1920, but that school would not evolve into a comprehensive School of Business Administration until the 1930s.[222] Across the Hudson River in New Jersey, Saint Peter's College opened the Hudson College of Commerce and Finance in 1932, mainly as a way to serve its working-class clientele. For similar reasons, Boston College opened its College of Business Administration in 1938. It was no coincidence that much of this innovation took place during the Great Depression, when many prospective students, particularly in poor urban areas, were under pressure to pursue gainful employment and would have viewed a traditional liberal arts education as a luxury their families could not afford. Georgetown stubbornly refused to follow suit until after the middle of the twentieth century, when it finally opened a formal business school in 1957.

In part to satisfy their own consciences, the Jesuits made some efforts to incorporate characteristics of their classical curriculum into their business schools, emphasizing ethics and critical thinking so that students would graduate with a well-rounded intellect. The Jesuits' great fear was that students would leave their campuses having learned nothing but rote commercial skills and having missed the opportunity to develop as moral human beings. Santa Clara's business school, for example, required all students to complete a "comprehensive course in in philosophy" to meld the liberal arts with the commercial.[223]

Today, business schools are almost ubiquitous at Jesuit colleges and universities. Holy Cross, which focuses exclusively on undergraduate education, is the only Jesuit institution that does not offer the Master of Business Administration. Spring Hill is the only other Jesuit college that lacks a formal business school, but it nonetheless has an MBA program. What began as a simple concession to student demand has finally become—or perhaps more accurately, is finally acknowledged—as an important part of a Jesuit university's mission.

Engineering Schools

Jesuit engineering schools, like Jesuit business schools, first took root in the practical, no-nonsense environments of the Midwest and the far west. Jesuit schools in Michi-

---

222. Shelley, *Fordham*, 291.
223. McKevitt, *University of Santa Clara*, 210.

gan, Wisconsin, Illinois, California, and Washington were the first to add schools of engineering to their repertoire; otherwise, they would have looked absurd next to the massive land-grant universities that dominated higher education in those states.

Gonzaga and other western schools located near mining communities had long offered classes on mineralogy, but these fell under the commercial divisions and focused more on assessing and selling precious metals than extracting them.[224] Marquette became the first Jesuit institution to add a formal engineering school in 1908. As might be expected, given its location in one of America's industrial capitals, the University of Detroit also became an early leader in the field, adding a school of engineering in 1911 and, ten years later, the country's first school of aeronautical engineering.[225] Loyola (Chicago) likewise experimented with an engineering school in 1911, although that particular incarnation of the school closed and is not directly continuous with the engineering programs that exist on the Loyola campus today.

In 1912, Santa Clara became the last Jesuit university to open an engineering school in the pre-World War I era. Loyola (New Orleans) toyed with an engineering school briefly in the 1920s, but more permanent engineering schools followed in the mid-twentieth century at Gonzaga, Seattle, Loyola Marymount, and Saint Louis Universities—all located in states where the very concept of university education was associated with the science-heavy, land-grant model. The much younger Fairfield University in Connecticut is the only Jesuit institution east of Detroit to sponsor a school of engineering today (though Boston College does offer an engineering *program*).

Social Work Schools

The Jesuits established law, business, and engineering schools where such degrees were most *wanted*; they established social work schools where such degrees were most *needed*. Social work programs emerged first at Jesuit universities in New York and Chicago, where urban poverty was greatest and where the need to connect the poor to resources was high.

Fordham University took the lead in this field. Its Graduate School of Social Service, now recognized as among the best in the United States, traces its origins to the early 1900s, when various Catholic interests in New York City began pushing for a school devoted to fighting urban poverty. Archbishop Patrick Hayes of New York suggested to Fordham that such a school would be a better use of its money than the ill-fated Fordham Medical School. The St. Vincent DePaul Society, which coordinated donations for the needy through New York's Catholic churches, along with the newly established Catholic Charities of the Archdiocese of New York, began exploring possibilities for a training school that would benefit their staff, their volunteers, and the causes for which they stood.[226]

---

224. McKevitt, *Brokers*, 215–216.
225. Garraghan, *Jesuits of the Middle U.S. Vol. III*, 485.
226. Shelley, *Fordham*, 190, 232–237.

An Irish-born Fordham Jesuit, Terence Shealy, SJ, became a notable figure in New York's antipoverty movement when he began leading retreats for laymen that combined Jesuit spirituality with lectures designed to educate the public on social issues. Building on his reputation as an intellectual and spiritual leader to New York's burgeoning charitable sector, Father Shealy opened a School of Social Studies at Fordham in 1911. Six years later, that school evolved into a School of Sociology and Social Service that, like most of Fordham's professional programs, operated out of the Woolworth Building in Manhattan. The new school enjoyed strong moral and financial support from the Archdiocese of New York, which sought to train its own corps of social workers to promote child welfare, combat homelessness, and improve the human condition in a city where such issues were visible daily.[227]

At about the same time, the Catholic interest in urban poverty led to the creation of a School of Sociology at Loyola University in Chicago. As in New York, the driving force behind the Chicago school was a Jesuit with a deep commitment to Catholic social teaching: Frederic Siedenburg, SJ. An alumnus of St. Xavier College in Cincinnati and Saint Louis University, Father Siedenburg was assigned to Chicago in 1911 and quickly organized a public lecture series designed to raise awareness of contemporary social issues. Topics covered included women's right to vote, workers' rights, and other issues inspired by the 1891 papal encyclical on labor, *Rerum Novarum*.[228]

As in New York, the local Archdiocese in Chicago took a special interest in Loyola's new school. Unfortunately for Father Siedenburg, the similarities ended there. While New York's archdiocesan officials threw strong support behind Father Shealy's school at Fordham, the archbishop of Chicago, George Cardinal Mundelein, disagreed with many of Father Siedenburg's decisions as dean. While recognizing the need for a school of applied social service in his archdiocese, Mundelein wanted it to operate according to his priorities—which is to say, he wanted it to focus almost exclusively on Chicago's Catholic community. He was reportedly unhappy that Father Siedenburg had taken a more ecumenical approach, enrolling large numbers of non-Catholics and engaging in resource-intensive cooperative work with Protestant and Jewish charities. Forty years later, after the Second Vatican Council, this ecumenism would have been seen as a virtue—but Father Siedenburg was too far ahead of his time. The result was that Siedenburg was forced out of Loyola in 1932 after an eighteen-year career in Chicago. He was reassigned to the University of Detroit, where he continued lecturing, writing, and working toward poverty amelioration in that city.[229] In 1932, he drew on his experience at Loyola (which had a thriving dental school) to lead the effort to open a much-needed dental school at Detroit.[230]

---

227. Ibid., 232–237.

228. Edward J. Gumz, "Frederic Siedenburg, SJ: The Journey of a Social Activist," *Social Work and Christianity* 39, no. 3 (2012): 275–276.

229. Gumz, "Frederic Siedenburg," 276–280.

230. Muller, *University of Detroit*, 187. Bennish, *Continuity*, 138.

Outside of New York and Chicago, the Jesuits opened a School of Sociology at Xavier University in Cincinnati in 1918, a version of which exists today as Xavier's College of Professional Sciences. After the First World War, social work programs also emerged at Saint Louis University (1930) and Boston College (1936).

Education Schools

As public education became compulsory in many areas of the country around the turn of the twentieth century, many states began to open "normal schools" that specialized in the training of teachers. However, mainstream American universities were slow to embrace education as an academic and professional field of study. Early pioneers, like the University of Iowa (1873) and the University of Michigan (1879), opened the first departments in the field, but Harvard University did not open its Graduate School of Education until 1920.[231]

Catholic immigrants at the time were building a bewildering number of parish elementary schools, most of which were staffed by women's religious orders. When the US bishops all but mandated an elementary school in every Catholic parish at the Third Plenary Council of Baltimore in 1884, they also urged each diocese to establish its own "normal school" that would train teachers to staff that growing educational network. Even though most dioceses charged forward with the construction of new elementary schools as directed, few diocesan teacher training programs opened.[232] More often, women's religious orders took it upon themselves to open colleges that would train their own members. These "sisters' colleges," as they became known, existed mainly to grant degrees to prospective nuns—mainly in education, but also in fields like nursing and social work.

There was, at first, little incentive for the Jesuits to duplicate these efforts. Few Catholic laypeople were involved in elementary education, and the Jesuits did not see it as their responsibility to train members of other religious orders. By far the biggest obstacle, however, was that a large segment of the education profession was female. Jesuit officials in Rome were still hesitant to allow women to enroll at American Jesuit colleges. They tolerated the small numbers of women enrolled at Jesuit law, medical, and other professional schools, and they even accepted the inevitability of nursing schools when the university owned a hospital; however, they were hesitant to permit any Jesuit university to open a school of education where female students would presumably be in the majority.[233] The Jesuits had no incentive to offer schools of education as long as few of their male students aspired (or had the option) to become Catholic elementary school teachers.

---

231. Brett Bertucio, "W(h)ither the Liberally Educated Teacher? An Historical Reflection," in *Leisure and Labor: Essays on the Liberal Arts in Catholic Higher Education*, ed. Anthony P. Coleman (New York: Lexington Books, 2020), 62.

232. Ibid., 63.

233. See Cook, *Founded on Faith*, 116.

As a result, some Jesuit colleges limited their involvement in teacher training to indirect sponsorship. They sometimes used their charters to award credit for courses delivered at convents, Catholic normal schools, and sisters' colleges—effectively treating those schools as branch campuses. In New Orleans, for example, prospective teachers who enrolled at Ursuline College technically received their credits from Loyola University. By the 1930s, this kind of arrangement was raising eyebrows in accrediting agencies, which frowned on universities awarding credit in their own names for work completed elsewhere. In 1938, Loyola started its own school of education rather than risk probation by rubber-stamping the coursework at Ursuline.[234]

Creighton opened a "pedagogy" program in 1907, leading to a teaching certificate; the University of Detroit and the forerunner of Xavier University in Cincinnati did the same in 1912 and 1914, respectively.[235] Fordham established its Teachers' College in its downtown home, the Woolworth Building, in 1916. Ironically, because of the ecclesial politics described above, Fordham's Teachers' College "had a closer connection with the public schools than with the parochial schools of New York City."[236] Boston College began offering programs in education in 1919.

Today, seventeen of the twenty-seven Jesuit colleges and universities sponsor schools of education, most of which originated between the 1930s and 1950s, when opposition to coeducation in the Jesuit hierarchy was weakening. Indeed, the rise of education programs at Jesuit colleges roughly corresponds with the rise in women students. It was an education program (at Marquette University) that led to one of the first instances of Jesuit coeducation in the United States. Several universities—including Marquette, Creighton, Loyola (New Orleans), Regis, and Saint Louis—eventually allowed female Catholic school teachers to enroll in their evening and weekend courses and earn credits toward state certification requirements. By the 1930s, these cracks in the glass ceiling were starting to erode the all-male character of the Jesuit colleges.

Other Professional Schools

A handful of other professional schools emerged in the early 1900s. Marquette (1910) and Xavier (1914) experimented with schools of journalism, although only Marquette's continues to exist today in the form of the College of Communication. Marquette also acquired the Wisconsin Conservatory of Music in 1910 and became the first Jesuit school to offer professional degrees in that field.[237] The only other Jesuit school to open a college of music was Loyola University in New Orleans, the birthplace of jazz, in 1932.

The most innovative professional school at a Jesuit university was Georgetown's School of Foreign Service, opened in 1919 in response to the need for better-trained

---

234. Ibid., 96–99, 116–117.

235. Muller, *University of Detroit*, 90. Mihelich, *History of Creighton*, 87.

236. Shelley, *Fordham*, 289.

237. Garraghan, *Jesuits of the Middle U.S. Vol. III*, 455.

American diplomats, foreign trade managers, and economists that World War I had so painfully illustrated. That school's history properly belongs in the next section and it will be given a fuller treatment there, but for now, suffice to say that the School of Foreign Service stands out as the one instance in which a Jesuit university set a precedent for academia as a whole. The experiment at Georgetown created an entirely new professional field of study—international affairs—that became widespread across the country. Unlike other professional schools, where the Jesuits copied what secular universities were already doing, the Georgetown School of Foreign Service stands out for its willingness to break the academic mold.

The First Women Students

Professional schools opened the door to coeducation at Jesuit universities. In virtually every case, the first women at any given Jesuit university enrolled in its professional degree programs. Coeducation was therefore a piecemeal process on most Jesuit campuses, with certain schools, departments, and degree programs within the university opening their doors to women before others. The undergraduate liberal arts college was typically the last unit of the university to admit women. In many cases, that milestone did not take place until the 1960s, but by that time, women had been earning graduate and professional degrees from Jesuit universities for more than fifty years. The last Jesuit college to admit women was, unsurprisingly, Holy Cross, which lacked any graduate or professional programs.

Catholic higher education for women was still in its infancy at the turn of the twentieth century. There were, of course, many Catholic girls' schools, often associated with convents and located in close proximity to boys' colleges. The very first Catholic girls' school in the country was Georgetown Visitation Academy, which the Sisters of the Visitation opened next door to Georgetown College in 1799. Even though many were quite old and respected, these girls' schools were essentially high schools and were not accredited to grant college degrees. Beginning in the late 1890s and continuing through the 1950s, some Catholic girls' high schools added college-level courses, which allowed them to offer two-year associate's degrees or four-year bachelor's degrees to women who stayed on campus to continue their studies beyond the high school curriculum. Apart from those that were founded as "sisters' colleges," virtually all Catholic women's colleges in the United States originated this way. The first Catholic girls' high school to elevate itself to collegiate status and confer a bachelor's degree was Notre Dame of Maryland University in Baltimore, which graduated six women in 1899. Today, that historic women's university shares a library with Loyola University (Maryland), although the two institutions remain separate.

Because those Catholic girls' high schools-cum-colleges only offered undergraduate degrees, Catholic women who wanted graduate or professional education had no choice but to turn to the men's colleges. Although the sexes were still segregated at the undergraduate level, it became common for Catholic men's universities to admit women in small numbers to their schools of law, business, and medicine, since the alternative was to lose those students to the public universities. Marquette University, through its programs in education, claims to have been the first all-male Catholic university in the United States to admit women, in 1909. Women had enrolled, however, in professional schools at Georgetown, Saint Louis, and Creighton Universities before that time.

The first women ever to *enroll* at a Jesuit university in the United States were most likely Jeannette Sumner and Annie Rice, both of whom enrolled at Georgetown's School of Medicine in 1880. At the time, the medical school was located apart from the main campus in downtown Washington, DC, and was mainly under the control of the doctors who taught there. There are no records to indicate that the doctors consulted the Jesuits prior to admitting the two women, or what deliberations might have followed their applications.[238]

After a year at Georgetown Medical School, both Sumner and Rice withdrew and enrolled instead at the Women's Medical College of Philadelphia, an all-female medical school that had opened 31 years earlier. Why they made this decision is unknown, but we can assume that it was not because they were struggling with their studies or because they had changed career plans. After graduating from the Philadelphia school, both returned to Washington to practice medicine in 1883.[239] Years later, in 1898, another woman named Louise Taylor applied to Georgetown Medical School, but was not admitted; instead, one Georgetown professor agreed to serve as her private tutor.[240] In Omaha, Creighton Medical School's inaugural class in 1892 included one woman, Kate Drake, who eventually left the program before finishing.[241]

The first woman to *graduate* from any Jesuit university was likely A.M. Griffith, who earned her medical degree at Creighton in 1898; five other women graduated from Creighton Medical School by 1900.[242] In 1906, the Georgetown Hospital Training School for Nurses (forerunner of Georgetown's modern-day School of Nursing), graduated its first class after opening three years earlier. Georgetown's nursing students, however, did not mix with the male undergraduates in the classroom, and those first graduates technically received diplomas rather than bachelor's degrees.

In 1907, Loyola University (New Orleans) went coeducational without realizing it. That year, the university sponsored an outreach program to local nuns in their convents. Father Patrick Ryan, SJ traveled to the historic Ursuline and Sacred Heart Convents in New Orleans to teach Latin and history to the sisters; in 1909, he trav-

---

238. Jon Reynolds, "The Unknown Women of Georgetown," Georgetown University Library: Booth Family Center for Special Collections, (undated), https://www.library.georgetown.edu/special-collections/archives/essays/unknown-women.

239. Patti North, "Georgetown University Medical Center's Trailblazing Women: Highlights from the Many Who Helped Shape History," *Georgetown Health Magazine* (Fall/Winter 2017), https://alumni.georgetown.edu/news/gumc/magazine/2017/fall-winter/gumc-trailblazing-women#:~:text=Annie%20Rice%2C%20MD%2C%20(1853,earned%20medical%20degrees%20in%201883.

240. Durkin, *Georgetown Middle Years*, 203.

241. Mihelich, *History of Creighton*, 75.

242. Ibid.

eled to San Antonio to teach the nuns at what is now the University of the Incarnate Word. At the time, Father Ryan's classes were viewed as personal enrichment for the sisters, but in 1924, Loyola University retroactively awarded college credit to all the women who had participated. Those nuns became, in effect, the first women to *earn undergraduate credits* from a Jesuit university, even though these credits were delayed by more than fifteen years.[243] Since the women were studying in off-campus locations and did not realize that they were earning college credits at the time, it would be spurious for Loyola to claim that they represent true coeducation.

In 1908, Saint Louis University admitted five women to its law school: Bertha Bruening, Adele Doyle, Mary Maguire, Rosie O'Boyle, and Anna Ross.[244] When they graduated, they were probably the first women to earn degrees from any Jesuit university outside of the medical field.

Marquette Breaks the Glass Ceiling

Marquette's claim to be the first coeducational Catholic university essentially ignores those prior instances of women's education at Georgetown, Creighton, Loyola, and Saint Louis. Still, some historians do give this honor to Marquette because its female students took classes on the main campus (albeit at a time of the year when their male counterparts were absent). This was coeducation only in the narrowest, most technical sense. During the summer of 1909, while the male students were away, Marquette president James McCabe, SJ, invited nuns teaching in Milwaukee's Catholic schools to take courses on campus, using classrooms that otherwise would have sat empty. These summer "teacher institutes," as such programs were usually called, were relatively common at the time at secular universities. Their target audience was mainly public school teachers early in their careers.[245] Marquette was attempting a Catholic version of the same, and even that was not unprecedented; two years earlier, Creighton had allowed the Sisters of Mercy in Omaha to use its empty summer classrooms for teacher certification.[246] Marquette, however, was the first Jesuit university to *advertise* its programs as being open to women and admit women as a matter of policy.

Even though Marquette's summer teacher's institute was originally meant only for nuns, some laywomen teaching in local Catholic schools also signed up, possibly because the admission criteria had not been made clear in the brochures. Marquette allowed those laywomen to participate. This mix of sisters and lay teachers became the first women to enroll on the Marquette campus.[247]

---

243. Cook, *Founded on Faith*, 42–43.

244. Saint Louis University, *Saint Louis Brief* 9, no. 2 (Spring 2008): 3, https://issuu.com/slulaw/docs/volume_9_issue_2.

245. Bertucio, "W(h)ither," 62.

246. Mihelich, *History of Creighton*, 87.

247. Power, *Catholic Higher Education*, 275–276.

These developments in Milwaukee scandalized the Missouri Province leadership in Saint Louis so dramatically that Father McCabe appealed to Rome for permission to continue the summer program. During the resulting delay in communication across the Atlantic, Marquette's summer teacher institute went forward as planned. It continued in a state of limbo for three years before the Jesuit authorities in Rome officially approved it, allowing Marquette to continue what it was already doing.[248] Marquette added more female students in 1911 when it created an undergraduate division for women, and in 1912, when it acquired Milwaukee's Trinity Hospital and its affiliated Training School for Nurses.

Other Coeducation through World War I

Loyola University of New Orleans (not by accident this time) began to enroll women in 1912. When it acquired the New Orleans College of Pharmacy, two female pharmacy students—Lucrecia Landa and Lillian Maloney—came along with the deal, becoming the first women to graduate from Loyola in 1913. By 1918, more than a fifth of Loyola's total enrollment consisted of women in its various professional schools. That same year, Mary Jane Howard graduated from Loyola's School of Dentistry, becoming the first woman to earn a Doctor of Dental Surgery from the large Jesuit dental network.[249] In addition to admitting small numbers of women to their doctoral degree programs, many Jesuit dental schools also started hygienist programs that enrolled significant numbers of undergraduate women by the 1930s. In Jesuit dental, law, and business schools, it became common to see a handful of women in each graduating class; the University of Detroit admitted women to these programs beginning in 1916, as did fellow Missouri Province schools Saint Louis, Marquette, and Loyola (Chicago).[250] Women represented fifteen percent of the entering class at Creighton's School of Pharmacy in 1918.[251]

At many of these schools, there were quotas for the number of women who could be admitted each year, and these quotas continued through the middle of the 1900s. At the same time, the nursing schools at Georgetown, Marquette, and elsewhere were officially closed to men. It was not until the 1940s that both Marquette and Georgetown elevated their nursing certificates to full Bachelor of Science in Nursing programs, and not until the 1960s that most Jesuit nursing schools began to admit male students. Nonetheless, the fact that women were already sharing classrooms with men at Jesuit universities by the 1910s meant that a line had been crossed, and the dominoes were already falling toward full coeducation a half-century later.

Women's contributions to Jesuit higher education during this period went beyond the impact of the first female students. Jesuit universities benefitted from an

---

248. Ibid., 276.
249. Cook, *Founded on Faith*, 52–53, 63.
250. Muller, *University of Detroit*, 117–118.
251. Mihelich, *History of Creighton*, 102.

unusually large number of female donors and benefactors who made transformative gifts. The most obvious of these were Sarah Emily and Mary Lucretia Creighton in Omaha, who helped to arrange the gifts that made Creighton University and its associated medical center possible. There were others—among them Ida Ryan, the mother of two Georgetown students who contributed funds to Georgetown Hospital in 1898 and built Ryan Hall as a dormitory in 1904. In Cincinnati, Susanna Hinkle, a benefactor of many Catholic institutions and causes in that city, donated the money that enabled Xavier University to build its signature building, Hinkle Hall, when it relocated to a new campus in 1919. In New Orleans, sugar-industry heiress Kate McDermott funded the construction of Holy Name of Jesus Church in memory of her brother, Thomas, resulting in one of the architectural gems of the Loyola University campus.

The Move to New Campuses

At about the same time new professional schools were proliferating at Jesuit universities, many of those universities were relocating to new campuses. Since they were originally conceived as day schools, most Jesuit colleges were located in the middle of congested downtown areas perfect for serving local students who lived a short walk or streetcar ride away. The single-building campuses were designed to be accessible for commuters, not for long-term growth. As those colleges developed into universities, virtually all of them felt a pressing need for more space and began to look to the suburbs and less-developed parts of the city to spread their wings.

Excluding those colleges that were downgraded to high schools, the only nineteenth-century Jesuit colleges that stayed put on their original campuses were Georgetown, Holy Cross, Spring Hill, Santa Clara, Fordham, Creighton, and Gonzaga (Spokane), along with the now-defunct St. Charles College of Louisiana and St. Mary's College of Kansas. Most of these were the oldest Jesuit colleges in their respective regions, and their founders had purchased large tracts of property from the beginning, always intending them to be residential boarding schools. By contrast, the colleges that originated as day schools often had no choice but to pack up and move as American students began to demand better facilities than a single-building, downtown commuter college could provide.

The need for bigger campuses did not strike the Jesuits suddenly. With a few exceptions, like Saint Louis University and Xavier University, the Jesuits had always intended their downtown college campuses to be temporary. Some colleges, like the University of Detroit and Loyola University (Baltimore), held their first classes in leased property. In other cases, like Canisius College in Buffalo and Loyola University in New Orleans, the Jesuits purchased land for a new campus decades before they had a workable plan or even a pressing need to relocate. Sacred Heart College (Regis University) in Colorado was unique in that it relocated from isolated mountain town of Morrison to the more urban environs of Denver, making it the only Jesuit school to move from the suburbs to the city.

Saint Louis University was the first Jesuit school to relocate. Its original 1820s-era campus (located on Ninth Street just a few blocks back from the Mississippi River) was built for the needs of a frontier town where dirt roads and horses were the main means of transportation. Over time, the surrounding neighborhood became one of the city's seedier sections, full of disreputable taverns that worried parents and tempted the boarding students to break curfew. On three separate occasions, the Jesuits bought property speculatively, expecting that someday their flagship Midwestern university would have to move. They settled on the present campus in the 1880s. Although Saint Louis University briefly stopped accepting boarding students after the move, the new campus improved public perception of the university and enrollment increased.[252]

The imperative was somewhat more urgent in San Francisco, where it became necessary to find a new campus for St. Ignatius College after the 1906 earthquake destroyed the original college buildings. St. Ignatius operated for more than a decade in rented quarters (about two blocks south of its current campus) before the Jesuits found a permanent home.

The fates of the original campuses varied. In some cases, the Jesuits repurposed the old college campus as a Jesuit high school. In others, the historic property was sold. In Baltimore, Buffalo, Cincinnati, and Seattle, the original campus was, first and foremost, a Catholic parish and continued to function as such even after the school relocated. In only one case (Detroit) did the Jesuits retain the original property for use in higher education; the University of Detroit Mercy still houses its law school on its original Riverfront Campus. Located one block from the Detroit Renaissance Center and the world headquarters of General Motors, the building sits on some of the most valuable real estate in the city.

The new campuses provided a blank slate for some exquisite architecture. Gasson Hall (1913) at Boston College and Barbelin Hall (1927) at Saint Joseph's University are magnificent examples of the collegiate gothic style. Xavier's Hinkle Hall (1919) is modeled after the medieval castle of the Xavier family in northern Spain. Western collegiate buildings tended to be more utilitarian, but many, like Saint Louis's DuBourg Hall (1888), Seattle's Garrand Hall (1894), and Marquette's Johnston Hall (1906), became local landmarks. Even at schools that did not relocate, it was a rich era for design. At Georgetown, the crests of every Jesuit college in the country (at the time) were carved into the walls of the Gaston Hall auditorium. Talented Jesuit Brother Francis Schroen hand-painted the interior of Gaston Hall with allegorical figures representing Georgetown's dual nature as a Catholic university committed to its Church and as an American university dutifully patriotic in its service to its country—an important message at a time when many would have seen those identities as irreconcilable.

---

252. Garraghan, *Jesuits of the Middle U.S. Vol. III*, 435–439.

RELOCATION OF JESUIT COLLEGES AND UNIVERSITIES

Date	School	Old Campus	New Campus
1888–1889	Saint Louis University	Ninth and Washington Streets, St. Louis	Grand Avenue, St. Louis
1888	Regis University	Morrison, Colo. and Las Vegas, NM	Northern Denver, donated by publishing mogul John Brisben Walker, 1887
1894	Seattle University	St. Francis Hall, Sixth & Spring Streets (Site of Women's University Club), downtown Seattle	Property of Arthur Denny, purchased 1890
1904	Loyola University (New Orleans)	Immaculate Conception Church (present site of Pere Marquette Building), Common & Baronne Streets, New Orleans. Continued to serve as the site of Jesuit High School until the high school relocated in 1926	Pierre Fouchet estate near World Cotton Exhibition fairgrounds/Audubon Park. Purchased 1889
1905–1907	Marquette University	Tenth and State Streets, Milwaukee	Grounds of Church of the Gesu
1908	Loyola University Chicago	Holy Family Church (present site of St. Ignatius College Prep), Roosevelt Paul Railroad	Rogers Park, purchased from Chicago, Milwaukee, & St. Paul Railroad
1909–1913	Boston College	Immaculate Conception Parish, South End (Harrison Ave.), Boston. Continued to serve as the site of Boston College High School until the high school relocated to its present site in 1950	Amos Adams Lawrence Farm, Chestnut Hill, Mass.
1911–1920	Xavier University	St. Francis Xavier Church, Sycamore Street, Cincinnati	Former Avondale Athletic Club, Cincinnati
1912	Canisius College	St. Michael Church, Washington Street, Buffalo	Hamlin Park, Former retreat house of Sisters of St. Joseph. Purchased 1874.
1914–1927	University of San Francisco	Leased property, Hays & Schrader Streets (present site of St. Mary's Medical Center), San Francisco	Grounds of St. Ignatius Church, San Francisco

continued on next page

RELOCATION OF JESUIT COLLEGES AND UNIVERSITIES (*continued*)

Date	School	Old Campus	New Campus
1922	Loyola University Maryland	St. Ignatius Church, North Calvert Street, Baltimore	Evergreen estate, northern Baltimore, purchased from Garrett family
1926–1927	Loyola Marymount University	Venice Boulevard, downtown Los Angeles (present site of Loyola High School)	Del Rey Hills (modern-day Westchester), donated by Harry Culver, real estate mogul
1927	Saint Joseph's University	Church of the Gesú (present site of St. Joseph's Prep School)	Overbrook neighborhood, Philadelphia (City Avenue)
1927	University of Detroit Mercy	Jefferson Avenue, present site of Ss. Peter & Paul Church and the university's Riverfront Campus	Martin Park, Livernois Street
1935	John Carroll University	Present site of St. Ignatius High School, Lorain Ave., Cleveland	Shaker Heights (University Heights). Purchased 1923.
1936	Saint Peter's University	Commerce Building, Jersey City	Edward Young estate, Kennedy Boulevard, Jersey City
Unfulfilled	St. John's University (Toledo)	Walnut & Superior Streets, Toledo	Ottawa Park property purchased 1921. University closed before move.

Athletics

As a side effect of the move to larger campuses, many Jesuit colleges could now put more emphasis on athletics. At the urban day schools, sports had consisted of whatever games the boys could play on city lots at recess. As they acquired more property, the Jesuit colleges could offer proper playing fields, and nearly all embraced the opportunity to join in the growing world of intercollegiate athletics.

At the boarding colleges, sports had always been an important part of student life outside of class. The great spectator sports of football and basketball had yet to be invented, so early nineteenth-century students mainly played handball, fencing, and other games on an intramural level. Baseball became popular in the mid-1800s, but again, most of the early games were intramural affairs. Students organized themselves into teams and played each other, sometimes pitting one class against another, but rarely venturing off campus to play against other colleges.

As intercollegiate football and other sports gained popularity in the 1870s, the Jesuits were ambivalent. On one hand, they embraced sports as a reflection of the Jesuit ideal, *mens sana in corpore sano* (healthy mind in a healthy body). St. Ignatius had urged his followers to take time for recreation, and the Jesuits were always happy to find an outlet for their teenage students' hormone-fueled energy. At the same time, however, they tried to keep their students' heads in the classroom. As games became more elaborate affairs and teams sought to travel around the country, Jesuit colleges and universities adopted a uniform policy on intercollegiate travel. Student athletes could not be away from campus for more than four school days to compete in road games.[253]

This strict travel policy, in place through the 1940s, limited potential rivalries between Jesuit schools. Teams could not schedule games outside of a four-day round-trip travel radius. As a result, games between Georgetown and Saint Louis were rare, despite the historic ties between those institutions; Georgetown teams could travel no further than Detroit without a special waiver from the Jesuit authorities. Many Jesuit schools, therefore, developed their most intense rivalries with other colleges in their own cities. In the west, Santa Clara frequently played against Stanford, Berkeley, and the Christian Brothers-affiliated St. Mary's College in Oakland. By the 1920s, the annual football game between Santa Clara and St. Mary's became known as the "Little Big Game" (a Catholic version of the "Big Game" between Stanford and Berkeley), and drew such large crowds that it had to be played at Kezar Stadium, future home of San Francisco's professional teams.[254]

Not surprisingly, the biggest and most popular athletics programs emerged first at the Jesuit schools that had the facilities to support them. Georgetown, Fordham, Holy Cross, Santa Clara, and (after its move to Chestnut Hill in 1913) Boston College had campuses big enough to offer practice facilities for rugby, football, baseball, and other outdoor sports. The eastern schools began to challenge traditional powerhouses like Harvard, Yale, Penn, Army, and Navy on the field, and since they were within a four-day round-trip of each other, they developed strong intra-Jesuit rivalries as well. Unlike many of their secular rivals, however, the Jesuit schools mostly lacked stadiums of their own. In a practice that would haunt them in future generations, they played many of their biggest games in large municipal stadiums that required hefty rent payments and drained the athletic budgets.

Baseball was the most popular sport in the late 1800s, but football was gaining ground quickly. Fordham (1882), Georgetown (1891), Holy Cross (1891), Marquette (1892), Boston College (1892), Santa Clara (1896), Saint Louis (1899), Creighton (1900), and Xavier (1900) were among the first American universities to field football teams at a major level, and they often challenged the best programs in the country— including schools that today compete in the Ivy League, Big Ten, and Pac-12. They also boasted strong local fan bases, especially among Catholics. The annual Georgetown-Fordham and Georgetown-Boston College games drew national attention, as did Boston College-Holy Cross—which challenged the Harvard-Yale game (at least in Catholic circles) as New England's greatest football rivalry. Loyola (Chicago) and

253. McKevitt, *University of Santa Clara*, 249.
254. Ibid., 190.

Loyola (New Orleans) had a popular rivalry fueled as much by their homonym as by their halfbacks. In Milwaukee, newspaper journalists dubbed Marquette's football team the "Golden Avalanche" because of the impressive sight of its golden helmets gleaming in the sun as the players ran out onto the field. Saint Louis University claims to have been the first college football program to execute a forward pass, in a 1906 game.

As football gained popularity, it came under greater scrutiny. The nineteenth-century version of football was more violent and less protected than today's game, and players risked serious injury or even death on the field. The Jesuits' ambivalence toward intercollegiate athletics was especially pronounced when it came to football, and the game's popularity could never overcome the Jesuits' concerns for the safety of their students. As a result, the very Jesuit schools that had been among the first to play football were also among the first to ban it.

In 1894, citing the danger of the sport, the superior of the Maryland-New York Province decreed that no Jesuit colleges under his jurisdiction—which included Boston College, Georgetown, Holy Cross, and Fordham—would be allowed to field intercollegiate football teams. Despite the order, football continued. At Georgetown, President J. Havens Richards, SJ, turned a blind eye when the students went ahead and scheduled games in violation of the provincial's order. Santa Clara banned the game between 1905 and 1919, but restored it under pressure from local alumni who wanted to see their school compete on the field.[255] This combination of civil disobedience and alumni lobbying kept football alive on Jesuit campuses for several generations, but the immense costs of playing football in off-campus municipal stadiums proved unsustainable by the 1950s and 1960s.

School Colors

The rise of intercollegiate athletics led directly to the American tradition of "school colors." Teams needed to identify themselves on the field, especially for the benefit of fans viewing the action from afar. The close historic and administrative ties among Jesuit universities led to many similarities in their color choices, which continue to serve as a reminder of their connections today. As already mentioned, Georgetown adopted blue and gray as its official colors after the Civil War to symbolize healing and reunification in the divided country; in the years ahead, many other Jesuit universities (especially on the East Coast) would incorporate Georgetown gray into their uniforms. Outside of the Jesuit network, gray is an uncommon color in American college athletics, but it features prominently on the jerseys at Saint Joseph's, Loyola (Baltimore), Xavier, and to a more limited degree, Fordham, Loyola Marymount, and Saint Louis. A hint of gray or silver on a jersey almost always indicates that the school in question is part of the Jesuit family.[256]

---

255. Curran, *History of Georgetown Vol. II*, 119. McKevitt, *University of Santa Clara*, 145.
256. See Varga, *Baltimore's Loyola*, 240–241.

Blue and white, the colors of the Virgin Mary, became the dominant colors in the schools that grew out of the Missouri Province. Originally used at Saint Louis University, the combination was adopted by many of Saint Louis's daughter institutions—including Creighton, Detroit, Rockhurst, and the now-defunct St. Mary's (Kansas). Outside the Missouri Province, the same color scheme also appears at Gonzaga (Spokane) and Saint Peter's.

Most of the colleges founded by the German Jesuits in Buffalo used blue and gold. Canisius, John Carroll, and the now-defunct St. John's ('Toledo) shared those colors, giving the three Jesuit schools on the shores of Lake Erie a common visual identity. Marquette coincidentally chose those colors as well, which meant that the Midwestern Jesuit schools were somewhat bifurcated—blue and white in the Great Plains, blue and gold on the Great Lakes. Regis University, which originally used brown and gold, later changed its color palette to blue and gold to match the others.[257]

Maroon and gold, the colors of the Loyola family crest in Spain, came into use at Loyola (Chicago) and Loyola (New Orleans) as well as at Boston College. Fordham, likewise, uses maroon, but pairs it with gray. St. Xavier College (now Xavier High School) in New York City uses maroon and light blue, combining the colors of Fordham and Columbia Universities.

Red, usually paired with white, is the dominant color at most western Jesuit schools, including Santa Clara (where it originated), Seattle, Loyola Marymount, and Brophy (now a high school). Loyola Marymount incorporates both red and gray—combining the colors of Georgetown and Santa Clara. Imperial purple is another common choice, appearing on the uniforms at Holy Cross, Spring Hill, Gonzaga (DC), and the University of Scranton.

Scientific Research: Astronomy and Seismology

Although the Jesuits emphasized teaching over research at their schools, they made important contributions to science around the turn of the twentieth century. The Jesuit colleges' research enterprises were tiny compared to those of the land grant universities, but many individual Jesuit scientists were conducting experiments as groundbreaking as anything being done at the public schools. Two areas in which the Jesuits had a particularly big impact were astronomy and seismology.

St. Ignatius had an interest in astronomy and often prayerfully meditated by gazing at the stars; in Rome, the Jesuits were the traditional curators of the Vatican Observatory. This interest crossed the Atlantic early. Georgetown built an astronomical observatory on its campus in 1843, equipping it with state-of-the art instruments that allowed the Jesuits to calculate the exact latitude and longitude of the nation's capital for the first time.[258] In St. Louis, a noted Jesuit astronomer, Charles Charroppin,

257. Stansell, *Regis*, 56.
258. Curran, *History of Georgetown Vol. I*, 150–156.

SJ, pioneered the new science of tracking and photographing eclipses. In Omaha, John Creighton donated an observatory to his namesake university in 1885—the second such facility ever built in Nebraska. One of the Creighton Observatory's early resident scientists was the French astronomer Jerome Sixtus Ricard, SJ, who later served on the faculty at Santa Clara. After arriving in California, Father Ricard achieved notoriety for his theories about the sun and its effects on the earth's weather patterns. Although many of those theories have since been disproven, Father Ricard became one of Santa Clara's most famous faculty members, often quoted in the press and sought out by California's agriculture industry for his meteorological predictions. In 1925, Santa Clara built him a state-of-the-art observatory to support his research.[259]

The Georgetown, Creighton, and Santa Clara observatories still exist today, although their use for scientific research has diminished because of the difficulty of seeing the night sky amid bright city lights. Holy Cross also built a small observatory, but it was much less sophisticated than the others and it was eventually demolished. The Jesuits opened the independent Weston Observatory outside of Boston in 1931, and it became affiliated with Boston College in 1949.

Loyola University in Chicago constructed an observatory in 1911, but it was seldom used for its intended purpose of stargazing. Instead, it housed a seismograph—the instrument used to measure earthquakes. Seismography became a major scientific focus for Jesuit universities.

To measure the movement of the earth accurately, it is necessary to make many different calculations from different points on the planet's surface. The Jesuits, with their network of colleges and universities spread across the country, were in a unique position to conduct research in this field. Using their huge geographic footprint to their advantage, they set up seismographic equipment from Washington, DC to Washington State, with each station communicating its data and measurements to the others.

The first station was in Cleveland, at what is now known as John Carroll University. Frederik Odenbach, SJ, one of the exiled German Jesuits who taught at the fledgling school, designed the lab himself based on his memory of other seismological stations he had seen during his scientific career in Europe. Recognizing that the Jesuits had a readymade infrastructure for gathering data across the North American continent, Father Odenbach convinced the American Jesuit leaders to latch onto seismography as a niche field in which they could compete with even the biggest state universities. It did not hurt that he made this pitch shortly after St. Ignatius College in San Francisco was destroyed by the 1906 earthquake.[260] The California Province jumped at the opportunity to invest in a strong seismography program at Santa Clara, hoping to prevent another disaster. By the 1920s, both Georgetown and Santa Clara were home to state-of-the-art, hyper-

---

259. McKevitt, *University of Santa Clara*, 225.

260. Agustin Udías and William Stauder, "The Jesuit Contribution to Seismology," *Seismological Research Letters* 67, no. 3 (May/June 1996): 10–19, https://www.seismosoc.org/inside/eastern-section/jesuit-contribution-seismology/.

sensitive Gallitzin seismographs, Georgetown being the first American university of any kind to own that sophisticated piece of equipment.[261]

In total, the Jesuits built thirty-eight seismographic research stations around the world, a little fewer than half of which were located at Jesuit colleges in the United States. Seismographs opened at (using modern university names) John Carroll in Cleveland (1900), Santa Clara in California (1907), Gonzaga in Spokane (1909), Holy Cross in Worcester (1909), Marquette in Milwaukee (1909), Regis in Denver (1909), Georgetown in Washington (1910), Canisius in Buffalo (1910), Saint Louis in Missouri (1910), Fordham in New York (1910), Loyola in New Orleans (1910), Spring Hill in Mobile (1910), Loyola in Chicago (1913), Xavier in Cincinnati (1927), the University of San Francisco in California (1950), and other Jesuit properties in Boston, Arkansas, southeastern Missouri, and elsewhere.[262]

Beginning in 1925, Saint Louis University served as the nerve center of this work, receiving measurements from Jesuit seismographs around the world, analyzing the data, and reporting the results to the scientific community. Saint Louis became home to the Jesuit Seismological Association, an organization that linked Jesuit and non-Jesuit researchers across the globe.[263] The head of Saint Louis University's Department of Geophysics, Father James Macelwane, SJ, became a renowned figure in both Jesuit and secular academic circles. He served as president of the American Geophysical Union and, in 1931, served as the first chair of the Jesuits' Commission on Higher Studies, which helped to bring American Jesuit higher education into the academic mainstream.[264]

For the most part, these seismographic stations no longer exist, although one of their legacies is the strong geophysics program at Saint Louis University. Gradually, the United States government became more involved in earthquake prediction through the National Oceanic and Atmospheric Administration (NOAA) and its affiliated National Weather Service. Taxpayer-funded NOAA research stations eventually rendered the Jesuit network obsolete. When Father Oldenbach of John Carroll University first lobbied his fellow Jesuits create a seismographic research network in 1909, he wrote, "Our Society can make a move which cannot be duplicated unless the Government should organize a bureau of seismology."[265] That was precisely what happened, and precisely what put the Jesuit network out of business. Nonetheless, the Jesuits played an important role in modernizing this critical branch of natural science and introducing it to the United States. The work of great Jesuit geologists, physicists, astronomers, and meteorologists was at the cutting edge of its day, and set the stage for the publicly funded research that came afterward.

---

261. McKevitt, *University of Santa Clara*, 363–364 (n. 27). "Obituary: Francis A. Tondorf, SJ," *Bulletin of the Seismological Society of America* 19, no. 4 (1929): 245–246.

262. Stansell, *Regis*, 78. Udías and Stauder, "Jesuit Contribution."

263. Udías and Stauder, "Jesuit Contribution."

264. Ibid. Fitzgerald, *Governance*, 26–27.

265. Stansell, *Regis*, 78.

Fundraising Challenges, 1865–1918

Jesuit college presidents of the late 1800s and early 1900s were acutely aware of the financial struggles their schools faced. Presidents often took it upon themselves to court donors and raise money, but Jesuit colleges were nowhere near as successful at attracting large donations as their Protestant counterparts. In the 1870s, Georgetown President Patrick Healy, SJ and Holy Cross President Joseph O'Hagan, SJ embarked on a joint nationwide speaking tour to raise money for their institutions. But O'Hagan died on the journey and Healy barely raised enough to cover his travel expenses.[266] On the West Coast, Santa Clara hosted a lavish celebration for its fiftieth anniversary in 1901, but despite large audiences of celebratory alumni on campus, there were virtually no donations, and "the college had little besides publicity to show for its efforts."[267]

Why the lack of success? There are a few reasons. First, American Catholics at the turn of the century were mainly poor, working-class immigrants with little disposable income. Despite their limited means, Catholics were establishing an entire parallel society within the United States—including Catholic elementary schools, Catholic hospitals, Catholic cemeteries, Catholic orphanages, and the Catholic parishes that stood at the center of all of these enterprises. Universities were just one part of a vast infrastructure of life-sustaining institutions that these immigrant communities were building from the ground up. Across the country, Italian stone masons, Irish laborers, Polish iron workers, and others donated their skills to build exquisite church buildings and elementary schools for their communities, but they had little spare cash to contribute to elite institutions like Georgetown and Holy Cross. Even in large and wealthy New York City, Fordham struggled to raise an endowment; New York's Catholics simply had nothing left after donating what they could from their limited wages to Catholic charities, parish soup kitchens, or Catholic hospitals.

To complicate matters, individual Catholic bishops had their own fundraising priorities as they built their dioceses. If a bishop decided that a new cathedral was a higher priority than a new building for the Jesuit college (as was the case in Louisville in the 1840s), he could make it extremely difficult for the Jesuits to hold a competing fund drive. Moreover, while the Jesuits were usually the first Catholic religious order to open a college in their respective cities, they were seldom the last; other orders, like the Christian Brothers and the Vincentians, opened their own schools that began asking the public for money, draining the already small Catholic donor pool even further.

Where the Jesuits did find willing donors like the Creighton family in Omaha, they proved themselves to be effective fundraisers. However, they struggled to raise money from their own alumni. Although many alumni offered moral support to the college and gladly returned to campus for reunions and football games, their enthusiasm did not always translate into cash donations. Perhaps one reason for this is the

---

266. Curran, *History of Georgetown Vol. I*, 307–308.
267. McKevitt, *University of Santa Clara*, 133.

sense of permanence and stability the Jesuits cultivated for their brand of education. Emphasizing the deep traditions of the *Ratio Studiorum*, the Jesuits happily promoted the idea that a Jesuit education was timeless—transcending the generations and even the centuries. Having dedicated their lives to the institutions in which they served, the priests projected a sense of stability that masked a behind-the-scenes reality marred by institutional debt and budget shortfalls. Most Jesuit college students never would have known that their institution was operating on shoestring, and after returning as alumni years later, they hardly would have believed it if the Jesuits had confessed that their presence was anything but eternal.

The Jesuits could, of course, shrewdly use this well-cultivated image of stability to their advantage. The Jesuits sometimes skirted the financial requirements of accrediting agencies by claiming their unpaid staff as part of a "living" endowment. Although their bank accounts were small, so were their expenses, and most of their faculty and staff worked for nothing more than room and board. The total value of the Jesuits' free labor, if paid out in competitive market-rate salaries, would have been worth an enormous sum in endowment funds.

Finally, Jesuit colleges were not simply fundraising for themselves. In addition to building classrooms for the students, they were building churches for the community and supporting other ministries that were only indirectly attached to the colleges, such as prison and hospital outreach. The Jesuit community at any given college needed money to travel to distant churches and rural areas, bringing the sacraments to far-flung missions and shut-ins. Only a portion of the money the Jesuits raised went to instruction or other line items that affected the college. In fact, the colleges, with their relatively steady tuition income, were often called upon to donate excess revenue to support the province's other priorities, as when Santa Clara University provided a $50,000 loan to prop up struggling Loyola High School in Los Angeles during World War II.[268]

Diversity and Race Relations, 1865–1918

Between the Civil War and World War I, Jesuit colleges became more Catholic and less religiously diverse than they had been.[269] This was in large part due to the huge influx of Catholic immigrants to the United States. A related effect was the decline in the proportion of Latin American and Caribbean students. Whereas students from Mexico and elsewhere south of the boarder had constituted a significant part of the early enrollment at Santa Clara, Saint Louis, Georgetown, and elsewhere, they were gradually eclipsed by Italian, Irish, and Eastern European immigrants who were settling closer to campus. There were exceptions—like Las Vegas College in New Mexico, where the student body, like the local community, was mainly Mexican-American. By and large, however, the "old" American Catholic population of Spanish and French descent was overwhelmed by the "new" ethnic mixture that came to dom-

---

268. Ibid., 232, 314.
269. Ibid., 146. Curran, *History of Georgetown Vol. I*, 137.

inate the American Catholic Church. There was no decision to de-emphasize recruitment of Hispanic Americans, and some Hispanic students continued to enroll; there was simply a shift in the demographics of the American Catholic population that made Hispanics a smaller overall proportion of the student body.

Few Jesuits at the time would have viewed these developments principally in terms of race. The overall mission of the Jesuit colleges had not changed, regardless of which Catholic immigrant groups they served. Like Latin American immigrants, most Italian- and Polish-American immigrants would have viewed themselves as part of an oppressed minority group in the United States, outside of mainstream US culture. A Cuban-American and a Polish-American were both Catholic, and both were unwelcome at many mainstream Protestant colleges. A Jesuit school provided refuge for both. This did not, of course, apply equally to dark-skinned Latin American students of African descent, who would have been seen as Black in the United States and would have been subject to the same segregationist policies as any African-American.

As before, race relations on campus depended largely on each school's location. In most western schools, like Gonzaga and Seattle, the main racial dynamic was between recent white settlers and longtime Native American residents. Despite the Jesuits' long history of ministering to the western Native Americans, Gonzaga University caved to local civic pressure and initially prohibited indigenous people from enrolling. Nonetheless, other Jesuit schools like St. Mary's College and St. Francis Institute at least briefly continued to educate limited numbers of Native Americans alongside white students. Western Jesuits also continued to operate many elementary schools for Native Americans, although those mission schools have recently faced criticism for the role they played in suppressing indigenous language and culture.

In the Southern colleges, including all of the institutions sponsored by the New Orleans Province, the primary racial dynamic was between white and African-American. Race relations on campus reflected the generally poor atmosphere of the Reconstruction era. Like other Southern colleges at the time, Jesuit colleges remained strictly segregated, and many of their students subscribed to the racist attitudes of the day. One particularly upsetting story comes from St. Charles College in Louisiana. After the Civil War, a young Jesuit seminarian from Europe, a Mr. Koch, came to St. Charles to study for the priesthood. Born in Latin America of mixed German and African ancestry, he had been sent to Louisiana by his European superiors, who obviously did not understand the severity of racial tensions in the American South. The lay students at St. Charles immediately labeled the new Jesuit in their midst as a "colored" man and demanded that he leave campus. A day after his arrival, Mr. Koch had to set sail again for Europe, where he successfully became a Jesuit priest and served as a missionary through the Belgian Province.[270]

Outside the South, many Jesuits continued to minister to Black Catholics. Although it would be some years before Jesuit colleges allowed Black students to

---

270. Platt, citing Albert Biever, SJ, *Sacrifice*, 69.

enroll, the Jesuits were not blind to the needs of African-Americans. In Missouri, the priests at Saint Louis University managed St. Elizabeth's Parish, the city's primary Black Catholic church, where the congregation consisted mainly of former slaves.[271] In Cincinnati, Jesuits from Xavier took responsibility for St. Ann's Parish, which opened in 1866 to serve Black Catholics. The parish sponsored an elementary school for Black children.[272]

The most important milestone in race relations came in 1877, when Father Patrick Healy became the first African-American president of a majority-white university. Healy was the Georgia-born son of an Irish plantation owner and a slave, who lived together as husband and wife but could not legally marry in antebellum America. Healy's race was rarely discussed publicly but was well-known to his Jesuit superiors, who (after a bit of hand wringing) appointed him to lead Georgetown University. He became Georgetown's most transformative nineteenth-century president. Despite their many missteps, this unique milestone in American history is something of which the Jesuits can be proud. The northern Jesuits, at least, were tolerant enough to ordain a priest who had been born legally into slavery and promote him to the presidency of their most important university—a university located in the District of Columbia no less, where slavery had been legal just fifteen years earlier.

Jesuit Colleges and World War I

When the United States entered World War I in 1917, it signaled the end of one era and the beginning of another in American higher education. Military recruiters descended onto college campuses, and the relationship between the federal government and private colleges would never be the same. In many cases, college campuses became virtual military bases.

Prior to this time, the United States military relied on the service academies at West Point and Annapolis to fill its officer corps— with help from land-grant colleges like Texas A&M and Virginia Tech, which emphasized military science. For a conflict the size and scale of World War I, however, the military had no choice but to expand its recruitment efforts to private universities. In 1916, as the conflict raged in Europe and American involvement looked increasingly likely, the federal government created the Reserve Officer Training Corps (ROTC) program, which established official reserve units on 115 college campuses. Jesuit schools, in general, were quick to respond to this opportunity; after all, the Jesuits themselves were fairly militaristic in their chain of command, so the discipline and structure of a military lifestyle fit nicely into the Jesuit ethos. Georgetown hosted one of the first ROTC units in the country, while Santa Clara's ROTC unit was among the first and the most robust on the West Coast.[273]

---

271. Millett, "Memory," 333, 336–337.
272. Bennish, *Continuity*, 79.
273. McKevitt, *University of Santa Clara*, 182. Curran, *History of Georgetown Vol. II*, 76.

The Great War's most immediate effect on Jesuit higher education was to deplete the available student pool. As college-age males entered the service, the resulting decline in demand for undergraduate education forced Seattle College in Washington State and Saint Peter's College in New Jersey to suspend their undergraduate divisions, becoming high schools in everything but name. In the long term, the strains of the First World War also contributed to the 1921 death of Brooklyn College and the 1922 reorganization of the New Orleans Province, which scaled back its educational projects in Shreveport and Tampa while permanently closing its colleges in Galveston and Grand Coteau. Sacred Heart College in Augusta, Georgia closed for good in the middle of the war in 1917, although that move had been planned for some time.

As the war effort expanded, President Woodrow Wilson signed into law another program, the Students Army Training Corps (SATC), as a wartime expansion of the original ROTC concept. Colleges and universities that participated in the SATC received payment from the War Department, and in exchange, they offered an approved curriculum that emphasized wartime skills like navigation and physical fitness. Students who enrolled/enlisted in the SATC were exempt from the draft until age twenty-one, at which point they would become military officers.[274]

To be eligible to participate in the SATC program, colleges had to enroll at least 100 male students over the age of eighteen. Over 500 colleges and universities nationwide met this threshold and hosted an SATC unit, including twenty-one Jesuit institutions. The influx of cash was a welcome development at struggling schools like Saint Joseph's (Philadelphia) and St. Ignatius (San Francisco), the latter of which was still rebuilding after the 1906 earthquake. In Chicago, where the Jesuits were in the process of transferring their undergraduate programs from the original St. Ignatius College campus to the new Loyola University campus, separate SATC units operated at both locations.

Ten Jesuit colleges did not participate, mainly because they were too small or too young to put in a respectable bid. On the East Coast, the Jesuits made the strategic decision to suspend the undergraduate programs at Loyola College in Baltimore and Gonzaga College in Washington, DC, concentrating the eligible students from those schools on the Georgetown campus as a way to strengthen Georgetown's SATC bid (and increase its government paycheck).[275]

Where they existed, SATC units affected campus life in a profound way for a short period. President Wilson established the SATC in the summer of 1917, which meant that most colleges could not get their units up and running until classes started in fall, 1918. By then, the conclusion of the war in Europe on November 11 was only two months away. Still, for the brief window when SATC existed, the overwhelming majority of the Jesuits' undergraduate students were enrolled in it, which meant that drilling and military discipline became as much a part of college life as the classes

---

274. Curran, *History of Georgetown Vol. II*, 82–84.

275. Ibid., 82. Varga, *Baltimore's Loyola*, 208.

themselves. In addition to the standard SATC units, a handful of American colleges and universities hosted special naval SATC divisions focused on preparing students for service at sea. Six Jesuit schools (Georgetown, Detroit, Holy Cross, Fordham, Marquette, and Saint Louis) were chosen for this honor.

The Jesuit colleges' enthusiasm for the war mirrored that of American Catholics as a whole. In general, Catholic immigrants saw World War I as an opportunity to prove their patriotism and show their fellow Americans that they were worthy citizens of their adopted country.[276] Fordham president Joseph Mulry, SJ embarked on a national speaking tour to drum up Catholic support for the war.[277] Twenty years earlier, Catholics' loyalties had been suspect during the Spanish-American War, which pitted the United States against one of the oldest Catholic imperial powers in Europe. Now, with a new and decisively non-religious conflict calling them into duty, many lay faculty and students at Jesuit colleges eagerly enlisted. Thirty-nine Jesuits enlisted as military chaplains.[278] The hope was that a solid wartime record could help Catholics assimilate and gain acceptance in American society.

ROTC programs and SATC programs were the first significant government investment in Jesuit higher education since the pre-Civil War era. The cash kept the colleges afloat during the challenging wartime years, but the reorganization of the curriculum along military lines, even if temporary, upended business as usual on Jesuit colleges. The thirty-nine enlisted Jesuits represented a sizeable chunk of the available Jesuit teaching staff, making it difficult to resume college-level instruction in Seattle and Baltimore. Another legacy of the war, the 1918 Spanish flu epidemic, kept classrooms empty and, at least at Saint Peter's College in Jersey City, ended any hope of resuming college instruction for a generation.

The war accelerated coeducation. While most Jesuits' undergraduate programs remained all-male, graduate and professional programs accepted women in small numbers to fill empty chairs. At St. Xavier College in Cincinnati, women were admitted to evening and summer courses for the first time in 1918, enrolling in the college's new business and social work degree programs.[279] The president of St. Xavier at the time was none other than Father James McCabe, who had been president of Marquette University when it first admitted women in 1909.

---

276. Curran, *History of Georgetown Vol. II*, 75–80.

277. Shelley, *Fordham*, 159.

278. Gerard F. Giblin, SJ, "Jesuits as Chaplains in the Armed Forces, 1917–1960," *Woodstock Letters* LXXXIX, no. 4 (1960): 326.

279. Bennish, *Continuity*, 126.

STUDENTS ENROLLED IN SATC PROGRAMS, 1918[280]

Boston College	750
Campion College	250
Creighton University	430
College of the Holy Cross	749
Fordham University	572
Georgetown University	487
Gonzaga University	150
Loyola University/St. Ignatius College (Chicago)	230
Loyola University (New Orleans)	300
Marquette University	825
Santa Clara University	103
St. Charles College (Louisiana)	110
St. Ignatius College (John Carroll University, Cleveland)	125
Saint Joseph's College (Philadelphia)	121
Saint Louis University	680
St. Mary's College (Kansas)	117
St. Xavier College (Xavier University, Cincinnati)	242
Spring Hill College	350
University of Detroit (Mercy)	209
Canisius College; St. Ignatius College (Univ. of San Francisco)	Participated in SATC, but did not report numbers.
Brooklyn College Gonzaga College (DC) Loyola College (Baltimore) Loyola College (Los Angeles) Rockhurst College Sacred Heart College (Denver) Saint Peter's College St. Mary's College (Galveston) St. John's University (Toledo) Seattle College	Did not participate in SATC

---

280. "Students in Our Colleges in the United States and Canada: October 10, 1918," *Woodstock Letters* XLVII, no. 3 (1918): unnumbered page.

Toward the Future

As they left the Great War behind and stepped blinking into the sunlight of the new world order, the Jesuit colleges attempted to return to normal, but much had permanently changed. The schools in 1919 had evolved significantly, especially compared to what they had been in 1865. They were still recognizable as Jesuit institutions, and their style of education remained rooted in the traditions of the men in black robes who lived on campus. However, they now had significantly more students (including some women) enrolled in a significantly larger menu of degree programs. The weekly schedule was evolving from a six-day week (with two half-days off) to the more familiar five-day week (with Saturdays and Sundays off). The "colleges" that had once enrolled students as young as eight years old were now serving an older population, and a sharper line was being drawn between students over and under the age of eighteen, the latter of whom were spinning off into separate divisions that looked something like the standard American high school. What had been a six-year plan of study to earn a bachelor's degree was transforming into a four-year plan. Lay faculty were playing a much bigger role on campus, particularly in the professional programs.

Most importantly, the standard plan of Jesuit education that had stood for more than three hundred years, the *Ratio Studiorum*, was losing steam. Faculty were specializing in a particular academic discipline. Students were being given more choice in what they studied. As the 1920s began, Jesuit colleges were self-consciously on the precipice of great change, and they entered the inter-war years determined to figure out how to navigate these unexplored waters. For more than twenty years, they would try to remake themselves as modern American universities that retained a distinctively Catholic, Jesuit identity. It was challenging, difficult work—and little did they know that, by 1945, all of their efforts would be turned on their heads once again.

Part V:

The Big Leap Forward (1919–1945)

Overview, 1919–1945

Having built (by far) the biggest network of Catholic colleges in the country, the Jesuits now faced the reality of managing it. As World War I ended, the Jesuits found themselves responsible for more schools than almost any other non-governmental organization in the United States. They managed more colleges than any branch of the Catholic Church and almost any Protestant denomination—with the possible exception of the Methodists, who were quickly losing influence over their rapidly secularizing institutions like Vanderbilt, Syracuse, and Wesleyan.

Post–World War I America was becoming a hostile environment for religiously affiliated colleges. Organizations like the Carnegie Foundation for the Advancement of Teaching pushed universities toward a standard way of operating that usually required some administrative distance between the school and whatever church or religious organization originally founded it. Trends that had started before the war—universal public education through high school, academic freedom for college faculty, buffet-style elective courses at the undergrad level, and a new emphasis on graduate and professional education—became even more pronounced in the 1920s and 1930s, permanently changing the way most universities functioned. A uniquely American invention—the accrediting agency—began to police higher education and shoehorn universities into the prevailing mold. Jesuit schools had resisted these trends longer than most, but like it or not, education in America was changing, and the Jesuits would have to adapt or watch everything they had built wither into irrelevance.

Fortunately, Jesuit leaders were up to the task. A new generation of American-born Jesuits was replacing the old, European-born Jesuits who had dominated the college faculties in the nineteenth century. If the Europeans had been staunchly conservative in their ways and slavishly loyal to tradition, many of the Americans ranged from moderate to liberal in their views. As they adapted to prevailing trends, the Jesuits began to shed their reputation as out-of-touch, conservative relics of the Old World and became one of the most progressive orders in the Catholic Church. Some individual Jesuits developed national reputations for their vociferous support of worker's rights, African-American rights, and social justice.

Keeping the universities healthy, modern, and true to their traditions was a difficult balancing act. At the same time that American academics were criticizing the Jesuit colleges for being too religious, authorities in the Catholic Church were accusing those same colleges of being too secular. In the midst of all of this regulatory uncertainty came the financial uncertainty of the Great Depression, which severely limited some of the Jesuits' grandest plans for further growth.

Forced to focus on the quality of their schools, the Jesuits finally relaxed their emphasis on quantity. This was a period of contraction, not expansion. In 1922, the New Orleans Jesuits closed St. Charles College in Grand Coteau and St. Mary's University in Galveston, while tabling the collegiate ambitions of the Jesuit high schools in Tampa and Shreveport. In the 1930s, financial pressures from the Depression forced the Midwestern Jesuits to close St. Mary's College in Kansas and St. John's University in Toledo. The East Coast Jesuits downgraded Brooklyn College to a prep school in 1921.

Only the western Jesuits attempted to build new colleges during this era, opening two small proto-colleges in Phoenix, Arizona and Tacoma, Washington (both in the late 1920s). Neither developed full-fledged undergraduate programs and both remained, in practice, high schools. The West Coast Jesuits, however, were able to revive the dormant undergraduate division at Seattle College in Washington State in the 1930s, and their eastern colleagues simultaneously revived Saint Peter's College in New Jersey. In 1942, the Maryland Jesuits also assumed control of the fifty-four-year-old University of Scranton in northeastern Pennsylvania, making it their only truly successful new expansion project of the era.

The twenty years between the two world wars were a relatively brief period in the history of Jesuit higher education, but they presented unique challenges and belong in a category of their own. The Jesuits did their best to modernize their colleges and performed admirably, given the circumstances. With little money, they transformed their small liberal arts schools into something recognizably American, while experimenting with new philosophies and pedagogies to keep a distinctively Catholic flavor in the education they offered. Swept up in national academic trends, they finally separated their colleges from their high schools and built prominent athletic programs far beyond their means.

Despite these efforts, World War II would soon upend the American education system once again, washing away many of the sandcastles the Jesuits had so carefully built. After reinventing themselves once, Jesuit colleges were called upon to do so again, and their world would never be the same.

The Push from Accreditation Agencies

All universities—including Catholic universities—faced pressure to conform to emerging national standards in the early 1900s. Often this pressure was informal, through organizations like the American Association of University Professors (which tried to institutionalize academic freedom as a norm across the country) and the Carnegie Teachers Pension Fund, which offered pensions to university employees as long as the university met certain standards in its management and governance.[1] But these organizations could only effect change through pull, not through push. The

---

1. Marsden, *Soul*, 281–282.

inter-war years saw the rise of a new kind of organization—the regional accrediting agency—with power to enforce standards. Created by governments and by the universities themselves, these agencies had the right to pass judgment on the quality of a school and, if necessary, revoke its right to award degrees.

Accreditation agencies were the means by which the secular academy imposed its sensibilities onto religiously affiliated schools, including those operated by Catholic religious orders. Different accrediting bodies emerged to cover each region of the country. Since most Jesuit colleges were concentrated in the northeast and the Midwest, two of these agencies had outsized influence over the Jesuit network: the Middle States Association (which covered the region from New York to Washington, DC) and the North Central Association (which covered Ohio to the Rocky Mountains.)

In 1917, of the ten colleges and universities sponsored by the Missouri Jesuits, only Saint Louis and Creighton were accredited by the North Central Association.[2] That so few Jesuit colleges passed muster—or even tried to get the agency's stamp of approval—was a source of embarrassment to Catholics and contributed to the perception that Catholic schools were academically inferior. This view had always been strong in academic circles, but the accreditation issue helped it to creep into public opinion.

Accrediting agencies had three major complaints about Catholic, and specifically Jesuit, colleges and universities:

1. **High School Affiliations.** Jesuit colleges continued to sponsor high school divisions, which was falling out of favor in academia and seen as beneath the dignity of a proper university.[3] The *Ratio Studiorum* curriculum was built around a six-year plan of study leading to the bachelor's degree. This European model no longer fit the American system. Around the turn of the twentieth century, most Jesuit colleges had adjusted their curriculum to a seven- or eight-year plan—that is, four years for the high school division, and four years for the undergraduate division. But the high schools and colleges were still tightly interwoven, in many cases sharing the same campuses, faculty, and facilities. Accreditors scoffed at the sight of thirteen-year-olds playing at recess just outside of what were supposed to be college classrooms. Catholic students, as well, increasingly preferred public colleges where they knew that the majority of their schoolmates would be their own age.[4] For some students, it was embarrassing to earn a college degree from an institution the public perceived mainly as a high school.

2. **Doctorates.** It becoming necessary to hold a PhD in order to teach at the college level, and accrediting agencies were beginning to measure a university's

---

2. Gleason, *Contending*, 57.

3. Joseph F. Rishel, *The Spirit that Gives Life: The History of Duquesne University, 1878–1996* (Pittsburgh: Duquesne University Press, 1997), 78–80.

4. Marsden, *Soul*, 358.

quality by the percentage of its faculty who held a doctorate. Unfortunately, the Jesuits—who still represented a significant chunk of the faculty in their own institutions, at least at the undergraduate level—generally lacked PhDs. Only a handful of Jesuit priests had attended a secular graduate school, even though they all had completed intense academic work in the seminary.

The Jesuits argued that their own lengthy formation process as priests should be considered at least the equivalent of a secular PhD.[5] Their seminary studies were certainly as long as, if not longer than, most doctoral programs. Unfortunately, the seminaries at which most Jesuit priests had been trained were not recognized by any secular authority to grant degrees. Their academic programs were recognized only by the Catholic Church, and they were not chartered graduate schools in the eyes of American law.[6]

The few professors at Jesuit institutions who did have PhDs (both lay and ordained), were mainly graduates of Catholic universities. This academic "inbreeding" was somewhat deliberate, because the universities were trying to develop a distinctively Catholic worldview among their faculty.[7] Unfortunately, only a handful of Catholic universities even offered the doctorate, and those that did were not known for their quality. In 1934, the American Council on Education, led by President Raymond Hughes of Iowa State, published the country's first comprehensive ranking of PhD programs in specific fields. No doctoral programs at any Jesuit university made the list. Only two Catholic universities were represented: The Catholic University of America (which was ranked in only five fields), and the University of Notre Dame (which was ranked in just one: chemistry).[8] Even that modest representation did not help much, because unlike many other religious orders, the Jesuits had resisted sending their priests to Catholic University for doctoral work, in part because of lingering resentment that the Vatican-approved institution was retarding the growth of the Jesuits' own universities on the East Coast.

This left the Jesuits with few options within the Catholic education network for their own priest-professors. In 1926, the same Raymond Hughes (then president of Miami University in Ohio), speaking on behalf of the North Central Association, suggested that professors at Catholic colleges would be well-advised to pursue graduate work at secular universities.[9] Although it was true that Catholic universities lagged behind state universities in the quality of their doctoral programs, such guidance, though well-intentioned, made it dif-

---

5. Fitzgerald, *Governance*, 11.
6. Ibid., 50.
7. Gleason, *Contending*, 189.
8. Ibid., 182. Fitzgerald, *Governance*, 36–37.
9. Gleason, *Contending*, 185.

ficult for the Catholic higher education system to reinforce a Catholic world-view in their teaching corps.[10]

3. **Endowments.** Accrediting bodies often set minimum financial requirements that universities had to meet to prove their solvency. At the very least, universities needed endowments sufficient to cover their debts and enough income to meet operating expenses. Many Jesuit schools were in such poor financial condition that they struggled even to meet those minimum standards. For years, they had gotten away with this penury because of their low overhead costs. Their Jesuit faculty and staff worked for nothing. However, when accrediting agencies began scrutinizing the colleges' books, the true value of the Jesuits' unpaid services was difficult to estimate on a balance sheet.[11]

Some Jesuit schools referred to the community of priests residing on campus as a "living endowment" to offset the fact that they lacked an actual endowment.[12] Saint Peter's College put an announcement in the New Jersey newspapers in 1932:

> The JESUITS supply the TEACHING STAFF. They receive no salary. For 53 years serving New Jersey gratis. If paid each $2,000 annually since 1878 (the date of the college's founding), average staff of 13 Jesuits would have received in salaries $1,378,000. At 5% this sum represents an endowment of $27,560,000. No boy ever turned away from St. Peter's because he could not pay tuition. These Jesuits are ready to teach in a tent, if necessary, to help deserving youth. Without money and without a building these Jesuit teachers have only their LIFE to give.[13]

At first, some regulators were willing to accept this argument as a concession to the unique nature of Catholic education. Canisius College in Buffalo received a state charter from the New York Board of Regents even though its finances fell well below the usual standards. But as time progressed, regulators became less likely to overlook the shoestring budgets of Jesuit colleges and began to insist on generally accepted accounting practices. It did not help that different Jesuit colleges and universities estimated the value of the priests' contributed services differently.[14]

As their standards became stricter, the accrediting agencies posed no idle threat. In 1929, the Southern Association temporarily suspended Loyola University (New

---

10. Ibid., 189.

11. Ibid., 185.

12. Ibid., 185.

13. As quoted in Alan Delozier, "The Society of Jesus and Academia in Nova Caesarea: Robert I. Gannon, SJ & the Re-Birth of St. Peter's College, 1930–1936," *New Jersey Studies: An Interdisciplinary Journal* 4, no. 1 (Winter, 2018): 108–109.

14. Gleason, *Contending*, 185, 166.

Orleans). 1934 was a particularly bad year for Jesuit higher education; the North Central Association revoked the accreditation of Regis College, Xavier University, and the University of Detroit, while the Southern Association put Loyola (New Orleans) on a one-year probation. The main issue, in almost all cases, was the schools' threadbare financial state. Both Xavier and Detroit had their accreditation restored within twelve months after showing improvement, but Regis was not fully reaccredited until 1952.[15] The final insult came in 1935, when the Association of American Universities removed Fordham from its list of approved schools. While the AAU was not an accrediting body, it was the gold standard in higher education and its censure arguably carried more serious repercussions. Specifically, the AAU criticized Fordham for inadequate library facilities and the supposedly poor performance of Fordham alumni in graduate schools, but the latter accusation seems to have been based on some faulty data. Fordham's new president, Robert Gannon, SJ, succeeded in remedying these issues and reobtained the AAU stamp of approval the following year.[16]

Hoping to develop some alternative form of accreditation that took their unique needs into account, Catholic universities briefly turned to the National Catholic Education Association (NCEA), which started to act as its own accrediting body. However, the NCEA was in reality a professional association, not the Catholic equivalent of a regional accreditor, and it stopped offering alternative accreditation in 1934.[17] This left Catholic universities at the mercy of the secular authorities.

The Pull from Rome

At the same time accreditors were pushing the Jesuit colleges in one direction, Catholic authorities in Rome were pulling them in the other. The global leader of the Jesuits at this time was Wlodimir Ledóchowski, SJ, a Polish national born to Austro-Hungarian imperial nobility. In office from 1915 to 1942, Ledóchowksi was known for his conservative European viewpoints and (at least early in his career) tended to view the innovations coming from his American provinces as a threat to tradition. Although in time his views mellowed and he became an important advocate for reform, the American Jesuits always had to tread lightly in his presence.[18]

One of Ledóchowski's chief concerns was the religious diversity of Jesuit colleges. Particularly in the professional schools, there were large numbers or even outright majorities of non-Catholics on the faculty, some of them in deanships and other positions of authority. This issue first came to Ledóchowski's attention in 1927, when a staunchly conservative member of the curia in Rome, Rafael Cardinal Merry del Val, summoned Ledóchowski to his office. The Spanish cardinal had read a scandalous report that accused American Jesuit colleges of being unfaithful to their Catholic

---

15. Ibid., 187. Cook, *Founded on Faith*, 94–95. Fitzgerald, *Governance*, 48. Stansell, *Regis*, 105.
16. Shelley, *Fordham*, 267–272.
17. Gleason, *Contending*, 188.
18. Fitzgerald, *Governance*, 5.

roots. According to his unnamed sources, the colleges were employing Protestants, Jews, and even atheists as faculty. They were even said to be admitting women in ever-larger numbers. Ledóchowski did his best to defend his fellow Jesuits, but quickly sent his American provincials a detailed questionnaire to confirm how many of the Vatican's accusations were true. The results of the survey showed that about seven percent of the Jesuit colleges' undergraduate professors, and more than fifty percent of their graduate and professional faculty, were non-Catholic. As for female and non-Catholic students—yes, they were present on campus, although the women were restricted to specific programs and a substantial portion were Catholic nuns.[19]

After receiving the results, Ledóchowski wrote to the American Jesuits, instructing them to hire only Catholics as deans, to limit the number of non-Catholic students and professors, and to end the practice of admitting women altogether.[20] Historian Paul Fitzgerald, SJ has described Ledóchowski's letter as "unfamiliar with the educational concomitants of a pluralistic society . . . (espousing) obsolete regulations that had been effective in another time and place."[21] Historian Philip Gleason takes an even blunter view:

> With the best will in the world, the American Jesuit superiors could not have followed the most rigorous of these guidelines. There were simply not enough Catholic professors and administrators to fill all the positions; coeducation was an established fact in several Jesuit institutions. . . .[22]

In the end, according to Fitzgerald, the American Jesuits simply "disregarded those injunctions which, anachronistic and unrealistic, were beyond the possibility of fulfillment."[23] In truth, most Jesuits got along well with the non-Catholic deans and professors they employed. In New Orleans, most early deans of Loyola Law School were Catholic, but the Jesuits were open-minded enough to employ an accomplished Louisiana judge, Mark Boatner, as law dean between 1924 and 1929. Boatner was both a Unitarian and a member of the Masons, but he was also a well-known civic leader and was willing to work without pay. His religious beliefs apparently did not prevent him from working well with the Loyola Jesuits during his five years in office.[24]

Some of the strongest pushback came from Jesuit schools that could not have survived had they followed Ledóchowski's orders to the letter. In the lean years of the Great Depression, a struggling Jesuit college or graduate school could not afford to exclude tuition-paying female students entirely. Seattle College, for one, became a pioneer in coeducation partly because it needed women to fill its classrooms. As it resurrected its long-dormant undergraduate programs, it inaugurated an "evening col-

---

19. Ibid., 21–23. Gleason, *Contending*, 178–179.
20. Fitzgerald, *Governance*, 23.
21. Ibid., 23.
22. Gleason, *Contending*, 179.
23. Fitzgerald, *Governance*, 24.
24. Cook, *Founded on Faith*, 73–74.

lege" in 1931 that enrolled significant numbers of women (including nuns). The college's leadership, Fathers Howard Peronteau, SJ, and James McGoldrick, SJ, jesuitically argued that these women posed no threat to the Seattle's single-sex status as long as they were confined to the evening college. But as Seattle historian Walt Crowley noted, "What (Peronteau) failed to report was the fact that on McGoldrick's watch, 'evening' classes began at noon."[25]

Another flashpoint in the controversy was in New York. At Fordham's School of Pharmacy, more than three quarters of the students were Jewish, as was the school's founding dean, Jacob Diner. Even though Diner had led the school since it opened its doors in 1912, Ledóchowski insisted that he be replaced by a Catholic. Fordham's Jesuits pushed back hard on this affront to their colleague, insisting that Dean Diner was fully committed to the traditions of Jesuit education and had developed a curriculum steeped in Jesuit tradition. Pharmacy students were required to take courses in ethics taught by respected Jesuit faculty members. Diner, they argued, was a better example of Jesuit ideals and principles than many Catholics, even putting his own money into the pharmacy school to ensure its success. Ultimately, Diner continued in his position and worked at Fordham for more than thirty years, during which he always remained fully committed to the school's Catholic and Jesuit identity.[26]

The Jesuit Response

In response to the new regulatory jungle on both sides of the Atlantic, the American Jesuits made four major attempts to reform their colleges during the inter-war years. The first was an Inter-Province Committee, which brought together representatives of the different Jesuit provinces annually from 1921 to 1931. The second was a Commission on Higher Studies, a similar but more authoritative body that met between 1931 and 1934. The third was an attempt to create a national point person for Jesuit higher education, who served between 1934 and 1937. Finally, from 1937 to 1946, this work coalesced with the creation of the Jesuit Educational Association, forerunner of today's Association of Jesuit Colleges and Universities. To varying degrees, these commissions and individuals became the first nationwide supervising bodies for Jesuit higher education.

The Inter-Province Committee on Studies (1921–1931)

On March 27, 1921, eleven Jesuits met at the now-defunct Campion College in Prairie du Chien, Wisconsin. The gathering had been almost a year in the making, and it represented a first-of-its-kind collaboration between the four American Jesuit Provinces: Maryland-New York, Missouri, New Orleans, and California. (A fifth province—New England—was in the works, but would not be formally established

---

25. Crowley, *Seattle University*, 46.
26. Shelley, *Fordham*, 196–199.

until five years later.) Their charge was to explore how to coordinate the activities of the vast Jesuit education network and ensure the quality of Jesuit schools.

Chairing the meeting was Albert Fox, SJ, the sitting president of Campion and future president of Marquette. Father Fox was a respected leader (even in secular circles) and sat on a number of committees in the North Central Association and the National Catholic Education Association. A realist, he was an irenic figure who brought the Catholic tradition and the emerging secular standards into dialogue like few others could. He also spoke candidly about the ways in which Catholic higher education had to reform itself to remain accessible to twentieth century audiences.[27]

Under Fox's leadership, the Inter-Province Committee adopted a slogan: "Every Jesuit college a standard college."[28] To achieve this end, it pushed for the separation of the colleges and their affiliated high schools. This process had already begun, but it accelerated quickly in the 1920s. Jesuit colleges spun off their high school divisions—both by physically separating the campuses and by legally incorporating the high schools as separate institutions. The Committee also urged the Jesuits to stop using the term "college" to describe lower-level schools that were not actively granting degrees. Jesuit schools that were only "colleges" in a legal or aspirational sense—like Tampa College in Florida, Gonzaga College in the District of Columbia, Brooklyn College in New York, and St. John Berchmans College in Louisiana (among others)—ran a risk of false advertising and diluted the Jesuit brand. Ironically, Campion College, which hosted the initial meeting, was an early casualty of this policy. It officially dropped its collegiate status and became Campion High School in 1925.

Despite this progress, real power remained in the hands of the provincials, not in the hands of the Inter-Province Committee members. The Committee could only make recommendations; each province ultimately still controlled the colleges within its jurisdiction. At its third meeting (in New Orleans in 1923), the Committee proposed the creation of a new, national association for Jesuit colleges and high schools. But the provincials rejected this idea on the grounds that there was already a National Catholic Education Association, and a separate club for Jesuit schools would make the Jesuits look elitist, uncooperative, or both to their Catholic colleagues.[29] Especially in these early years of the Ledóchowski era, it was vital to avoid any perception that the Jesuits were distancing themselves from the rest of the Church.

The Inter-Province Committee was an important first step, but it lacked any real teeth to back up its recommendations. Its chief contribution was its ability to bring the different provinces into meaningful dialogue with each other. The conservative Maryland-New York Province, the young California Province, the overextended New Orleans Province, and the aggressively modern Missouri Province could all learn from each other's strengths and weaknesses. It was the first time Jesuit colleges in the United States cooperated horizontally on a national level rather than vertically with

27. Gleason, *Contending*, 186.
28. Garraghan, *Jesuits of the Middle U.S. Vol. III*, 511.
29. Fitzgerald, *Governance*, 9.

the Jesuit leadership in Rome. As they tackled issues like PhDs for Jesuit faculty and even the need to establish a pan-Jesuit alumni association, they created a precedent for future collaboration and, ultimately, modernity.[30]

The Commission on Higher Studies (1931–1934)

After consulting with American colleagues and reflecting on their views, Father Ledóchowski in Rome softened his stance toward the American Jesuit colleges. It was a remarkable reversal; in the span of a few years, Ledóchowski went from a conservative force to a committed reformer, and his views evolved from suspicion to a near-complete embrace of American trends. He came to realize that Jesuit institutions had to play the academic game if they were to have any influence on American intellectual life. He also came to understand that, by limiting their audience to Catholics and by focusing on insular traditions, Jesuit colleges all but guaranteed that a Catholic perspective would be absent from mainstream American thought.[31] Surely, it was better for Jesuit colleges if the country's educational leadership took them seriously.

Ledóchowski suggested a four-pronged approach to improving Jesuit higher education in the United States:

1) Improve cooperation among Jesuit colleges.
2) Study and learn from the successes of America's leading secular universities.
3) Work to meet the accreditation agencies' standards.
4) Train Jesuits properly as college professors and researchers—that is, by sending them back to school to earn PhDs.[32]

It was hard to believe that this plan was written by the same person who had proposed such reactionary policies just a few years earlier. To help implement this agenda, Ledóchowski appointed a new committee of American Jesuits known as the Commission on Higher Studies. It functioned much like the old Inter-Province Committee (and indeed, included some veterans of that committee), but had the added weight of Ledóchowski's endorsement. Whereas the Inter-Province Committee had been a toothless ad-hoc cooperative body, the Commission on Higher Studies would have real power to influence Ledóchowski's decisions. Members of the Commission included:[33]

- Charles Carroll, SJ, regent of the University of San Francisco School of Law, former president of Seattle College, and former dean at Gonzaga University in Spokane.
- Charles Deane, SJ, dean at Fordham University.

---

30. Ibid., 11–19.
31. Ibid., 25.
32. Ibid., 24–25.
33. Ibid., 26, 31.

- Albert Fox, SJ, former president of Campion College and Marquette University, former chair of the Inter-Province Committee, and (at the time) dean at John Carroll University.
- John Hynes, SJ, President of Loyola University (New Orleans) who held a doctorate from the Gregorian University in Rome.
- Edward Tivnan, SJ, former president of Fordham University and former professor at Boston College. He held a PhD in chemistry from Georgetown University.
- James Macelwane, SJ, graduate dean at Saint Louis University and arguably the best-known Jesuit academic in the country at the time. He held a PhD in physics from Berkeley and his leading roles in the Jesuit Seismological Association and the Seismological Society of America have already been described.[34]

The Commission led a short but influential life. It met six times in 1931 and 1932, after which it produced a written report for Ledóchowski that pulled no punches. The report described the current state of graduate education—and even upper-level undergraduate education—at Jesuit universities as alarmingly inadequate. Too few Jesuits had PhDs and too few actually understood modern American education. Doctoral programs at Jesuit universities lacked rigor and awarded PhDs to students who did not merit the honor. Jesuit university presidents and deans lacked proper training as administrators and were often ill-prepared for the responsibilities entrusted to them. All of this was made worse by the presence of the Catholic University of America, which remained a thorn in the Jesuits' side by discouraging high-quality graduate programs at Jesuit universities.[35]

To solve these problems, the Commission recommended that virtually all Jesuits earn a PhD as a normal part of their priestly formation. It was a logical proposal for priests who could expect to work in academia at some point in their careers, but it was also expensive. The Jesuit provinces would have to pay thousands of dollars in graduate school tuition, and many priests and seminarians realistically would have to be sent to secular universities for their doctorates.[36] It also demanded quite a bit of the seminarians. By themselves, seminary formation and doctoral work were intense experiences; trying to do both in a roughly ten-year period would require a special kind of individual.

The Commission's most significant recommendation was that Father Ledóchowski establish a strong, authoritative administrator to oversee all Jesuit higher education in the United States. This individual, known as a "commissarius," would have real power to make decisions that affected the universities without going through the provincials. He would report directly to Ledóchowski and speak with the authority of the superior general's representative.[37]

---

34. Ibid., 3, 16, 26–27.
35. Gleason, *Contending*, 179–180.
36. Ibid., 181.
37. Ibid., 181.

This was sweeping power to entrust to one person, but Ledóchowski responded favorably to the suggestion. So began the next stage in the efforts to bring all Jesuit colleges and universities under a single umbrella.

The *Instruction on Studies and Teaching* (1934) and the Commissarius, 1934–1937

In 1934, armed with the recommendations of the Commission on Higher Education, Ledóchowski sent a formal document to his American colleagues entitled the *Instruction on Studies and Teaching*. In it, he fully endorsed the notion that Jesuits should be trained as scholars according to the best American standards. They should conduct research, publish scholarly books and articles, participate in academic conferences, and hold leadership positions in scholarly societies just like any professor at any secular university.[38] Although the American Jesuits had already identified this path forward, the *Instruction* was the first time such a directive had come from Rome. It was now official policy: Jesuits would train as modern academics as well as priests.

Ledóchowski's *Instruction* also encouraged American Jesuit universities to adhere to the standards of the accreditors. To help improve their standing, he encouraged them to dive full-force into graduate education.[39] It was the first time that Jesuit leaders had openly disregarded the privileged place of the Catholic University of America in graduate study. Twenty years earlier, Superior General Franz Xavier Wernz, SJ, had de-emphasized graduate work at Georgetown so as not to offend the papal authorities behind Catholic University. Now, Ledóchowski unapologetically encouraged Jesuit universities to establish competing programs for the sake of their own reputations. So much for a unified Catholic higher education system in the United States.

As for the critical post of "Commissarius," Ledóchowski already had someone in mind. Father Daniel O'Connell, SJ, was serving as the head of studies for the newly created Chicago Province, which had been carved out of the eastern half of the massive Missouri Province in 1928. O'Connell had earned his undergraduate degree from St. Mary's College in Kansas and his PhD from Fordham University, and had been both a professor and administrator at St. Xavier College in Cincinnati before assuming his crucial new role.[40]

O'Connell had power and he intended to use it. He visited every Jesuit college and university in the United States, making decisions as he went to encourage strategic growth and eliminate redundant or weak programs. He ordered Boston College to cut all of its PhD programs, which were sub-par compared to those at neighboring schools in Massachusetts. He questioned the need for graduate programs at Georgetown, but did not outright ban them. In Fordham, he saw great potential, and hoped that someday hundreds of young Jesuits could come to the Bronx campus to earn

---

38. Fitzgerald, *Governance*, 38.
39. Ibid., 40.
40. Ibid., 39–40.

their PhDs as a normal part of their training. Unfortunately, the same year that O'Connell visited, Fordham received the devastating news that it was being removed from the Association of American Universities' list of approved institutions. This was a nightmare scenario. O'Connell held the AAU in the highest possible esteem, and the Association's official censure put a stop to whatever grand vision he may have had for Fordham as the Jesuits' premier research university.[41] Although Fordham recovered from the embarrassment, it never again seriously competed with Georgetown as the top-ranked Catholic university on the East Coast.

In the Midwest, O'Connell hoped to consolidate academic resources at Saint Louis University—a plan that obviously did not sit well with Marquette, Loyola (Chicago), Detroit, and Creighton. Although O'Connell ultimately was not able to stem the growth of those four emerging research universities, his decisions arguably retarded the development of smaller Missouri Province schools like Regis in Denver, Rockhurst in Kansas City, Xavier in Cincinnati, and John Carroll in Cleveland. O'Connell actually recommended closing Regis, since he saw it as a drain on resources that the Missouri Province could no longer afford. In his vision, it was also best that Rockhurst remain a small undergraduate liberal arts college.[42] This was an unfortunate move, since the general paucity of higher education in the Kansas City area meant that Rockhurst probably had much more potential. With the right investment, Rockhurst could have been to Kansas City what Marquette was to Milwaukee—the dominant local research university, even outshining the local public schools. In Denver, Regis was spared the axe largely because the Missouri Province did not want to assume its enormous debt.[43]

In the end, most of the Midwestern colleges and universities continued according to the status quo. The small colleges remained small and Xavier's once-promising growth was cut short after it lost its law school in 1934. In fairness, the local Jesuit provinces were not awash with cash, so even without O'Connell's intervention it would have taken moves of administrative genius for the smaller colleges to develop drastically differently. The only college that actually closed on O'Connell's watch was St. John's University in Toledo. O'Connell's visit to the South and the west were relatively uneventful and largely maintained the status quo, although his somewhat brash style did earn him some enemies there.[44]

It was ironic that, after experiencing how hard it had been to coordinate their own academic programs with those of the Catholic University of America a generation earlier, the Jesuits (under O'Connell) would attempt the same kind of heavy-handed centralization within their own network. In the end, just as Catholic University was unable to stamp out competing programs, the Jesuits were unable to coordinate their own work on a national level for very long. In short order, Boston College and Georgetown

---

41. Ibid., 41–45.
42. Ibid., 46–47, 51. Stansell, *Regis*, 106.
43. Stansell, *Regis*, 107.
44. Fitzgerald, *Governance*, 48–49.

continued to develop their PhD programs, and the smaller regional colleges continued to do what was best for them. It proved difficult to convince any college president or provincial to put the interests of the Jesuit network above the interests of the institution they managed. As Philip Gleason wrote, "If meaningful coordination was a vain hope in a supposedly centralized body like the Jesuits it was utterly beyond the realm of possibility among Catholic institutions generally."[45]

O'Connell stepped down as commissarius in 1936 after two years in the position. His reign had been brief, but it resulted in improvements. On his recommendation, previously independent, lower-level Jesuit seminaries started to affiliate with accredited Jesuit universities so that they could award academic credits legitimately under civil law.[46] More importantly, the groundwork had been lain for the next big development, one that Ledóchowski himself had encouraged: the creation of a national Jesuit Educational Association.

The Executive Committee and the Rise of the Jesuit Educational Association (1937–1946)

Just before Father O'Connell lost his title and lost the authority to speak on behalf of the superior general in Rome, he began the process of creating a "Jesuit Educational Association" by convening a small group of Jesuits in Chicago in 1935. This was the direct ancestor of today's Association of Jesuit Colleges and Universities, although as the original name implied, it was then open to Jesuit high schools as well. Leading the group was an Executive Committee consisting of representatives from the different provinces, and over time, this group collectively played a role similar to the one O'Connell had performed single-handedly. For continuity's sake, O'Connell served as the committee's first chair.[47]

Although the Executive Committee's charge was comprehensive, much of its time was spent working out new templates for graduate education. Father Macelwane, the noted seismologist from Saint Louis, chaired its committee on graduate studies and authored a set of norms for Jesuit graduate schools in 1937. The biggest issue, predictably, was whether to develop a handful of Jesuit universities into truly great graduate institutions, or (as Macelwane preferred) to allow all universities to start modest graduate programs as a way to improve their own reputations.[48] Ultimately, the Jesuits adopted Macelwane's more laissez-faire approach almost by default, because as always in academia it proved too difficult to herd the cats, so to speak.

After a bullish career as a national authority, O'Connell was replaced as chair of the Executive Committee in 1937. His successor, Father Edward Rooney, SJ, was

---

45. Gleason, *Contending*, 198.
46. Fitzgerald, *Governance*, 50.
47. Ibid., 54–56.
48. Gleason, *Contending*, 198.

more measured in his approach and helped to establish the Jesuit Educational Association as a national player. Rooney led the effort to write the new organization's bylaws, structure, and constitution, and his diplomatic skill enabled him to obtain the approval of the American provincials. In his new role as head of the JEA, Rooney became a kind of intermediary between the Jesuit Superior General in Rome and the American colleges and universities. In its early stages from the 1940s through the 1960s, the JEA held significant power over Jesuit schools, and Rooney's approval—along with the superior general's—became necessary to make any significant change (such as adding a new school or degree program). Even though the JEA essentially added a layer of bureaucracy to Jesuit education at the national level, it was a form of progress because it enabled the colleges to bring their concerns to Rooney, who could act as their spokesperson to the superior general. The JEA also facilitated an impressive and unprecedented level of communication among the colleges. Taking advantage of a new technology—commercial air travel—Jesuit college presidents and other officials began to meet on a regular basis under JEA auspices. By the 1960s, these JEA conferences took place multiple times a year. The JEA also began publishing a national newsletter, *Jesuit Education Quarterly*, in 1938.[49]

By the time Father Ledóchowski died in Rome in 1942, the American Jesuits were well on their way to a workable, national framework for cooperation. The Jesuit Educational Association was less centralized, perhaps, than the superior general had first envisioned, but it was probably the best that could be expected in the notoriously laissez-faire world of American higher education. The Jesuits now had a national association to promote communication, if not outright cooperation.

Keeping a Catholic Perspective I: Theology Departments

As they developed their priests into legitimate scholars and built stronger graduate programs, Jesuit universities began to organize themselves into academic departments. This, of course, was a big departure from the uniformity of the old *Ratio Studiorum*. The mantra, "Every Jesuit college a standard college" meant that the schools finally had to bite the bullet they had so far resisted and offer specialized majors instead of a single curriculum for every student.

There had been internal departments within Jesuit universities before. Law schools and medical schools had operated as distinct departments since the middle of the 1800s. Loyola University (New Orleans) had attempted to organize all of its programs into departments in 1910, only to be ordered to end the practice by its Jesuit provincial.[50] It was not until the 1920s and 1930s, however, that many Jesuit universities organized departments for English, history, chemistry, astronomy, philosophy, and other liberal arts fields. At the same time, they began to organize their classes

49. Fitzgerald, *Governance*, 58–65.
50. Cook, *Founded on Faith*, 44–45.

according to credit hours, which enabled them to give students a transcript that made sense to outsiders.[51] Latin, though still required for many undergraduates, became part of a long list of core courses in the humanities and sciences. Ancient Greek became an elective, not a central part of every student's daily experience.

Although electives were not unheard of prior to this time (Jesuit colleges had offered optional courses in subjects like music, calligraphy, and foreign languages since the 1700s) they now took up more space in the academic program. It was still a far cry from the free-for-all elective system at Harvard, but students at Jesuit colleges now had some choice in what they studied.

One question that emerged during this time was how to keep a distinctively Catholic flavor to a Jesuit education. It had always been taken for granted that the *Ratio Studiorum* provided an ideal mix of intellectual rigor and moral formation. Now that the *Ratio* was falling by the wayside, how could the Jesuits keep its spirit alive in a modern curriculum?

Religious education proved to be a flashpoint. Even though the *Ratio* was imbued with religious themes and sensibilities, it had not included courses in theology *per se*. Jesuit schools had long offered a weekend catechism lesson for Catholic students, but these "Sunday school" lectures looked increasingly out of place as the average age of the students increased and as the college curriculum became more sophisticated. Thus, as they began to organize themselves into departments, many Jesuit universities created a department of theology or religious studies for their undergraduates.

In taking this step, Jesuit colleges were influenced by the writings of St. John Henry Newman, the English cardinal and Oxford professor whose seminal work, *The Idea of a University*, was first published in 1873. In it, Newman argued that no university worthy of the name could exclude theology from its list of course offerings. Universities claim to expose students to the sum total of human knowledge, and since theology was a legitimate branch of knowledge, Newman criticized any university that neglected to teach it alongside physics and chemistry. Theology, in fact, was the queen of the sciences since it alone could find deeper meaning in the big questions that other fields of study took for granted, bringing all subjects into dialogue with each other and with the ultimate purpose of human existence. Newman viewed theology as the glue that held the academy together, even in an age when faculty were developing ever-narrower fields of expertise.[52]

Such heady arguments aside, it made sense for a Catholic university to have at least one department devoted to religion. But the steps the American Jesuit universities took in this direction were surprisingly cautious. Catholic theology, traditionally, had been studied only by aspiring priests in the seminary; offering it to laypeople at

---

51. Dorothy Brown, "Learning, Faith, Freedom, and Building a Curriculum" in *Georgetown at 200: Faculty Reflections on the University's Future*, ed. William C. McFadden (Washington: Georgetown University Press, 1990), 82–83.

52. See Edward Hahnenberg, "Theodore M. Hesburgh, Theologian: Revisiting Land O'Lakes Fifty Years Later," *Theological Studies* 78, no. 4 (December 2017): 942.

the undergraduate level was practically unheard of.[53] Since the Church already had plenty of seminaries, there was no real need for most of the new theology departments at "regular" universities to offer graduate courses. They simply had to adapt esoteric seminary subjects for a broad lay audience of non-specialist undergraduates.

Many Jesuit colleges debated what to name these new departments. Developments at Georgetown during this time are illustrative. Just past the turn of the century, Georgetown students were required to take courses in what the university called "Christian Doctrine," and by 1912 that title had morphed into "Evidences of Religion." In 1919, Georgetown created a "Department of Apologetics" to manage the teaching of religion. Over a decade later, in 1932, that department changed its name to the "Department of Religion" and did not become the "Department of Theology" until 1957.[54] This shifting nomenclature reflected that, while "theology" was a more correct academic term, "religion" or "religious studies" better reflected the department's original purpose in cultivating religious literacy among laypeople. Similar debates took place across the country, and to this day, Jesuit colleges differ in the terminology they use. At Georgetown, the department now refers to itself as the "Department of Theology *and* Religious Studies."

Keeping a Catholic Perspective II: The Rise of Neoscholasticism

An even bigger issue facing Jesuit schools was how to maintain the cohesion of the old *Ratio Studiorum* in a modern academic environment. One of the *Ratio's* key strengths was that lessons built logically upon each other, in sequence, so that by the end of the six-year experience a student theoretically should have developed a deep, well-defined understanding of the world—including the connections between morality, science, the humanities, and philosophy. The Jesuit college graduate was supposed to be an eloquent and erudite citizen-scholar in command of the wisdom of the past and capable of articulating his worldview to anyone. (Never mind, of course, that hardly any students actually completed the full six-year plan of study. McKevitt estimates that only about 2 percent of the approximately six thousand students enrolled in the classical curriculum at Jesuit colleges in the late 1800s actually graduated.)[55] That reality aside, how could the Jesuits maintain that same spirit in the modern era and encourage students to see the "big picture" behind their studies?

As historian Dorothy Brown describes it, "New terms like 'organic unity,' 'synthetic vision,' 'integral Catholicism,' and 'Catholic culture' became buzz words" in the 1920s and 1930s.[56] To try to glue the entire academic experience together, the Jesuits of the inter-war years settled onto a particular philosophy—neoscholasticism. Although not entirely new, neoscholasticism was enjoying a surge in popularity in the

---

53. Ibid., 933.
54. McFadden, "Catechism," 148–149.
55. McKevitt, *University of Santa Clara*, 122.
56. Brown, "Learning," 83.

early twentieth century after a series of popes endorsed it as an ideal framework to combine traditional Catholic thought with modernity.[57] It was based on the writings of St. Thomas Aquinas, a thirteenth-century Dominican philosopher, whose particular worldview is often described as "scholastic." Accordingly, the twentieth-century adaptation of Aquinas's thought took on the prefix "neo-" as Catholic scholars attempted to apply it to their contemporary intellectual scene. Occasionally, in deference to its original source, the same philosophy was also known as "neo-Thomism."

As a philosophical worldview, neoscholasticism tried to find the deeper meaning behind all branches of human thought, and operated on the assumption that all human knowledge was connected to the goodness of God's creation. Aquinas's writings suggested that God's very existence made human knowledge possible and that science and research were merely ways of getting closer to a fuller, more enlightened understanding of God's purpose for the world. When academics lost sight of that bigger picture, the philosophy held, scientific knowledge could be corrupted and used for evil purposes like developing weapons of war. However, when framed by the tradition of the Catholic Church and refined by the Church's teaching authority, human reason could be used for good and could solve real-world problems, such as labor inequalities and social injustices. The Catholic tradition brought a moral component to the search for truth that secular universities tended to overlook in their misguided, results-driven research focused narrowly on the bottom line.[58]

Since the Jesuits were the intellectual leaders of the Catholic education system, many other Catholic schools adopted neoscholasticism as a paradigm. Catholic leaders hoped that this approach to education would instill a distinctive "Catholic culture" into students and distinguish both the student experience and the research output at Catholic universities.[59] As Patrick Byrne has noted, "alumni who were educated during the late stages of that period . . . still testify that (neoscholasticism) gave them a greatly cherished orientation for the rest of their lives."[60] Furthermore, neoscholasticism and its principles inspired a number of important Catholic intellectuals at the time. Byrne sees its influence in the writings of great social justice writers and peace philosophers like Flannery O'Connor, Thomas Merton, and Dorothy Day.[61]

As a philosophy, however, neoscholasticism did have weaknesses. Because it was vague enough to apply to almost any situation, it sometimes failed to give meaningful answers to important questions. When they were unable to resolve an intellectual debate through neoscholasticism, scholars and students were inevitably told to consult an expert somewhere in the Church hierarchy—the very kind of authoritarianism that American academics tend to reject in knee-jerk fashion. As such, neoscholasti-

---

57. Gleason, *Contending*, 105–113.

58. Ibid., 114–123. Patrick H. Byrne, "The Good under Construction and the Research Vocation of a Catholic University," *Journal of Catholic Education* 7, no. 3 (March 2004): 324–326.

59. Brown, "Learning," 83.

60. Byrne, "Good," 326.

61. Ibid., 326.

cism reinforced the stereotype that professors at Catholic universities did not and could not enjoy complete academic freedom. Such accusations were poison in academic culture and ultimately neoscholasticism failed to calm the anti-Catholic prejudices in the scholarly world.

The desire to find deeper meaning behind a college education was not unique to Catholics. As electivism spread and a bachelor's degree became little more than a random collection of unrelated courses, even secular schools started to push back and argue for more cohesion in the curriculum. One major critic was Robert Maynard Hutchins, president of the University of Chicago from 1929 to 1945. In his 1936 book, *The Higher Learning in America*, he attacked American universities for emphasizing financial and professional considerations ahead of the search for personal enlightenment and philosophical truth. Hutchins fought against the hyper-specialization of academic life and was sympathetic to Catholic universities for their willingness to resist prevailing trends by providing an education that at least attempted to shape students into well-rounded, moral human beings.

Ultimately, however, neither Hutchins nor the Catholic institutions he admired would succeed in swinging the pendulum back in the other direction. Historian George Marsden writes,

> The affinities of Hutchins's views to Catholicism were also a major strike against him. . . . Catholic thinkers were likely to hail his critique. . . . Catholic thinkers, however, were seldom given a serious voice in mainstream American intellectual culture and most of those who controlled that culture were ready to dismiss Hutchins's views just because of their parallels to Catholicism.[62]

A generation later, Mt. Holyoke College faculty member Peter Viereck would put it more bluntly, arguing that anti-Catholicism was becoming "the anti-Semitism of the intellectuals."[63]

The search for meaning in college curricula continued after World War II. In 1945, a Harvard committee proposed an undergraduate curriculum based on "great books" as a way to give some common meaning to the college experience. A year later, a presidential commission convened by Harry Truman argued that all education should be characterized by an allegiance to democratic values and patriotic duty.[64] These efforts, in effect, tried to achieve by secular means what the Catholic universities were trying to achieve through neoscholasticism.[65] In the end, individual faculty members' academic freedom made it virtually impossible to unite any large university's curriculum with a common theme, but traditionalists of the 1920s and 1930s certainly tried.

---

62. Marsden, *Soul*, 379.
63. As quoted in Larry Tye, *Bobby Kennedy: The Making of a Liberal Icon* (New York: Random House, 2017), 223.
64. Marsden, *Soul*, 389, 393.
65. Rizzi, "Newman's *Idea*," 43.

Separating from the High Schools

The separation of Jesuit colleges from their high school divisions was a gradual process, but the phenomenon as a whole reached its peak in the inter-war years. Virtually all Jesuit colleges eventually shed their high schools, which legally incorporated as separate nonprofit organizations with their own presidents, their own boards of trustees, and occasionally their own Jesuit communities. Sometimes this was accompanied by a physical separation of the two campuses, but in other cases, physical separation and legal separation took place years or even decades apart.

There were emotional and practical reasons for holding onto the high schools, and some colleges took longer than others to cut the umbilical cord. In truth, most nineteenth-century Jesuit schools had been more like modern-day high-schools than modern-day colleges in terms of the age of their students and the atmosphere on campus. More often than not, the high school division could claim closer continuity with the institution's history than the college division. At many schools, the large, revenue-producing high schools had long subsidized the small undergraduate programs. By the 1920s, that imbalance had shifted clearly in favor of the colleges, and the high schools came to be seen as obstacles for accreditation and reputational liabilities.

The first Jesuit college to separate its older and younger students was St. Xavier College in Cincinnati, which briefly moved the lowest grade levels to their own building on a rural property outside the city in the 1840s.[66] Still, this was just a physical separation; legally speaking, St. Xavier was still one school with two campuses. It was not until the early 1900s that most Jesuit colleges began offering an eight-year, American-style plan of study rather than the six-year, European-style curriculum of the *Ratio Studiorum*. They had few other options, since the old-fashioned six-year curriculum no longer matched the normal educational life cycle in the United States. Under the old system, Jesuits had to admit students to "college" after eighth grade, or had to recruit students who had already completed a year or two of high school elsewhere. This became unsustainable by the 1920s, as most Americans began to attend public "high schools" through age eighteen. The experience of Canisius College in Buffalo illustrates the rough timeline that many Jesuit schools followed in their evolution. Canisius began offering an eight-year plan of study between 1894 and 1896, officially describing the first four years as its "high school" and the second four years as its "college."[67] The two divisions physically separated in 1912 and legally separated in 1928.

In general, the spinoff high schools continued to use the college's name, colors, athletic team nicknames, and branding. This allowed the Jesuits to get the best of both worlds. Colleges could legally claim that they nothing to do with the high schools, which satisfied accreditors. At the same time, the high schools could cultivate a strong

---

66. Bennish, *Continuity*, 50.
67. Dunn, "Gymnasium," 433–434.

reputation among parents who drooled at the idea of sending their teenage children to an elite college prep program.

The table below provides a rough overview of when this process happened in each case.

Date of Separation	College (Modern-day Names)	High School (Modern-day Names)	Notes
1874	Gonzaga College (discontinued) *Washington, DC*	Gonzaga College High School *Washington, DC*	Gonzaga conferred its last college degree in 1874 but continued to enroll students who finished their degrees at Georgetown until the early twentieth century[68]
1907	Marquette University *Milwaukee, WI*	Marquette University High School *Milwaukee, WI*	College relocated 1907, high school remained on original campus until it, too, relocated in 1922
1911	Loyola University *New Orleans, LA*	Jesuit High School *New Orleans, LA*	The Jesuits consolidated college programs at Loyola and high school programs at Immaculate Conception, which relocated and adopted present name 1926
1912	Canisius College *Buffalo, NY*	Canisius High School *Buffalo, NY*	High school became a separate department in 1883, college relocated 1912. High school independently chartered by New York State in 1928
1912	College of St. Francis Xavier (discontinued) *New York, NY*	Xavier High School *New York, NY*	St. Francis Xavier College folded all degree programs into Fordham
1913	Boston College *Chestnut Hill, MA*	Boston College High School *Boston, MA*	College relocated to Chestnut Hill 1913; legally separated 1927
1914	College of the Holy Cross *Worcester, MA*	None	High school discontinued
1919	Xavier University *Cincinnati, OH*	St. Xavier High School *Cincinnati, OH*	Maintained some common business operations until 1934
1919	Georgetown University *Washington, DC*	Georgetown Preparatory School *Bethesda, MD*	Prep School moved to Bethesda 1919. Legally separated in 1927.
1921	Brooklyn College (discontinued) *Brooklyn, NY*	Brooklyn Preparatory School *Brooklyn, NY*	College discontinued 1921; high school closed 1972

---

68. Francis Patrick Cassidy, *Catholic College Foundations and Development in the United States (1677–1850)* (Washington: Catholic University of America Press, 1924), 34.

Date of Separation	College (Modern-day Names)	High School (Modern-day Names)	Notes
1921	Loyola University *Baltimore, MD*	Loyola Blakefield *Towson, MD*	Loyola High School changed its name after a donor, George Blake, enabled it to move to a new campus in 1941
1922	Loyola University *Chicago, IL*	St. Ignatius College Preparatory School *Chicago, IL*	St. Ignatius briefly continued operations as a downtown college after Loyola moved to Rogers Park campus.
		Loyola Academy *Wilmette, IL*	The Jesuits opened a second Chicago high school, Loyola Academy, on Loyola University's "new" Rogers Park campus in 1909. That school relocated to suburban Wilmette, Illinois in 1957.
1922	St. John Berchmans College (discontinued) *Shreveport, LA*	Loyola College Preparatory School *Shreveport, LA*	Tabled plans to develop into a college after de Boynes visit, 1922
1924	Saint Louis University *St. Louis, MO*	Saint Louis University High School *St. Louis, MO*	
1925	Santa Clara University *Santa Clara, CA*	Bellarmine College Preparatory School *San Jose, CA*	Originally named University of Santa Clara High School, changed to present name in 1928
1925	Campion College (discontinued) *Prairie du Chien, WI*	Campion High School *Prairie du Chien, WI*	College division closed 1925; high school closed 1975.
1927	Saint Joseph's University *Philadelphia, PA*	Saint Joseph's Preparatory School *Philadelphia, PA*	College relocated 1927; Legally separated 1967
1929	University of San Francisco *San Francisco, CA*	St. Ignatius College Preparatory School *San Francisco, CA*	High school department separated 1927, relocated again 1969
1929	Seattle University *Seattle, WA*	Seattle Preparatory School *Seattle, WA*	Legally separated when college relocated back to original campus, leaving prep school at Interlaken Blvd.
1929	Loyola Marymount University *Los Angeles, CA*	Loyola High School *Los Angeles, CA*	College relocated
1929	Tampa College (discontinued) *Tampa, FL*	Jesuit High School	High school obtained collegiate charter in 1929, but never developed into a true college. Present name adopted 1940

Date of Separation	College (Modern-day Names)	High School (Modern-day Names)	Notes
1930	Saint Peter's University *Jersey City, NJ*	Saint Peter's Preparatory School *Jersey City, NJ*	Dormant college restored 1930; legally separated 1955
1931	University of Detroit Mercy *Detroit, MI*	University of Detroit Jesuit High School and Academy *Detroit, MI*	Legally separated 1948
1935	John Carroll University *University Heights, OH*	St. Ignatius High School *Cleveland, OH*	College relocated
1935	Spring Hill College *Mobile, AL*	None	High school closed
1935	Brophy College *Phoenix, AZ*	Brophy College Preparatory School *Phoenix, AZ*	Entire school closed 1935; high school reopened 1952
1937	Fordham University *The Bronx, NY*	Fordham Preparatory School *The Bronx, NY*	New York State recognized high school as separate 1937; legally separated 1970
1954	Gonzaga University *Spokane, WA*	Gonzaga Preparatory School *Spokane, WA*	High school became a separate department 1922
1958	Creighton University *Omaha, NE*	Creighton Preparatory School *Omaha, NE*	
1962	Rockhurst University *Kansas City, MO*	Rockhurst High School *Kansas City, MO*	High School became a separate department 1923, relocated and legally separated 1962
1977	University of Scranton *Scranton, PA*	Scranton Preparatory School *Scranton, PA*	High school opened in unused university buildings, 1944
1979	Regis University *Denver, CO*	Regis Jesuit High School *Aurora, CO*	High school became a separate department 1921. Plans to relocate in 1960 fell through due to lack of funds.[69] Legally separated 1979, high school relocated to Aurora, Colorado 1989
Ongoing	Fairfield University *Fairfield, CT*	Fairfield Preparatory School *Fairfield, CT*	Founded 1942, still affiliated

---

69. Stansell, *Regis*, 191–192.

Only two Jesuit colleges discontinued their high schools: Holy Cross (1914) and Spring Hill (1935). Holy Cross could afford to do this, in part, because it was the largest Catholic undergraduate college in the United States at the time, with more than 1,000 students.[70] The opposite happened in places like Brooklyn College and Campion College, where it was more logical to phase out the small bachelor's degree programs and focus exclusively on educating high school students.

For the large boarding colleges like Georgetown and Santa Clara, relocating the high school divisions freed up much-needed space on campus, but came at a cost. It was expensive to acquire property and build new campuses for the high schools, and in some cases, the Jesuits used revenue from the colleges themselves to pay those bills. Santa Clara University assumed a third of the debt necessary to rid itself of its high school.[71] At Georgetown, the university transferred $47,000 from its hospital to help pay the more than quarter-million dollar price tag for the new Georgetown Prep campus in Maryland.[72]

The tradition of associating a Jesuit high school with each Jesuit college ran so deep that the practice continued later in the century, even when it was no longer necessary for historic or practical reasons. Shortly after they assumed control of the University of Scranton in 1942, the Jesuits opened Scranton Prep nearby and did not formally separate the two institutions until 1977. As part of their efforts to found Fairfield University in Connecticut, the Jesuits began by founding Fairfield Prep, which is the only Jesuit high school that has never legally separated from its parent institution.

Today, even though most Jesuit high schools are separately incorporated, they maintain good relations with the nearby Jesuit colleges and often serve as important feeders for student recruitment. The colleges, which own the copyrights to the athletic logos and other intellectual property, often willingly allow the high schools to use those symbols. Boston College High School uses the same fight song as Boston College. Sports teams at Saint Louis University High School are known as the "Junior Billikens" in homage to the team nickname at the university across town.

Some high schools bear vestiges of old college traditions that the colleges themselves have abandoned. Marquette University High School still refers to its athletic teams as the "Hilltoppers," even though Marquette University stopped using that name decades ago. In Baltimore, Loyola (Blakefield) High School continued to use the original school colors (blue and gold) even after Loyola College changed its colors to green and gray. In many cases, the names of the high schools preserve the original names of the colleges. When St. Xavier College in Cincinnati dropped the word "Saint" from its name and became Xavier University in 1930, St. Xavier High School preserved the old moniker. The various "St. Ignatius" high schools in Cleveland,

70. Gleason, *Contending*, 84.

71. McKevitt, *University of Santa Clara*, 208.

72. Curran, *History of Georgetown Vol. II*, 424 (n. 64).

Chicago, and San Francisco recall the original names of John Carroll University, Loyola University, and the University of San Francisco, respectively. Moreover, the large majority of the spinoff high schools remain all-male.

The only two twentieth-century Jesuit colleges that never sponsored high schools of any kind were the two youngest: Le Moyne College in Syracuse (founded 1946) and Wheeling University in West Virginia (founded 1954).

The First Professional School of International Affairs

As the Jesuit universities were shedding their prep divisions on the lower end of the spectrum, they were rapidly expanding their graduate and professional schools on the upper end. As mentioned earlier, most of the Jesuit schools of law, business, engineering, etc. that took shape during this period were Catholic versions of the kinds of professional schools that mainstream American universities had already perfected. Jesuit schools were sometimes the first in the city or state to offer a specific kind of professional degree, but generally not the first in the country. However, there was one major exception to this rule—a Jesuit-run professional school that was not only the first of its kind in the United States, but which also set a global academic standard by defining an entirely new field of study and offering an entirely new kind of degree. This was the School of Foreign Service at Georgetown University, founded in 1919.

The idea for a specialized school designed to prepare students for international careers seems to have originated outside of the Jesuit network. Constantine McGuire, a Catholic economist with close ties to the US Treasury Department and reported connections to the Vatican, began pitching the concept to several different universities in 1918. World War I had proven that the United States lagged embarrassingly behind Europe in terms of the skill of its diplomats and the expertise of its business leaders in matters of foreign trade. McGuire envisioned a school that would train students in negotiation, foreign languages, shipping, commerce, and other trappings of globalization that the Great War had brought into the public consciousness. Having recently been denied a faculty position at his own alma mater, Harvard, "because of an unwritten rule against hiring Catholics to teach medieval history,"[73] McGuire went elsewhere with his proposal. He enlisted the financial backing of another prominent Catholic, James Farrell, CEO of the US Steel Corporation in Pittsburgh, and their connections quickly brought them to Georgetown.[74]

Georgetown President John Creeden, SJ, initially balked at the idea, considering it too expensive. But he reconsidered after another Jesuit, Father Richard Tier-

---

73. Georgetown University Edmund A. Walsh School of Foreign Service and Washington Custom Media, *SFS 100: A Century of Service* (Washington: Georgetown University Press, 2019), 016, 34–35, quote from p. 35.

74. Ibid., 016.

ney of *America* magazine, intervened to change his mind. Washington, DC, was the ideal location for such a school, and the unique concept of a broad liberal arts curriculum with a professional, international focus fit perfectly with the character of a global teaching order like the Jesuits. With a faculty corps that still included large numbers of foreign-born Jesuits, and given its proximity to the nation's seat of power, Georgetown would have no trouble finding qualified teachers. Father Creeden agreed to the proposal.[75]

The new school was to be called the School of Foreign Service—an inventive term at the time, because the US Department of State did not yet have a branch known as the "Foreign Service." It was not until Congress passed the Rogers Act of 1924 that the old Diplomatic and Consular Services united under that name. Father Creeden appointed a young Jesuit, Father Edmund Walsh, SJ, to be the first "regent"—the position above "dean" in the hierarchy of most Jesuit-run professional schools. Father Walsh, an Irish-American Bostonian by birth and a graduate of Boston College High School, had been a member of the national board of directors of the short-lived Student Army Training Corps during World War I, in which capacity he supervised SATC programs throughout New England.[76]

Thus began an almost forty-year reign in which Father Walsh shaped the School of Foreign Service, interrupted only briefly from 1922 to 1924, when the Vatican tapped him to lead the Papal Relief Mission to the famine-stricken Soviet Union, which was still reeling from World War I and the Bolshevik Revolution. His experiences in Russia and in subsequent diplomatic missions for the Vatican convinced the young priest of the dangers of communism—a viewpoint that the School of Foreign Service curriculum would come to reflect. In his later years, Walsh became fond of walking the halls of the school in his customary black cape and became a larger-than-life personality—both in the eyes of the students and in the halls of power in Washington, DC, where many alumni wound up working.[77]

The school was an almost instant success, attracting 70 students in its first (experimental) year and enabling Walsh to hire Roy MacElwee, a prominent former bureau director in the Commerce Department, as its first dean. Three years later, it awarded its first "Bachelor of Foreign Service," an entirely new degree in American academia.[78] Although the curriculum initially focused on shipping and trade, it came to include cutting-edge courses in geopolitics, foreign languages, history, and government. By the middle of the century, it had spun off a School of Business and School of Languages and Linguistics at Georgetown, and had attracted prominent faculty members like Henry Kissinger, Jeane Kirkpatrick, Madeleine Albright, and others who were tapped for federal government service before, during, or after their teach-

---

75. Ibid., 34–35.

76. Seth Tillman, *Georgetown's School of Foreign Service: the First 75 Years* (Washington: Georgetown University, 1994), 2–3.

77. Ibid., 6. Georgetown University & Washington Custom Media, *SFS 100*, 138–141.

78. Georgetown University & Washington Custom Media, *SFS 100*, 36, 64.

ing careers. Alumni, including future President of the United States Bill Clinton, credited the school's unique blend of liberal arts and professional studies with shaping their worldview.[79]

Plenty of Americans were uneasy that the nation's oldest, largest, and most prominent school of foreign affairs was located within a Catholic university. In the 1920s, the Scottish Rite Masons reacted with alarm to rumors that America's diplomatic corps could soon be dominated by Catholics who, they feared, might use US power to promote Vatican interests. The Masons donated $1 million in 1928 to Georgetown's local rival, the secular George Washington University, to establish a School of Government (known today as the Elliott School for International Affairs). The bequest stipulated that the gift would be revoked if the George Washington University ever adopted a religious affiliation.[80]

In one respect, the fear-mongers were right; Georgetown did indeed become the largest feeder school for the US Foreign Service and many similar agencies, outranking even the Ivy League institutions. On the other hand, reports of a Catholic "mafia" in the government were overstated. As early as 1940, the School of Foreign Service's student body was almost 40% non-Catholic, and its faculty was 52% non-Catholic.[81]

As the School of Foreign Service flourished and globalization brought more attention to international issues, many universities followed Georgetown's lead and established similar programs. Copycat schools included Princeton University's School of Public and International Affairs (1930), Tufts University's Fletcher School of Law and Diplomacy (1933), Harvard University's John F. Kennedy School of Government (1936), the Johns Hopkins University's Nitze School of Advanced International Studies (1943), Columbia University's School of International and Public Affairs (1946), and the University of Pittsburgh's Graduate School of Public and International Affairs (1957). They and others formed the Association of Professional Schools of International Affairs in the 1980s, which today boasts almost 70 full and affiliate members worldwide, all of which offer professional degrees based largely on the model that Georgetown brought into existence in 1919.

False Starts in Phoenix and Tacoma

The Great Depression foiled a number of Jesuit projects. During the boom years of the 1920s, the California Province made plans to expand to Phoenix, Arizona and Tacoma, Washington, and those plans came to fruition by the end of the decade when new "colleges" opened in both cities. Each was, in Jesuit parlance, a *collegium inchoatum*—a high school that the Jesuits intended to develop into a proper college when the time was ripe. Both schools were legally incorporated as colleges even before classes

---

79. Bill Clinton, *My Life* (New York: Knopf, 2004), 76–78.

80. Tillman, *Georgetown's School of Foreign Service*, 18.

81. Ibid., 18.

began. Unfortunately, the catastrophic effects of the Depression meant that neither ever developed into a true college.

According to articles of incorporation signed and notarized in December 1927, the Phoenix school was to be called William Henry Brophy College. Its namesake was an Irish immigrant who settled in Arizona and made a fortune in banking before his death in 1922. His widow, Ellen Amelia Goodbody Brophy, became a philanthropist with a preference for Arizona Catholic causes. Her gifts supported a Catholic orphanage in Tucson and a girls' school in Douglas, and in 1927–1928, she joined the long list of transformative female donors in Jesuit history by funding the new Jesuit school.[82] Brophy College joined Creighton University as one of only two American Jesuit colleges named after a donor, and indeed, the circumstances in Arizona resembled those in Nebraska exactly fifty years earlier. Both schools were made possible by generous women who had been recently widowed.

Ellen Amelia Brophy was present when the school laid its cornerstone with great fanfare in 1928, and for a time it seemed that the proto-college was on its way to success.[83] But the Depression hit it hard, and in 1932 a Jesuit newsletter reported that Brophy had "suspended its College department for the time being."[84] By 1935, even the high school was forced to close. This was unfortunate because Arizona lacked any other Catholic colleges, and remains generally underserved by higher education today. As Mexican immigration brought thousands more Catholics to the state over the next several decades, the lack of any Catholic colleges in Arizona looked even more inexcusable.

In 1957, the Jesuits reopened Brophy as a high school using the original buildings. Today, while Brophy remains one of Arizona's most prestigious prep schools, its beautiful, expansive campus serves as a visual reminder that it was originally intended to be much more. Nonetheless, the dream of a Jesuit university in Phoenix got new life in the twenty-first century through the work of Brophy's spiritual next-of-kin, Creighton. In 2009, Creighton University Medical School established a branch campus at Arizona's St. Joseph's Hospital, and has since embarked on ambitious expansion plans to offer a variety of medical degrees in Phoenix. As a result, there is finally a Jesuit university presence in the Grand Canyon State.

The California Province's expansion to Tacoma, Washington was on a smaller scale than its efforts in Phoenix. The Jesuits assumed control of St. Leo Parish in Tacoma in 1911, and a year later opened an elementary school on the parish property. In 1927, they filed to incorporate under the title, "The Jesuit Fathers of Bellarmine College of Tacoma," and the articles of incorporation state:

---

82. Ann Knake, Jesuit Archives and Research Center, St. Louis, Missouri, personal correspondence, October 28, 2020. "MS 1225 Brophy Family Papers, 1882–1976," Arizona Historical Society, http://www.arizonahistoricalsociety.org/wp-content/upLoads/library_Brophy-Family.pdf.

83. "Varia," *Woodstock Letters* LVII, no. 3 (1928): 539–540.

84. "Varia," *Woodstock Letters* LXI, no. 1 (1932): 162.

The object for which the said corporation is formed is to establish . . . in the City of Tacoma, Washington, an Educational Institution to be known as BEL-LARMINE COLLEGE, in which young men will be taught and instructed in High School and Collegiate courses of education, in conformity with the laws of the State of Washington, and the system commonly used by Jesuit educators.[85]

The namesake of the college was Robert Bellarmine, SJ, a seventeenth-century Italian cardinal and scholar who was then three years away from sainthood. It, too, opened with fanfare on September 23, 1929—just as the stock market was collapsing 3,000 miles away in New York.[86] Although the school did not close, the financial pressures of the Depression meant that the Jesuits never developed it into a college. Moreover, in the 1930s, nearby Seattle College rebuilt its own undergraduate programs and certainly did not need the competition. Today, the Jesuit school in Tacoma is known as Bellarmine Prep.

Other Casualties of the Great Depression

In 1931, at about the same time that Brophy College discontinued its fledgling undergraduate program, the Missouri Jesuits made the difficult decision to discontinue the undergraduate program at St. Mary's College in rural Kansas. It was hard to justify the existence of the isolated school now that there were proper Jesuit colleges in both Omaha and Kansas City. The blow was softened by the decision to relocate Saint Louis University's theology programs to the old St. Mary's campus. St. Mary's continued to function as a Jesuit seminary for over thirty years, but in 1967 the seminarians and theology faculty returned to Saint Louis, and the Kansas property was eventually sold.

St. John's University in Toledo, which had once seemed like a promising project of the Buffalo Jesuit Mission, closed in 1936. The downtown school had purchased land for a new campus as late as 1921, but the funds to develop that property disappeared with the stock market crash. Across the state, a year before St. John's closed, John Carroll University had relocated to its own new campus in the Cleveland suburbs, and the province lacked the means to do the same in Toledo. Being a smaller and less economically diverse city than Cleveland, Toledo could not supply enough tuition-paying students to keep the school afloat, and the Jesuits withdrew. The property that they had acquired for the new campus (near the city's Ottawa Park) is today home to St. Francis de Sales High School and the Gesu Church, which was originally staffed by Jesuits but is now in the hands of the Oblates of St. Francis de Sales.

---

85. "Bellarmine Preparatory School—Jesuit Fathers Of Bellarmine College Of Tacoma. Washington State Corporation Records, 1855–2004," Washington State Archives, accessed October 31, 2020, https://digitalarchives.wa.gov/DigitalObject/Download/c6a4dbd9-d8e3-4da2-92be-3103f0137ad9.

86. "Varia," *Woodstock Letters* LVIII no. 1 (1929): 233–234.

Robert Gannon, SJ, and the Resurrection of Saint Peter's College, New Jersey (1930)

Amid all of the closures and contractions of the 1930s, there were two bright spots in the Jesuit network. Both Seattle College in Washington State and Saint Peter's College in New Jersey restored the undergraduate programs that they had cut during the challenging years of the First World War. These were not technically "new" Jesuit colleges, but both were rebuilt almost from scratch. The only major advantages they had were strong local name recognition and pre-existing state charters that they could dust off when they resumed offering degrees. Both of those factors eased the administrative burden somewhat, but everything else—from the faculty to the curriculum—had to be recreated from the ground up.

Seattle College, at least, could return to its mothballed old campus just east of downtown, and re-occupy historic Garrand Hall. Saint Peter's had bigger challenges. It had been one of the three New York-area colleges that the Jesuits closed in the 1910s and 1920s as they consolidated their resources at Fordham University—a long-planned process accelerated by World War I. The loss was a blow to Jersey City, where the population continued to grow and Catholic immigrants squeezed out of Manhattan settled in large numbers. Saint Peter's High School continued to operate, but its graduates had to look across the Hudson to Fordham or across the marshy Hackensack River to Seton Hall when it came time to pursue a college degree. Many of the boys were too poor to afford even those relatively short commutes, especially during the Depression.

The bishop of Newark, Thomas Walsh, saw great need for a Catholic college in Jersey City and pleaded with the Jesuits to reopen Saint Peter's, even though it would compete for students with the diocesan-run Seton Hall. Walsh's lobbying convinced Wlodemir Ledóchowski to authorize the restoration from Rome.[87] Tapped to lead the project was an up-and-coming young Jesuit, Robert I. Gannon, SJ.

Father Gannon was arguably the greatest American Jesuit leader of the inter-war years. Born in Staten Island to Irish-American parents who obviously held the Jesuits in high esteem (his middle initial, "I," stood for "Ignatius"), Gannon earned his high school diploma from the Loyola School in Manhattan, his undergraduate degree from Georgetown, and his doctorate from the Gregorian University in Rome. His was a complete Jesuit education, save for some post-doctoral studies at Cambridge University in England after his ordination. At the relatively young age of 36, he was appointed dean of Fordham's downtown college in the Woolworth Building in 1929. His success in that post led the Jesuits to entrust him with rebuilding Saint Peter's College in 1930.[88]

Although Gannon was the man most associated with resurrecting Saint Peter's, he never served as its president. An older Jesuit, Joseph Dinneen, SJ, was president of the

---

87. Delozier, "Society of Jesus," 104.
88. Ibid., 99–100.

entire Saint Peter's operation (including the high school) while Gannon himself was dean of the college for a period of six years. However, Gannon acted with a great deal of leeway during his deanship, and his superiors seem to have trusted his judgment. Knowing that the high school's existing facilities were obsolete for higher education, his first move was to secure rented space in the Chamber of Commerce Building in downtown Jersey City. The site was convenient to rail transportation and replicated some of the best features of Fordham's Woolworth Building location. He also assembled an impressive faculty of eleven of the best Jesuits the province had to offer, determined that the local boys would not be deprived of a quality education because of their poverty.[89] He described the Jersey City college as an "everyman's Cambridge" meant to combat the unjust reality, as true in those days as it is today, that a student's educational opportunity was determined largely by circumstances of birth.[90]

Since Saint Peter's was essentially the first Jesuit college built during the age of the accreditation agency, Gannon could tailor its curriculum to modern standards from the start. Still, as he built a cutting-edge undergraduate college, he took pains to incorporate Jesuit traditions, like an extracurricular religious sodality and a debating club (the Bellarmine Debating Society), along with an annual convocation to award prizes to the top students.[91] The plan that he put in place at the small New Jersey college became a blueprint for how other East Coast Jesuit colleges could adapt to modernity.

Saint Peter's implemented a number of true innovations during Gannon's tenure as dean. In 1932, it opened a large business school that it called the "Hudson College of Commerce and Finance." Although Fordham had begun operating a School of Accounting in the Woolworth Building twelve years earlier, the Hudson College at Saint Peter's was the first modern Jesuit business college on the East Coast. Father Gannon promoted Hudson College to prospective students by citing its practical curriculum, convenient location, low tuition, and Catholic character. Nowhere else in New Jersey could students hope to earn such a marketable degree, backed by the elite reputation of the Jesuits, for such a reasonable price.[92] Under Gannon's leadership, Saint Peter's also broke the color barrier by enrolling a Black student, Hudson Oliver, in 1934.

In the later years of his deanship, Father Gannon planned and orchestrated the relocation of Saint Peter's College from its rented home in the Chamber of Commerce Building to its permanent campus on the estate of Edward Young, a Jersey City banker and politician. Unfortunately, Gannon himself barely got to enjoy the new space because his successes at Saint Peter's landed him a promotion. He was appointed president of Fordham University in 1936, at a time when Fordham badly needed his steady leadership. A year earlier, it had suffered its devastating censure by the Association of American Universities. Without a quick fix, the long-term consequences to Fordham's reputation would have been immense.

---

89. Ibid., 109–110.
90. Ibid., 102.
91. Ibid., 121–125.
92. Ibid., 120–121.

Fortunately, Gannon succeeded in righting the ship and mended relations with the AAU in his first year. He apologized for his predecessors' shortcomings, fixed the issues that the AAU had identified with Fordham's library, and rebuilt the university's image with the help of a public relations firm. Later in his tenure, he shepherded Fordham Law School through the American Bar Association's accreditation process and breathed new life into Fordham's graduate programs.[93] It is no exaggeration to say that, through a combination of leadership skill and a willingness to work with accreditors, Gannon became the second founder of one Jesuit college and the savior of another in a span of seven years. He stepped down as president of Fordham in 1949 and spent the rest of his life serving at Jesuit high schools, parishes, and spiritual centers in the New York City area.

Jesuit College Sports: Fight Songs, Mascots, and Nicknames

One of Father Gannon's most enduring legacies at Saint Peter's College was his decision to adopt the peacock as the school mascot. It was a fitting symbol for the resuscitated college, since the peacock (like the mythical phoenix) is a symbol of resurrection.[94] Although some college sports teams had begun using mascots much earlier, it was not until the inter-war years that many American colleges formally adopted these unofficial symbols. Often, local sportswriters and journalists first coined nicknames for college teams, and over time, the colleges themselves embraced the imagery.

There are a number of ways (even today) in which Jesuit college mascots, fight songs, and sports traditions reflect their shared history. One example is "hoya," a word that appears in traditional songs and yells at Georgetown, Holy Cross, and Marquette. Although there is no documented evidence for this, the term is presumed to have originated at Georgetown in the late 1800s and early 1900s among students who chanted, "Hoya Saxa" at football games, combining a Greek term (properly transliterated as "Hoia") with a Latin term (Saxa) to form a cheer that translates loosely as, "What Rocks!" Whether the students simply confused the two languages that they studied every day or deliberately mixed them, the phrase stuck, and in 1927 the *Washington Star* began referring to Georgetown teams as "the Hoyas." The paper's editors liked the name because it took up less space on a headline than "Georgetown" or the alternative team nickname then in vogue, "the Hilltoppers."[95] Years later, when Eugenio Cardinal Pacelli (future Pope Pius XII) visited Georgetown in 1936, the students greeted him with, "Hoya, Hoya, Saxa! Hoya Georgetown! Pacelli, Pacelli, Pacelli!"[96]

---

93. Shelley, *Fordham*, 270, 272–273.
94. Delozier, "Society of Jesus," 107.
95. Curran, *History of Georgetown Vol. II*, 435 (n. 61).
96. Ibid., 161.

The word "Hoya" or "Hoiah" was so catchy that it migrated north to Worcester, where it appears in three different early-1900s Holy Cross fight songs. One is simply titled "Hoiah Holy Cross!" while another begins, "Then we'll give another Hoiah as we go down Linden Lane." A third fight song (and the most commonly sung today) begins, "Ring out then your Hoiah with a Chu! Chu! Rah! Rah! . . . / Give another Hoiah and a Chu! Chu! Rah! Rah! / A Chu! Chu! Rah! Rah! for Holy Cross!"[97] The last of these three cheers migrated west to Marquette, where it evolved into, "Ring out Ahoya with an M.U. Rah! Rah!"

In a kind of circular symmetry, the Georgetown fight song cleverly mocks Holy Cross's appropriation of the term, ending with the verses: "Chu! Chu! Rah! Rah! is dear to Holy Cross . . . / But the yell of all the yells, the yell that wins the day / Is the Hoya! Hoya! Saxa! for the dear old Blue and Gray."

These sorts of playful college yells and chants were common in the early 1900s, and many are still used in one form or another today. Examples from non-Catholic colleges include the University of Kansas ("Rock Chalk! Jayhawk! K.U.!"), Virginia Tech ("Hokie, Hokie, Hokie, Hi!"), the University of Virginia ("Wa Hoo Wa!"), Bucknell University ("Ray, Bucknell!"), the University of Pittsburgh ("Allegheny, Genac, Genac, Genac!"), and Yale University ("Boola, Boola!"). Within the Jesuit network, frequent exchange of faculty between schools no doubt facilitated the viral spread of certain cheers across the country.

In addition to Georgetown's "Hoyas," there are several other Jesuit college teams that use unusual or one-of-a-kind nicknames and mascots. Saint Louis University's teams have been known as the "Billikens" since about 1910. A "Billiken" was a cherubic good-luck charm faddishly popular at the time, often sold as a bank or a keychain. It had a distinctive face with a mischievous grin. As with the term "Hoya," there is no definitive answer as to how it became associated with the university, but the tradition reportedly began when fans noticed that the Saint Louis football coach, John Bender, bore a resemblance to the waggish character.

The Loyola (Chicago) Ramblers took their unusual name in 1926 because of the football team's reputation for traveling far and wide for away games. Prior to that date, the school briefly referred to its teams as the "Grandees"—a title for a Spanish nobleman—in an attempt to pay homage to the Spanish lineage of St. Ignatius Loyola. Because the nickname "Ramblers" does not lend itself well to a concrete mascot, Loyola (Chicago), is today one of four Jesuit colleges (the others being Loyola of New Orleans, John Carroll, and the University of Scranton) to use a wolf as its official mascot. As previously mentioned, the lupine imagery recalls the original meaning of the word "Loyola"—a contraction of the Spanish "Lobo y Olla" or "wolf and kettle."

Spanish nobility also played a role in the University of San Francisco's decision to name its teams, "the Dons" in 1932, replacing the previous nickname, "The Grey Fog." The school's mascot, Don Francisco, bears a resemblance to the mythical Zorro

---

97. Holy Cross Bands. *Marching Band Handbook 2016/2017*, 34.

figure of the southwest. Other unusual nicknames include the Canisius Golden Griffins, the Loyola (Maryland) Greyhounds, the John Carroll Blue Streaks, the Spring Hill Badgers, and the Xavier Musketeers—a name suggested by Xavier trustee (and Alexandre Dumas enthusiast) Francis Finn, SJ, in 1925.[98]

Marquette University's teams have had a number of nicknames over the years. Early Milwaukee sportswriters dubbed the school's football team "the Golden Avalanche." The university's teams were successively known as the "Hilltoppers" and the "Warriors" later in the twentieth century, but the latter name became associated with imagery of a Native American warrior and was deemed inappropriate, especially given Wisconsin's large indigenous population. The nickname was changed to the "Golden Eagles" in 1994. Later, in 2005, the university briefly announced its intention to adopt a new nickname, "the Marquette Gold" before alumni backlash forced it to reconsider. After a voting campaign that considered several nicknames, including "Golden Avalanche" and "Wolves," the university settled on the familiar "Golden Eagles."

It was not the only time that a Jesuit team nickname caused controversy. Seattle University changed its team name from the "Chieftains" to "Redhawks" in 2000. The original name, adopted in 1938, had been intended as a kind of tribute to Chief Seattle, the university's namesake and an important Catholic figure in the history of the Pacific Northwest. Over time, however, the name and the Native American imagery associated with it came to be seen as disrespectful and offensive. Likewise, Holy Cross has long referred to its teams as "the Crusaders," making use of what was once a very popular mascot for Catholic schools. However, attitudes had changed by the twenty-first century, and the medieval Crusaders were seen less as Catholic heroes than as symbols of the historic animosity between Islam and Christianity. In 2018, Holy Cross President Philip Boroughs, SJ, announced that the college would keep the "Crusader" name but would no longer use the imagery of a mounted medieval knight. Several other Jesuit colleges also used the "knight" as a mascot—possibly in reference to St. Ignatius's background as a soldier. All of them, however, have either closed or reverted to high school status.

Many American colleges used live animal mascots in the early-to-mid 1900s. Saint Peter's College kept live peacocks on campus, while Loyola University (New Orleans) kept a wolf cub named Fang who was eventually donated to the nearby Audubon Zoo after he grew to adulthood. Fordham kept a series of live rams (all named Rameses) on campus between 1925 and 1978. The costs of feeding these animals and maintaining their health was significant, and rival schools sometimes tried to sneak onto campus and kidnap the mascots before big games. As a result, these traditions became difficult to maintain unless the animal in question belonged to a species normally kept as a pet. Among Jesuit schools today, only Georgetown maintains a live mascot—a bulldog that traditionally lives either with a Jesuit or with a staff member in one of the university-owned row houses.

---

98. Bennish, *Continuity*, 137.

Costumed mascots (usually a student in a suit) did not emerge until roughly the 1980s, at which time many mascots became more cartoonish or downright silly. Perhaps the strangest was the "Blue Blob" at Xavier University, an amorphous creature that looks like a furry, animated sack of potatoes with eyes and a mouth. Three Jesuit schools (Loyola Marymount, Loyola Maryland, and Scranton) named their costumed mascots "Iggy" after St. Ignatius Loyola.

The table below shows all modern-day Jesuit colleges and their current mascots.

School	Team Nickname	Mascot
Boston College *Chestnut Hill, MA*	Eagles	Baldwin the Eagle
Canisius College *Buffalo, NY*	Golden Griffins	Petey the Griffin, named for St. Peter Canisius
Creighton University *Omaha, NE*	Blue Jays	Billy Bluejay
Fairfield University *Fairfield, CT*	Stags	Lucas the Stag, named for alumnus and employee William Lucas
Fordham University *The Bronx, NY*	Rams	Same
Georgetown University *Washington, DC*	Hoyas	Jack the Bulldog, named for a live bulldog used as a mascot in the 1960s
Gonzaga University *Spokane, WA*	Bulldogs (also Zags)	Spike the Bulldog
John Carroll University *University Heights, OH*	Blue Streaks (formerly, Saints)	Lobo the Wolf
Le Moyne College *Syracuse, NY*	Dolphins	Same. Note: the dolphin appears on the ancient coat of arms of the Catholic bishop of Syracuse, Sicily, namesake of the city in Upstate New York.[99]
Loyola Marymount University *Los Angeles, CA*	Lions	Iggy the Lion, named for St. Ignatius Loyola
Loyola University *Chicago, IL*	Ramblers	LU Wolf
Loyola University *Baltimore, MD*	Greyhounds	Iggy the Greyhound, named for St. Ignatius Loyola
Loyola University *New Orleans, LA*	Wolfpack	Havoc the Wolf
Marquette University *Milwaukee, WI*	Golden Eagles	Same

---

99. Le Moyne College Office of Mission and Identity, *The Le Moyne College Green Book* (Syracuse: Le Moyne College, 2011), 22.

School	Team Nickname	Mascot
Regis University *Denver, CO*	Rangers	Regi the Ranger (an anthropomorphic fox)
Rockhurst University *Kansas City, MO*	Hawks	Same
Saint Joseph's University *Philadelphia, PA*	Hawks	Same
Saint Louis University *St. Louis, MO*	Billikens	Same
Saint Peter's University *Jersey City, NJ*	Peacocks	Same. Note: the colonial-era Dutch settlement in northern New Jersey was known as Pavonia, which translates from Latin as "Land of the Peacock."
Santa Clara University *Santa Clara, CA*	Broncos	Bucky the Bronco
Seattle University *Seattle, WA*	Redhawks	Rudy the Redhawk
Spring Hill College *Mobile, AL*	Badgers	Same
University of Detroit Mercy *Detroit, MI*	Titans	Tommy Titan
University of San Francisco *San Francisco, CA*	Dons	Don Francisco, named for Don Francisco de Haro, the city of San Francisco's first *alcalde* (mayor).
University of Scranton *Scranton, PA*	Royals	Iggy the Royal Wolf, named for St. Ignatius Loyola
Xavier University *Cincinnati, OH*	Musketeers	D'Artagnan the Musketeer (primary) The Blue Blob (secondary)

Many Jesuit colleges closed their doors before the tradition of college athletics and mascots became widespread, but former Jesuit colleges that did (or do) have official mascots are listed below.

School	Team Nickname
Bellarmine Prep (Bellarmine College) *Tacoma, WA*	Lions
Brophy College Prep School *Phoenix, AZ*	Broncos
Brooklyn Prep (Brooklyn College) *Brooklyn, NY*	Eagles
Campion College *Prairie du Chien, WI*	Knights

School	Team Nickname
Gonzaga College High School *Washington, DC*	Eagles
Jesuit High School (College of the Immaculate Conception) *New Orleans, LA*	Blue Jays
Jesuit High School (Tampa College) *Tampa, FL*	Tigers
Loyola College Prep (St. John Berchmans College) *Shreveport, LA*	Flyers
St. John's University *Toledo, OH*	Saints
St. Mary's College *St. Marys, Kansas*	Knights
Wheeling University *Wheeling, WV*	Cardinals
Xavier High School (St. Francis Xavier College) *New York, NY*	Knights

The Golden Age of Jesuit Football

The all-male environments at Jesuit colleges (and most Catholic colleges) made it almost inevitable that they would be swept up in the twentieth-century craze for inter-collegiate football. College football had been growing in popularity before World War I, but concerns about the safety of the game (as well as the outbreak of war itself) led many schools to suspend their teams. After the war, the Jesuits gradually overcame the reservations they had about football's danger to the health of their students.

Jesuit football teams were among the most prominent in the country, and played against teams from much larger public universities. In an era when professional football was still in its infancy, the fact that most Jesuit schools were located in large cities gave them an enviable amount of newspaper and radio coverage, as well as a fan base that extended beyond their own students and alumni. The most popular intra-Jesuit rivalry continued to be the annual game between Boston College and Holy Cross, but Fordham and Georgetown also drew large crowds whenever they met. Similar rivalries emerged in the west, where Santa Clara, San Francisco, and Loyola (Los Angeles) clashed regularly on the gridiron.

Many Jesuit college alumni, including Vince Lombardi (Fordham), Don Shula (John Carroll), Pete Rozelle (San Francisco), and Paul Tagliabue (Georgetown) went on to shape the game of football in profound ways. As a student, Lombardi had been part of the legendary 1936 Fordham linebacker corps that earned the nickname, "The Seven Blocks of Granite." Jesuit teams also amassed some unusually strong win-loss records. The Loyola (New Orleans) Wolfpack went undefeated in 1926 and scored a total of 355 points in the season—more than any other team in the country.[100] Between 1922 and 1950, seven Jesuit football teams appeared in a combined thirteen postseason bowl games, with an overall record of 6–7. Considering that fewer than ten major college bowl games were typically played in each of these years, this was a significant presence:

Year	Bowl Game	Champion	Runner-Up
1922	San Diego East-West Christmas Classic	West Virginia 21	**Gonzaga 13**
1937	Sugar Bowl	**Santa Clara 21**	Louisiana State 14
1938	Sugar Bowl	**Santa Clara 6**	Louisiana State 0
1940	Cotton Bowl	Clemson 6	**Boston College 3**
1941	Cotton Bowl	Texas A&M 6	**Fordham 12**
1941	Orange Bowl	Mississippi State 14	**Georgetown 7**
1941	Sugar Bowl	**Boston College 19**	Tennessee 13
1942	Sugar Bowl	**Fordham 2**	Missouri 0
1943	Orange Bowl	Alabama 37	**Boston College 21**
1946	Orange Bowl	Miami (Florida) 13	**Holy Cross 6**
1950	Orange Bowl	**Santa Clara 21**	Kentucky 13
1950	Sun Bowl	Texas Western (Texas-El Paso) 33	**Georgetown 20**
1950	Salad Bowl	**Xavier 33**	Arizona State 21

This list of bowl games would have been longer by one if not for an admirably principled stance taken by the University of San Francisco in 1951. The Dons went undefeated in the regular season (including victories against Fordham, Santa Clara, and Loyola of Los Angeles), after which they received an invitation to the prestigious Orange Bowl in Miami. There was, however, a catch: because the game was to be played in the still-segregated South, the Orange Bowl committee insisted that the Dons leave behind two African-American players, Ollie Matson and Burl Toler. Rather than accept this injustice, the team declined the bid altogether. A year later, facing financial difficulties, the University of San Francisco discontinued its football program—a decision that almost certainly could have been avoided (or at least postponed) if the team had accepted the Orange Bowl bid and the big cash payout that came with it. It was a remarkable expression of the true meaning of the word "team" and a refreshing example of a university sports program putting principle ahead of the bottom line.

As most Jesuit colleges were located in large cities, they rarely had the space to build grandiose on-campus stadiums. Consequently, Jesuit schools often had to pay exorbitant rents at off-campus municipal stadiums that they shared with professional baseball teams, horse racing, and other civic events. Georgetown played high-profile

---

100. Cook, *Founded on Faith*, 81.

games at Washington's Griffith Stadium, Fordham played at New York's Polo Grounds, Saint Louis played at Sportsman's Park, Loyola (Chicago) played at Soldier Field, and Boston College played at Fenway Park when the local professional teams were out of town. In the west, Loyola (Los Angeles) rented out the gargantuan Rose Bowl for home games, and both San Francisco and Santa Clara played frequently at Kezar Stadium, the 55,000-seat municipal stadium in Golden Gate Park.

Unfortunately, with small student bodies of 1,000 undergraduates or fewer, Jesuit colleges had to rely on local fans without a direct connection to the university to fill the seats in those cavernous stadiums. Ticket sales were solid, but rarely robust enough to cover the high rents. With only limited control over when the stadiums would be available, Jesuit college football teams often had to cede prime weekends to the professional tenants.

Only a handful of Jesuit colleges built large on-campus football stadiums in the inter-war years. Holy Cross, the University of Detroit, and Marquette built facilities large enough to seat more than 20,000 fans in the 1920s, but of those, only Holy Cross's Fitton Field still stands today. The stadiums in Detroit and Milwaukee became reasonably important civic venues and occasionally hosted professional teams, but both were obsolete by the 1970s and were torn down. Smaller on-campus venues included Gonzaga Stadium in Spokane (1922), Creighton Stadium in Omaha (1924), Loyola University Stadium in New Orleans (1928), and the 15,000-seat Corcoran Stadium at Xavier University in Cincinnati (1929). Most of these facilities have been demolished and their valuable campus real estate has been repurposed (usually for academic buildings).

As popular as college football was, it was not sustainable for small, private schools in urban areas, where construction costs were high and space was limited. Many Jesuit colleges heroically tried to maintain football programs through World War II and beyond, but they were living on borrowed time as the sport came to be dominated by rural, state-sponsored universities with access to almost limitless taxpayer dollars. Urban, private schools that had ruled college football in the first half of the twentieth century (like Harvard, Yale, Penn, Pacific, the University of Chicago, and St. Mary's of California) gradually fell into obscurity or irrelevance in the second half.

In a sign of things to come, Loyola University (Chicago) discontinued its football team in 1930, followed by Regis in 1931, Loyola (Baltimore) in 1933, Loyola (New Orleans) in 1939, and Saint Joseph's of Philadelphia in 1939. The pressures of World War II forced both Gonzaga and Spring Hill to discontinue football in 1941. As the costs of competing in football continued to grow after World War II, virtually all Jesuit colleges would have no choice but to follow suit.

Jesuit Labor Schools and the Labor Movement

The Great Depression reignited Jesuit interest in labor and workers' rights, especially in the New York City area. More than two decades had passed since Father Terence Shealy, SJ had led the workers' retreats that grew indirectly into the

Fordham School of Social Service in New York, and Father Frederic Siedenburg, SJ had founded what is today the Loyola University School of Social Work in Chicago. As the American economy shrank, as the role of labor unions changed, and as communist ideology gained traction abroad, many New York-area Jesuits became concerned about the future of the Catholic working class. There was a real danger that Catholic laborers could fall victim to job cuts, fall under the sway of godless Marxism, or both. The Jesuits believed that Catholic social teaching, with its respect for workers' rights and its less extreme solutions to labor problems, could be a moderating influence in an increasingly secular, polarized environment. To spread this message, they created several adult education programs that collectively became known as the Jesuit labor schools.[101]

A generation earlier, the Jesuits might have simply started these programs on their own university campuses. But now that accreditation agencies were watching, universities had to be more cautious about how their facilities were being used, who was sitting in their classrooms, and what courses were being taught with or without credit. As a clever work-around to this issue, many Jesuit labor schools simply set up shop at Jesuit high schools. The first such school opened at Xavier High School in Manhattan in 1936 and eventually became known as the Xavier Institute of Industrial Relations. In 1938, a similar program opened on the campus of Brooklyn Prep, calling itself the Crown Heights School of Catholic Workmen.[102] Although neither of the host campuses was an accredited college, both had been accredited colleges in living memory, which gave some gravitas to the new outreach initiatives. A third school opened in 1946 in Jersey City, and although it was loosely affiliated with Saint Peter's College, it was actually housed at Saint Peter's Prep.[103] There were also several satellite locations at parishes and other facilities throughout the New York City region.

The classes offered by these labor schools attracted hundreds of workers and managers, although their enrollment fluctuated as employment conditions changed and World War II and its aftermath reversed some of the economic damage of the Depression. Their objective was to encourage respect for Catholic social teaching in the labor disputes of the day, but the Jesuits who designed the curriculum sometimes faced criticism from Rome that the schools' religious character was being dumbed down in order to appeal to as broad an audience as possible.[104]

At the time, the serious academic study of labor and labor unions was gaining traction. Cornell University founded its famous School of Industrial and Labor Relations in 1945. However, the Jesuits seem to have viewed their own schools first and foremost as a social ministry and not as a scholarly undertaking. They measured suc-

---

101. This section is based heavily on Joseph M. McShane, SJ, "A Survey of the History of the Jesuit Labor Schools in New York: An American Social Gospel in Action," *Records of the American Catholic Historical Society of Philadelphia* 102, no. 4 (Winter 1991): 37–64.

102. Ibid, 43, 61.

103. Ibid., 54.

104. Ibid., 56.

cess by the number of people they served and the real-world impact of their outreach on local labor conditions, not on the number of articles published by their (largely volunteer) faculty.

When the New York Jesuits opened Le Moyne College in Syracuse (a mere sixty miles from Cornell) in 1946, the local bishop asked them to incorporate a Catholic-inspired Institute of Industrial Relations in the new school.[105] A similar program independently opened at Holy Cross in Massachusetts. The Holy Cross Institute of Industrial Relations began in 1943, seeking to facilitate dialogue between workers and managers in the Worcester area. It continued for more than forty years, until 1984.[106] In the South, Loyola University (New Orleans) opened an Institute of Industrial Relations in 1947; its founder, Father Louis Twomey, SJ, used it as a forum to promote racial integration in Louisiana workplaces and even hosted foreign policy workshops designed to promote democratization in Latin America.[107]

Back in the greater New York City area, the Brooklyn school was discontinued in 1952 and the Saint Peter's school followed suit in 1974. The Xavier school, however, continued to operate until 1988—a longevity mainly attributable to the sheer will of its director, Father Philip Carey, SJ, who died just a few months after it closed. In the end, the labor schools were a creative and, in their day, important outreach effort by the Jesuits to utilize the power of education to effect real social change. They also served as proving grounds for some Jesuits who went on to leadership roles elsewhere, including Philip Dobson, SJ, who directed both Xavier and Saint Peter's labor schools before being named president at Canisius College in Buffalo.[108]

Race Relations in the Inter-War Years

Jesuit colleges gingerly broke the color barrier in the 1920s and 1930s. In addition to Hudson Oliver, who enrolled at Saint Peter's College in 1934, Boston College admitted its first Black student, Casper Augustus Ferguson, in 1933. Even earlier, in 1922, a Black woman named Mabel Raimey enrolled at Marquette Law School, taking classes in the popular night division before moving on to a successful law practice in Milwaukee.[109] Still, progress remained spotty, and it would not be until after World War II that most Jesuit schools made more concerted efforts to recruit and enroll African-Americans.[110]

For obvious demographic reasons, Jesuit schools on the West Coast took the lead in enrolling Asian-Americans. Seattle College enrolled (and employed as staff members) a number of Japanese-Americans at the onset of World War II. It even hosted

---

105. Bender, *Brief History of the New York Province*, 42–43.
106. Kuzniewski, *Thy Honored Name*, 307–308.
107. Cook, *Founded on Faith*, 161–162.
108. McShane, "Survey," 59.
109. Phoebe Weaver Williams, "A Black Woman's Voice: The Story of Mabel Raimey, 'Shero,'" *Marquette Law Review* 74, no. 3 (1991): 345–376.

exchange students from Sophia University, the Jesuit school in Tokyo. In 1942, when the federal government ordered Japanese-Americans to relocate to internment camps until their wartime loyalties could be assessed, Seattle College provided a refuge for those in its own community as long as it legally could.[111]

Records are sparse regarding the presence of Native Americans, Asian-Americans, Pacific Islanders, and Hispanics on campus at this time, but the Jesuit schools did carefully document the religion of their students, and those records consistently show an unusually diverse mix of Jews, Protestants, Catholics, and others of no particular religion. That was significant at a time when America's top universities discriminated against Jews and Catholics, and it reflects that Jesuit schools defined their social justice mission primarily in terms of immigrants, first-generation Americans, and religious minorities rather than in terms of race. Immigrant rights and immigrant poverty, of course, remained serious issues in the United States, particularly in the Catholic community.

Nonetheless, the Jesuits, like the rest of the country, were beginning to reckon with America's race issues. If there was a discernable "turning point," it was a Mass that took place on February 11, 1944 at St. Francis Xavier College Church on the campus of Saint Louis University. Because of the paucity of male students during World War II, most of the students gathered in the pews that cold winter day were women.[112] The homilist was Father Claude Heithaus, SJ, a Saint Louis faculty member and a native son of Missouri who taught classics and archaeology. He delivered a blistering sermon that sent shockwaves through the city of St. Louis and the Jesuit education network, attacking racism and challenging the Jesuits to integrate African-American students into their schools.

Heithaus's homily was radical by 1944 standards. He threw down the gauntlet and declared bluntly that no true Christian could possibly discriminate against fellow children of God based on the color of their skin. He invoked the teachings of Jesus, asserting that Christ "incorporated all races and colors into His Mystical Body," and "denounced injustice." He reminded the congregation that Catholics themselves had been victims of discrimination (and had even been enslaved) throughout history, which made it unconscionable that they should perpetuate any form of "diabolical prejudice" against Blacks. Urging the university to integrate as soon as possible, he proclaimed that "scholars know no color" and argued:

> St. Louis University admits Protestants and Jews, Mormons and Moham-medans, Buddhists and Brahmins, Pagans and atheists, without even looking at their complexions. Do you want us to slam our doors in the face of Catholics, because their complexion happens to be brown or black?

---

110. Even earlier than these examples, William M. Gordon became the first Black graduate of Creighton Medical School in 1901.

111. Crowley, *Seattle University*, 48, 56.

112. Faherty, *Saint Louis University*, 31.

Heithaus punctuated his sermon with an act of contrition: "Lord Jesus, we are sorry and ashamed for all the wrongs that white men have done to Your Colored children. We are firmly resolved never again to have any part in them, and to do everything in our power to prevent them. Amen."[113]

Heithaus's homily was printed verbatim in the Saint Louis University student newspaper and given prominent coverage in the local media. The Missouri Jesuits had already been considering admitting Black students to their universities, but the 1944 sermon brought the issue rather uncomfortably to the forefront. Less than three months later, Saint Louis University announced that it would integrate its student body—making it the first American university in any former slave state to do so.[114] However, like many prophets, Heithaus paid a price for speaking truth to power; the bishop of St. Louis condemned the homily and the outspoken priest was temporarily reassigned to less visible ministries in the rural Midwest.[115] After a short exile, he resumed his teaching career, first at Marquette and then once again at Saint Louis, where he retired as a campus icon.

The First Women Deans

The inter-war years also saw important milestones in women's equality. Although women continued to earn seats in the classroom (especially in professional programs), the 1930s were most notable for the rise of female deans.

The schools of nursing at both Georgetown and Marquette had been led by women prior to the 1930s, but because both were diploma programs and did not have the status of co-equal schools within the university, those women did not yet have the title "dean." The first female dean was Sister Berenice Beck, OSF, a Franciscan who served as director of the St. Joseph's Hospital School of Nursing in Milwaukee. Since the hospital was affiliated with the Marquette Medical School, its nursing program was technically part of the university network. Sister Berenice worked to integrate it more fully under the Marquette umbrella so that it could offer bachelor's degrees. In 1936, she succeeded, and the St. Joseph's Hospital School of Nursing officially became the College of Nursing at Marquette University, with Sister Berenice as its first "dean." It was just one of her many accomplishments. Prior to assuming that role, she had been one of the first female graduates of Marquette (where she earned both bachelor's and master's degrees) and held a PhD in nursing from the Catholic University of America.

113. Text found at Claude H. Heithaus, SJ, "The Sermon that, 62 Years Ago, Denounced Discrimination," *The University News* (12 April 2006), https://unewsonline.com/2006/04/tesermonthatyearsa godenounceddiscrimination/. See also Millett, "Memory," 335–336.

114. Faherty, *Saint Louis University*, 32. See also "SLU Legends and Lore: The Heithaus Homily," Saint Louis University (26 February 2020), https://www.slu.edu/news/2020/february/slu-legends-lore-heithaus-homily.php.

115. Millett, "Memory," 343.

In 1939, Anna King became the first lay female dean at a Jesuit university when she assumed leadership of Fordham's School of Social Service. The Fordham president who approved King's appointment was the progressive Father Robert Gannon, SJ, who faced criticism from his superiors in Rome for the decision. Nonetheless, King proved herself to be more than worthy of the responsibility, and was soon elected national president of the American Association of Schools of Social Service.[116]

At Georgetown, the leaders of the nurses' training school held the title "superintendent" from 1903 to 1929 and "principal" from 1929 to 1945. Six Franciscan sisters (beginning with Sister Geraldine, OSF, in 1903) helmed the school during those years. Its first lay leader was Anne Mary Murphy, who served from 1945 to 1947 with the title "director of nursing education." The first to hold the title "dean" was Sister Agnes Miriam, SCN, a Sister of Charity who assumed the role in 1947.[117]

When the Saint Louis University School of Nursing opened in 1928, it was originally led by a Jesuit, Father Alphonse Schwittala, SJ, who simultaneously served as dean of the university's School of Medicine. By 1934, Sister Mary Athanasia Brune, SSM became associate dean of the nursing school, and given the immense pressures on Father Schwittala's time (which included high-level responsibilities in the Missouri Province), it seems probable that Sister Brune may have acted as dean in every meaningful day-to-day sense of the word. In 1941, Sister Mary Geraldine Kulleck, SSM, became the school's first official female dean. Both women were members of the Sisters of Mary, known today as the Franciscan Sisters of Mary, with whom Father Schwittala partnered in creating a Catholic healthcare network in the St. Louis area.[118]

In Chicago, Sister Helen Jarrell, RHSJ, became the first "dean" of the School of Nursing at Loyola University in 1939, after servings as its founding "director" for five years. Under her leadership, six different Chicago-area hospitals joined forces to combine their nurses' training programs into a single, degree-granting school affiliated with the university.[119]

In Seattle, the Sisters of Providence operated a nurses' training school at their Providence Hospital, and in the 1920s, that school affiliated with the University of Washington to enable it to offer bachelor's degrees. However, as Seattle College restored itself as a proper undergraduate institution in the 1930s, the Sisters reasoned that a Catholic college would make a better home for their nursing program. Between 1935 and 1941, the nursing school transferred from the public university to the Jesuit college, with Sister John Gabriel Ryan, SP, serving as its head.[120] Although Sister John Gabriel did not technically hold the title dean, she deserves to be included in this list because her leadership was as transformative as the others'.

---

116. Shelley, *Fordham*, 248.

117. Curran, *History of Georgetown Vol. II*, 403.

118. Saint Louis University School of Nursing, "Carrying Commitment Forward," passim, esp. 5–7.

119. Loyola University Chicago, "Niehoff School of Nursing Golden Jubilee Celebration."

120. Crowley, *Seattle University*, 39.

At a time when few women had such professional opportunities, these women (mostly, but not exclusively, Catholic nuns) were earning doctorates and managing the modern equivalent of multimillion-dollar nonprofit organizations. Jesuit universities provided unique outlets for their ambitions and the benefit was mutual.

Some Jesuit universities responded to their increasing numbers of female students by hiring high-level female administrators for the first time. Outside of nursing degree programs, Marquette University, Saint Louis University, and Seattle College were the three Jesuit schools that most deliberately and determinedly opened their undergraduate classrooms to women in the inter-war years. All three hired "deans of women" to advise and mentor the female collegians. Mathilda Steinbrecher at Marquette (1923), Anna Proutz at Seattle (1935), Nancy McNeir Ring at Saint Louis (1941) all held the title "dean" even though they did not have administrative responsibility over a school and a faculty.[121] Some of their successors in the mid-twentieth century, like Marie Leonard at Seattle and Dame Mary Bruemmer at Saint Louis (the latter of whom received a papal knighthood for her service), became campus icons in their own rights.

The Jesuits Start Broadcasting: WWL in New Orleans

The Jesuits' growing expertise in science enabled one university to become a pioneer the new field of broadcasting. In 1913, Loyola University (New Orleans) obtained a broadcast license to operate one of the country's first training programs in radio technology. During World War I, tech-savvy Jesuits on the Loyola faculty helped to train radio operators for the military. By 1922, Loyola's operation had evolved into the first licensed radio station in New Orleans, WWL. Father Orie Abell, SJ—a physicist and a graduate of Regis College in Denver—led the station between 1924 and 1932, developing it into a regional icon for the entire South.[122]

By the 1930s, WWL was producing its own original programming and was generating a signal powerful enough to be heard across much of North America. Advertising revenue from the station exceeded tuition revenue by 1940 and accounted for about 40% of the university's income. Its programming included locally produced radio dramas and live music, but also featured weekly Catholic Mass broadcast live from Loyola's Holy Name of Jesus Church and educational shows featuring Loyola faculty.[123] What had started as a science project was now generating so much money that Jesuit officials in Rome started to question whether the New Orleans Jesuits were engaged in a for-profit enterprise—something strictly forbidden within the order. After traveling to Rome to explain himself, Loyola's president "was able to argue that

---

121. Ibid., 48.
122. Cook, *Founded on Faith*, 120–124.
123. Ibid., 130, 134–135, 156.

the commercial success of the station was a beneficial accident and entirely secondary to its religious and educational mission."[124]

In 1957, WWL branched out into the new field of television broadcasting, and eventually grew into one of the most commercially successful CBS affiliates in the country. Loyola University now owned a broadcast empire that dwarfed the university itself in the number of people it reached each day. As time passed, however, the campus leaders "decided it was unwise to allow the university to be so financially dependent on a single investment."[125] It had never been common for universities to own commercial broadcast stations, especially in large markets like New Orleans, but the few that did eventually sold off those businesses to focus solely on their educational missions. Loyola sold its two stations for more than $115 million in 1989, putting most of the money into its endowment.[126]

Over the course of the twentieth century, many people educated at Jesuit colleges around the country left their marks on the broadcasting and entertainment fields, including pioneers like Bing Crosby (Gonzaga of Spokane), Bob Newhart (Loyola of Chicago), Bob Keeshan (Fordham), Carl Reiner (Georgetown), Denzel Washington (Fordham), Bob Denver (Loyola of Los Angeles), and Tim Russert (John Carroll).

The Changing Role of Catholics in America

By the inter-war years, Jesuit colleges faced a new and unprecedented reality: Catholics were no longer completely unwelcome at mainstream American universities. In large part, this was due to the rise of public universities, which by law did not discriminate on religious grounds. Catholics attending a public institution might still face prejudice from their classmates (especially in certain regions of the country), but they would have no trouble earning admission. This was a big departure from the days in which private universities, heavily Protestant in both outlook and tradition, maintained a stranglehold on American higher education. Schools like Harvard remained closed to all but the wealthiest and best-connected Catholics (like the Kennedy family), but for the first time, the Jesuit colleges were not the only reasonable alternative. Many Catholic immigrants were attracted to the low tuition and, frankly, better facilities at public universities. By 1919, the University of Illinois enrolled more Catholic students than all of the Catholic colleges and universities in Illinois combined.[127]

The Catholic Church found it difficult to respond to these developments with a unified voice. On one side were the bishops, who naturally wanted to serve the Catholic students at public universities by assigning priests to campus ministry. The dioceses spent enormous sums of money building Catholic centers (often called Newman Centers in honor of educational philosopher and future saint John Henry

---

124. Ibid., 133.
125. Ibid., 140.
126. Ibid., 140.
127. Marsden, *Soul*, 358.

Newman) on secular college campuses. On the other side were the Jesuits, Christian Brothers, Vincentians, and other teaching orders who argued that that money would be better invested in Catholic universities.[128]

Generally speaking, Catholic bishops during this era paid closer attention to campus ministry at non-Catholic universities than at Catholic ones. It was a bishop's responsibility to ensure that every Catholic in his diocese received proper spiritual care, and that included local public college students. But bishops were more likely to take a hands-off approach to Catholic colleges, on the presumption that the community of priests on each campus was capable of handling the religious dimensions of the school. The result was that many bishops only stepped in when they felt the Catholic colleges had overreached or underperformed, even though closer cooperation between the dioceses and the colleges might have been beneficial.[129]

Outside of academia, nothing symbolized how far Catholics had come in American society—or how far they had yet to go—like the 1928 presidential campaign of Al Smith. Born in Manhattan to Irish-, Italian-, and German-American parentage, Smith was elected governor of New York in 1918 and served non-consecutively in that office for the next ten years. In 1928, he became the Democratic candidate for president of the United States—the first Catholic ever to receive the nomination of a major American political party. The national electorate proved to be much less open to Smith's religious background than the more diverse voters of New York, and he lost to Herbert Hoover in a landslide, 444 electoral votes to 87. Anti-Catholic bigotry was still alive and well in the United States, and it would be more than a generation before Catholic candidates could seriously contend for national office.

The "New" Jesuit College President

As the 1930s came to a close, one thing was obvious: Jesuit universities were vastly larger, more complex institutions than ever before. Their leadership model, though, had not changed in 150 years. At the top was the rector-president, whose role had both civil and canonical responsibilities. To the outside world, this chief executive was simply the president of the university. In the eyes of the Catholic Church, however, he was also the rector of the Jesuit community—the religious superior of all of the Jesuits living on campus, responsible for their welfare and spiritual development. Although this book has used the term "president" to describe the leaders of Jesuit universities up to this point, most of those men would have seen themselves first and foremost as "rectors."

Under civil law, most Jesuit universities were required to have boards of trustees in order to maintain their charters from the state governments. Often, however, these

---

128. Ibid., 358.

129. See Joseph H. Lackner, "Campus Ministry on Catholic Campuses," in *Handbook of Research on Catholic Higher Education*, ed. Thomas C. Hunt, Ellis A. Joseph, Ronald J. Nuzzi, and John O. Geiger (Greenwich, CT: Information Age Publishing, 2003), 293–324.

boards did not have any meaningful oversight power over the president. They mainly consisted of the Jesuits living on campus, all of whom saw the rector as their immediate supervisor. Not surprisingly, open criticism from board members was rare. Therefore, the rector-president had near total de facto control over the campus and the Jesuit faculty, and the only superiors to whom he was truly accountable were his provincial and the Jesuit general in Rome. Meanwhile, he was responsible not only for making decisions that affected the university, but also for solving disputes that arose among the Jesuits themselves, mentoring young Jesuits, hearing confessions, and supervising the community.[130]

It was an enormous amount of responsibility to place on the shoulders of one man, and it became increasingly anachronistic as the role of college president became more demanding. The arrangement had been workable when a group of ten or so Jesuits could run an entire college and the total student enrollment numbered in the hundreds. But as the universities evolved into large bureaucratic organizations with over 1,000 students, professional schools scattered across the city, scores of Jesuits, and dozens of lay faculty, it became clear that the old model had to change.

Perhaps the biggest issue was term limits. Each rector served a standard three-year term. Talented rectors could be assigned a maximum two consecutive terms, which meant that the longest any Jesuit could hope to lead a university was six years. In rare cases (as at Creighton University, where Father Michael Dowling's relationship with the Creighton family kept the donations flowing) the Jesuits were able to keep presidents in office beyond the limit by requesting exceptions from Rome. By and large, however, they followed the rules. This meant that talented Jesuit rectors with a deep affinity for a specific school (like Father Anthony Ciampi at Holy Cross) sometimes had to step down, only to be reappointed three years later. Ciampi served as Holy Cross president for a total of nine years in three non-consecutive three-year spurts. In between his second and third term in Worcester, he served a term as president of Loyola (Baltimore). That constant reshuffling and relocation could take its toll on the men as well as the institutions.

There were some advantages to the old system. It forced the Jesuits to emphasize a standard "Jesuit" way of doing things and prevented any one man from deviating too far in quixotic experiments. It minimized the damage that an incompetent president could do to an institution. It also maximized the number of institutions that could benefit from the skills of a good president, who could be assigned to multiple schools at different points in his career. Lastly, it emphasized equity, in keeping with the Jesuit principle that all students, regardless of background or status, deserved equal access to quality education. Father Coleman Nevils, for example, served as one of Georgetown's most transformative presidents in the early 1930s—and, despite his success designing and executing a brilliant campus master plan for Georgetown during the height of the

---

130. Michael Rizzi, "Cooperation after Independence: Lessons from Politics," *Journal of Catholic Higher Education* 39, no. 2 (2020): 150.

Great Depression—he stepped down after seven years and eventually became the first Jesuit president of the University of Scranton. It speaks volumes that the Jesuits, in assigning their best talent, gave no more priority to the sons of diplomats and presidents in Washington than they gave to the sons of coal miners and railroad workers in northeastern Pennsylvania.

Nonetheless, it was time for a change. Jesuit universities could not afford to share their best leaders with high schools, retreat centers, and parish churches much longer. Complex institutions needed vision and stability in the front office. As was so often the case in Jesuit history, the first innovations came out of Marquette University, which briefly separated the offices of rector and president in 1922. Still, the Marquette experiment lasted only a few months, and it accomplished little beyond drawing attention to the problem.[131]

Real progress began in the 1930s, when Wlodemir Ledóchowski in Rome agreed to try a long-term separation of the rector/president offices on an experimental basis. If ever there was a Jesuit university that needed stable leadership, it was Fordham, which had just lost the Association of American Universities' stamp of approval. And if ever there was a Jesuit deserving of a long-term leadership appointment, it was Father Robert Gannon, who had recently distinguished himself by bringing Saint Peter's College back from the grave. When Gannon assumed the Fordham presidency in 1936, he filled both traditional roles. Four years later, however, he was allowed to remain president after a different Jesuit, Father John Harding Fisher, SJ, was appointed rector of the Fordham community. In that capacity, Fisher worked as religious superior to the Fordham Jesuits (Gannon included), but Gannon acted largely as his own man in the president's office. As simple as this arrangement seems to modern ears, it was highly controversial at the time and generated significant debate in Rome. Here was an acknowledgement that the university was at least administratively outside of the normal Church hierarchy, and a splice was being inserted into the traditional chain of command.[132]

By the end of the decade, similar experiments were undertaken at Loyola University (Chicago), with Father Joseph Egan, SJ as rector and Father James Hussey, SJ as president; and at the University of San Francisco, with Father Carroll O'Sullivan, SJ as rector and Father William Dunne, SJ as president. It soon became clear that the success or failure of the arrangement was at least in part a function of the personalities of the two men involved.[133] The Jesuits were creating two-headed leadership teams at their universities, and the jury was still out as to how such an arrangement would work in the long term.

The death of Wlodimir Ledóchowski in 1942 and the chaos of the Second World War halted progress. Nonetheless, the stage was set for major reforms destined to take place in the 1950s and 1960s in the way Jesuit universities were managed.

---

131. Gleason, *Contending*, 386 (n. 70).
132. Fitzgerald, *Governance*, 110–114.
133. Ibid., 114, 116.

The Provinces Split

The rector-president problem was not the only administrative issue facing American Jesuits in the inter-war years. The sheer size of the provinces was making them difficult to govern. During World War I, there were four Jesuit provinces in the United States: Maryland-New York on the East Coast; Missouri in the Midwest, New Orleans in the South, and California in the far west. They were becoming unwieldy, either because of the number of Jesuits (as in the Maryland-New York Province) or because of geography (as in the Missouri Province, which stretched from Cleveland to Denver).

In 1926, a separate New England Province was carved out of the Maryland-New York Province, with jurisdiction over all six New England states. This meant that Boston College and Holy Cross were administratively separate from the other East Coast schools for the first time in their history.

In 1928, the Jesuits created a Chicago Province from the eastern half of the Missouri Province's territory. This new province had jurisdiction over Loyola (Chicago), the University of Detroit, Xavier, and John Carroll, along with the ill-fated St. John's University in Toledo. The Missouri Jesuits retained control over Marquette, Saint Louis, Rockhurst, Creighton, Regis, and the ill-fated St. Mary's College of Kansas.

In 1932, the northern half of the California Province spun off into the new Oregon Province, with control over Gonzaga and Seattle Universities as well as the still-substantial Jesuit mission network in the northern Rockies and Alaska. The smaller California Province retained control over Santa Clara, Loyola (Los Angeles), and the University of San Francisco.

Finally, in the midst of the war in 1943, the Maryland-New York Province (*sans* New England) split again. The resulting New York Province was essentially centered on Fordham and the other Jesuit activities in New York City, but it also had control over Saint Peter's College in New Jersey and Canisius College in Buffalo. The Maryland Province, now back to its historic original name, sponsored Georgetown, Loyola (Baltimore), and Saint Joseph's (Philadelphia).

As a side effect of these changes to the map (which continued after World War II with the creation of new provinces in Detroit and Wisconsin), the Jesuits found opportunities to expand and build new colleges. Because each province had less territory to cover, each was able to focus on smaller cities under its jurisdiction that a larger province might have overlooked. During the 1940s and 1950s, these conditions brought about the last great wave of Jesuit expansion in higher education. The New England Province expanded to southern Connecticut with Fairfield University in 1942. The New York Province, focused almost exclusively on New York State, built Le Moyne College in Syracuse in 1946. The Maryland Province likewise expanded to the University of Scranton in 1942 and Wheeling College in 1954 (although the Scranton expansion slightly preceded the province split).

A second side effect was that the "exchange network" of Jesuit faculty and presidents became smaller. The provinces became more insular and the flow of faculty from one institution to another took place within smaller groupings of schools. After the split, for example, Georgetown and Loyola (Baltimore) shared administrators at a high rate—including men like Lawrence Gorman, SJ and Edward Bunn, SJ, both of whom served in leadership posts at Loyola before being promoted to the Georgetown presidency. However, Georgetown and Holy Cross, now two provinces removed from each other, no longer shared Jesuits as often as they once did.

Broadly, this reorganization also meant that most Jesuit provinces were now centered on one major university (Georgetown in the Maryland Province, Fordham in New York Province, Loyola in the Chicago Province, etc.). Alongside that anchor university, each province sponsored a constellation of smaller, more modest satellite colleges (Canisius, John Carroll, Saint Joseph's, Rockhurst, etc.) that mainly focused on undergraduate education. In the east, this helped to alleviate the resource war between Georgetown and Fordham. It also contributed to the rise of Boston College as a research institution, since the New England Province could prioritize that school's development in ways that the Maryland-New York Province never did. This was less true on the West Coast, where most of the young universities were developing at roughly the same rate, but it did mean that emerging giants like Loyola (Los Angeles) and Seattle got more attention from their provincials than otherwise might have been the case.

Jesuit Colleges and World War II

No war—including the Civil War—has ever had a more profound or longer-lasting impact on American colleges and universities than World War II. If the previous eighty years had seen the government gradually creep into higher education through the land-grant colleges, World War II ushered in an era in which the government became an essential partner for virtually all colleges, public and private.

When Adolf Hitler invaded Poland in 1939, most Americans (including a majority of Catholic college students, according to a survey by the Jesuit magazine, *America*) hoped that the United States could stay out of the conflict.[134] However, by necessity and by choice, Jesuit colleges enthusiastically supported the war effort after the 1941 attack on Pearl Harbor rapidly changed public opinion. Like World War I before it, this was an opportunity for Catholics to prove their mettle as patriotic Americans and consummate the dream (so precious to their ancestors who had come to the country by boat) of finally assimilating into US culture.

On a practical level, colleges across the country saw their prospective student pool plummet to dangerous levels as college-age males were drafted. Jesuit colleges that had already started to admit women (like Seattle, Marquette, Saint Louis, and the University of Detroit) woke up one morning to discover that women were suddenly in the majority in some degree programs.[135] To avoid a total shutdown of their operation,

---

134. Varga, *Baltimore's Loyola*, 296–297.
135. Crowley, *Seattle University*, 54.

most Jesuit colleges had to join forces with the War Department and transform their campuses (quite literally) into bona fide military bases, where dorms became barracks, most male students became reservists, and old curriculum plans (like neoscholasticism) were thrown out the window to accommodate the military's preferred plan of study. School calendars were accelerated and summer sessions added to allow students to graduate more quickly and reach the battlefields faster. In exchange for all of this accommodation, the federal government provided massive paychecks, without which many colleges almost certainly would not have survived.

There were two principal programs through which the US military inserted itself (financially and academically) into American higher education during World War II. The first was the Army Special Training Program (ASTP), whereby the War Department contracted with universities to provide training for reserve soldiers in fields like foreign language, geography, and engineering. Students were seventeen years old, and after a year in the program, when they reached the draft age of eighteen, they would be expected to serve in the Army. The second was the Navy's V-12 program, which was similar to the modern-day Naval Reserve Officer Training Corps (ROTC). It allowed students to enroll in a reasonably normal (if accelerated) college experience and earn a bachelor's degree (most often in naval science) with a government subsidy. The Roosevelt administration announced both programs in 1942.

The ASTP program favored schools that already had a well-established Army ROTC unit on campus. Therefore, the universities selected to host an ASTP unit were disproportionately large, public land-grant colleges. However, some private universities successfully applied to participate, among them Boston College, Georgetown, Fordham, Xavier, and the University of Detroit. As the War Department negotiated how much it would reimburse the Jesuit colleges for their services, the fact that Jesuit faculty members normally received no salary at all became a sticking point. Government lawyers at first argued that faculty who worked for room and board should only be reimbursed the actual cost of their living expenses, but the colleges eventually convinced the War Department to pay market-rate salaries for all Jesuit ASTP instructors.[136]

The V-12 program, by contrast, favored small colleges that were feeling the enrollment pinch the hardest and that would be in serious danger of shutting down without government help. This, as it turned out, was a long list. More than 1600 colleges applied to host a V-12 unit, of which 131 were successful.[137] Holy Cross, Gonzaga (Spokane), John Carroll, and Marquette all made the cut.

Smaller government programs also helped to keep the colleges afloat. Georgetown's federal connections helped it to land valuable contracts from the War Department (to help assign and classify prospective servicemen through a so-called STAR unit), and from the US Public Health Service (to train wartime nurses). Xavier

---

136. Varga, *Baltimore's Loyola*, 320. Curran, *History of Georgetown Vol. II,,* 221. Bennish, *Continuity*, 165.

137. Kuzniewski, *Thy Honored Name*, 302–303.

hosted an Army Air Corps reserve unit.[138] All told, hundreds of thousands of dollars flowed from federal coffers into Jesuit colleges and universities, without which their classrooms would have been almost empty and their tuition income reduced to a life-threatening trickle.

The colleges, for their part, more than earned what they were paid. Thousands of Jesuit-educated young men stepped up to join the fighting forces, while the five Jesuit nursing schools sent hundreds of women to military hospitals at home and abroad. Female students who were not studying nursing contributed in other ways, such as by joining the Navy WAVES program. Faculty who did not themselves volunteer for uniformed service provided much-needed expertise, teaching foreign languages and other high-demand skills that the military had to develop rapidly during wartime.

Jesuit schools that were not lucky enough (or politically connected enough) to land these lucrative government contracts had to be more creative in their survival tactics. They expanded their evening colleges and adult education programs, adding courses at odd hours of the day to accommodate the schedules of factory workers pressed into the job market by the need for wartime goods.[139] These part-time commuter students by no means replaced the revenue that was lost when the full-time boarding students disappeared, but it softened the blow. At Saint Joseph's in Philadelphia, where the facilities on the roughly fifteen-year-old campus were still too small to be of interest to the military, enrollment fell from about 500 to just 62 in three years. Saint Joseph's College received financial help from Saint Joseph's Prep during those lean years.[140] Regis College in Colorado was also judged to be too small for military use, but it successfully partnered with the University of Denver to bid jointly for a government contract that kept both institutions alive.[141]

Wartime necessity accelerated racial integration, religious diversity, and coeducation. Loyola (Baltimore) admitted its first Black students in 1946—very early for a school in a former slave state. Schools that still had a policy against female undergraduates beefed up the number of women in their graduate schools. At Holy Cross, the one Jesuit college that had traditionally limited its enrollment to Catholics, there were now significant numbers of Protestants and Jews enrolled in the V-12 program. At Georgetown, Jewish students were not unusual even before the war, but one particular young Jewish man in the ASTP program would go on to a legendary career in comedy. Carl Reiner hosted a 1943 Christmas pageant in Georgetown's Gaston Hall, during which he wowed the crowd by doing hilarious impressions of the Jesuit faculty members. (Reportedly, the Jesuits victims of Reiner's satirical sketches were laughing hardest of all.)[142]

---

138. Bennish, *Continuity*, 162–163. Curran, *History of Georgetown Vol. II*, 221.

139. Varga, *Baltimore's Loyola*, 316.

140. Contosta, *Saint Joseph's*, 172–174.

141. Stansell, *Regis*, 148–149.

142. Kuzniewski, *Thy Honored Name*, 303. Varga, *Baltimore's Loyola*, 316. Curran, *History of Georgetown Vol. II*, 220, 226.

The war effort was so massive and involved so many people (including those who made the ultimate sacrifice) that it would be impossible to list all of the heroes by name here. We will have to rely on a small sample. As in other conflicts, many Jesuits enlisted as military chaplains, including Georgetown religion professor Martin O'Gara, SJ, and Holy Cross mathematics professor Joseph O'Callahan, SJ. O'Gara died tragically in 1945 when his flight home (after which he was scheduled to be discharged) caught fire. As the plane went down, there were not enough parachutes for all of the passengers to leap to safety, and O'Gara selflessly gave his own parachute to another soldier. O'Callahan became the first military chaplain ever to be awarded the Medal of Honor; his heroic actions on board the USS Franklin helped to prevent what would have been a devastating explosion of onboard munitions during a Japanese bombing attack. The USS O'Callahan and the USS Georgetown Victory were among the ships later commissioned by the Navy to honor Jesuit contributions.[143]

It was a transformative four-year period—and yet, when World War II ended, its biggest and most lasting impact on American higher education was still to come. As millions of newly minted young veterans returned from the frontlines or otherwise resumed civilian life, they benefitted from the 1944 G.I. Bill—through which the federal government paid for their education. This meant that a bachelor's degree was now a realistic goal for many young people who otherwise would have lacked the means. It also meant that nationwide demand for a college education was about to shoot through the roof, resulting in an enrollment boom that pushed the small Jesuit colleges to their absolute limits. Student headcounts would double, triple, or even quadruple in a span of a few years, forcing the Jesuit colleges to hire unprecedented numbers of lay faculty, erect new buildings, and completely rethink old traditions (like the curriculum and daily schedule) that had been designed for schools a fraction of the size.

For the first time in their long histories, the Jesuits colleges became almost wholly reliant on taxpayer dollars to exist. This raised new issues in Church-state relations that forever changed how the colleges were managed and how they interacted with both Church and country. What followed was a period of rapid change in which pioneer educators felt their way forward with no map or compass to guide them.

---

143. Kuzniewski, *Thy Honored Name*, 307.

Part VI:

The Search for Identity (1945–1990)

Overview, 1945–1990

On September 26, 1963, in the middle of one of the busiest years in Vatican history, Pope Paul VI stepped away from the Second Vatican Council to deliver a live address via television to Georgetown University. Across the ocean, students and faculty gathered together in Georgetown's McDonough Gymnasium to watch the pope on a giant screen. The occasion was Georgetown's 175th anniversary and, by corollary, the 175th anniversary of Catholic higher education in America. Paul VI echoed the words of one of his predecessors, Pius XI, in describing Georgetown as "the alma mater of Catholic colleges in the United States of America"[1] before returning to the Council that would transform the Church. It was celebration amid change—a fitting metaphor for Catholic higher education at the time.

If the nineteenth century was like an extended childhood for Jesuit colleges and universities, the early twentieth century (especially the era between the two World Wars) was a coming-of-age moment during which they left that childhood behind. Using Catholic terminology, we might say that Jesuit colleges and universities were "baptized" in the 1800s and "confirmed" in the years leading up to World War II.

Following that war, Jesuit higher education entered into full-blown adolescence that lasted roughly until 1990. Like any teenager, Jesuit colleges and universities were slightly rebellious, prone to questioning authority, and eager to spread their wings. At the same time, like anyone who successfully navigates the awkward teen years, they also took more responsibility for their own health and livelihood, maturing and growing into themselves while experimenting with the trappings of independent adulthood.

The men (and now, women) who helped to lead the universities through these turbulent years were in truly uncharted territory. They were building on solid foundations but without clear blueprints. Their schools were now many times bigger and more complex than they had ever been. New problems—like how to cope with record enrollments and how to cooperate with the Church and the government—presented major challenges (especially when the very nature of that Church and that government was changing in real time). These educators were pioneers of a different sort. They were no less innovative than the Jesuit missionaries who travelled on foot to frontier settlements like St. Louis, Bardstown, and San Francisco a century earlier, but the

---

1. Paul VI, "Message of Pope Paul VI to Georgetown University," September 26, 1963, http://www.vatican.va/content/paul-vi/en/speeches/1963/documents/hf_p-vi_spe_19630926_georgetown-university.html. See also Durkin, *Georgetown University, First in the Nation's Capital*, dust jacket and 136.

threats they faced were intellectual, not physical, and their biggest challenges were not mob violence and war, but politics and deep-seated inequalities that bubbled to the surface of American society in the 1960s and beyond.

The issues they faced were many, and built off each other. Because of the G.I. Bill and the post-World War II baby boom, Jesuit college campuses designed to accommodate a few hundred students suddenly had to accommodate a few thousand. Ironically, as the pool of potential students became larger, competition for those students became fiercer. In the 1950s and 1960s, governments around the country began opening community colleges to offer accessible education—especially for students who could not afford to leave their hometowns to earn degrees. Reputable public universities opened branch campuses in every corner of their states. These new public schools replicated, almost to a T, the original mission of most Catholic and Jesuit universities—but the community colleges could now fulfill that mission more cheaply and conveniently. Jesuit schools had to rethink their very purpose and redefine themselves as modern private universities, not as the community colleges of the nineteenth century.

But the Jesuits were not mere spectators as new colleges and universities went up across the country; they, too, still knew how to build. In one last great wave of expansion, new Jesuit colleges sprang up in midsized industrial cities in Pennsylvania, Connecticut, New York, and West Virginia. This, along with the rapid growth at existing schools, meant that new professors (mainly laypeople) had to be hired at unprecedented rates. Unlike previous generations, these laypeople demanded a livable salary as well as some say in university governance. The chummy Jesuit college run by a handful of priests was a thing of the past, but the schools tried desperately to maintain its spirit while doubling or tripling in size.

Much about the students was changing as well. By the 1970s, all Jesuit colleges were both fully coeducational and racially integrated. Those decisions, when they finally came, required much more than a vote by the boards of trustees. New dorms went up and new campus amenities were added (after 1972, as a matter of law) to accommodate women. Moreover, simply bringing the races together did not end racism; it merely began a long dialogue that continued for generations.

All of this was happening concurrently with, and at times because of, major changes in the outside world. In Rome, the Second Vatican Council reimagined what it meant to be Catholic and redefined how a Catholic institution should be managed. American Catholics entered into an unprecedented era of prosperity symbolized by the 1960 election of John F. Kennedy as president. The subsequent Civil Rights Act of 1964, Title IX legislation of 1972, and the Americans with Disabilities Act of 1990 changed who could and should pursue higher education. And all of this took place amid the backdrop of the Cold War, during which colleges and universities were called upon to serve as frontline agents in the space race and the (largely government-funded) scientific duel with the Soviet Union.

Jesuit colleges responded with their boldest and most important move yet. Beginning in the late 1960s and mirroring a process taking place at virtually every Catholic college in the country, they legally separated from the Society of Jesus and from each other, incorporating as independent non-profit institutions. Henceforth, each Jesuit college would stand on its own, and its relationship to the Jesuit order would be fundamentally different—based on sponsorship and cooperation, but not direct control.

Meanwhile, Jesuit colleges got really good at basketball.

Fortunately, this generation of Jesuit leaders was up to the challenges it faced. Shortly after World War I, the Jesuits had decided to send their best young priests to graduate school, encouraging them to earn PhDs and become true scholars. That generation was now in charge, and it shaped Jesuit higher education in remarkable ways.

The G.I. Bill: From Famine to Feast

In 1944, as the Allied victory in World War II started to look inevitable and imminent, President Roosevelt signed into law the Servicemen's Readjustment Act, better known as the G.I. Bill. The government feared that millions of veterans returning from war all at once could overwhelm the US labor market and spark another depression, so it offered to pay for those veterans to go to school, keeping them off the unemployment rolls for a few more years. Meanwhile, it invested in a massive public works program that created jobs and built a new national infrastructure designed to accommodate the car rather than the passenger train. These strategies worked, and resulted in an era of unprecedented prosperity in the United States.[2]

Colleges and universities that had been surviving on table scraps just a few years earlier now drank from a firehose as thousands of returning soldiers applied for admission. Within the Jesuit college network, the total combined enrollment skyrocketed from just over 28,000 in 1944 to more than 98,000 in 1948.[3] This brought unprecedented tuition revenue, but it also brought infrastructure problems, because most Jesuit colleges had nowhere near the dorm space or the classroom space necessary to accommodate such crowds. Many Jesuit schools took a portion of the government money they were now receiving and gave it right back to the government, buying surplus military buildings, barracks, or other hastily built wartime structures and relocating them to the school grounds. These new buildings were cheaply made—easy to disassemble and reassemble—and they gave a kind of austere, Spartan look to the campuses that reminded the veterans of Army life. Always intended to be temporary, most of these buildings fell to the wrecking ball within a few years, but they served their purpose.[4]

Human infrastructure was harder to build. By themselves, the Jesuits could never hope to teach all of the courses that now had to be added to the schedule, so the universities hired record numbers of laypeople. In Rome, the newly elected Jesuit general, the Belgian-born Jean-Baptiste Janssens, SJ, recognized the practical necessity of

---

2. Varga, *Baltimore's Loyola*, 327.

3. Fitzgerald, *Governance*, 79.

4. McKevitt, *University of Santa Clara*, 265.

diluting the Jesuit teaching corps, but urged his colleagues to train lay faculty as best they could in the traditions of Jesuit education and the objectives of Jesuit pedagogy.[5] This was easier said than done. The Jesuits themselves normally spent years learning those traditions in the seminary, and no guidebook described how to condense that long formation process into a crash course for newly hired lay professors. The Jesuits had to improvise.

In this environment, it became virtually impossible to give all students a common experience, and old attempts at curricular cohesion like neoscholasticism quietly faded away. The student schedule also became more lax. With such large student bodies, it became impossible to enforce mandatory wake-up times, daily Mass attendance for Catholics, or restrictions on free time off campus. Even though most students were accustomed to a military regimen, they were also older and more mature, and it seemed ridiculous to force adults in their mid-twenties or older to follow archaic campus rules designed for teenagers.[6] All of these changes took time, and many began in embryonic form even before World War II, but the war and its aftermath fast-tracked them.

Besides, strict lifestyle restrictions were already out of vogue at public universities and community colleges, and those schools threatened to eat the Jesuits' lunch if they did not keep up with the times. Not since the nineteenth century had so many new public colleges opened in such a short period. Jesuit colleges had grown comfortable in their role as providers of accessible education, mainly offering degrees to underprivileged immigrants and working-class students for whom travel was not an option. But as public and community colleges usurped that role in the 1950s and beyond, private universities came to be seen as a somewhat more "elite" option. It was the first time that many Jesuit schools had thought of themselves in this way, and it required a reimagining of their missions and of the image they presented to the outside world.

The 1944 G.I. Bill expired after twelve years, but later versions, like the Montgomery G.I. Bill of 1984 and the Post-9/11 G.I. Bill of 2008, have kept the government checks flowing and made veterans an indispensable part of the student pool for most colleges and universities. Military service became a gateway to education for millions of Americans who otherwise never could have afforded a college degree. These programs also helped to make most private colleges dependent on government funding—a dependence that only increased with the introduction of federal student loans, federal work-study programs, Pell Grants, and other taxpayer-supported revenue sources that emerged in the following decades. At Jesuit and other Catholic colleges, this would eventually raise questions about the separation of church and state that dramatically affected how Catholic higher education governed itself.[7]

---

5. Fitzgerald, *Governance*, 103.

6. Varga, *Baltimore's Loyola*, 412–413.

7. Rizzi, "We've Been Here Before," 165–166.

The Baby Boom Colleges:
Scranton, Fairfield, Le Moyne, and Wheeling

The new, smaller Jesuit provinces that emerged just before 1945 facilitated a wave of expansion in the northeast. The old Maryland-New York Province split in three, which meant that the now-separate New England, New York, and Maryland Provinces each had less territory to cover and more opportunity to focus their efforts on midsize cities that had escaped the attention of earlier generations of Jesuits. The glut of demand generated by the G.I. Bill, combined with a sustained jump in the birthrate as veterans settled down and had families, meant that forecasters predicted a robust student market for the foreseeable future. The Maryland Province added new schools in Scranton, Pennsylvania and Wheeling, West Virginia; the New York Province expanded Upstate with a new school in Syracuse; and the New England Province expanded south to the New York suburbs in Connecticut.

The University of Scranton (1942), Scranton, Pennsylvania

Long before it became a pop culture icon as the fictional setting for NBC's sitcom, "The Office," Scranton was an economic hub for northeastern Pennsylvania. Along with its twin city, Wilkes-Barre, it became an important center for coal mining, iron and steel production, and the railroad industry. In the late nineteenth century, this economic bait attracted a typically Catholic blend of Polish, Italian, Irish, and Eastern European immigrants.

Although the Scranton/Wilkes-Barre area has long been overshadowed in its own state by the much larger population centers in Philadelphia, Pittsburgh, Harrisburg, and the Lehigh Valley, it punched above its weight politically. The Scranton family from which the city takes its name included a number of prominent business and government leaders—one of whom, Bill Scranton, served as governor of Pennsylvania in the 1960s. Native sons Bob Casey, Sr. and Bob Casey, Jr. (both of whom were Jesuit-educated at Scranton Prep and the College of the Holy Cross) served Pennsylvania respectively as governor and US senator. Both pro-life, pro-labor Democrats, the Caseys represented a distinctively Catholic political viewpoint nurtured in a culturally Catholic city. Another Scranton native, President Joe Biden, also espoused many such old-school, working-class Catholic values during his political career.

Catholic influence in northeastern Pennsylvania was strong. Despite its relatively small size, the Scranton/Wilkes-Barre area is today home to four Catholic colleges—the University of Scranton (Jesuits), King's College (Congregation of Holy Cross), Misericordia University (Sisters of Mercy), and Marywood University (Sisters, Servants of the Immaculate Heart of Mary). All date their origins to the first half of the twentieth century or earlier, but the University of Scranton is the oldest and the best known.

When the Jesuits took the helm of the University of Scranton in 1942, the school was already 54 years old. Until that point, it had followed the familiar Catholic college origin story. In 1888, the first bishop of Scranton, William O'Hara, opened what he called St. Thomas College (named for St. Thomas Aquinas). Per the usual pattern, the little college was originally more like a modern-day high school, and was successively staffed by diocesan priests, the Xaverian Brothers, and the Christian Brothers during its first five decades. Always small, it did not even qualify for an SATC unit during World War I because it lacked a collegiate charter from the state. Prior to the 1920s, it awarded degrees in the name of one of the Christian Brothers' other nearby colleges, including LaSalle College in Philadelphia and the now-defunct St. John's College in Washington, DC. The Christian Brothers finally secured a state charter for St. Thomas College in 1922; full accreditation came in 1927, followed by the adoption of its current name in 1938.

As was the case elsewhere in America's industrial heartland, Scranton was approaching its all-time peak population around the time of World War II. During this time of prosperity, one of the patriarchs of the Scranton family, Worthington Scranton (an Episcopalian by practice but a strong supporter of all of the city's civic institutions), donated his large urban estate to the University of Scranton in early 1942. The property sat just a few blocks from the university's original buildings and provided one of the best campus growth opportunities within the city limits. Despite all of these positive developments, the Christian Brothers informed the local diocese that they intended to withdraw from Scranton that same year, hoping to concentrate their personnel at LaSalle College. The local bishop, William Hafey, began his search for another religious order with the resources and the energy to develop this diamond in the rough. Naturally, the Jesuits were first on his list.[8]

Former Georgetown President W. Coleman Nevils, SJ arrived in Scranton in 1942 to lead the revamped university. Even though this was the middle of World War II, the Jesuit expansion to Scranton was, essentially, a post-war endeavor. During the quiet wartime years, Father Nevils seized the opportunity to devote himself more fully to planning, working on strategies to develop the Worthington Scranton estate and transform the university into a recognizably Jesuit institution. The old Christian Brothers' curriculum had, per usual, emphasized trades and practical skills; Nevils elevated the standards to include more classics and humanities, modeling the new curriculum after the adapted versions of the *Ratio Studiorum* then in vogue at other Jesuit colleges. In 1944, he also opened a high school, Scranton Prep, in an unused university building that had formerly served as a charity hospital. By the time the war ended the following year, all of that planning had paid off, and a steady stream of students enrolled in the revitalized university.

By quirk of history, Father Nevils was not, technically, the first Jesuit president of the University of Scranton. In 1895, while St. Thomas College was still under diocesan control, the local bishop appointed Father Daniel MacGoldrick to the school presidency—a position he held for five years. Father MacGoldrick was a former Jesuit who

---

8. Richard Grady, "Scranton University," *Jesuit Educational Quarterly* V, no. 2 (September 1942): 145–147.

had taught at Georgetown before leaving the order to become a diocesan priest, which enabled him to accept the job in Scranton. It was he who oversaw the school's first transition into the hands of the Xaverian and then the Christian Brothers.[9]

As heavy industry declined in the 1970s and 1980s, northeastern Pennsylvania (along with most of the Rust Belt) suffered staggering job losses, but the University of Scranton remained a bright spot in the local economy. For years, it has been the largest non-medical, non-governmental employer in Lackawanna County, and its more than 5,000 students bring an important vitality to the downtown area. It remains one of the anchor cultural institutions that keeps the city vibrant. Few other American cities take such collective civic pride in being home to a Jesuit university.

Fairfield University (1942), Fairfield, Connecticut

Not long after the New England Province came into existence in 1926, the Boston-based Jesuits began contemplating expansion. With responsibility for just two colleges (Boston College and Holy Cross), they had men to spare. Providence, Rhode Island was the second-largest city in New England and a tempting target, but the Dominicans had already opened Providence College in that city in 1917. That left Hartford, Connecticut as the most logical option. Despite its importance in American history, Connecticut had long been underrepresented in Catholic higher education. Its residents had easy access to the many Catholic colleges in New York City, but only a handful of Catholic colleges (all women's schools run by nuns) actually operated within the Constitution State.

During the 1930s, the New England Jesuits repeatedly sought permission of the Bishop of Hartford, Maurice McAuliffe, to build a college in his diocese. The bishop agreed in 1941, but to the Jesuits' surprise, recommended against putting the college in Hartford itself. The state capital was already crowded with secular colleges and relatively little space was available for a proper campus; city officials would be hesitant to let another tax-exempt nonprofit organization acquire large amounts of property. Instead, McAuliffe recommended Bridgeport, an industrial city in southern Connecticut with a large and growing concentration of Catholics. Although the city was just down the road from New Haven, Yale University may as well have been on another planet considering how few working-class Catholic students it admitted each year.[10]

For more than 100 years, the Jesuits had grown accustomed to being "first on the scene" wherever they built a college. On the American frontier, they were often the first to open a college in any city, which enabled them to snag prime real estate and watch the city and the college grow together. Bridgeport presented an unfamiliar problem. The New England Jesuits quickly discovered that it was much harder to open a college in a mature city, where little land was available and where the local gov-

---

9. Ibid., 145.

10. Joseph MacDonnell, SJ, *If these Stones Could Speak: The Phenomenal Growth of the Fairfield University Campus* (Fairfield, CT: Fairfield University, 1996), 8.

ernments were not desperate to provide education. Unable to find a suitable campus in Bridgeport itself, the Jesuits looked instead to nearby Fairfield, a wealthy New York suburb in the Connecticut panhandle. There, they acquired the estate of the Jennings family—local business leaders who were associated with Standard Oil and moved in the same circles as the Rockefellers—in 1941. A few months later, the Jesuits supplemented that purchase by buying the neighboring estate of Walter Lasher, more than doubling the total acreage. Having acquired an ideal physical space, the Jesuits next ran into political difficulties; Connecticut regulators initially denied a charter for the new school on the grounds there were already plenty of colleges in the state.[11] Because this decision came in the middle of the lean wartime years, it is reasonable to assume that regulators feared the effect that a new college—especially a men's college—would have on the already depleted male student pool.

To overcome these challenges, the New England Jesuits returned to the old Jesuit playbook and began their work in Fairfield with a *collegium inchoatum*—a high school. As their predecessors had done for more than 100 years, they planned to establish themselves in the community first with a modest high school before adding a college division—hoping that, in time, regulators would recognize the high school's value and have a change of heart. Fairfield College Preparatory School opened its doors in 1942, even though, by that time, most Jesuit colleges were dissociating from their affiliated high schools. Although it ran counter to prevailing trends, this strategic chess move had the desired effect. In 1945, as the tidal wave of veterans was about to crash onto America's shores, the Connecticut legislature approved a charter for "Fairfield University of St. Robert Bellarmine."[12] Full accreditation followed four years later. Strikingly, this makes Fairfield the first and only Jesuit university to describe itself as a "university" (rather than an "academy" or "college") from the day it opened its doors. According to Fairfield historian Joseph MacDonnell, this was important to the New England Jesuits because, decades earlier, they had been burned when Boston College lost out on the name "Boston University" to its crosstown rival, despite being the first of the two institutions to be chartered.[13]

Barely twenty years had passed since the days when the Jesuits cannibalistically operated four colleges in the New York City area. In the 1910s and 1920s, they had tried to stop shooting themselves in the foot by consolidating St. Francis Xavier, Brooklyn, and Saint Peter's Colleges into Fordham. Now, in the 1940s, Saint Peter's was back in business and an entirely new Jesuit college—Fairfield—was operating in the New York metro area's eastern fringe. It was a net loss of just one institution. Fortunately, population growth and the G.I. Bill meant that New York could now comfortably support three Jesuit colleges, and the physical distance between them—punctuated by three different state borders—helped to keep them at peace with each other.

---

11. Ibid., 9–10, 14–15.
12. Ibid., 14–18.
13. Ibid., 17.

Fairfield University's first two rector-presidents, John McEleney, SJ and James Dolan, SJ (the latter of whom had been head of the New England Province during the original negotiations with Bishop McAuliffe), put it on solid footing. By 1953, responding to growth in the local Catholic population, the Vatican erected a new diocese for southern Connecticut—the Diocese of Bridgeport. While this brought Fairfield closer to the seat of the local bishop, it also brought more competition. Ten years later, the young diocese opened its own college nearby—Sacred Heart University—designed from the beginning as a coeducational, lay-led institution. Fairfield University, which was still all-male at the time, would not admit women until 1970. The two schools have managed to coexist, albeit with a healthy and sometimes spirited rivalry.

Today, Fairfield University maintains a beautifully manicured suburban campus just a short train ride from New York City. In a crowded New England educational scene, it has carved out an excellent reputation in less than an average human lifetime. In 1999, it became the first Jesuit school in half a century to open a school of engineering, after acquiring the Bridgeport Engineering Institute. While it is located in one of the wealthiest neighborhoods and wealthiest counties in the country, it has not forgotten its original mission and continues to sponsor outreach programs to inner-city Bridgeport.

Le Moyne College (1946), Syracuse, New York

As was the case in Scranton, the Jesuit expansion to Syracuse has origins that slightly predate the 1943 Maryland-New York Province split. In 1940, Syracuse Bishop Walter Foery asked the Jesuits to open a college in his diocese, which (much like Scranton) had a booming manufacturing economy and a growing Catholic population. There were, as yet, no Catholic colleges in the large Upstate city along the Erie Canal. The New York Jesuits were receptive to the idea, hoping to avoid the perception that their ministry in the state was "a tale of two cities"—Buffalo and New York City.[14]

Bishop Foery, however, put an unusual and forward-thinking condition on his offer: the college was to be coeducational from the start. This would save the expense of building two separate schools, one for men and one for women—a formula that (elsewhere in the country) all too often had limited the growth of both. Since other colleges within the Jesuit network were already enrolling women at the time, this proved to be less controversial than it would have been a few decades earlier, and Superior General Janssens in Rome gave his approval. Nonetheless, it meant that the Syracuse school would be the first American Jesuit college to admit women to all of its programs from the day it opened its doors.[15]

Local Catholics responded in force to the subsequent fundraising efforts, which took a big leap forward when a local landowner, William Cahill, donated a small plot

---

14. Bender, *Brief History of the New York Province*, 41.
15. Ibid., 42–43.

of land in town to the Diocese of Syracuse. Bishop Foery quickly purchased a neighboring parcel and sold the combined properties—which amounted to nearly 120 acres—to the Jesuits. While construction was underway, Le Moyne College commenced classes in a diocesan office building downtown in 1947, relocating to its permanent campus the following year.[16] Initially, the Jesuits planned to operate Le Moyne under Canisius College's charter, which would have made it legally a branch campus of Canisius. However, that became unnecessary after Le Moyne successfully obtained its own provisional charter from the state in 1946, followed by a full charter in 1950.[17]

The school's name evoked the memory of Simon Le Moyne, SJ, a seventeenth-century French-Canadian Jesuit missionary who became a respected emissary between the Europeans and the Haudenosaunee (whom the French called the Iroquois) in what is today Upstate New York. Father Le Moyne was among the first Europeans to visit the region and to identify the local salt deposits that became an early economic driver in Syracuse.[18]

At the time Le Moyne College opened in the 1940s, the New York Jesuits were already developing a reputation for the "labor schools" that they conducted downstate. Bishop Foery of Syracuse insisted that the new college in his diocese offer similar outreach to local union members and managers.[19] The Le Moyne Institute of Industrial Relations opened concurrently with the college, offering courses on workers' rights and Catholic social thought comparable to those the Jesuits were teaching in New York City. Because it was formally affiliated with a college (and was located close to the New York State School of Industrial-Labor Relations at Cornell University, which had opened two years earlier), the Le Moyne Institute had a slightly more scholarly flavor than the other Jesuit labor schools, which were mainly outreach programs. Le Moyne College continued to offer courses on labor relations for generations, sometimes hiring faculty who had earned their doctorates at Cornell.

As Upstate New York, like other industrial regions of the United States, declined in population over the next seventy years, many of its Catholic colleges were forced to close, merge, or reinvent themselves for other purposes. This was not the case at Le Moyne, which is today the only four-year Catholic college between the outskirts of Albany and the outskirts of Buffalo. Befitting a school that has enrolled women since the beginning, Le Moyne set a precedent when it chose a woman, Linda LeMura, as its president in 2014. LeMura was only the second woman—and first lay woman—to lead an American Jesuit college.

---

16. Ibid., 43. Le Moyne College, *Le Moyne College Green Book*, 14.

17. William J. Bosch, SJ, Personal Correspondence, October 6, 2020. "Varia: New York Province, Le Moyne College," *Woodstock Letters* LXXV, no. 1 (1946): 82.

18. Weiss, "Jesuit Mission Years," 1–9.

19. Bender, *Brief History of the New York Province*, 42–43.

Wheeling University (1954), Wheeling, West Virginia

Near the tip of West Virginia's northern panhandle, fenced in by Pennsylvania to the east and Ohio to the west, lies Wheeling. If one were to sail a boat down the Ohio River from Pittsburgh to Cincinnati, Wheeling (and its sister city, Steubenville, located slightly upriver in Ohio) would be the first significant metro area encountered along the route. In the nineteenth century, this region rose to some prominence as the original western terminus of the National Road—America's first highway—which connected the C&O Canal in Cumberland, Maryland to the Ohio River at Wheeling. Because the C&O Canal also connected to the Potomac River near the Georgetown University campus, the National Road made it possible to move goods from the Potomac to the Ohio, and Wheeling became an important stopping point for westward expansion.

Over time, Wheeling's role as a transportation hub, combined with abundant local coal and mineral deposits, helped it to develop a robust manufacturing economy. Wheeling became a "Pittsburgh in miniature," with booming glass and steel industries that attracted the same kinds of nineteenth-century Catholic immigrants who settled elsewhere in the industrial Midwest. This made it demographically and economically different from the rest of Virginia prior to the Civil War. Because they lived at the northernmost tip of "the South," Wheeling residents generally mirrored northern opinions on slavery. The city became the epicenter of the movement to secede from Virginia during wartime; beginning in 1861, pro-Union representatives from Virginia's western counties gathered in Wheeling to debate separation, culminating in the creation of West Virginia as a state in 1863. The downtown building in which those debates took place is preserved as a historic landmark and known today as "West Virginia Independence Hall." For more than twenty years after West Virginia achieved statehood, Wheeling shared duties with Charleston as the state capital before all government offices concentrated in the latter city.

Wheeling's unique demographics meant that it was home to the vast majority of the Catholics in West Virginia, an overwhelmingly Protestant state. Wheeling was, therefore, a natural choice as the seat of the state's only Catholic diocese. For a small city, it also had an unusually diverse mix of cultural institutions. Its easy accessibility and proximity to the mountains attracted wealthy industrial barons from Pittsburgh and Cleveland, who sometimes holidayed in Wheeling and established high-quality arts organizations like the Wheeling Symphony and the Oglebay Institute—a notable complex of museums located in the city's Oglebay Park resort.

One thing that Wheeling lacked at midcentury, however, was a proper college. This became an issue as the postwar baby boom produced a demographic bulge of young people. Across the river, the Bishop of Steubenville successfully lured Franciscan priests from Pennsylvania to establish the College of Steubenville in 1946. Bishop John Swint of Wheeling hoped to do the same on his side of the state line. Beginning in 1951, he reached out to the Maryland Jesuits in hope that they could staff West Virginia's first Catholic college.

The Jesuits were interested, both because this project would fit nicely into the optimistic, expansionist spirit of the times and because it would give them a presence in the greater Pittsburgh area. Pittsburgh had largely escaped the attention of the Maryland Jesuits, which is surprising considering that it had one of the largest Catholic populations in the country. In the vacuum created by the Jesuits' absence, Spiritan priests from Germany (fleeing the same *Kulturkampf* persecutions that drew Jesuit refugees to Buffalo in the 1870s) built Duquesne University into one of America's largest and most comprehensive Catholic institutions. Since Pittsburgh itself had no need for another Catholic college, Wheeling provided a convenient back door for a Jesuit presence in the region.

The Maryland Jesuits assigned Clifford Lewis, SJ (a native of western Pennsylvania) to lead the feasibility study in Wheeling. Although Lewis never served directly as president of the resulting college, he is recognized as its de facto founder and became an iconic presence on campus for the remainder of his adult life. That adult life began with an immense tragedy; in his twenties, he had married a Pittsburgh-area college professor named Catherine O'Keefe, who died in a car accident less than a year after the wedding. O'Keefe had convinced her new husband, who was born Baptist, to convert to Catholicism prior to the nuptials. Stricken with grief, Lewis found comfort in his new faith and entered the Jesuit order two years later.[20]

Father Lewis pushed the Wheeling project to completion even as Bishop Swint himself became discouraged by the costs involved. For a campus, the diocese acquired 61 acres of surplus land from the Mount de Chantal Visitation Academy, a historic girls' high school operated by the Sisters of the Visitation.[21] The sisters had a long history of cooperating with the Jesuits, dating all the way back to Father Leonard Neale's term as Georgetown University president in the 1790s. On Father Neale's invitation, the sisters opened Georgetown Visitation Academy—the oldest Catholic girls' school in the country—adjacent to Georgetown University in 1799. Visitation sisters from Georgetown later came to Mobile, Alabama to open the female counterpart to Spring Hill College. In 1848, a third group of nuns from the Georgetown convent set out for Wheeling and opened the girls' high school that would, in a kind of poetic parallelism, eventually provide the land for the Jesuit school in West Virginia.

After Father Lewis personally supervised the campus plan and construction, Wheeling College incorporated in 1954, opened its doors to students (male and female) in 1955, and received a state charter in 1957. In the meantime, Lewis successfully lobbied for an amendment to the G.I. Bill that enabled the new college to enroll veterans and collect federal payments even before it was fully accredited.[22]

Lewis continued to serve the university until his death in 1983 and became an important civic figure in Wheeling, championing causes that drew scholarly (and gov-

20. John C. Bates, "Rev. Clifford M. Lewis, SJ—Journalist, Husband, Priest, College Co-Founder and Historian," *Gathered Fragments* XXVII, no. 1 (Fall 2017): 68–70.

21. Ibid., 70–71.

22. Ibid., 72.

ernment) attention to the city's unique place in American history.[23] The Jesuits memorialized him in 2002 when they created the Clifford M. Lewis, SJ Appalachian Institute in Wheeling, which serves as both a research institute and a community service program promoting the interests of one of America's poorest and most forgotten regions. The institute has drawn much-needed attention to a part of the United States that frequently lacks basic medical care and where millions of Americans survive with limited education and employment opportunities. Appalachia, as a whole, remains criminally under-studied by American academics and overlooked by others in positions of power, but Wheeling Jesuit University did much to work against this unfortunate reality. It provided education to thousands of students in a state where only a small fraction of the population attends college, and coordinated thousands of volunteer hours in rural, isolated mountain communities.

The nearby College of Steubenville changed its name to the Franciscan University of Steubenville in 1986. That same year, to emphasize its own identity, Wheeling College became Wheeling Jesuit College and achieved university status ten years later. It was the first time in the nearly 200-year history of Jesuit higher education in the United States that a college had used the term "Jesuit" in its name.[24]

The university arguably peaked under Jesuit leadership in the 1990s and early 2000s. Due in part to the efforts of long-serving West Virginia Senators Robert Byrd and Jay Rockefeller—who never missed an opportunity to lard federal spending bills with pork to support their home state—Wheeling Jesuit University landed some important federal contracts, including a multimillion-dollar research grant from NASA that supported construction of a new science building on campus.

In spite of its accomplishments, Wheeling Jesuit remained, throughout its life, the poorest and the smallest of the twenty-eight American Jesuit colleges and universities. With fewer than 30,000 residents in the early 2000s, Wheeling was the smallest city to host a Jesuit university since St. Marys, Kansas in the 1930s. Although the metro area (including Steubenville) was home to around 150,000 residents, it was shrinking. Over time, Wheeling Jesuit began to operate as something of a charity, heavily discounting its tuition for needy Appalachian residents and operating at a financial loss. As population declines continued in the twenty-first century, the situation finally became unsustainable, and Wheeling Jesuit fell victim to the same economic forces that seriously weakened other small, private colleges in the northeast and Midwest.

In 2019, the university's lay leaders announced a major cost-saving campaign that restructured the entire institution, eliminating most humanities programs and refocusing almost exclusively on business and health care degrees. The Jesuits, noting that such an education was not within the Jesuit liberal arts tradition, withdrew from Wheeling. Sponsorship of the university reverted to the local diocese, and the school renamed itself "Wheeling University." It was the first time since 1868—when the

---

23. Ibid., 73–75.
24. Ibid., 72.

Jesuits left St. Joseph's College in Bardstown, Kentucky in the aftermath of the Civil War—that the American Jesuits had walked away from one of their sponsored colleges while the college was still operational.

Peaks and Challenges in the 1950s: John Tracy Ellis Throws down the Gauntlet

The successful opening of Wheeling College in 1955 meant that the roster of Jesuit colleges and universities for the rest of the twentieth century was complete. The Jesuit network was at its all-time high, with twenty-eight "true" degree granting institutions (not just glorified high schools) in eighteen states and the District of Columbia. No other Catholic religious order came close. Across the country, the Catholic Church was entering into an unprecedented time of prosperity as second- and third-generation Americans, including many veterans, were able to achieve home ownership and raise large families. Seminaries were full, and the number of priests and other religious vocations in the United States were approaching their all-time records. Because of the hard work of previous generations, most Catholic children had access to a neighborhood Catholic school, and thanks to the abundant cheap labor of teaching sisters and brothers, most could attend for a pittance in tuition. After a long campaign in which voters and journalists rigorously questioned his faith, a Catholic, John F. Kennedy, was narrowly elected president in 1960.

Many Catholics today look back on the halcyon days of the 1950s and early 1960s as the "peak" of Catholic culture. Judging strictly by the numbers of priests and the numbers of Catholic institutions in operation, they are correct, but behind the scenes there were serious issues within the Church. Future generations would learn that a small, but not insignificant percentage of the men ordained to the priesthood during this time did not belong there, as they either engaged in misconduct during their careers or voluntarily left religious life in later decades. In its fervor to staff its huge infrastructure of hospitals, schools, orphanages, and other charities, the Catholic Church recruited young men and women in their teens to what were meant to be life-long vocations—even before some were mature enough to make such a commitment. These practices and others would be reconsidered during the Second Vatican Council in the early 1960s, but they were commonplace earlier.

In 1955, Catholic higher education also had a major self-reckoning. That year, Monsignor John Tracy Ellis, a prominent scholar who had earned his doctorate from the Catholic University of America, published a provocative essay in the journal *Thought* (a publication of Fordham University Press). The essay was adapted from an equally provocative speech that Ellis had given at Maryville College in St. Louis earlier that year at a conference of Catholic educators. Entitled, "American Catholics and the Intellectual Life," Ellis's article asked why Catholics had contributed so little to mainstream American thinking despite their numbers, and why Catholics remained so underrepresented in the scholarly world despite operating hundreds of American colleges and universities. US Catholics (in the pre-Kennedy era) were punching seriously below their demographic weight when it came to their influence on politics, media, and especially the academy.

Despite the fact that there were more Catholics in the United States than in almost any country on earth, Ellis argued, "the American intellectual climate has been aloof and unfriendly to Catholic thoughts and ideas, when it has not been openly hostile."[25] Although he attributed some of this hostility to lingering anti-Catholic bias in American society, Ellis mainly pointed the finger at Catholics themselves, who had failed to produce in their own ranks intellectual leaders on par with those of the ruling classes. For generations, the Church and most of its energy had been devoted to improving the position of immigrants, and "Not until this generation has the Church been given time (with the cessation of mass immigration) to take a breath and take stock."[26] During what was ostensibly a time of prosperity, Catholic universities were struggling to find teachers capable of articulating a distinctively Catholic worldview. This was partly because the Church had failed to train such scholars, but also partly because Catholic universities had failed to develop a meaningfully "Catholic" approach to research. At home, many working-class Catholic families still encouraged their children to enter the workforce and earn money as early as possible rather than pursue a life of the mind. As a result, Catholics were still overrepresented on the union rolls in Midwestern steel mills and trade schools but were painfully underrepresented in coastal universities, intellectual associations, and government agencies that steered the direction of the country.

There was a simple yet unstated explanation for the shortcomings that Ellis identified. In the Catholic higher education system, a career as a college professor and a religious vocation were largely inseparable, which meant that few Catholic laypeople could aspire to scholarly life. For generations, the teaching profession in Catholic colleges and universities was effectively limited to Catholic priests, brothers, and nuns. Many of these men and women were outstanding educators, but their training was primarily in ministry, not in scholarship. Even though they left a major impact on the lives of the individuals they taught, they did not leave much impact in the publishing world or on the direction of American academia as a whole. The Catholic education system was designed to help people, not to advance the frontiers of knowledge.

Moreover, Catholic universities had indeed tried to articulate a distinctive worldview through neoscholasticism in the 1920s and 1930s, but that movement had not worked (partly because of flaws in neoscholasticism itself, and partly because Catholics had so few graduate schools capable of training professors in that way of thinking). When it came to research, Catholic universities were playing a game in which the rules had already been set by secular schools with no consideration for Catholic tradition.

---

25. John Tracy Ellis, "American Catholics and the Intellectual Life," *Thought* 30, no. 3 (Autumn 1955): 354.

26. Ellis, quoting D.W. Brogan in Ibid., 355.

By contrast, American Protestants had separated the teaching profession from the ministry profession since the late 1800s, meaning that a scholarly career had long been a realistic goal for laypeople (at least those born into the right social class). Protestant higher education, however, was doing some soul-searching of its own in the 1950s—for the exact opposite reason. Protestants were concerned that their best research universities were not religious *enough* and had veered too far in the direction of scholarly productivity, largely abandoning their original mission to shape students' lives in meaningful, moral ways. In 1951, Yale alumnus William F. Buckley, Jr. published his ground-shaking book, *God and Man at Yale*, in which he described the Christian influence at his (still officially Protestant) alma mater as laughably superficial. In the name of "academic freedom," professors promoted atheism or other values contradictory to Yale's stated mission. Buckley's book caused a stir in New Haven and in the old boys' network in East Coast academia, but its harshest accusations were dismissed by those in power, in part because Buckley was a Catholic. One incredulous Episcopal bishop wondered why Buckley had not attended Fordham if he was looking for an education that conformed to his religious worldview.[27]

Back in the Catholic world, when Monsignor Ellis threw down the gauntlet to his fellow Catholics in his 1955 article, the reaction was as swift as it could be in academia. The essay served as a wake-up call to modernize Catholic higher education even further and rapidly expand Catholic graduate programs. As some of the largest and best-resourced Catholic universities in the country, the twenty-eight Jesuit institutions were in a much better position than the others to lead these efforts.

The Jesuits Respond

Ellis's article accelerated a process that was already in motion at Jesuit schools. The first generation of Jesuits to earn PhDs as a routine part of its formation was coming of age, and the universities were putting a great deal of stock into that group's scholarly potential. Once in power, these priest-scholars pushed major reforms in the classroom and in the front office.

In 1940, the Jesuits sought to develop a new approach for teaching theology to undergraduates, after years of complaints from students who found the neoscholastic approach boring or unrelatable. John Courtney Murray, SJ, one of the most prominent Jesuit theologians at the time, was entrusted with the task. Murray was a Boston College alumnus who had risen to prominence as a professor at the Jesuit seminary in Woodstock, Maryland; his publishing career had garnered attention even at non-Catholic universities, leading to a faculty appointment at Yale. Murray's revamped approach to theology education emphasized Catholic social teaching and used faith as a call to action, making the topic more approachable for the average layperson.[28] His

---

27. Marsden, *Soul*, 10–15.
28. Curran, *History of Georgetown Vol. II*, 158.

1965 book, *The Problem of God*, became the basis for required theology courses at Georgetown and elsewhere.

Administratively, the Jesuits were streamlining their campus bureaucracies to encourage innovation. In 1954, a committee within the Jesuit Educational Association recommended discontinuing the office of "regent" in graduate and professional schools. Most Jesuit schools of law, medicine, dentistry, etc. were still overseen by a Jesuit "regent" who ranked above the dean. The regent ensured some form of Jesuit control over the school, since relatively few Jesuits actually taught in the professional programs and since the deans themselves were often laypeople. In the most modest interpretation of the job, the regent simply served as the central university's representative. However, there was little consistency in the way that regents approached their role. As historian Paul Fitzgerald, SJ observed, "In theory, the lines were clearly drawn; in practice there could be gray areas. A strong dean might ignore the regent; a strong regent could intimidate a dean."[29] One example of the latter was Edmund Walsh, SJ, the regent of Georgetown's School of Foreign Service, who reigned with near impunity over a succession of deans for more than thirty years.

The committee's recommendation was controversial because many Jesuit university presidents still valued regents, who could ensure that the professional schools stayed true to the Jesuit mission.[30] Nonetheless, by the end of the 1960s most of the positions had been phased out. Often the incumbent Jesuit retained the title "regent," as long as he wanted, but after he stepped down or retired, he was not replaced. The position had come to be seen as an unnecessary level of bureaucracy that created two-headed monsters atop the professional schools and made decision-making more difficult.

The Chimera of National Cooperation

While the Jesuits were trying to reduce red tape within their campuses, they were (with good intentions) adding it at a national level. The Jesuit Education Association (JEA), under the leadership of Edward Rooney, SJ, was doing its best to coordinate graduate programs among the twenty-eight institutions. The original hope was that each Jesuit graduate school could develop strong doctoral programs in a handful of niche fields. The top Jesuit scholars in, say, literature would concentrate at one university while the top scholars in economics would all be assigned to another. This would reduce competition among the graduate schools and facilitate the rise of a few truly great doctoral programs that could supply the entire network with professors, all of whom had been trained by the best Catholic minds in their field.[31]

As good as this sounded in theory, it was next to impossible to coordinate in practice. As Paul Fitzgerald has noted, individual Jesuit university presidents were not eager to sacrifice their best professors to another school in the name of the greater good, and

---

29. Fitzgerald, *Governance*, 120.
30. Ibid., 121.
31. Ibid., 131–132.

it was hard to explain to a prospective student in New York why the only doctoral program available was in St. Louis.[32] College presidents were prone to do what was best for their institutions' survival, no matter what the Jesuit hierarchy had to say.

As head of the JEA, Father Rooney had significant power, and his approval was officially necessary to add new degree programs. But in trying to coordinate and improve the universities' development, Rooney also slowed it down. Some Jesuit college presidents skirted this red tape. Seattle University President Albert Lemieux, SJ, started a graduate program without Rooney's knowledge in 1958.[33] Seattle (the University) and Seattle (the city) were both growing rapidly, and Father Lemieux simply bypassed the Jesuit bureaucracy in order to meet the immediate needs of both.

In Paul Fitzgerald's definitive telling of the story, Jesuit authorities in Rome at the time were mainly concerned about three issues. As the American universities exploded in size, they would have to address 1) the large number of lay professors they were hiring, 2) the role of philosophy in the modern student experience, and 3) the overall Catholic and Jesuit mission of the universities. The first issue was deceptively straightforward. Laypeople were clearly here to stay, because there were not enough Jesuits to fill all teaching positions, but the Jesuits would have to decide how much decision-making power they would share with their lay co-workers. In time, non-Jesuit faculty members would demand input into how their institutions were managed, and the universities would be forced to create faculty senates and other deliberative bodies that had heretofore been completely absent on Jesuit campuses. Gone were the days in which virtually all professors had taken vows of obedience to the college president, so managing faculty became much more complicated.[34]

On the second issue (philosophy), the Jesuits held an important conference in Los Angeles in 1962 that helped to establish philosophy and theology as pillars of the "new," post-*Ratio Studiorum* undergraduate curriculum.[35] On the third issue—Catholic and Jesuit mission—a solution proved more difficult to articulate. By 1964, however, a coherent vision was emerging. That year, the JEA sponsored two transformative conferences (one at Georgetown in January and the other at Santa Clara in August) that addressed the "mission" issue. During the January meeting, Father Michael Walsh, SJ, (then-president of Boston College and future president of Fordham) argued that Jesuit universities could be truly *Jesuit* as long as they ensured, in Fitzgerald's words, "the caliber, training, and strategic location of Jesuits in the university community." This could be accomplished by keeping a Jesuit in the president's office and by strategically assigning one or two Jesuit faculty members to each university department. Jesuit identity was a matter of distribution, not numerical majorities.[36]

---

32. Ibid., 132–133.
33. Ibid., 146.
34. Ibid., 150–151.
35. Ibid., 156–157.
36. Ibid., 166.

At the Santa Clara meeting in August, the dominant view was that Jesuit college presidents should be allowed handle these issues themselves, without extensive supervision from Father Rooney, the JEA, or the local provincial. The universities were too big to be managed centrally. Decision-making had to be kept as close to the ground as possible, and the individual presidents (all of whom were Jesuits in good standing) should be trusted to handle their own affairs. This view was reinforced a few months later at a 1965 meeting in St. Louis. The Jesuits then set out to re-write the bylaws of the JEA to remove most of Father Rooney's authority and empower individual campus presidents to make their own decisions.[37]

The attitudes expressed at those 1964–65 meetings are notable in that they largely equated Jesuit *mission* with Jesuit *presence*. The key to maintaining a Jesuit identity was keeping Jesuits themselves on campus. It was not exactly a new idea; after all, in the nineteenth century, Jesuits occupied virtually all of the teaching positions in their small colleges. Now that the growth of the colleges had made that level of dominance impossible, Jesuit schools could ensure the authenticity of their mission by reserving specific positions on campus for priests. It was a reasonable solution, but it came at a time when vocations to the priesthood were at an all-time high and a steady supply of new Jesuits was taken for granted. It did not directly address what might happen in future generations if the pool of vocations became so small that it was impossible to find enough Jesuits willing and able to serve.

Jesuits were, however, already thinking about the longer-term implications of these decisions. The top education official in the Chicago Province, Father Robert Harvanek, SJ, argued as early as 1961 that the Jesuits would have no choice but to hand over control of their universities to laypeople as long as they continued to grow so quickly.[38] Even at this early date, the future direction of Jesuit higher education was obvious to those who stopped to think about it. But the high vocation rates of the 1960s may have given the Jesuits a false sense of security, or at least made the issue of lay control seem so distant that they felt comfortable kicking the can down the road. Many longer-term questions remained unanswered, but debates about the finer points of Jesuit college and university mission would have to wait until another day. After years of experimenting with different bureaucratic structures, the Jesuit college presidents were happy to have won the autonomy to make their own decisions without several layers of supervision up the Jesuit chain of command. It would take a few years for the implications of these decisions to play out, but by the end of the decade, American Jesuit colleges and universities would become fundamentally independent of the Jesuit hierarchy.[39]

37. Ibid., 165–168, 188. Varga, *Baltimore's Loyola*, 426.
38. Varga, *Baltimore's Loyola*, 442.
39. Ibid., 426. Fitzgerald, *Governance*, 188.

Vatican II (1962–1965)

Meanwhile, in Rome, historic changes were afoot. In 1958, the cardinals elected seventy-six-year-old Angelo Roncalli to the papacy, hoping tacitly that the frail old man would have a short and uncontroversial tenure. Short it was, lasting only five years, but Roncalli surprised almost everyone when, as Pope John XXIII, he led perhaps the most transformative papacy in modern history.

Sensing the spirit of change throughout the world in the 1960s and heeding calls for reform in the global church, Pope John XXIII called an ecumenical council—the highest form of church governance that, when in session, is more powerful even than the pope himself. It had been nearly 100 years since Pope Pius IX convened what came to be known as the First Vatican Council. (Despite its name, that gathering was, in fact, the twentieth ecumenical council in Church history; it was simply the first to take place at the Vatican.) In 1962, Pope John XXIII charged the Second Vatican Council with re-evaluating Catholic practices in light of modern society.

In its overall spirit, the Council sought to bring the Church closer to the people—redefining "the Church" to mean "the people of God," not the administrative apparatus centered in Rome. Priests would now celebrate Mass in the vernacular rather than in Latin, and would face the congregation rather than facing the altar. These and other symbolic changes sought to emphasize each priest's role as a shepherd accessible to his flock. Dioceses would be smaller so that bishops could interact more directly with the people. As a whole, the Church re-emphasized its social justice mission and engaged in more constructive dialogue with other religions and other Christian denominations, including Protestants and Jews, with which it had had confrontational relationships in the past.

Catholic education was only one part of the gargantuan agenda of Vatican II, but the Council sought to frame education in the same overall spirit of engagement and openness. It produced a *Declaration on Christian Education* that very generally encouraged Catholic schools (at all levels) to embrace the world as it truly is and to meet the people of God where they live.[40] The problems of an imperfect world could best be solved by teaching the people to act within it, not shielding them from it. One might say that the Catholic Church as a whole had finally embraced the traditional Jesuit philosophy of education four centuries after Ignatius and his colleagues introduced it.

On the subject of colleges and universities, the *Declaration on Christian Education* was characteristically vague, but it supported openness and modernity. It encouraged Catholic universities to teach and conduct research on all "individual subjects . . . according to their own principles, method, and liberty of scientific inquiry, in such a way that an ever deeper understanding of these fields may be obtained." It also encouraged the universities to promote "the harmony of faith and science," drawing upon the rich Catholic philosophical tradition and keeping a Catholic perspective relevant in

---

40. Fitzgerald, *Governance*, 189.

the modern world. Ideally, students would leave the Catholic university prepared to "undertake weighty responsibilities in society and witness to the faith in the world."[41]

The *Declaration* also urged Catholic universities to add theology departments "suited to lay students," develop world-class research institutes, and make themselves accessible to any student with ambition and promise.[42] In that respect, the document gave official Vatican approval to some major goals that Jesuit universities already were pursuing. Jesuits had (almost to a fault) long sought to make their schools accessible to as many students as possible, and they were already building their research capacity and experimenting with undergraduate theology programs. After Vatican II, many other Catholic universities run by other religious orders would follow suit.

Apart from the *Declaration*, Vatican II produced few policy statements that directly addressed higher education. Its most sweeping reforms came in other areas of Catholic life. However, the Council did introduce a number of changes that affected Jesuit colleges and universities indirectly. It called for more lay involvement in the management of Catholic institutions, which officially opened the door to for laypeople to lead Catholic universities. (Indeed, the Catholic University of America hired its first lay president in 1969, shortly after the Council concluded and long before any Jesuit university did so.) The Council also made the wearing of a religious uniform—or habit—optional for priests, nuns, and others with religious vocations. It was left up to each order to determine how its own members should dress. In the case of the Jesuits, the old floor-length black cassock and biretta cap soon went the way of the dodo. It became commonplace to see Jesuits in casual street clothes or in standard Roman collars that looked no different from those worn by diocesan priests. 120 years earlier, the Jesuits in New York, St. Louis, and elsewhere had worn everyday street clothes when they wanted to go into town *incognito* and avoid attracting mobs; now they wore such clothes as a matter of choice.

Vatican II also emphasized freedom of conscience. This meant that compulsory Mass attendance for Catholic students—which had already been on the decline at Catholic colleges—quickly disappeared at the few colleges that still had such rules in place. Nobody, least of all grown adults, could be forced to receive a sacrament, and authentic worship required the free will of the participants. As adults in their twenties replaced teenagers on college campuses, and as the Church hierarchy officially took a stand against such old practices, mandatory Mass became a thing of the past at virtually all Catholic universities.[43]

---

41. Paul VI, "Declaration on Christian Education, Gravissimum Educationis," The Holy See, October 28, 1965, http://www.vatican.va/archive/hist_councils/ii_vatican_council/documents/vat-ii_decl_19651028_gravissimum-educationis_en.html.

42. Ibid.

43. Varga, *Baltimore's Loyola*, 412–413.

Exodus of Priests

In the immediate wake of Vatican II, there was a mass exodus of Catholic priests from the priesthood. It was accompanied by an even greater wave of brothers and nuns who sought release from their religious vows or simply walked away. Reliable statistics on this phenomenon are difficult to find and most of the data that does exist has been pieced together through surveys and other unofficial sources, but it has been estimated that more than 3,400 American men left the priesthood in the four years immediately after Vatican II. Nearly 5,000 in total had walked away by 1975, ten years later.[44] New vocations, which had peaked in the years leading up to Vatican II, "slowed to a trickle for reasons that have been endlessly debated for the past fifty years with few agreed-upon conclusions."[45]

This phenomenon went far beyond the Jesuits, but the Jesuits certainly felt its effects. Their numbers in the United States fell from about 8,000 to about 5,000—a drop of almost 40%—in twenty-five years through a combination of older men leaving the order and fewer young men joining it.[46] Nationally, the total number of priests in the United States fell from almost 60,000 in 1970 to just under 36,000 in 2019. The declines were even more significant on the women's side of the Church, where the number of nuns fell from almost 161,000 to about 44,000 during the same period—a drop of nearly 73%. All of this came at a time when the country's Catholic population was growing.[47]

Ex-Jesuits, in general, had more marketable professional skills than most other ex-priests because they had earned PhDs (often at the Jesuit order's expense). Many were more than qualified to work at secular universities and could continue to pursue careers in academia. There were also cases in which men left the Jesuits but chose to remain priests, transferring their vows to a diocese or a different religious order. All of this was permissible under Church law as long as the proper procedures were followed and the proper dispensations were granted, but rarely in Church history has there been a time like the late 1960s, when so many cases presented themselves in such a short period of time. By 1969, a Jesuit researcher, Paul Reiss, SJ, predicted that within ten years only 5 percent of the professors at Jesuit colleges would be Jesuits. That prediction was accurate in at least some cases.[48]

Thus, Jesuit college administration between the 1960s and the early 2000s became an exercise in managing unprecedented growth at the student level while simultaneously managing unprecedented decline in the clerical level. Even without the

---

44. Gleason, *Contending*, 319.

45. Shelley, *Fordham*, 431.

46. Gleason, *Contending*, 319. Contosta, *Saint Joseph's*, 278.

47. Center for Applied Research in the Apostolate, "Frequently Requested Church Statistics," 2020, https://cara.georgetown.edu/frequently-requested-church-statistics/.

48. Varga, *Baltimore's Loyola*, 442. Center for Applied Research in the Apostolate, "Frequently Requested Church Statistics."

exodus from the priesthood, the Jesuits colleges would have had no choice but to hire large numbers of lay faculty and staff, but the exodus certainly accelerated the process.

Pedro Arrupe, SJ: A New Leader

While their Church and country were in the throes of change during the 1960s, the American Jesuit colleges also had to contend with the uncertainty of a new leader in Rome. In 1964, just as the American Jesuits were working out a new, less centralized management model for their schools, Superior General Jean-Baptiste Janssens, SJ, died. Elected as his replacement was the relatively young 57-year-old Pedro Arrupe, SJ, of Spain, whose leadership of the Society of Jesus would be transformative.

Father Arrupe was a committed progressive in the mold of Vatican II, and he embraced its reformist ideology wholeheartedly. It was he who coined the mantra, "Men for others," used so often to describe the mission of Jesuit higher education today. Arrupe was no stranger to the United States; as a young man, he had studied for the priesthood at St. Mary's College in Kansas (which was, at the time, functioning as the theological school of Saint Louis University). Early in his career, he was assigned to Japan, where he taught at a school near Hiroshima and rushed into the city almost immediately after it was destroyed by the atomic bomb to provide medical care to the victims.[49] That experience and others gave him a strong focus on the needs of the poor and marginalized, and under his leadership, the Society of Jesus reoriented itself heavily toward social justice issues. Symbolic of this change in priorities was a transition that took place in San Jose, California, in 1991. That year, the Jesuits relinquished control of the exquisite St. Joseph's Church to the local diocese, which quickly turned it into a Cathedral. In a trade deal, the diocese allowed the Jesuits to take control of Most Holy Trinity Church, an immigrant parish in a poor neighborhood across town. The Jesuits gave up control of the city's grandest and most historic parish in order to work with some of the city's most forgotten residents.

The Jesuit order under Arrupe developed a reputation for being progressive in its views. This did not sit well with some older Jesuits who still remembered a time, about sixty years earlier, when Jesuit schools were known for their ultra-conservative approach to education. Particularly during the 1960s and 1970s, there were "fierce polarities" within some Jesuit communities that pitted the older generation against the younger.[50] To be sure, similar generational divides were taking shape elsewhere around the country as the baby boomers reached young adulthood, but it was strikingly uncomfortable for older Jesuits accustomed to order and discipline. Thomas Shelley tells the story of a 1971 incident on the Fordham campus, where two young Jesuits protested the Vietnam War during their ordination ceremony. Terence Cardinal Cooke, the Archbishop of New York, had no sooner ordained the young men to the priesthood when one of them grabbed the microphone out of the cardinal's

---

49. Fitzgerald, *Governance*, 190.
50. Shelley, *Fordham*, 432.

hand and "launched into a denunciation of Cooke as a warmonger" because of his role as a vicar to the military. This brazen act of disrespect horrified the older Jesuits, but the cardinal kept his cool and simply offered messages of love and support for both the newly ordained men and for the military.[51]

Publish or Parish? Should the Jesuits Get Out of Higher Education?

Some "baby-boomer" Jesuits were so committed to social justice causes that they openly questioned whether the order should continue to sponsor colleges at all. After joining the Jesuits, many young men engaged principally in pastoral work in homeless shelters, hospitals, and other charities; they envisioned a ministry career more like that of a social worker than a university professor.[52] Volunteerism was in vogue; the Peace Corps had come into existence in 1961, and the Jesuits were busy creating a network of regional service programs that would evolve into today's Jesuit Volunteer Corps. Some young Jesuits felt that Catholic priests could do more good as managers in soup kitchens or as missionaries in remote foreign villages than as college professors locked in their ivory towers.[53] Even though the Jesuits had once seen their parish ministry and academic ministry as complementary, a new "publish or parish" dichotomy was taking shape. In Philip Gleason's words, "Some Jesuits . . . dismissed the colleges as 'practically useless,' and Daniel Berrigan, SJ, the most famous 'Catholic radical' of the day, carried the social reformers' anti-intellectualism to an extreme by characterizing scholarship as 'raw sewerage.'"[54]

The spirit of the younger Jesuits was not terribly radical in the grand scheme of Jesuit history. The Jesuits had been interested in helping the poor and promoting social equality since the time of St. Ignatius. Indeed, they had first gotten into the business of education as a means to that end. Through the nineteenth century, Jesuits had seen education primarily as a way to improve the lives of the poor and marginalized. In America, this meant that they opened schools in remote cities where access to education was severely lacking, and where they could provide education to boys who otherwise never would have received it. As those cities grew, that mission evolved, and the Jesuit schools refocused their efforts on providing free or low-cost college degrees to disadvantaged Catholic immigrants.

It was the business of higher education—not the Jesuits—that had changed most drastically. By the 1960s, most Americans had access to higher education and Jesuit colleges were no longer providing an essential service to the poor. Indeed, as private institutions, they were more expensive than community colleges and attracted a wealthier clientele. Catholics were increasingly assimilating into American society and the old immigrant mindset was beginning to fade. The traditional *raison d'etre* of Jesuit colleges was being turned on its head.

---

51. Ibid., 432–433, quote from 433.
52. Contosta, *Saint Joseph's*, 277.
53. Shelley, *Fordham*, 432. Varga, *Baltimore's Loyola*, 442.
54. Gleason, *Contending*, 319.

Previous generations of Jesuit college professors had spent most of their time teaching and mentoring students, but this generation was being pressured to conduct academic research. Some Jesuits embraced the scholarly lifestyle, but others openly questioned whether a priest's time was best spent publishing scientific papers that few would ever read. The Jesuits had not started colleges because they wanted to wear white coats in labs—they had started colleges because they wanted to wear black frocks among everyday people who needed their help. As academia continued to emphasize research productivity over student welfare, some Jesuits started to doubt whether St. Ignatius's old missionary order still belonged in academia.

Realistically, the Jesuits were never going to abandon the colleges that they had worked so hard to build. They had spent thirty years and untold sums of money training an entire generation of priests with PhDs, and the young voices who spoke out against the scholarly lifestyle were never more than a vocal fringe. Nonetheless, after branching out to Wheeling in 1954, the Jesuits stopped building colleges and refocused their expansionist energy toward high schools. Not only were high schools still relatively cheap to build, but they also allowed the Jesuits to focus completely on teaching and working with students—a ministry much closer to the traditional Jesuit comfort zone. Among the Jesuit high schools that opened during this era were Strake Jesuit in Houston (1960), Brebeuf Jesuit in Indianapolis (1962), St. John's Jesuit in Toledo (1965), and DeSmet Jesuit near St. Louis (1967).

In summary, even though most Jesuits remained committed to the future of Jesuit higher education, serious personnel challenges stood in their way. Although their commitments had never been higher (with twenty-eight rapidly growing colleges and universities under their control), they were losing unprecedented numbers of their own men to the post-Vatican II exodus, and some of their new vocations had little interest in higher education. One did not need a crystal ball to understand what this meant for the future. To remain viable, Jesuit colleges and universities would have to accept laypeople into positions of leadership and completely rethink their relationship to the Jesuit order. Just a few years after achieving unprecedented highs in both size and scope, Jesuit higher education was on the verge of unprecedented change.

Separate Incorporation

In the late 1960s, more than forty years of gradual decentralization in Jesuit higher education reached its logical conclusion. Jesuit universities—and indeed, virtually all Catholic universities in the United States—began to separate legally from the Church and from each other, incorporating as independent nonprofit institutions. Until then, most Jesuit colleges had been legally the property of the local Jesuit province (or at least, a broader corporation that included nearby Jesuit parishes and other ministries, as was the case in Philadelphia, Louisiana, New Mexico, and elsewhere). Now, the Society of Jesus and its universities would be separate legal entities.

The boards of trustees at most Jesuit colleges had, until then, consisted entirely of Jesuits. There were rare exceptions; in its early days in the 1850s, Santa Clara University had a board of trustees that included significant numbers of laypeople, but otherwise the laity had been almost completely absent from the schools' legal governing boards. Some Jesuit schools, like Seattle University and Regis University, experimented in the 1950s by creating advisory boards that included laypeople, but these boards only made recommendations to the Jesuits, who still wielded ultimate power.[55] That was all about to change. As independent institutions, each Jesuit college would incorporate under its own board of trustees.

Saint Louis University was ground zero. In 1967, President Paul Reinert, SJ, announced that the university would formally separate from the Missouri Province of the Society of Jesus and would no longer function under the province's ownership. Saint Louis and the University of Notre Dame in Indiana were the first two Catholic universities to cross that threshold in 1967, but within a handful of years virtually all American Catholic colleges and universities (including all twenty-eight Jesuit institutions) would follow. By the mid-1970s, there were virtually no Catholic colleges or universities left in the United States, Jesuit or otherwise, that were still owned and directly managed by the Catholic Church.

The changes that began in St. Louis redefined the legal relationship between the Jesuits and their universities. Specifics varied somewhat from institution to institution, but the basic principles were the same. Moving forward, the university president would be elected by vote of the board of trustees rather than appointed by the Jesuit provincial. Jesuits would be represented on those boards, but the majority of the voting trustees (and in virtually every case, the board chairs) would be lay.

The buildings in which the Jesuits lived on campus would legally separate from the rest of the university. Those buildings would remain the property of the local Jesuit province or would incorporate as a separate nonprofit organization, while the university would retain control over the remainder of the campus, including small chapels and other sacred spaces designed for student use. However, there was also the delicate fact that many Jesuit universities had large Catholic churches on their campuses that functioned not just as student chapels, but as parishes for the surrounding neighborhoods. Because it was inappropriate for a Catholic parish to fall under the control of laypeople, these large churches would separate from the rest of the university and function as independent parishes with their own pastoral staff. Priests assigned to the parish would not necessarily play any role at the university—a marked contrast from the days in which Jesuit college faculty doubled as pastors in the local community. Sometimes, this meant that the Jesuits established two separate communities of priests—one to staff the university and one to staff the parish—within walking distance of each other.[56]

The university would no longer provide direct financial support to the on-campus parish or to the Jesuit community. Instead, Jesuits who worked at the university

---

55. Crowley, *Seattle University*, 61. McKevitt, *University of Santa Clara*, 110. Stansell, *Regis*, 195.
56. Rizzi, "Cooperation," 152–153.

would be paid salaries, just like any other employee. The Jesuits' vows of poverty meant that they could not own anything, so any salaries they earned went into a common pool that the entire community, including retirees, could use. Although the universities would try to hire Jesuits whenever possible, the Jesuits were not guaranteed jobs; they would apply for open faculty and staff positions like any other candidate, albeit with some tacit special consideration.[57]

Although the universities could no longer rely on the Jesuits' free labor, the presence of Jesuit faculty still proved to be a financial boon to most schools. After meeting their own expenses, many Jesuit communities generously donated a portion of their collective income back to the universities. In 1977, the Fordham Jesuits returned almost a quarter-million dollars from their combined salaries to the university.[58] Some Jesuits refused to take a salary—including university presidents, who would have been paid an enormous sum if they had been compensated at market rates. Well into the twenty-first century, some Jesuit presidents—such as Boston College's William Leahy, SJ, Holy Cross's Philip Boroughs, SJ, Seattle University's Stephen Sundborg, SJ, and Xavier University's Michael Graham, SJ—worked for little or no direct compensation.[59]

These administrative changes did *not* mean that the universities were no longer Catholic or Jesuit. It simply meant that the Jesuits were now *sponsoring* the universities without *owning* them. This was a tricky concept to understand, even in the 1960s. In Rome, Pedro Arrupe asked his American colleagues for some clarification on this point before he approved the changes. The Catholic and Jesuit identity of the universities had been taken for granted when the Jesuits owned all property and centrally controlled all decisions. Now that even the university president was answerable to a lay-dominated board rather than the Jesuit hierarchy, what exactly defined the university as a Jesuit institution?[60]

The Catholic Church had never laid out minimum standards for what constituted a Catholic university, and it would not do so for another thirty years. Nor had it ever defined what responsibilities were incumbent upon a religious order that chose to "sponsor" any kind of school. However, the presumption was that a university remained "Catholic" as long as the Jesuits, a canonically recognized branch of the Catholic Church, identified it as one of the order's official ministries. The Jesuits who lived and worked on campus would serve as both the university's connection to the Church and the Church's immediate representatives to the university. Working with the lay faculty and staff, the Jesuit community would have collective responsibility for ensuring the university's Catholicity.[61]

---

57. Ibid., 153.
58. Shelley, *Fordham*, 446.
59. Rizzi, "Cooperation," 153.
60. Fitzgerald, *Governance*, 202.
61. Robert Emmett Curran, *A History of Georgetown University, Volume III* (Washington: Georgetown University Press, 2010), 9. Rizzi, "Cooperation," 154.

There were hiccups as Catholic religious orders and their universities started to work together as co-equal partners. At Georgetown, there was an ongoing dispute (which predated the 1960s) between the university and neighboring Holy Trinity Parish about which institution should have control of the parish's dilapidated burial ground, Holy Rood Cemetery. The result of this impasse was that Georgetown University (to this day) owns a large cemetery in Washington, DC, and it was not until 2018 that the university and parish embarked on a cooperative plan to maintain the property. In Baltimore, St. Ignatius Church was located on Loyola College's former campus on Calvert Street. Even after the church became independent of the college and the college relocated to more spacious quarters, Loyola still technically owned many of the vacated classroom buildings surrounding the church. As those structures deteriorated, neither the college nor the parish had the means or need to maintain them, and some of the property practically had to be given away to a third-party buyer.[62]

Naturally, some Jesuits opposed separate incorporation, believing that that the order had given up too much, too fast. The Society of Jesus had owned some of America's most recognized educational institutions, not to mention some extremely valuable real estate in the biggest cities in the country; its direct assets were now reduced to a few scattered buildings.[63]

Nonetheless, for the generation of Jesuits who pushed these reforms through in the 1960s and 1970s, separate incorporation brought tremendous benefits. First, it protected the Jesuit interest in the universities. For the first time, the Jesuit community owned property that belonged solely to the Society of Jesus, and was not simply reserved for its use by fickle university officials. This meant that the Jesuits were protected from any future attempts by the university to acquire their residence or force them off campus in the name of expansion. In an increasingly litigious society, it also meant that anyone with a grievance against the university would file lawsuits against the university itself, not against the Jesuit province.[64]

The same held true in reverse; separate incorporation meant that the universities were financially immune from future bankruptcies that would affect struggling Jesuit provinces. Moreover, the universities could keep all of their tuition revenue for themselves. In the past, the universities had subsidized other Jesuits ministries, as when Santa Clara University financially supported its spinoff Jesuit high schools in San Jose and Los Angeles during the 1920s through 1940s, or when revenue from Georgetown Hospital helped to pay construction costs for Georgetown Prep School in the 1920s. Previous Jesuit provincials had drawn upon the colleges' cash reserves for other charitable causes, since the colleges were some of the only Jesuit ministries that generated income.[65] Now, under separate incorporation, each university's finances were squarely in its own hands. Not surprisingly, many Jesuit universities began to professionalize

---

62. Varga, *Baltimore's Loyola*, 499.
63. Curran, *History of Georgetown Vol. III*, 9.
64. Ibid., 8. Kuzniewski, *Thy Honored Name*, 407. Rizzi, "Cooperation," 153, 155–156.
65. McKevitt, *University of Santa Clara*, 314. Rizzi, "Cooperation," 150.

their fundraising offices and hire full-time fundraising staff around this time. The Jesuits had done their best to raise money in the past, but it took separate incorporation to bring the colleges into the modern world of fundraising.

Separate incorporation also solved the persistent president-rector problem. The campus presidency was now a purely university-level position and carried no canonical responsibilities whatsoever. If a Jesuit were hired as a college president, he would simply seek his provincial's permission before accepting the position, and that permission would be freely given. Meanwhile, the provincial would appoint a rector to lead the Jesuit community on each campus, and that position would be strictly a Jesuit appointment with no responsibility to the university (though many rectors freely donated their time as adjunct professors or part-time counselors). Campus presidents at long last enjoyed the autonomy that their predecessors had coveted for decades and could make decisions as they saw fit. It was the equivalent of a modern-day public university suddenly learning that the state governor and legislature were stepping back and reducing their oversight authority. Moreover, presidents could now serve as long as they wanted (unless voted out by the board of trustees) and were no longer bound by a three-year term. In the second half of the twentieth century, it became common for Jesuit college presidents to serve for ten years or more. Eleven different men led Georgetown as president from 1898 to 1952, but only six different presidents served from 1952 to 2000.

Finally, it is important to remember that the finer legal arguments associated with separate incorporation seemed almost "academic" in the late 1960s. The Catholic mission and identity of the schools appeared secure because Jesuits remained solidly entrenched in the presidents' offices of all twenty-eight institutions, and because the postwar baby boom had produced a seemingly endless supply of Catholic students to populate the classrooms. Although there were some questions about how to live out a Jesuit mission in this new environment, the "on-the-ground" reality for most faculty, staff, and students did not noticeably change.

Separate incorporation was inevitable. The Jesuits had been working toward this goal implicitly or explicitly for decades, and it was no longer possible for a small club of about five thousand men to run twenty-eight colleges and universities by itself. After years of managing their education network internally, the Jesuits had shepherded those universities to a point of growth, complexity, and prestige that demanded a different leadership model. Moving forward, the Jesuits would be a supportive resource for the universities, not a privileged club of administrators. In the words of historian Robert Emmett Curran, "It was, in fact, the legal recognition that the familial university was no more."[66] Paul Fitzgerald, SJ, observes, "Having slipped their Roman moorings, these Jesuit institutions glided smoothly into the mainstream of American academic life and discovered that their vessels were seaworthy."[67]

---

66. Curran, *History of Georgetown Vol. III*, 9.
67. Fitzgerald, *Governance*, 188.

Most universities needed only a few years to iron out the basic details, which demonstrates how necessary the reforms were and how committed the Jesuits were to enacting them. In every case, two separate legal processes had to take place. First was the overhaul of the board of trustees from an all-Jesuit body to a larger board including laypeople, which (at minimum) required a revision of the documents the school had submitted to the state when it originally applied for its charter. Second was the separate incorporation of the Jesuit community and/or parish church as a non-profit organization independent of the university. Georgetown added laypeople to its board in 1966 and its Jesuit community separately incorporated in 1968.[68] Saint Louis passed the two milestones in reverse order, separately incorporating its Jesuit community in 1967 (which still qualifies it as the first to do so) and adding laymen to its board in 1968.[69] Holy Cross transitioned in 1969, and Marquette and the University of Detroit followed in 1970. Other schools started the negotiations in the late 1960s but needed a few more years to work out the details, such as Saint Joseph's of Philadelphia (1972), Boston College (1972), Saint Peter's (1972), Loyola of New Orleans (1972), and Fairfield (1973).

Legal Challenges to Catholic Education

Separate incorporation came, not coincidentally, at about the same time that a series of high-profile court cases challenged the constitutionality of government aid to religiously affiliated schools. These cases threatened the very lifeblood of Catholic colleges. Secularists in American society had mostly looked the other way when Catholic colleges benefitted from emergency military funds during World War II, but twenty years later, the colleges were becoming more and more reliant on federal student aid and research grants. It was only a matter of time before courts started to question whether tax dollars could be used in this way. The three most significant cases were *Horace Mann League v. Board of Public Works of Maryland* (1966), *Lemon v. Kurtzman* (1971), and *Tilton v. Richardson* (1971).

The *Horace Mann* case came down as a defeat for Catholic schools. The State of Maryland had provided construction grants for new buildings at four religious colleges—St. Joseph's College (now defunct), the College of Notre Dame, Western Maryland College (known today as McDaniel College), and Hood College. Secularists challenged the constitutionality of those grants in Maryland court. The judges ruled that Hood College, a Protestant institution, could accept the state money because its religious identity was fairly weak and inconsequential in the classroom, but that the other three colleges were too sectarian and therefore ineligible for the public funds. The Supreme Court of the United States refused to hear an appeal, which meant that precedent remained on the side of the secularists.

---

68. Curran, *History of Georgetown Vol. III*, 7–8.
69. Faherty, *Saint Louis University*, 44.

Loyola College in Baltimore was not party to the case, but the ruling made many Jesuits uneasy.[70]

In *Lemon v. Kurtzman*, the Supreme Court struck down attempts by state governments in Pennsylvania and Rhode Island to provide taxpayer money to non-public K-12 schools. Among other things, the funds were to be used to pay portions of teachers' salaries. While the case did not directly touch on Catholic higher education, it had vast implications for Catholic schools at lower levels, and the resounding 8–0 and 8–1 decisions (striking down the Pennsylvania and Rhode Island laws, respectively) offered clear warning that public funding for Catholic colleges could soon be in jeopardy.

The third case, *Tilton v. Richardson*, involved a Jesuit institution directly. A group of Connecticut social activists, including eight faculty members from the state's secular universities, filed a legal challenge to the Higher Education Facilities Act of 1963. On the basis of that law, Fairfield University and three other Catholic colleges in Connecticut (Albertus Magnus, Sacred Heart, and the now-defunct Annhurst) had accepted federal money for campus construction projects. In a narrow 5–4 decision, the Supreme Court ruled in favor of the Catholic schools, upholding the constitutionality of the 1963 law. Moving forward, this precedent meant that religiously affiliated colleges could legally use federal money to build classroom buildings, dormitories, and other facilities that had non-religious purposes. Even though Fairfield University's dorms contained small chapels, the court ruled that they were principally used for student housing, and that purpose was sufficiently secular to make Fairfield eligible for the government grants.[71]

In both the *Horace Mann* and *Tilton* cases, the attorneys for the Catholic schools were Jesuit-educated. Frank Gallagher, who argued on behalf of the religious colleges in *Horace Mann*, was a Loyola (Baltimore) alumnus. Edward Bennett Williams, who successfully represented the defendants in *Tilton*, held a bachelor's degree from Holy Cross and a law degree from Georgetown. However, the victory in the *Tilton* case was so narrow that few Catholic school administrators could sleep well in its aftermath. The courts were an eyelash away from denying public funding for Catholic schools, which could have disastrous implications for veterans and others who used government aid to pay tuition. In the aftermath of the *Horace Mann* case, Gallagher advised the Jesuit colleges to step up efforts to include laypeople on their boards, thereby avoiding the charge that they were directly controlled by church authorities. In Connecticut, in the midst of *Tilton*, Fairfield University of St. Robert Bellarmine removed the words "of St. Robert Bellarmine" from its seal so as not to draw attention to its religious nature.[72]

---

70. Varga, *Baltimore's Loyola*, 442–443. Fitzgerald, *Governance*, 294 (n. 11).

71. MacDonnell, *If These Stones Could Speak*, 14. Fitzgerald, *Governance*, 294–295 (n. 11).

72. Varga, *Baltimore's Loyola*, 443. Fitzgerald, *Governance*, 294–295 (n. 11). McDonnell, *If these Stones Could Speak*, 14.

The Land O'Lakes Statement (1967)

Even though separate incorporation provided some legal protection from judges and those who took a hardline view on the separation of church and state, it also introduced a new set of issues. Most importantly, how would Catholic universities maintain their religious mission? The laypeople who now served on the boards were thoroughly dedicated to the universities' Catholic identity, but history had shown that Protestant universities began to secularize shortly after reducing clerical control. Earlier in the century, universities like Chicago, Duke, Stanford, Vanderbilt, Northwestern, Southern California, Syracuse, Wake Forest, and much of the Ivy League, had already introduced lay governance, and in all of those cases, the new leadership model led to a gradual de facto or de jure secularization of the entire campus. Catholic schools hoped to avoid a similar fate.

The race was on to develop some sort of theory or mission statement that could guide the work of modern Catholic research universities at a time when lay control was the norm and old traditions like the *Ratio Studiorum* existed only in spirit. In 1967, a small group of Catholic university leaders and other Church officials met at Land O'Lakes, Wisconsin to draft such a position paper. Seven of the most prominent American Catholic research institutions were represented, including the Catholic University of America, the Catholic University of Puerto Rico, Seton Hall, Notre Dame, and four Jesuit institutions: Boston College, Fordham, Georgetown, and Saint Louis. Present were the archbishop of Atlanta and the auxiliary bishop of Newark (the latter of whom was also president of Seton Hall) and representatives of two foreign Catholic universities: Université Laval in Québec and the Pontificia Universidad Católica del Perú in Lima.[73]

The document they produced, known as the Land O'Lakes Statement, proved to be one of the most significant (and controversial) milestones in the history of Catholic higher education. The statement identified ten principles designed to bridge the gap between Catholic tradition and modern research. Most of these principles seem commonplace and uncontroversial today, but were innovative at the time. Most of the document urged Catholic universities to establish theology departments oriented toward teaching, research, and interdisciplinary dialogue. Even as late as 1967, remarkably few Catholic universities were doing so, and theology was still seen as a new, even faddish addition to the undergraduate curriculum outside of seminaries.[74] The statement called on Catholic universities to serve as "think tanks" for the Catholic Church—pursuing research on topics that matter to the Church and to the people it serves. It also drew attention to the university's role in forming responsible young

---

73. "Land O'Lakes Statement: The Nature of the Contemporary Catholic University" in *American Catholic Higher Education: Essential Documents, 1967–1990*, ed. Allice Gallin (Notre Dame, IN: University of Notre Dame Press, 1992), 12.

74. Hahnenberg, "Theodore M. Hesburgh," 933.

adults, preparing ethical citizens for public service in a diverse world. These ideas are uncontroversial and helpful in framing the mission of a Catholic research university.

Article One of the Land O'Lakes Statement, however, has generated six decades of debate. It declared, "The Catholic University today must be a university in the full modern sense of the word . . . (and) must have a true autonomy and academic freedom in the face of authority of whatever kind, lay or clerical, external to the academic community itself."[75] Philip Gleason famously described this line as a "declaration of independence" from the Church.[76] It was, certainly, an assertion that Catholic universities no longer needed direct management by the Church to have an authentically religious mission.

Some scholars identify the Land O'Lakes Statement as a "symbolic turning point" after which Catholic universities began to prioritize academic freedom over fidelity to their religious roots.[77] Many conservative Catholics consider the statement a serious blow to the authenticity of the universities' religious mission by circumventing the Church's role as a teaching authority. However, the impact of the statement is sometimes exaggerated: Catholic universities had their fair share of disagreements with the Church even when they *were* under direct Church control.[78] Recall that Father Peter Kenney was appalled when he visited Saint Louis University in the 1830s and discovered that the frontier Jesuits were taking extreme liberties with the *Ratio Studiorum* curriculum. Another Jesuit inspector, Father Felix Sopranis, had the same reaction when he visited St. Ignatius College in San Francisco in the 1850s. Recall also that Jesuit colleges sometimes ignored direct orders from provincial authorities—as when Georgetown continued to play football in the early 1900s after its provincial banned the sport, or when Seattle University started new graduate programs without approval from the Jesuit Educational Association. For that matter, Jesuits had founded *entire colleges* (like St. Aloysius College in Louisville and Santa Clara University in California) against the wishes of their Roman superiors. It would be wrong, therefore, to assume that Catholic universities would be more obedient if only they remained under direct Church management.

The 1960s marked a turning point in Catholic higher education, but we should not attribute too much influence to a three-day conference that took place at that time. Generations of dedicated Catholic educators had pushed for the reforms of the late 1960s, and those reforms would have been necessary with or without the Land O'Lakes Statement. Moreover, the 1950s and 1960s were not "typical" decades for the Catholic Church in the United States. At no time in American history have Catholics represented a bigger proportion of the population, nor have there ever been more priests and nuns available to teach, nor had there been (to that point) so many Catholic young people with the means to attend college. In the decades following the

---

75. "Land O'Lakes Statement," 7.
76. Gleason, *Contending*, 317.
77. Ibid., 317.
78. Rizzi. "We've Been Here Before," 166–167.

Land O'Lakes Statement, many Catholic universities did indeed begin to look differ-ent; among other things, they became more diverse they had been at midcentury. This, however, was mainly because the demographics of America—especially in the large cities where most Catholic schools were located—were changing. To a generation that only had the 1950s as a reference point, these changes seemed unusual, but they were not unprecedented. In fact, with the exception of the baby boom era of the 1950s and the immigrant boom around the turn of the twentieth century, the enrollment at many Catholic universities has been religiously diverse more often than it has been overwhelmingly Catholic.[79]

The Land O'Lakes Statement was a pragmatic attempt to adapt Catholic tradition to modern academic culture, and its main goal was not to upend that tradition, but to keep it viable and ensure that it survived. Many of the statement's recommendations, like the need to sponsor theology departments and the importance of interdisciplinary dialogue, have become so second-nature to Catholic universities that it can be easy to forget how groundbreaking they were at the time. It is unfortunate that the controversy over Article One tends to overshadow the wisdom in the overall statement, especially because this "declaration of independence" neither caused independence from the Church nor cut any lines of authority that had worked particularly well in the past.[80]

The Denver Workshop (1969)

Although it is not nearly as famous as the Land O'Lakes Conference of 1967, the Jesuit Educational Association hosted its own conference two years later to map out the future of Jesuit higher education. Ninety-three delegates, including presidents, provincials, faculty members, deans, and students (including some women) converged in Denver in August, 1969. The conference was officially titled, "Jesuit Universities and Colleges: Their Commitment in a World of Change," but informally it came to be known as the "Denver Workshop." As one attendee wrote, "The last meeting of this kind was in 1962, and it might as well have been 1562—so much has changed."[81]

The documents and recommendations that emerged from the Denver Workshop reflect a sense of optimistic adaptation. The participants knew they were living in a time of great change, saw that change as both positive and inevitable, and believed that Jesuit tradition could successfully adapt to a new reality. One attendee reported "a remarkable degree of unanimity on such things as separate incorporation, lay trustees, (and) the social and civic orientation of liberal arts programs."[82]

Participants in the Denver Workshop expressed an overarching belief that Jesuit tradition could and did fit into modern paradigms for education. St. Ignatius

---

79. Ibid., 171–172.

80. Ibid., 167. Rizzi, "Newman's *Idea*," 39, 43–44.

81. James M. Somerville, "Commitment in a World of Change," *Jesuit Educational Quarterly* 32, no. 2 (October 1969): 61–64, quote and data from p. 61.

82. Ibid., 61.

had always urged his followers to be flexible and adapt to the customs of the country in which they worked, so it was entirely in character for Jesuit universities to change with the times. What the Jesuits were attempting was new, but it fit easily within the Ignatian legacy. Saint Louis University's reformist president, Paul Reinert, SJ, pointed out that "delegation and diffusion of authority is really in accordance with the spirit of the Society and our earliest traditions. Saint Ignatius urged, and in his own administrative practice demonstrated that decisions should be made at the level of close contact with reality."[83]

At the same time, Jesuit universities had something unique to contribute to American academia because of St. Ignatius's "world-affirming spirituality," which emphasized the importance of finding God in all things.[84] Modern research could itself be a religious act, a form of "secular mysticism" wholly compatible with the best of the Ignatian spiritual tradition. The changes taking shape in the Church and in the United States were seen as evidence of God's work in the world, and Jesuit universities would embrace those changes, helping to shape them in a positive direction that affirmed the inherent goodness of creation and the dignity of all people.[85]

To be sure, the participants in the Denver Workshop had many serious concerns, including the projected decline in priests (which ended up being far more severe than they imagined), and uncertainty about whether the Jesuits could maintain a network of twenty-eight large and autonomous institutions.[86] The conference concluded, however, with a sense of "grand hopefulness."[87]

Following the Denver Workshop, the Jesuits charged forward with their plans for modernization. They were so confident in their reformist agenda that they implemented it across the board, even at small colleges with no ambition to become research institutions. Nicholas Varga observes that the Denver Workshop marks the point at which "the Jesuits extended the principles enunciated at Land O'Lakes to their colleges as well as to their universities. These developments made academic freedom, tenure, and faculty participation in governance the general rule."[88]

Later in 1969, the Jesuit Educational Association published and widely circulated a report, *Guidelines for Jesuit Higher Education: The Consensus Statements, Recommendations, and Committee Reports of the J.E.A. Denver Workshop on Jesuit Universities and Colleges.* It became a guidebook for Jesuit college presidents and trustees seeking to modernize their campuses.

---

83. Paul Reinert, SJ, "The Imperatives Determining the Future of Jesuit Higher Education," *Jesuit Educational Quarterly* 32, no. 2 (October 1969): 65–66.

84. Joseph A. O'Hare, SJ, "Jesuit Education in America," in *The Jesuit Tradition in Education and Missions: A 450-Year Perspective*, ed. Christopher Chapple (Scranton: University of Scranton Press, 1993), 153.

85. Brown, "Learning," 79–108, 89–90.

86. Charles F. Donovan, "The Liberal Aims of Jesuit Higher Education," *Jesuit Educational Quarterly* 32, no. 2 (October 1969): 94–95.

87. Brown, "Learning," 105.

88. Varga, *Baltimore's Loyola*, 438.

The JEA Becomes the AJCU

The final administrative hurdle to clear as the Jesuit colleges moved toward autonomy was the Jesuit Educational Association, which still had bylaws that gave it approval power over new degree programs and other details on all twenty-eight campuses. The JEA put up no resistance. After the powerful Father Edward Rooney stepped down from the JEA presidency in 1966, he was succeeded by Paul Reinert, SJ, the reform-minded Saint Louis University president. Under Father Reinert's leadership, the JEA would never stand in the way of modernization he saw as urgent and essential.

In 1969, the Jesuits began serious talks to replace the JEA with something looser and less powerful. A year later, they formally dissolved the JEA and spun off two main successor organizations—the Association of Jesuit Colleges and Universities (AJCU), and the Jesuit Secondary Education Association. The AJCU was designed from the beginning to be an association, not a governing body—one that would provide a framework for dialogue and cooperation in Jesuit higher education without exerting direct power. Its role would be mainly consultative, not authoritative—and to ensure that this remained the case, its governing board would consist of the college presidents themselves. For the first few decades of the AJCU's existence, the college presidents ensured that it stayed small, with minimal staff and limited activity. In the 1990s and beyond, however, the AJCU developed into an excellent support network for Jesuit higher education, organizing annual conferences for all types of professionals—from campus ministers to registrars. In general, the scarcer Jesuits became on campus, the more active—and proactive—the AJCU became in developing strategies, publishing guidebooks, and hosting events designed to keep the Ignatian spirit alive at the universities. The Jesuits had a significant head start in these efforts compared to other Catholic religious orders; while the Association of Catholic Colleges and Universities had existed since 1899, the Franciscans, Benedictines, Sisters of Mercy, and others did not form independent associations for their own institutions until the 1990s or later.

Father Paul Reinert's progressive agenda, in a sense, made this rapid change possible. He formally stepped down as president of Saint Louis University in 1974, but his presence continued to loom large. In fact, it became nearly impossible to find a Jesuit willing to take his place at Saint Louis, since most assumed (correctly, as it turned out) that the larger-than-life Reinert would still have a great deal of power on campus. During Reinert's tenure in office, Saint Louis University had not just pioneered a new governance model; it had also become the first American university in any former slave state to integrate African-Americans and had gone fully coeducational by admitting women to all of its programs. Reinert's career therefore encapsulated all three of the major changes that took place at Jesuit universities in the mid-1900s. In retirement, he worked mainly to revitalize the city of St. Louis's urban slums and became a respected civic leader. However, not all of his legacies were positive; twenty-five years of his aggressive and ambitious leadership virtually bankrupted

Saint Louis University, and his administration made the controversial decision to remove most of the religious symbols from the Saint Louis University classrooms. His successors reversed those mistakes, but only at great cost.[89]

Full Coeducation

By the 1960s, it was not unusual to see women on Jesuit campuses. For most Jesuit universities, coeducation was a gradual process that took shape incrementally, not in one dramatic turn. It began with the graduate and professional schools, even as the undergraduate liberal arts colleges remained exclusively male. At first, most Jesuit law schools, dental schools, and other professional schools admitted women only in small quotas or limited them to evening courses. By the 1970s, these quotas had disappeared and women were enrolling in every program on campus.

Piecemeal coeducation was administratively awkward and academically hard to justify. Women were on the same campus as men but were only allowed to enroll in certain degree programs. At Georgetown in 1950, for example, the Graduate School and the Schools of Medicine, Dentistry, and Foreign Service were all coeducational; the Law School and undergraduate liberal arts College were all-male; and the Nursing School was all-female. Yet even in the College and the Nursing School, male and female students saw each other daily on campus and were allowed to cross-register and take classes together. Women were therefore sitting in the same undergraduate classes as their male counterparts, but unable to earn the same degrees. This arrangement began to seem ridiculous and unjust. At times, it was openly duplicitous; during the 1920s and 1930s, Saint Louis University allowed women to take regular undergraduate courses and earn bachelor's degrees, but technically registered all female students in its School of Education so that it could report that its college division remained exclusively for men.[90] A number of other Jesuit universities used similar methods to keep women on campus while reporting to their superiors that the all-male tradition remained alive and well.

Even before World War II, many Jesuit universities were coeducational in everything but name. Women were small minorities in some degree programs, but as early as 1938 they represented about 10,500 of the 41,800 students enrolled in Jesuit higher education, or 25%.[91] The last single-sex bastions were the undergraduate colleges and the nursing schools, and those barriers began to disappear by the 1950s. In a process that peaked in the 1960s, Jesuit nursing programs started to admit men and liberal arts programs started to admit women.

---

89. Faherty, *Saint Louis University*, 46–54.

90. Curran, *History of Georgetown Vol. III*, 73–74. Adrianna Smith, "Fifty years of Women at Georgetown College," *Georgetown Magazine* 51, no. 2 (Spring 2020): 32–33. William P. Leahy, SJ, *Adapting to America: Catholics, Jesuits, and Higher Education in the Twentieth Century* (Washington: Georgetown University Press, 1991), 83.

91. Leahy, *Adapting*, 77.

Although it is sometimes difficult to pinpoint the exact year when a university went "fully" coeducational, the date its undergraduate programs admitted women is generally a good representation. Marquette University pioneered in this category. The university had made history when it first enrolled women in a summer training program for teachers in 1909, but that was only the first of many quick and surprisingly comprehensive steps toward coeducation. Its president, Father James McCabe, opened a permanent undergraduate division for women (staffed by the Sisters of Charity) in 1911—making Marquette the first Catholic men's university in the United States to sponsor dedicated bachelor's degree programs for women.[92]

Outside of Milwaukee, coeducation took root earliest in the relatively liberal west—where most states had guaranteed women the right to vote long before the federal government had done so—and somewhat surprisingly in the conservative South. Catholic women's colleges (and Catholics in general) were rare in the South, so coeducation was a practical necessity; Jesuit colleges needed the students, and Catholic women (including nuns) needed the educational opportunity. Spring Hill College in Alabama sought permission from Rome to enroll women in the 1930s, claiming that it could not find enough local Catholic men to fill its classrooms. Jesuit General Wlodimir Ledóchowski denied the request, advising Spring Hill to close rather than admit female students. Fortunately, Spring Hill kept itself afloat by compromising and allowing women to enroll in Saturday classes.[93]

Loyola University (New Orleans) used the same method to grant bachelor's degrees to women as early as the 1920s, even though it technically registered all of them in its evening and weekend division. In fact, women accounted for an enormous percentage of Loyola's graduates during that decade, including "all 13 A.B.s awarded in 1922, and 12 of the 14 awarded in 1923."[94] Quite a few of Loyola's female students were nuns drawn from the large convents in and around New Orleans, but laywomen were well represented. Including professional schools, women made up a third of Loyola's total enrollment in 1927. By the 1930s, Loyola had a sorority, a homecoming queen, and multiple women on its student council; women in its School of Education had unfettered access to virtually all classes on campus. And yet, the university was still assuring Wlodemir Ledóchowski and other Jesuit authorities in Rome that its undergraduate college was all-male.[95]

Seattle College was more brazen in its moves toward coeducation; it admitted women to its bachelor's degree programs unilaterally in 1931, without approval from Rome or the local bishop. Seattle's decision raised eyebrows throughout the Church

---

92. Ibid., 73–74. Before Marquette opened its women's division, both Duquesne and DePaul Universities admitted some women individually to their bachelor's degree programs. They may, therefore, have some claim to being the first coeducational Catholic undergraduate programs, but Duquesne's decision was ad hoc and records of DePaul's decision are vague. See Rishel, *Spirit*, 32, 40.

93. Leahy, *Adapting*, 79.

94. Cook, *Founded on Faith*, 75.

95. Ibid., 75, 85, 111, 117.

hierarchy, but the college initially skirted those objections by invoking the usual loop-hole: it claimed that all of its female students were enrolled in its evening extension school (even though there were hardly any restrictions on what classes they could take). By 1933, Seattle openly acknowledged that it was fully co-educational.[96] With less fanfare, the University of Detroit also began admitting women to its bachelor's degree programs in 1931, initially limiting them to majors in education and social sciences. Detroit was already admitting women liberally to its law school and business school, and in the midst of the Great Depression, it desperately needed extra tuition revenue. The university's leaders agreed that women were "to be encouraged to attend . . . Catholic women's colleges. But it was felt that the University could not close its doors to Sisters and lay women who insisted on coming."[97] By the mid-1930s, women were competing on Detroit's elite debate teams and, by the wartime year of 1944, forty percent of Detroit's students were female.[98]

Although Seattle and Marquette were forthright about enrolling women, schools including Detroit, Loyola, and Spring Hill remained almost secretive about it until the late 1940s, when the Society of Jesus formally dropped its objections to coeducation as a matter of policy.[99] Gonzaga (Spokane) became fully co-ed in 1948, Saint Louis in 1949, Creighton in 1951, Spring Hill in 1952, Loyola (New Orleans) in 1956, and Santa Clara in 1961. Most other Jesuit schools, however, took substantially longer to cross that threshold and did not fully open their doors to women until after Vatican II. The last to transition in the early 1970s were the more conservative schools on the East Coast—including Holy Cross, which had no graduate or professional programs and therefore no tradition of enrolling women.

Although many Jesuit universities initially planned to recruit women only in limited numbers, the undergraduate programs were soon overwhelmed with female applicants.[100] Universities scrambled to build women's dorms in the 1970s, but given the limited space on the mostly urban campuses, many Jesuit colleges found that the only solution was to make their existing dorms co-ed. In 1969, Campion Hall at Seattle University became the first co-ed dorm at any American Jesuit college.[101] By the 1990s, women outnumbered men on virtually every Jesuit campus.

The list below indicates when each Jesuit college or university became *fully* coeducational, even though, in almost all cases, women had enrolled in specific degree programs much earlier. Included are LeMoyne College and Wheeling University, which were coeducational from the day they opened in 1946 and 1955, respectively. Both deserve some credit for anticipating a trend that was not fully developed elsewhere in the Jesuit network.

---

96. Crowley, *Seattle University*, 45–46.
97. Muller, *University of Detroit*, 172.
98. Ibid., 203, 211.
99. Leahy, *Adapting*, 85. Crowley, *Seattle University*, 52.
100. Shelley, *Fordham*, 382–385. Curran, *History of Georgetown Vol. III*, 74–75.
101. Crowley, *Seattle University*, 84.

Date	School	Notes
1911	Marquette University, *Milwaukee, WI*	First fully co-ed Catholic university in the United States
1931	Seattle University, *Seattle, WA*	
1931	University of Detroit, *Detroit, MI*	Women initially limited to specific majors within the bachelor's degree
1946	Le Moyne College, *Syracuse, NY*	Coeducational from the day it opened
1948	Gonzaga University, *Spokane, WA*	
1949	Saint Louis University, *Saint Louis, MO*	
1951	Creighton University, *Omaha, NE*	Women admitted to summer school since 1913. A majority-female evening school, the University College, was organized in 1932.[102]
1952	Spring Hill College, *Mobile, AL*	
1955	Wheeling University, *Wheeling, WV*	Coeducational from the day it opened
1956	Loyola University, *New Orleans, LA*	Women had been awarded bachelor's degrees on an individual basis since the 1920s.
1961	Santa Clara University, *Santa Clara, CA*	
1964	University of San Francisco, *San Francisco, CA*	
1964	Fordham University, *New York, NY*	Operated separate undergraduate college for women on campus 1964–1974; men's and women's colleges merged 1974.
1965	Canisius College, *Buffalo, NY*	
1966	Loyola University, *Chicago, IL*	
1966	Saint Peter's University, *Jersey City, NJ*	
1968	John Carroll University, *Cleveland, OH*	
1968	Loyola Marymount University, *Los Angeles, CA*	Formally merged with Marymount College in 1973 after sharing a campus for five years.
1968	Regis University, *Denver, CO*	
1969	Georgetown University, *Washington, DC*	
1969	Rockhurst University, *Kansas City, MO*	
1969	Xavier University, *Cincinnati, OH*	
1970	Boston College, *Chestnut Hill, MA*	

102. Mihelich, *History of Creighton*, 166–169.

Date	School	Notes
1970	Fairfield University, *Fairfield, CT*	
1970	Saint Joseph's University, *Philadelphia, PA*	
1970	University of Scranton, *Scranton, PA*	
1971	Loyola University Maryland, *Baltimore, MD*	Became co-ed after merger with Mount St. Agnes College
1972	College of the Holy Cross, *Worcester, MA*	Last American Jesuit college to admit women

Merging with Women's Colleges

As Jesuit universities went coeducational, some Catholic bishops worried about the long-term effects that decision would have on Catholic women's colleges.[103] Colleges run by nuns faced the same challenges as those run by priests—dwindling vocations, separate incorporation, and pressure to grow rapidly—but they often had no endowments to speak of and were in even worse condition than the men's colleges financially. Now, they were losing hundreds if not thousands of potential students.

Some Catholic women's colleges responded by going coeducational in their own right, although many did not do so immediately. By the early 2000s, the overwhelming majority had started to admit men. For many Catholic women's colleges, however, the pressures were too great, and the only viable options were to close or to merge with a better-financed men's college nearby.

Several Jesuit universities absorbed Catholic women's colleges, and in some cases, that merger was the trigger that led to full coeducation. The terms of the agreements and their long-term legacies varied widely. In Detroit and Los Angeles, the nuns joined the Jesuits as co-equal sponsors of the resulting university. In other cases, as in Boston and New Orleans, a few buildings on the physical campus are all that remain of the former women's college.

Early Experiments in St. Louis and Omaha

The first meaningful partnerships between Jesuit universities and nearby Catholic women's colleges emerged in the Midwest. Beginning in 1926, Saint Louis University entered into a "corporate college" arrangement with Fontbonne College (Sisters of St. Joseph), Maryville College (Religious of the Sacred Heart of Jesus), and Webster College (Sisters of Loretto), which gave the women at those schools access to Saint Louis University facilities and enabled them to participate in extracurricular activities like drama alongside the men. Two Catholic junior colleges and a Catholic teacher's college in the St. Louis area (all now defunct) were also part of the grouping. While most

---

103. See McKevitt, *University of Santa Clara*, 285.

of their actual instruction took place on their own campuses, the women formally received degrees from Saint Louis University alongside degrees from their home institutions. Faculty at the six partner colleges technically became faculty at Saint Louis. This relationship continued for about two decades but fizzled out after Saint Louis University itself went fully co-educational.[104]

In Omaha, Creighton University entered into a similar relationship with two local women's colleges in the 1920s: the College of St. Mary (Sisters of Mercy) and Duchesne College (Religious of the Sacred Heart of Jesus), the latter of which is today a high school. Because Creighton, like Saint Louis, was accredited by the North Central Association, the women's colleges could offer degrees under Creighton's umbrella. Both schools briefly constituted all-women's divisions of Creighton University, but the arrangement ended in 1936. By then, the women's colleges had grown strong enough to seek accreditation independently, which required them to dissociate from the university.[105]

Although they were innovative, these "corporate college" experiments did not result in any permanent affiliations among the schools in Missouri or Nebraska.

Loyola University (Los Angeles), Marymount College, and St. Joseph's College (1968)

The first (and perhaps the most complex) true merger between a Jesuit college and a women's institution took place in Los Angeles. By the 1960s, there were four Catholic women's colleges in the greater Los Angeles area: Immaculate Heart College (Sisters of the Immaculate Heart of Mary), Marymount College (Religious of the Sacred Heart of Mary), Mount St. Mary's College (Sisters of St. Joseph of Carondolet), and St. Joseph's College (Sisters of St. Joseph of Orange). Immaculate Heart and its sponsoring order were fiercely independent and clashed often with the local archbishop, James Cardinal McIntyre, who opposed many of the reforms of Vatican II and made it difficult for nuns in his archdiocese to implement them. The college closed in 1981. Mount St. Mary's is now a university and is one of the few remaining women's colleges on the West Coast. Marymount and St. Joseph's ultimately joined forces with the Jesuits' Loyola University to form Loyola Marymount University.

Marymount College traced its roots to a junior college that the Religious of the Sacred Heart of Mary (RSHM Sisters) opened in 1933. It started to offer four-year degrees in 1948. St. Joseph's College, which was always a small institution, began life as a school exclusively for nuns shortly after the Sisters of St. Joseph built a motherhouse in Orange County in the 1920s. By the 1960s, it was enrolling lay women. The

---

104. Tracy Schier and Cynthia Russett, eds., *Catholic Women's Colleges in America* (Baltimore: Johns Hopkins University Press, 2002), 348–349. See also Faherty, *Saint Louis University*, 23–24. Garraghan, *Jesuits of the Middle U.S. Vol. III*, 443.

105. Mihelich, *History of Creighton*, 169–171.

RSHM Sisters and Sisters of St. Joseph joined forces in 1967 and began to operate the two women's colleges as a single institution under the Marymount name. The combined school offered two-year associate's degrees and four-year bachelor's degrees on both campuses.

The two communities of sisters wanted their most ambitious students to have access to the resources of a major Catholic university, and negotiated with the Jesuits at Loyola about creating a new partnership. In 1968, the sisters consolidated all four-year bachelor's degree programs for women into a single location, moving them to the spacious Loyola campus overlooking Marina del Rey. At first, Marymount College remained independent, but its students could take classes at Loyola and benefitted from access to the Loyola libraries and other amenities. In addition to the four-year campus that it shared with Loyola, Marymount continued to offer two-year programs on its two original campuses in Orange County and the Palos Verdes Peninsula.

The old St. Joseph College campus rebranded as Marymount College of Orange, but eventually closed. At Loyola, the men's and women's schools shared a campus for five years before acknowledging that they could save money by combining their operations and eliminating the need for two sets of administrators. In 1973, Loyola University merged with the four-year division of Marymount College, and Loyola Marymount University was born. The RSHM Sisters and the Sisters of St. Joseph joined the Jesuits as co-sponsors of the combined school, making Loyola Marymount one of the few Catholic universities sponsored by three different religious orders.

The 1973 merger did not, however, include the two-year Marymount campus in Palos Verdes. That campus continued to operate as an independent junior college under RSHM auspices, and by the 1980s, it expanded its offerings to include bachelor's degrees. It became known as Marymount California University, and despite the similarities between their names, it had no connection to the Jesuit institution across town. In 2022, its enrollment weakened by the coronavirus pandemic, Marymount California University announced plans to close after an attempt to merge with an out-of-state university fell through.

Loyola College (Baltimore) and Mount St. Agnes College (1971)

In Baltimore, Loyola College was already cooperating with two women's colleges by the 1960s: the College of Notre Dame, which sat on an adjacent campus, and Mount St. Agnes College, located about three miles north in the city's Mount Washington neighborhood. The three schools began merger discussions, but negotiations were complicated because the women's colleges had much less money to contribute to any potential partnership than Loyola.[106]

Mount St. Agnes College was a project of the Sisters of Mercy and dated to 1870. Although it initially hoped to be a co-equal partner in any merger, its enormous debt and operating deficits ultimately made such a deal impossible. In 1970, Loyola offered

---

106. Varga, *Baltimore's Loyola*, 472–476.

to acquire the school's human resources—which included about 400 students and twenty-five faculty and staff for whom it could find room on its payroll. Mount St. Agnes had little choice but to accept this offer, since the alternative was closure. More than a dozen Sisters of Mercy came along with the deal, but since it was more an acquisition than a merger, the Sisters did not become co-sponsors of Loyola as had happened in Los Angeles. They merely became Loyola employees, some of them for many years. Loyola thus became a coeducational institution all at once in 1971, and the original Mount St. Agnes campus was sold to cover debts. That property is today a branch campus of the Johns Hopkins University.[107]

Ironically, the College of Notre Dame (now known as Notre Dame of Maryland University) never merged with Loyola despite being located directly adjacent to it. Sponsored by the School Sisters of Notre Dame, the historic institution was the first Catholic women's college to award a bachelor's degree in the United States in 1899. Although it entered into merger discussions with Loyola on multiple occasions, the talks always fell through because of financial disparities, differences in the way the schools defined tenure, or other reasons. The still-separate schools do, however, share a library, which they built jointly in 1973 on the land between them.

Fordham University, the Thomas More College for Women (1974), and Marymount College (2000)

Fordham's experience with coeducation was unique. In 1964, it opened Thomas More College as a separate college for women on its campus in The Bronx. This arrangement was similar in spirit to the relationship between Columbia University and Barnard College in Manhattan; men would enroll at Fordham College and women would enroll at Thomas More College, and they would take classes near each other but typically not together. Unlike Barnard, Thomas More would be a constituent unit of Fordham University led by a Jesuit dean, not a loosely affiliated school led by its own president.

Coming slightly before the end of Vatican II, Fordham's decision to open Thomas More College was barely ahead of its time. Jesuit authorities in Rome questioned whether it was appropriate for the Society of Jesus to run a women's college. The hierarchy had just recently (and somewhat begrudgingly) accepted coeducation, but it was almost unheard of for the Jesuits to operate any school exclusively for women. Despite the controversy, Thomas More College thrived. It existed for ten years before the Fordham administration decided to merge the men's and women's colleges in 1974 as a cost-saving measure. Thus, 1964 marks the point at which Fordham went fully co-ed, but 1974 was the milestone year in which it fully integrated its classes. Ironically, because Fordham was ahead of other Jesuit institutions in the first regard, it was behind other institutions in the latter.[108]

---

107. Ibid., 475.
108. Shelley, *Fordham*, 382–385.

The 1972 Title IX legislation, which mandated equal opportunities for women in (among other areas) college sports, presented a problem for Fordham. Fordham's athletic teams were traditionally known as the Rams, which by definition are male. The university had to decide whether to refer to its women's teams as the Ewes (which did not seem particularly intimidating), as the Lady Rams (an oxymoron), or some other appellation. Ultimately, Fordham called all of its teams by a single name—Rams. Other universities, like Saint Peter's (Peacocks), Syracuse (Orangemen), Duquesne (Dukes), and Virginia Tech (Gobblers—that is, male turkeys), wrestled with the same problem.

Fordham's merger with Thomas More College was an exclusively internal affair, but the university pursued an external merger as well. In 2000, it announced that it was acquiring Marymount College, a women's college located in New York's Hudson Valley. As the similarity in its name implies, this Marymount was, like the one in Los Angeles, sponsored by the Religious of the Sacred Heart of Mary. The RSHM Sisters established it in 1907, but by the early 2000s, it was facing serious financial and enrollment problems much like other women's colleges that had refused to admit men. Fordham pledged to continue to operate Marymount as an all-female branch campus as long as possible, but after five years, the merger had not led to any significant increase in enrollment. Fordham formally closed the campus in 2007 and sold the property to a company, EF Education, for $27 million the following year.

Boston College and Newton College of the Sacred Heart (1974)

The Religious of the Sacred Heart of Jesus (RSCJ Sisters) founded Newton College of the Sacred Heart in the suburbs of Boston in 1946. It was located just two miles from Boston College in Chestnut Hill. Decades earlier, when Boston College was still located in the South End, the RSCJ Sisters operated a girls' high school nearby. When the Jesuits moved to the suburbs, the RSCJ Sisters followed, so the two institutions were always in close proximity.

Boston, however, was awash in women's colleges, including secular institutions like Wellesley College and Catholic institutions like Anna Maria, Emmanuel, Labouré, Regis, and (the now-defunct) Marian Court Colleges. It was inevitable that some schools would be squeezed out of such a crowded market. In 1974, Boston College acquired Newton, and the property has been known as its Newton Campus ever since. Today, it is principally home to athletic fields and Boston College Law School. Newton Country Day School of the Sacred Heart, an all-girls' high school affiliated with the RSCJ Sisters network, still exists next door.[109]

---

109. James M. O'Toole, "Jesuits and Madames: The Life and Death of Newton College of the Sacred Heart, 1945–75," in *Crossings and Dwellings: Restored Jesuits, Women Religious, American Experience, 1814–2014*, ed. Kyle B. Roberts and Stephen Schloesser (Leiden, Boston: Brill, 2017), 603–617.

University of San Francisco and Lone Mountain College (1978)

Just four years after the Jesuits and RSCJ Sisters finished their negotiations in Boston, their counterparts at the other end of the country entered into a merger of their own. The RSCJ Sisters sponsored Lone Mountain College in San Francisco, which traced its roots to a girls' high school founded in 1898 in what is today Silicon Valley. After adding a two-year degree program, that school became Menlo Park Junior College, and after relocating to San Francisco, it became the San Francisco College for Women.

The circumstances in Boston and San Francisco were remarkably parallel. The Bay Area, too, had an over-supply of women's colleges, including the secular Mills College and the Catholic-affiliated Dominican, Holy Names, and Notre Dame de Namur Colleges. In order to set itself apart, the San Francisco College for Women became coeducational and renamed itself Lone Mountain College in 1969, but the small influx of male students that resulted was not enough to solve its budgetary issues. It was located in such close proximity to the better-known Jesuit university that it could not successfully compete. The University of San Francisco acquired it in 1978. Today, the property is known as the University of San Francisco's Lone Mountain Campus (even though it is only one block from the main campus) and houses the university's School of Education, dorms, a Jesuit residence, and graduate study offices. The beautifully wooded property is a striking oasis in the bustling San Francisco cityscape.

Xavier University and Edgecliff College (1980)

The Sisters of Mercy established Edgecliff College (originally under the name Our Lady of Cincinnati College) in 1935. It was two miles from Xavier University's campus in Avondale. In 1980, Edgecliff's president, Sister Margaret Anne Molitor, RSM, announced plans to join forces with the Jesuit institution, mainly as a way to solve Edgecliff's financial problems. Xavier officials were careful to explain that this was not a true merger; instead, the Edgecliff College corporation would be dissolved and all of its assets would transfer to Xavier University.

Like many women's colleges operated by the Sisters of Mercy, Edgecliff had particular strengths in art, music, and social work. Collectively, those programs became the Edgecliff College of Fine Arts and Community Services, a constituent college of Xavier University. At least initially, that college continued to operate on its original campus, but in 1986, the university sold the property and brought all of the Edgecliff faculty and students to Avondale. The College of Fine Arts and Community Services ceased operations as a distinct unit within Xavier, but its degree programs continued through other schools and departments.[110]

The original Edgecliff campus is today home to the University of Cincinnati's Victory Parkway Campus, as well as private homes.

---

110. Bennish, *Continuity*, 204–205.

Loyola University (New Orleans), Ursuline College (1956), and St. Mary's Dominican College (1984)

The Ursuline Sisters came to the French colony of New Orleans in 1727, making them the first Catholic nuns to serve in what is today the United States. The city's Ursuline Academy, a high school for girls, dates to that year. By the 1920s, like many Catholic girls' schools, it had expanded to include a small college division.

The Dominican Sisters opened a girls' high school in New Orleans just before the Civil War in 1860. By 1910, it had begun to offer bachelor's degrees under the name St. Mary's Dominican College, located on a campus in the city's trendy Uptown neighborhood about three blocks from Loyola University and the still-developing campus of Tulane University.

Loyola University had a longstanding relationship with both institutions. At a time when Ursuline College lacked accreditation in the 1920s, Loyola recognized Ursuline students and faculty as its own, which allowed Ursuline to award credits under Loyola's charter. In 1956, Ursuline discontinued its college division to redefine itself solely as a high school, and its displaced collegians enrolled at Loyola. Although there were already plenty of women studying at Loyola at the time, the absorption of the Ursuline women marks the point at which Loyola's undergraduate programs became "unambiguously co-ed."[111]

St. Mary's Dominican College's excellent location did not spare it from the same fate, and by the 1980s, the college was in dire condition. In 1984, shortly after it announced plans to close, Loyola University purchased its campus. This was real estate deal, not a merger, but the former buildings of the women's college became important assets to Loyola. The former women's campus is now Loyola University's Broadway Campus, home to the Loyola College of Law and other university departments. St. Mary's Dominican High School, the only surviving division of the old college, still operates in a separate location in New Orleans approximately a mile away from Loyola University.

Regis University and Loretto Heights College (1988)

The Sisters of Loretto opened Loretto Heights College on the outskirts of Denver in 1891, after more than thirty years of ministry in the area. It was the only Catholic women's college ever to operate in Colorado.

The college enjoyed a good reputation and began to admit men in the 1970s. Less than two decades later, however, it was struggling. Because Colorado had never been an especially good environment for Catholic education due to its limited Catholic population, the state's two Catholic colleges recognized that it made sense to cooperate rather than compete. In 1988, Loretto Heights College merged with the Jesuits' Regis College, bringing its notable nursing and healthcare programs under the aegis

---

111. Cook, *Founded on Faith*, 174.

of Regis. The addition of the new professional schools enabled Regis to attain university status three years later.

The original campus of Loretto Heights College was too distant from Regis to be of use, and it was sold in 1989 to a Japanese educational conglomerate, which renamed it Teikyo Loretto Heights College and used the property primarily to provide English-language education to non-native speakers. That school rebranded briefly as Colorado Heights University before closing permanently in 2017. The legacy and alumnae of the original Loretto Heights College, however, remain part of the Regis University network.

University of Detroit and Mercy College of Detroit (1990)

By the middle of the twentieth century, the city of Detroit proper had two Catholic women's colleges. The first, Marygrove College, moved into the city from the suburbs in 1927 and was sponsored by the Servants of the Immaculate Heart of Mary. The second, Mercy College of Detroit, opened its doors in 1935 as a specialized nursing school under the leadership of the Sisters of Mercy; by 1941, it had grown into a comprehensive undergraduate college, though it was known primarily for its healthcare programs. The two women's colleges had a history of cooperating with the Jesuit-sponsored University of Detroit; since 1972, all three institutions had been in an academic consortium that allowed students to cross-register for classes at any of the three campuses.[112]

In 1987, Father Robert Mitchell, SJ and Sister Maureen Fay, OP—respectively the presidents of the University of Detroit and Mercy College—began an informal dialogue about consolidation. It began almost by accident when the two presidents attended a conference together and spoke about their common challenges. Their schools were located less than five miles apart, and were facing similar recruitment problems brought on by Detroit's economic woes following the decline of the auto industry. Back in Michigan, Fay and Mitchell continued to bounce ideas off each other, relying largely on the good personal rapport between them to move the process along. When they finally approached their boards and faculty about the concept of a merger, most were receptive. Meanwhile, Marygrove College soon got word of the discussions and asked to be included. After a feasibility study, the two women's colleges and the University of Detroit began serious talks about consolidation in 1988.[113]

Marygrove College withdrew from the negotiations two years later, announcing its intention to remain independent. Mercy College and the University of Detroit persisted, however, and formally united in 1990. Mercy College hoped to avoid a lopsided deal like the one that had taken shape in ten years earlier in Cincinnati, where

---

112. Herman J Muller, SJ, "Advancing the U of D Legacy—University of Detroit, 1978–1990," in *Legacy of Excellence: A Continuing history of Jesuit and Mercy Higher Education in Detroit*, ed. Herman J. Muller, Mary Justine Sabourin, and Shari S. Cohen (Detroit: University of Detroit Press, 2003), 27.

113. Cohen, "University of Detroit Mercy," 246–248.

its former sister school, Edgecliff College, was already fading into a distant memory. Although it was smaller than the University of Detroit, Mercy College was solvent and was not facing impending closure, which gave it much stronger negotiating stance than many other women's colleges at the time. Since the merger in Detroit was designed to strengthen both institutions, Mercy felt that it could be more assertive in the discussions.

The resulting university took on a new name, first suggested by a local marketing agency: the University of Detroit Mercy. Much like the situation at Loyola Marymount University in Los Angeles, the Sisters of Mercy and the Jesuits decided to be equal co-sponsors of the combined institution, and both communities committed to contribute faculty and staff. The thirty-six members of the governing board would include six trustees selected by the Jesuits and six selected by the sisters.[114] Fortunately, the charisms of the two orders were complementary; the Sisters of Mercy, like the Jesuits, preferred to live and work closely with the people they served, and were particularly dedicated to education, health care, and the needs of the poor. Among Catholic religious orders, they were second only to the Jesuits in the number of colleges and universities they sponsored in the United States.

Sister Fay became the president of the combined university. Father Mitchell, who was already planning to retire from the Detroit presidency, took on the mostly ceremonial role of university chancellor.[115] This made Sister Fay the first woman to serve as president of any Jesuit university. She was a Dominican nun, not a Sister of Mercy, but her resume left no doubt that she was the most qualified person for the job. She had earned a master's degree in English from the University of Detroit and a PhD from the University of Chicago before becoming president of Mercy College in 1983, and her leadership was widely recognized. She continued to serve as president of the united university until 2004, when she was succeeded by a Jesuit, Father Gerard Stockhausen, SJ.

Initially, the combined institution maintained both campuses, with nursing and health-related programs (including the old University of Detroit Dental School) consolidating at the Mercy location and liberal arts departments consolidating at the original Jesuit campus. As a cost-saving measure, in 2003 the university sold the former Mercy campus to Wayne County Community College for $14 million. Most healthcare programs relocated to the main campus, while the Dental School found a new home in Detroit's Corktown neighborhood.

As for Marygrove College, which pulled out of the original merger talks in 1990, the future was not bright. It continued to operate as a co-ed institution until 2017, when low enrollment forced it to shutter its undergraduate division in an attempt to refocus exclusively on its more profitable graduate degrees. That experiment did not last long, and the entire college closed permanently in 2019.

---

114. Ibid., 255, 261.
115. Ibid., 224.

Loyola University (Chicago) and Mundelein College (1991)

In 1929, the Sisters of Charity of the Blessed Virgin Mary established Mundelein College—named for the sitting Archbishop of Chicago, George Cardinal Mundelein. The school originally occupied a stunning art deco skyscraper near the southern edge of Loyola University's lakefront campus in Rogers Park. Over the years, it acquired a handful of satellite buildings nearby, but the core of the campus remained its signature tower.

Because of their proximity, it was inevitable that the fates of Loyola and Mundelein would be intertwined. By the 1960s, Mundelein had grown to become one of the largest women's colleges in the United States, but it was about to face serious competition from across the street. Loyola had long admitted women to its downtown programs, but when its main campus at Rogers Park went fully co-ed in 1966, many of the women who otherwise might have applied to Mundelein began to look instead to Loyola because of its better facilities and more diverse degree programs. That pressure eventually took its toll, and by the early 1990s, Mundelein's enrollment had fallen below 1,000.

All of the other Catholic women's colleges in the Chicago area—including St. Xavier College (Sisters of Mercy), Barat College (Religious of the Sacred Heart of Jesus), and Rosary College (now known as Dominican University in honor of its sponsoring order)—were admitting men by 1990. Mundelein was the last all-women's college in the State of Illinois. In 1991, Loyola and Mundelein announced plans to merge, with Loyola assuming Mundelein's debt and absorbing its academic programs. Initially, both sides hoped that the Mundelein name would survive as the weekend college of Loyola University, but over time that ceased to be the case.

Several Sisters of Charity from Mundelein accepted long-term positions at Loyola. Perhaps the most famous was Sister Jean Dolores Schmidt, BVM, who became a campus icon as the chaplain for the Loyola men's basketball team. In 2018, she became a national celebrity when, at age 98, she accompanied the Ramblers through their improbable run to the semifinals of the NCAA tournament. The Mundelein name remains attached to several physical features of the Loyola campus, including the original art deco skyscraper—now known as the Mundelein Center for the Fine and Performing Arts, the university's largest classroom building.

Mergers that Did Not Take Place

In some cities, a merger between the Jesuit college and a neighboring women's college might have been logical or even desirable, but never took place. Georgetown Visitation Academy, the all-girls high school adjacent to Georgetown University, discontinued its college division in 1967 rather than merge with its neighbor. In Kansas City, Rockhurst College enjoyed a friendly relationship with the all-female St. Teresa's College nearby, but the women's school (known today as Avila University) relocated across town and both went co-educational independently in 1969. In Buffalo, the Sisters of St. Joseph operated Medaille College down the street from Canisius College, but despite their proximity the two institutions remained independent.

On various occasions, they have discussed opportunities to share services as a way to cut costs, but those talks have not yet led to a merger.

Racial Integration

Just as it is often difficult to pinpoint the exact year a college went co-educational, it can be hard to identify when a college racially integrated. Very few universities had a clear turning point or a watershed moment like the fiery anti-racist sermon that Father Claude Heithaus, SJ preached at Saint Louis University in 1944. Instead, many universities began admitting African-Americans and other racial groups piece-meal and without any dramatic declaration that they were doing so.

It is tempting to date a school's integration from the year the first African-American student enrolled on campus, but the presence of a single student certainly does not indicate that a university was integrated. By that logic, Holy Cross has been inte-grated since the Healy brothers enrolled in the 1850s. Other African-American pio-neers deserve mention more for their personal accomplishments than for any grand policy change they represent on the part of the university: William M. Gordon, who graduated from Creighton Medical School in 1901; Mabel Raimey, who first enrolled at Marquette Law School in 1922; Jerry Dixon, who graduated from Detroit Law School in 1926; and Willis Nathaniel Huggins, who earned a doctorate in education from Fordham in 1932.

The story of Hudson Oliver is illustrative. A graduate of the Jesuits' Xavier High School in Manhattan, Oliver was denied admission to Fordham because of his race. He found a more welcoming environment across the river at Saint Peter's College, where he enrolled in 1934. Fordham's resistance to the integration of its undergradu-ate college is especially puzzling because it had admitted African-Americans to its graduate schools for more than ten years by that time.[116] As Oliver's experience indi-cates, integration was often determined not by centralized policy within the Jesuit order or even within each university, but by the quirky individual decisions of the people in charge of admissions.

By the late 1940s, though, African-Americans were present on most Jesuit cam-puses, albeit in small numbers—collectively amounting to about one percent of all students.[117] By the 1960s, virtually all Jesuit colleges were not only admitting African-Americans, but actively recruiting them and encouraging their enrollment through scholarships and other means. Santa Clara, for example, increased its population of African-American and Mexican-American students from a combined 3 percent of the student body in 1968 to 16 percent in 1976 by directing about one-third of its schol-arship budget toward that goal.[118] At Holy Cross, Father John Brooks, SJ (who would

---

116. Shelley, *Fordham*, 326.
117. Varga, *Baltimore's Loyola*, 358.
118. McKevitt, *University of Santa Clara*, 300.

later become president of the college) personally traveled to dozens of high schools to recruit African-American students. His efforts resulted in the enrollment of twenty African-American men in 1968—one of whom, Clarence Thomas, became a Supreme Court justice.

Some universities never had official policies prohibiting Black students from enrolling, but at least one had such a policy on the books without realizing it. In the 1960s, Xavier University in Cincinnati applied for a federal loan, which required it to submit a copy of its original articles of incorporation. Unbeknownst even to the Xavier administration, those original 1840 documents stated that the college was dedicated to the "education of white youth." Xavier had been unwittingly violating its own written policy for years by admitting non-white students.[119] Naturally, the college changed that bylaw after the government pointed it out.

In 1944, Saint Louis University became the first American university (of any kind) located within a former slave state to admit African-Americans. Loyola (Baltimore) was not far behind, in 1946. Both, however, were located in relatively open-minded border states that had never joined the Confederacy, which made their decisions somewhat easier. For schools in the Deep South, racial integration faced additional hurdles, but the Jesuit colleges still integrated ahead of non-Catholic schools. As early as 1948, Spring Hill College in Mobile published a pamphlet in which its president, Father Patrick Donnelly, SJ, called for racial integration and vowed to make Spring Hill a beacon of true equality for Alabama. In 1954, under the presidency of Father Andrew Smith, SJ, the college welcomed nine African-American students (including both men and women), making it the first college of any kind in Alabama to desegregate. This brave decision brought attention from civil rights opponents and advocates alike. The local branch of the Ku Klux Klan attempted to burn a cross in protest on the Spring Hill campus in 1957; alert students confronted the bigots and foiled the plan. Martin Luther King, Jr. mentioned Spring Hill by name in his famous 1963 Letter from a Birmingham Jail, praising Alabama Catholics for their commitment to desegregation.[120]

Not surprisingly, integration proved to be trickiest in the staunchly segregated city of New Orleans, where, in 1962, Loyola University became the last of the American Jesuit colleges to fully integrate. Louisiana had strict laws on segregation and was also home to the nation's only historically Black Catholic college, Xavier University of Louisiana; Loyola long justified its exclusion of Black students on the grounds that they could attend Xavier across town. Nevertheless, Loyola gradually integrated its programs, beginning with its law school and evening division in the early 1950s. Loyola benefitted when Spring Hill's progressive presidents—Fathers Donnelly and Smith—became presidents of Loyola after leaving Mobile. The two men successively

---

119. Bennish, *Continuity*, 195.

120. Gentry Holbert, "A Historical Moment: Spring Hill College," *Conversations on Jesuit Higher Education* (22 December 2016), http://www.conversationsmagazine.org/web-features/2016/12/22/a-historical-moment-spring-hill-college.

led Spring Hill from 1946 to 1959, and then, in the same order, they led Loyola from 1952 to 1966, bringing their commitment to integration with them.[121]

Loyola's Jesuits had been divided on integration in the 1940s and 1950s, but there were several priests in the community who pushed hard to integrate African-Americans—including Father Joseph Fichter, SJ (a professor of sociology) and Father Louis Twomey, SJ (who led Loyola's Institute of Industrial Relations). In 1947, Father Fichter organized an interracial committee of students from Loyola, Xavier, and the two Catholic women's colleges in New Orleans; the group became known as the South East Regional Interracial Commission (SERINCO), and it hosted events and published materials opposing segregation.[122] Father Twomey, who served as regent of Loyola's law school, personally encouraged two of the most promising Black students from Xavier to apply for law degrees: Harry Alexander in 1949 and Richard Gumbel in 1951. Against the regent's recommendations, Loyola's admissions committee rejected both men because of their race; Twomey then pulled strings within the Jesuit network and got both of the disappointed applicants into Georgetown Law School. Nonetheless, his persistence eventually paid off, and in 1952, Loyola Law School accepted two African-Americans: Norman Francis and Benjamin Johnson.[123]

Athletics proved to be a vehicle for integration, not least because of the face they presented to the outside world. The Loyola (Chicago) Ramblers won a national basketball championship in 1963 with a starting lineup that included four Black players—virtually unheard of at the time.[124] Georgetown hired John Thompson, Jr., as its men's basketball coach in 1972, and during his nearly three-decade career, he not only served as the most visible African-American university employee, but also recruited dozens of talented inner-city athletes to Georgetown, developing a reputation as a national authority on racial equity in college sports. In 1984, he became the first Black head coach in college basketball history to lead a team to a national championship. He rarely reveled in that accomplishment, arguing that others would have preceded him had the sport not been unjustly segregated in the days of his ancestors. In 1989, his vociferous opposition led the NCAA to drop a proposed rule change that would have made student athletes ineligible for scholarships if they did not earn minimum scores on standardized tests—a move he saw as discriminatory to those from underprivileged backgrounds. Thompson's insistence on scholastic achievement (he employed a former nun as a tutor for the players and kept a deflated basketball on his desk as a reminder that professional sports careers were fleeting) resulted in impressive graduation rates for his teams. Thompson's death in 2020 prompted an outpouring of support from an entire generation of Black coaches and athletes who credited him as a role model.

---

121. Cook, *Founded on Faith*, 179, 193.

122. Ibid., 163–164.

123. Ibid., 165, 174–175, 179.

124. See Michael Lenehan, *Ramblers: Loyola-Chicago 1963—The Team that Changed the Color of College Basketball* (Chicago: Midway Books, 2013).

The 1951 University of San Francisco football team made headlines when it refused to play in the Orange Bowl after bowl organizers banned the Dons' African-American players. Regrettably, not all Jesuit athletic programs behaved similarly. In 1962, the Xavier University men's basketball team received an invitation to play in the Sugar Bowl Tournament in New Orleans, which insisted that the Musketeers leave their Black players behind. Despite widespread calls to boycott the tournament, Xavier President Paul O'Connor, SJ allowed the team accept the invitation, explaining that he felt it was better for northern, integrated universities to engage the South in dialogue rather than isolate it in protest.[125]

To be sure, there were incidents of racism on campus as Jesuit colleges integrated, but they did not stop progress. By and large, African-American students enrolled at Jesuit campuses earlier than at many secular universities. Jesuit colleges were by no means national trendsetters in this regard, but they were at least in step with the Civil Rights Movement and, in places, ahead of the local curve. Their religious nature provided a moral justification for integration and freed them from some of the segregationist laws that still applied to many public universities.

At a time when their traditional audience, white Catholics, were assimilating into the American mainstream, Jesuit colleges remained cognizant of the discrimination that American Catholics and other first-generation immigrants had faced. Many consciously tried to develop non-discriminatory admissions policies. They continued to enroll Hispanic, Native American, Jewish, and Asian-American students, even though those populations varied from school to school. Often, however, it took deliberate effort by campus leaders like Father Brooks of Holy Cross to accelerate integration and make it a conscious effort, not simply a piecemeal process.

The work goes on. Integration began in isolated instances in the early 1900s, became a deliberate policy in the 1950s and 1960s, and continues to this day. True integration is an ever-evolving challenge, but one toward which the universities continue to strive.

The Decline of Jesuit Football

The post-World War II era saw the demise—either permanently or temporarily—of most remaining Jesuit college football programs. In a sense, the war killed Jesuit football, damaging many teams beyond repair by forcing them to suspend their seasons and forgo what little revenue they might have generated. By the 1950s and 1960s, the costs of playing in rented urban stadiums and transporting dozens of players across the country far outpaced ticket sales. Jesuit teams often struggled to attract fans in major cities where professional sports were becoming more popular and more readily available. Without the benefit of taxpayer dollars to build and maintain stadiums or recruit top athletes, Jesuit schools, like most private colleges, ceded their place at the top of the sport to the large public universities.

---

125. Bennish, *Continuity*, 191–192.

The decision to drop football was painful for almost everyone—except the presidents and administrators who paid the bills. In Cincinnati, for example, Xavier University temporarily lost accreditation in 1934 in part because of its huge football operating deficits.[126] Any university administrator who saw the red ink understood that nothing short of a miracle could enable small, independent colleges to compete in college football at the highest level. Nationwide, only a handful of wealthy private universities like Miami, Southern California, Stanford, and Vanderbilt were able to sustain their football programs, sometimes absorbing significant financial losses in the process. Even the well-endowed Ivy League schools, which dominated the sport prior to World War II, fell into obscurity because they declined to offer athletic scholarships.

The best-known Catholic football program, Notre Dame, avoided the fate of other Catholic schools in part because its spacious rural campus enabled it to build its own stadium. In location and scope, Notre Dame was a highly atypical Catholic university. Most Catholic institutions were located in cities, and they rarely had the space to build stadiums like the 54,000-seat bowl (later expanded to over 80,000) that Notre Dame erected in 1930. Even in its original 1930 configuration, Notre Dame Stadium was more than twice as large as the biggest Jesuit-owned stadiums at the time (at Boston College, Detroit, Marquette, and Holy Cross). With no rental expenses, Notre Dame did not suspend its football program during the lean wartime years, and instead won four national championships against depleted competition in the 1940s. Its success on the football field redefined the university's financial priorities and public image for decades. Although Notre Dame's rural location did cause enrollment problems at times, especially during the war, it also presented unique opportunities. Whereas most urban Catholic schools served local inner-city students, Notre Dame's twentieth-century leaders strategically turned the campus's isolation into an asset, taking advantage of its proximity to Chicago, Detroit, Cincinnati, and other fast-growing centers of Catholic wealth in the Midwest. Notre Dame recruited students from all of those cities, using its football team to maintain visibility. Because only students wealthy enough to travel to South Bend were generally able to enroll, the university tended to attract a well-to-do clientele capable of paying full tuition. Unlike other Catholic universities, which specialized in the humanities and low-pay service professions like nursing and social work, Notre Dame academically emulated the public, land-grant institutions that surrounded it. Earlier than most Catholic schools, it specialized in lucrative academic fields like engineering, science, architecture, and business, attracting corporate and government grants, and producing graduates with the capacity to donate large sums of money to sustain its football program. By prioritizing institutional assets that generated revenue, Notre Dame was able to amass one of the largest endowments of any university in the country, exceeding $11 billion today. By contrast, most Catholic colleges raised only what they needed to survive; the

126. Bennish, *Continuity*, 148–149.

second-largest endowment at any Catholic university is Boston College's $2.5 billion, and few others have ever topped the $1 billion mark.[127]

After World War II, virtually all of the remaining Jesuit football programs were discontinued, including those at Saint Louis (1949), Canisius (1949), Saint Peter's (1950), Georgetown (1951), San Francisco (1952), Santa Clara (1952), and Fordham (1955). A handful of Jesuit schools held out slightly longer, often because they owned their own stadiums, but in due time Marquette (1960), Scranton (1960), Detroit (1963), Loyola Marymount (1973), and Xavier (1973) made the same decision. The most extreme case was Loyola (New Orleans), which discontinued all intercollegiate sports in 1972 as a cost-saving measure, not to resume competition until 1991.[128]

The only Jesuit colleges that have continuously fielded football teams since World War II are Boston College, Holy Cross, and John Carroll. In a move counter to prevailing trends, Boston College built its own on-campus stadium in 1957, bringing its team home from Fenway Park and other off-campus venues it had rented until that point. The programs at both Holy Cross and John Carroll were spared only because both decided to drop to lower levels of competition. In 1955, the Cleveland school stopped competing at a high intercollegiate level and began scheduling games against local liberal arts colleges (in what is known today as NCAA Division III), cutting costs significantly. Holy Cross gave up its right to offer football scholarships in 1986 when it joined a handful of prestigious liberal arts colleges like Bucknell and Colgate to create the Patriot League—an athletic conference that initially replicated the "academics-first" philosophy of the Ivy League. This decision marked the end of the Boston College-Holy Cross football rivalry, and after 1986, the two schools' football teams did not play each other for thirty-two years.

This left Boston College as the only Jesuit school (and one of only two Catholic schools, along with Notre Dame) still competing at the highest level of intercollegiate football, known today as the Football Bowl Subdivision (FBS). The Eagles have been successful, appearing in 25 bowl games from 1980 to 2020. A handful of Jesuit schools, including Canisius, Georgetown, Fordham, Saint Peter's, San Francisco, and Santa Clara, resumed football in or around the 1960s, but the new teams were a shadow of what they once were, both in their competitiveness on the field and the caliber of the opponents they played. Many have since been discontinued. Today, apart

---

127. In 1839, Bishop Simon Bruté of Vincennes had invited the Jesuits to build a college in Indiana and had offered them the enormous parcel of land that eventually became the Notre Dame campus. The Jesuits declined because they were otherwise engaged at Saint Louis University and St. Mary's College in Kentucky, and were considering more promising offers in Detroit and Cincinnati. Bishop Bruté's successor later offered the same parcel in South Bend to the Congregation of Holy Cross, which founded Notre Dame in 1842. The Holy Cross fathers built a much smaller national network of colleges than the Jesuits and poured most of their financial resources into Notre Dame. They also had a less rivalrous relationship with the Catholic University of America, where they sent many priests to earn PhDs and gain experience in a research university setting—experience that they later brought back to Indiana. See Garraghan, *Jesuits of the Middle U.S. Vol. III*, 112–113 and Power, *Catholic Higher Education*, 368–369.

128. Cook, *Founded on Faith*, 208–209, 227.

from Boston College, only Georgetown, Fordham, and Holy Cross field football teams at the Division I level, all three as members of the Patriot League in the Football Championship Subdivision (FCS).

The Rise of Jesuit Basketball

Despite the loss of football, athletics remained popular at Jesuit universities, which at midcentury were still predominantly male. Many schools turned their attention to basketball, which was growing in popularity and had many positive qualities that football lacked. Basketball courts required little space—a major advantage on cramped city campuses. Games were played indoors during the heart of the school year, which kept players and fans occupied during the winter—an especially attractive feature in the frigid northern cities where most Jesuit schools were located. Most importantly, with small team rosters and only ten players on the court at a time, basketball was one of the few team sports in which a small, private college stood a real chance to defeat a large and better-funded public university. Just as baseball gave way to football on Jesuit campuses early in the 1900s, so football yielded to basketball in the middle of the century.

Jesuit schools enjoyed remarkable success on the basketball court, developing strong local and even national fan bases. Many became near-annual staples in the NCAA men's basketball tournament, and five—Georgetown, Holy Cross, Loyola (Chicago), Marquette, and San Francisco—won national championships, with San Francisco accomplishing the feat twice. Under coach Phil Woolpert, the Dons won sixty consecutive games in the mid-1950s—a remarkable run that ranks as the second-longest unbeaten streak in NCAA history (after UCLA's 88-game run in the 1970s). Between 1943 and 1985, more than one-third of the NCAA men's basketball tournaments featured a Jesuit school in the final or semi-final game.

Because of their popularity, some Jesuit basketball programs, including Georgetown and Marquette, began to play their home games in large arenas normally home to professional teams, often filling them to capacity. The fact that Jesuit basketball teams were located in some of the country's biggest television markets meant that advertisers were eager to sponsor them and buy commercial airtime during games. During the 1970s and 1980s, television networks began to see live sports as a reliable way to attract audiences, and broadcasters hyped games featuring urban Catholic schools. To capitalize on their success, many Jesuit schools began to align with other urban, basketball-centric universities to form conferences that could market and sell broadcast rights. As a result, the main Jesuit basketball conferences grew in step with the growth of televised sports.

Georgetown and Boston College became charter members of the Big East conference in 1979, aligning themselves with fellow basketball powers Connecticut, Seton Hall, St. John's, and others. Holy Cross was invited to join the Big East as well, but declined; at the time, it was strategically investing in academics over athletics and found a better fit in the Patriot League. While Boston College is no longer a member, Marquette, Creighton, and Xavier joined the Big East in the new century. In the west, San Francisco and Santa Clara aligned with traditional rival St. Mary's College in 1953 to form the core of today's West Coast Conference (WCC); Gonzaga, Loyola (Los Angeles), and Seattle joined the conference by the 1970s, though Seattle temporarily withdrew from NCAA Division I in 1980. Midwestern Jesuit schools changed league affiliations often from the 1950s onward, but the major schools like Saint Louis, Loyola (Chicago), and Detroit were often associated with each other in the Missouri Valley Conference, Midwestern City Conference (today's Horizon League), and Conference USA. Today, outside of the Big East and WCC, most Division I Jesuit schools compete in the Atlantic 10, Patriot League, or Metro Atlantic Athletic Conference.

All of these conferences became popular with fans. The Big East in particular became a national power, and by the 1980s, it was arguably the preeminent men's college basketball league in the country, playing games at a sold-out Madison Square Garden in New York and other high-profile venues.

Jesuit universities produced an impressive number of professional basketball players, including many who became household names. The so-called "Dream Team" in the 1992 Olympics included Patrick Ewing (Georgetown) and John Stockton (Gonzaga). Other names familiar even to casual basketball fans include Alonzo Mourning, Dikembe Mutombo, and Allen Iverson (Georgetown); Dwyane Wade and Doc Rivers (Marquette); David West and Tyrone Hill (Xavier); Dick Vitale (a Detroit coach); and Bill Russell (San Francisco).

Georgetown's 1984 championship was the last NCAA title won by a Jesuit basketball team in the twentieth century, but many teams have remained nationally prominent. Gonzaga emerged as a national power in the 1990s, appearing in twenty consecutive NCAA tournaments between 1999 and 2019 before the coronavirus pandemic brought the 2020 season to a premature end. Xavier, Creighton, Marquette, Saint Joseph's, Saint Louis, Saint Peter's, and Loyola (Chicago) also enjoyed success with multiple tournament appearances.

The table below includes all Jesuit champions, finalists, and semi-finalists in the NCAA men's basketball tournament to date.

JESUIT NCAA MEN'S BASKETBALL TOURNAMENT FINALISTS AND SEMI-FINALISTS

1943	Georgetown	Runner-up	Lost to Wyoming in title game
1947	**Holy Cross**	**National champion**	**Defeated Oklahoma in title game**
1948	Holy Cross	Semi-finalist	
1952	Santa Clara	Semi-finalist	
1955	**San Francisco**	**National champion**	**Defeated LaSalle in title game**
1956	**San Francisco**	**National champion**	**Defeated Iowa in title game**
1957	San Francisco	Semi-finalist	

1958	Seattle	Runner-up	Lost to Kentucky in title game
1961	Saint Joseph's	Semi-finalist	Relinquished record after some players were revealed to be involved in a gambling scandal
1963	**Loyola Chicago**	**National champion**	**Defeated Cincinnati in title game**
1974	Marquette	Runner-up	Lost to North Carolina State in title game
1977	**Marquette**	**National champion**	**Defeated North Carolina in title game**
1982	Georgetown	Runner-up	Lost to North Carolina in title game
1984	**Georgetown**	**National champion**	**Defeated Houston in title game**
1985	Georgetown	Runner-up	Lost to Villanova in title game
2003	Marquette	Semi-finalist	
2007	Georgetown	Semi-finalist	
2017	Gonzaga	Semi-finalist	
2018	Loyola Chicago	Semi-finalist	
2021	Gonzaga	Finalist	Lost to Baylor in title game

In addition to these titles, five Jesuit men's basketball teams have claimed the National Invitation Tournament (NIT) championship. The NIT is less prestigious today but was, originally, the equivalent of the NCAA tournament. Jesuit winners are: Saint Louis (1948), San Francisco (1949), Holy Cross (1954), Xavier (1958 and 2022), and Marquette (1970). The 1949 NIT featured an all-Jesuit title game, pitting San Francisco against Loyola (Chicago). At lower levels of competition, the University of Scranton and Loyola (New Orleans) have also won national championships. No Jesuit college to date has won an NCAA Division I women's basketball title, but Creighton, Gonzaga, and Xavier have advanced as far as the quarterfinals of the women's NCAA tournament, and Creighton (2004) and Marquette (2008) have won the postseason Women's NIT. Scranton has enjoyed ongoing success in the women's Division III tournament, including the 1985 national title.

Other Sports

Outside of basketball, Saint Louis University and the University of San Francisco became major powers in men's soccer, winning fourteen national championships between them in the 1960s and 1970s. The 1969 championship game pitted the Billikens against the Dons, with Saint Louis coming out on top, 4–0. As with football and basketball, the Jesuit dominance of men's soccer waned as better-financed public universities invested money in their programs, catching up to the visionary Jesuit schools. Nonetheless, the Santa Clara men's soccer team tied in the national championship in 1989, and Georgetown claimed the national title in 2019. The Santa Clara women have won two national soccer championships (2001 and 2020).

Holy Cross is the only Jesuit baseball team ever to win the College World Series (in 1952), but Creighton's softball team won five national titles between the 1960s and 1980s. Boston College has claimed five national men's ice hockey championships to date, four of them since 2001. Loyola (Chicago) has won national championships in men's volleyball, and Boston College in women's lacrosse. Le Moyne College has emerged as a major power in Division II lacrosse, winning a total of seven national titles between its men's and women's teams since 2004.

Jesuit Colleges and the Cold War

The Catholic Church and the United States government were both intensely anticommunist in the middle of the twentieth century. Even before the Polish-born Pope John Paul II ratcheted up the Church's fight against Marxism in the 1980s, previous popes viewed the Soviet Union and its atheist ideology as an existential threat to the Western world. After President Harry Truman identified anticommunism as the central, guiding principle of American foreign policy in 1947, several government agencies, including the FBI and CIA, became strange bedfellows with the Catholic Church in America. For Irish-Americans and other Catholics accustomed to marginalization in the governing classes, this attention from some of the nation's top law enforcement agencies was both flattering and a welcome indication that they had finally assimilated.

Universities replaced weapons factories as the arsenals of the Cold War. As the space race escalated in the 1960s and as scientists grappled with atomic energy, it became clear that the conflict between communism and capitalism would be won with ideas and technology, not with conventional arms. The United States and the Soviet Union both began to pour immense sums of money into university research, especially in science and engineering. The Jesuits hoped to tap into that revenue both as a matter of patriotic duty and as a competitive necessity. In 1958, a year after the Soviets launched Sputnik into orbit, the Jesuit Educational Association established the Jesuit Research Council of America (JRCA). Initially, the organization was based at the University of Detroit (one of the best Jesuit engineering schools in the country), and its goal was to help Jesuit institutions apply more effectively for federal grants by cataloguing their scientific equipment and keeping records of their research capacity. In 1962, the JRCA offices relocated to Washington, DC, to be closer to grant-making officials. Robert Henle, SJ, dean of the Saint Louis University Graduate School and future president of Georgetown University, chaired the association.[129]

Although their scientific contributions paled in comparison to the nuclear research taking place at the University of California and University of Chicago, Jesuit universities still had an impact on America's Cold War efforts, especially in the ranks of the federal government. Central to these efforts were the School of Foreign Service and School of Languages and Linguistics at Georgetown—both of which trained

---

129. Fitzgerald, *Governance*, 122–123.

thousands of federal government employees, graduating top diplomats who maintained the peace at a time when the global powder keg was close to exploding. Father Edmund Walsh, SJ, Regent of the School of Foreign Service, designed a cutting-edge curriculum to prepare Cold Warriors in their fight against the communist threat. Walsh had been a critic of the Soviet Union ever since he led the Vatican's efforts to deliver humanitarian aid to the country in the 1920s, witnessing firsthand the starvation and suffering that followed the Bolshevik Revolution. In 1947, Georgetown's reputation in this field caught the attention of the federal government, which selected it to host the 404th Strategic Intelligence Detachment, the country's first intelligence-focused military reserve unit on a university campus. The Georgetown campus also (secretly) hosted the 1951 diplomatic talks that led to the creation of a permanent democratic government for West Germany.[130]

McCarthyism

One of the most controversial American political figures of the Cold War had some Jesuit ties. Senator Joseph McCarthy of Wisconsin, whose name became a shorthand for the Congressional investigations into domestic communism in the United States, was a Catholic and a Marquette University graduate. According to legend, McCarthy was seeking a persuasive central issue for his re-election campaign, and raised the topic during a January 1950 dinner with Father Walsh of Georgetown. Because McCarthy began his public crusade against American communists one month later, some in the Washington media speculated that Father Walsh must have put the idea in the senator's head. Walsh denied doing anything of the sort, and Drew Pearson, the journalist who originally wrote the story, never offered convincing proof of his version of events. Still, the tale was widely circulated and widely believed in Washington.[131]

Lingering anti-Catholic sentiment helped to fuel the rumors about the Jesuit origins of McCarthyism, as some observers concluded that their worst fears about the Jesuits had come true; the secret cabal of priests was infiltrating the American government just as it had infiltrated European royal courts centuries earlier. However, those rumors were unfounded. Historian Robert Emmett Curran summarizes the scholarly judgment on Walsh's 1950 dinner with McCarthy this way:

> (T)he meeting (between Walsh and McCarthy) certainly took place, but it was completely out of character for Walsh to raise the issue of domestic subversion as a fit campaign topic. His writings and speeches barely touched the subject; his overriding concern was the threat of external communism and the measures the United States needed to take to defend itself and the western world against this totalitarian menace. Other critics of the story have shown that McCarthy had engaged in antisubversive charges long before his dinner with Walsh.[132]

---

130. Curran, *History of Georgetown Vol. II*, 262–263.
131. Ibid., 261–262.
132. Ibid., 262.

The Georgetown School of Foreign Service, meanwhile, continued to produce graduates (and employ retired government officials) who really did have an impact on government—a positive one. An army of diplomats, military officers, and intelligence officials with Georgetown connections helped to lead the efforts against nuclear proliferation and prevented the Cold War from becoming a hot one. In 1970, Dr. Peter Krogh began his legendary 25-year deanship of the School of Foreign Service, cultivating future government officials in the Jesuit humanistic tradition. Krogh became widely respected in the Washington establishment and made Georgetown a destination for retired foreign policymakers seeking an academic career.

J. Edgar Hoover's FBI

The story of Jesuit alumni in federal government was not limited to Georgetown graduates or to the State Department. Other federal agencies, especially the Department of Justice, developed strong ties to the broader Jesuit network. J. Edgar Hoover, the longtime director of the Federal Bureau of Investigation (FBI) from 1924 to 1972, was a Presbyterian by practice but developed a famously warm relationship with the Catholic Church while in office.

Under Hoover, beginning in the 1940s, the FBI targeted Catholic universities in its efforts to recruit new agents and analysts. Georgetown naturally produced many recruits, but other Jesuit colleges, particularly Fordham, also began to send large numbers of graduates into the Bureau every year. From Hoover's point of view, there were natural synergies between the FBI and Jesuit colleges; a hyper-masculine, disciplined culture thrived at both ends of the pipeline. Jesuit-educated young men learned strict moral codes and respect for authority—qualities the FBI valued.[133] In Catholic university graduates, Hoover found a reliable pool of squeaky-clean, idealistic men who were simultaneously eager to prove their mettle as patriotic Americans, willing to take orders, capable of passing government background checks with flying colors, and reliably unwilling to leak classified information. As one historian wrote, paraphrasing a famous quip by New York Senator Daniel Patrick Moynihan, "during the McCarthy era, as Harvard men were investigated for their alleged un-Americanism, it was 'Fordham men' who did the checking."[134]

Hoover maintained a close professional relationship with Fordham president Robert Gannon, SJ, but also developed strong ties to the Church hierarchy outside of academia. Most notable was his relationship with Richard Cardinal Cushing, the Archbishop of Boston and an alumnus of Boston College. Cushing promoted Hoover's books and anti-communist ideology in his circles (including in the national Catholic press), and Hoover offered FBI agents to protect the archbishop during his

---

133. See Steve Rosswurm, *The FBI and the Catholic Church, 1935–1962* (Amherst: University of Massachusetts Press, 2009).

134. Patrick McNamara, William Dinges, and Joseph A. McCartin, Untitled review of *The FBI and the Catholic Church, 1935–1962* by Steve Rosswurm, *U.S. Catholic Historian* 29, no. 2 (Spring 2011): 77.

travels, even providing transportation to and from airports.[135] Still, the relationship between the two men was less about quid pro quo than about mutual admiration and the converging priorities of the FBI and Catholic Church. Archbishop Michael Curley of Baltimore and auxiliary Bishop Fulton Sheen of New York were also publicly known to be Hoover associates.[136]

While Hoover's pro-Catholic feelings extended to the Church as a whole, the Jesuits played an outsized role in the courtship because of the number of students they sent into Hoover's FBI ranks. At least one Jesuit also became a secret FBI informant. Father Edward Conway, SJ was an alumnus of Holy Cross and Saint Louis University, as well as a professor at Regis College in Denver. In the 1940s, he served as treasurer of the National Committee for Atomic Information (NCAI), in which capacity he met regularly with the FBI to inform on suspicious or undemocratic activity within the NCAI. At the time, the FBI was seriously concerned about the loyalties of scientists and others within the American nuclear program—most famously investigating Dr. J. Robert Oppenheimer of the Manhattan Project. Father Conway was a relatively minor player in this story, but his actions contributed to the firing of Daniel Melcher, Director of the NCAI, under suspicion of communist sympathies.[137]

The Vietnam War and the End of the Jesuit-FBI Alliance

The marriage of convenience between the US Department of Justice and Jesuit higher education arguably reached its peak when Richard Nixon appointed John N. Mitchell, a two-time Fordham graduate, as attorney general in 1969. By then, however, strains in the relationship were beginning to appear. After Vatican II, Jesuit colleges (like the Jesuits themselves) were becoming less rigid and less reliably conservative, making them a less fertile recruiting ground for federal agents.

Like many college campuses, Jesuit schools were gripped by anti-war protests during the 1960s and 1970s, as students spoke out against US military action in Vietnam. A few Jesuit priests joined in with the protests—something that would have been unthinkable a generation earlier. The radical Father Daniel Berrigan, SJ, was arrested by the FBI after he and other antiwar protesters destroyed the records of the Catonsville, Maryland draft board with a homemade explosive in 1968. Berrigan received a three-year federal prison sentence for his actions. Along with his brother, activist Father Philip Berrigan, he was featured on the January 25, 1971

---

135. James Garneau, "The Director and His Eminence: The Working Relationship and Questions of Church and State as Reflected in Cardinal Cushing's FBI Files," *American Catholic Studies* 114, no. 2 (Summer 2003): 45–48.

136. Sheen later became bishop of Rochester and Curley became the first archbishop of Washington.

137. Rosswurm, *FBI and the Catholic Church*, 180–225. McNamara et al. untitled review, 78. Jessica Wang, "Scientists and the Problem of the Public in Cold War America, 1945–1960," *Osiris* Second Series, Vol. 17, Science and Civil Society (2002): 337–338.

cover of *Time* magazine, which dubbed them the "Rebel Priests." Philip Berrigan was a Josephite priest, not a Jesuit, but he held degrees from Holy Cross and Loyola (New Orleans).

Another well-known Jesuit antiwar activist was Father Richard McSorley, SJ, a Georgetown faculty member perhaps best known for his 1977 piece, *It's a Sin to Build a Nuclear Weapon.* The post-Vatican II generation of Jesuits had so many leftist members that at least one conservative Jesuit asked Attorney General John Mitchell and the FBI to investigate the New England Province leadership for "supposedly subversive activities."[138] In this environment, the direct pipeline between Jesuit campuses and the FBI sprang leaks, especially after J. Edgar Hoover's death in 1972.

Nonetheless, Jesuit graduates continued to enter public service, military service, and national security work in large numbers. Many Jesuit schools were also well-represented in the newly established Peace Corps, initially led by John F. Kennedy's brother-in-law, Sargent Shriver. Though himself a Yale graduate, Shriver was a Catholic deeply familiar with Jesuit education, sending two of his five children to Georgetown and one to Holy Cross.

Urban Decay in the 1970s and 1980s

The 1960s saw so much change in Jesuit higher education that the following decades seem tame by comparison. However, the 1970s and 1980s brought challenges of their own. The post-World War II prosperity that empowered more Americans to go to college also enabled them to abandon their tightly packed urban neighborhoods and relocate to sprawling suburbs. Simultaneously, the collapse of the American industrial economy took jobs away from the old urban core of most cities, forcing even more families to uproot themselves. By the 1970s, cities were losing population, and city neighborhoods that were once predominantly Catholic began to lose their Italian, Polish, or other ethnic identities, becoming more diverse and often more impoverished.

For the predominantly urban Jesuit universities, this presented unforeseen problems. Homes near campus that once housed five- or six-child Catholic families were now occupied by elderly retirees—or worse, sat vacant and deteriorating. The racial mix of the cities changed as well, as African-Americans from the rural South moved north during the Great Migration, and as immigration brought new residents from all corners of the globe. Often poor, these first-generation Americans were exactly the audience many Jesuit schools were originally designed to serve, but private-university tuition had become so high in the intervening years that many Jesuit colleges were now unaffordable for residents of their own neighborhoods. Jesuit parishes on campus struggled to maintain their exquisite church buildings now that the local Catholic population was dwindling and the few remaining parishioners relied on Social Secu-

---

138. Shelley, *Fordham*, 433.

rity for income. The result was that many Jesuit university campuses became pockets of relatively privileged students reared in the suburbs, while the surrounding neighborhoods sent fewer and fewer students, languishing in poverty.

Some Jesuit universities, like Saint Joseph's, Boston College, Xavier, and Loyola Marymount, had already relocated to suburban or near-suburban environments, which largely shielded them from this phenomenon. John Carroll University, now located in the wealthy Shaker Heights area, was particularly far from the urban decay of downtown Cleveland. Many other universities, however, found themselves in the heart of inner-city neighborhoods where poverty was on the rise. The Jesuit schools in Buffalo, Syracuse, Scranton, Baltimore, Milwaukee, and Chicago felt the effects as the industrial economies of those cities collapsed. Even the elegant Georgetown neighborhood in the nation's capital saw declines in its population, property values, and average income.

Nowhere was this phenomenon truer than in Detroit and in The Bronx. Poverty rates skyrocketed in the immediate vicinity of Fordham University, and much of The Bronx became an urban slum. The University of Detroit struggled to recruit students amid the perception that its city was dying, and in the early 1980s, it sought a lifeline when it opened a branch campus in the wealthy Oakland County suburb of Clarkston, Michigan. Since 1959, Clarkston had been home to Colombiere College, the Jesuit seminary for the Detroit Province. Using existing facilities at the old seminary, the University of Detroit operated a "Colombiere Campus" for lay students from 1982 to 1989, but the hoped-for enrollment never materialized. Ultimately, the University of Detroit abandoned the project and refocused its attention on its 1990 merger with Mercy College, hoping to improve its viability in the struggling city. Loyola College in Baltimore likewise opened a suburban campus in Columbia, Maryland in 1967, and that branch survives to this day.[139]

The University of San Francisco happened to be located a few blocks north of the famous Haight-Ashbury district, which became ground zero for the nation's hippie culture in the 1960s. When the California Jesuits chose that neighborhood for their rebuilt school after the 1906 earthquake, they could hardly have imagined that it would eventually become the global epicenter of psychedelic drug culture and (along with Memphis, Detroit, and New York) one of the hubs of the rock and roll youth movement. As the 1960s came to a close and the rest of the country left hippie counterculture in the past, Haight-Ashbury retained its reputation as a promiscuous drug haven—not at all the kind of environment many Jesuits (and parents) wanted for their college-age students.

Jesuit schools did attempt to fight the poverty emerging on their doorsteps. As the urban areas around Saint Louis University deteriorated, the Missouri Jesuits—led by Saint Louis president Paul Reinert, SJ—began ambitious outreach initiatives to the city's poorest communities. In many cases, neighborhoods like Rogers Park in

---

139. Varga, *Baltimore's Loyola*, 493–494.

Chicago and Evergreen in Baltimore were spared the worst of the poverty that gripped the rest of their cities, and this was due in part to the stabilizing economic presence of the Jesuit university. College campuses continued to provide good-paying jobs even as the factories closed.

In time, gentrification brought new waves of wealthy, young urban professionals to long-neglected neighborhoods, and in the long term many cities saw their populations rebound. Meanwhile, Jesuit schools remained committed to their hometowns, and none abandoned their urban campuses. In fact, some seized the opportunity to expand. Taking advantage of historically low urban real estate prices, many Jesuit universities bought up property that proved to be outstanding investments in the long term. In 1968, Fordham became an anchor tenant of the new Lincoln Center development on Manhattan's Upper West Side. Having purchased some of the best real estate in the country for just over $2 million, Fordham built a state-of-the-art facility for its law school and other professional programs in what became one of New York's most desirable areas.[140] In Washington, Georgetown purchased property mere blocks from the Supreme Court in 1968, also for just over $2 million. In 1971, that prime location became home to its law school.[141]

Back to the Courts:
Roemer v. Board of Public Works

Jesuit universities remained constantly under fire from legal activists and agitators determined to deny them access to tax money. Rulings in previous court cases like *Tilton v. Richardson* had come down so narrowly in the universities' favor that many secularists continued to press the issue. In 1971, the State of Maryland began offering nearly unconditional cash grants to private colleges, leading to a lawsuit by activists who hoped that such state aid to religious schools would finally be declared unconstitutional. The case would go down in history as *Roemer v. Board of Public Works of Maryland*.[142]

During the trial and depositions, many officials at Loyola College in Baltimore were called to testify. The plaintiffs tried to establish that Loyola and other sectarian colleges in Maryland were proselytizing their students, and should therefore be disqualified from receiving state money even though they were now incorporated separately from the Church. Attorneys pointed out that some professors at the colleges opened class with a prayer. During testimony, Father Joseph Sellinger, Loyola's president, was pressed on whether he could separate his role as a priest from that of college administrator. Would his vow of obedience obligate him to take orders from the Jesuit hierarchy, even in matters of college management? Father Sellinger countered

---

140. Shelley, *Fordham*, 349–350.
141. Curran, *History of Georgetown Vol. III*, 97.
142. Varga, *Baltimore's Loyola*, 501–502.

that his Jesuit superiors only held authority over him in spiritual matters and would never interfere with his day job, stating moreover that his only "superior" as college president was the Loyola board of trustees. Sellinger and other witnesses also emphasized that Loyola faculty enjoyed full academic freedom, pointing out that Vatican II had defined religious faith as a matter of individual conscience, not as a mandate to be imposed. Loyola faculty members, including two who were Jewish, testified that they had never been pressured to teach according to the precepts of the Catholic Church and that the Jesuits and Sisters of Mercy on the faculty were academically qualified to be there.[143]

In the end, the lower courts (in 1974) and the United States Supreme Court (in 1976) once again sided with the colleges. Both rulings held that the educational mission of the religious schools was comparable to that of secular universities, and that their main objective was to provide high-quality degree programs, not to proselytize. Even prayer in classroom was allowable as long as it was a matter of the professor's academic freedom, not imposed by the institution.[144]

Once again, however, the ruling was close. In the lower court, the final judgment was 2–1, and in Washington, it was 5–4. The Methodist-affiliated Western Maryland College (known today as McDaniel College) was the sole Protestant institution implicated in the original lawsuit; on that campus, school officials decided to remove all crosses and religious symbols from college buildings—even from the school chapel— rather than contest the appeal.[145] The four Maryland colleges that continued to fight all the way to the Supreme Court—Loyola, Notre Dame of Maryland, Mount St. Mary's, and the now-defunct St. Joseph's—were all Catholic. Their victory was, by extension, a victory for all Catholic higher education. In Nicholas Varga's words, "It is probably no exaggeration to say that the *Roemer* decision made the difference between life and death for many church-related institutions" by affirming that government aid to religious colleges was legal for a broad range of discretionary purposes.[146]

The *Roemer* case did not mean the end of such lawsuits against Jesuit universities, but it established a clear, broad precedent that served the universities well in those future legal challenges. In 2007, the Missouri Supreme Court heard arguments in a lawsuit challenging Saint Louis University's eligibility, as a Catholic institution, to receive $8 million in state financing for its new Chaifetz Arena. That ruling came down decisively in the university's favor, 6–1. The fact that the universities were now incorporated separately from the Church proved to be one of their saving graces in the American legal system.

---

143. Ibid., 503–505.
144. Ibid., 507–511.
145. Ibid., 508.
146. Ibid., 511.

Universities Adrift:
Rethinking Mission in the 1970s and 1980s

As if they were not busy enough dealing with lawsuits and urban decay on their doorsteps, Jesuit universities simultaneously had to rethink their entire approach to education. At a time when even the courts had concluded that Catholic universities closely resembled their secular counterparts, how would the universities maintain a distinctive, Catholic identity? The Land O'Lakes Statement and similar documents had articulated some strategies for doing so, but how well would those strategies work in practice?

Through the efforts of noted Georgetown theology professor Monika Hellwig and other pioneering thinkers, a new scholarly field began to emerge in the 1970s and 1980s: the study of Catholic identity in higher education. Faculty (lay and clerical) began to think seriously about the mission of Catholic universities in their current form. Organizations like the Association of Catholic Colleges and Universities held conferences and circulated guidebooks to help Catholic institutions reevaluate their mission and live it under modern circumstances. Academic journals like the *Journal of Catholic Higher Education* and the *Journal of Catholic Education* began to publish scholarly articles on this topic. A small, but not insignificant, number of doctoral students around the country began to study Catholic higher education as a niche subfield. Seeds planted in the 1970s and 1980s began to flourish by the early 2000s as the scholarly literature matured and grew.

For the time being, it was possible for casual observers to take the universities' Catholic identity for granted, but the number of Jesuits in the classroom and the administration steadily declined each year. It became obvious that Jesuit universities eventually would have to hire laypeople as presidents (something that other Catholic universities were already doing). The Jesuits' decades-long efforts to train their priests as academics had paid off, giving them a deeper pool of potential university presidents than many other Catholic religious orders. Still, it would be a tall order to staff a network of twenty-eight large (and growing) institutions in the long term.

One thing was clear: to improve their quality and reputation, the universities had to hire quality faculty. Often, this meant hiring graduates of secular doctoral programs. Sometimes, the best scientist or economist available for an open teaching position had no background at all in Catholic higher education. Non-Catholic faculty members were nothing new at Jesuit institutions, but never before had the universities hired so many professors who were complete outsiders to the Jesuit network. Some of these professors were genuinely open-minded and interested in learning about Jesuit pedagogy and spirituality, but others were (at best) apathetic to the Jesuit tradition or (at worst) openly hostile to it. Universities had to wrestle with how to orient faculty toward the goals and methods of Jesuit education without setting off alarm bells by doing anything that might be construed as pressure or censorship. Faculty are sensitive to any perceived limits on their academic freedom, and it would take only one or two unhappy professors to convince secular activists to file another lawsuit, alleging that the universities were, in fact, proselytizing. Universities had to find a way to promote their Jesuit tradition as a positive quality, not a limitation, to faculty trained in a secular American education system that encouraged skepticism about such things.

Rumors began to circulate that the Vatican was going to get involved. In the 1980s, Vatican officials made it known that they would soon issue a document explaining the goals of Catholic higher education and clarifying some longstanding confusions about what, exactly, qualified a university as "Catholic." They circulated drafts of the document in the United States and around the world, seeking comment. American university presidents naturally reviewed the drafts with one eye on the courts, hoping that whatever the Vatican proposed would not undermine their recent hard-fought legal victories. The document that resulted from these discussions, the apostolic constitution *Ex corde Ecclesiae*, was promulgated by Pope John Paul II in 1990 and will be given fuller treatment in the next section.

Throughout these decades of soul-searching, the Jesuits (and Jesuit schools) increasingly latched onto social justice as a defining goal. In December, 1974, under the leadership of Pedro Arrupe, Jesuits from around the world gathered in Rome for a General Congregation to plan out their priorities for the future. After three months of meetings in which they debated the most pressing needs of their contemporary world, the Jesuits resolved, among other things, to emphasize "serving faith and promoting justice" in their ministry.[147] As Fordham President Joseph O'Hare, SJ explained in a 1993 essay, it was initially unclear how this re-emphasis on social justice would affect Jesuit higher education. Should the Jesuits only hire scholars who would advocate for social justice? Should Jesuit scholarship be biased toward those particular views?[148]

Some Jesuits looked to the past as a model. It had been more than half a century since most Jesuit colleges shed ties to their high schools, but high school outreach was still an effective way to serve needy students. In 1975, Seattle University began a cooperative experiment with Seattle Prep, creating a six-year combined high school/college curriculum under the name "Matteo Ricci College," a new unit of Seattle University. In effect, Matteo Ricci College recreated the old model of the six-year Jesuit undergraduate curriculum, but that model had become such a distant memory that, by the 1970s, it was seen as a radical new experiment and was even funded by the Carnegie Foundation. A number of underprivileged local students enrolled in the six-year program.[149] It has since ceased to operate as a separate college and is now the Matteo Ricci Institute in Seattle University's College of Arts and Sciences. Although the six-year plan of study has faded away over the years, the department still offers college-in-high-school credit at five Catholic high schools in the Seattle area and administers unique, humanities-based bachelor's degree programs.

---

147. O'Hare, "Jesuit Education," 151.

148. Ibid., 151.

149. Crowley, *Seattle University*, 97–98.

Pedro Arrupe died in 1981. Concerned about the state of the Jesuit order, Pope John Paul II intervened in the usual process to select Arrupe's successor, appointing his preferred candidate, the Italian Paolo Dezza, SJ, on an interim basis. When the Jesuits ultimately convened in Rome in 1983, the Dutch-born Peter Hans Kolvenbach, SJ emerged as the new superior general. Although Arrupe had spent time in the United States as a seminarian, Kolvenbach was the first permanent superior general with teaching experience at an American Jesuit university, having served on the faculty at Georgetown. He saw synergies between social justice and education, encouraging the Jesuits to integrate those two sides of their ministry so that, in O'Hare's words, "a healthy exchange between the university and the activist could ensue. . . . (R)esearch and understanding are essential to effective social change."[150]

1989: A Bicentennial Celebration

To celebrate the 200th anniversary of its founding (and thus, of Jesuit higher education in the United States), Georgetown hosted a series of activities in 1989, reflecting on its past and planning for its future. The year culminated in "Assembly '89: Jesuit Ministry in Higher Education"—a conference that drew about nine hundred participants (750 Jesuits and 180 laypeople) from all twenty-eight Jesuit colleges and universities in the United States.

Georgetown's previous anniversary celebrations had been largely internal affairs that did not engage the broader Jesuit network.. At its centennial in 1889, it had awarded medals to President Grover Cleveland and James Cardinal Gibbons, Archbishop of Baltimore.[151] Its 175th anniversary in 1964 featured an address by Pope Paul VI via telecast and a scheduled speech by John F. Kennedy (actually delivered by Lyndon Johnson after Kennedy's assassination). In both cases, the audiences at these celebrations were mainly Georgetown faculty and students. The bicentennial in 1989, however, was a broad celebration of the entire Jesuit network—not just of Georgetown. Even allowing that travel to Washington, DC was much easier in 1989 than in those earlier years, it is notable the Jesuit schools celebrated this milestone together only after they had legally separated from each other. Back in the days when Georgetown was formally united to other Jesuit colleges (through the Jesuit province and ultimately through the Society of Jesus in Rome), its celebrations were more limited in scope. Once cooperation became voluntary rather than mandatory, the Jesuit universities found a new desire to celebrate their shared history together.

Father General Kolvenbach flew from Rome to attend the conference, where he spoke to the faculty and university presidents assembled. According to one Jesuit who witnessed the speech, Kolvenbach used the opportunity to offer a hopeful, realistic view of Jesuit higher education:

---

150. O'Hare, "Jesuit Education," 152.
151. Curran, *History of Georgetown Vol. I*, 349.

In the past three decades . . . the entire context of Jesuit education has changed "irrevocably." He (Kolvenbach) urged his fellow Jesuits not to spend time lamenting this fact or trying to deny it. They should recognize that "this changed world of ours is the only one in which we are called to work out our mission. How best to exercise our apostolic influence in the present is the only question worthy of our attention.[152]

Another keynote speaker was Cornell University President Frank H. T. Rhodes, who urged the Jesuits to remember their unique approach to higher education, which he saw as a valuable addition to the intellectual diversity of the American academy. Speaking as a Protestant and as president of an avowedly secular institution, Rhodes praised the Jesuit colleges for their history of training immigrants, helping them "contribute to American life while keeping the tenets of their faith in a land of largely Protestant heritage." He described their work as a "heroic story of dedication and scholarship," but he challenged them to maintain their distinctiveness, so that their Jesuit identity remained a living and vibrant part of their mission, not simply a historical reference to their origins. He urged the Jesuits to draw upon their tradition of adaptability and keep themselves engaged in the world as it is, not as "quaint critics of a bygone era" but as active scholars bringing their unique voices to the conversation. Most provocatively, he challenged them: "Probably no single Jesuit institution now qualifies as among the very top 20 or so US institutions in terms of scholarly excellence. It is appropriate, I think, to ask why not and also to ask whether an appropriate goal might be one superb Jesuit institution."[153]

Such was the task that awaited Jesuit universities as they strove, not just toward excellence, but toward a uniquely Jesuit form of excellence in the twenty-first century.

---

152. McFadden, "Introduction," xv.

153. Frank H. T. Rhodes, "The Mission and Ministry of Jesuits in Higher Education," *America* (5 August 1989), as reprinted by Boston College Office of University Mission and Ministry, 5, 6, 10, https://www.bc.edu/content/dam/files/offices/mission/pdf1/ju10.pdf.

Part VII:

Modern Universities (1990–Present)

Overview, 1990–Present

By the 1990s, universities had become like small cities, and the role of university president was akin to that of a city mayor. Once upon a time, Jesuit colleges had been nothing more than small communities of a few dozen students and a handful of faculty. Now, they operated their own police departments, their own fleets of buses, and in four cases, multimillion-dollar hospital networks. Students numbered in the thousands. In 1910, the total combined enrollment of all Jesuit colleges and universities nationwide (including their affiliated high schools) had been less than 15,000.[1] By 2010, there were six *individual* universities (Boston College, Fordham, Georgetown, Loyola of Chicago, Marquette, and Saint Louis) that *each* enrolled close to 15,000 students.

In the distant past, a Jesuit college campus required nothing more than a few classrooms, a chapel, and an optional open area for sleeping (if it was a boarding school). Now, the campuses included health clubs, apartment complexes, and high-tech laboratories with sophisticated equipment. Universities increasingly had to be all things to all people, providing not just an education, but counseling and psychiatric services, legal services, immigration support, and computer support, to name just a few of their responsibilities. In addition, they were simultaneously managing huge library complexes, professional fundraising operations, radio and television stations, academic presses, and sports media empires that rivaled the professional leagues in popularity. It was enough to make any college president's head spin.

Decades had now passed since the Jesuits decided to send most of their young priests to graduate school to earn PhDs. Many Jesuits had now become respected scholars, and the secular academy was paying attention to their work. Some Jesuits were so highly regarded in their fields that non-Catholic universities sought to hire them. During this era, individual Jesuits became tenured professors or deans at Harvard, the University of Virginia, and elsewhere. Jesuit philosopher Patrick Heelan, SJ served as vice president of the State University of New York at Stony Brook in the 1970s and 1980s before accepting a similar position at Georgetown in the early 1990s. Former Georgetown President Timothy Healy, SJ served as president of the New York Public Library from 1989 to 1992. By any measure, Jesuits were some of the best-educated people in America, and many became respected civic as well as religious leaders.

Yet their numbers continued to fall precipitously. Between 2011 and 2020, in response to declining membership, the ten Jesuit provinces merged into four—

---

1. "Students in our colleges, in the United States and Canada, Oct. 1, 1910," *Woodstock Letters* XXXIX, no. 3 (1910): unnumbered page.

roughly comparable to the four provinces that had existed in the early 1900s. These mergers brought many Jesuit institutions (like Georgetown and Holy Cross) back into the same provincial networks for the first time in decades. Laypeople began to replace Jesuits in the college presidents' offices. The centuries-old criticism that Jesuit universities were "not Catholic enough" suddenly took on new meaning as the Jesuits themselves became small minorities on their own campuses. New guidelines from the Vatican, in the form of Pope John Paul II's *Ex corde Ecclesiae*, sought to help Catholic universities understand and maintain their Catholic identity in this new reality. Jesuit universities became proactive about that identity and sought ways to express it in modern terms.

In addition to all of this change, several Jesuit colleges found themselves caught in the crosshairs of national tragedies. The terrorist attacks of September 11, 2001 took place within eyesight of the campuses of Georgetown, Fordham, and Saint Peter's Universities. Four years later, Hurricane Katrina struck New Orleans, forcing Loyola University to suspend classes for the fall 2005 semester. In a remarkable gesture of solidarity, all Jesuit colleges opened their doors to Loyola undergraduates after the hurricane, welcoming them as guest students for the fall term so that they could continue their education uninterrupted. Loyola's law students were likewise offered seats at any Jesuit law school for the semester. In 2021, when Hurricane Ida struck New Orleans and left Loyola University without power, busloads of Loyola students found refuge at Spring Hill College in Mobile, which housed them just as it had housed students from fire-stricken St. Charles College in 1907.

The demographics of America were changing. Catholic families who traced their roots to places like Italy, Ireland, France, and Eastern Europe were assimilating as the old immigrant generations died out and baby boomers—who had not grown up bilingual and who had been encouraged by their parents to blend into American society—raised largely Americanized families of their own. The Northeast and the Midwest, where most Jesuit colleges were located, grayed and lost population. It was a booming time for Catholic senior care centers and Catholic cemeteries, but not for Catholic education. The only major growth in the Catholic Church in America was taking place in the Southwest and (for the first time since the Civil War) in the South, where Latin American immigrants brought their largely Catholic faith to a region almost devoid of Catholic colleges and universities.

Catholics were also making major inroads into national politics. When Fordham Law graduate Geraldine Ferraro ran for vice president of the United States in 1984, she faced sharper criticism from Church leaders unhappy with her stance on abortion than from American Protestants unhappy with the prospect of a Catholic so close to the presidency. By 1993, the United States had a Jesuit-educated president—Bill Clinton, who was himself a Southern Baptist but often spoke of his Georgetown degree when courting the Catholic vote.[2] (Decades earlier, Lyndon Johnson had

---

2. Clinton, *My Life*, 76.

briefly attended Georgetown Law School, but never graduated.) When Boston College Law alumnus John Kerry ran for president in 2004 and when Rockhurst High School alumnus Tim Kaine ran for vice president in 2016, critics hardly mentioned their Catholic faith, although Kaine in particular emphasized his Ignatian values as his motivation for pursuing a public service career. Catholics also became a majority on the United States Supreme Court, including Georgetown-educated Antonin Scalia and Holy Cross-educated Clarence Thomas.

Jesuit college alumni pursued public service careers at a notable rate. They became so numerous in the United States Congress that the AJCU began tracking them and publishing a list after every federal election; the 117th Congress included 13 senators and 41 members of the House of Representatives with Jesuit degrees.[3] Other notable public servants include presidential advisor Anthony Fauci (Holy Cross) and several state governors, such as Alaska's Frank Murkowski (Seattle and Santa Clara), Arizona's Janet Napolitano (Santa Clara), California's Gavin Newsom (Santa Clara), and Oklahoma's Frank Keating (Georgetown). Outside of government, Jesuit alumni achieved fame in a wide variety of fields. The list includes broadcasters Norah O'Donnell (Georgetown), Tim Russert (John Carroll), Maria Shriver (Georgetown), and Chris Matthews (Holy Cross); actors Alan Alda (Fordham), Linda Cardellini (Loyola Marymount), Bradley Cooper (Georgetown), Chris Farley (Marquette), Jim Gaffigan (Georgetown), Amy Madigan (Marquette), Bill Murray (Regis), Bob Newhart (Loyola of Chicago), Chris O'Donnell (Boston College), Amy Poehler (Boston College), Denzel Washington (Fordham), and George Wendt (Rockhurst); and authors Tom Clancy (Loyola of Baltimore) and Elmore Leonard (Detroit), to name but a few. As the many ethnic surnames in this paragraph suggest, most of these people were descended from Catholic immigrants for whom such influential careers would have been impossible generations earlier. It had taken time, but Catholics and other Jesuit-educated individuals were finally contributing their voices to American politics, media, and the intellectual zeitgeist in ways that John Tracy Ellis and others of his generation had only dreamed.

In 2019, the imbalance between Catholic demographic growth (concentrated in the South) and Catholic education (concentrated in the aging north) claimed a victim in the Jesuit network. Wheeling Jesuit University, the youngest of the Jesuit colleges, downsized dramatically in response to declining enrollment. With most of its humanities departments eliminated, it no longer offered a recognizably Jesuit education, and the Jesuits ended their affiliation with the school. The university continues as a diocesan institution—which is more than can be said for many other small, northern colleges (Catholic and non-Catholic) that had no choice but to close permanently in the 2010s. These enrollment pressures only intensified during the coronavirus pandemic that struck the United States in 2020 and forced virtually all American colleges to

---

3. "Jesuit Alumni in Congress," Association of Jesuit Colleges and Universities, 2021, https://www.ajcunet.edu/alumni-in-congress.

teach classes remotely via the internet. Losing millions of dollars in revenue as dorms sat empty and students deferred admission, many of the small colleges that did survive were forced to implement drastic cost-saving measures.

In sum, although by some measures Catholics and Catholic education in the United States had never been stronger, Catholic colleges and universities faced new versions of familiar issues, and they remained engaged in a yearly struggle to compete with better-financed public and private universities across the country. Their challenge now was to hold their own in that environment and maintain a Jesuit spirit without Jesuits in charge.

Ex corde Ecclesiae (1990)

St. John Paul II was elected pope in 1978, and soon thereafter began to prioritize a stronger relationship between the Church and its universities. Although the Vatican had a number of concordats (or diplomatic agreements) with individual countries that addressed Catholic higher education, it had never drafted a clear, universal statement on the nature of Catholic universities. Such statements existed, but had been written by universities themselves through the efforts of the International Federation of Catholic Universities or similar organizations. As such, they emphasized academic freedom and other issues that were more important to the universities than to the Church authorities. John Paul II sought to issue a statement that clearly defined the Catholic university and applied equally to all institutions across the globe. In 1980, he charged the Congregation for Catholic Education with drafting such a document.

This was no easy task. The Vatican was attempting to write a set of standards and guidelines for a worldwide audience, but the nature of higher education differed widely from country to country. There were some countries in which the government tightly controlled all education and forced the Catholic Church into what amounted to a junior partnership at its own universities; there were others in which Catholic universities operated with impunity and virtually no state oversight. Different cultures had wildly different ideas about the appropriate age of "college" students and the nature of the work necessary to earn a bachelor's degree. Drafting a general statement that applied equally to education systems as diverse as those of Brazil, Congo, India, Japan, Poland, and the United States seemed a near impossibility.

Nonetheless, by 1985, a working draft of the document was ready for review. The Vatican circulated it to Catholic university presidents and others, requesting feedback. Called the "Draft Schema of a Pontifical Document on Catholic Universities," the proposal echoed much of what the universities had written in their own position papers up to that point. It referred to importance of modern science, religious pluralism, and service to the Church. However, the Schema also asserted explicit Church control over the universities and defined a limited oversight role for local bishops. It charged local bishops with ensuring that "the principles of Catholic doctrine are faithfully observed" on campus (particularly in theology departments), and it empowered the bishops to "declare the university to be no longer Catholic" if the "Catholic character of the university continues to be compromised in a serious way."[4] It also sought to establish a norm that the president of a Catholic university must be a practicing Catholic.

The reaction from American Catholic universities was resoundingly negative. University presidents responded with alarm to the suggestion that the Vatican or local bishops might assert even limited authority over internal campus issues. Sister Alice Gallin, OSU, a Fordham alumna and president of the Association of Catholic Colleges and Universities (ACCU), summarized the universities' reactions in a letter to the Vatican in early 1986. Emphasizing the highly decentralized nature of American academia, she wrote, "You will understand . . . why most of those responding would find it more advantageous to the work of the Church in American Higher Education if this kind of juridical document were not issued at all."[5] She further objected to the notion that bishops should exercise significant authority over theology professors. Gallin argued that, while bishops have a legitimate teaching authority, it was "the theologians whose task it is to explore new insights and push beyond present understandings of the faith. The university is the home of the theologian, not the bishop, and the bishop must respect that fact."[6]

In other words, there was a difference between the kind of teaching done by bishops from the pulpit on Sundays and the kind done by university professors in the classroom on weekdays. In the former, the message was vetted, official, and designed to promote clarity; in the latter, new ideas could be proposed, challenged, and questioned. Sister Gallin also pointed out that, "While ninety-nine percent of the Catholic colleges and universities have Catholic presidents, it would be unfortunate to state that it must always be so. . . . These things are better left to the wisdom and prudence of the board of trustees."[7]

To emphasize the point, the Board of Directors of the ACCU almost simultaneously sent its own letter to the Vatican in 1986, arguing against a stronger role for bishops in academic affairs. "The very life of our colleges and universities," the board wrote, ". . . is one of academic freedom and self-regulation by the academic community." The ACCU pointed out that American Catholic universities represented the largest and most influential block of universities within the global Church, so the American way of doing things in higher education should be given more consideration in any global policy statement.[8]

---

4. "Draft Schema of a Pontifical Document on Catholic Universities," in *American Catholic Higher Education*, ed. Gallin, 206.

5. Alice Gallin, "Synthesis of Responses received from U.S. Catholic College and University Presidents to the Pontifical Document on Catholic Universities," in *American Catholic Higher Education*, ed. Gallin, 264.

6. Ibid. 270.

7. Ibid., 271.

8. "Response of the Board of Directors of the Association of Catholic Colleges and Universities on 'Proposed Schema for a Pontifical Document on Catholic Universities,'" in *American Catholic Higher Education*, ed. Gallin, 274.

In a third letter, the presidents of thirteen of the largest and most prestigious American Catholic research universities raised objections to the Draft Schema in 1986, arguing that it would do more harm than good if published. Among the thirteen American signatories of the letter were eight Jesuits: the presidents of Boston College, Detroit, Georgetown, Marquette, Santa Clara, and Saint Louis, as well as Father William Byron, SJ, who was then serving as president of the Catholic University of America. Joining them were the presidents of DePaul, Notre Dame, Villanova, the University of Dayton, and the University of San Diego (the only layman on the list). This illustrious group argued that, if the Schema were published as written:

> Secularistic critics of Catholic education would find that their most searing critiques of Catholic universities had been confirmed by the Vatican itself. For if the relationship of these universities to the Church, as defined in this Schema, must necessarily involve control by the Church, then Catholic universities cannot respect academic freedom, and cannot enjoy true institutional autonomy. . . . This, at least, would be the view of most of the academic communities in North America and a good part of our general public.

> Our critics would charge that such direct ecclesiastical control means that our institutions are not universities at all but places of narrow sectarian indoctrination; hence they have no right to claim public monies to support what would be described as their proselytizing mission. If such a view prevailed in our courts, then decades of sacrifice by generations of faculty, students, and benefactors of Catholic universities in North America would have been squandered.[9]

John Paul II proved to be responsive to these concerns. The final document no longer contained the provision requiring the president of a Catholic university to be a Catholic. The Apostolic Constitution, known as *Ex corde Ecclesiae* ("From the Heart of the Church") also guaranteed that a Catholic university "possesses that institutional autonomy necessary to perform its functions effectively and guarantees its members academic freedom, so long as the rights of the individual person and of the community are preserved within the confines of the truth and the common good."[10]

Despite its overall tone of open-mindedness, however, *Ex corde* proved to be a lightning rod for controversy. Against the wishes of some critics, the final version preserved a provision giving local bishops the right to determine whether or not universities in their diocese were "Catholic." This in and of itself would not have been terribly controversial, since it merely codified what had been done in practice since at least the 1700s. Far more contentious was *Ex corde's* reference to a concept known as the *mandatum*.

The *mandatum* quickly and perhaps unfairly came to be seen as the defining feature of *Ex corde*. If professors knew nothing else about *Ex corde*, they typically knew

---

9. "Statement of Presidents of Leading Catholic Universities of North America on the Schema for a Proposed Document on the Catholic University," in *American Catholic Higher Education*, ed. Gallin, 279–280.

10. "Ex corde Ecclesiae" in *American Catholic Higher Education*, ed. Gallin, 417.

that it "required" theology professors at Catholic universities to obtain a mandate—or *mandatum*—from the local bishop approving their right to teach. This essentially meant that the bishops had the right to "approve" or verify that Catholic theology professors at Catholic universities were in compliance with Church doctrine.

The concept of the *mandatum* and its relationship to *Ex corde* is sometimes misunderstood. In fact, *Ex corde* mentions the word *mandatum* only once—and only in a footnote near the end of the document. Furthermore, *Ex corde* did not introduce the notion that Catholic theologians are answerable to their local bishop; that principle already existed in canon law, though it was a relatively recent addition. At the time *Ex corde* was promulgated, there were already canons that gave bishops authority over theology professors—specifically, canon 810, which states that bishops can (at least take steps to) remove professors who inaccurately represent Catholic doctrine, and canon 812, which states that professors who teach theology must have a *mandatum* from Church authorities.

Both of these laws were designed primarily to meet the needs of Catholic universities in Europe. During the Revolutions of 1848, the various governments of what is today Germany took control of Church-sponsored universities and secularized them; German Catholic bishops insisted on having some say in the appointment of theology faculty because otherwise there was no way to ensure that the newly secular institutions would represent Catholic belief correctly. The Vatican negotiated with the German governments to maintain some level of influence over the theology departments of what were, by then, thoroughly public universities.[11] Naturally, there was never a need for such an agreement with the United States, where theologians were protected from government interference by both the Constitution and by the norms of academic freedom.[12]

For many years, these rules about the *mandatum* applied only to a few specific European countries with which the Vatican had negotiated accords. There was no standard by which to apply it globally. In fact, the code of canon law in effect worldwide between 1917 and 1983 barely mentioned Catholic higher education, apart from a few laws about seminaries. However, when John Paul II revised the code of canon law in 1983, the revamped rules included several broad references to Catholic universities, including canons 810 and 812.

Ex corde Ecclesiae merely drew attention to these laws when it was published seven years later. Its references were not overt; the only mentions of canons 810 and 812 come in the form of footnotes. Earlier drafts had been much blunter and more direct about bishops' authority over theologians; the final version of *Ex corde* was much toned-down on this issue, but the reference to the *mandatum* was still there, buried deep.

---

11. Alice Gallin, "Construction of the Code of Canon Law of 1983, 1977–1983," in *American Catholic Higher Education*, ed. Gallin, 153. "Code of Canon Law: Commentary on Canons 807–814," in *American Catholic Higher Education*, ed. Gallin, 184.

12. "Code of Canon Law: Commentary," 177.

In 2001, the United States Conference of Catholic Bishops released guidelines on how the *mandatum* would be implemented in America. Those guidelines clarified that the *mandatum* was simply a bishop's acknowledgement that theologians were not misrepresenting Catholic teaching in their teaching and writing. It applied only to Catholic faculty members teaching Catholic theology; all other professors in all other departments on campus were entirely exempt. Even theology professors were exempt if they were not Catholic or if they taught courses on other religions. Moreover, it was the responsibility of each individual theologian, not the university, to pursue and obtain a *mandatum*. The entire process was so limited in scope that it bordered on being inconsequential to most universities and their faculty.

Nonetheless, reaction from the academic community was strong. Theology professors, including many priests, expressed dismay at the notion that their work was subject to any kind of quality control beyond normal peer review. Many questioned why this extremely limited form of bureaucracy was even necessary. In effect, the *mandatum* simply verified that a professor was not presenting personal opinion as official Catholic doctrine. In the end, only a handful of theology departments at Catholic universities ever required their professors to obtain the *mandatum*, and the vast majority left the matter up to individual faculty members, many of whom ignored the requirement. American bishops, by and large, did not enforce the *mandatum* requirement, nor did they draw undue attention to what they realized was a controversial issue. The rules remained in effect, but there were few, if any, consequences for theology professors who did not comply.

In the end, the controversy over the *mandatum* obscured much of the value in *Ex corde Ecclesiae*. In the same way that conservative Catholics tend to reject the Land O'Lakes Statement solely because of its stance on academic freedom, liberal Catholics tend to reject *Ex corde* because of its stance on bishops' authority. Both groups do so to their own detriment. The Land O'Lakes Statement is, at its heart, a conservative document that tries to preserve the best of the Catholic educational tradition in a modern context; *Ex corde* is, at its core, a liberal document that affirms virtually all of the principles that universities value, including academic freedom, interreligious dialogue, and pluralism.[13] Both, if read in their entirety, offer wisdom and strategic thinking to help Catholic universities maintain both academic excellence and a strong religious identity.

Lay Presidents

After Jesuit universities separately incorporated in the late 1960s and early 1970s, selecting a Jesuit as the university president became mostly a matter of tradition and not a requirement. Marquette, Loyola (New Orleans), Santa Clara, and a handful of other schools originally adopted bylaws that required the president to be a

---

13. See Rizzi, "Newman's *Idea*." Rizzi, "We've Been Here Before," 166–167.

Jesuit, while the bylaws at Saint Joseph's in Philadelphia merely said that a Jesuit president was "desirable."[14] Even where they existed, most such rules eventually had to be amended because of the limited number of Jesuit priests available. Many observers tacitly wondered: how long would it be, after separate incorporation opened the door, before a Jesuit university hired a lay president? The answer, as it happened, was about thirty years.

By the early 2000s, there were fewer than 4,000 Jesuits in the United States, and that number would fall below 3,000 by 2010. Moreover, the *average* age of these men was over 60.[15] Although Jesuits' active, meaningful, and relatively stress-free lives often kept them in the workforce well past normal retirement age, it became extremely difficult to find qualified young Jesuits with the skills and stamina to take on a university presidency. Finding one such leader was a challenge; finding twenty-eight at any given time was a near impossibility. The job of university president is so multi-faceted, so complex, and so unforgiving that only a *rara avis* can do it successfully. In the twenty-first century, the average tenure of all university presidents in the United States declined to just over six years, reflecting the difficulty of the job.[16] Leading a small, intimate liberal arts college like Spring Hill was hard enough; leading a massive, comprehensive university like Georgetown or Saint Louis required a rare skill set indeed.

At the turn of the twentieth century, lay presidents were no longer a rarity at Catholic colleges and universities. Many colleges sponsored by other religious orders had made the transition decades earlier. Yet Jesuit schools maintained a reputation for keeping Jesuits in the front office. In 2000, there was only one Jesuit university with a non-Jesuit president: the University of Detroit Mercy, still led by Sister Maureen Fay, OP. None were led by laypeople. Inevitably, any Jesuit with leadership experience automatically became a prime candidate in the eyes of presidential search committees. Some Jesuits were hired as presidents despite having limited administrative backgrounds; many proved competent once entrusted with the job, but there was sometimes little in their past work experience to prepare them for the financial, managerial, and other responsibilities inherent in the role.

In 2001, Georgetown hired John DeGioia as president, making him the first layperson to lead a Jesuit university in the United States. A lay president was not entirely inevitable at the time; many other universities hired Jesuit presidents in the early 2000s, and there were several Jesuits on the Georgetown faculty—including Scott Pilarz, SJ, Michael Garanzini, SJ, and Kevin Wildes, SJ—who would go on to become respected presidents of other Jesuit institutions before the end of the

---

14. Contosta, *Saint Joseph's*, 276. See also McKevitt, *University of Santa Clara*, 297.

15. Center for Applied Research in the Apostolate, "The Changing Jesuit Geography," Nineteen Sixty-Four Blog (1 February 2011), http://nineteensixty-four.blogspot.com/2011/02/changing-jesuit-geography.html.

16. Andy Thomanson, "Is College President 'the Toughest Job in the Nation'?" *Chronicle of Higher Education* (1 May 2018), https://www.chronicle.com/article/is-college-president-the-toughest-job-in-the-nation/#:~:text=The%20tenure%20of%20college%20presidents,8.5%20years%20a%20decade%20before.

decade. John DeGioia, however, was clearly a qualified candidate, and he outlasted all of those other men in his time in office. He was a two-time Georgetown alumnus who had served previously as Georgetown's senior vice president; his appointment came by unanimous vote of Georgetown's board of directors and carried the strong, vocal support of Georgetown's Jesuit community. Familiar with the Jesuit tradition and dedicated to preserving it, he often referenced Georgetown's Jesuit identity in his speeches and created a number of presidential-level initiatives, such as the Initiative on Catholic Social Thought and Public Life, to keep that identity visible and relevant.

As the twentieth century wore on, other Jesuit universities followed Georgetown's precedent. Many lay presidents came from within the Jesuit network, since presidential search committees often made familiarity with the Jesuit tradition a prerequisite for the job. Spring Hill College's Christopher Puto was a former dean of the business school at Georgetown. Fred Pestello, an alumnus of John Carroll University, served as president of Le Moyne College for six years before becoming president of Saint Louis University in 2014. Saint Joseph's University President Mark Reed was an alumnus of both Fairfield University and Boston College.

In 2010, Loyola Marymount became the first Jesuit university to hire a non-Catholic president, though he was no stranger to Jesuit education. David Burcham was an alumnus and former dean of Loyola Law School in Los Angeles. He served as university president until 2015, when he was succeeded by Timothy Law Snyder—a Catholic formerly on the faculty at Georgetown, Fairfield, and Loyola (Baltimore).

The rise of lay presidents made it possible for more women to lead Jesuit colleges and universities, following in the footsteps of the first trailblazer, Sister Maureen Fay of Detroit. In 2014, Linda LeMura became the first laywoman to serve as a Jesuit college president, taking the helm of Le Moyne College after serving as a Le Moyne dean and provost. Jo Ann Rooney rose to the presidency of Loyola University (Chicago) in 2016, and Louisiana attorney Tania Tetlow became president of Loyola University (New Orleans) two years later. In 2022, Tetlow was announced as the next president of Fordham University, making her the first woman to be named to the top executive role at two Jesuit institutions. Between 2021 and 2022, women also served as president or acting president at Loyola (Baltimore), Regis, Santa Clara, and Xavier.

There were logistical issues associated with the transition to lay presidents. Many American universities provide free housing for their presidents, but at Jesuit institutions, most presidents had traditionally lived in simple accommodations in the Jesuit residence along with their fellow priests. Now that the universities were hiring laypeople with spouses and sometimes children, many Jesuit institutions had to purchase a house somewhere near campus to serve as their official presidential residence. That, along with the president's salary, often represented a significant financial investment for the university. Some Jesuit presidents had declined to accept a salary during their time in office, and while this saved their institutions a substantial amount of money, it made the shock to the budget even more dramatic when the universities had to add a six-figure presidential salary to their expenses.

Recently, Jesuit universities have also looked to priests outside of the Society of Jesus in their presidential searches. In 2006, Rockhurst University hired Father Thomas Curran as president; Curran was a member of the Oblates of St. Francis de Sales, but later transferred his vows to the Society of Jesus and became a Jesuit while in office.

As of the 2021–2022 academic year, a majority of Jesuit colleges and universities (twenty-one of twenty-seven) were led by lay presidents.

A New Approach to Mission

The rise of lay presidents arguably improved the visibility of the universities' Jesuit identity. As long as a Jesuit priest occupied the president's office, it was easy for faculty, staff, and students to take their institution's Jesuit mission somewhat for granted, assuming that the trappings of that mission were handed down from the top. When lay presidents came into office, the university's Jesuit mission became, to an extent, everyone's responsibility. The Jesuits living on campus became a special resource rather than a privileged clique. They were present to serve the university rather than manage it—offering workshops on Jesuit pedagogy and spirituality, counseling faculty and students, and serving as chaplains—making them a kind of live-in resource that secular universities lacked.

Jesuit universities had always been run like family businesses, but the increasing role of laypeople in the administration extended the "family" far beyond the Jesuit community. It was no longer a mere platitude for a Jesuit leader to say that everyone on campus shared responsibility for the university mission; lay presidents could now emphasize that imperative by personal example, demonstrating how laypeople could embrace and live out the Ignatian spirit. In their writing, speeches, and public appearances, lay presidents like John DeGioia continually reminded their campus communities of the value of the Jesuit approach to education and deliberately invested university resources in programs that reflect and support that tradition.

In the 1990s and early 2000s, many Jesuit universities created a new position specifically to oversee activities related to their Jesuit mission. Often called "vice president for mission," these new positions reflected a desire to be more proactive about mission issues and ensure that upper-level decision making reflected Jesuit values. These individuals advocate for the institution's Jesuit identity and promote awareness of it, in the same way that a "vice president for diversity and inclusion" might advocate for and promote awareness of the needs of underrepresented students on campus. The University of San Francisco created a University Council for Jesuit Mission.[17]

These new officers worked with the human resources staff to orient new employees to the Jesuit tradition and to promote mission-driven hiring practices; they spoke

17. Michael T. Rizzi, "Defining Catholic Higher Education in Positive Terms," *Journal of Catholic Education* 22, no. 2. (2019): 20.

at student orientations and supervised campus ministry offices, retreat programs, community service initiatives, and volunteer programs. Many produced videos, brochures, and other media about Ignatian spirituality or conducted workshops on Jesuit pedagogy for faculty. Virtually all worked closely with the university president and other high-level administrators. Many, but by no means all, of the individuals who held these positions were Jesuit priests; laypeople served as the point person (or at least one of the point people) for Jesuit mission in at least ten of the twenty-eight universities in 2015.[18]

The LGBTQ Rights Movement

The movement toward LGBTQ equality emerged as one of the defining civil rights issues of the early twenty-first century, leading to the legalization of same-sex marriage through the 2015 Supreme Court case, *Obergefell v. Hodges*. Colleges and universities—both Catholic and non-Catholic—responded to this movement as it gained momentum.

Catholic teaching on homosexuality is sometimes misunderstood. Although the Catholic Church disapproves of sexual behavior outside of marriage, it does not view homosexuality itself as inherently sinful; merely being homosexual does not put an individual at odds with Church teaching or incapable of receiving the sacraments. To the contrary, the Church has repeatedly affirmed that LGBTQ individuals are human beings worthy of dignity, respect, and love, and many Catholic dioceses have organized LGBTQ ministry and outreach programs.

LGBTQ rights issues periodically came up in Jesuit higher education in the mid-to-late 1900s, but the universities were not yet warm to the idea of officially recognized LGBTQ student groups. Some such groups existed unofficially on campus for decades without receiving university funding. At Fordham, the group FLAG (Fordham Lesbians and Gays) traced its roots to the late 1970s and applied for recognition by the university in 1990; that application was rejected—not by the Jesuits in the administration, but by the student leaders in Fordham's student government.[19]

Attitudes toward LGBTQ groups and resource centers on campus changed in the early 2000s. This was due in part to changing attitudes in society at large, although there were some Jesuits—most notably prolific author and speaker James Martin, SJ—who became vocal advocates for LGBTQ issues. Among the twenty-eight Jesuit colleges and universities, Loyola (Baltimore) was an early pioneer in this field. Loyola's LGBTQ student organization traced its roots to 1995, and in 2003, the college established "Stonewall House" as a resource for LGBTQ students. An LGBTQ organization for Loyola faculty and staff followed in 2004. Georgetown opened a resource center in 2008.

---

18. Association of Jesuit Colleges and Universities, "AJCU Mission and Identity Survey, 2014–2015," https://static1.squarespace.com/static/55d1dd88e4b0dee65a6594f0/t/56043592e4b043d49b5d54c2/1443116434506/AJCUMissionSurveyFinal_10-14.pdf.

19. Shelley, *Fordham*, 484–485.

By the end of the 2010s, most Jesuit colleges (and many Catholic colleges sponsored by other religious orders) would do the same and officially recognized groups and/or resource centers or programs designed to serve LGBTQ students. Many cited such initiatives as an example of their commitment to the Jesuit principle of *cura personalis*—care for the whole person.

Merging with Theological Schools

As the number of Jesuits declined, it became difficult for each Jesuit province to maintain seminaries for their young priests-in-training. By the early 2000s, only two stand-alone Jesuit graduate schools of theology remained in the United States: the Weston Jesuit School of Theology in Cambridge, Massachusetts, and the Jesuit School of Theology at Berkeley in Berkeley, California.

Both of those seminaries accepted lay students as a way to keep themselves afloat, but as time progressed, it became increasingly difficult to maintain the human infrastructure necessary to run independent graduate theological schools. The two seminaries needed registrars, secretaries, librarians, IT support, and human resource officers, not to mention faculty. Many independent seminaries in the United States were facing similar challenges at that time, and many were affiliating with established universities as a way to save costs. This enabled them to keep their records in the university's existing archives and take advantage of the university's support services without duplicating staffing.

In 2008, the Weston Jesuit School of Theology affiliated with Boston College and formed the core of what became known as the Boston College School of Theology and Ministry. It relocated from Cambridge to a new campus diagonally across the street from Boston College in Chestnut Hill; formerly, the property had been the Boston Archdiocesan seminary before Boston College purchased it two years earlier. The school's original building in Cambridge, located just blocks from the Harvard campus, was sold and is now used for offices.

Likewise, the Jesuit School of Theology at Berkeley affiliated with Santa Clara University in 2009, renaming itself the Jesuit School of Theology of Santa Clara University. The seminary, however, remained on its original campus in Berkeley, located a few blocks from the University of California campus.

The remnants of the old Woodstock College, after a brief stay in New York in the 1970s, relocated to the Georgetown University campus, becoming the Woodstock Theological Center. While it existed, the center became a well-known think tank on theological issues, but it closed in 2013 after the Jesuits concluded that they could no longer staff or support it due to their declining personnel. All that remains of Woodstock is its impressive theological library, one of the largest in the world, housed in Georgetown's Lauinger Library.

Today, the theological schools in Boston and Berkeley continue to educate Jesuits and lay students alike, and both have been strengthened by their affiliations with recognized universities. This outcome is not a little ironic. For over two hundred years, the Jesuits had separated their seminaries from their lay colleges, often at enormous cost. Ever since John Carroll established Georgetown College and St. Mary's Seminary as separate institutions in the 1790s, the Jesuits spent the modern-day equivalent of millions of dollars to build an enormous infrastructure of seminaries—some of which siphoned much-needed resources away from the core universities. Although these seminaries certainly played an important role in the lives of the priests who studied there, in the end, none of them survived as independent educational institutions. Some, like St. Charles College in Louisiana and Colombiere College in Michigan, evolved into Jesuit retreat centers that are still used at some stages of Jesuit training, but most of the Jesuits' seminary education today takes place at Jesuit universities. Had the Jesuits organized their educational network along those lines from the beginning—keeping their seminarians and their lay students on the same campuses—they would have saved enormous amounts of time, energy, and money that ultimately could have been put to better use in the institutions that did survive.

As of 2020, most Jesuit seminarians complete their preliminary studies at Fordham, Saint Louis, or Loyola (Chicago) before moving on to advanced training at one of the two graduate theological schools at Boston College or Santa Clara. Independently, two other Jesuit universities offer some form of seminary training. Creighton sponsors an Institute of Priestly Formation, which offers programs for diocesan priests from around the country. Gonzaga hosts on its campus the Bishop White Seminary, the undergraduate seminary for the Diocese of Spokane.

Jesuit Colleges on September 11, 2001

When *al Qaeda* terrorists attacked the United States using four hijacked civilian airplanes in 2001, universities from coast to coast cancelled classes and held prayer services for the victims. While all Jesuit institutions were in some way affected, Fordham, Georgetown, and Saint Peter's were particularly close to the tragedy.

In New York, the collapse of the World Trade Center made travel into Manhattan virtually impossible. Students and employees at Fordham's campus in The Bronx were prohibited from leaving unless they were traveling to the northern suburbs. Those who lived in Manhattan or further south had no choice but to spend the night of September 11 on campus, where the university set up cots and other makeshift accommodations in the library and other buildings. Many commuter students overnighted with friends in the dorms. Fordham's Lincoln Center campus in Manhattan was especially close to the World Trade Center site, and its students and staff, effectively trapped in their buildings, hastily organized a prayer service led by the campus undergraduate dean, Father Robert Grimes, SJ.[20] Similarly, students and faculty at Saint Peter's were trapped in New Jersey, unable to return to their homes across the Hudson.

---

20. Shelley, *Fordham*, 480–481.

When a third plane crashed into the Pentagon, smoke from the fires filled the sky above Arlington, Virginia and wafted across the Potomac River to the Georgetown campus. On a clear day, the Pentagon is normally visible from Georgetown, giving the university a front-row seat to the tragedy. Within a few minutes of the plane crash, a crowd of students and Jesuits had gathered on the rooftop of Village A, the building closest to the river, to stare at the funnel-shaped plume of ashes. The Jesuits, who were as stunned as the rest of the campus, did their best to show leadership and keep the students calm. Within a few hours, campus ministry organized a Catholic Mass celebrated by nearly the entire Jesuit community in a packed Gaston Hall auditorium, along with Protestant, Jewish, and Muslim prayer services in their respective worship spaces. Just a few years earlier, Georgetown had become the first American university (of any kind) to hire a full-time Muslim chaplain in its campus ministry office: Imam Yahya Hendi. Imam Hendi proved to be a reassuring presence for Georgetown's Muslim students in the weeks following September 11, joining with other clergy at the university to preach unity and empathy across faiths.

So many Georgetown students rushed to Georgetown University Hospital to donate blood that the hospital issued a statement asking volunteers to stay away, keeping the roads and parking lots accessible to victims of the attack. Similarly, Fordham students from Lincoln Center donated supplies to neighboring Roosevelt Hospital.[21] When stunned Americans tuned in to hear President George W. Bush address the nation that evening, they learned that the United States government would be open for business on Wednesday, September 12. Universities that had been planning or at least considering an extended shutdown largely followed the president's lead, and class was in session the next day. Predictably, many professors found it difficult to teach under these circumstances, and many classes became makeshift support groups for students who had just started the semester and were just getting to know each other.

Jesuit Colleges and the Sexual Abuse Crisis in the Catholic Church

In the early 2000s, the *Boston Globe* published a series of investigative articles exposing decades of sexual abuse by priests in the Archdiocese of Boston. In 2018, the Pennsylvania Attorney General published a grand jury report detailing similar abuse allegations against priests from the state's seven Catholic dioceses. Hundreds of priests were implicated in allegations dating to the mid-1900s. Although those men represented only a small fraction of the tens of thousands of priests who lived and worked during those decades, the reports were scandalous in part because they revealed how few of the accused priests had ever faced criminal justice during their lifetimes. The Catholic Church had handled most cases internally without reporting

---

21. Shelley, *Fordham*, 481.

them to civil authorities. Worldwide, Catholic bishops and leaders of religious orders faced pressure to release their records on this subject and publicly identify clergy, brothers, and sisters credibly accused of abuse.

In 2018 and early 2019, the Jesuit provinces released the names of credibly accused priests and brothers dating back to the 1950s. The initial lists included 42 names from the Central and Southern Province, 65 from the Midwestern Province, 19 from the Maryland Province, 50 from the Northeast Province, and 111 from the Western Province. The majority of the men named were already dead; most of the remainder had been either dismissed from the priesthood or removed from ministry.[22]

A substantial number of the allegations came from Jesuit parishes, retreat centers, and high schools; comparatively fewer allegations emerged from the universities. Nonetheless, some Jesuit universities were affected both directly and indirectly. In 2018, an investigative report discovered that the former Oregon Province had housed several elderly priests accused of sexual misconduct at the Cardinal Bea retirement home on the campus of Gonzaga University. Like all Jesuit residences, that retirement home was Jesuit property—not university property—although it was essentially on the Gonzaga campus. In 2018, Gonzaga released a statement explaining that the university had never been informed of the accusations against the men at the time they lived there; all had since been moved to a different residence.[23]

It was a painful period for Catholics around the world. While the men accused of misconduct represented, in most cases, only a small percentage of the priests actively engaged in ministry in the various dioceses, their crimes were nonetheless a scar on the entire Church. As of this writing, the full impact of the scandal is still unfolding.

Changing Demographics, a Crisis in Wheeling, and a Coronavirus Pandemic

Higher education in America faced a distribution problem of sorts in the 2010s. Most colleges and universities—particularly small, private colleges—were concentrated in northern states like Pennsylvania, New York, Ohio, and their neighbors. Yet the country's population growth was overwhelmingly concentrated in the South and southwest—the "Sun Belt"—where states like Arizona, Texas, Florida, and Nevada became destinations for millions of immigrants as well as domestic migrants drawn by year-round warmth and booming job opportunities.

---

22. Jack Jenkins, "U.S. Jesuit provinces release names of priests accused of abuse," *America* (19 December 2018), https://www.americamagazine.org/faith/2018/12/19/us-jesuit-provinces-release-names-priests-accused-abuse. Michael J. O'Loughlin, "USA Northeast Province releases names of Jesuits credibly accused of sexual abuse," *America* (15 January 2019), https://www.americamagazine.org/faith/2019/01/15/usa-northeast-province-releases-names-jesuits-credibly-accused-sexual-abuse.

23. Thayne McCulloh and Gonzaga University, "Statement from President McCulloh Regarding National News Story" (17 December 2018), https://www.gonzaga.edu/about/president-leadership/messages-media/2018/statement-from-president-mcculloh-regarding-national-news-story.

Higher education did not keep pace with these demographic changes. The process of starting a new college or university had become prohibitively complicated, and relatively few universities opened in the Sun Belt to meet the local demand. Even though the population of Arizona exceeded that of Massachusetts, Arizona at the turn of the century had only three major nonprofit, four-year institutions: the University of Arizona, Arizona State University, and Northern Arizona University. The booming city of Las Vegas, with about two million people in its vicinity, had only one major four-year institution: a branch campus of the University of Nevada. Not surprisingly, community colleges and for-profit institutions like the University of Phoenix flourished in those states. The few public universities that existed became astronomically large to meet local demand; Arizona State enrolled more than 50,000 students on its Tempe campus alone.

For Catholic higher education, the distribution problem was particularly acute. Catholic colleges were over-represented in the northeastern and Midwestern states where there were fewer students to enroll and more competing institutions, but they were largely absent from the country's growth regions. There were no Catholic colleges at all in many Southern and southwestern states (with the exception of a few small satellite campuses, such as Creighton University's medical branch in Phoenix).

These market conditions all but ensured that some small, tuition-dependent universities would collapse under enrollment pressure. Many Catholic colleges in the northeast and Midwest closed in the 2010s, particularly those, like St. Catherine College in Kentucky and the College of St. Joseph in Vermont, that had been founded by women's religious orders. Many of these colleges were located in rural areas and had served the poor and underprivileged students of their communities for more than a century. They could no longer survive at a time when expenses were high and tuition exceeded what local students were capable of paying.

Wheeling Jesuit University was the Jesuit institution most vulnerable to these developments. Located in a small city and lacking a large endowment, it had no choice but to discount tuition, and that charity reached unsustainable levels in the 2010s. The school's financial problems were so acute that in 2017 it sold its own campus to the Diocese of Wheeling-Charleston, agreeing to lease the property back. Over the next several years, the diocese donated or pledged millions of dollars to shore up the struggling university, but by 2019, it became clear that more drastic measures were necessary. The university announced plans to eliminate most departments and majors with the exception of some health care and business programs.

There were only a handful of Jesuits living on campus at the time, but a number of them lost their jobs in the cuts. The Maryland Province shortly thereafter announced that it was withdrawing its sponsorship of the university, noting that an education devoid of the humanities was not a true Jesuit education. The university changed its name to "Wheeling University" and became a diocesan institution, with the diocese initially donating millions of dollars in an attempt to sustain the only brick-and-mortar Catholic university in West Virginia. The Jesuits had closed and/or sold numerous colleges during their history, but not since the aftermath of the Civil

War had they withdrawn from a college (St. Joseph's in Kentucky) that continued to operate after their departure.

Nationwide, the 2020 COVID-19 pandemic added fuel to an already dire situation in higher education. The loss of many international students and the need to move classes online brought dramatic declines in tuition revenue, forcing many small, private colleges to make deep cuts. In July, 2020, Canisius College in Buffalo announced that it would lay off dozens of employees and eliminate several majors, including a number of humanities disciplines, such as classics and religious studies. Also in 2020, Spring Hill College announced that it would cut its tuition in half in an attempt to attract more students. The extent of these cuts and their long-term effects throughout the Jesuit network remain to be seen.

What is certain is that demographic change and the COVID-19 pandemic exposed serious structural issues in the American higher education system. Jesuit colleges and universities will have to navigate these issues to survive, just as they have in the past. They will need to figure out how to respond to the changing nature of the Catholic Church in America, which is becoming more Hispanic and more Southern. They will also need to think seriously about how a Jesuit education can take place online rather than in-person. These challenges need not spell the end of Jesuit higher education, but they will require adaptation.

A Jesuit Community College: Arrupe College (2015)

Despite their declining numbers and despite their bewildering list of existing obligations, the Jesuits continued to expand. During the 1990s and early 2000s, the traditional Jesuit enthusiasm for education as a vehicle for social change remained constant, and found new forms of expression. Many Jesuit provinces found a renewed interest in secondary education, lending their expertise to a network of inner-city high schools known as the Cristo Rey schools. The prototype was Cristo Rey Jesuit High School in Chicago, which opened in 1996 to serve low-income urban students. Other Cristo Rey schools soon followed around the country, and many defrayed the cost of tuition by negotiating work and internship opportunities for their students with local businesses. For the first time, the Jesuits also got into the business of operating middle schools like the Washington Jesuit Academy, which serves low-income inner-city boys in the nation's capital.

It was perhaps inevitable that this spirit would find some expression in Jesuit higher education. In 2015, Father Stephen Katsouros, SJ founded what was billed as the world's first Jesuit community college—Arrupe College, a constituent unit of Loyola University (Chicago). The new college offers two-year associate's degrees mainly to disadvantaged students from Chicago's inner city, specifically targeting those who otherwise might not have pursued a college degree at all, let alone at a private institution like Loyola. With a combination of low tuition and intensive mentorship from advisors, Arrupe College developed a model that allowed at-risk students to graduate with minimal debt. After completing their first two years of college in a supportive environment, many students were better accustomed to the expectations of undergraduate study and better prepared to pursue a bachelor's degree at Loyola or elsewhere.

Arrupe College received significant attention in the national media, in part because of its impressive graduation rates and in part because it was so rare for a private university to go to such lengths to accommodate the needs of poor, often underprepared students. In 2017, Father Katsouros published a memoir about the college's inaugural year entitled, *Come to Believe: How the Jesuits Are Reinventing Education (Again)*.[24] He stepped down as dean in 2020, having been charged by the Jesuits to replicate the Arrupe model elsewhere around the country.

Arrupe College was, in many ways, a blend of the old and the new. It replicated the mission of the very first Jesuit colleges by serving a disadvantaged population and, like the early Jesuit schools, it was mainly designed to offer access to education. Its audience was local, and it fulfilled a legitimate need in its hometown that existing universities and community colleges were overlooking. At the same time, it did all of this within a modern context—attaching itself to a prestigious private university to provide its students with modern resources and to avoid the complexities of accrediting a new college from scratch. It remains to be seen how the Arrupe College model will translate into other contexts and how sustainable it will be, but in Chicago, it has quickly become an example of an authentically Catholic and Jesuit education adapted to the twenty-first century.

---

24. Stephen N. Katsouros, SJ, *Come to Believe: How the Jesuits Are Reinventing Education (Again), Inside the First Year of the New Arrupe College* (New York: Orbis Books, 2017).

Epilogue

What is our final assessment of Jesuit higher education in America, considering all the sweat and struggle, success and failure, good decision-making and bad decision-making described in these pages? Alone among the various arms of the Catholic Church, the Jesuits have been part of our country from the colonial era to the present. They have witnessed and participated in the successes and failures of the United States, and their schools have reflected the country's evolving circumstances, attitudes, and needs for more than two centuries.

We must acknowledge—if not marvel at—the sheer scope of what a small group of a few thousand priests accomplished. They built, usually from scratch, a network of colleges that reached almost every corner of the United States. They nurtured and cultivated those colleges into modern universities, even when that process inevitably meant that they had to sacrifice their own control, sharing power with laypeople for the good of the institutions. Twenty-eight of the schools they built still operate as colleges and universities today, enrolling nearly a quarter-million students and directly employing more than 30,000 people, almost all of them non-Jesuits. A great many people owe their education and/or their livelihoods to this legacy.

That the Jesuits were able to do this while building an equally vast network of parish churches, high schools, middle schools, charities, and nonprofit organizations like the Jesuit Volunteer Corps is nothing short of remarkable. That they were able to do this while anti-Catholic forces in the United States (as well as Roman skepticism of American values) sometimes actively sought to prevent them from succeeding is nothing short of astounding.

At their core, the Jesuits are essentially a service organization—a group of individuals who dedicate their lives to helping others. Few, if any, other service organizations can claim a comparable long-term impact on the American higher education sector or the American economy. If an organization like the Peace Corps or Teach for America were directly responsible for creating twenty-eight colleges and universities, that organization would rightly be acknowledged as one of the greatest economic assets the United States has ever had. If it had built such a vast network even though armed street mobs often protested whenever its members came to town, and even though activists repeatedly filed lawsuits against it in a deliberate attempt to undermine its work, that would be a notable accomplishment indeed. The Jesuits deserve to be acknowledged for the unique civic and religious asset that they were (and still are), improving students' lives and combating some of America's earliest, most virulent forms of prejudice.

Anti-Catholic prejudice has been an important theme in American history, but Jesuit colleges have done their part to combat it—both by opening their doors to non-Catholics and by empowering Catholics to participate fully in American society. This approach to social justice actually *worked*. Working-class Catholics and other first-

447

generation college students (who otherwise never would have had the opportunity to go to college) were able to become lawyers, business executives, doctors, dentists, and other professionals because of the accessibility of the local Jesuit school. At a time when higher education was dominated by America's wealthy elite, the Jesuits provided a back door to the middle class. They were not alone in this regard; other Catholic colleges did the same. But no single college came close to the scale and impact of the Jesuit network. The fact that an Irish-American lawyer, a Polish-American college professor, or an Italian-American politician are no longer oddities in American culture reflects the fact that the Jesuits succeeded in their goals.

Catholics in America today still face implicit discrimination, but this is mild compared to the violence and overt intolerance that their immigrant ancestors faced. The fact that many Catholics have effectively assimilated into American culture reflects, to a large extent, the success of Jesuit higher education. Still, for all of their accomplishments, many Jesuit colleges still grapple with the lingering effects of anti-Catholic discrimination of the past. We can only imagine how much stronger Saint Louis University would be today if it had not been forced to give up its pioneering medical school, in effect, to nearby Washington University, which eventually supplanted it as the city's dominant educational institution.

The Jesuits themselves did make mistakes and missteps. Some wounds were self-inflicted, and some decisions were unjust. The Maryland Jesuits' 1838 slave sale was anathema to the order's mission. Some Jesuit schools were slow to confront racial injustice in America for fear of drawing attention to themselves and redirecting the crosshairs of intolerance in their own direction. Still, for every Jesuit school like Loyola (New Orleans) that embraced racial integration late, there were others like Saint Louis and Spring Hill that embraced it early—setting precedents by integrating their students well ahead of other colleges in their areas. For every Jesuit school like Gonzaga (Spokane) that excluded Native Americans, there were others that enrolled indigenous people in limited numbers at various points in history.

It is, therefore, difficult to judge the Jesuit educational network as a whole on issues of race and justice. As with the country as a whole, the Jesuits' progress was gradual and uneven. At any given time, there were individual Jesuits who pushed for what was right and others who advocated for what was wrong, but right ultimately won the day—in step with, and sometimes ahead of, the American norm. In judging the Jesuit colleges' record on tolerance, we must also acknowledge that tolerance was integral to their very existence from the beginning. The tolerance they showed toward early American immigrants, toward Hispanics, and toward international students—all of which put them light-years ahead of most American colleges—slowly but inexorably expanded to include other marginalized groups. Even the Jesuit colleges' legacy of openness toward women is much deeper and more nuanced than is normally acknowledged. The barriers to women's admission that fell in the 1960s were the very last, not the first, to come down.

Administratively, the Jesuits certainly could have been more judicious with their resources. They spent vast amounts of money building seminaries and duplicative colleges close to their existing schools. At great cost, they acquired property for failed institutions like Regis College in Illinois and Allouez College in Wisconsin. The construction costs associated with the ill-fated Brooklyn College in the 1900s and Woodstock College in the 1860s each exceeded $200,000—the equivalent of many millions of dollars today.[1] It would be wrong to call all of those quixotic projects complete wastes of money, because while they existed many of these failed schools meant a great deal to the students they served. But in the grand scheme, those schools were not necessary, and their impact was only temporary. The money could have been better spent shoring up the struggling Jesuit colleges that already existed. If all of those funds had been invested into endowments to support the colleges instead of poured into needless expansion, the overall Jesuit network could have been much healthier financially.

In making this judgment, however, it is important to remember that quantity, not quality, was the Jesuits' goal for most of their history in education. Nineteenth-century Jesuits typically were not seeking to build the best colleges possible; they were seeking to serve the largest number of people possible, and colleges and universities were just part of their enormous web of social projects, missions, parishes, charities, and outreach initiatives. Had the Jesuits been content with pouring all of their money into Georgetown and Saint Louis Universities, both schools would be far wealthier today, but schools like Boston College and Marquette University would not even exist and far fewer people would have received a Jesuit education.

Like many Catholic universities, Jesuit schools have often done what was best for individual students rather than what was best for the long-term health of the institution. This sets them apart from secular institutions like Harvard that have amassed enormous wealth by courting elite students and donors while, for much of their existence, excluding average Americans. Jesuit schools sought only the resources they needed to survive, nothing more, even to the point of turning down worthy investments that would have distracted them from their core educational mission. This was an excellent strategy for helping people in the short-term but not for building stable institutions in the long-term. The Jesuits' principles were strong, and their pocketbooks suffered as a result. It was not until the 1900s that the Jesuits focused on the quality of their institutions over quantity—first by opening professional schools in the 1910s, and then by modernizing their faculty and research capacity in the 1930s through 1960s. At the very moment they did so, it is telling that some individual Jesuits started to push back—urging the schools to return to their old ways, emphasizing accessibility over scholarship and affordability over extravagance.

Although Jesuit colleges spent a great deal of the twentieth century "catching up" to their secular counterparts, they are not followers. On the contrary, they were leaders in many of the ways that truly mattered; Jesuits perceived a need for education where others, including the government, did not. Jesuit colleges awarded the first bachelor's degrees west of the Mississippi and on the Pacific coast. They were the first

---

1. Curran, *History of Georgetown Vol. I*, 277. Bender, *Brief History of the New York Province*, 22.

permanent schools of any kind in many of America's greatest cities—including Washington, St. Louis, San Francisco, and Omaha. The Jesuits rank not only among the country's greatest educators, but also among its greatest pioneers.

In time, the government caught up to the Jesuits by opening public universities and community colleges in all of those cities, and such institutions could often provide education more cheaply and accessibly. Even the Jesuits' greatest scientific research project—the seismology network of the early 1900s—was ultimately rendered obsolete by more efficient government programs. While these developments undermined the Jesuits' influence in the long term, they also underscore how far ahead of the curve the early Jesuits were. The Jesuits accurately perceived the need for an educational infrastructure in America, and they built an early prototype of that infrastructure (at great cost and personal sacrifice) when no one else dared do so. To put it succinctly, the Jesuits were the first to do many things that the American government eventually perfected.

This means that many Jesuit colleges were simultaneously first on the scene and yet outside of the American mainstream. Paradoxically, they set the standard early, but they remained outsiders—eventually facing stifling competition from the more dominant factions in American academic culture that followed them. By the mid-1900s, this had forced Jesuit colleges into a role that was not entirely comfortable for them—the role of the elite, private American university. The irony was that their early success and the deep roots of their tradition made it somewhat more difficult for them to adapt to the mainstream as time went on. The titles of many of the excellent books on this topic—*Contending with Modernity*, *Continuity and Change*, *Adapting to America*, etc.—reflect this unusual dichotomy.

The Future of Jesuit Higher Education

Now more than ever, America needs the Jesuit ethos of education. In an era when misinformation, internet conspiracy theories, and nonsensical "fake news" find wide audiences, the best hope for the future is a strategy that the Jesuits have been pursuing since 1547—educating as many people as possible. They taught paupers to talk with princes and brought the power that comes from education to the masses. In Europe, they ensured that knowledge was not the exclusive domain of the privileged nobles. In America, they empowered whole generations of underprivileged citizens to contribute to a democratic, civil society. Education is the key to civil discourse and the democratization of education—making it accessible as widely as possible—is the best way to achieve this goal.

At a time when religion and science are often wrongly seen as at odds with one another, the Jesuits bridge that gap as few others can. They prove through example that one need not be anti-intellectual to be religious, nor anti-religion to be an intellectual. The United States political system is increasingly defined by a divide between (on the one hand) rich, urban, educated, seculars who ignore or dismiss matters of faith and (on the other) poor, rural, uneducated people who embrace religion as the defining feature of their lives—even to the point of rejecting modern science outright. This dichotomy is false, especially considering that many great American universities are rooted in religion and many great scientific discoveries, from genetics to health care, came from religious sources. The Jesuits show by their lives and careers that it is possible to unite reason and faith, and that the outcome of that marriage can be enlightening and beautiful. If more Americans were exposed to this way of thinking, our country would benefit.

Arrupe College in Chicago, the first Jesuit community college, is the latest Jesuit attempt to respond to this need in the modern world. But the same values still motivate other schools in the Jesuit network. Even Georgetown, the most selective Catholic university in the country with an acceptance rate of less than 15%, has taken steps to serve first-generation and low-income students through its Georgetown Scholars Program, widely viewed as a model for elite college accessibility. It also sponsors a Prison Scholars Program to award bachelor's degrees to inmates at Washington-area jails. The challenge, as has been the case throughout Jesuit history, is how to balance the need for accessibility with the long-term health of the institution. Jesuit schools cannot provide education for free, but at the same time, the high tuition rates necessary for their survival are already beyond the reach of most students they hope to serve.

By expanding their accessibility, Jesuit colleges face another problem—one they have grappled with since the end of World War II. Their sheer size makes it difficult for them to have a meaningful impact on the life of every student they enroll. The number of Jesuits in this country continues to decline. Some colleges have only a dozen or so Jesuits on campus to serve thousands of students. In many cases, the number of Jesuits on campus today is comparable to the number who lived on that same campus in the nineteenth century, when only a few hundred students were enrolled. A student today can graduate from a Jesuit university without ever having met a Jesuit, let alone having developed a meaningful mentoring relationship with one.

Nonetheless, we still talk about Jesuit education in the present tense, not the past tense, and with the right decision-making that will continue well into the future. I do not claim to have the answers to this dilemma, but in a 2019 article, I argued in favor of a handful of strategies that universities can use to keep their Catholic identity relevant, visible, and meaningful.[2]

The Jesuit educational tradition is now in the hands of laypeople, and those laypeople must be empowered to feel ownership of that tradition. The Jesuits on campus should teach their lay colleagues about the goals and objectives of Jesuit education, offering workshops and other opportunities to learn about the unique advantages of Jesuit pedagogy. Those advantages apply, and have always applied, to all faculty and students regardless of their religious preferences. The Jesuit mission emphasizes care for the whole person, equality, justice, service, critical thinking, per-

---

2. Rizzi, "Defining Catholic Higher Education."

sonal responsibility, morality, academic rigor, and effective communication; it is a mission that all students—Catholic and non-Catholic, religious and irreligious—can support. The fact that secular universities increasingly hold similar values does not make those values any less authentically Catholic or Jesuit. These principles have animated Jesuit higher education for centuries, and in staying true to those principles, Jesuit schools are staying true to their identity. As I wrote in 2019, "One need not be Catholic to appreciate the benefits of studying and working at a Catholic university, or the ways in which Catholic institutions can outperform their secular counterparts in many aspects of research, teaching, and student life."[3] A Jesuit identity is a positive feature that colleges and universities should proudly promote to prospective students and employees.

At the same time, it is not enough simply to emphasize the quality of Jesuit education. Jesuit colleges must constantly remind their faculty, staff, and students about how and why they choose these values. Presidents should refer often to the school's Ignatian mission in public statements, and the school should make its identity clear in its marketing materials and other publications. Universities should be proactive about establishing research centers, speaker series, and academic programs that reflect their Jesuit identity. Some examples include the Institute for Advanced Jesuit Studies at Boston College and the Hank Center for the Catholic Intellectual Heritage at Loyola University (Chicago). Many Jesuit schools already offer degrees or minors in Catholic studies and sponsor important initiatives on interreligious dialogue. Jesuit schools should be centers for the Catholic voice in America, ensuring by their research and teaching that Catholic contributions to the United States are not forgotten. They should keep the Catholic intellectual tradition alive, relevant, and connected to modern academic thought. They should also be centers of research and discovery for issues that matter to American Catholics and to the future of the Catholic Church.[4]

A Jesuit identity must be lived, not confined to the dusty shelves of the university archives. If Jesuit universities continue to work toward this goal in a deliberate way, thinking about their Ignatian mission and using it to inform every decision—from finances to extracurricular activities to pedagogy—it will remain relevant. In academia, the answer to almost any question is "more dialogue." The history, present, and future trajectory of Jesuit higher education is an extraordinarily rich topic that warrants dialogue and can only live as long as it is actively discussed. Students, employees, and faculty at Jesuit schools should be able to articulate how and why their community service projects, scholarship priorities, research initiatives, and other activities are informed by their school's Jesuit mission.

In this way, a school can have a vibrant Jesuit mission with or without the presence of actual Jesuits on campus. Hopefully the day will never come when the Jesuits' numbers fall so low that they can no longer assign priests to all twenty-seven colleges

---

3. Ibid., 22.
4. Ibid., 9–13.

and universities—but if it does, even that need not signal the end of the schools' Jesuit identity. A Jesuit education without Jesuits is possible as long as the people in the community regularly think about, discuss, and live the Ignatian mission. Bishop Canevin High School, a Catholic high school in Pittsburgh, recently decided to adopt an Ignatian charism as part of its core identity. Bishop Canevin High School has never been formally affiliated with the Jesuits; no Jesuit has ever taught there. However, its lay faculty and staff have embraced Ignatian spirituality and pedagogy and made the Jesuit heritage a central part of the student experience. If a school with no Jesuit heritage can build this identity from scratch, so too can a school with decades of actual Jesuit tradition.

In many ways, the Jesuit network is stronger today than ever before, because the fruits of the network and its camaraderie extend to all students, faculty, and staff, not just the club of priests who once managed it all. This will continue as long as all members of the campus community feel connected to that identity. As long as they keep talking about their mission, as long as they continue to encourage that camaraderie, the American Jesuit schools will preserve the spirit that has collectively animated them for more than two centuries. My hope is that this book has contributed in some small way to this dialogue and helped to facilitate more.

I will close with a personal story. When Jorge Cardinal Bergoglio, SJ was elected Pope Francis in March 2013 (becoming the first Jesuit to hold that office), I was in my office at the University of Pittsburgh. My work-study assistant at the time, who sat outside my office at a reception desk in the main hallway, was a graduate student who held her undergraduate degree from Fairfield University. We had both attended Jesuit colleges, many miles and several years apart, but we spoke often about the impact the Jesuits had had on our lives and came to realize that many of our formative experiences in college had been similar. The professors who had taught us—Jesuit and lay—and the spirit they embodied clearly transcended time and space.

When the news came in that Cardinal Bergoglio had been elected pope, my assistant exclaimed, "Michael, he's a Jesuit!" which brought me out of my office to give her a high-five. I have no doubt that similar celebrations took place around the world that day among the hundreds of thousands of people whose lives have been touched for the better by this extraordinary group of educators. Not a bad legacy for a small group of priests who built one of the largest, best, and most influential higher education networks in the history of the United States.

AMDG

Appendix

Chronological List of Jesuit Colleges and Universities by Founding Date

Legend:
Gray: College is closed
Gray with Bold/Italic Font: College today operates as a high school

Name	Founded (Closed)	Chartered	Jesuits Took Control (Left)	Location	Founded By
Georgetown University	1789	1815	1814	Washington, DC	Diocese of Baltimore
New York Literary Institute	1808(1813)	N/A	Immediately	New York, New York	Jesuit Maryland Mission
Saint Louis University	1818	1832	1829	St. Louis, Missouri	Diocese of Louisiana and the Floridas
St. Joseph's College	1819(1889)	1825	1848 (1868)	Bardstown, Kentucky	Diocese of Bardstown
Gonzaga College	*1821*	*1858*	*1821/1848*	*Washington, DC*	*Jesuit Maryland Mission*
St. Mary's College	1821(1976)	1837	1831 (1846)	Lebanon, Kentucky	Father William Byrne
St. John's Literary Institute	*1829*	*1850*	*Immediately (1903)*	*Frederick, Maryland*	*Jesuit Maryland Mission*
Spring Hill College	1830	1836	1847	Mobile, Alabama	Diocese of Mobile
Xavier University	1831	1842	1840	Cincinnati, Ohio	Diocese of Cincinnati
St. Charles College	1837 (1922)	1852	Immediately	Grand Coteau, Louisiana	Jesuit Province of Lyon (France)
St. Ignatius Literary Institute	1841 (1846)	N/A	Immediately	Louisville, Kentucky	Jesuit Province of Lyon (France)
Fordham University	1841	1846	1846	New York, New York	Diocese of New York
St. Joseph's College	1843 (1849)	N/A	1848 (1849)	St. Paul, Oregon Territory	Catholic Oregon pioneers
College of the Holy Cross	1843	1865	Immediately	Worcester, Massachusetts	Jesuit Maryland Province
College of St. Francis Xavier	*1847 (1912)*	*1861*	*Immediately*	*New York, New York*	*Jesuit New York-Canada Mission*

Name	Founded (Closed)	Chartered	Jesuits Took Control (Left)	Location	Founded By
St. Mary's College	1848 (1931)	1869	Immediately	St. Marys, Kansas	Jesuit Missouri Vice Province
St. Aloysius College	1849 (1852)	1851	Immediately	Louisville, Kentucky	Jesuit Missouri Vice Province
College of the Immaculate Conception	*1849 (1911)*	*1852*	*Immediately*	*New Orleans, Louisiana*	*Jesuit New Orleans Mission*
College of Ss. Peter and Paul	1850 (1856)	1852	Immediately	Baton Rouge, Louisiana	Jesuit New Orleans Mission
Saint Joseph's University	1851	1852	Immediately	Philadelphia, Pennsylvania	Jesuit Maryland Province
Santa Clara University	1851	1855	Immediately	Santa Clara, California	Jesuit Rocky Mountain (Oregon) Mission
University of San Francisco	1855	1859	Immediately	San Francisco, California	Jesuit California Mission (Turin Province)
Loyola University Maryland	1852	1853	Immediately	Baltimore, Maryland	Jesuit Maryland Province
St. Mary's University	1855 (1922)	1856	1884	Galveston, Texas	Diocese of Galveston
Boston College	1858	1863	Immediately	Boston, Massachusetts	Jesuit Maryland Province
Loyola University Chicago	1870	1870	Immediately	Chicago, Illinois	Jesuit Missouri Province
Canisius College	1870	1883	Immediately	Buffalo, New York	Jesuit Buffalo Mission
St. Francis Institute	1871 (1891)	1871	Immediately	Osage Mission, Kansas	Jesuit Missouri Province
St. Peter's University	1872	1872	Immediately	Jersey City, New Jersey	Jesuit New York-Canada Mission
University of Detroit Mercy	1877	1881	Immediately	Detroit, Michigan	Jesuit Missouri Province
Las Vegas College	1877 (1888)	1878	Immediately	Las Vegas, New Mexico Territory	Jesuit New Mexico Mission (Naples Province)
Creighton University	1878	1879	Immediately	Omaha, Nebraska	Jesuit Missouri Province

Name	Founded (Closed)	Chartered	Jesuits Took Control (Left)	Location	Founded By
Campion College	1880 (1925)	1881	Immediately	Prairie du Chien, Wisconsin	Jesuit Buffalo Mission
Marquette University	1881	1864	Immediately	Milwaukee, Wisconsin	Jesuit Missouri Mission
St. Joseph's College	1884 (1898)	N/A	Immediately	San Jose, California	Jesuit California Mission
John Carroll University	1886	1890	Immediately	Cleveland, Ohio	Jesuit Buffalo Mission
Gonzaga University	1887	1894	Immediately	Spokane, Washington	Jesuit Rocky Mountain Mission (Turin Province)
Regis University	1888	1893	Immediately	Morrison/Denver, Colorado	Jesuit Southwest Mission (Naples Province)
University of Scranton	1888	1922	1942	Scranton, Pennsylvania	Diocese of Scranton
St. John's University	1898 (1936)	1900	Immediately	Toledo, Ohio	Jesuit Buffalo Mission
Tampa College	*1899*	*1929*	*Immediately*	*Tampa, Florida*	*Jesuit New Orleans Mission*
Seattle University	1891	1898	Immediately	Seattle, Washington	Jesuit Rocky Mountain Mission (Turin Province)
Sacred Heart College	1900 (1917)	1902	Immediately	Augusta, Georgia	Jesuit New Orleans Mission
St. John Berchmans College	*1902*	*N/A*	*Immediately (1982)*	*Shreveport, Louisiana*	*Jesuit New Orleans Mission*
Loyola University New Orleans	1904	1912	Immediately	New Orleans, Louisiana	Jesuit New Orleans Province
Brooklyn College	1908 (1921)	1908	Immediately	Brooklyn, New York	Jesuit Maryland-New York Province
Rockhurst University	1910	1910	Immediately	Kansas City, Missouri	Jesuit Missouri Province
Regis College	1910 (1913)	1910	Immediately	East St. Louis, Illinois	Jesuit Missouri Province
Loyola Marymount University	1911	1918	Immediately	Los Angeles, California	Jesuit California Province

Name	Founded (Closed)	Chartered	Jesuits Took Control (Left)	Location	Founded By
Bellarmine College	1929	1927	Immediately	Tacoma, Washington	Jesuit California Province
Brophy College	1929	1927	Immediately	Phoenix, Arizona	Jesuit California Province
Fairfield University	1942	1945	Immediately	Fairfield, Connecticut	Jesuit New England Province
Le Moyne College	1946	1946	Immediately	Syracuse, New York	Jesuit New York Province
Wheeling University	1954	1957	Immediately (2019)	Wheeling, West Virginia	Jesuit Maryland Province

Bibliography

"AJCU Mission and Identity Survey, 2014–2015." Association of Jesuit Colleges and Universities. Accessed 2017. https://static1.squarespace.com/static/55d1dd88e4b0dee65a6594f0/t/56043592e4b043d49b5d54c2/1443116434506/AJCUMissionSurveyFinal_10-14.pdf.

"The American Mission: Maryland Jesuits from Andrew White to John Carroll." Georgetown University Library Booth Family Center for Special Collections. Accessed 2019. https://www.library.georgetown.edu/exhibition/american-mission-maryland-jesuits-andrew-white-john-carroll.

"Articles of Incorporation of Jesuit Fathers of Bellarmine College of Tacoma." Washington State Digital Archives. Washington State Corporation Records, 1855–2004. Accessed 2020. https://digitalarchives.wa.gov/DigitalObject/Download/c6a4dbd9-d8e3-4da2-92be-3103f0137ad9.

Bashnal, L. G., SJ. "The Flood at Augusta, Georgia." *Woodstock Letters* XXXVIII, no. 1 (1909): 65–72.

Bates, John C. "Rev. Clifford M. Lewis, SJ—Journalist, Husband, Priest, College Co-Founder and Historian." *Gathered Fragments* XXVII, no. 1 (Fall 2017): 65–78.

Beckett, Edward F., SJ. "Listening to Our History: Inculturation and Jesuit Slaveholding." *Studies in the Spirituality of the Jesuits* 28, no. 5 (November, 1996).

Bender, Arthur C., SJ. *A Brief History of the New York Province.* New York: New York Province of the Society of Jesus, undated.

Bennish, Lee J., SJ. *Continuity and Change: Xavier University, 1831–1981.* Chicago: Loyola University Press, 1981.

Bertucio, Brett. "W(h)ither the Liberally Educated Teacher? An Historical Reflection." In *Leisure and Labor: Essays on the Liberal Arts in Catholic Higher Education,* edited by Anthony P. Coleman, 59–68. New York: Lexington Books, 2020.

Boroughs, Philip L., SJ. "President's Response to Report of the Mulledy/Healy Legacy Committee." College of the Holy Cross, 16 June 2016. https://news.holycross.edu/blog/2016/06/16/presidents-response-to-report-of-the-mulledyhealy-legacy-committee/.

Brown, Dorothy. "Learning, Faith, Freedom, and Building a Curriculum." In *Georgetown at 200: Faculty Reflections on the University's Future,* edited by William C. McFadden, SJ, 79–105. Washington: Georgetown University Press, 1990.

Brown, Thomas. "Letter from Thomas Brown, an Enslaved Man at St. Louis University, 1833." The Georgetown Slavery Archive, Georgetown University. https://slaveryarchive.georgetown.edu/items/show/39. Accessed 2020.

Burke, James L., SJ. *Jesuit Province of New England: The Formative Years.* College of the Holy Cross Libraries. https://crossworks.holycross.edu/nenprovhistory/1/. Accessed 2020.

Byrne, Patrick H. "The Good under Construction and the Research Vocation of a Catholic University." *Journal of Catholic Education* 7, no. 3 (March 2004): 320–328.

Canaris, Michael M. "*Alma Mater, Mater Exulum*. Jesuit Education and Immigration in America: A Moral Framework Rooted in History and Mission." In *Undocumented and in College: Students and Institutions in a Climate of National Hostility*, edited by Terry-Ann Jones and Laura Nichols, 84–103. New York: Fordham University Press, 2017.

Cassidy, Francis Patrick. *Catholic College Foundations and Development in the United States (1677–1850)*. Washington, Catholic University of America Press, 1924.

The Catholic Educational Exhibit at the World's Columbian Exposition, Chicago, 1893, edited by a well known Catholic writer, under the special supervision of the Rev. Brother Maurelian. Chicago: JS Highland and Company, 1896. https://luc.access.preservica.com/uncategorized/digitalFile_1c1d59f7-4c74-4d85-9463-8db53035ecf0/.

"The Changing Jesuit Geography." Nineteen Sixty Four Blog. Center for Applied Research in the Apostolate, February 1, 2011. http://nineteensixty-four.blogspot.com/2011/02/changing-jesuit-geography.html.

Chapple, Christopher. "Introduction." In *The Jesuit Tradition in Education and Missions*, edited by Christopher Chapple. Scranton: University of Scranton Press, 1993.

Clancy, Thomas H., SJ. "After the Suppression." Loyola University New Orleans Office of Mission and Ministry. http://mm.loyno.edu/jesuit-community/after-suppression. Accessed 2020.

Clinton, Bill. *My Life*. New York: Knopf, 2004.

"Code of Canon Law: Commentary on Canons 807–814." In *American Catholic Higher Education: Essential Documents, 1967–1990*, edited by Alice Gallin, 175–190. Notre Dame, IN: University of Notre Dame Press, 1992.

Cohen, Shari S. "University of Detroit Mercy—Renewal and Change for a New Century." In *Legacy of Excellence: A Continuing History of Jesuit and Mercy Higher Education in Detroit*, edited by Herman J. Muller, SJ, Mary Justine Sabourin, RSM, and Shari S. Cohen, 241–295. Detroit: University of Detroit Mercy Press, 2003.

Contosta, David R. *Saint Joseph's: Philadelphia's Jesuit University: 150 Years*. Philadelphia: Saint Joseph's University Press, 2000.

Cook, Bernard A. *Founded on Faith: A History of Loyola University New Orleans*. New Orleans: Loyola University, 2012.

Cook, Bernard A. "Jesuit Priest Advised not to Purchase Tulane's Land." *The Maroon*, September 8, 2011. https://loyolamaroon.com/100992/features/jesuit-priest-advised-not-to-puchase-tulanes-land/.

Cordara, Giulio Cesare, SJ. *On the Suppression of the Society of Jesus: A Contemporary Account*, translated by John P. Murphy, SJ. Chicago: Loyola Press, 1999.

Critchley-Menor, William, SJ. "Interview: How the Jesuits are Working to Confront their History of Slavery." *America*, February 26, 2021. https://www.americamagazine.org/politics-society/2021/02/26/black-history-slavery-jesuits-catholic-reconciliation-240100.

Crowley, Walt. *Seattle University: A Century of Jesuit Education*. Seattle: Seattle University, 1991.

Curran, Robert Emmett. *A History of Georgetown University Volumes I, II, and III*. Washington: Georgetown University Press, 2010.

Curran, Robert Emmett. "'Wave Her Colors Ever': Writing Georgetown's History." *US Catholic Historian* 28, no. 3 (2010): 65–78.

Daley, John M., SJ. *Georgetown University: Origin and Early Years*. Washington: Georgetown University Press, 1957.

Delozier, Alan. "The Society of Jesus and Academia in Nova Caesarea: Robert I. Gannon, SJ & the Re-Birth of St. Peter's College, 1930–1936." *New Jersey Studies: An Interdisciplinary Journal* 4, no. 1 (Winter, 2018): 98–129.

Devitt, Edward I., SJ. "History of the Maryland-New York Province IX: The Province in the Year 1833." *Woodstock Letters* LXII, no. 3 (1933): 309–348.

Devitt, Edward I., SJ. "History of the Maryland-New York Province XVI: Boston College and Church of the Immaculate Conception." *Woodstock Letters* LXIV, no. 3 (1935): 401–402.

Dickens, Charles. *American Notes*. New York: St. Martin's Press, 1984.

Donovan, Charles F. "The Liberal Aims of Jesuit Higher Education." *Jesuit Educational Quarterly* 32, no. 2 (October 1969): 81–98.

"Draft Schema of a Pontifical Document on Catholic Universities." In *American Catholic Higher Education: Essential Documents, 1967–1990*, edited by Alice Gallin, 191–215. Notre Dame, Indiana: University of Notre Dame Press, 1992.

Dunn, Edward, SJ. "A Gymnasium in Buffalo: The Early Years of Canisius College." *Urban Education* 18, no. 4 (January 1984): 426–437.

Durkin, Joseph T., SJ. *Georgetown University: First in the Nation's Capital*. Garden City, New York: Doubleday & Company, 1964.

Durkin, Joseph T., SJ. *Georgetown University: The Middle Years (1840–1900)*. Washington: Georgetown University Press, 1963.

Ellis, John Tracy. "American Catholics and the Intellectual Life." *Thought* 30, no. 3 (Autumn 1955): 351–388.

F.J.K., SJ. "The Badge of Loyola: An Emblem for the Colleges of the Society." *Woodstock Letters* XXIX, no. 1 (1900): 1–5.

Fagan, James P., SJ. "The Loyola School, New York." *Woodstock Letters* XXXIII, no. 1 (1904): 75–92.

Faherty, William Barnaby, SJ. *Better the Dream: Saint Louis University and Community, 1818–1968*. St. Louis: Saint Louis University, 1968.

Faherty, William Barnaby, SJ. "Nativism and Midwestern Education: The Experience of Saint Louis University, 1832–1856." *History of Education Quarterly* 8, no. 4 (Winter, 1968): 447–458.

Faherty, William Barnaby, SJ. *Saint Louis University: A Concise History*. St. Louis: Gas House Books, 2009.

Fields, Stephen M., SJ. "Newman's Challenge to the Contemporary Academy." *Christian Higher Education* 2, no. 3 (2003): 251–67.

Fitzgerald, Paul A., SJ. *The Governance of Jesuit Colleges in the United States, 1920–1970*. Notre Dame: University of Notre Dame Press, 1984.

Flexner, Abraham. *Medical Education in the United States and Canada*. New York: Carnegie Foundation for the Advancement of Teaching, 1910. http://archive.carnegiefoundation.org/publications/pdfs/elibrary/Carnegie_Flexner_Report.pdf.

"Frequently Requested Church Statistics," Center for Applied Research in the Apostolate, 2020. https://cara.georgetown.edu/frequently-requested-church-statistics/.

Gallin, Alice, OSU. "Construction of the Code of Canon Law of 1983, 1977–1983." In *American Catholic Higher Education*, edited by Alice Gallin, 153–154. Notre Dame, IN: University of Notre Dame Press, 1992.

Gallin, Alice, OSU. "Synthesis of Responses received from U.S. Catholic College and University Presidents to the Pontifical Document on Catholic Universities." In *American Catholic Higher Education, Essential Documents, 1967–1990*, edited by Alice Gallin, 259–278. Notre Dame, IN: University of Notre Dame Press, 1992.

Ganss, George, SJ. *The Spiritual Exercises of St. Ignatius: A Translation and Commentary.* Chicago: Loyola Press, 1992.

Garneau, James. "The Director and His Eminence: The Working Relationship and Questions of Church and State as Reflected in Cardinal Cushing's FBI Files." *American Catholic Studies* 114, no. 2 (Summer 2003): 37–53.

Garraghan, Gilbert J., SJ. *The Jesuits of the Middle United States Volumes I, II, and III.* Chicago: Loyola University Press, 1983.

Geger, Barton T. "Cura Personalis: Some Ignatian Inspirations." *Jesuit Higher Education* 3, no. 2 (2014): 6–20.

Georgetown University Edmund A. Walsh School of Foreign Service and Washington Custom Media. *SFS 100: A Century of Service.* Washington: Georgetown University Press, 2019.

Giblin, Gerard F., SJ. "Jesuits as Chaplains in the Armed Forces, 1917–1960." *Woodstock Letters* LXXXIX, no. 4 (1960): 325–338.

Gleason, Philip. *Contending with Modernity: Catholic Higher Education in the Twentieth Century.* New York: Oxford University Press, 1995.

Gleason, Philip. "The First Century of Jesuit Higher Education in America." *US Catholic Historian* 25, no. 2 (Spring 2007): 37–52.

Gorman, Margaret, RSCJ. "Influence of Ignatian Spirituality on Women's Teaching Orders in the United States." In *The Jesuit Tradition in Education and Missions*, edited by Christopher K. Chapple, 182–202. Scranton: University of Scranton Press, 1993.

Grady, Richard. "Scranton University." *Jesuit Educational Quarterly* V, no. 2 (September 1942): 145–147.

Grendler, Paul F. *The Jesuits and Italian Universities, 1548–1773.* Washington: Catholic University of America Press, 2017.

Gumz, Edward J. "Frederic Siedenburg, SJ: The Journey of a Social Activist." *Social Work and Christianity* 39, no. 3 (2012): 273–293.

Hahnenberg, Edward. "Theodore M. Hesburgh, Theologian: Revisiting Land O'Lakes Fifty Years Later." *Theological Studies* 78, no. 4 (December 2017): 930–959.

Heithaus, Claude H., SJ. "The Sermon that, 62 Years Ago, Denounced Discrimination." *The University News*, April 12, 2006. https://unewsonline.com/2006/04/tesermonthatyears agodenounceddiscrimination/.

"Highly Decorated: The Work of Brother Francis Schroen, SJ." Georgetown University Library Booth Family Center for Special Collections, 2006. Accessed 2022. https://library.georgetown.edu/exhibition/highly-decorated-work-brother-francis-c-schroen-sj.

Hogan, J.A., SJ. "Reminisces of the Galveston Storm." *Woodstock Letters* XXIX, no. 3 (1901): 428–447.

Holbert, Gentry. "A Historical Moment: Spring Hill College." *Conversations on Jesuit Higher Education* (December 22, 2016). http://www.conversationsmagazine.org/web-features/2016/12/22/a-historical-moment-spring-hill-college

Holy Cross Bands. *Marching Band Handbook 2016/2017.* Worcester: College of the Holy Cross, 2016.

Hughes, M. T., SJ. "New Mexico." *Woodstock Letters* IX, no. 2 (1880): 134–140.

Ignatius of Loyola. *The Autobiography of St. Ignatius of Loyola*, edited by John C. Olin. New York: Fordham University Press, 1992.

Jablonsky, Thomas J. *Milwaukee's Jesuit University: Marquette, 1881–1981.* Milwaukee: Marquette University Press, 2007.

Jenkins, Jack. "U.S. Jesuit provinces release names of priests accused of abuse." *America*, December 19, 2018. https://www.americamagazine.org/faith/2018/12/19/us-jesuit-provinces-release-names-priests-accused-abuse.

"Jesuit Alumni in Congress." Association of Jesuit Colleges and Universities, 2021. https://www.ajcunet.edu/alumni-in-congress.

John Paul II. "Ex corde Ecclesiae." In *American Catholic Higher Education: Essential Documents, 1967–1990*, edited by Alice Gallin, 413–437. Notre Dame, Indiana: University of Notre Dame Press, 1992.

Katsouros, Stephen N., SJ. *Come to Believe: How the Jesuits Are Reinventing Education (Again), Inside the First Year of the New Arrupe College.* New York: Orbis Books, 2017.

Kersher, Jim. "Zag History 101." *The Spokesman Review*, July 8, 2007. https://www.spokesman.com/stories/2007/jul/08/zag-history-101/.

Kuzniewski, Anthony J., SJ. "'Our American Champions': The First American Generation of American Jesuit Leaders after the Restoration of the Society." *Studies in the Spirituality of Jesuits* 46, no. 1 (Spring 2014).

Kuzniewski, Anthony J., SJ. *Thy Honored Name: A History of the College of the Holy Cross, 1843–1994.* Washington: Catholic University of America Press, 1999.

Lackner, Joseph H. "Campus Ministry on Catholic Campuses." In *Handbook of Research on Catholic Higher Education*, edited by Thomas C. Hunt, Ellis A. Joseph, Ronald J. Nuzzi, and John O. Geiger, 293–324. Greenwich, CT: Information Age Publishing, 2003.

"Land O'Lakes Statement: The Nature of the Contemporary Catholic University." In *American Catholic Higher Education: Essential Documents, 1967–1990*, edited by Alice Gallin, 7–12. Notre Dame, IN: University of Notre Dame Press, 1992.

Le Moyne College Office of Mission and Identity. *The Le Moyne College Green Book.* Syracuse: Le Moyne College, 2011.

Leahy, William P., SJ. *Adapting to America: Catholics, Jesuits, and Higher Education in the Twentieth Century.* Washington: Georgetown University Press, 1991.

Lenehan, Michael. *Ramblers: Loyola-Chicago 1963—The Team that Changed the Color of College Basketball.* Chicago: Midway Books, 2013.

"MS 1225 Brophy Family Papers, 1882–1976." Arizona Historical Society. Accessed 2020. http://www.arizonahistoricalsociety.org/wp-content/upLoads/library_Brophy-Family.pdf.

MacDonnell, Joseph, SJ. *If these Stones Could Speak: The Phenomenal Growth of the Fairfield University Campus.* Fairfield, CT: Fairfield University, 1996.

Mahoney, Kathleen A. *Catholic Higher Education in Protestant America: The Jesuits and Harvard in the Age of the University.* Baltimore: Johns Hopkins University Press, 2003.

Maitrugues, J., SJ. "St. Charles College, Grand Coteau, La." *Woodstock Letters* V, no. 1 (1876): 17–29.

Marsden, George M. *The Soul of the American University: From Protestant Establishment to Established Nonbelief.* New York: Oxford University Press, 1996.

McCulloh, Thayne. "Statement from President McCulloh Regarding National News Story." Gonzaga University, December 17, 2018. https://www.gonzaga.edu/about/president-leadership/messages-media/2018/statement-from-president-mcculloh-regarding-national-news-story.

McFadden, William C., SJ. "'Catechism at 4 for All the Schools': Religious Instruction at Georgetown." In *Georgetown at Two Hundred: Faculty Reflections on the University's Future*, edited by William C. McFadden, 143–168. Washington: Georgetown University Press, 1990.

McFadden, William C., SJ. "Introduction." In *Georgetown at Two Hundred: Faculty Reflections on the University's Future*, edited by William C. McFadden, xiii–xviii. Washington: Georgetown University Press, 1990.

McKevitt, Gerald, SJ. *Brokers of Culture: Italian Jesuits in the American West, 1848–1919*. Palo Alto: Stanford University Press, 2007.

McKevitt, Gerald, SJ. "Jesuit Higher Education in the United States." *Mid-America: An Historical Review* 73, no. 3 (October 1991): 209–226.

McKevitt, Gerald, SJ. "The Jump that Saved the Rocky Mountain Mission: Jesuit Recruitment and the Pacific Northwest." *Pacific Historical Review* 55, no. 3 (1986): 427–453.

McKevitt, Gerald, SJ. *The University of Santa Clara: A History, 1851–1977*. Palo Alto: Stanford University Press, 1979.

McNamara, Patrick, William Dinges, and Joseph A. McCartin. Untitled review of *The FBI and the Catholic Church, 1935–1962* by Steve Rosswurm. *U.S. Catholic Historian* 29, no. 2 (Spring 2011): 77–79.

McShane, Joseph M., SJ. "A Survey of the History of the Jesuit Labor Schools in New York: An American Social Gospel in Action." *Records of the American Catholic Historical Society of Philadelphia* 102, no. 4 (Winter 1991): 37–64.

Mihelich, Dennis N. *The History of Creighton University: 1878–2003*. Omaha: Creighton University Press, 2006.

Millett, Nathaniel. "The Memory of Slavery at Saint Louis University." *American Nineteenth Century History* 16, no. 3 (2015): 329–350.

Mitchell, David. *The Jesuits: A History*. New York: F. Watts, 1981.

Monzell, Thomas I. "The Catholic Church and the Americanization of the Polish immigrant." *Polish American Studies* 26, no. 1 (1969): 1–15.

Morris, Frank. "Regis . . . The College the Pioneers Built." *Roundup Magazine*, Spring 1958. https://epublications.regis.edu/cgi/viewcontent.cgi?article=1018&context=roundup.

Mulhern, Joseph, C., SJ. "Spring Hill Observes Centennial." *Woodstock Letters* LIX, no. 3 (1930): 335–346.

Mulledy/Healy Legacy Committee. "What We Know: Report to the President of The College of The Holy Cross." College of the Holy Cross, 18 March 2016. https://www.holycross.edu/sites/default/files/files/mulledy-healy/mulledycommitteereportfinal.pdf.

Muller, Herman J., SJ. "Advancing the U of D Legacy—University of Detroit, 1978–1990." In *Legacy of Excellence: A Continuing history of Jesuit and Mercy Higher Education in Detroit*, edited by Herman J. Muller, SJ, Mary Justine Sabourin, RSM, and Shari S. Cohen, 7–55. Detroit: University of Detroit Press, 2003.

Muller, Herman J., SJ. *The University of Detroit, 1877–1977: A Centennial History*. Detroit: University of Detroit, 1976.

Nalezyty, Susan. "The History of Enslaved People at Georgetown Visitation." *US Catholic Historian* 37, no. 2 (Spring 2019): 23–48.

"Niehoff School of Nursing Golden Jubilee Celebration." Loyola University Archives and Special Collections. NSON- Golden Jubilee records UA1985.16. Loyola University Chicago. Accessed 2020. https://www.luc.edu/media/lucedu/archives/pdfs/nson_jubilee.pdf.

North, Patti. "Georgetown University Medical Center's Trailblazing Women: Highlights from the Many Who Helped Shape History." *Georgetown Health Magazine*, Fall/Winter 2017. https://alumni.georgetown.edu/news/gumc/magazine/2017/fall-winter/gumc-trailblazing-women#:~:text=Annie%20Rice%2C%20MD%2C%20(1853,earned%20medical%20degrees%20in%201883.

Nuesse, C. Joseph. *The Catholic University of America: A Centennial History.* Washington: Catholic University of America Press, 1990.

O'Hare, Joseph A., SJ. "Jesuit Education in America." In *The Jesuit Tradition in Education and Missions: A 450-Year Perspective*, edited by Christopher Chapple, 143–154. Scranton: University of Scranton Press, 1993.

O'Loughlin, Michael J. "USA Northeast Province releases names of Jesuits credibly accused of sexual abuse," *America* (15 January 2019). https://www.americamagazine.org/faith/2019/ 01/15/usa-northeast-province-releases-names-jesuits-credibly-accused-sexual-abuse

O'Malley, John W., SJ. "How the First Jesuits Got Involved in Education." In *The Jesuit Ratio Studiorum: 400th Anniversary Perspectives*, edited by Vincent J. Duminuco, SJ, 56–74. New York: Fordham University Press, 2000. Reprinted online by Boston College. https://www.bc.edu/content/dam/files/top/church21/pdf/HowtheFirstJesuitsBecame InvolvedinEducation.pdf. Accessed 2020.

O'Toole, James M. "Jesuits and Madames: The Life and Death of Newton College of the Sacred Heart, 1945–75." In *Crossings and Dwellings: Restored Jesuits, Women Religious, American Experience, 1814–2014*, edited by Kyle B. Roberts and Stephen Schloesser, 603–617. (Leiden, Boston: Brill, 2017).

Paul VI. "Declaration on Christian Education, Gravissimum Educationis." The Holy See, October 28, 1965. http://www.vatican.va/archive/hist_councils/ii_vatican_council/documents/vat-ii_decl_19651028_gravissimum-educationis_en.html.

Paul VI. "Message of Pope Paul VI to Georgetown University." The Holy See, September 26, 1963. http://www.vatican.va/content/paul-vi/en/speeches/1963/documents/hf_p-vi_spe_19630926_georgetown-university.html.

Pavur, Claude Nicholas. *The Ratio Studiorum: the Official Plan for Jesuit Education.* St. Louis: Institute of Jesuit Sources, 2005.

Platt, R. Eric. *Sacrifice and Survival: Identity, Mission, and Jesuit Higher Education in the American South.* Tuscaloosa: University of Alabama Press, 2014.

Posey, Walter B. Review of *The French Jesuits in Lower Louisiana (1700–1763)* by Jeane Delanglez. *Church History* 4, no. 4 (December, 1935): 314–315.

Power, Edward J. *Catholic Higher Education in America: A History.* New York: Appleton Century Crofts, 1972.

Reinert, Paul, SJ. "The Imperatives Determining the Future of Jesuit Higher Education." *Jesuit Educational Quarterly* 32, no. 2 (October 1969): 65–80.

"Response of the Board of Directors of the Association of Catholic Colleges and Universities on 'Proposed Schema for a Pontifical Document on Catholic Universities.'" In *American Catholic Higher Education*, edited by Alice Gallin, 273–278. Notre Dame, IN: University of Notre Dame Press, 1992.

Reynolds, Jon. "The Unknown Women of Georgetown." Georgetown University Library. https://www.library.georgetown.edu/special-collections/archives/essays/unknown-women. Accessed 2020.

Rhodes, Frank H.T. "The Mission and Ministry of Jesuits in Higher Education." *America*, August 5, 1989. Reprinted by Boston College Office of University Mission and Ministry. https://www.bc.edu/content/dam/files/offices/mission/pdf1/ju10.pdf. Accessed 2020.

Rishel, Joseph F. *The Spirit that Gives Life: The History of Duquesne University, 1878–1996.* Pittsburgh: Duquesne University Press, 1997.

Rizzi, Michael. "Cooperation after Independence: Lessons from Politics." *Journal of Catholic Higher Education* 39, no. 2 (2020): 147–165.

Rizzi, Michael. "Defining Catholic Higher Education in Positive Terms." *Journal of Catholic Education* 22, no. 2 (2019): 1–25.

Rizzi, Michael. "*Newman's Idea of a University* in Dialogue with the Land O'Lakes Statement of 1967." *Newman Studies Journal* 16, no. 2 (2019): 34–50.

Rizzi, Michael. "A Typology/Change Model for US Catholic Universities: Expressing a Catholic, American Identity." *Journal of Catholic Higher Education* 36, no. 2 (Summer 2017): 171–191.

Rizzi, Michael. "We've Been Here Before: A Brief History of Catholic Higher Education in America." *Journal of Catholic Higher Education* 37, no. 2 (Summer 2018): 153–174.

Roothaan, Jan, SJ. "Fr. Roothaan, SJ Lays Out the Conditions for the Sale of Enslaved Persons, 22 December 1836." Georgetown Slavery Archive, Georgetown University. Accessed 2020. https://slaveryarchive.georgetown.edu/items/show/94.

Rosswurm, Steve. *The FBI and the Catholic Church, 1935–1962.* Amherst: University of Massachusetts Press, 2009.

Ryan, John J., SJ. "St. John's College, Frederick: Half a Century Ago." *Woodstock Letters* XXX, no. 2 (1901): 231–246.

St. Joseph's College. "Prospectus, St. Joseph's College, San Jose, California, For the Scholastic Year 1892–3." Jesuit Archives and Research Center, St. Louis, MO.

Saint Louis University. "Catalog—1898." Saint Louis University Digital Archives. Accessed 2020. http://digitalcollections.slu.edu/digital/collection/catalogs/id/3551/.

Saint Louis University. *A Debate by the Philalethic Society of Saint Louis University on Monday, February 21, 1870.* St. Louis: George Knapp & Co. 1870.

Saint Louis University. *Saint Louis Brief* 9, no. 2 (Spring 2008): 3. https://issuu.com/slulaw/docs/volume_9_issue_2.

Saint Louis University. "SLU Legends and Lore: The Heithaus Homily." February 26, 2020. https://www.slu.edu/news/2020/february/slu-legends-lore-heithaus-homily.php.

Saint Louis University School of Nursing. "Carrying Commitment Forward: School of Nursing Celebrates 90 Years." *Cura Personalis*, Spring 2018. https://www.slu.edu/nursing/about/cura-pdfs-jpgs/curapersonalis2018.pdf.

Salter, J. M., SJ. "Our College at Augusta, Georgia." *Woodstock Letters* XXXIV, no. 3 (1905): 381–385.

Schier, Tracy, and Cynthia Russett, eds. *Catholic Women's Colleges in America.* Baltimore: Johns Hopkins University Press, 2002.

Schmidt, Kelly L., Sean Ferguson, and Claire Peterson, "Enslaved People in the Jesuits' Missouri Province," Slavery, History, Memory, and Reconciliation Project, 2020. https://www.jesuits.org/our-work/shmr/what-we-have-learned/missouri/.

Seismological Society of America. "Obituary: Francis A. Tondorf, S.J." *Bulletin of the Seismological Society of America* 19, no. 4 (1929): 245–246.

Shelley, Thomas J. *Fordham: A History of the Jesuit University of New York, 1841–2003.* New York: Fordham University Press, 2016.

Sibila, Nick. "The Court Case that Could Finally Take Down Antiquated Anti-Catholic Laws." *The Atlantic*, January 12, 2020. https://www.theatlantic.com/ideas/archive/2020/01/espinoza-montana-bigoted-laws/604756/.

Smith, Adrianna. "Fifty years of Women at Georgetown College." *Georgetown Magazine* 51, no. 2 (Spring 2020): 32–33.

Solari, Agnes and Margaret Zero. "St. Joseph's College and Rectory Building, 1892–1977." Jesuit Archives and Research Center, St. Louis, MO, October 10, 1977.

Somerville, James M. "Commitment in a World of Change." *Jesuit Educational Quarterly* 32, no. 2 (October 1969): 61–64.

Stansell, Harold L., SJ. *Regis: On the Crest of the West.* Denver: Regis University, 1977.

"State Buys 4,400 Acres of Waterfront from Jesuits." *Washington Examiner*, January 29, 2009. https://www.washingtonexaminer.com/state-buys-4-400-acres-of-waterfront-from-jesuits.

"Statement of Presidents of Leading Catholic Universities of North America on the Schema for a Proposed Document on the Catholic University." In *American Catholic Higher Education, Essential Documents1967–1990,* edited by Alice Gallin, 279–283. Notre Dame, IN: University of Notre Dame Press, 1992.

"Students Army Training Corps: Second Edition. Descriptive Circular." University of Colorado Archives, October 14, 1918. https://cudl.colorado.edu/MediaManager/srvr?mediafile=MISC/UCBOULDERCB1-58-NA/1511/i7375352x.pdf.

Swarns, Rachel L. "Is Georgetown's $400,000-a-Year Plan to Aid Slave Descendants Enough?" *New York Times,* 30 October, 2019. https://www.nytimes.com/2019/10/30/us/georgetown-slavery-reparations.html.

Thomanson, Andy. "Is College President 'the Toughest Job in the Nation'?" *Chronicle of Higher Education* (May 1, 2018). https://www.chronicle.com/article/is-college-president-the-toughest-job-in-the-nation/#:~:text=The%20tenure%20of%20college%20presidents, 8.5%20years%20a%20decade%20before.

Tillman, Seth. *Georgetown's School of Foreign Service: the First 75 Years.* Washington: Georgetown University, 1994.

Tye, Larry. *Bobby Kennedy: The Making of a Liberal Icon.* New York: Random House, 2017.

Udías, Agustin and William Stauder. "The Jesuit Contribution to Seismology." *Seismological Research Letters* 67, no. 3 (May/June 1996): 10–19. https://www.seismosoc.org/inside/eastern-section/jesuit-contribution-seismology/.

Varga, Nicholas. *Baltimore's Loyola, Loyola's Baltimore, 1851–1986.* Baltimore: Maryland Historical Society, 1990.

Villiger, Burchard, SJ. "Autobiography of Father Burchard Villiger." *Woodstock Letters* XXXII, no. 1 (1903): 75.

Wang, Jessica. "Scientists and the Problem of the Public in Cold War America, 1945–1960," *Osiris* Second Series, vol. 17, Science and Civil Society (2002): 323–347.

Warner, William. *At Peace with All Their Neighbors: Catholics and Catholicism in the National Capital, 1787–1860.* Washington: Georgetown University Press, 1994.

Weiss, Arthur A., SJ. "Jesuit Mission Years in New York State 1654–1879." *Woodstock Letters* LXXV, no. 1 (1946): 7–25.

Widman, C. M. "Springhill College (1830–1898)." *Woodstock Letters* XXVII, no. 3 (1898): 267–278.

Williams, Phoebe Weaver. "A Black Woman's Voice: The Story of Mabel Raimey, 'Shero.'" *Marquette Law Review* 74, no. 3 (1991): 345–376.

Wimmer, Boniface, OSB. "Concerning the Missions." In *Boniface Wimmer: Visions of a Founder*. Latrobe, PA: St. Vincent College, undated.

Woods, Henry, SJ. "California Mission of the Society of Jesus." *Woodstock Letters* XIII, no. 2 (1884): 157–164.

Woodstock Letters. "The Buffalo Mission: 1869–1969." *Woodstock Letters* 98, no. 4 (1969): 465–466.

Woodstock Letters. "Death of Father John McElroy." *Woodstock Letters* VI, no. 3 (1878): 178–186.

Woodstock Letters. "Galveston, St. Mary's University." *Woodstock Letters*, XIX, no. 1 (1890): 75–80.

Woodstock Letters. "The Jubilee of the Province, 1833." *Woodstock Letters* XII, no. 2 (1883): 205–258.

Woodstock Letters. "Las Vegas College, New Mexico." *Woodstock Letters* VII, no. 1 (1878): 40–43.

Woodstock Letters. "New Mexico." *Woodstock Letters* XIII, no. 1 (1884): 42–50.

Woodstock Letters. "Students in Our Colleges in the U. States and Canada, 1890–'91." *Woodstock Letters* XX, no. 3 (1891): unnumbered page.

Woodstock Letters. "Students in Our Colleges in the U. States and Canada, 1894–'95." *Woodstock Letters* XXIV, no. 3 (1895): unnumbered page.

Woodstock Letters. "Students in Our Colleges in the United States and Canada. October 1, 1900." *Woodstock Letters* XXIX, no. 3 (1901): unnumbered page.

Woodstock Letters. "Students in Our Colleges in the United States and Canada, Oct. 1, 1901." *Woodstock Letters* XXIX, no. 3 (1901): unnumbered page.

Woodstock Letters. "Students in our Colleges, in the United States and Canada, Oct. 1, 1910." *Woodstock Letters* XXXIX, no. 3 (1910): unnumbered page.

Woodstock Letters. "Students in Our Colleges in the United States and Canada, October 1, 1915." *Woodstock Letters* XLIV, no. 3 (1915): unnumbered page.

Woodstock Letters. "Students in Our Colleges in the United States and Canada, October 10, 1917." *Woodstock Letters* XLVI, no. 3 (1917): unnumbered page.

Woodstock Letters. "Students in Our Colleges in the United States and Canada: October 10, 1918." *Woodstock Letters* XLVII, no. 3 (1918): unnumbered page.

Woodstock Letters. "Students in Our Colleges in the United States and Canada, October 10, 1920." *Woodstock Letters* XLIX, no. 3 (1920): unnumbered page.

Woodstock Letters. "Varia." *Woodstock Letters* VII, no. 2 (1878): 132–133.

Woodstock Letters. "Varia." *Woodstock Letters* LVII, no. 3 (1928): 539–540.

Woodstock Letters. "Varia." *Woodstock Letters* LVIII, no. 1 (1929): 233–234.

Woodstock Letters. "Varia." *Woodstock Letters* LXI, no. 1 (1932): 162.

Woodstock Letters. "Varia." *Woodstock Letters* LXXV, no. 1 (1946): 82–83.

Worcester, Thomas, ed. *The Cambridge Companion to the Jesuits*. Cambridge: Cambridge University Press, 2008.

Index